Y0-AGJ-063

— The Unofficial Guide® to
Walt Disney World®
& EPCOT® —

Also available from Macmillan Travel:

The Unofficial Guide® to
Walt Disney World®
& EPCOT®

1996 Edition

Bob Sehlinger

Macmillan • *USA*

Macmillan Travel
A Simon & Schuster Macmillan Company
1633 Broadway
New York, New York 10019-6785

Copyright © 1985, 1987, 1989, 1990, 1991, 1992,
1993, 1994, 1995, 1996
by Robert W. Sehlinger
1996 edition

All rights reserved, including the right of
reproduction in whole or in part in any form

Produced by Menasha Ridge Press
Design by Barbara E. Williams

Macmillan is a registered trademark
of Macmillan, Inc.

The Unofficial Guide is a registered
trademark of Robert W. Sehlinger.

ISBN 0-02-860663-9

ISSN 1059-3578

Manufactured in the United States of America

10 9 8 7 6 5 4 3 2

For Trent, Marva, and Nicholas

Trademarks.   The following attractions, shows, components, entities, etc., mentioned or discussed in this guide are registered trademarks of the Walt Disney Company, Inc.:

Adventureland	Magic Kingdom
AudioAnimatronics	New Orleans Square
Captain EO	PeopleMover
Disneyland	Space Mountain
EPCOT	Walt Disney
Fantasyland	Walt Disney World

New trademarks are applied for almost continuously. These will be recognized as and when appropriate in subsequent editions of this guide.

Contents

List of Maps

Acknowledgments

Special thanks to our field research team who rendered a Herculean effort in what must have seemed like a fantasy version of Sartre's *No Exit* to the tune of "It's a Small World." We hope you all recover to tour another day.

Caroline Blondy
Allison Grizzle
Betsy Amster
Leslie Cummins
Molly Burns
Holly Brown
Barbara Williams
Taylor O'Bryan (the Human Probe)
Trent Sehlinger
Mary Mitchell

Peals of laughter and much appreciation to nationally renowned cartoonist Tami Knight for her brilliant and insightful work.

Mike Jones, Lee Wiseman, Marie Hillin, and Patt Palmer all energetically contributed to shaping this latest edition. Marjorie Hudson provided invaluable counsel regarding the organization of the guide. Psychologists Dr. Karen Turnbow, Dr. Gayle Janzen, and Dr. Joan Burns provided much insight concerning the experiences of small children at Walt Disney World. "Hotel Women" Molly Burns and Holly Brown inspected many dozens of hotels.

Many thanks also to Barbara Williams and Caroline Nasrallah for design and production, and to Alexa Dilworth, Erin Willder, and Pam Morrison for editorial work on this book. Tseng Information Systems earned our appreciation for their fine work and for keeping tight deadlines in providing the typography. Cartography was provided by Tim Krasnansky. The index was prepared by Ann Cassar.

Finally, some of John Finley's comments and descriptions, which originally appeared in *Central Florida Attractions* (coauthored by Finley and Bob Sehlinger, Menasha Ridge Press, 1983), are reproduced in this guide.

INTRODUCTION

How Come "Unofficial"?

—— Declaration of Independence

The author and researchers of this guide specifically and categorically declare that they are and always have been totally independent of the Walt Disney Company, Inc., of Disneyland, Inc., of Walt Disney World, Inc., and of any and all other members of the Disney corporate family not listed.

The material in this guide originated with the author and researchers and has not been reviewed, edited, or in any way approved by the Walt Disney Company, Inc., Disneyland, Inc., or Walt Disney World, Inc.

This guidebook represents the first comprehensive *critical* appraisal of Walt Disney World. Its purpose is to provide the reader with the information necessary to tour Walt Disney World with the greatest efficiency and economy, and with the least amount of hassle and standing in line. The authors of this guide believe in the wondrous variety, joy, and excitement of the Disney attractions. At the same time, we recognize realistically that Walt Disney World is a business, with the same profit motivations as businesses the world over.

In this guide we have elected to represent and serve you, the consumer. Its contents were researched and compiled by a team of evaluators who were, and are, completely independent of Walt Disney World and its parent corporation. If a restaurant serves bad food, or a gift item is overpriced, or a certain ride isn't worth the wait, we can say so, and in the process, hopefully make your visit more fun, efficient, and economical.

—— The Importance of Being Goofy

A group of Disney executives, clean-shaven (because of a company policy banning all facial hair) and impeccably attired in dark suits, gather around a polished black walnut table. There is an almost palpable tension. Everyone speaks in hushed tones, carefully measuring their words:

"I don't want to be blindsided by this at the shareholders' meeting."

3

"No one's raised the issue yet. Let's just sit on it. The last thing we want is to stir something up."

"Too late; I've heard the *Post* is working on a story. There are even rumors about a paternity suit."

"What's Donald saying?"

"He's stonewalling. Won't return my calls."

"Well, he's going to have to come clean. Our people need to know what to tell the press."

"Right. And we need to know, too. If he doesn't have a brother and he doesn't have a sister, where *did* Huey, Dewey, and Louie come from?"

And so it goes. . . .

What really makes writing about Walt Disney World fun is that the Disney people take everything so seriously. Day to day they debate momentous decisions with far-ranging consequences: Will Goofy look swishy in a silver cape? Have we gone too far with the Little Mermaid's cleavage? At a time when the whole nation is concerned about the drug problem, can we afford to have a dwarf named "Dopey"?

Unofficially, we think having a sense of humor is pretty important. This guidebook has a sense of humor and it is probably necessary that you do too. Not to use this book, but more significantly, to have fun at Walt Disney World. Disney World (in the popular phrasing) is the mother of all tourist attractions. A certain amount of levity is required simply to survive. Think of the *Unofficial Guide* as a private trainer to help get your sense of humor in shape. It will help you understand the importance of being Goofy.

An Apology of Sorts

The first edition of *The Unofficial Guide to Walt Disney World* was considerably less than 200 pages, a mere shadow of its present massive size. In the years since the first edition, Disney World has grown considerably; adding the Disney-MGM Studios, Pleasure Island, Typhoon Lagoon, Blizzard Beach, several new attractions in EPCOT and the Magic Kingdom, and about 16,500 new hotel rooms. The *Unofficial Guide* has grown to match this expansion.

We have no idea where it will all end. In 30 years we may be selling an alphabetized 26-volume edition, handsomely packaged in its own imitation oak bookcase. In the meantime, we offer a qualified apology for the tome that is our current edition. We acknowledge that it may be too heavy to be comfortably carried without the assistance of a handcart, llama, or

Sherpa, but defend the inclusion of all the information presented. Not every diner uses the catsup, the A-1 Sauce, and the Tabasco, but it's nice to have all three on the table.

The Death of Spontaneity

One of our all-time favorite letters came from a man in Chapel Hill, North Carolina:

> Your book reads like the operations plan for an amphibious landing. . . . Go here, do this, proceed to Step 15. . . . You must think that everyone [who visits Walt Disney World] is a hyperactive, Type-A, theme-park-commando. Whatever happened to the satisfaction of self-discovery or the joy of spontaneity? Next you will be telling us when to empty our bladders.

As it happens, we researchers for the *Unofficial Guide* are a pretty existential crew. We are big on self-discovery if the activity is walking in the woods or watching birds. Some of us are able to improvise jazz without reading music, while others can whip up a mean pot of chili in the absence of a recipe. When it comes to Walt Disney World, however, we all agree that you either need a good plan or a frontal lobotomy. The operational definition of self-discovery and spontaneity at Walt Disney World is the "pleasure" of heat prostration and the "joy" of standing in line.

It's easy to spot the free spirits at Walt Disney World, particularly at opening time. While everybody else is stampeding to Space Mountain, they are the ones standing in a cloud of dust puzzling over the park map. Later, they are the people running around like chickens in a thunderstorm trying to find an attraction with less than a 40-minute wait. Face it, Walt Disney World is not a very existential place. In many ways it's the quintessential system, the ultimate in mass-produced entertainment, the most planned and programmed environment imaginable. Spontaneity and self-discovery work about as well at Walt Disney World as they do on your tax return.

We are not saying that you can't have a great time at Walt Disney World. Bowling isn't very spontaneous either, but lots of people love it. What we are saying is that you need a plan. You do not have to be compulsive or inflexible about it, just think about what you want to do before you go. Don't delude yourself by rationalizing that the information in this bulky guide is only for the pathological and the superorganized. Ask not for whom the tome tells, Bubba, it tells for thee.

The Attraction That Ate Florida

Before Walt Disney World, Florida was a happy peninsula of many more-or-less equal tourist attractions. Distributed around the state in great proliferation, they constituted the most perennially appealing vacation opportunity in the United States. There was the Monkey Jungle, the Orchid Jungle, venerable Marineland, the St. Augustine Alligator Farm, Silver Springs, the Miami Wax Museum, the Sunken Gardens, the Coral Castle, and the Conch Train Tour. These, along with Cypress Gardens, Busch Gardens, and others, were the attractions that ruled Florida. Now like so many dinosaurs, those remaining survive precariously on the droppings of the greatest dinosaur of them all, Walt Disney World. With doors still open, the old standbys continue to welcome tourists, thank you, but when was the last time you planned your vacation around a trip to Jungle Larry's Safari Park?

When Walt Disney World arrived on the scene, Florida tourism changed forever. Before Disney (B.D.), southern Florida was the state's and the nation's foremost tourist destination. Throngs sunned on the beaches of Miami, Hollywood, and Fort Lauderdale and patronized such nearby attractions as the Miami Serpentarium and the Parrot Jungle. Attractions in the Ocala and St. Augustine area upstate hosted road travelers in great waves as they journeyed to and from their southern Florida destinations. At the time, Orlando was a sleepy little central Florida town about an hour's drive from Cypress Gardens, and with practically no tourist appeal whatsoever.

Then came Disney, and it was not as if Walt had sneaked up on anyone. To the contrary, he came openly and bargaining hard, asking for improved highways, tax concessions, bargain financing, and community support. So successful had been his California Disneyland that whatever he requested, he received.

Generally approving, and hoping for a larger aggregate market, the Florida attractions industry failed to discern the cloud on the horizon. Walt had tipped his hand early, however, and all the cards were on the

7

table. When Disney bought 27,500 central Florida acres, it was fairly evident that he did not intend to raise cattle.

The Magic Kingdom opened on October 1, 1971, and was immediately successful. Hotel construction boomed in Orlando and Kissimmee and around Walt Disney World. Major new attractions popped up along recently completed Interstate 4 to cash in on the wellspring of tourists arriving to tour Disney's latest wonder. Walt Disney World became a destination, and suddenly nobody cared as much about going to the beach. The Magic Kingdom was good for two days, and then you could enjoy the rest of the week at Sea World, Cypress Gardens, Circus World, Gatorland Zoo, Busch Gardens, the Stars Hall of Fame Wax Museum, and the Kennedy Space Center.

These various satellite attractions, all practically new and stretching from east coast to west coast, formed what would come to be called the Orlando Wall. No longer did tourists pour into Miami and Fort Lauderdale. Rather, they held up at the Orlando Wall and exhausted themselves and their tourist dollars in the shiny modern attractions arrayed between Cape Canaveral and Tampa. In southern Florida venerable old attractions held on by a parrot feather and more than a few closed their doors. Flagship hotels on the fabled Gold Coast went bust or were converted to condominiums for legions of retirees.

When Walt Disney World opened, the very definition of a tourist attraction changed. Setting standards for cleanliness, size, scope, grandeur, variety, and attention to detail, Walt Disney World overnight relegated the majority of Florida's headliner attractions to positions of comparative insignificance. Newer attractions such as Sea World and the vastly enlarged Busch Gardens strove successfully to achieve the new standard. Cypress Gardens, Weeki Wachi, and Silver Springs expanded and modernized. Most other attractions, however, slipped into a limbo of diminished status from which they never recovered. Far from being headliners or tourist destinations, they plugged along as local diversions, pulling in the curious, the bored, and the sunburned for two-hour excursions.

Many of the affected attractions were and are wonderful places to spend a vacation day, but even collectively, as has been sadly demonstrated, they do not command sufficient appeal to lure many tourists beyond the Wall. We recommend them, however, not only for their variety of high-quality offerings, but as a glimpse of Florida's golden age, a time of less sophisticated, less plastic pleasures, before the Mouse. Take a day or two and drive three-and-a-half hours south of Orlando. Visit the Miami Seaquarium or Ocean World, try Vizcaya, Fairchild Tropical Gardens, and Lion Country Safari. Drive Collins Avenue along the Gold Coast. You'll be glad you did.

When EPCOT Center opened in Walt Disney World on October 1, 1982, another seismic shock reverberated through the Florida attractions industry. This time it was not only the smaller and more vulnerable attractions that were affected, but the newer large-scale attractions along the Orlando Wall. Suddenly, with EPCOT Center, Walt Disney World had swallowed up another one to two days of each tourist's vacation week. When the Magic Kingdom stood alone, most visitors had three or four days remaining to sample other attractions. With the addition of EPCOT Center, that available time was cut to one or two days.

Disney ensured its market share by creating the multiday admission passes, which allow unlimited access to both the Magic Kingdom and EPCOT Center. More cost-efficient than a one-day pass to a single park, these passes had the effect of keeping the guest on Disney turf for three to five days.

The Kennedy Space Center and Sea World, by virtue of their very specialized products, continued to prosper following the opening of EPCOT Center. Most other attractions, however, were forced to focus more of their energy on local markets. Some, like Busch Gardens, did very well, with increased local support replacing the decreased numbers of Walt Disney World destination tourists coming over for the day. Others, like Cypress Gardens, suffered badly but worked diligently to improve their product. Some, like Circus World and the Hall of Fame Wax Museum, passed into history.

Though long an innovator, Disney turned in the mid-80s to copying existing successful competitors, except that copying is not exactly the right word. What Disney did was to take a competitor's product concept, improve it, and reproduce it in Disney style on a grand scale.

The first competitor to feel the heat was Sea World when Disney added The Living Seas pavilion to the Future World section of EPCOT Center. Sea World, however, had killer whales, the Shark Encounter, and sufficient corporate resources to remain preeminent among marine exhibits. Still, many Walt Disney World patrons willingly substituted a visit to The Living Seas for a visit to Sea World.

Disney had one of its own products threatened when the Wet 'n Wild water theme park took a shot at the older, smaller, but more aesthetically pleasing River Country. Never one to take a challenge sitting down, Disney responded in 1989 with the opening of Typhoon Lagoon, the largest swimming theme park in the world.

Also in 1989 Disney opened Pleasure Island, a one-admission multi-nightclub entertainment complex patterned on Orlando's successful Church Street Station. In the several years Pleasure Island has been oper-ating, it has robbed Church Street Station of much of its destination tourist traffic.

Finally, and most significantly of all, in 1989 Walt Disney World opened the Disney-MGM Studios, a combination working motion picture and television production complex and theme park. Copying the long-heralded Universal Studios tour in southern California, the Disney-MGM Studios were speeded into construction and operation after Universal announced its plans for a central Florida park.

This newest of the Walt Disney World theme parks, however, affected much more than Universal's plans. With the opening of Disney-MGM, the 3-Day World Passport was discontinued. Instead, Disney patrons were offered either a single-day pass or the more economical multiday passports, good for either four or five days. With the three theme parks on a multiday pass, plus two swimming parks, several golf courses, various lakes, and a nighttime entertainment complex, Disney effectively swal-lowed up the average family's entire vacation. Break away to Sea World or the Kennedy Space Center for the day? How about a day at the ocean (remember the ocean)? Fat chance.

With the opening of the Walt Disney World Swan and Dolphin hotels, and the Conference Center, Disney took a quantum leap toward monopo-lizing the business and convention traveler as well. With over 250,000 square feet of exhibit space, the Conference Center is one of the largest in the Southeast.

In 1995 Disney opened Blizzard Beach, a third swimming park, and began plans for a fourth major theme park, a zoological park designed to compete directly with Busch Gardens. During the same year, the first phase of Disney's All-Star Resorts came on line, featuring (by Disney standards) budget accommodations. The location and rates of the All-Star Resorts are intended to capture the market of the smaller independent and chain hotels situated along US 192. Disney has even discussed con-structing a monorail to the airport so that visitors will not have to set a single foot in Orlando.

I regret the passing of an era in Florida tourism. The old attractions were more intimate, more personal, more human. The live alligators were more interesting (if less predictable) than the Disney robotic version, and I found I could stomach the pungent odor of a real cougar. Each modest attraction embodied the realization of some maverick's dream, a dream he longed to share with anyone who passed through the turnstile.

But dreams are only as grand as the people who create them, and only the truly visionary endure. Such was the dream of Walt Disney, come to fruition in Walt Disney World. Is his dream a cancer in the breast of tourism? Possibly, but it is also a testimony to careful planning, harboring of resources, precise timing, and adherence to a standard of quality unprecedented in the entertainment industry. Walt Disney World represents the delivery of a product that amazes and delights, that exceeds the expectations of almost every visitor.

From an entrepreneurial seed, a cartoon mouse, and a California amusement park years ahead of its time has risen an entertainment giant, a giant that sometimes moves clumsily and sometimes with cold, hard determination but always with a commitment to quality. Walt Disney World represents the kind of imagination, industry, and farsighted thinking that might have preserved American leadership in steel, automobiles, and electronics.

I am not sure that I like the idea of the Walt Disney Company monopolizing and orchestrating a Florida visitor's entire vacation, but that seems to be the handwriting on the wall, if not the present reality. And there is this: a tourist could do a lot worse. The bottom line, however, is that Disney has a grip on Florida unprecedented in the history of tourism. As the grip tightens, it will be interesting to see whose interests are served.

How This Guide Was Researched and Written

While much has been written concerning Walt Disney World, very little has been comparative or evaluative. Most guides simply parrot Disney World's own promotional material. In preparing this guide, however, nothing was taken for granted. Each theme park was visited at different times throughout the year by a team of trained observers. They conducted detailed evaluations and rated each theme park with all its component rides, shows, exhibits, services, and concessions according to a formal, pretested rating instrument. Interviews with attraction patrons were conducted to determine what tourists — of all age groups — enjoyed most and least during their Disney World visit.

While our observers were independent and impartial, we do not claim special expertise or scientific backgrounds relative to the types of exhibits, performances, or attractions. Like you, we visit Walt Disney World as tourists, noting our satisfaction or dissatisfaction. We do not believe it necessary to be an agronomist to know whether we enjoyed the agricultural exhibits in the EPCOT Center Land pavilion. Disney offerings are marketed to the touring public, and it is as the public that we have experienced them.

The primary difference between the average tourist and the trained evaluator is in the evaluator's professional skills in organization, preparation, and observation. The trained evaluator is responsible for much more than simply observing and cataloging. While the tourist seated next to the evaluator is being entertained and delighted by the *Tropical Serenade* (*Enchanted Tiki Birds*) in the Magic Kingdom, this professional is rating the performance in terms of theme, pace, continuity, and originality. He or she is also checking out the physical arrangements: Is the sound system clear and audible without being overpowering; is the audience shielded from the sun or from the rain; is seating adequate; can everyone in the audience clearly see the staging area? And what about guides and/or performers: Are they knowledgeable, articulate, and professional in their presentation; are they friendly and engaging? Does the performance begin and end on time; does the show contain the features described in Disney World's promotional literature? These and many other considerations figure prominently in the rating of any staged performance. Similarly, detailed and relevant checklists were prepared and applied by observer teams to rides, exhibits, concessions, and to the theme parks in general. Finally, observations and evaluator ratings were integrated with audience reactions and the opinions of patrons to compile a comprehensive quality profile of each feature and service.

In compiling this guide, we recognize the fact that a tourist's age, sex, background, and interests will strongly influence his or her taste in Walt Disney World offerings and will account for a preference of one ride or feature over another. Given this fact we make no attempt at comparing apples with oranges. How indeed could a meaningful comparison be made between the priceless historic artifacts in the Mexican pavilion of EPCOT Center and the wild roller coaster ride of the Magic Kingdom's Space Mountain? Instead, our objective is to provide the reader with sufficient description, critical evaluation, and pertinent data to make knowledgeable decisions according to individual tastes.

The essence of this guide, therefore, consists of individual critiques and descriptions of each feature of the Magic Kingdom, EPCOT Center, and Disney-MGM Studios, along with detailed Touring Plans to help you avoid bottlenecks and crowds. Also included are in-depth descriptions for Typhoon Lagoon, Blizzard Beach, Pleasure Island, and nearby Universal Studios Florida.

—— Letters, Comments, and Questions from Readers

Many of those who use *The Unofficial Guide to Walt Disney World* write to us asking questions, making comments, or sharing their own strategies for visiting Walt Disney World. We appreciate all such input, both positive and critical, and encourage our readers to continue writing. Readers' comments and observations are frequently incorporated in revised editions of the *Unofficial Guide* and have contributed immeasurably to its improvement. If you write us or return our reader survey form, rest assured that we will not release your name and address to any mailing list companies, direct mail advertisers, or any other third party.

Reader Questionnaire and Restaurant Survey

At the back of this guide, you will find a short questionnaire that you can use to express opinions concerning your Walt Disney World visit. The questionnaire is designed to allow each member of your party, regardless of age, to tell us what they think. There is also a separate restaurant survey that you can use to describe your Walt Disney World dining experiences. Clip the questionnaire and the restaurant survey out along the dotted lines and mail to:

Reader Survey
The *Unofficial Guide* Series
P.O. Box 43059
Birmingham, AL 35243

How to Write the Author

Bob Sehlinger
The Unofficial Guide to Walt Disney World
P.O. Box 43059
Birmingham, AL 35243

When you write, be sure to put your return address on your letter as well as on the envelope. Sometimes envelopes and letters get separated. It is also a good idea to include your phone number. And remember, as travel writers, we are often out of the office for long periods of time, so forgive us if our response is a little slow.

Questions from Readers

Questions frequently asked by readers in their letters to the author are answered in an appendix at the end of the *Unofficial Guide*.

Field Research Internship

A small number of qualified graduate students are selected each year to participate in a field research internship held in conjunction with semiannual revision work at the Disney parks and in relation to consulting projects at other American theme parks. The internships focus on theme park planning and design, attraction product design and engineering, vehicular and pedestrian traffic engineering, and the functional areas of marketing and operations. Internships are four days to a week in duration. Applicants must be 21 years of age or older and currently enrolled in an accredited graduate program, preferably in a relevant field of study (business, statistics, engineering, architecture, etc.), and be available at one month's notice for dates in June, July, and August. Those selected will be expected to pay all of their own expenses, including transportation to the research site, lodging, and meals. To apply, send vita with cover letter and SASE to:

Field Research Internship
c/o The *Unofficial Guide* Series
P.O. Box 43059
Birmingham, AL 35243

Walt Disney World: An Overview

If you are selecting among the tourist attractions in Florida, the question is not whether to visit Walt Disney World but how to see the best of the various Disney offerings with some economy of time, effort, and finances.

Make no mistake, there is nothing on earth quite like Walt Disney World. Incredible in its scope, genius, beauty, and imagination, it is a joy and wonder for people of all ages. A fantasy, a dream, and a vision all rolled into one, it transcends simple entertainment, making us children and adventurers, freeing us for an hour or a day to live the dreams of our past, present, and future.

Certainly we are critics, but it is the responsibility of critics to credit that which is done well as surely as to reflect negatively on that which is done poorly. The Disney attractions are special, a quantum leap beyond and above any man-made entertainment offering we know of. We cannot understand how anyone could visit Florida and bypass Walt Disney World.

—— What Walt Disney World Encompasses

Walt Disney World encompasses forty-three square miles, an area twice as large as Manhattan Island, or roughly the size of Boston. Situated strategically in this vast expanse are the Magic Kingdom, EPCOT Center, and the Disney-MGM Studios theme parks, three swimming theme parks, a botanical and zoological park, a nightlife entertainment area, a competitive sports complex, several golf courses, hotels and campgrounds, almost 100 restaurants, four large interconnected lakes, a shopping complex, a convention center, a permanent nature preserve, and a complete transportation system consisting of four-lane highways, elevated monorails, and a system of canals.

Most tourists refer to the entire Florida Disney facility as Walt Disney World, or more simply, as Disney World. The Magic Kingdom, EPCOT Center, and Disney-MGM Studios are thought of as being "in" Disney

World. Other visitors refer to the Magic Kingdom as Disney World and EPCOT Center as EPCOT, and are not sure exactly how to label the entity as a whole. In our description we will refer to the total Disney facility as Walt Disney World according to popular tradition, and will consider the Magic Kingdom, EPCOT Center, and everything else that sits on that 43-square-mile chunk of real estate to be included in the overall designation.

The Major Theme Parks

The Magic Kingdom

The Magic Kingdom is what most people think of when they think of Walt Disney World. It is the collection of adventures, rides, and shows symbolized by the Disney cartoon characters and Cinderella Castle. Although the Magic Kingdom is only one element of the Disney attraction complex, it remains the heart of Disney World. The Magic Kingdom is divided into seven subareas or "lands," six of which are arranged around a central hub. First encountered is Main Street, U.S.A., which connects the Magic Kingdom entrance with the central hub. Moving clockwise around the hub, other lands are Adventureland, Frontierland, Liberty Square, Fantasyland, and Tomorrowland. Mickey's Starland, the first new land in the Magic Kingdom since the park opened, is situated along the Walt Disney Railroad on three acres between Fantasyland and Tomorrowland. Access is through Fantasyland or via the railroad. Main Street and the other six lands will be described in detail later. Three hotel complexes (the Contemporary Resort, Polynesian Resort, and Grand Floridian Beach Resort) are located close to the Magic Kingdom and are directly connected to it by monorail and by boat. Two additional hotels, Shades of Green (formerly the Disney Inn) and Disney's Wilderness Lodge Resort, are located nearby, but are not serviced by the monorail.

EPCOT Center

EPCOT (Experimental Prototype Community of Tomorrow) Center opened in October of 1982. Divided into two major areas, Future World and World Showcase, the park is twice the size of and is comparable in scope to the Magic Kingdom. Future World consists of a number of futuristic pavilions, each relating to a different theme concerning man's

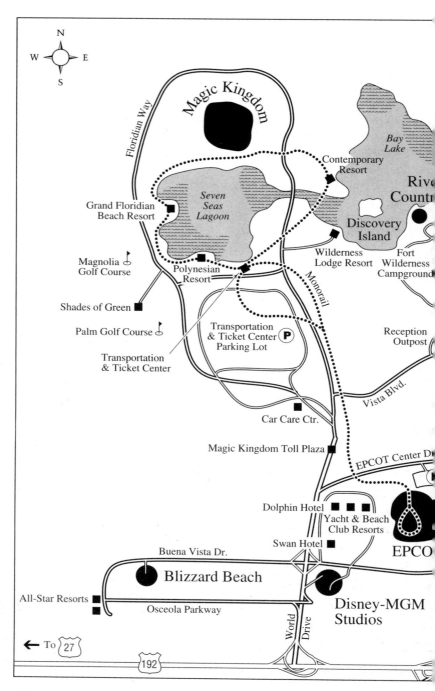

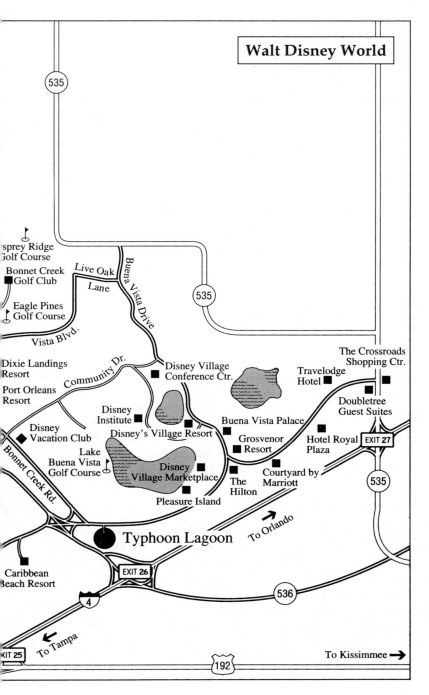

Walt Disney World

535

Osprey Ridge
Golf Course

Bonnet Creek
Golf Club

Live Oak
Lane

Buena Vista Drive

535

Eagle Pines
Golf Course

Vista Blvd.

The Crossroads
Shopping Ctr.

Dixie Landings
Resort

Community Dr.

Disney Village
Conference Ctr.

Travelodge
Hotel

Port Orleans
Resort

Doubletree
Guest Suites

Disney
Institute

Buena Vista Palace

Disney
Vacation Club

Disney's Village Resort

Bonnet Creek Rd.

Lake
Buena Vista
Golf Course

Grosvenor
Resort

Hotel Royal
Plaza

EXIT 27

Disney
Village Marketplace

The
Hilton

Courtyard by
Marriott

535

Pleasure Island

To Orlando

Typhoon Lagoon

Caribbean
Beach Resort

EXIT 26

536

4

To Tampa

EXIT 25

To Kissimmee →

192

19

creativity and technological advancement. World Showcase, arranged around a 41-acre lagoon, presents the architectural, social, and cultural heritages of almost a dozen nations, with each country represented by famous landmarks and local settings familiar to world travelers. EPCOT Center is generally more educationally oriented than the Magic Kingdom and has been repeatedly characterized as a sort of permanent world's fair. Unlike the Magic Kingdom, which Disney spokesmen represent as being essentially complete, EPCOT Center is portrayed as a continually changing and growing entity.

There are five EPCOT Center resort hotels: Disney's Beach Club, Disney's Yacht Club, Disney's Boardwalk Resort, the Walt Disney World Swan, and the Walt Disney World Dolphin. All are within a 5- to 15-minute walk of the International Gateway entrance to the EPCOT Center theme park. The hotels are also linked to the park by canal and tram. EPCOT Center is connected to the Magic Kingdom and its resort hotels by monorail.

The Disney-MGM Studios

This $300 million, 100-plus-acre attraction, which opened in 1989, is divided into two areas. The first is a theme park relating to the past, present, and future of the motion picture and television industries. This section contains movie-theme rides and shows and covers about half of the Disney-MGM complex. Highlights here include a re-creation of Hollywood and Sunset Boulevards from Hollywood's Golden Age, audience participation shows on TV production and sound effects, movie stunt demonstrations, a children's play area, and three high-tech rides: the Twilight Zone Tower of Terror, Star Tours, and The Great Movie Ride, which takes guests for a journey through the movies' greatest moments.

The second area, encompassing the remaining half, is a working motion picture and television production facility comprised of three sound stages, a back lot of streets and sets, and creative support services. Public access to this area is limited except for studio tours, which take visitors behind the scenes for crash-courses on Disney animation and movie making, including (on occasion) the opportunity to witness the actual shooting of a feature film or television show.

The Disney-MGM Studios are connected to other Walt Disney World areas by highway and canal, but not by monorail. Guests can park in the Studios' own pay parking lot or commute by bus from EPCOT Center, the Transportation and Ticket Center, or from any Walt Disney World lodging. Patrons staying in the EPCOT Center resort hotels can also reach the Studios by boat.

The Water Theme Parks

There are three major swimming theme parks in Walt Disney World: Typhoon Lagoon, River Country, and Blizzard Beach. Typhoon Lagoon is the world's largest park of its kind and is distinguished by a wave pool capable of making six-foot waves. River Country, a pioneer among water theme parks, is much smaller but very well done. Since Typhoon Lagoon's opening in 1989, River Country has catered primarily to Walt Disney World campground and resort hotel guests. Blizzard Beach is the newest Disney water park and features more slides than the other two swimming parks combined. All three parks are beautifully arranged and landscaped, with great attention paid to atmosphere and aesthetics. Typhoon Lagoon and Blizzard Beach have their own adjacent parking lots. River Country can be accessed on foot for campground guests, or by Disney boat or bus for others.

The Minor Theme Parks

Pleasure Island

Part of the Walt Disney World Village, Pleasure Island is a six-acre nighttime entertainment center where one cover charge will get a visitor into any of seven nightclubs. The clubs have different themes and feature a variety of shows and activities. Music ranges from pop-rock to country and western to jazz. For the more sedentary (or exhausted) there is a ten-screen movie complex, or for the hungry, several restaurants, including a much-hyped Planet Hollywood.

Discovery Island

Discovery Island is a small zoological park situated on an island in Bay Lake. Featuring birdlife and tropical plants, Discovery Island can be accessed by boat from the Magic Kingdom or Fort Wilderness docks. Low-key and quite scenic, the tiny park offers a number of short, circular trails that guests can explore at their own pace. Discovery Island also offers three educational shows featuring resident birds and wildlife.

—— Should I Go to Walt Disney World If I've Been to Disneyland in California?

Walt Disney World is a much larger and more varied entertainment complex than is Disneyland. There is no EPCOT Center, Disney-MGM Studios, Blizzard Beach, or Typhoon Lagoon at Disneyland. To be specific, Disneyland is roughly comparable to the Magic Kingdom theme park at Walt Disney World. Both the Magic Kingdom and Disneyland are arranged by "lands" accessible from a central hub and connected to the entrance by a Main Street. Both parks feature many rides and attractions of the same name: Space Mountain, Jungle Cruise, Pirates of the Caribbean, It's a Small World, and Dumbo, the Flying Elephant, to name a few. Interestingly, however, the same name does not necessarily connote the same experience. Pirates of the Caribbean at Disneyland is much longer and more elaborate than its Walt Disney World counterpart. Space Mountain is somewhat wilder in California, and Dumbo is about the same in both places.

Disneyland is more intimate than the Magic Kingdom since it doesn't have the room for expansion enjoyed by the Florida park. Pedestrian thoroughfares are more narrow, and everything from Big Thunder Mountain to the Castle is scaled down somewhat. Large crowds are less taxing at the Magic Kingdom since there is more room for them to disperse.

At Disneyland, however, there are dozens of little surprises: small unheralded attractions tucked away in nooks and crannies of the park, which give Disneyland a special charm and variety that the Magic Kingdom lacks. And, of course, Disneyland has more of the stamp of Walt Disney's personal touch.

For additional information on Disneyland, see *The Unofficial Guide to Disneyland* by Bob Sehlinger, Macmillan U.S.A.

PART ONE: Planning
Before You Leave Home

Gathering Information

In addition to this guide, we recommend that you obtain copies of the following:

1. The Disney Travel Company Florida Brochure. This full-color booklet describes Walt Disney World in its entirety and lists rates for all Disney resort hotels and campgrounds. Also described are Walt Disney World package vacations. The brochure is available from most full-service travel agents, or can be obtained by calling the Walt Disney Travel Company at (800) 327-2996.

2. The Official Map of the Walt Disney World Resort. Also called the Walt Disney World Property Map, this large folding map contains detailed layouts of the Magic Kingdom, EPCOT Center, and the Disney-MGM Studios on one side, and a good road map of Walt Disney World on the opposite side. The map can be obtained for the asking by calling Walt Disney World Information at (407) 824-4321.

3. Walt Disney World Guidebook for Guests with Disabilities. If members of your party are sight or hearing impaired, or partially or wholly nonambulatory, you will find this small guide very helpful. To receive a copy, call (407) 824-4321.

4. Orlando MagiCard. If you are considering lodging outside of Walt Disney World, or if you think you might patronize some of the attractions and restaurants outside of Walt Disney World, it is worthwhile to obtain an Orlando MagiCard, a Vacation Planner, and the Orlando Official Accommodations Guide from the Orlando/Orange County Convention & Visitors Bureau at (800) 255-5786 or (407) 363-5874. The MagiCard makes you eligible for discounts at area hotels, restaurants, and attractions (excluding Walt Disney World). When you call the above number, you will have to endure various recorded menu options. At the end of the recording, press "0" to get a live person on the line. Request a MagiCard, a Vacation Planner, and an Orlando Official Accommodations Guide (all free). The line is manned during weekday business hours. Allow four weeks for delivery.

5. Florida Traveler Discount Guide. Another good source of lodging, restaurant, and attraction discounts throughout the state of Florida, the Florida Traveler Discount Guide can be obtained by calling (904) 371-3948, Monday–Friday, 8 A.M. to 5 P.M., EST. Published by Exit Information Guide, the discount guide is free, but you will be charged $3 ($5 U.S. to Canada) for postage and handling. Similar guides to other states are available at the same number.

6. Kissimmee–St. Cloud Tour & Travel Sales Guide. This full-color directory of hotels and attractions is one of the most complete available, and is particularly of interest to those who intend to book accommodations outside of Walt Disney World. In addition to hotels and motels, the directory also lists rental houses, timeshares, and condominiums. To receive a copy, contact the Kissimmee–St. Cloud Convention and Visitors Bureau at (800) 327-9159.

Request information as far in advance as possible and allow about four weeks for delivery. Make a checklist of the information you have requested and be prepared to follow up if you have not received your material within six weeks. Sometimes, as a Garland, Texas man notes, persistence is the key:

> Per your advice, I called WDW to get the "Florida Vacation
> Guide." They never sent it. Called back two more times, and
> finally got it the week before we left — in fact, got two."

Disney Info On-Line

A lot of late-breaking news is available on-line through Prodigy, CompuServe, America Online, and other on-line user services, including the Internet. Much of this information is supplied by recently returned Disney vacationers and even Walt Disney World employees. There is a newsgroup on usenet called rec.arts.disney that provides up-to-date information and answers questions concerning just about anything at Walt Disney World.

Additional information concerning Walt Disney World can be obtained at the public library, at travel agencies, from AAA, or by calling or writing any of the following:

Important Walt Disney World Telephone Numbers

General Information   (407) 824-4321

When you call the main information number you will be offered a menu of options for recorded information on theme park operating hours, recreation areas, shopping, entertainment complexes, tickets and admissions, resort reservations, and directions by highway and from the airport. If you are using a rotary dial telephone, your call will be forwarded to a Disney information representative. If you are using a touchtone phone and have a question that is not covered by recorded information, press zero (0) at any time to speak to a Disney representative.

Accommodations/Reservations	(407) 934-7639
	or (407) 824-8000
All-Star Resorts	(407) 939-5000
Beach Club Resort	(407) 934-8000
Blizzard Beach	(407) 560-3400
Boardwalk Resort	N/A
Caribbean Beach Resort	(407) 934-3400
Contemporary Resort	(407) 824-1000
Convention Information	(407) 828-3200
Dining Reservations for Walt Disney World Lodging Guests	(407) 939-3463
If calling from:	
Home	(407) 939-3463
WDW guest room	Dial 55 for same day
	Dial 56 for 1–3 day advance
WDW campground	Dial 44 for same day
	Dial 45 for 1–3 day advance
Discovery Island Information	(407) 824-3784
Disney Institute	(800) 746-5858
Disney Village Marketplace	(407) 828-3800
Dixie Landings Resort	(407) 934-6000
Educational Programs	(407) 354-1855
Fishing Reservations	
& Information	(407) 824-2621
Fort Wilderness Campground	(407) 824-2900
Grand Floridian Beach Resort	(407) 824-3000
Guided Tour Information	(407) 824-4321
Horseback Tours Reservations	(407) 824-2832
Learning Programs	
Business Programs	(407) 824-7997
Other Programs	(407) 354-1855
Lost and Found for articles lost:	
Yesterday or before	
(All parks)	(407) 824-4245

Today at Magic Kingdom	(407) 824-4521
Today at EPCOT Center	(407) 560-6105
Today at Disney-MGM	(407) 560-4668
Medical Care in WDW	(407) 648-9234
Merchandise Mail Order	(407) 363-6200
	or (800) 272-6201
Movie Information	
AMC Pleasure Island	(407) 827-1300
Disney films at hotels	(407) 824-4321
Ocala Information Center	(904) 854-0770
Pleasure Island Information	(407) 934-6374
Polynesian Resort	(407) 824-2000
Port Orleans Resort	(407) 934-5000
Resort Dining and	
Recreational Information	(407) 939-3463
River Country Information	(407) 824-2760
Shades of Green	
U.S. Armed Forces Hotel	(407) 934-7639
Tee Times and Golf Studio	(407) 824-2270
Telecommunication for the Deaf	(407) 827-5141
Tennis Reservations/Lessons	(407) 824-3578
Typhoon Lagoon Information	(407) 560-4141
Vacation Club Resort	(407) 827-7700
Village Resort	(407) 827-1100
Walt Disney Travel Company	(407) 828-3232
Walt Disney World Dolphin	(407) 934-4000
Walt Disney World Swan	(407) 934-3000
Wilderness Lodge Resort	(407) 824-3200
Yacht Club Resort	(407) 934-7000

Important Walt Disney World Addresses

Walt Disney World Information/Guest Letters
P.O. Box 10040
Lake Buena Vista, FL 32830-0040

Walt Disney World Central Reservations
P.O. Box 10100
Lake Buena Vista, FL 32830-0100

Convention and Banquet Information
P.O. Box 10000
Lake Buena Vista, FL 32830-1000

Walt Disney World Educational Programs
Wonders of Walt Disney World (Ages 10–15)
The Disney Learning Adventure (Adults)
P.O. Box 10000
Lake Buena Vista, FL 32830-1000

Merchandise Mail Order (Guest Service Mail Order)
P.O. Box 10070
Lake Buena Vista, FL 32830-0070

Walt Disney World Ticket Mail Order
P.O. Box 10030
Lake Buena Vista, FL 32830-0030

When to Go to Walt Disney World

—— *Selecting the Time of Year for Your Visit*

Walt Disney World is busiest of all Christmas Day through New Year's Day. Thanksgiving weekend, the week of Washington's Birthday, spring break for colleges, and the two weeks around Easter are also extremely busy. To give you some idea of what busy means at Walt Disney World, up to 92,000 people have toured the Magic Kingdom alone on a single day! While this level of attendance is far from typical, the possibility of its occurrence should forewarn all but the ignorant and the foolish from challenging this mega-attraction at its busiest periods.

The least busy time of all is from after the Thanksgiving weekend until the week before Christmas. The next slowest times are September through the weekend preceding Thanksgiving, January 4th through the first half of February, and the week following Easter through early June. March is dicey. Crowds ebb and flow depending on spring break schedules. At the risk of being blasphemous, our research team was so impressed with the relative ease of touring in the fall and other "off" periods that we would rather take our children out of school for a week than battle the summer crowds.

Many readers share their thoughts about the best time of year to visit Walt Disney World. The following two letters are fairly representative. First, from a Centerville, Ohio, family:

> Catching on to the "off season," we took the kids out of school and went to WDW in mid-May. So did a lot of other people. In fact, there were enough people there for me to think crowds must be increasing in the off-season as more people wise up about avoiding the masses. If I'm wrong, and this really was half the summer crowd, "high season" these days must be total and complete gridlock. I wouldn't wish it on my worst enemy.

And from a West Plains, Missouri, mom:

> We have visited WDW 3 times in the past 8 years, each time in the second week of June. Each time the crowds were worse, and

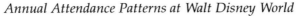

Annual Attendance Patterns at Walt Disney World

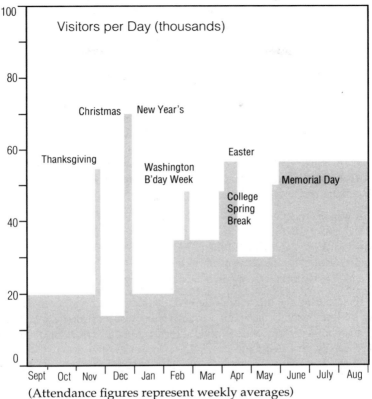

(Attendance figures represent weekly averages)

this time they were so big that we won't go at this time of year anymore.

The Down Side of Off-Season Touring

Though we strongly recommend going to Walt Disney World in the fall or spring, you should understand that there are certain trade-offs. The parks often open late and close early on fall and spring days. When the parks open as late as 10 A.M., everyone arrives at about the same time, making it hard to beat the crowd. A late opening coupled with an early closing drastically reduces the number of hours available to tour. Even when crowds are small, it is difficult to see a big park like the Magic

Kingdom or EPCOT Center between 10 A.M. and 6 P.M. Early closing (before 8 P.M.) also usually means that evening parades or fireworks are eliminated. And, because these are slow times of the year at Walt Disney World, you can likewise anticipate that some rides and attractions may be closed for maintenance or renovation. Finally, you should know that central Florida temperatures fluctuate wildly during the late fall, winter, and early spring; daytime lows in the 40's are not uncommon.

Given the choice, however, we would never go to Walt Disney World in the summer or during a holiday period. To us, small crowds, bargain prices, and stress-free touring are well worth risking a little cold weather or a couple of closed attractions.

Most readers who have tried Walt Disney World at varying times of year agree. A gentleman from Ottawa, Ontario, who toured in early December wrote:

> It was the most enjoyable trip [to Walt Disney World] I have ever had, and I can't imagine going [back] to Disney World when it is crowded. Even without the crowds we were still very tired by afternoon. Fighting crowds certainly would have made a hellish trip. We will never go again at any other time.

Even during the off-season, the size of the crowd on a given day can vary enormously. Usually this variance is the result of some special program or admission incentive aimed at locals. A mother from Bridgewater, New Jersey, reported that:

> Although you mentioned the fact that school trips are [common] in EPCOT during September and October, we were unprepared for the impact these groups had, especially since the kids are often unsupervised. From what I can see, the park can literally be enjoyed only on weekends during these months. Our visit was completely destroyed by unsupervised hordes of 10 to 12 year olds.

A Staten Island, New York, family found weekdays tranquil, but ran into a mess at the Magic Kingdom on Saturday, stating:

> Saturday (at MK) was rather horrifying. There were what seemed to be hordes of "day trippers" (Scout troops, church groups, the Demolay Temple from Tampa, etc.). Even Tom Sawyer's Island was no idyllic oasis at 11:30 A.M. We left at about 1:30 P.M. for a swim and nap back at our motel, and returned at 8 P.M. (the MK was open until midnight that night) to discover that the crowds had not thinned appreciably.

Walt Disney World Weather

	Average Daily Low	Average Daily High	Average Daily Temperature	Avg. Daily Humidity (%)	Avg. Rainfall per Month (inches)	No. Days of Rain per Month
January	49°	72°	61°	74	2.1	6
February	50°	73°	62°	71	2.8	7
March	55°	78°	67°	71	3.2	8
April	60°	84°	72°	69	2.2	6
May	66°	88°	77°	72	3.9	9
June	71°	91°	81°	77	7.4	14
July	73°	92°	82°	79	7.8	17
August	73°	92°	82°	80	6.3	16
September	73°	90°	81°	80	5.6	14
October	65°	84°	75°	77	2.8	9
November	57°	78°	68°	76	1.8	6
December	51°	73°	62°	76	1.9	6

Hurricane Season

The likelihood of tangling with the locals in September and October can be significantly reduced by avoiding the Magic Kingdom on Saturday and EPCOT Center on weekdays. Usually the presence of large groups tapers off in all of the parks by the beginning of November.

—— *Selecting the Day of the Week for Your Visit*

Selecting the best day of the week to visit a specific Walt Disney World theme park requires analysis of several variables. Entering into the equation are:

1. The time of year of your visit (holiday, summer, or off-season);

2. Attendance patterns for each day of the week at the respective parks;

3. Whether you are staying in a Walt Disney World hotel or campground (thereby making yourself eligible for early entry to the theme parks on specified days of the week);

4. The traveling habits of people coming to Walt Disney World from outside of Florida.

A typical vacation scenario during the summer would be for a family to arrive in the Orlando area on Sunday, visit the Magic Kingdom and EPCOT Center on Monday and Tuesday, visit Disney-MGM Studios on Wednesday, and go to Typhoon Lagoon or a non-Disney area attraction on Thursday. Friday is often reserved for heading home or to another Florida destination. If this was all we had to consider, we could recommend Fridays and Sundays as the best days all year long to avoid crowded conditions at the theme parks.

During the off-season, however, the Disney people initiate dozens of special promotions to attract the local population to Walt Disney World. Because these folks are not on vacation, they tend to visit the theme parks on the weekend. During the fall, late winter, and spring, you might encounter larger crowds on a weekend than on a weekday, especially at the Magic Kingdom.

In addition to its special promotions, Disney also operates a cooperative program with local school administrations that brings tens of thousands of school children to EPCOT Center for field trips in March and September. Similarly, in the late spring, the Disney theme parks are full of high school students on "senior days" or prom nights. Many of these programs are held on weekdays.

The most significant shift in daily attendance patterns is the result of an early-entry program for guests staying at Walt Disney World resort hotels and campgrounds (but not for guests at Disney Village Hotels). Initiated in 1993, the program originally applied only to the Magic Kingdom and operated on four days of the week. In 1994, the program was amended to include EPCOT Center and the Disney-MGM Studios. Each day of the week, Disney World lodging guests are invited to enter a designated theme park one hour before the general public is admitted. Although the early-entry program is frequently changed, and may possibly be abandoned altogether, here is how it looked at the time we went to press:

Monday	Magic Kingdom
Tuesday	EPCOT Center
Wednesday	Disney-MGM Studios
Thursday	Magic Kingdom
Friday	EPCOT Center
Saturday	Magic Kingdom
Sunday	Disney-MGM Studios

During the early-entry hour, Disney resort guests can enjoy certain attractions opened early for their benefit. At the Magic Kingdom, for example, attractions in Fantasyland, as well as Space Mountain and the Grand Prix Raceway in Tomorrowland, are usually open to the early arrivals. At EPCOT Center, The Living Seas, The Land, and Journey Into Imagination open early, and at the Disney-MGM Studios early entrants can enjoy the Twilight Zone Tower of Terror, The Great Movie Ride, and Star Tours. The specific attractions scheduled for early entry change from time to time.

How Early Entry Affects Attendance at the Theme Parks

The effect of the early-entry program on attendance is pronounced at all three of the major theme parks, especially during the busier times of the year. Each day, a vast number of Walt Disney World resort guests, not unexpectedly, tour whichever theme park is designated for early entry. If the Magic Kingdom is designated for early entry on Monday, for example, this means that the Magic Kingdom will be more crowded than usual on that day, and that EPCOT Center and the Disney-MGM Studios will be less crowded (because most of the Walt Disney World lodging guests will be at the Magic Kingdom). Accordingly, you can expect EPCOT Center and the Disney-MGM Studios to be more crowded on the days when those parks are respectively slated for early entry.

During holiday periods and the summer, when Disney hotels are full, the early-entry program makes a tremendous difference in crowd levels at each of the parks. The program funnels so many people into whichever park is scheduled for early entry that the park fills by about 10 A.M. and is practically gridlocked by noon. Whatever advantage you gain by taking advantage of early entry first thing in the morning is completely offset by horrendous crowds later in the day. Our advice during the busier times of year, for both those lodging inside Walt Disney World and for those staying outside of Walt Disney World, is to avoid whichever park is scheduled for early entry.

An alternative strategy for those eligible for early entry is to take advantage of early entry, but only until the designated park begins to get crowded. At that time, exit the early-entry park and head for one of the other parks. This plan works particularly well at the Magic Kingdom for families with small children who love the attractions in Fantasyland. If you elect to use your early-entry privileges, be sure to be among the first early entrants in the park.

A mother of three from Lee Summit, Missouri, wrote sharing her experiences with early entry:

Our first full day at WDW, we went to the Magic Kingdom. This was on a Monday, an early entry day for resort guests. We were there at 7:30 and were able to walk onto all the rides in Fantasyland with no wait. At 8:45 we positioned ourselves at the Adventureland rope and ran towards Splash Mountain when the rope dropped. We were able to ride Splash Mountain with no wait (switching off), and then Big Thunder with about a 15 minute wait (switching off). We then went straight to the Jungle Cruise and the wait was already 30 minutes, so we skipped it. The park became incredibly crowded as the day progressed, and we were all exhausted from getting up so early to get there for early entry. We left the park around noon. After that day, I resolved to avoid early entry days and instead be at a non-early entry park about 1/2 hour before official opening time. This worked much better for us.

A lady from Ann Arbor, Michigan (who is clearly working overtime trying to figure all this stuff out) had this to say:

We are starting to think that reverse-reverse psychology might work: Disney opens one park earlier for all their guests, so all the guests go to that park, but then, everyone buys your book in which you tell them not to go to that park because all Disney guests are

there, so no-one goes to that park, therefore we can go to that park because people think it's going to be packed and they avoid it.
What do you think?

Because the Disney people have changed the early-entry program numerous times in the past three years, we suggest you call Walt Disney Information at (407) 824-4321 before you leave home to verify the early-entry schedule during your stay.

Assuming the early-entry days do not change, we recommend the following:

Off-Season Touring.   If you are a Disney resort or campground guest visiting Walt Disney World during the off-season and other less busy times of year, by all means take advantage of your early-entry privileges. You will get a jump on the general public and add an extra hour to what, in the off-season, is already a short touring day. If you stay outside Walt Disney World and are not eligible for early entry, avoid whichever park is scheduled for early entry and visit one of the other two parks instead.

Summer and Holiday Touring.   If you visit during the summer or over a holiday period, *avoid* whichever park is scheduled for early entry. This is true regardless of whether you stay in or out of Walt Disney World or are eligible or ineligible for early entry. For all theme park visitors, the best days to visit the respective theme parks during the summer and holiday periods are as follows:

Best Days to Visit During Summer & Holiday Periods

Magic Kingdom	1	Friday
	2	Sunday
	3	Wednesday
	4	Tuesday
EPCOT Center	1	Sunday
	2	Saturday
	3	Thursday
	4	Monday
Disney-MGM Studios	1	Saturday
	2	Friday
	3	Monday
	4	Thursday

If you visit Walt Disney World over a major holiday period, you can expect huge crowds at each of the parks every day. If you have early-entry privileges, use them in the early morning and then head for another park around 10 A.M. If you are not accorded early-entry privileges, avoid any park for which early entry is in effect. During longer holidays like Easter and Christmas, crowds build almost exponentially as the big day approaches, culminating on the holiday itself.

If Disney changes the early-entry days and you have to puzzle this out on your own, remember the following:

1. Weekend days (Friday, Saturday, Sunday) will usually be less crowded than weekdays during the summer (except on holiday weekends).

2. Weekends often tend to be more crowded during the off-season, particularly in the spring and fall when the weather is nice. For the most part, however, off-season weekends cannot compare (in terms of crowd levels) to weekdays or weekends during the summer or holiday periods.

3. All days, but particularly weekend days, are crowded during Thanksgiving, Christmas and New Years, and Easter. Also expect huge crowds over three-day weekends for national holidays like Presidents' Day.

4. You must balance the least crowded days of the week (for the time of year of your visit) with an estimation of the impact of early entry. Early entry has a greater effect on the Magic Kingdom and the Disney-MGM Studios than on EPCOT Center. Regardless, as a rule of thumb, all guests should avoid whichever theme park is operating on an early-entry schedule during the summer and holiday periods. For both Disney resort guests and for guests staying outside of Walt Disney World, the idea is to anticipate which of the three parks will be least crowded on a given day, and then be one of the first guests through turnstiles when that park opens.

5. During the busier times of year, Disney resort guests who insist on taking advantage of their early-entry privileges should be on hand at the park where early entry is scheduled 1½ hours before the official opening time. Tour until the park becomes crowded, and then depart to spend the rest of the day at one of the other parks.

—— Packed Park Compensation Plan

The thought of teeming, jostling throngs jockeying for position in endless lines under the baking Fourth of July sun is enough to wilt the

will and ears of the most ardent Mouseketeer. Why would anyone go to Walt Disney World during a major holiday period? Indeed, if you have never been to Walt Disney World, and you thought you would just drop in for a few rides and a little look-see on such a day, you might be better off shooting yourself in the foot. The Disney folks, however, being Disney folks, feel kind of bad about those long, long lines and the basically impossible touring conditions on packed days and compensate their patrons with a no-less-than-incredible array of first-rate live entertainment and happenings.

Throughout the day the party goes on with shows, parades, concerts, and pageantry. In the evening, particularly, there is so much going on that you have to make some tough choices. There are concerts, parades, light shows, laser shows, fireworks, and dance productions occurring almost continually in all the parks. No question about it, you can go to Walt Disney World on the Fourth of July (or on any other extended hours, crowded day), never get on a ride, and still get your money's worth five times over. Admittedly, it's not the ideal situation for a first-timer who really wants to see the theme parks, but for anyone else it's a great party.

If you decide to go on one of the parks' "big" days, we suggest that you arrive an hour and 20 minutes before the stated opening time. Use the Walt Disney World one-day touring plan of your choice until about 1 P.M. and then take the monorail to a Disney resort hotel for lunch and relaxation. Local Floridians visiting Walt Disney World on holidays often chip in and rent a room for the group (make reservations well in advance) in one of the Disney hotels, thus affording a place to meet, relax, have a drink, or change clothes prior to swimming. A comparable arrangement can be made at other nearby hotels as long as they furnish a shuttle service to and from the parks. After an early dinner, return to the park of your choice for the evening's festivities, which get cranked up about 8 P.M.

*PART TWO: Making the Most of
Your Time and Money*

Allocating Money

How much you spend depends on how long you stay at Walt Disney World. During Walt Disney World's first decade, a family with a week's vacation could enjoy the Magic Kingdom and River Country and still have several days for the beach or other area attractions. Since the opening of EPCOT Center in 1982, however, Walt Disney World has steadily been enlarging to monopolize the same family's entire week. Today, with the addition of Blizzard Beach, Typhoon Lagoon, the Disney-MGM Studios, and Pleasure Island, you had best allocate five days for a whirlwind tour (or seven days if you're old-fashioned and insist on a little relaxation during your vacation). If you do not have five or seven days, or think you might want to venture beyond the edge of "The World," be prepared to make some hard choices.

The theme parks, studios, and swimming attractions are **huge,** require a lot of walking, and sometimes a lot of waiting in lines. Moving in and among typically large crowds all day is exhausting. The unrelenting central Florida sun often zaps the most hearty traveler, making tempers short. In our many visits to Walt Disney World we observed, particularly on hot summer days, a dramatic transition from happy, enthusiastic tourists upon arrival to zombies plodding along later in the day. Visitors who began their day enjoying the wonders of the Disney imagination lapsed into an exhausted, production-line mentality ("We've got two more rides in Fantasyland, then we can go back to the hotel.").

We recommend that you approach Walt Disney World the same way you would approach an eight-course Italian dinner: with plenty of time between courses. The best way not to have fun is to attempt to cram too much into too little time.

—— *Prices Subject to Change without Notice*

Book reviewers who complain that prices quoted in guidebooks are out of date should note that Walt Disney World ticket prices seem to change about as often as the prime rate. If we were publishing a daily newspaper, maybe we could keep up. But since we are covering Walt Disney World in a book, we've decided to throw in the towel; no more listing admission prices. We will tell you this much: expect to pay about $40 for an adult 1-Day/One-Park Only Ticket, about $132 for a 4-Day Value Pass, about $146 for a 4-Day Park-Hopper Pass, $198 for a 5-Day World-Hopper Pass. Annual Passports cost about $246, and a Florida Resident's Seasonal Passport runs around $139. All of the admission cost estimates above include tax.

—— Walt Disney World Admission Options

There are basically seven Walt Disney World admission options (several with silly names):

1. 1-Day/One-Park Only Ticket
2. 4-Day Value Pass
3. 4-Day Park-Hopper Pass
4. 5-Day World-Hopper Pass
5. Be Our Guest Pass
6. Annual Passport
7. Florida Resident's Passport

The **1-Day Ticket** is good for admission and unlimited use of "attractions and experiences" at the Magic Kingdom *or* EPCOT Center *or* the Disney-MGM Studios, but does *not* provide same-day admission to more than one of the three.

The **4-Day Value Pass** provides four days of separate admissions: a one-day/one-park admission each to the Magic Kingdom, EPCOT Center, and the Disney-MGM Studios, plus an additional one-day "wild card" admission that can be used to revisit one park of your choice. The Magic Kingdom part of the pass can only be used at the Magic Kingdom. Similarly, the EPCOT Center part of the pass is limited specifically to EPCOT Center, and the Disney-MGM Studios part of the pass is good only at the Studios. With the 4-Day Value Pass, you could visit the Magic Kingdom on Monday (using the Magic Kingdom admission) and EPCOT Center on Tuesday (using the EPCOT Center admission). If you wanted to return to EPCOT Center on Wednesday, you would have to use the "wild card" admission. At that point, you would have one admission remaining on your 4-Day Value Pass, a Disney-MGM Studios admission good only at the Studios. A guest who visits the Magic Kingdom in the morning and then goes to EPCOT Center for dinner, would have to use two of the four admissions included in the 4-Day Value Pass on the same day. You can, however, come and go as you please at the *same* theme park on a given day as long as you get your hand stamped for reentry as you leave the park.

The **4-Day Park-Hopper Pass** provides same-day admission to the Magic Kingdom, EPCOT Center, and the Disney-MGM Studios. With this admission you can tour the Studios in the morning, eat dinner at EPCOT Center, and stop by the Magic Kingdom for the evening parades and fireworks.

The **5-Day World-Hopper Pass** provides same-day admission to all three of the major theme parks, unlimited use of the transportation systems, plus admission to Pleasure Island, Blizzard Beach, Typhoon Lagoon, River Country, and Discovery Island. Admission to the minor parks is unlimited for a seven-day period beginning the day the pass is first used at one of the three major parks. With the 5-Day World-Hopper Pass, you can bounce from park to park all day long and use only one of your five days' admission.

The 4-Day Value and Park-Hopper passes, and the 5-Day World-Hopper Passes do not have to be used on consecutive days and are, in fact, good forever. 4-Day Park-Hopper Passes can be upgraded to 5-Day World-Hopper Passes as long as they have at least one day's admission remaining, by paying the difference between the four-day and five-day pass price.

If you buy the 4-Day Park-Hopper Pass or 5-Day World-Hopper Pass at the Transportation and Ticket Center or at the entrance to the theme parks, you must have your photograph taken and laminated on the pass. Needless to say, this procedure slows down the ticket purchasing process. The purpose of this additional bureaucracy, according to Disney, is to inhibit the resale of passes on the black market.

The **Be Our Guest Pass** is another admissions program for Walt Disney World lodging and campground guests. It provides the same benefits as the World-Hopper Pass (described above), but can be purchased for *any* length of stay from one night to two days or longer. The Be Our Guest program is the first time Walt Disney World has offered a comprehensive admission option (all major and minor parks) for stays shorter than four days. Be Our Guest Passes additionally provide a cost savings of about 7% compared to the four- and five-day passes. On the negative side, Be Our Guest Passes are good only for the guest's inclusive length of stay, while unused days on the Value Passes and the Hopper Passes are good forever.

The **Annual Passport** is good for unlimited use of the major theme parks for one year. An add-on option can be purchased that also provides unlimited use of the minor theme parks. In addition to theme park admission, Annual Pass holders are accorded a number of perks, including complimentary parking and the privilege of making advance reservations at Walt Disney World restaurants.

The **Florida Resident's Passport.** In 1995, Walt Disney World expanded the admission options for Florida residents. For the time being Florida residents can select from a veritable menu of choices, including:

Florida Resident's Seasonal Passport. This is a cut-rate pass (about $140 for adults) that allows the holder to enjoy unlimited use of the three major theme parks during specific, quieter times of the year.

Florida Resident's EPCOT After 4 P.M. Passport. At about $75 for adults, this pass allows Florida residents to visit EPCOT Center on any day after 4 P.M.

Florida Resident's One-Park Annual Passport. This pass, at around $105 for adults, provides Florida residents with annual passport privileges to their choice of any one of the three major theme parks.

Florida Resident's Annual Passport. Annual passports are available to Florida residents at about 9% off the regular price.

Florida Resident's One-Day Discounts. At certain slower times of the year Florida residents are offered discounts on One-Park/One-Day passes. In 1995 these discounts ran about 28% off the regular price of a one-day pass for those under 55 years old, and a whopping 43% off for seniors (55 years and older).

While applicants must prove Florida residency to be eligible, it is not necessary to have a Florida driver's license or live in Florida year-round. A utility bill in your name for a Florida address will suffice.

—— Which Admission Should You Buy?

If you only have one day to spend, select the park that most interests you and buy the One-Day/One-Park Only Ticket. If you have two days and do not plan to return to Florida for a couple of years, buy two 1-Day Tickets (or a Be Our Guest Pass if you are a Disney lodging guest). If you think you might be passing through the area again in the next year or two, go ahead and spring for a four- or five-day pass. Use two days of admission to see as much as you can and save the remaining days for another trip. Remember that with the five-day passes, admission to Pleasure Island, Blizzard Beach, Typhoon Lagoon, River Country, and

Discovery Island expires within seven days of the first time you use your pass at the Magic Kingdom, EPCOT Center, or the Disney-MGM Studios.

If you plan to spend three or more days at Walt Disney World, buy a four- or five-day pass. If you live in Florida or plan to spend seven or more days in the major theme parks, the Annual Passport at about $246 is a good buy. If you live in Florida, and do not mind being restricted to visiting Walt Disney World at designated off-peak times of year, the Florida Resident's Seasonal Pass should be considered.

If you visit Walt Disney World every year, here's a way to save big bucks on admission. Let's say you usually take your vacation during the summer months. This year, plan your Disney vacation for July and buy an Annual Passport. Next year, schedule your trip in June. Because the Annual Passports start on the date of purchase, the passports you buy this year will still be good for next year's vacation if you go a month earlier! If you spend four days each year at Walt Disney World (8 days altogether for the two consecutive years), you'll knock your daily admission cost down to about $30 per adult per day. The longer your Disney vacation, of course, the more you save with the Annual Passport. If you visit the theme parks for seven days each year, your admission charge will be less than $18 per day.

—— *The Black Market*

Many readers write asking if they can use remaining admissions on partially redeemed four- and five-day passes brought home by relatives. The facts are as follows:

1. The pass is sold to the purchaser on a non-transferable basis. The pass states on the back, "To be valid this Pass must be used by the same person for all days."

2. On passes sold prior to February 1994, there is nothing on the pass that in any way identifies the purchaser. On multi-day, all-park passes sold subsequent to that date, the pass bearer's photograph and signature appear on the pass.

3. Disney admission attendants do not request a receipt or any other proof of purchase for admission passes.

A corollary question concerns what to do with any unused admissions on four- or five-day passes that you purchase legally during your Disney vacation. Our advice is to put the passes someplace safe and hang onto them. For starters, the resale of unused multi-day passes is a misdemeanor, and the friendly guy offering you cash for your unused ticket may be a security officer. Secondly, because Disney raises admission prices almost every year, using an old pass during your next visit will save you some bucks.

—— Where to Buy Your Admission in Advance

You can buy your admission at a Disney Store before you leave home or, if you're driving, at Disney's Ocala Information Center at exit 68 on I-75. If you plan to fly to Walt Disney World, you will be able to purchase tickets at the airport Disney Store.

Tickets are also available through the mail from the Walt Disney World Ticket Mail Order Service (see page 29). In addition, you can purchase tickets at most of the Walt Disney World hotels.

—— Where Not to Buy Your Admission in Advance

Because admission passes to Walt Disney World are not discounted, any offers of free or cut-rate tickets should trigger warning signals. Anyone offering free tickets to any attraction in the Orlando/Kissimmee area is probably selling real estate or time-share condominiums. You may actually receive a free ticket, but you will have to subject yourself to a lengthy site inspection and/or high-pressure sales pitch.

Many hotels outside of Walt Disney World make tickets to area attractions available through independent travel brokers who maintain a kiosk or desk in the hotel's lobby. While these brokers are legitimate operators, the only advantage to buying from them is convenience. In the case of Disney admission passes, expect to pay normal Disney prices or a little more for your tickets if you purchase them from an independent.

—— How Much Does It Cost to Go to Walt Disney World for a Day?

Let's say we have a family of four, Mom and Dad, Tim (age 12), and Sandy (age 8), driving their own car and staying outside of Walt Disney World. Since they plan to be in the area for a week they intend to buy 4-Day Park-Hopper Passes. Here is how much a typical day would cost, excluding lodging and transportation:

Breakfast for four at Denny's with tax & tip	$21.50
EPCOT Center parking fee	5.00

One day's admission on a 4-Day Park-Hopper Pass

Dad:	Adult 4-Day with tax = $146 divided by four (days)	36.50
Mom:	Adult 4-Day with tax = $146 divided by four (days)	36.50
Tim:	Adult 4-Day with tax = $146 divided by four (days)	36.50
Sandy:	Child 4-Day with tax = $117 divided by four (days)	29.25

Morning break (soda or coffee)	6.75
Fast-food lunch (sandwich or burger, fries, soda), no tip	26.00
Afternoon break (soda and popcorn)	14.35
Dinner at Italy (no alcoholic beverages), with tax & tip	86.00
Souvenirs (Mickey T-shirts for Tim and Sandy) with tax*	33.50
One-day Total (does not include lodging or transportation)	$331.85

*Cheer up, you won't have to buy souvenirs every day.

Allocating Time

Which Park to See First?

This question is less academic than it appears at first glance, especially if there are children or teenagers in your party. Children who see the Magic Kingdom first expect more of the same type of entertainment at EPCOT Center and the Disney-MGM Studios. At EPCOT Center they are often disappointed by the educational orientation and more serious tone (many adults react the same way). Disney-MGM offers some pretty wild action, but here, too, the general presentation is educational and more adult.

For first-time visitors especially, see EPCOT Center first; you will be able to enjoy it fully without having been preconditioned to think of Disney entertainment as solely in the fantasy/adventure genre. Parties that include children should definitely see EPCOT Center first. Children will be more likely to judge and enjoy EPCOT Center on its own merits if they see it first, and will be more relaxed and patient in their touring.

Next, see the Disney-MGM Studios. The Studios help both young and old make a fluid transition from the imposing EPCOT Center to the fanciful Magic Kingdom. Also, because the Studios are smaller, you will not have to walk as much or stay as long. Save the Magic Kingdom for last.

Operating Hours

It cannot be said that the Disney folks are not flexible when it comes to hours of operation for the parks. They run a dozen or more different operating schedules during the year, making it advisable to call (407) 824-4321 for the **exact** hours of operation the day before you arrive. In the off-season, the parks may be open only from 10 A.M. to 6 P.M. At busy times of the year, by contrast, the parks may be open from 8 A.M. until 2 A.M. the following morning.

—— *Official Opening Time vs. Real Opening Time*

The hours of operation that the Disney folks will give you when you call are "official hours." In actuality the parks will open earlier. If the official hours of operation are 9 A.M. to 9 P.M., for example, the Main Street section of the Magic Kingdom will open at 8 or 8:30 A.M. and the remainder of the park will open at 8:30 or 9 A.M. If the official opening time for the Magic Kingdom is 8 A.M., and you are eligible for early entry, you will actually be able to enter the park at 6:30 A.M.

Many visitors, relying upon the accuracy of the information disseminated by Disney Guest Relations, arrive at the stated opening time to find the park packed with people. If you visit the Magic Kingdom, for example, on an early-entry day and enter the park when the general public is admitted, you will always find the park swarming with Walt Disney World lodging guests.

The Disney folks publish their hours of operation well in advance, but allow themselves the flexibility to react to gate conditions on a day-by-day basis. Based on a survey of local hotel reservations, Disney traffic controllers estimate how many visitors to expect on a given day. To avoid bottlenecks at the parking facilities and ticket windows, the theme parks frequently open early, absorbing the crowds as they arrive.

If you do not have early-entry privileges, plan to tour a park where early entry is *not* in effect, arriving 50 minutes before the official opening time regardless of the time of year of your visit. If you happen to go on a major holiday, arrive an hour and 20 minutes in advance of the official opening time.

If you are a Disney resort guest and want to take advantage of early entry, arrive at the resort for which early entry is in effect one hour and 30 minutes before the time the park is scheduled to open for the general public. If you are depending on Disney transportation, you will find that buses, boats, and monorails serving the early-entry park will initiate operations about two hours before the published opening time (when the general public is admitted).

At the end of the day, the Disney people usually shut down all rides and attractions at approximately the official closing time. Main Street in the Magic Kingdom remains open a half hour to an hour after the rest of the park has closed.

—— *The Vacation That Fights Back*

Though a vacation is what you make it, visits to Walt Disney World require a level of industry and stamina more traditionally associated with running marathons or picking a thousand acres of cotton. A mother from Middletown, New York spells it out:

> A vacation at WDW is not a vacation in the usual sense—sleeping late, total relaxation, leisurely meals, etc. It is a doing vacation that's frankly exhausting, but definitely worth doing. It's a magical place, where the visitor feels welcomed from the minute they arrive at their accommodations to the last second before boarding the shuttle bus back to the airport (what a bummer!).

An Indianapolis mother of two adds the following:

> My main thought throughout our time at WDW was, "It's so much work to have so much fun!" I can't imagine going without your touring plans in hand—I'm sure we'd have only seen half as much and we'd have become so angry with each other over trying to decide what to see next. Even with generally careful following of the 1 day plans and arriving an hour early, we missed at least one "not to be missed" feature per [theme park], mostly due to brain death in the heat.

Here's the point: at Walt Disney World *less is more*. Take Walt Disney World in small doses a little at a time with plenty of swimming, napping, reading, and relaxing in between. Plus, we have it on good authority that Walt Disney World is *not* going to be packed up and shipped to Tibet next year. Do you get it? If you don't see everything this year, you can come back! The whole shooting match will still be sitting right in the middle of Florida next year. Honest.

—— *Optimum Touring Situation*

An optimum touring situation at Walt Disney World requires a good itinerary, a minimum of five days on site (i.e., not including travel time), and a fair amount of money. It also requires a fairly prodigious appetite for Disney-type entertainment. We will provide the itinerary; the rest is up to you.

The essence of an Optimum Touring Situation is to see the various attractions of Walt Disney World in a series of shorter, less exhausting visits during the cooler, less crowded parts of the day, with plenty of rest and relaxation between visits.

Since an Optimum Touring Situation calls for leaving and returning to the theme parks on most days, it obviously makes for easier logistics if you are staying in one of the Walt Disney World resort hotels connected by the monorail. Also, if you stay in Walt Disney World you are accorded early-entry privileges at one of the major theme parks each day of the week, as well as the option of making advance reservations for the *Hoop-Dee-Doo Musical Revue* and the various dinner shows performed nightly at the resort hotels. In-World guests also have freer use of the bus, boat, and monorail transportation system, and have more alternatives for baby-sitting and children's programs. Sound good? It is, but be prepared to pay.

If you do not plan to stay at a Walt Disney World property, you can still use the day-by-day plan listed below. The plan will not be as efficient owing to increased commuting time, but it will be a whole lot less expensive.

Buy a 5-Day World-Hopper Pass or a Be Our Guest Pass if you are staying in a Disney hotel. These passes will allow you to come and go as you desire at all of the major and minor theme parks. If you are lodging outside of Walt Disney World, buy the 5-Day World-Hopper Pass.

If you visit Walt Disney World during a busy period (see pages 30–32), you need to get up early to beat the crowds. Short lines and stress-free touring are basically incompatible with sleeping in. If you want to sleep late *and* enjoy your touring experience, visit Walt Disney World during a time of year when attendance is lighter.

We do not believe that there is one ideal itinerary. Tastes, levels of energy, and basic perspectives on what constitutes entertainment and relaxation vary. This understood, what follows is our personal version of an optimum Walt Disney World vacation week. It is the itinerary we use when asked to host a tour or guide a dignitary.

Before You Go

1. Make reservations as far in advance as possible for the Grand Floridian Beach Resort. If you cannot afford the Grand Floridian, go for the Contemporary Resort or the Polynesian Resort. If your party is all adult, or if you do not intend to spend much time at the Magic Kingdom, try the Yacht Club, the Beach Club, or the Vacation Club. Honeymooners or others on a romantic getaway should consider

the new Wilderness Lodge Resort or the Polynesian Resort. If all of the hotels mentioned above are too expensive, try Port Orleans, the Dixie Landings, the Caribbean Beach, or the All-Star Resorts.

2. When you book your accommodations, try to make reservations for the *Hoop-Dee-Doo Musical Revue*, a dinner show performed nightly in Pioneer Hall at the Fort Wilderness Campground. Try to obtain reservations for one of the days you do not visit EPCOT Center or the Magic Kingdom.

3. Reserve a rental car if you want to try local (off-World) restaurants or other attractions such as Universal Studios Florida, Sea World, or the Kennedy Space Center.

On Site

Day 0 — Travel Day

1. Arrive and get settled. Explore the features and amenities of your hotel.

2. If you get checked in by 3 P.M. or earlier, and the Magic Kingdom is open until 9 P.M. or later, go ahead and run the itinerary for Day 4. If you arrive later in the day and are looking for something to do, this would be a perfect night for the *Hoop-Dee-Doo Musical Revue.*

3. Before 9 P.M., dial 55 or 56 and make next-day reservations for the EPCOT restaurants of your choice (Walt Disney World resort guests can now make advance reservations for any Disney-MGM, EPCOT Center, or Magic Kingdom full-service restaurant up to 60 days in advance with their confirmation number by calling (407) 939-3463). Try for a 1 P.M. lunch seating and a 7 or 8 P.M. dinner seating.

Day 1

1. Tour EPCOT Center using the touring plans provided in this guide. Break off the plan after lunch and return to the hotel for a nap and some beach time.

2. Return to EPCOT Center between 4 and 5 P.M., visiting any attractions in the Future World section of the park that you missed during the morning. Tour until dinner time.

3. After dinner, tour the World Showcase section of EPCOT Center until dark. Then find a good vantage point for watching IllumiNations, a fireworks, music, and laser spectacular performed nightly on the World Showcase Lagoon.

Day 2

1. Tour the Disney-MGM Studios according to the touring plans in this guide. You should be able to see everything by mid-afternoon.

2. Return to your hotel for rest and rejuvenation.

3. Try a quiet dinner in or out of Walt Disney World and then enjoy a performance of the Electrical Water Pageant at the waterfront of the Polynesian Resort. This is another good night for the *Hoop-Dee-Doo Musical Revue* or one of the other Walt Disney World or local dinner shows. Early to bed.

Day 3

1. Visit Typhoon Lagoon or Blizzard Beach using the "Planning Your Day" section provided in this guide. Once again, be on hand when the park opens.

2. Return to the hotel sometime after lunch for campers' quiet time.

3. Eat a relatively early dinner in or out of the World and then visit Pleasure Island for a night of Disney family-style nightclubbing. If you have children with you, there are several babysitting/children's program alternatives available to choose from (see pages 180–83).

Day 4

1. Sleep late after your big night out. Eat lunch at the hotel and then take the monorail to the Magic Kingdom. If your party includes young children, use the Magic Kingdom One-Day Touring Plan for Parents with Small Children, starting at Step 13. If your group consists of adults and children over eight, use Day 2 of the Magic Kingdom Two-Day Touring Plan A.

2. Between 6 and 7 P.M., catch the monorail to one of the resort hotels for dinner. Before or after dinner, call 56 (campground guests,

45) and make next-day dinner reservations for the EPCOT Center restaurant of your choice. Go for a 7 or 8 P.M. seating.

3. Return to the Magic Kingdom after dinner. Continue touring according to the Touring Plan, taking breaks to watch the evening parade and Fantasy in the Sky fireworks.

Day 5

1. Get up early and return to the Magic Kingdom, arriving early. If your party includes young children, use the Magic Kingdom One-Day Touring Plan for Parents with Small Children starting with Step 1 and continue until you have seen everything. If your group is made up of adults and children over eight, use Day 1 of the Magic Kingdom Two-Day Touring Plan A.

2. Have a late lunch and get some rest at your hotel. In the late afternoon take the monorail to EPCOT Center. Visit any of the attractions you missed on Day 1 and have dinner.

—— Seeing Walt Disney World on a Tight Schedule

Many visitors do not have five days to devote to Disney attractions. Some are en route to other destinations or may wish to spend time sampling the attractions of Orlando and central Florida. For these visitors, efficient, time-effective touring is a must. They cannot afford long waits in line for rides, shows, or meals.

Even the most efficient touring plan will not allow the visitor to cover two or more of the major theme parks in one day, so plan on allocating at least an entire day to each park (an exception to this rule is when the theme parks close at different times, allowing the visitor to tour one park until closing time and then proceed to another park). If your schedule permits only one day of touring overall, we recommend concentrating your efforts on only one of the theme parks and saving the others for a subsequent visit.

One-Day Touring

A comprehensive tour of the Magic Kingdom, EPCOT Center, or the Disney-MGM Studios in one day is possible but requires a knowledge of the park, good planning, and no small reserve of energy and endurance.

One-day touring does not leave much time for leisurely meals in sit-down restaurants, prolonged browsing in the many shops, or lengthy rest periods. Even so, one-day touring can be a fun, rewarding experience.

Successful one-day touring of either the Magic Kingdom or EPCOT Center, or of the Disney-MGM Studios, hinges on **three cardinal rules**:

1. Determine in Advance What You Really Want to See

What are the rides and attractions that appeal to you most? Which additional rides and attractions would you like to experience if you have any time left? What are you willing to forgo?

2. Arrive Early! Arrive Early! Arrive Early!

This is the single most important key to efficient touring and avoiding long lines. First thing in the morning there are no lines and relatively few people. The same four rides that you can experience in one hour in the early morning can take as long as three hours to see after 10:30 A.M. Have breakfast before you arrive so you will not have to waste your prime touring time sitting in a restaurant. Avoid the park where early entry is scheduled, arriving at one of the other parks 45 minutes or more before the official opening time.

Taking our advice about arriving early will work in your favor most of the time, particularly if you are vacationing at Walt Disney World over any holiday period (including National Education Association breaks or spring break) or during the summer. Because Disney opening procedures are flexible, however, you may occasionally suffer a few extra minutes waiting to be admitted. Rest assured that this investment in time is well spent.

The Disney folks vary opening procedures according to the number of visitors they anticipate on a given day. Simply stated, they open up as early as required to avoid crowds overwhelming the parking facilities, ticket sellers, and transportation systems. On busier days this almost always translates into admitting visitors a half hour to an hour before the officially stated opening time in the parks not slated for early entry.

3. Avoid Bottlenecks

Helping you avoid bottlenecks is what this guide is all about. Bottlenecks occur as a result of crowd concentrations and/or less than optimal crowd management. Concentrations of hungry people create bottlenecks at restaurants during the lunch and dinner hours; concentrations of people moving toward the exit near closing time create bottlenecks in the gift shops en route to the gate; concentrations of visitors at new and unusually popular rides create bottlenecks and long waiting lines; rides that are slow in boarding and disembarking passengers create bottlenecks and long waiting lines.

Avoiding bottlenecks involves being able to predict where, when, and why they occur. To this end we provide **touring plans** for the Magic Kingdom, EPCOT Center, and the Disney-MGM Studios, as well as for Pleasure Island, to assist you in avoiding bottlenecks. In addition we provide detailed information on all rides and performances, which allows you to estimate how long you may have to wait in line, and which also allows you to compare rides in terms of their capacity to accommodate large crowds. Touring plans for the Magic Kingdom begin on page 401, touring plans for EPCOT Center begin on page 499, and the touring plan for Disney-MGM Studios begins on page 557. The Pleasure Island touring plan may be found on pages 626–29. For your convenience we have also included one-day touring plans for Universal Studios Florida on pages 584–88.

In response to many reader requests, we have also added clip-out versions of the touring plans at the end of this book.

—— Touring Plans: What They Are and How They Work

When we interviewed Walt Disney World visitors who toured the theme parks on slow days, say in early December, they invariably waxed eloquent about the sheer delight of their experience. When we questioned visitors who toured on a moderate or busy day, however, they spent much of the interview telling us about the jostling crowds and how much time they stood in line. What a shame, they said, that you should devote so much time and energy to fighting the crowds in a place as special as Walt Disney World.

Given this complaint, we descended on Walt Disney World with a team of researchers to determine whether a touring plan could be devised that would move visitors counter to the flow of traffic and allow them to see any of the theme parks in one day with only minimal waits in line. On some of the busiest days of the year, our team monitored traffic flow into and through the theme parks, noting how the parks filled and how the patrons were distributed among the various attractions. Likewise, we observed which rides and attractions were most popular and where bottlenecks were most likely to form.

After many long days of collecting data, we devised a number of preliminary touring plans, which we tested during one of the busiest weeks of the entire year. Each day individual members of our research team would tour the park according to one of the preliminary plans, noting how long it took to walk from place to place and how long the wait in line was for each ride or show. Combining the knowledge gained through these trial runs, we devised a master plan that we retested and fine-tuned. This plan, with very little variance from day to day, allowed us to experience all of the major rides and attractions, and most of the lesser ones, in one day, with an average wait in line at each ride or show of less than five minutes.

From this master plan we developed a number of alternative plans that take into account the varying tastes and personal requirements of different Walt Disney World patrons. Each plan operates with the same efficiency as the master plan but addresses the special needs and preferences of its intended users.

Finally, after all of the plans were tested by our staff, we selected (using convenience sampling) a number of everyday Walt Disney World patrons to test the plans. The only prerequisite for being chosen for the test group (the visitors who would test the touring plans) was that the guest must be visiting a Disney park for the first time. A second group of ordinary patrons was chosen for a "control group," first-time visitors who would tour the park according to their own plans but who would make notes of what they did and how much time they spent waiting in lines.

When the two groups were compared, the results proved no less than amazing. On days when EPCOT Center's and the Magic Kingdom's attendance exceeded 48,000, visitors touring on their own (without the plan) **averaged** $3\frac{2}{3}$ hours more waiting in line per day than the patrons touring according to our plan, and they experienced 37% fewer rides and attractions.

General Overview of the Touring Plans

The Walt Disney World touring plans are step-by-step plans for seeing as much as possible with a minimum of time wasted standing in line. They are designed to assist you in avoiding crowds and bottlenecks on days of moderate to heavy attendance. On days of lighter attendance (see "Selecting the Time of Year for Your Visit," page 30), the plans will still save you time but will not be as critical to successful touring.

Will the Plans Continue to Work Once the Secret Is Out?

Yes! First, all of the plans require that a patron be on hand when the theme parks open. Many vacationers simply refuse to make the sacrifice of rising early, but could see more in the one hour just after the parks open than in several hours once the parks begin to fill. Second, it is anticipated that less than 1% of any given day's attendance will have been exposed to the plans, not enough to bias the results. Last, most groups will interpret the plans somewhat, skipping certain rides or shows as a matter of personal taste.

How Frequently Are the Touring Plans Revised?

Because the Disney folks are always adding new attractions and changing operations, we revise the touring plans every year. Most of the complaints we receive concerning the touring plans come from readers who are using older, out-of-date editions of the *Unofficial Guide*. Be prepared, however, for surprises. Opening procedures and show times for theater productions, for example, are subject to change, and you never know when an attraction might break down.

Touring Plans and the Obsessive/ Compulsive Reader

We suggest that you follow the touring plans religiously, especially in the mornings, if you are visiting Walt Disney World during busier, more crowded times of year. The consequence of touring spontaneity in peak season is literally hours of otherwise avoidable standing in line.

During the quieter times of year, as our readers point out, there is no need to be compulsive about following the touring plans.

From a mom in Atlanta, Georgia:

Emphasize perhaps *not* following [the touring plans] in off-season. There is no reason to crisscross the park when there are no lines.

From a Marlboro, New Jersey, father:

The time we went in November, the longest line was about a five minute wait. [At this time of year], your readers do not have to be so neurotic about running into the park and then to various attractions.

From a mother in Minneapolis:

I feel you should let your readers know to stop along the way to various attractions to appreciate what else may be going on around them. We encountered many families using the *Unofficial Guide* [who] became too serious about getting from one place to the next, missing the fun in between.

Even on days when the parks are crowded, we realize that the touring plans can contribute to some stress and fatigue. A mother wrote us from Stillwater, Maine, saying:

We were thankful for the Touring Plan and were able to get through the most popular rides early before the lines got long. One drawback was all the bouncing around we did backtracking through different parts of the Magic Kingdom in order to follow the Touring Plan. It was tiring and a bit hectic at times.

What can we say? It's one of those *lesser of two evils* situations. If you choose to visit Walt Disney World at a busy time of year, you can either get up early and hustle around, or you can sleep in and take it easy, consequently seeing less and spending a lot of time standing in lines.

When using the touring plans, however, try to relax and always be prepared for some surprises and possible setbacks. When you feel your blood pressure going up and your Type-A brain starts doing cartwheels, reflect on the advice of a woman from Trappe, Pennsylvania:

You cannot emphasize enough the dangers of using your Touring Plans that were printed in the back of the book, especially if the person using them has a compulsive personality. I have a compulsive personality. I planned for this trip for two years, researched it by use of guidebooks, computer programs, video tapes and information received from WDW. I had a two-page itinerary for our one-week trip in addition to your Touring Plans of the theme parks.

On night three of our trip, I ended up taking a non-scheduled trip to the emergency room of Sand Lake Hospital in Lake Buena Vista. When the doctor asked what seemed to be the problem, I responded with "I don't know, but I can't stop shaking, and I can't stay here very long because I have to get up in a couple hours to go to MGM according to my itinerary." Diagnosis: an anxiety attack caused by my excessive itinerary. He gave me a shot of something, and I slept through the first four attractions the next morning. This was our third trip to WDW (not including one trip to Disneyland); on all previous trips I used only the Steve Birnbaum book and I suffered no ill effects. I am not saying your book was not good. It was excellent! However, it should come with a warning label for people with compulsive personalities.

A Word about Early Entry and the Touring Plans

If you are a Disney resort guest and elect to take advantage of your early-entry privileges, complete your early-entry touring *before* the general public (Disney's term) is admitted and get in position to begin the Touring Plan. At EPCOT Center, the Disney-MGM Studios, and the Magic Kingdom, the general public will usually be admitted a half hour before the officially stated opening time. A mother from Wilmington, Delaware, explains what happens when the Visigoths break through while you're in the middle of an early-entry attraction:

The early-entry times went like clockwork. We were finishing up The Great Movie Ride when Disney-MGM opened [to the public], and [we] had to wait in line quite awhile for *Voyage of the Little Mermaid,* which sort of screwed up everything thereafter. Early opening attractions should be finished up well before regular opening time so you can be at the plan's first stop as early as possible.

Tour Groups from Hell

We have discovered that tour groups of up to 200 people sometimes use our touring plans. A lady from Memphis writes:

When we arrived at The Land [pavilion at EPCOT], a tour guide was holding your book and shouting into a bullhorn, "Step 7. Proceed to Journey into Imagination." With this, about 65 Japanese tourists in red T-shirts ran out the door.

Unless your party is as large as the above tour group, this development should not cause you undue stress. Because there are so many in a touring group, they move slowly and have to stop periodically to collect stragglers. The tour guide also has to accommodate the unpredictable needs of five dozen or so individual bladders. In short, you should have no problem passing a group after the initial encounter.

"Bouncing Around"

A lot of readers object to crisscrossing a theme park as sometimes called for in our touring plans. A lady from Decatur, Georgia, said that she "got dizzy from all the bouncing around" and that the "running back and forth reminded [her] of a scavenger hunt." We empathize, but here's the rub, park by park.

In the Magic Kingdom the most popular attractions are positioned all the way across the park from one another. This, of course, is no accident, nor is it some malicious Disney plot. Simply put, it's good theme park planning, a method of more equally distributing guests throughout the park. If you want to experience the most popular attractions in one day without long waits, you can either arrive early before the park fills and knock off those attractions first thing (which requires crisscrossing the park); or, you can enjoy the main attractions on one side of the park first thing in the morning, and try the popular attractions on the other side of the park during the hour or so before closing, when attendance has presumably thinned. All other approaches will subject you to awesome waits at some attractions if you tour during the busier times of year.

The absolute best way to minimize "bouncing around" when touring the Magic Kingdom is to use the Magic Kingdom Two-Day Touring Plan B, which spreads the more popular attractions over two mornings and which also works beautifully even when the park closes early (8 P.M. or earlier).

At EPCOT Center we have revised the touring plans to eliminate most of the "bouncing around," and have added some special instructions to assist those who seek to further minimize the walking required.

The Disney-MGM Studios layout is configured in a way that precludes an orderly linear approach to touring, or to a clockwise or counterclockwise rotation. Orderly touring is further confounded by a live entertainment schedule that essentially prompts guests to interrupt their touring from time to time in order to head to whichever theater is about to crank up. The bottom line at the Studios, therefore, is that you are stuck with a lot of "bouncing around" whether you use the touring plan or not. In our opinion, when it comes to Disney theme parks, it's best to have a plan.

A Clamor for Customized Touring Plans

We are inundated with mail from readers requesting that we develop additional touring plans. Plans we have been asked to create include: a plan for ninth and tenth graders, a plan for rainy days, a senior's

*Max is annoyed because he can't find
a touring plan for cross-dressing
unicyclists.*

plan, a plan for folks who sleep late, a plan that omits rides that "bump, jerk, and clonk," a plan for gardening enthusiasts, and a plan for single women.

The touring plans presented in this book are intended to be flexible. The idea is to adapt them to the preferences of your group. If you do not want to go on rides that bump and jerk, simply skip any such attractions when they come up in a touring plan. If you wish to sleep in and not go to the park until noon or so, use the afternoon part of a Plan. If you are a ninth grader and want to ride Space Mountain three times in a row, go ahead and ride. Will it decrease the effectiveness of the touring plan? Sure, but the Plan was only created to help you have fun. Don't let the tail wag the dog. It's your day.

Variables That Will Affect the Success of the Touring Plans

How quickly you move from one ride to another; when and how many refreshment and rest room breaks you take; when, where, and how you eat meals; and your ability (or lack thereof) to find your way around will all have an impact on the success of the plans. Smaller groups almost always move faster than larger groups, and parties of adults can generally cover more ground than families with young children. Switching off (see page 166), among other things, inhibits families with little ones from moving expeditiously from attraction to attraction. Plus, some children simply cannot conform to the "early to rise" conditions of the Touring Plans. A mom from Nutley, New Jersey, had this to say:

[Although] the Touring Plans all advise getting to parks at opening, we just couldn't burn the candle at both ends. Our kids (10, 7, and 4) would not go to sleep early and couldn't be up at dawn and still stay relatively sane. It worked well for us to let them sleep a little later, go out and bring breakfast back to the room while they slept, and still get a relatively early start by not spending time on eating breakfast out. We managed to avoid long lines with an occasional early morning, and hitting popular attractions during parades, mealtimes and late evenings.

And a family from Centerville, Ohio, volunteered this:

The toughest thing about your tour plans was getting the rest of the family to stay with them, at least to some degree. Getting them to pass by attractions in order to hit something across the park was no easy task (sometimes impossible).

While we realize that following the touring plans is not always easy, we nevertheless recommend continuous, expeditious touring until around 11:30 A.M. After that hour, breaks and so on will not affect the plans significantly.

Some variables that can have a profound effect on the touring plans are beyond your control. Chief among these are the manner and timing of bringing a particular ride to full capacity. For example, Big Thunder Mountain Railroad, a roller coaster in the Magic Kingdom, has five trains. On a given morning it may begin operation with two of the five, and then add the other three if and when needed. If the waiting line builds rapidly before the Disney operators decide to go to full capacity, you could have a long wait, even early in the morning. This often happens at 20,000 Leagues Under the Sea in the Magic Kingdom, causing our team to label the ride as the biggest bottleneck in "the World."

Another variable relates to the time that you arrive for a Disney theater performance. Usually, your wait will be the length of time from your arrival to the end of the presentation then in progress. Thus, if *Country Bear Jamboree* is 15 minutes long, and you arrive one minute after a show has begun, your wait for the next show will be 14 minutes. Conversely, if you happen to arrive just as the ongoing show is wrapping up, your wait will be only a minute or two. It's luck of the draw.

What to Do If You Lose the Thread

Anything from a blister to a broken-down attraction can throw off a Touring Plan. If unforeseen events interrupt a Touring Plan, try the following:

1. Skip one step on the Touring Plan for every 25 minutes you are delayed. If you lose your billfold, for example, and spend about an hour finding it, skip two steps on the Touring Plan and pick up from there.

2. Forget the Touring Plan and organize the remainder of your day using the *Optimum Touring Times* clip-out charts at the back of this guide. These charts summarize the best times of day to visit each attraction.

Touring Plan Clip-out Pocket Outlines

For your convenience, we have prepared outline versions of all the touring plans presented in this guide. The pocket outline versions present the same touring itineraries as the detailed touring plans, but with vastly abbreviated directions. First, select the touring plan which is most appropriate for your party, then familiarize yourself with the detailed version of the touring plan. Once you understand how the touring plan works, clip out the pocket outline version of your selected touring plan from the back of this guide, and carry it with you as a quick reference when you visit the theme park.

Understanding Walt Disney World Attractions

Walt Disney World's primary appeal is in its rides and shows. Understanding how these rides and shows are engineered to accommodate guests provides some information that, aside from being interesting, is invaluable in developing an efficient itinerary.

All the attractions at Walt Disney World, regardless of the theme park in which they are located, are affected by two overriding elements: capacity and popularity. Capacity is simply how many guests the attraction can serve at one time, in an hour, or in a day. Popularity is a comparative term describing how well visitors like a particular attraction.

Capacity can be adjusted for some attractions. It is possible, for instance, to add additional trams at the Disney-MGM Backstage Studios Tour, or to put a couple of extra boats on the water at the Jungle Cruise in the Magic Kingdom. For the most part, however, capacity remains relatively fixed.

From a designer's perspective, the idea is to match capacity and popularity as closely as possible. A big high-capacity ride that is not very popular is a failure of sorts. Lots of money, space, and equipment have been poured into the attraction, yet there are always empty seats. Dreamflight, a newer ride in the Magic Kingdom, comes closest to fitting this profile.

While it is extremely unusual for a new Disney attraction such as Dreamflight not to measure up, it is fairly common for an older ride to lose its appeal. The Magic Kingdom's *Tropical Serenade*, for example, often plays to half-full audiences.

In general, Disney attractions are immensely popular when they are new. Some, like Space Mountain (Magic Kingdom), have sustained great appeal years beyond their debut while others, like EPCOT Center's The Living Seas and El Rio del Tiempo, have declined in popularity after just a few years of operation. Most attractions, however, work through the honeymoon and then settle down to handle the level of demand for which they were designed. When this happens, there are enough interested guests during peak hours to fill almost every seat, but not so many as to develop a prohibitively long line.

Sometimes Disney properly estimates an attraction's popularity but then fouls up the equation by mixing in a third variable such as location. Spaceship Earth, the ride inside the huge geosphere at EPCOT Center, is a good example. Placing the ride squarely in the path of every tourist entering the park assures that it will be inundated during the morning hours when the park is filling up. On the other side of the coin, *The American Adventure,* located at the extreme opposite end of EPCOT Center, has a huge capacity but plays to a partially filled theater until about noon, when guests finally work their way into that part of the park.

If demand is high and capacity is low, large lines will materialize. Dumbo, the Flying Elephant in the Magic Kingdom has the smallest capacity of almost any Walt Disney World attraction, yet it is probably the most popular ride among young children. The result of this mismatch is that children and parents must often suffer long, long waits for a one-and-a-half-minute ride. Dumbo is a simple yet visually appealing midway ride. Its capacity (and that of many other attractions, including Space Mountain) is limited by the very characteristics that contribute to its popularity.

Capacity design is always predicated on averages: the average number of people in the park, the normal distribution of traffic to specific areas within the park, and the average number of staff required to operate the ride. On a holiday weekend when all the averages are exceeded, all but a few attractions operate at maximum capacity, and even then are overwhelmed by the huge crowds. On low-attendance fall days full capacity is often not even approximated and guests can literally walk onto most rides without any wait whatsoever.

The Magic Kingdom offers the greatest variety in both capacity and popularity, offering rides and shows of vastly differing sorts. Only the Magic Kingdom offers low-capacity midway rides, spook-house genre "dark" rides, and roller coasters. Technologically, its product mix ranges from state of the art to the antiquated. This diversity makes efficient touring of the Magic Kingdom much more challenging. If guests do not understand the capacity/popularity relationship and plan accordingly, they might spend most of the day waiting in line.

While EPCOT Center and the Disney-MGM Studios have fewer rides and shows than the Magic Kingdom, almost all of their attractions are major features and rank on a par with the Magic Kingdom's Pirates of the

Caribbean and Jungle Cruise in scope, detail, imagination, and spectacle. All but one or two of the EPCOT Center and Disney-MGM rides are fast-loading, and most have large carrying capacities. Because EPCOT Center and Disney-MGM attractions are on average well-engineered and very efficient, lines may appear longer than those in the Magic Kingdom, but usually move more quickly. There are no amusement park rides at EPCOT Center or the Disney-MGM Studios and few attractions that are specifically intended for children.

In the Magic Kingdom, crowded conditions are more a function of the popularity and engineering of individual attractions. At EPCOT Center, traffic flow and crowding is much more affected by the park layout. For touring efficiency, it is important to understand how the Magic Kingdom rides and shows operate. At EPCOT Center this knowledge is decidedly less important.

Crowds at the Disney-MGM Studios have been larger than anticipated since it opened in 1989. Greater-than-expected attendance coupled with a relatively small number of attractions has resulted in long lines, long waits, and frustrated guests. Disney plans to double the size of the theme park, but in the meantime a well-considered touring plan is essential.

It is necessary to understand how the rides and shows are designed and how they function to develop an efficient touring plan. We will examine both.

Cutting Down Your Time in Line by Understanding the Rides

There are many different types of rides at Walt Disney World. Some rides, like The Great Movie Ride at the Disney-MGM Studios, are engineered to carry more than 3,000 people every hour. At the other extreme, such rides as Dumbo, the Flying Elephant can only accommodate around 400 persons in an hour. Most rides fall somewhere in between. Lots of factors figure into how long you will have to wait to experience a particular ride: the popularity of the ride; how it loads and unloads; how many persons can ride at one time; how many units (cars, rockets, boats, flying elephants, etc.) are in service at a given time; and how many staff personnel are available to operate the ride. Let's take them one by one:

1. *How popular is the ride?*

Newer rides like the Tower of Terror at the Disney-MGM Studios, and Splash Mountain at the Magic Kingdom attract a lot of people, as do longtime favorites such as the Jungle Cruise. If you know a ride is popular, you need to learn a little more about how it operates to determine when might be the best time to ride. But a ride need not be especially popular to form long lines; the lines can be the result of less than desirable traffic engineering (i.e., it takes so long to load and unload that a line builds up anyway). This is the situation at the Mad Tea Party and Cinderella's Golden Carrousel in Fantasyland. Since mostly children and teens ride the Mad Tea Party, it only serves a small percentage of any day's attendance at the Magic Kingdom. Yet, because it takes so long to load and unload this comparatively less popular ride, long waiting lines form.

2. How does the ride load and unload?

Some rides never stop. They are like a circular conveyor belt that goes around and around. We call these "continuous loaders." The Haunted Mansion in the Magic Kingdom is a continuous loader, as is Spaceship Earth at EPCOT Center. The number of people that can be moved through in an hour depends on how many cars, "doom buggies," or whatever are on the conveyor. The Haunted Mansion and Spaceship Earth have lots of cars on the conveyor belt and consequently can move more than 2,000 people an hour.

Still other rides are "interval loaders." This means that cars are unloaded, loaded, and dispatched at certain set intervals (sometimes controlled manually and sometimes by a computer). Space Mountain in Tomorrowland is an interval loader. It has two separate tracks (in other words the ride has been duplicated in the same facility). Each track can run up to 14 space capsules, released at 36-second, 26-second, or 21-second intervals. (The bigger the crowd, the shorter the interval.)

In one kind of interval loader, like Space Mountain, empty cars (space capsules) are returned to the starting point where they line up for reloading. In a second type of interval loader, one group of riders enters the vehicle while the last group of riders departs. We call these "in-and-out" interval loaders. Splash Mountain is a good example of an in-and-out interval loader. As a boat pulls up to the dock, those who have just completed their ride exit to the left. At almost the same time, those waiting to ride enter the boat from the right. The boat is released to the dispatch point a few yards down the line where it is launched according to whatever time interval is being used.

Interval loaders of both types can be very efficient at moving people if (1) the dispatch (launch) interval is relatively short and (2) the ride can accommodate a large number of vehicles in the system at one time. Since many boats can be floating through Pirates of the Caribbean at a given time, and since the dispatch interval is short, almost 3,000 people an hour can see this attraction. 20,000 Leagues Under the Sea is an in-and-out interval loader that can only run a maximum of nine submarines at a time with a fairly long dispatch interval. Thus 20,000 Leagues can only handle up to 1,600 people an hour.

A third group of rides are "cycle rides." Another name for these rides is "stop-and-go" rides. Here, those waiting to ride exchange places with those who have just ridden. The main difference between in-and-out interval rides and cycle rides is that with a cycle ride the whole system shuts down when loading and unloading is in progress. While one boat is loading and unloading in It's a Small World (an interval loader), many other boats are advancing through the ride. But when Dumbo, the Flying Elephant touches down, the whole ride is at a standstill until the next flight is launched. Likewise, with Cinderella's Golden Carrousel, all riders dismount and the Carrousel stands stationary until the next group is mounted and ready to ride. In discussing a cycle ride, the amount of time the ride is in motion is called "ride time." The amount of time that the ride is idle while loading and unloading is called "load time." Load time added to ride time equals "cycle time," or the time expended from the start of one run of the ride until the start of the succeeding run.

Cycle rides are the least efficient of all rides in terms of traffic engineering. The only cycle rides at Walt Disney World are in the Magic Kingdom.

3. *How many persons can ride at one time?*

This figure is defined in terms of "per ride capacity" or "system capacity." Either way the figures allude to the number of people who can be riding at the same time. Our discussion above illustrates that the greater the carrying capacity of a ride (all other things being equal), the more visitors it can accommodate in an hour. Also, as mentioned previously, some rides can add extra units (cars, boats, etc.) as crowds build to increase carrying capacity, while others like the AstroOrbiter in Tomorrowland have a fixed capacity (it being impossible to add additional rockets).

4. *How many "units" are in service at a given time?*

A "unit" is simply our term for the vehicle you sit in during your ride. At the Mad Tea Party the unit is a tea cup, at 20,000 Leagues it's a submarine, and at the Grand Prix Raceway it's a race car. On some rides (mostly cycle rides), the number of units in operation at a given time is fixed. Thus, there are always 16 flying elephant units operating on the Dumbo ride, 90 horses on Cinderella's Golden Carrousel, and so on. What this fixed number of units means to you is that there is no way to increase the carrying capacity of the ride by adding more units. On a busy day, therefore, the only way to carry more people each hour on a fixed-unit cycle ride is to shorten the loading time (which, as we will discuss next, is sometimes impossible) or by decreasing the riding time, the actual time the ride is in motion. The bottom line on a busy day for a cycle ride is that you will wait longer and possibly be rewarded for your wait with a shorter ride. This is why we try to steer you clear of the cycle rides unless you are willing to ride them early in the morning or late at night. The following are cycle rides, all located in the Magic Kingdom:

Fantasyland:	Dumbo, the Flying Elephant
	Cinderella's Golden Carrousel
	Mad Tea Party
Tomorrowland:	AstroOrbiter

Many other rides throughout Walt Disney World can increase their carrying capacity by adding more units as the crowds build. Big Thunder Mountain Railroad in Frontierland is a good example. If attendance is very light, Big Thunder can start the day by only running one of their five available mine trains from one of two available loading platforms. If lines start to build, the other loading platform is opened and more mine trains placed into operation. At full capacity a total of five trains can carry about 2,400 persons an hour. Likewise Star Tours at Disney-MGM Studios can increase its capacity by adding more simulators, and the Maelstrom boat ride at EPCOT Center can add more Viking ships. Sometimes a long queue will disappear almost instantly when new units are brought on line. When an interval-loading ride places more units into operation, it usually shortens the dispatch intervals, so more units are being dispatched more often.

5. *How many staff personnel are available to operate the ride?*

Allocation of additional staff to a given ride can allow extra units to be placed in operation, or additional loading areas or holding areas to be opened. In the Magic Kingdom, Pirates of the Caribbean and It's a Small World can run two separate waiting lines and loading zones. The Haunted Mansion has a one-and-a-half-minute preshow which is staged in a "stretch room." On busy days a second stretch room can be activated, thus permitting a more continuous flow of visitors to the actual loading area.

Additional staff make a world of difference in some cycle rides. Often there is only a single attendant operating the Mad Tea Party. This one person must clear visitors from the ride just completed, admit and seat visitors for the upcoming ride, check that all tea cups are properly secured (which entails an inspection of each tea cup), return to the control panel, issue instructions to the riders, and finally activate the ride (whew!). A second attendant allows for the division of these responsibilities and has the effect of cutting loading time by 25 to 50%.

By knowing the way a ride loads, its approximate hourly capacity, and its relative popularity, we can anticipate which rides are likely to develop long lines, and more importantly how long we will have to wait to ride at any given time of day.

—— *Cutting Down Your Time in Line by Understanding the Shows*

Many of the featured attractions at Walt Disney World are theater presentations. While not as complex as rides from a traffic engineering viewpoint, a little enlightenment concerning their operation may save some touring time.

Most of the theater attractions at Walt Disney World operate in three distinct phases:

1. There are the guests who are in the theater viewing the presentation.
2. There are the guests who have passed through the turnstile into a holding area or waiting lobby. These people will be admitted to the theater as soon as the presentation in progress is concluded. Several attractions offer a preshow in their waiting lobby to entertain guests until they are admitted to the main show. Among these are *Tropical Serenade* (*Enchanted Tiki Birds*) and *Time Voyager* in the Magic Kingdom, The Living Seas and Universe of Energy at EPCOT Center, and *Monster Sound* and *MuppetVision 4-D* at the Disney-MGM Studios.
3. There is the outside line. Those waiting here will enter the waiting lobby when there is room, and will ultimately move from the waiting lobby to the theater.

The theater capacity and the popularity of the presentation, along with the level of attendance in the park, determine how long the lines will be at a given theater attraction. Except for holidays and other days of especially heavy attendance, the longest wait for a show usually does not exceed the length of one complete performance.

Since almost all Walt Disney World theater attractions run continuously, only stopping long enough for the previous audience to leave and the waiting audience to enter, a performance will be in progress when you arrive. If a showing of *Impressions de France* in the French pavilion at EPCOT Center is 18 minutes in duration, the longest wait under normal circumstances should be about 18 minutes if you were to arrive just after the show had begun.

All Walt Disney World theaters (except the Main Street Cinema in the Magic Kingdom and various amphitheater productions) are very strict when it comes to controlling access. Unlike a movie theater at home, you cannot just walk in during the middle of a performance. This being the case, you will always have at least a short wait.

Most of the theaters at Walt Disney World hold a lot of people. When a new audience is admitted, the outside line (if there is one) will usually disappear. Exceptions are *Country Bear Jamboree* in the Magic Kingdom; *The Making of Me* in the Wonders of Life pavilion, *Honey, I Shrunk the Audience* in the Imagination pavilion at EPCOT Center; and the *Voyage of the Little Mermaid* and *Muppet Vision 4-D* at the Disney-MGM Studios. Because these shows are so popular (or have a small seating capacity like *The Making of Me*), you may have to wait through two or more shows before you are admitted (unless you go early in the morning).

—— *How to Deal with Obnoxious People*

At every theater presentation at Walt Disney World, visitors in the preshow area elbow, nudge, and crowd one another in order to make sure that they are admitted to the performance. Not necessary—if you are admitted through the turnstile into the preshow area a seat has automatically been allocated for you in the theater. When it is time to proceed into the theater don't rush; just relax and let other people jam the doorways. When the congestion has been relieved simply stroll in and take a seat.

Attendants at many theaters will instruct you to enter a row of seats and move completely to the far side, filling every seat so that each row can be completely filled. And invariably some inconsiderate, thick-skulled yahoo will plop down right in the middle of the row, stopping traffic or forcing other visitors to climb over him. Take our word for it—there is no such thing as a bad seat. All of the Disney theaters have been de-

signed to provide a near-perfect view from every seat in the house. Our recommendation is to follow instructions and move to the far end of the row.

The Disney people also ask that visitors not use flash photography in the theaters (the theaters are too dark for the pictures to turn out, *plus* the flash is disruptive to other viewers). Needless to say, this admonition is routinely ignored. Flashers are more difficult to deal with than row-blockers. You can threaten to turn the offenders over to Disney security, or better yet, simply hold your hand over the lens (you have to be quick) when they raise their cameras.

PART THREE: *Selecting Your Hotel*

Selecting Your Hotel

We have found lodging to be a primary concern of those visiting Walt Disney World. In general, the Magic Kingdom resort hotels and EPCOT Center resort hotels are the most expensive, while rooms at other Walt Disney World hotel properties run slightly less. The least expensive lodging is located outside of Walt Disney World. Also out of the World, however, are some of the area's most luxurious hotels.

In addition to proximity and a certain number of guest privileges, there is special magic and peace of mind associated with staying inside Walt Disney World. "I feel more a part of everything and less like a visitor," is the way one guest described it.

There is no real hardship, however, in staying outside Walt Disney World and driving (or taking the often available hotel shuttle) to the theme parks for your visit. Meals can be had less expensively, too, and there is this indirect benefit: rooming outside "The World" puts you in a more receptive mood toward other Orlando area attractions and eating establishments. Universal Studios Florida, the Kennedy Space Center, Sea World, and Cypress Gardens, among others, are well worth your attention.

Prices for accommodations are subject to change, but our research team lodged in an excellent (though not plush) motel surrounded by beautiful orange groves for one third the cost of staying in the least expensive Walt Disney World hotel. Our commuting time was 17 minutes one way to the Magic Kingdom or EPCOT Center parking lots.

If there are small children in your party, review the section, *Walt Disney World with Kids* (see pages 139–84) before making your lodging selection. Similarly, seniors, couples on a honeymoon or romantic holiday, and disabled guests should refer to the applicable sections of *Special Tips for Special People* (see pages 185–206) before choosing a hotel.

—— Benefits of Staying in the World

The specific privileges and amenities of staying in a Walt Disney World lodging property (listed below) are these:

1. Convenience. Decreased commuting time made possible by close proximity to the theme parks, and by easy access to the Walt Disney World bus, boat, and monorail transportation system. This is especially advantageous if you stay in one of the hotels connected by the monorail or by the lake/canal system (boat service).

2. Early Entry at the Theme Parks. Walt Disney World lodging guests (excluding guests at the independent hotels of the Disney Village Hotels) are invited to enter a designated theme park one hour earlier than the general public each day. Occasionally Walt Disney World lodging guests are offered special deals on admission, for instance, a passport good for the exact number of days of your visit or discounted admission to the water theme parks. These benefits and extras are subject to change without notice and are generally put in effect for a limited time and for a specific purpose, such as promoting a new Walt Disney World theme park or attraction. The early-entry program, however, is now in its fourth year.

3. Preferential Treatment in Making Dinner Show Reservations. Disney resort guests are accorded special privileges in making advance reservations to the *Hoop-Dee-Doo Musical Revue* and other Walt Disney World dinner shows.

4. Lunch and Dinner Reservations. Disney resort guests can make lunch and dinner, as well as character dining or dinner show, reservations over the phone, up to 60 days in advance (with their lodging confirmation number), at EPCOT Center, Disney-MGM Studios, and Magic Kingdom full-service restaurants. During the past year, interestingly, Disney restaurant reservationists have stopped asking for lodging confirmation numbers. Though this new policy has been kept quiet and may change at any time, the practical consequence for the time being is that *anybody* (not only Disney resort guests) can make advanced dining and show reservations.

5. Babysitting and Childcare Alternatives. A number of alternatives for babysitting, childcare, and special children's programs are offered to Disney hotel and campground guests. Each of the resort hotels connected by the monorail, as well as several other Disney hotels, offers "clubs," or themed childcare centers where potty-trained children, 3 to 12 years, can be left while the adults go out. Also available are the Fairy Godmother and Kinder-Care in-room babysitting services (see pages 182–83).

6. Overnight Kennel Privileges. Only Walt Disney World resort guests may leave pets overnight in the kennels.

7. Guaranteed Theme Park Admissions. On days of particularly heavy attendance, Walt Disney World resort guests are guaranteed admission to the theme parks.

8. Children Sharing a Room with Their Parents. There is no extra charge per night for children under 18 sharing a room with their parents.

9. Free Parking. Walt Disney World resort guests with cars do not have to pay for parking in the theme park lots.

10. Recreational Privileges. Walt Disney World resort guests are accorded preferential treatment for tee times at the golf courses.

—— Staying In or Out of the World: Weighing the Pros and Cons

1. Cost. The primary consideration in deciding whether to stay in or out of Walt Disney World is the cost of your hotel room. Disney resort hotel rooms start at about $75 a night (including tax), spiraling upward to over $300 per night. Rooms outside of Walt Disney World range from $25 to $240 per night with a broad range of choices in the $35–60 category. Check our hotel quality and value ratings on pages 119–26) to compare specific hotels both in and out of the World.

2. Ease of Access. Even if you stay in Walt Disney World you are dependent on some mode of transportation. Hotels on the monorail line cut time commuting to the Magic Kingdom, but that's all. You must take a bus (or boat) everywhere else. The EPCOT resorts provide easy access to EPCOT Center, but only through the International Gateway, located at the opposite end of the park from where you need to initiate your touring. The EPCOT resorts also provide boat service to the Disney-MGM Studios. All other Disney World lodging properties depend on bus service. It may be less stressful to use the Disney transportation system, but with the single exception of commuting to the Magic Kingdom, the fastest, most efficient, and most flexible way to get around is usually a car. If you have been touring EPCOT Center, for example, and want to take the kids back to Disney's Grand Floridian Beach Resort for a nap, forget the monorail. You'll get back much faster if you have your own car.

A reader from Raynham, Massachusetts, who stayed at the Caribbean Beach Resort (and liked it very much) described her transportation experience:

> Even though the resort is on the Disney bus line, I recommend renting a car if it [fits] one's budget. The buses do not go directly to many destinations and often you have to switch at the Transportation and Ticket Center. Getting a [bus] seat in the morning is no problem [because] they allow standees. Getting a bus back to the hotel after a hard day can mean a long wait in line.

To present a complete picture, it must be said that the Disney transportation system, particularly the bus system, is about as efficient as humanly possible. No matter where you are going, you rarely have to wait more than 15 to 20 minutes for a bus, monorail, or boat. While only for the use and benefit of Disney guests, it *is* nonetheless public transportation, with "public" as the operative word. In other words, you are relegated to accepting the inconveniences inherent in any transportation system: conveyances that arrive and depart according to their schedule as opposed to yours; the occasional necessity of transfers; multiple stops; time lost while loading and unloading large numbers of passengers; and, generally, the challenge of understanding and utilizing a large, complex transportation network.

3. Small Children. Although the actual hassle of commuting to most off-World hotels is only slightly (if at all) greater than that of commuting to Disney World hotels, a definite peace of mind results from staying in Walt Disney World. If you are traveling with small children and have a few bucks, go for the Polynesian Resort on the monorail line. If the Polynesian is too expensive but you can handle $94–119 a night, try to book the Caribbean Beach, Dixie Landings, or Port Orleans resorts. The new All-Star Resorts offer rooms in the $70–80 range.

4. Splitting Up. If you are in a party that will probably be splitting up (as frequently happens in families with children of widely varying ages), staying in the World offers more transportation options and therefore more independence. Mom and Dad can take the car and return to the hotel for a relaxed dinner and an early bedtime while the teens remain in the park for the evening parades and fireworks.

5. Feeding the Army of the Potomac. If you have a large crew that chows down like cattle on a finishing lot, you might be better off staying outside the World where food is far less expensive.

6. Visiting Other Orlando Area Attractions. If you plan to visit Sea World, Spaceport USA, Universal Studios Florida, or other area attractions, it may be more convenient to stay outside the World.

7. Homesickness. If you get homesick and make a lot of phone calls to Mom 'n' 'em, you do not want to be calling from a Disney hotel. Walt Disney World hotels charge 75¢ for local calls and tack on a hefty 50% surcharge to direct dial long distance calls. *Tip:* If you use a calling card there is no surcharge.

—— How to Get Discounts on Lodging at Walt Disney World

There are so many guest rooms in and around Walt Disney World that competition has become brisk, and everyone, including Disney, is having to wheel and deal to keep the rooms filled. This has led to a more flexible discount policy for Walt Disney World hotels. Actually getting the discounts, however, remains a confusing and somewhat Machiavellian task in the best Disney tradition. In any event, here are some tips which should be of help.

1. Value Season vs. Regular Season. The same room is $20–40 cheaper in Value Season than in Regular Season.*

1996 Value Season	*1996 Regular Season*
January 2–February 9	December 19, 1995–January 1, 1996
April 23–June 7*	February 10–April 22
August 11– December 18	June 8–August 10 December 19–January 1, 1997

*The Caribbean Beach, Port Orleans, and Dixie Landings resorts operate on a similar, but slightly different calendar. The All-Star Resorts offer the same rates year-round.

2. Travel Agents. Travel agents, once ineligible for commissions on Disney bookings, are now active players and particularly good sources for information on time-limited special programs and discounts.

3. Disney's Ocala Information Center. The Disney Information Center off I-75 in Ocala, Florida, routinely books Disney hotel rooms at discounts of up to 43%! The discounts are offered as an incentive to walk-in travelers who may not have considered lodging at a Disney property or even going to Walt Disney World. The number of rooms available at specific hotels varies according to date and season, but you can almost always count on getting a good deal. Because the discount program is designed to snare uncommitted, walk-in travelers, you must reserve your room in person at the Information Center. If you call the center in advance, however, and tell them you are on your way down, they will usually tell you what they have available and what the discounts are. The phone number is (904) 854-0770. The Information Center is open daily from 9 A.M. until 6 P.M. Finally, as with all things Disney, there is no telling how long this discount program will last.

4. Disney Shareholder Discounts. The discount program for Walt Disney Company shareholders has been effectively dismantled. Disney shareholders are currently offered only a modest discount on the purchase of a Magic Kingdom Club Gold Card, available to the general public for about $65. For information, call the Walt Disney Company's shareholder relations office at (818) 505-7040.

5. Magic Kingdom Club. The Magic Kingdom Club is offered as a benefit by employers, credit unions, and organizations. Membership entitles you to a 10–30% discount on Disney lodging and a 5–7% discount on theme park tickets, among other things. Almost all state and federal government employees are Magic Kingdom Club members (though a lot of them don't know it). If you work for a large company or organization, ask your personnel department if the Magic Kingdom Club benefit is provided. Those not signed up through their work can buy a two-year individual membership in the Magic Kingdom Club Gold Card program for about $65. For information call (714) 520-2500 or write:

> Magic Kingdom Club
> Gold Card
> P.O. Box 3850
> Anaheim, CA 92803-3850

6. Organizations and Auto Clubs. As Disney has become more aggressive about selling guest rooms, it has developed time-limited programs with a number of auto clubs and other organizations. Recently, for instance, AAA members were offered 10–20% savings on Walt Disney hotels, preferred parking areas at the theme parks, and discounts on Disney package vacations. While these deals come and go, the market suggests that there will be more coming than going for the next year. If you are a member of AARP, AAA, or any travel or auto club, check to see if your association has a program before shopping elsewhere.

7. *Room Upgrades.* Sometimes a room upgrade is as good as a discount. If you are visiting Walt Disney World during a slower time of year, try booking the least expensive room in the Disney hotel of your choice using as many of the aforementioned discounts as applicable. When checking in, inquire very politely about being upgraded to a "water-" or "pool-view" room. A fair percentage of the time, you will be accommodated at no additional charge.

8. *Extra Nights Discounts.* During slower times of year, try booking your Disney hotel for half the period you intend to stay. Quite often, the hotel will offer you extra nights at a nicely discounted rate in an effort to get you to prolong your stay.

—— *Walt Disney World Lodging**

The Grand Floridian, Polynesian, Contemporary, Wilderness Lodge, and Shades of Green resorts are all located near the Magic Kingdom. The Walt Disney World Swan and Dolphin Hotels, along with the Yacht and Beach Clubs, and Disney's Boardwalk, are situated near EPCOT Center. Disney's Village Resort is located on the northeast side of Walt Disney World with the All-Star Resorts occupying a similar position on the southwest side. Centrally located are the Caribbean Beach Resort, as well as the Vacation Club, Port Orleans, and Dixie Landings arrayed along Bonnet Creek.

The Disney Resort Hit Parade

Most Convenient to Theme Parks

1. Polynesian
2. Yacht & Beach Clubs
3. Boardwalk
4. Contemporary
5. Caribbean Beach

Best Atmosphere and Theme Presentation

1. Wilderness Lodge
2. Polynesian
3. Grand Floridian
4. Caribbean Beach
5. Dixie Landings

*Rates vary depending on room location (view) and/or season, and are subject to change.

**Best for Activities
and Recreation**

1. Fort Wilderness
2. Polynesian
3. Contemporary
4. Grand Floridian
5. Vacation Club

Most Romantic

1. Wilderness Lodge
2. Polynesian
3. Grand Floridian
4. Contemporary
5. Vacation Club

Best Hotel Restaurants

1. Yacht & Beach Clubs
2. Swan & Dolphin
3. Grand Floridian
4. Contemporary
5. Wilderness Lodge

**Best for Families
with Children**

1. Polynesian
2. Fort Wilderness
3. Caribbean Beach
4. Vacation Club
5. Dixie Landings

The Magic Kingdom Resort Hotels

Monorail Resorts. Expensive, but most convenient, are the hotels situated around the Seven Seas Lagoon or Bay Lake and connected to the Magic Kingdom and EPCOT Center by monorail. These include the giant A-frame hotel, Disney's Contemporary Resort; Disney's Polynesian Resort; and Disney's Grand Floridian Beach Resort, modeled after the fabled Florida grand hotels of the nineteenth century. Accommodations in any of these hotels make touring Walt Disney World easier and more relaxing. Commuting to and from the Magic Kingdom via monorail is quick and simple, allowing visitors to return at leisure to their hotel for a nap or a dip. Additionally, the Seven Seas Lagoon and Bay Lake offer a variety of boating, swimming, and other water sports. Restaurants at the Grand Floridian and Contemporary are average to good. Restaurants at the Polynesian are improved with the addition of 'Ohana.

We rank the Polynesian Resort as the most convenient of all Walt Disney World Resorts. Not only can you commute directly to the Magic Kingdom by monorail, but you can also, by walking to the Transportation and Ticket Center (about a five to eight minute walk), catch a direct monorail to EPCOT Center. This feature makes the Polynesian the only Disney resort with direct monorail access to two theme parks. To minimize your walk to the TTC, try to reserve a room in the Pago Pago, Moorea, or Oahu guest buildings.

The Polynesian is also a great choice for couples and honeymooners. Book a waterfront room in the Moorea building: You will have a perfect view of Cinderella's Castle and the Magic Kingdom fireworks across the Seven Seas Lagoon. For families with small children, the Polynesian offers the best of all the Disney childcare facilities, the Neverland Club.

Contemporary Resort
1,050 rooms	lakefront	monorail service	$195–435 per night

Polynesian Resort
863 rooms	lakefront	monorail service	$189–360 per night

Grand Floridian Beach Resort
900 rooms	lakefront	monorail service	$245–440 per night

Disney's Wilderness Lodge Resort, located on Bay Lake, is close to both the Magic Kingdom and the Fort Wilderness Campground, but is not on the monorail line. The newest Disney luxury property, the Wilderness Lodge is modeled on rustic National Park Service lodges erected just before and after the First World War. Romantic and isolated, the Wilderness Lodge is a great choice for romantic couples or for seniors.

The Magic Kingdom and Bay Lake attractions can be reached by launch. All other Walt Disney World destinations are serviced by bus. Concerning Disney transportation, we have received many letters from readers complaining about boat and bus service to the Wilderness Lodge. The following is typical:

> I suggest that you advise your readers that although the Wilderness Lodge is truly a beautiful hotel, in order to have a happy and relaxing experience there, they should either have a car of their own or else the luxury of a lot of time to waste on boring travel through uninteresting countryside, multiple times daily. Even though a map shows you to be in the middle of the action, you are no closer in travel time than the hotels that are much farther away and much cheaper. Without perfect timing, even the "direct" boat to the Magic Kingdom takes a half hour. It is an extremely aggravating tease to be so near and yet so far away while staying at the hotel. Maybe that is how Disney defines a "wilderness experience," but it is my definition of frustration!

According to readers, the routes are long, indirect, and constantly changing, and written transportation system instructions provided to guests are confusing. When we visited the Wilderness Lodge in 1995, we were given a listing of "Recommended Transportation Routes." One of these indicated that to return to the Wilderness Lodge from Discovery

Island, we should "walk to the Pioneer Hall Depot and board the Crockett Bus." Not feeling Biblical, we thought better of walking across the lake and opted for the boat.

In addition to complaints about Wilderness Lodge transportation, several readers, including this woman from Grosse Pointe, Michigan, have had their fill of the hotel's heroic background music:

> Only a few things were out of sync—I was bothered by the rather loud western music "soundtrack" that served as background music through the Lodge (but, then, the music at EPCOT was even creepier!). At least the Disney folks should rotate more than 5 songs for the lodge music. I must have heard "The Magnificent Seven" fifty times in four days.

Disney's Wilderness Lodge Resort

729 rooms	lakefront	bus/bus service	$149–260 per night

Shades of Green (formerly the Disney Inn), was acquired on a long-term lease in 1994 by the U.S. Armed Forces as a recreational resource for active and retired service members. Though no longer open to the public, nonmilitary guests will continue to have access to the 45-hole golf course surrounding the hotel. One of the most luxurious, and possibly the most sedate and restful of the Disney resorts, Shades of Green will be sorely missed by seniors and couples traveling without children. Located near the Grand Floridian, Shades of Green is accessible by private car or the Disney bus system. Room rates vary according to military rank, with higher-ranking personnel paying more.

Shades of Green

288 rooms	golf course	shuttle bus service	rates for military personnel vary

The EPCOT Resort Hotels

Disney's Yacht Club Resort and Disney's Beach Club Resort are located between the Dolphin and EPCOT Center and across a lake from the Disney's Boardwalk Resort (opens 1996). EPCOT Center is within walking distance and the Disney-MGM Studios can be reached by boat. Other Walt Disney World destinations are serviced by bus. Modeled after the great New England seaside resorts of the nineteenth century, the Yacht and Beach Clubs feature the best restaurants to be found in the Disney hotels and the most imaginative hotel swimming areas at Walt Disney

World. Now that Shades of Green (Disney Inn) has been leased to the U.S. Armed Forces, the Yacht and Beach Clubs, along with the Grand Floridian, are among our recommended accommodations for seniors and for couples traveling without children.

Yacht and Beach Club Resorts
1,215 rooms   lakefront   boat/bus service $205–390 per night

Disney's Boardwalk Resort   Scheduled to open in the summer of 1996, Disney's Boardwalk Resort will be modeled after the vacation cottages of the early twentieth-century New England coast. The property will combine 378 deluxe hotel rooms with an adjacent 383 unit time-share development. There will be two full-service restaurants, and three night-spots in the complex. Located near the Beach and Yacht Clubs, the Boardwalk Resort is within easy walking distance of EPCOT Center; the Disney-MGM Studios can be reached by boat and other Walt Disney World locations by bus.

Disney's Boardwalk Resort
761 rooms   on lake   bus & boat service $200–355 per night

The Walt Disney World Swan, Walt Disney World Dolphin, and Conference Center is one of the largest convention/resort complexes in the southeastern United States. Built on the shore of a 50-acre lagoon, the complex is connected by canal to the Disney-MGM Studios, and by tram and walkway to EPCOT Center, as well as by bus and highway to other areas of Walt Disney World. In addition to extensive meeting and convention facilities, the Swan (a Westin property) and the Dolphin (a Sheraton property) offer several of the best restaurants in all of Walt Disney World. Guest rooms at the Swan and Dolphin are a little too trendy (garish?) for some, while others consider the zippy styling to be a breath of fresh air.

Swan Resort
758 rooms   lakefront   boat/bus service $195–335 per night
Dolphin Resort
1,510 rooms   lakefront   boat/bus service $185–375 per night

The Disney Vacation Club is a new property with an "old Key West" feel that offers nice guest rooms as well as luxurious one-, two-, and three-bedroom homes and villas with full kitchens. The Vacation Club, situated squarely in the middle of Walt Disney World, is a timeshare program; it is possible to acquire partial ownership in the property. Rooms and units not being used by timeshare owners are available for rental by nonowners. The Vacation Club has a restaurant, several pools, and other amenities including a workout room. The resort is served by the Disney bus system. We like the vacation club particularly for its quiet remoteness. First-class kitchens and roomy living areas make the Vacation Club a great choice for families who prefer to eat in.

Disney Vacation Club

| 275 rooms | golf course | shuttle bus service | $190–755 per night |

Other Themed Resort Hotels & Campgrounds In Walt Disney World

Disney's Village Resort is about six minutes from EPCOT Center by car and close to I-4. A huge entertainment, dining, lodging, and shopping complex, the Disney Village Resort offers a variety of lodging. The villas in this resort are one of two hotel accommodations in Walt Disney World proper that offer kitchen facilities. A relatively expensive grocery is located conveniently in the shopping complex. In 1995, some of the accommodations in Disney's Village Resort were incorporated into the new Disney Institute, which offers participative, educational vacation programs.

Fairway Villas	64 units	bus service	$355–375 per night
Treehouse Villas	60 units	bus service	$335–355 per night
Vacation Villas	119 units	bus service	$250–320 per night
Club Lake Villas	324 units	bus service	$185–290 per night

Budget Accommodations Disney Style. The best lodging deals in Walt Disney World for the economy conscious are the All-Star Resorts, with year-round rates of $70–80 per night. The All-Star Resorts are comprised of 20 three-story, T-shaped hotels offering a total of almost 4,000 guest rooms. In all, there are ten themed areas; five celebrate sports (surfing, basketball, tennis, football, and baseball) and the other five have musical motifs. The resort's design, which incorporates entrances shaped like musical notes and footballs, is pretty adolescent, sacrificing grace and beauty for energy and novelty. The guest rooms, although small, are thankfully less gimmicky. Other features include food courts, pools, and arcades. Despite the sports theme, there are no tennis, basketball, or other sports facilities. Transportation from the All-Star Resorts to the theme parks is by Disney bus.

Though most families like the All-Star Resorts, complaints like the following from a Falmouth, Massachusetts, family are common:

> The new All-Star Resorts are a great value but the rooms are very small (double beds, tiny table and two chairs). The food court is jammed from 8 to 10 P.M. when the parks close, as are all the local eateries.

All-Star Resorts
3,840 rooms   bus service $70–80 per night

Port Orleans, the Dixie Landings, and the Caribbean Beach Resorts. The second-best lodging deals in Walt Disney World are the Caribbean Beach, Port Orleans, and Dixie Landings resorts. All three offer nice accommodations at nightly rates of $90–119. The Caribbean has a colorful island theme, while Port Orleans and the Dixie Landings blend old New Orleans with a Mississippi River plantation motif. The Caribbean Beach Resort is situated on a 42-acre lake not far from EPCOT Center. The Port Orleans and Dixie Landings resorts are located side-by-side on one of the Disney canals. Of the three, the Caribbean Beach is the most centrally located and offers the best swimming and play areas for children. None of the three are serviced by monorail, but getting around Walt Disney World is easy by private car or the Disney bus system. The Dixie Landings and the Caribbean Beach resorts have multiple bus stops. At Port Orleans, however, there is only one stop. Port Orleans guests with rooms far from the bus station must endure quite a hike to catch a Disney bus.

Port Orleans and Dixie Landings both have passable full-service restaurants. The Caribbean Beach, however, offers only counter-service restaurants.

Caribbean Beach Resort
2,112 rooms   lakefront   shuttle bus service $90–119 per night
Port Orleans Resort
1,008 rooms   on canal   shuttle bus service $90–119 per night
Dixie Landings Resort
2,048 rooms   on canal   shuttle bus service $90–119 per night

Fort Wilderness Campground is a spacious resort campground for both tent and RV camping. Fully equipped, air-conditioned trailers are also available for rent. Campsites, classified as either "preferred" or "regular," are arranged on loops emanating from three main thoroughfares. The only difference between a preferred and regular campsite is that the preferred sites are closer to the campground amenities, i.e., swimming pools, restaurants, and shopping. All campsites have a 110- and 220-volt outlet, a picnic table, and a grill. Most RV sites have sanitary hook-ups. The campsites are roomy by eastern U.S. RV standards, but will probably feel a little cramped to tent campers. On any given day, about 90% of the campers will be RV folks. When making reservations, tent campers should request a campsite on Loop 1500, Cottontail Curl, or Loop 2000, Spanish Moss Lane. The better loops for RV campers are Loops 200, 400, 500, and 1400. All loops have a comfort station with showers, toilets, phones, an ice machine, and a coin laundry.

Aside from economy accommodations, some features of the Fort Wilderness Campground include a group camping area, full RV hook-ups, evening entertainment, horseback riding, bike trails, jogging trails, swimming, and a petting farm. River Country, a water theme park, is near Fort Wilderness Campground. Access to the Magic Kingdom and Discovery Island is by boat from the Fort Wilderness landing on Bay Lake, or to any other destination in Walt Disney World by private car or shuttle bus.

Fort Wilderness Campground

827 campsites	boat/bus service	$35–52 per night
363 trailers (sleeps 4–6)	boat/bus service	$180–195 per night

Walt Disney World Village Hotels.   In addition to the Village Resort, seven hotels offering a total of 3,825 rooms and suites are located in the Walt Disney World Village. Although commodious, some rooms are more expensive than the hotels serviced by the monorail. We found few bargains among the Walt Disney Village Hotels, and felt less of that special excitement you have when you stay inside "The World." While technically part of Walt Disney World, it is like visiting a colony instead of the mother country. Early-entry privileges to the Magic Kingdom are not accorded to guests at the Village Hotels, nor is free parking at the theme park pay lots. What's more, several of the Disney Village Hotels are dropping their contract with the Disney bus service that provides guest transportation to and from the parks. These developments make lodging at the Disney Village Hotels somewhat problematic. If you are considering one of the following hotels, be sure to clarify the transportation situation before making your reservations.

The Hilton	814 rooms	bus service	$185–245 per night
Courtyard Disney Village	323 rooms	bus service	$89–115 per night
Hotel Royal Plaza	396 rooms	bus service	$97–150 per night
Guest Doubletree Suites	229 rooms	bus service	$129–145 per night
Travelodge Hotel	325 rooms	bus service	$119–169 per night
Grosvenor Resort	630 rooms	bus service	$99–160 per night
Buena Vista Palace	808 rooms	bus service	$130–250 per night
	220 suites	bus service	$235–350 per night

—— *How to Evaluate a Walt Disney World Travel Package*

Hundreds of Walt Disney World package vacations are offered to the public each year. Some are created by the Walt Disney Travel Company, others by airline touring companies, and some by independent travel agents and wholesalers. Almost all Walt Disney World packages include lodging at or near the respective Disney facility and theme park admissions. Packages offered by the airlines include air transportation.

Package prices vary seasonally; mid-June to mid-August and holiday periods are most expensive. Off-season, forget packages: There are plenty of empty rooms and you can negotiate great discounts (at non-Disney properties) yourself. Similarly, airfares and rental cars are cheaper at off-peak times.

Almost all package ads feature a headline stating "5 Days at Walt Disney World from $605" (or some such). The key word in the ads is "from." The rock-bottom package price connotes the least desirable hotel accommodations. If you want better or more conveniently located digs, you'll have to pay more, often much more.

Walt Disney World packages offer a wide selection of hotels. Some, like the Disney-owned resorts, are very dependable. Others unfortunately run the quality gamut. If you consider a non-Disney–owned hotel, check its quality as reported by an independent rating system such as those offered by the *Unofficial Guides, AAA Directories, Mobil Guides,* or *Frommer's America on Wheels.* Checking two or three independent

NOTE: Incidentally, the Disney folks call the seven-hotel complex (which includes The Hilton and Buena Vista Palace) by four different names in their brochures and maps. It is referred to as the Walt Disney World Village, the Disney Village Resort, the Village Hotel Plaza, and Disney Village Hotels. And you thought you were confused?

sources is better than depending on one. Also, before you book, ask how old the hotel is and when the guest rooms were last refurbished. Locate the hotel on a local street map to verify its proximity to Walt Disney World. If you will not have a car, make sure the hotel has a shuttle service that satisfies your needs.

Packages with lodging in non-Disney hotels are much less expensive. On the flip side, guests staying in Disney hotels and campgrounds are accorded special privileges such as free parking and entry to the theme parks an hour before the general public on selected days. At Walt Disney World, you must stay at a Disney hotel or the Walt Disney World Swan (Westin) or Dolphin (Sheraton) Resorts to enjoy early-entry privileges. Curiously, the seven independent hotels located on property at the Walt Disney World Village (collectively known as "The Official Hotels of Walt Disney World") do not merit early entry or free parking benefits. Go figure. These hotels include the Buena Vista Palace, Grosvenor Resort, Guest Doubletree Suites, Hilton, Marriott Disney Village, Hotel Royal Plaza, and the Travelodge.

Packages should be a win/win proposition for both the buyer and the seller. The buyer only has to make one phone call and deal with a single salesperson to set up the whole vacation: transportation, rental car, admissions, lodging, meals, and even golf and tennis. The seller, likewise, only has to deal with the buyer one time, eliminating the need for separate sales, confirmations, and billing. In addition to streamlining selling, processing, and administration, some packagers also buy air fares in bulk on contract like a broker playing the commodities market. Buying a large number of air fares in advance allows the packager to buy them at a significant savings from posted fares. The same practice is applied also to hotel rooms. Because selling vacation packages is an efficient way of doing business, and because the packager can often buy individual package components (air fare, lodging, etc.) in bulk at discount, savings in operating expenses realized by the seller are sometimes passed on to the buyer so that, in addition to convenience, the package is also an exceptional value. In any event, that is the way it is supposed to work.

All too often, in practice, the seller realizes all of the economies and passes nothing in the way of savings on to the buyer. In some instances, packages are loaded additionally with extras which cost the packager next to nothing, but which run the retail price of the package sky-high. As you might expect, the savings to be passed along to customers are still somewhere in Fantasyland.

When considering a package, choose one that includes features you are sure to use. Whether you use all the features or not, you will most certainly pay for them. Second, if cost is of greater concern than convenience, make a few phone calls and see what the package would cost if you booked its individual components (air fare, rental car, lodging, etc.) on your own. If the package price is less than the a la carte cost, the package is a good deal. If the costs are about the same, the package is probably worth it for the convenience.

An Example. A popular package offered by the Walt Disney Travel Company is *Disney's All-Inclusive Deluxe Plan,* which includes:

1. Three, four, five, or seven nights' accommodation at your choice of the Grand Floridian Beach Resort, Yacht and Beach Club Resorts, Polynesian Resort, Contemporary Resort, Disney's Village Resort, Vacation Club Resort, or Fort Wilderness Resort Trailer Homes. Rates vary with choice of lodging between the Grand Floridian, most expensive, and the Fort Wilderness Resort Trailer Homes, least expensive.
2. Unlimited use of the Walt Disney World transportation system.
3. Admission and unlimited use of the Magic Kingdom, EPCOT 95, and the Disney-MGM Studios theme parks for the duration of your stay.
4. Admission and unlimited use of Pleasure Island (nighttime entertainment complex), River Country, Typhoon Lagoon, and Blizzard Beach (themed swimming parks), and Discovery Island (zoological park) for the duration of your stay. Admission becomes effective on check-in and is valid until midnight of your check-out day.
5. Unlimited use of Walt Disney World recreational facilities and activities.
6. Breakfast, lunch, and dinner each day at a variety of Disney World restaurants, gratuities included.
7. Round-trip transfers from the Orlando Airport or a rental car.
8. Admission to *Wonders of Walt Disney World* children's learning programs for children ages 10–15.
9. A private photo session with Mickey.
10. Free parking.
11. Birnbaum's *Official Guide to Walt Disney World* (one per party).

This package is interesting because it is one of Walt Disney World's most popular packages and is loaded with benefits and amenities. It is also interesting because you can come out a winner or a loser depending on how you use it. The package price varies with your choice of hotel and room, and with your length of stay. Our analysis is done for a Denver couple on a five-night package, traveling in July, and arriving in Orlando by air. The couple's choice of hotels is Disney's Polynesian Resort, connected to the Magic Kingdom by monorail. Because check-in time at the Polynesian is 3 P.M. or later, the couple plans to arrive at Walt Disney World in the late afternoon and to begin touring the theme parks the next day. Their itinerary calls for additional touring on their check-out day prior to departing for the airport. They chose a room with a "standard view" and took the rental car. The package costs $1,430 for each adult (two to a room) or $2,860 for the couple, tax included. The cost of their round-trip air fare from Denver will be in addition to the package price.

The five days' use of the transportation system is no big deal. Anyone who buys a regular four- or five-day admission can ride around all day on the buses and monorails. Besides, the package includes a rental car.

The package provides five days' admission to the Magic Kingdom, EPCOT Center, Disney-MGM Studios, River Country, Blizzard Beach, Typhoon Lagoon, Discovery Island, and Pleasure Island. Since it takes at least four days to see the three major theme parks, that doesn't leave much time to take advantage of Typhoon Lagoon, Blizzard Beach, River Country, Discovery Island, and Pleasure Island.

Another problem with the five days' admission provided in the package is that whatever you don't use you lose. Your admission options are good only for the days of your package, unlike the regular (non-package) five-day admission, the 5-Day World Hopper Pass. Unused days on the World Hopper Pass are good forever. If you come back next month or three years from now you will be able to finish using your World Hopper Pass. Not so with the package admission.

The package provides admission to Discovery Island, Pleasure Island, Typhoon Lagoon, Blizzard Beach, and River Country for the duration of your hotel stay. With the World Hopper Pass you have seven days from the date the pass is first used to enjoy these four smaller parks.

Unlimited use of Walt Disney World recreational facilities and activities are included in the package. This is a big deal if you want to golf, play tennis, boat, fish, and horseback ride. If you golf all morning, for instance, and visit the theme parks in the late afternoon and evening, you'll be walking on your tongue by the third day, but at least will be taking advantage of the recreational benefits. If you are vacationing at Walt Disney World primarily to enjoy the theme parks and do not intend to golf, horseback ride, etc., you will spend a lot of money on package features you won't be using. No matter how you cut it, you can't be in two places at once, and there is not enough time in five days to do all the stuff you're paying for. If you decided to buy a seven-night package in order to have more time for the recreational activities, it would cost you $1,887 per person, or $3,774 for two.

If you are a big eater, the inclusion of breakfast, lunch, and dinner each day is a major plus. Not only are these meals included, but you can eat as much as you want—appetizers, desserts, the works. Even tips are included (but not alcoholic beverages). You must eat all of your meals in full-service restaurants (no fast-food counter service or room service). While this ensures nicer meals, the time it takes to have a big sit-down breakfast and lunch every day bites into your touring and recreational schedule. On the bright side, you can select dinner shows like the *Hoop Dee Doo Revue* (providing space is available) or Disney character breakfasts as part of your meal package.

As far as the rest is concerned, the Wonders of Walt Disney World program is great if you have children of the appropriate age. In this example, however, we are dealing with an adult couple. Birnbaum's *Official Guide to Walt Disney World* is available at bookstores if you want to buy it exclusive of the package. Finally, the private photo session with Mickey may be more of a liability than an asset according to a gentleman from Texas who commented:

> Included in our vacation package was a photograph session with Mickey at You & Me Kid, a shop in the Disney Village Marketplace (aka WDW Village). Two *caveats emptor* here: First, the procedure for the photo session was very poorly arranged and executed with molasses-like speed (much to the ire of a gaggle of bedraggled parents). Second, we suspect that the delay was at least partially intentional: the more hours you were detained at the Disney Village before your appointment with The Mouse, the more steadily your billfold could be emptied on the relentless parade of Disney merchandise. Indeed, since this shopping center was the only location given for this special photo-op, our hunch is that the whole affair is little more than a lure to draw families off the beaten path to a nice but *tres* Disney Marketplace.

In the final analysis, the *All-Inclusive Deluxe Plan* is best suited to vacationers who have lots of energy and big appetites, and who like to play tennis and golf and go boating. It's for people who plan to be on the go from dawn until midnight and visit the theme parks every day. And finally, as you may have figured out, the package is set up in a way that makes it almost impossible not to waste many of its benefits.

Getting Down to Dollars and Cents.   If you leave out the golf, tennis, boating, and other recreational extras provided by the package, here is how the package compares to going it on your own:

Option A: Disney's All-Inclusive Deluxe Plan for two people in July, sharing a room with a standard view at the Polynesian Resort. $1,430 per person × 2	$2,860
Option B: Creating your own vacation with the same basic features as in Disney's All-Inclusive Deluxe Plan.	
The Polynesian Resort (with same room as in the package) for five nights with tax included. Total for two adults	$1,193
Two 5-Day World Hopper Passes (unlimited admission to three major and five minor parks) *plus* two 1-Day, 1-Park admissions, all with tax	472
$60 per person, per day meal allowance ($12 for breakfast, $18 for lunch, and $30 for dinner) for two people, for five days	600
Comparable rental car for the duration of the stay, with tax	124
Photo session with Mickey, plus prints	35
Birnbaum's *Official Guide to Walt Disney World*	13
Grand total for two people	$2,437
Amount saved by arranging things yourself	$423

Since only Option A (the package) includes the recreational facilities and activities, you could say that the difference between going it alone and buying the package is the charge for the recreational extras. In this case, the golf, tennis, boating, and horseback riding that you do or don't do in your five days costs you $423.

A less expensive version of the Deluxe Plan is *Disney's Resort Magic Plan,* which excludes meals and some recreational privileges such as golf, powerboat rental, and horseback riding, but offers the same admissions benefits plus a character breakfast. For identical dates and accommodations, the *Resort Magic Plan* will cost our couple $896 each, or $1,792 for both of them. If the couple purchases the same benefits as in the *Resort Magic Plan* a la carte, they will spend $1,833, $41 more than the package.

Another Example. Most Delta Dream Vacations offer exactly the same features as *Disney's Resort Magic Plan,* plus round-trip air transportation. If our couple buys a Delta Dream Vacation package for the same dates and accommodations, they will pay $1,360 per person, or $2,720 for two. If they book the same components themselves the cost will once again be $1,833 *before* buying airline tickets.

If you subtract the a la carte costs of all components from the total package price ($2,720 minus $1,833), the remainder ($887) amounts to what the couple is being charged for air fare, in this case $443.50 per person ($887 divided by two). If they can fly round-trip to Orlando from Denver for less than $443.50 a person, the package is not such a great deal. If air fares from Denver equal or exceed $443.50 per person, then the package makes sense.

Certified Vacations, the tour operator that packages Delta Dream Vacations, also runs the American Express Vacations program. If our couple buys a package with the same features from American Express with round-trip air from Denver, it will cost them $1,379 each, or $2,758 altogether. This time airfare costs our couple $925 ($2,758 minus $1,833), or $462.50 each.

O.K., Delta and American Express packages are both operated by Certified Vacations, and all three companies are officially tied to Disney by various sponsorships and other relations. Let's see what we come up with by trying to buy the same package from an operator more independent of Disney. Kingdom Tours, a large independent tour operator, charges $2,809 for the same package, air inclusive. In this case the couple will be paying $976 total ($2,809 minus $1,833), or $488 each for airfare.

MLT Vacations and Northwest World Vacations, both subsidiaries of Northwest Airlines, sell packages with the same features as those offered by the Disney Travel Company, Delta Dream Vacations, and American Express, plus some admissions to other area attractions such as Water Mania (swimming park), and the Church Street Station nighttime entertainment complex in downtown Orlando. Buying from MLT/Northwest, our couple will pay $1,324 apiece or $2,648 total, including round-trip air from Denver on Northwest. This time the flight is worth $755 ($2,648 minus $1,893), or $377.50 per person. Given that admissions to the Disney nightclub complex and the Disney swimming parks are included, it is doubtful that our couple will make use of the "out-of-the-World" admissions.

United Airlines offers vacation packages to Walt Disney World, but books rooms only in the Swan Hotel, an excellent property in Walt Disney World that is not owned by Disney. The United package includes round-trip air, accommodations at the Swan, a rental car, and park admissions for $1,265 per person, or $2,530 for our couple. If they book themselves and have to pay rack rate, they will pay $1,941 total before airfare. Subtracting the $1,941 do-it-yourself price from the package price of $2,530 leaves them an airfare cost of $589 or $294.50 each.

All tour operators, with the exception of Disney Travel Company, offer Orlando packages. Orlando packages feature hotels outside of, but near Walt Disney World, with admissions to Walt Disney World theme parks charged extra.

If you buy a package from Disney, do not expect Disney reservationists to offer suggestions or help you sort out your options. As a rule they will not volunteer information, but will only respond to specific questions you pose, adroitly ducking any query that calls for an opinion. A reader from North Riverside, Illinois, wrote to the *Unofficial Guide*, complaining:

> I have received various pieces of literature from WDW and it is very confusing to try and figure everything out. My wife made two telephone calls and the representatives from WDW were very courteous. However, they only answered the questions posed and were not very eager to give advice on what might be most cost effective. [The] WDW reps would not say if we would be better off doing one thing over the other. I feel a person could spend eight hours on the telephone with WDW reps and not have any more input than you get from reading the literature.

Another reader, also from Illinois, had this to say:

> I called Disney's reservations number and asked for availability and rates. . . . [Because] of the *Unofficial Guide* warning about Disney reservationists answering only the questions posed, I specifically asked, "Are there any special rates or discounts for that room during the month of October?" She replied, "Yes, we have that room available at a special price . . ." [For] the price of one phone call, I saved $440.

If you cannot get the information you need from the Disney people, try a good travel agent. Chances are the agent will be more forthcoming in helping you sort out your options. A dad from Valley Stream, New

York, used the Disney Travel Company, travel wholesalers, and travel agents in a successful round of comparison shopping:

Nothing pays off greater dividends than planning in advance. A year before our vacation we joined the Magic Kingdom Club. Some 8–9 months before our vacation I secured a package price from the Magic Kingdom Club, which I was able to use to negotiate a lower package with my travel agent. Yes, the travel agent packages are negotiable (much to my own surprise). What I now realize is that travel agents get WDW packages from different wholesalers and may not be immediately inclined to give you a package offered through the lowest-priced wholesaler. The first quotes I received were from AAA and Liberty Travel but, unbeknownst to me, both packages were, in fact, purchased through Delta Airlines. It was only after I was able to obtain a lower land package price by booking directly through Disney (as a Magic Kingdom Club member) that I was assured by each agent that they could beat the price I was able to secure — and they did, saving me several hundred dollars in the process. The air package was another reason to book through a travel agent. Our agent reserved seats for us on one airline only to call us three weeks later to tell us of discounts being offered through another airline. We acted quickly and bought the discounted tickets, saving another $200 on our air package.

Information Needed for Evaluation. For quick reference and to save on phone expenses, write or call Walt Disney World accommodations reservations at (407) 934-7639 or (407) 824-8000 and ask that you be mailed a current Walt Disney Travel Company Florida Brochure containing descriptions and room rates for all Walt Disney World lodging properties. Ask also for a rate sheet listing admission options and prices for all Walt Disney World theme parks including Pleasure Island, Typhoon Lagoon, Blizzard Beach, Discovery Island, and River Country, as well as the three major theme parks. This in hand, you are ready to evaluate any package that appeals to you. Remember that all packages are quoted on a per person basis, two to a room (double occupancy), and there is an 11% combined sales and room tax. For about everything else you buy in Florida (except groceries and prescription medicine), a 6% or 7% sales tax applies. Good luck.

Selecting and Booking a Hotel Outside of Walt Disney World

Lodging costs outside of Walt Disney World vary incredibly, as do amenities and services. If you shop around, you can find a nice, clean motel with a pool within 20 minutes of Walt Disney World for as low as $25 a night. You can also find luxurious, plush, expensive hotels with all the extras. Because of all the competition, discounts abound, particularly for members of AAA and AARP.

There are three primary "out-of-the-World" areas to consider:

1. International Drive area. This area about 15 to 20 minutes east of Walt Disney World parallels I-4 on its southern side, and offers a wide selection of both hotels and restaurants. Accommodations range from $30–200 per night. The chief drawbacks of the International Drive area are its terribly congested roads, countless traffic signals, and inadequate access to westbound I-4. The biggest bottleneck on International Drive is at its intersection with Sand Lake Road. In some sections of International Drive, the horrendous traffic can be circumvented by using local streets one or two blocks to the southeast (i.e., away from I-4).

Traffic aside, a gentleman from Ottawa, Canada, wrote extolling his International Drive experience:

International Drive is the place to stay when going to Disney. Your single paragraph description of this location failed to point out that [there are] several discount stores, boutiques, restaurants and mini-putts, and other entertainment facilities, all within walking distance of remarkably inexpensive accommodations and a short drive away from WDW. Many of the chain motels and hotels are located in this area, and the local merchants have created a mini-resort to cater to the tourists. It is the ideal place to unwind after a hard day visiting WDW at prices that allow you to spend your hard-earned vacation dollars where you want to—at Disney World itself. I have recommended this location for years and have never heard anything but raves about the wisdom of this advice.

Hotels in the International Drive area are listed in the Orlando Official Accommodations Guide published by the Orlando/Orange County

Convention and Visitors Bureau. To receive a copy, call (800) 255-5786 or (407) 363-5874.

2. Lake Buena Vista and the I-4 Corridor. There are a number of hotels situated along FL 535 and north of I-4 between Walt Disney World and I-4's intersection with the Florida Turnpike. These properties are easily reached from the Interstate, and are near a large number of restaurants, including those on International Drive. Driving time to Walt Disney World ranges from 5 to 15 minutes. Most hotels in this area are listed in the Orlando Official Accommodations Guide cited above.

3. US 192. This is the highway to Kissimmee, southeast of Walt Disney World. In addition to a number of large, full-service hotels, there are many small, privately owned motels in this area that are a good value. Several dozen properties on US 192 are actually closer to the Magic Kingdom, EPCOT Center, and the Disney-MGM Studios than the more expensive hotels in Walt Disney World Village and the Disney Village Hotel Plaza (in Walt Disney World). Traffic on US 192 is extremely heavy, but usually moves smoothly without much congestion. Though the food situation is rapidly improving, US 192 is somewhat inferior to the other areas in terms of number and quality of restaurants.

A senior citizen from Brookfield, Connecticut, was surprised and pleased with lodging in the US 192/Kissimmee area:

> We were amazed to find that from our cheaper and superior accommodations in Kissimmee it took only 5 minutes longer to reach the park turnstiles than it did from the Disney accommodations. Kissimmee is the way to go in our opinion.

Hotels located along US 192 and in Kissimmee are listed in the Kissimmee–St. Cloud Tour & Travel Sales Guide, available at (800) 333-5477.

Driving Time to the Theme Parks for Visitors Lodging Outside Walt Disney World

For those staying outside of Walt Disney World, we've calculated the approximate commuting time to the major theme parks' parking lots from each of several off-World lodging areas. Add a few minutes to pay your parking fee and actually park. Once parked at the Transportation and Ticket Center (Magic Kingdom parking lot), it takes an average of 20 additional minutes to reach the entrance to the Magic Kingdom. To

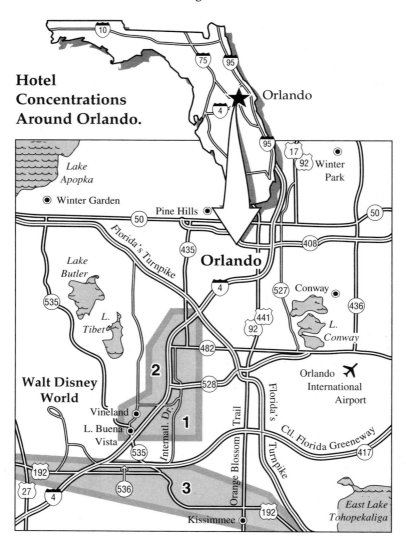

get to the EPCOT Center main entrance from the EPCOT Center parking lot, add 7 to 10 minutes. At the Disney-MGM Studios, expect to spend about 5 to 10 minutes getting from your car to the entrance. If you have not purchased your theme park admission in advance, tack on another 10 to 20 minutes.

Minutes From To	Magic Kingdom Parking Lot	EPCOT Center Parking Lot	Disney-MGM Studios Parking Lot
Downtown Orlando	26	23	24
North International Dr. and Universal Studios	20	17	18
Central International Dr. —Sand Lake Road	18	15	16
South International Dr. and Sea World	15	12	13
FL 535	10	7	8
FL 192, north of I-4	10–15	7–12	5–10
FL 192, south of I-4	10–18	7–15	5–13

—— *Getting a Good Deal on a Room Outside Walt Disney World*

The new hotel development at Walt Disney World has sharpened the competition among lodging properties throughout the Disney World/ Orlando/Kissimmee area. Hotels outside of Walt Disney World, in particular, are having to struggle to keep their guest rooms filled. Unable to compete with Disney resorts on the basis of convenience or perks, off-World hotels lure patrons with bargain room rates. The extent of the bargain, of course, depends on the season, the day of the week, and what else is going on in the area. In high season, during holiday periods, and when large conventions are being held at the Orange County Convention Center, even the most modest lodging properties are sold out. That having been said, below are some tips and strategies for getting a good deal on a room outside of Walt Disney World.

Though the following list may seem a bit intimidating, and may refer to players in the travel market that are unfamiliar to you, acquainting yourself with these concepts and strategies will serve you well in the long run. Simply put, many tips we provide for getting a good deal in or near Walt Disney World will work equally well at just about any other place where you need a hotel. Once you have invested a little time and have experimented with these strategies, you will be able to routinely obtain rooms at the best hotels, and at the lowest possible rates.

1. Orlando MagiCard. Orlando MagiCard is a discount program sponsored by the Orlando/Orange County Convention and Visitors Bureau. Card holders are eligible for discounts of 10–40% at approximately 75 participating hotels. The MagiCard is also good for discounts at certain area attractions, including Sea World, Cypress Gardens, Universal Studios, several dinner theaters, Church Street Station, and even Disney's Pleasure Island. Valid for up to six persons, the card is not available for groups or conventions.

To obtain an Orlando MagiCard and a list of participating hotels and attractions, call (800) 255-5786 or (407) 363-5874. Anyone over 18 years of age is eligible and there is no charge for the card. If you miss getting a card before you leave home, you can pick one up by stopping at the Convention and Visitors Bureau at 8445 International Drive in Orlando. When you call for your MagiCard, also ask for the Orlando Official Accommodations Guide and for the Orlando Vacation Planner.

2. Exit Information Guide. A company called EIG (Exit Information Guide) publishes a book of discount coupons for bargain rates at hotels throughout the state of Florida. These books are available free of charge in many restaurants and motels along the main interstate highways leading to the Sunshine State. Since most folks make reservations prior to leaving home, picking up the coupon book en route does not help much. For two dollars, however, EIG will mail you a copy (third class) before you make your reservations. If you call and use a credit card, EIG will send the guide first class for $3 ($5 U.S. for Canadian delivery). Write or call:

> Exit Information Guide
> 4205 N.W. 6th Street
> Gainesville, FL 32609
> (904) 371-3948

3. Special Weekend Rates. If you are not averse to a half hour drive to Walt Disney World, you can get great weekend rates on rooms in downtown Orlando. Most hotels that cater to business, state government, and convention travelers offer special weekend discounts, which range from 15–40% below normal weekday rates. You can find out about weekend specials by calling the hotel or by consulting your travel agent.

4. Getting Corporate Rates. Many hotels offer discounted corporate rates (5–20% off). Usually, you do not need to work for a large company or have a special relationship with the hotel to obtain these rates. Simply call the hotel of your choice and ask for their corporate rates. Many hotels will guarantee you the discounted rate on the phone when you make your reservation. Others may make the rate conditional on your providing some sort of *bona fides,* for instance a fax on your company's letterhead requesting the rate, or a company credit card or business card when you check in. Generally, the screening is not rigorous.

5. Half-Price Programs. Larger discounts on rooms (35–60%), in the Disney World area or anywhere else, are available through half-price hotel programs, often called travel clubs. Program operators contract with an individual hotel to provide rooms at deep discount, usually 50% off the rack rate, on a "space available" basis. In practice, space available generally means that you can reserve a room at the discounted rate whenever the hotel expects to be at less than 80% occupancy. A little calendar sleuthing will help you avoid high season, big conventions, holidays, and special events and increase your chances of chosing a time for your visit when the discounts are available.

Most half-price programs charge an annual membership fee or directory subscription charge of $25–125. Once enrolled, you are mailed a membership card and a directory listing all the hotels participating in the program. You will notice immediately that there are a lot of restrictions and exceptions. Some hotels, for instance, "black out" certain dates or times of year. Others may only offer the discount on certain days of the week, or require you to stay a certain number of nights. Still others may offer a much smaller discount than 50% off the rack rate.

Programs specialize in domestic travel, international travel, or both. The more established operators offer members up to 4,000 hotels to chose from in the United States. All of the programs have a heavy concentration of hotels in California and Florida, and most have a very limited selection of participating properties in New York City or Boston. Offerings in other cities and regions of the United States vary considerably. The programs with the largest selection of hotels in the Disney World area are Encore, at (800) 638-0930, and Travel America at Half Price (Entertainment Publications), at (800) 285-5525.

One problem with half-price programs is that not all hotels offer a full 50% discount. Another slippery problem is the base rate against which the discount is applied. Some hotels figure the discount on an exaggerated rack rate that nobody would ever have to pay. A few participating hotels may deduct the discount from a supposedly "superior" or "upgraded" room rate, even though the room is the hotel's standard accommodation. Though hard to pin down, the majority of participating properties base discounts on the published rates in the *Hotel & Travel Index* (a quarterly reference journal used by travel agents) and work within the spirit of their agreement with the program operator. As a rule, if you travel several times a year, you will more than pay for your program membership with your savings.

A noteworthy addendum to this information is that deeply discounted rooms through half-price programs are not commissionable to travel agents. In practical terms, this means that you must ordinarily make your own inquiry calls and reservations. If you travel frequently, however, and run a lot of business through your travel agent, he or she will probably do your legwork, lack of commission notwithstanding.

6. Preferred Rates.　If you cannot book the hotel of your choice through a half-price program, you and your travel agent may have to search for a lesser discount, often called a preferred rate. A preferred rate could be a discount made available to travel agents to stimulate booking activity, or a discount initiated to attract a certain class of traveler. Most preferred rates are promoted through travel industry publications and are often accessible only through an agent.

We recommend sounding out your travel agent about possible deals. Be aware, however, that the rates shown on travel agents' computerized reservations systems are not always the lowest rates obtainable. Zero in on a couple of hotels that fill your needs in terms of location and quality of accommodations, and then have your travel agent call for the latest rates and specials. Hotel reps are almost always more responsive to travel agents because they represent a source of additional business. There are certain specials that hotel reps will disclose *only* to travel agents. Travel agents also come in handy when the hotel you want is supposedly booked. A personal appeal from your agent to the hotel's director of sales and marketing will get you a room more than half the time.

7. Wholesalers, Consolidators, and Reservation Services.　If you do not want to join a program and buy a discount directory, you can take advantage of the services of a wholesaler or consolidator. Wholesalers and consolidators buy rooms, or options on rooms (room blocks), from hotels at a low negotiated rate. They then resell the rooms at a profit through travel agents, tour packagers, or directly to the public. Most wholesalers and consolidators have a provision for returning unsold rooms to participating hotels, but are disinclined to do so. The wholesaler's or consolidator's relationship with any hotel is predicated on volume. If they return rooms unsold, the hotel might not make as many rooms available to them the next time around. So wholesalers and consolidators often offer rooms at bargain rates, anywhere from 15–50% off the rack rate, occasionally sacrificing profit margin in the process, to avoid returning the rooms to the hotel unsold.

When wholesalers and consolidators deal directly with the public, they frequently represent themselves as "reservation services." When you call, you can ask them for a rate quote for a particular hotel or, alternatively, for their best deal in the area where you'd like to stay. If there is a maximum amount you are willing to pay, say so. Chances are the service will find something that works for you, even if they have to shave a dollar or two of their own profit. Sometimes you have to pay for your room by credit card when you make your reservation. Other times you pay as usual, when you check out. Listed below are two services that frequently offer substantial discounts:

Central Reservation Service	(800) 548-3311
Room Exchange	(800) 846-7000

8. *If You Make Your Own Reservation.* As you poke around trying to find a good deal, there are several things you should know. First, always call the hotel in question, not to the hotel chain's national 800 number. Quite often, the reservationists at the national 800 number are unaware of local specials. Always ask about specials before you inquire about corporate rates. Do not be reluctant to bargain. If you are buying a hotel's weekend package, for example, and want to extend your stay into the following week, you can often obtain at least the corporate rate for the extra days. Do your bargaining, however, before you check in, preferably when you make your reservations.

9. *Condominium Deals.* There are a large number of condo resorts and timeshares in the Kissimmee/Orlando area that rent to vacationers for a week or even less. Bargains can be found, especially during off-peak periods. Reservations and information can be obtained from the following reservation services:

Condolink	(800) 733-4445
Kissimmee–St. Cloud Reservations Center	(800) 333-5477

A majority of area condos that rent to visitors also work with travel agents. In many cases the condo owners pay an enhanced commission to agents who rent the units for *reduced consumer rates*. It's worth a call to your travel agent.

In the following section, "Hotels and Motels: Rated and Ranked," we compare hotels situated in three main areas outside Walt Disney World, described above, with those inside Walt Disney World. This evaluation will help you identify the best rooms and values, both in and out of the World.

In addition to Walt Disney World and the three lodging areas, there are also hotels at the intersection of US 27 and I-4, on US 441 (Orange Blossom Trail), and in downtown Orlando. All of these, however, require more than 20 minutes commuting time to Walt Disney World, and are not included in our comparative ratings. We've also excluded lodging properties south of Siesta Lago Road on US 192.

Hotels and Motels:
Rated and Ranked

—— What's in a Room?

Except for cleanliness, state of repair, and decor, most travelers do not pay much attention to hotel rooms. There is, of course, a discernible standard of quality and luxury that differentiates Motel 6 from Holiday Inn, Holiday Inn from Marriott, and so on. However, many hotel guests fail to appreciate that some rooms are better engineered than others.

Contrary to what you might suppose, designing a hotel room is (or should be) a lot more complex than picking a bedspread to match the carpet and drapes. Making the room usable to its occupants is an art, a planning discipline that combines both form and function.

Decor and taste are important, certainly. No one wants to spend several days in a room with decor that is dated, garish, or even ugly. But beyond the decor, how "livable" is the hotel room? In Orlando, for example, we have seen some beautifully appointed rooms that simply are not well designed for human habitation. The next time you stay in a hotel, pay attention to the details and design elements of your room. Even more than decor, these are the things that will make you feel comfortable and at home.

It takes the *Unofficial Guide* researchers about 40 minutes to inspect a hotel room. Here are a few of the things we check:

Room Size. While some smaller rooms are cozy and well designed, a large and uncluttered room is generally preferable, especially for a stay of more than three days.

Temperature Control, Ventilation, and Odor. The guest should be able to control the temperature of the room. The best system, because it's so quiet, is central heating and air conditioning, controlled by the room's own thermostat. The next best is a room module heater and air conditioner, preferably controlled by an automatic thermostat, but usually operated by manual button controls. The worst system is central heating and air without any sort of room thermostat or guest control.

The vast majority of hotel rooms have windows or balcony doors that have been permanently secured shut. Though there are some legitimate safety and liability issues involved, we prefer windows and balcony doors that can be opened to admit fresh air. Hotel rooms should be odor free, smoke free, and not feel stuffy or damp.

Room Security. Better rooms have locks that require a plastic card instead of the traditional lock and key. Card and slot systems allow the hotel to change the combination or entry code of the lock with each new guest. A burglar who has somehow acquired a room key to a conventional lock can afford to wait until the situation is right before using the key to gain access. Not so with a card and slot system. Though larger hotels and hotel chains with lock and key systems usually rotate their locks once each year, they remain vulnerable to hotel thieves much of the time. Many smaller or independent properties rarely rotate their locks.

In addition to the entry lock system, the door should have a deadbolt, and preferably a chain lock. A chain by itself is not sufficient. Doors should also have a peephole. Windows and balcony doors, if any, should have secure locks.

Safety. Every room should have a fire or smoke alarm, clear fire instructions, and, ideally, a sprinkler system. Bathtubs should have a nonskid surface, and shower stalls should have doors that open outward or slide side-to-side. Bathroom electrical outlets should be high on the wall and not too close to the sink. Balconies should have sturdy, high rails.

Noise. Most travelers have been kept awake by the television, partying, or amorous activities of people in the next room, or by traffic on the street outside. Better hotels are designed with noise control in mind. Wall and ceiling construction are substantial, effectively screening routine noise. Carpets and drapes, in addition to being decorative, also absorb and muffle sounds. Mattresses, mounted on stable platforms or sturdy bed frames, do not squeak even when challenged by the most acrobatic lovers. Televisions enclosed in cabinets, and with volume governors, rarely disturb guests in adjacent rooms.

In better hotels, the air conditioning and heating system is well maintained and operates without noise or vibration. Likewise, plumbing is quiet and positioned away from the sleeping area. Doors to the hall, and to adjoining rooms, are thick and well fitted to better keep out noise.

Darkness Control. Have you ever been in a hotel room where the curtains would not quite come together in the middle? Thick, lined curtains which close completely in the center and which extend beyond the dimensions of the window or door frame are required. In a well-planned room, the curtains, shades, or blinds should almost totally block light at any time of day.

Lighting. Poor lighting is an extremely common problem in American hotel rooms. The lighting is usually adequate for dressing, relaxing, or watching television, but not for reading or working. Lighting needs to be bright over tables and desks, and alongside couches or easy chairs. Since so many people read in bed, there should be a separate light for each person. (A room with two queen beds should have four individual lights.) Better bedside reading lights illuminate a small area, so if you want to sleep and someone else prefers to stay up and read, you will not be bothered by the light. A single lamp on a table between beds is the worst situation by far. In each bed, only the person next to the lamp will have sufficient light to read. This deficiency is often compounded by low-wattage light bulbs.

In addition, closet areas should be well lit, and there should be a switch near the door that turns on lights in the room when you enter. A seldom seen, but desirable, feature is a bedside console that allows a guest to control all or most lights in the room from bed.

Furnishings. At bare minimum, the bed(s) must be firm. Pillows should be made with nonallergic fillers and, in addition to the sheets and spread, a blanket should be provided. Bed clothes should be laundered with a fabric softener and changed daily. Better hotels usually provide extra blankets and pillows in the room or on request, and some use a second topsheet between the blanket and the spread.

There should be a dresser large enough to hold clothes for two people during a five-day stay. A small table with two chairs, or a desk with a chair, should be provided. The room should also be equipped with a luggage rack and a three-quarter- to full-length mirror.

The television should be color, cable-connected, and ideally have a volume governor and remote control. It should be mounted on a swivel base, and preferably enclosed in a cabinet. Local channels should be posted on the set and a local TV program guide should be supplied.

The telephone should be touchtone, conveniently situated for bedside use, and should have on or near it, easily understood dialing instructions and a rate card. Local white and yellow pages should be provided. Better hotels have phones in the bath and equip room phones with long cords.

Well-designed hotel rooms usually have a plush armchair or sleeper sofa for lounging and reading. The best headboards are padded for comfortable reading in bed, and there should be a nightstand or table on each side of the bed(s). Nice extras in any hotel room include a small refrigerator, a digital alarm clock, and a coffeemaker.

Bathroom. Two sinks are better than one, and you cannot have too much counter space. A sink outside the bathroom is a great convenience when two people are bathing and dressing at the same time. Sinks should have drains with stoppers.

Better bathrooms have both tub and shower with nonslip bottoms. Tub and shower controls should be easy to operate. Adjustable shower heads are best. The bath needs to be well lit and should have an exhaust fan and a guest controlled bathroom heater. Towels should be large, soft, and fluffy and provided in generous quantities, as should hand towels and washcloths. There should be an electrical outlet for each sink, conveniently and safely placed.

Complimentary shampoo, conditioner, and lotion are a plus, as are robes and bathmats. Better hotels supply their bathrooms with tissues and extra toilet paper. Truly luxurious baths feature a hair dryer, a small television, or even a jacuzzi.

Vending. There should be complimentary ice and a drink machine on each floor. Welcome additions include a snack machine and a sundries (combs, toothpaste) machine. The latter are seldom found in large hotels that have restaurants and shops.

—— *Room Ratings*

To evaluate properties according to their relative quality, tastefulness, state of repair, cleanliness, and size of their **standard rooms**, we have grouped the hotels and motels into classifications denoted by stars. Star ratings in this guide apply to Orlando area properties only, and do not necessarily correspond to ratings awarded by Frommer, Mobil, AAA, or other travel critics. Because stars have little relevance when awarded in the absence of commonly recognized standards of comparison, we have tied our ratings to expected levels of quality established by specific American hotel corporations.

★★★★★	*Superior Rooms*	Tasteful and luxurious by any standard
★★★★	*Extremely Nice Rooms*	What you would expect at a Hyatt Regency or Marriott

★★★	*Nice Rooms*	Holiday Inn or comparable quality
★★	*Adequate Rooms*	Clean, comfortable, and functional without frills —like a Motel 6
★	*Super Budget*	

Star ratings apply to *room quality only,* and describe the property's standard accommodations. For most hotels and motels a "standard accommodation" is a hotel room with either one king bed or two queen beds. In an all-suite property, the standard accommodation is either a one- or two-room suite. In addition to standard accommodations, many hotels offer luxury rooms and special suites, which are not rated in this guide. Star ratings for rooms are assigned without regard to whether a property has restaurant(s), recreational facilities, entertainment, or other extras.

In addition to stars (which delineate broad categories), we also employ a numerical rating system. Our rating scale is 0 to 100, with 100 as the best possible rating, and zero (0) as the worst. Numerical ratings are presented to show the difference we perceive between one property and another. Rooms at the Hyatt Orlando, Wyndham Garden Hotel, and Courtyard Disney Village are all rated as three and a half stars (★★★½). In the supplemental numerical ratings, the Hyatt is rated an 82, the Wyndham Garden an 81, and the Courtyard a 77. This means that within the three-and-a-half-star category, the Hyatt and Wyndham Garden are comparable, and both have slightly nicer rooms than the Courtyard.

The location column identifies the area around Walt Disney World where you will find a particular property. The designation "WDW" means that the property is located inside Walt Disney World. A "1" means that the property is located on or near International Drive. Properties on US 192 (aka Irlo Bronson Memorial Highway, Vine Street, and Space Coast Parkway) are indicated by a "3." All others are marked number "2," and for the most part, are located along the I-4 corridor, though some are in isolated locations that do not meet any other criteria.

Properties along US 192 also carry location designations with their names, such as the Holiday Inn Maingate East. The consensus in Orlando seems to be that the main entrance to Walt Disney World is the broad interstate-type road that runs off of US 192. This is called Maingate. Properties located along US 192 call themselves Maingate East or West to differentiate their positions along the highway. So, coming from US 27 toward the Maingate area, the properties before you reach the Maingate turnoff are called Maingate West, while the properties after you pass the Maingate turnoff are called Maingate East.

—— *How the Hotels Compare*

Cost estimates are based on the hotel's published rack rates for standard rooms. Each "$" represents $30. Thus a cost symbol of "$$$" means a room (or suite) at that hotel will be about $90 a night.

Here is a hit parade of the nicest rooms in town. We've focused strictly on room quality, and excluded any consideration of location, services, recreation, or amenities. In some instances, a one- or two-room suite can be had for the same price or less than that of a hotel room.

If you used an earlier edition of this guide, you will notice that many of the ratings and rankings have changed. In addition to the inclusion of new properties, these changes are occasioned by such positive developments as guest room renovation or improved maintenance and housekeeping. A failure to properly maintain guest rooms, or a lapse in housekeeping standards, can negatively affect the ratings.

Finally, before you begin to shop for a hotel, take a hard look at this letter we received from a man in Hot Springs, Arkansas:

> We cancelled our room reservations to follow the advice in your book [and reserved a hotel highly ranked by the *Unofficial Guide*]. We wanted inexpensive, but clean and cheerful. We got inexpensive, but [also] dirty, grim, and depressing. I really felt disappointed in your advice and the room. It was the pits. That was the one real piece of information I needed from your book! The room spoiled the holiday for me aside from our touring.

Needless to say, this letter was as unsettling to us as the bad room was to our reader. Our integrity as travel journalists, after all, is based on the quality of the information we provide our readers. Even with the best of intentions and the most conscientious research, however, we cannot inspect every room in every hotel. What we do, in statistical terms, is take a sample: we check out several rooms selected at random in each hotel and base our ratings and rankings on those rooms. The inspections are conducted anonymously and without the knowledge of the property's management. Although unusual, it is certainly possible that the rooms we randomly inspect are not representative of the majority of rooms at a particular hotel. Another possibility is that the rooms we inspect in a given hotel *are* representative, but that by bad luck a reader is assigned a room that is inferior. When rechecking the hotel our reader disliked so intensely, we discovered our rating was correctly representative, but that he and his wife had unfortunately been assigned to one of a small number of threadbare rooms scheduled for renovation.

The key to avoiding disappointment is to do some advance snooping around. We recommend that you ask the hotel to send a photo of their standard guest room before you book, or at least get a copy of the hotel's promotional brochure. Be forewarned, however, that some hotel chains use the same guest room photo in their promotional literature for *all* hotels in the chain, and that the guest room in a specific property may not resemble the photo in the brochure. When you or your travel agent call, ask how old the property is and when the guest room you are being assigned was last renovated. If you arrive and are assigned a room inferior to that which you had been led to expect, demand to be moved to another room.

How the Hotels Compare

Hotel	Location	Room Star Rating	Room Quality Rating	Cost	Phone (A/C 407)
WDW Grand Floridian Resort	WDW	★★★★★	97	$$$$$$$$$$$–	934-7639
WDW Beach Club Resort	WDW	★★★★½	95	$$$$	934-7639
WDW Yacht Club Resort	WDW	★★★★½	95	$$$$$$$$–	934-7639
Shades of Green	WDW	★★★★½	94	open to military only	824-3400
Marriott Orlando World Center	2	★★★★½	92	$$$$$+	239-4200
Stouffer Orlando Resort	2	★★★★½	92	$$$$$$$	351-5555
Peabody Orlando	1	★★★★½	91	$$$$$$$	352-4000
WDW Dolphin Resort	WDW	★★★★½	91	$$$$$$$$$–	934-7639
WDW Swan	WDW	★★★★½	91	$$$$$$$$$–	934-7639
Best Western Buena Vista Suites	1	★★★★½	90	$$$$–	239-8588
Homewood Suites Maingate	3	★★★★	88	$$$+	396-2229

How the Hotels Compare (continued)

Hotel	Location	Room Star Rating	Room Quality Rating	Cost	Phone (A/C 407)
WDW Contemporary Resort	WDW	★★★★	88	$$$$$$$	934-7639
WDW Polynesian Resort	WDW	★★★★	88	$$$$$$$$	934-7639
Doubletree Guest Suites	WDW	★★★★	87	$$$$$−	934-1000
Hawthorn Suites Orlando	1	★★★★	87	$$$$+	351-6600
Hilton Inn Gateway (tower rooms)	3	★★★★	87	$$$$−	396-4400
Hyatt Regency Grand Cypress	2	★★★★	87	$$$$$$$$	239-1234
Summerfield Suites	1	★★★★	87	$$$$$$−	352-2400
WDW Wilderness Lodge	WDW	★★★★	87	$$$$$$+	934-7639
Embassy Suites Orlando International	3	★★★★	86	$$$$	352-1400
Embassy Suites Resort	2	★★★★	86	$$$$$$+	239-1144
Summerfield Suites Lake Buena Vista	2	★★★★	86	$$$$$$+	238-0777
WDW Port Orleans Resort	WDW	★★★★	86	$$$+	934-7639
Sol Orlando Village Resort	3	★★★★	84	$$$$	397-0555
Villas at Resort World	2	★★★★	84	$$$$$−	800-423-8604
WDW Dixie Landings Resort	WDW	★★★★	84	$$$+	934-7639
Best Western Grosvenor Resort	WDW	★★★★	83	$$$+	828-4444
Buena Vista Palace	WDW	★★★★	83	$$$$$	827-2727
Enclave Suites	1	★★★★	83	$$$	351-1155
Embassy Suites Plaza International	1	★★★½	82	$$$$$$	800-362-2779

How the Hotels Compare (continued)

Hotel	Location	Room Star Rating	Room Quality Rating	Cost	Phone (A/C 407)
Heritage Inn Orlando	I	★★★½	82	$$$+	352-0008
Hilton Disney Village	WDW	★★★½	82	$$$$$$+	827-4000
Hyatt Orlando	3	★★★½	82	$$$+	396-1234
Residence Inn Lake Cecile	3	★★★½	82	$$$−	396-2056
Clarion Plaza Hotel	I	★★★½	81	$$$$+	352-9700
Radisson Twin Towers Hotel	I	★★★½	81	$$$$+	800-327-2110
Wyndham Garden Hotel	2	★★★½	81	$$+	239-8500
Holiday Inn Sun Spree Resort	2	★★★½	80	$$$	239-4500
Orlando Marriott	I	★★★½	80	$$$+	351-2420
Westgate Lakes	2	★★★½	80	$$$+	352-8051
Residence Inn Orlando	I	★★★½	79	$$$$	345-0117
WDW Caribbean Beach Resort	WDW	★★★½	79	$$$+	934-7639
Travelodge Hotel Disney Village	WDW	★★★½	78	$$$	828-2424
Courtyard by Marriott	I	★★★½	77	$$$−	351-2244
Courtyard Disney Village	WDW	★★★½	77	$$$	828-8888
Courtyard Maingate	3	★★★½	75	$$$	396-4000
Hilton Inn Gateway (garden rooms)	3	★★★½	75	$$$	396-4400
Hampton Inn International Drive	I	★★★	74	$$$−	345-1112
Howard Johnson Universal Tower	I	★★★	74	$$+	351-2100
Quality Suites Maingate East	3	★★★	74	$$$	396-8040
Radisson Inn Lake Buena Vista	2	★★★	74	$$	239-8400

How the Hotels Compare *(continued)*

Hotel	Location	Room Star Rating	Room Quality Rating	Cost	Phone (A/C 407)
Ramada Resort Maingate at the Parkway	3	★★★	74	$$$	396-7000
WDW All-Star Resort	WDW	★★★	74	$$$−	939-5000
Hampton Inn Maingate	3	★★★	73	$$+	396-8484
Ramada Resort Florida Center	1	★★★	73	$$+	351-4600
Days Inn Lake Buena Vista Resort	2	★★★	72	$$	800-423-3297
Hampton Inn Universal Studios	1	★★★	72	$$+	351-6716
Holiday Inn International Resort	1	★★★	72	$$$	351-3500
Quality Inn Lake Cecile	3	★★★	72	$$	396-4455
Travelodge Maingate East	3	★★★	72	$$$	396-4222
Radisson Inn International	1	★★★	71	$$+	345-0505
Travelodge Suites Eastgate	3	★★★	71	$$+	396-7666
Comfort Suites Orlando	2	★★★	70	$$$	351-5050
Days Inn Lake Buena Vista Village	2	★★★	70	$$$−	239-4646
Holiday Inn Maingate East	3	★★★	70	$$+	396-4488
Radisson Inn Maingate	3	★★★	70	$$+	396-1400
Sheraton World Resort	1	★★★	70	$$+	352-1100
Holiday Inn Universal Studios	1	★★★	69	$$$−	351-3333

How the Hotels Compare (continued)

Hotel	Location	Room Star Rating	Room Quality Rating	Cost	Phone (A/C 407)
Howard Johnson Fountain Park	3	★★★	69	$$+	396-1111
Floridian of Orlando	1	★★★	68	$$+	351-5009
Holiday Inn Express	1	★★★	68	$$	351-4430
Hotel Royal Plaza	WDW	★★★	68	$$$−	828-2828
Howard Johnson Park Square	2	★★★	68	$$$+	239-6900
Sheraton Lakeside Inn	3	★★★	68	$$	396-2222
Wellesley Inn	1	★★★	68	$$+	345-0026
Holiday Inn Maingate West	3	★★★	67	$$	396-1100
La Quinta Inn International	1	★★★	67	$$+	351-1660
Ramada Inn Westgate	3	★★★	67	$$−	800-365-6935
Westgate Towers	3	★★★	67	$$+	396-2500
Days Suites Maingate East	3	★★★	66	$$$$	396-7900
Delta Orlando Resort	1	★★★	66	$$$+	351-3340
MIC Lakefront Inn	1	★★★	66	$$	345-5340
Ramada Resort Maingate	3	★★★	66	$$+	396-4466
Wynfield Inn Westwood	1	★★★	66	$$+	800-346-1551
Days Inn Lake Buena Vista	2	★★★	65	$$+	239-4441
Las Palmas Hotel	1	★★★	65	$$	351-3900
Riande Continental Royal	1	★★★	65	$$+	800-895-2648
Comfort Inn International	1	★★½	64	$$$−	800-327-1366
Days Inn Maingate West	3	★★½	64	$$	396-1000
Econo Lodge Maingate West	3	★★½	64	$$−	396-9300

How the Hotels Compare (continued)

Hotel	Location	Room Star Rating	Room Quality Rating	Cost	Phone (A/C 407)
International Gateway Inn	1	★★½	64	$+	800-327-0750
Larson's Lodge Maingate	3	★★½	64	$$+	396-6100
Red Roof Inn Kissimmee	3	★★½	64	$$−	396-0065
Wynfield Inn Maingate	3	★★½	64	$$+	800-346-1551
Best Western Maingate	3	★★½	63	$$−	396-0100
Best Western Plaza International	1	★★½	63	$$$−	345-8195
Days Inn Orlando Lakeside	1	★★½	63	$$−	351-1900
Gateway Inn	1	★★½	63	$$	351-2000
Quality Inn Plaza	1	★★½	63	$$−	345-8585
Fairfield Inn International	1	★★½	62	$$+	363-1944
Ho Jo Inn	3	★★½	62	$+	800-446-5669
Howard Johnson Maingate	3	★★½	62	$$−	800-638-7829
Inns of America International	1	★★½	62	$+	800-826-0778
Inns of America Maingate	3	★★½	62	$+	800-826-0778
Famous Host Inn	3	★★½	61	$+	396-8883
Holiday Inn Maingate	3	★★½	61	$$	396-7300
Howard Johnson South Int'l Drive	1	★★½	61	$$+	351-5100
Ramada Limited Universal Maingate	1	★★½	61	$+	354-3996
Riande Continental Plaza	1	★★½	61	$$−	352-8211
Wilson World Maingate	3	★★½	61	$$$−	396-6000

How the Hotels Compare (continued)

Hotel	Location	Room Star Rating	Room Quality Rating	Cost	Phone (A/C 407)
Best Western Eastgate	3	★★½	60	$+	396-0707
Choice Suites	3	★★½	60	$+	396-1780
Comfort Inn at Lake Buena Vista	2	★★½	60	$$−	239-7300
Comfort Inn Maingate	3	★★½	60	$$−	396-7500
Howard Johnson Lodge	1	★★½	60	$$− .	351-2900
Buena Vista Motel	3	★★½	59	$+	396-2100
Days Inn Civic Center	1	★★½	59	$$$−	352-8700
Days Inn International Drive	1	★★½	59	$$$−	351-1200
Days Inn Universal Studios	1	★★½	59	$$+	351-3800
Park Inn International	3	★★½	59	$$+	396-1376
Sleep Inn Maingate	3	★★½	59	$+	396-1600
Travelodge Maingate West	3	★★½	59	$$	396-1828
International Inn	1	★★½	58	$$−	351-4444
Knights Inn Maingate	3	★★½	58	$+	396-4200
Quality Inn International	1	★★½	58	$$+	351-1600
Knights Inn Maingate East	3	★★½	57	$+	396-8186
Ramada Limited	3	★★½	57	$+	396-2212
Red Carpet Inn East	3	★★½	57	$	396-1133
Crystal Tree Inn	1	★★½	56	$$−	352-8383
Econo Lodge Maingate Central	3	★★½	56	$$−	396-4343
Golden Link Motel	3	★★½	56	$+	396-0555
Ho Jo Inn Maingate	3	★★½	56	$$+	396-1748
Sun Motel	3	★★½	56	$	396-2673

How the Hotels Compare (continued)

Hotel	Location	Room Star Rating	Room Quality Rating	Cost	Phone (A/C 407)
Travelodge Orlando Flags	1	★★½	56	$$+	800-722-7462
Rodeway Inn Eastgate	3	★★½	55	$+	396-7700
Central Motel	3	★★	55	$	396-2333
Monte Carlo	3	★★	55	$+	396-4700
Motel 6 International Drive	1	★★	55	$−	351-6500
Red Roof Inn Orlando	1	★★	55	$$−	352-1507
Traveler's Inn	3	★★	55	$+	396-1668
Days Inn Maingate East	3	★★	54	$$+	396-7900
Economy Inns of America	3	★★	54	$+	396-4020
Embassy Super 8 Motel	3	★★	54	$+	396-1144
Key Motel	3	★★	54	$	396-6200
King's Motel	3	★★	52	$+	396-4762
Econo Lodge Maingate Hawaiian	3	★★	51	$$−	396-2000
Motel 6 Maingate East	3	★★	51	$	396-6333
Motel 6 Maingate West	3	★½	45	$	396-6427

—— Good Deals and Bad Deals

Having listed the nicest rooms in town, let's reorder the list to rank the best combinations of quality and value in a room. As before, the rankings are made without consideration of location or the availability of restaurant(s), recreational facilities, entertainment, and/or amenities. Once again, each lodging property is awarded a value rating on a 0–100 scale. The higher the rating, the better the value. You will note that the Polynesian Resort at Walt Disney World has a relatively low value rating. This is because for the same price you can get a *nicer room* at another property. The Polynesian, however, is one of the most popular hotels in the area and many guests are willing to pay a higher rate for the convenience, service, and amenities.

We recently had a reader write us to complain that he had booked one of our top-ranked rooms in terms of value and had been very disappointed in the room. We noticed that the room the reader occupied had a quality rating of ★★½. We would remind you that the value ratings are intended to give you some sense of value received for dollars spent. A ★★½ room at $30 may have the same value rating as a ★★★★ room at $85, but that does not mean the rooms will be of comparable quality. Regardless of whether it's a good deal or not, a ★★½ room is still a ★★½ room.

Listed below are the best room buys for the money, regardless of location or star classification, based on averaged rack rates. Note that a suite can sometimes cost less than a hotel room.

Good Deals and Bad Deals

Hotel	Location	Room Value Rating	Room Star Rating	Cost
International Gateway Inn	1	99	★★½	$+
Red Carpet Inn East	3	99	★★½	$
Sun Motel	3	98	★★½	$
Radisson Inn Lake Buena Vista	2	95	★★★	$$
Ramada Inn Westgate	3	95	★★★	$$−
Motel 6 International Drive	1	95	★★	$−
Choice Suites	3	93	★★½	$+
Buena Vista Motel	3	91	★★½	$+
Wyndham Garden Hotel	2	89	★★★½	$$+
Golden Link Motel	3	89	★★½	$+

Good Deals and Bad Deals *(continued)*

Hotel	Location	Room Value Rating	Room Star Rating	Cost
Ho Jo Inn	3	89	★★½	$+
Knights Inn Maingate	3	87	★★½	$+
Inns of America International	1	86	★★½	$+
Knights Inn Maingate East	3	86	★★½	$+
Inns of America Maingate	3	84	★★½	$+
Howard Johnson Maingate	3	82	★★½	$$−
Best Western Buena Vista Suites	1	81	★★★★½	$$$$−
Enclave Suites	1	81	★★★★	$$$
Ramada Limited	3	81	★★½	$+
Central Motel	3	80	★★	$
WDW Port Orleans Resort	WDW	79	★★★★	$$$+
Residence Inn Lake Cecile	3	79	★★★½	$$$−
Days Inn Lake Buena Vista Resort	2	79	★★★	$$
WDW Dixie Landings Resort	WDW	78	★★★★	$$$+
Best Western Eastgate	3	78	★★½	$+
Sleep Inn Maingate	3	78	★★½	$+
Key Motel	3	78	★★	$
WDW Beach Club Resort	WDW	77	★★★★½	$$$$
Homewood Suites Maingate	3	77	★★★★	$$$+
Travelodge Orlando Flags	1	76	★★½	$$+
Motel 6 Maingate East	3	76	★★	$
Sheraton Lakeside Inn	3	75	★★★	$$
Holiday Inn Express	1	74	★★★	$$
Holiday Inn Maingate West	3	74	★★★	$$
Famous Host Inn	3	74	★★½	$+
Ramada Limited Universal Maingate	1	74	★★½	$+
Best Western Grosvenor Resort	WDW	73	★★★★	$$$+
MIC Lakefront Inn	1	73	★★★	$$
Heritage Inn Orlando	1	72	★★★½	$$$+
Las Palmas Hotel	1	72	★★★	$$
Travelodge Suites Eastgate	3	72	★★★	$$+
Courtyard by Marriott	1	70	★★★½	$$$−
Holiday Inn Maingate East	3	70	★★★	$$+

Good Deals and Bad Deals *(continued)*

Hotel	Location	Room Value Rating	Room Star Rating	Cost
Howard Johnson Universal Tower	I	70	★★★	$$+
Radisson Inn Maingate	3	70	★★★	$$+
Days Inn Orlando Lakeside	I	70	★★½	$$−
Hilton Inn Gateway (tower rooms)	3	69	★★★★	$$$$−
Westgate Lakes	2	69	★★★½	$$$+
Comfort Inn Maingate	3	69	★★½	$$−
Floridian of Orlando	I	68	★★★	$$+
Hampton Inn Maingate	3	68	★★★	$$+
Ramada Resort Florida Center	I	68	★★★	$$+
Monte Carlo	3	68	★★	$+
Traveler's Inn	3	68	★★	$+
Holiday Inn Sun Spree Resort	2	67	★★★½	$$$
Travelodge Hotel Disney Village	WDW	67	★★★½	$$$
Quality Inn Lake Cecile	3	66	★★★	$$
Ramada Resort Maingate	3	66	★★★	$$+
Riande Continental Royal	I	66	★★★	$$+
Howard Johnson Lodge	I	66	★★½	$$−
Riande Continental Plaza	I	66	★★½	$$−
Hampton Inn Universal Studios	I	65	★★★	$$+
Hotel Royal Plaza	WDW	65	★★★	$$$−
Howard Johnson Fountain Park	3	65	★★★	$$+
Comfort Inn at Lake Buena Vista	2	65	★★½	$$−
Embassy Super 8 Motel	3	65	★★	$+
WDW Caribbean Beach Resort	WDW	64	★★★½	$$$+
Embassy Suites Orlando International	3	63	★★★★	$$$$
Hyatt Orlando	3	63	★★★½	$$$+
Wellesley Inn	I	63	★★★	$$+
Westgate Towers	3	63	★★★	$$+
Howard Johnson Park Square	2	62	★★★	$$$+
Radisson Inn International	I	62	★★★	$$+
Sheraton World Resort	I	62	★★★	$$+

Good Deals and Bad Deals *(continued)*

Hotel	Location	Room Value Rating	Room Star Rating	Cost
Best Western Maingate	3	62	★★½	$$−
Econo Lodge Maingate Central	3	62	★★½	$$−
Quality Inn Plaza	1	62	★★½	$$−
Sol Orlando Village Resort	3	61	★★★★	$$$$
La Quinta Inn International	1	61	★★★	$$+
WDW All-Star Resort	WDW	61	★★★	$$$−
Wynfield Inn Westwood	1	61	★★★	$$+
Crystal Tree Inn	1	61	★★½	$$−
Red Roof Inn Kissimmee	3	61	★★½	$$−
Hawthorn Suites Orlando	1	60	★★★★	$$$$+
Hampton Inn International Drive	1	59	★★★	$$$−
Economy Inns of America	3	59	★★	$+
Marriott Orlando World Center	2	58	★★★★½	$$$$$+
Villas at Resort World	2	58	★★★★	$$$$$−
Days Inn Maingate West	3	58	★★½	$$
Gateway Inn	1	58	★★½	$$
Rodeway Inn Eastgate	3	58	★★½	$+
Holiday Inn Universal Studios	1	57	★★★	$$$−
Econo Lodge Maingate West	3	57	★★½	$$−
International Inn	1	57	★★½	$$−
Courtyard Disney Village	WDW	56	★★★½	$$$
Days Inn Lake Buena Vista	2	56	★★★	$$+
Days Inn Lake Buena Vista Village	2	56	★★★	$$$−
King's Motel	3	56	★★	$+
Hilton Inn Gateway (garden rooms)	3	55	★★★½	$$$
Holiday Inn Maingate	3	55	★★½	$$
Travelodge Maingate West	3	55	★★½	$$
Doubletree Guest Suites	WDW	54	★★★★	$$$$$−
Quality Suites Maingate East	3	54	★★★	$$$
Ramada Resort Maingate at the Parkway	3	54	★★★	$$$
Orlando Marriott	1	53	★★★½	$$$+
Holiday Inn International Resort	1	53	★★★	$$$

Good Deals and Bad Deals (continued)

Hotel	Location	Room Value Rating	Room Star Rating	Cost
Travelodge Maingate East	3	53	★★★	$$$
Comfort Suites Orlando	2	51	★★★	$$$
Howard Johnson South Int'l Drive	1	51	★★½	$$+
Motel 6 Maingate West	3	51	★½	$
Residence Inn Orlando	1	50	★★★½	$$$$
Delta Orlando Resort	1	50	★★★	$$$+
Quality Inn International	1	50	★★½	$$+
Wynfield Inn Maingate	3	50	★★½	$$+
Clarion Plaza Hotel	1	49	★★★½	$$$$+
Buena Vista Palace	WDW	48	★★★★	$$$$$
Fairfield Inn International	1	48	★★½	$$+
Red Roof Inn Orlando	1	48	★★	$$−
Courtyard Maingate	3	46	★★★½	$$$
Radisson Twin Towers Hotel	1	46	★★★½	$$$$+
Days Inn Universal Studios	1	46	★★½	$$+
Larson's Lodge Maingate	3	46	★★½	$$+
Park Inn International	3	46	★★½	$$+
Summerfield Suites	1	45	★★★★	$$$$$$−
Comfort Inn International	1	44	★★½	$$$−
Stouffer Orlando Resort	2	43	★★★★½	$$$$$$$
Best Western Plaza International	1	43	★★½	$$$−
Days Inn International Drive	1	43	★★½	$$$−
Peabody Orlando	1	42	★★★★½	$$$$$$$
Wilson World Maingate	3	42	★★½	$$$−
WDW Wilderness Lodge	WDW	41	★★★★	$$$$$$+
Ho Jo Inn Maingate	3	41	★★½	$$+
Econo Lodge Maingate Hawaiian	3	41	★★	$$−
WDW Yacht Club Resort	WDW	40	★★★★½	$$$$$$$$−
Days Inn Civic Center	1	40	★★½	$$$−
WDW Dolphin Resort	WDW	39	★★★★½	$$$$$$$$−
Summerfield Suites Lake Buena Vista	2	39	★★★★	$$$$$$+
WDW Swan	WDW	38	★★★★½	$$$$$$$$−
Embassy Suites Resort	2	38	★★★★	$$$$$$+
WDW Grand Floridian Resort	WDW	36	★★★★★	$$$$$$$$$$−

Good Deals and Bad Deals (continued)

Hotel	Location	Room Value Rating	Room Star Rating	Cost
Days Suites Maingate East	3	36	★★★	$$$$
Embassy Suites Plaza International	1	35	★★★½	$$$$$$
Hilton Disney Village	WDW	33	★★★½	$$$$$$+
WDW Polynesian Resort	WDW	32	★★★★	$$$$$$$$
Days Inn Maingate East	3	32	★★	$$+
Hyatt Regency Grand Cypress	2	31	★★★★	$$$$$$$$
WDW Contemporary Resort	WDW	31	★★★★	$$$$$$$

The Best Deals on Four- and Five-Star Rooms

Hotel	Location	Room Value Rating	Room Star Rating	Cost
Best Western Buena Vista Suites	1	81	★★★★½	$$$$–
Enclave Suites	1	81	★★★★	$$$
WDW Port Orleans Resort	WDW	79	★★★★	$$$+
WDW Dixie Landings Resort	WDW	78	★★★★	$$$+
WDW Beach Club Resort	WDW	77	★★★★½	$$$$
Homewood Suites Maingate	3	77	★★★★	$$$+
Best Western Grosvenor Resort	WDW	73	★★★★	$$$+
Hilton Inn Gateway (tower rooms)	3	69	★★★★	$$$$–
Embassy Suites Orlando International	3	63	★★★★	$$$$
Sol Orlando Village Resort	3	61	★★★★	$$$$
Hawthorn Suites Orlando	1	60	★★★★	$$$$+
Marriott Orlando World Center	2	58	★★★★½	$$$$$+
Villas at Resort World	2	58	★★★★	$$$$$–
Doubletree Guest Suites	WDW	54	★★★★	$$$$$–
Buena Vista Palace	WDW	48	★★★★	$$$$$
Summerfield Suites	1	45	★★★★	$$$$$$–
Stouffer Orlando Resort	2	43	★★★★½	$$$$$$

The Best Deals on Four- and Five-Star Rooms (continued)

Hotel	Location	Room Value Rating	Room Star Rating	Cost
Peabody Orlando	I	42	★★★★½	$$$$$$$
WDW Wilderness Lodge	WDW	41	★★★★	$$$$$$+
WDW Yacht Club Resort	WDW	40	★★★★½	$$$$$$$$−
WDW Dolphin Resort	WDW	39	★★★★½	$$$$$$$$−
Summerfield Suites Lake Buena Vista	2	39	★★★★	$$$$$$+
WDW Swan	WDW	38	★★★★½	$$$$$$$$−
Embassy Suites Resort	2	38	★★★★	$$$$$$+
WDW Grand Floridian Resort	WDW	36	★★★★★	$$$$$$$$$$−
WDW Polynesian Resort	WDW	32	★★★★	$$$$$$$$
Hyatt Regency Grand Cypress	2	31	★★★★	$$$$$$$$
WDW Contemporary Resort	WDW	31	★★★★	$$$$$$$

The Best Deals on Three-Star Rooms

Hotel	Location	Room Value Rating	Room Star Rating	Cost
Radisson Inn Lake Buena Vista	2	95	★★★	$$
Ramada Inn Westgate	3	95	★★★	$$−
Wyndham Garden Hotel	2	89	★★★½	$$+
Residence Inn Lake Cecile	3	79	★★★½	$$$−
Days Inn Lake Buena Vista Resort	2	79	★★★	$$
Sheraton Lakeside Inn	3	75	★★★	$$
Holiday Inn Express	I	74	★★★	$$
Holiday Inn Maingate West	3	74	★★★	$$
MIC Lakefront Inn	I	73	★★★	$$
Heritage Inn Orlando	I	72	★★★½	$$$+
Las Palmas Hotel	I	72	★★★	$$
Travelodge Suites Eastgate	3	72	★★★	$$+
Courtyard by Marriott	I	70	★★★½	$$$−
Holiday Inn Maingate East	3	70	★★★	$$+
Howard Johnson Universal Tower	I	70	★★★	$$+
Radisson Inn Maingate	3	70	★★★	$$+
Westgate Lakes	2	69	★★★½	$$$+

The Best Deals on Three-Star Rooms (continued)

Hotel	Location	Room Value Rating	Room Star Rating	Cost
Floridian of Orlando	I	68	★★★	$$+
Hampton Inn Maingate	3	68	★★★	$$+
Ramada Resort Florida Center	I	68	★★★	$$+
Holiday Inn Sun Spree Resort	2	67	★★★½	$$$
Travelodge Hotel Disney Village	WDW	67	★★★½	$$$
Quality Inn Lake Cecile	3	66	★★★	$$
Ramada Resort Maingate	3	66	★★★	$$+
Riande Continental Royal	I	66	★★★	$$+
Hampton Inn Universal Studios	I	65	★★★	$$+
Hotel Royal Plaza	WDW	65	★★★	$$$−
Howard Johnson Fountain Park	3	65	★★★	$$+
WDW Caribbean Beach Resort	WDW	64	★★★½	$$$+
Hyatt Orlando	3	63	★★★½	$$$+
Wellesley Inn	I	63	★★★	$$+
Westgate Towers	3	63	★★★	$$+
Howard Johnson Park Square	2	62	★★★	$$$+
Radisson Inn International	I	62	★★★	$$+
Sheraton World Resort	I	62	★★★	$$+
La Quinta Inn International	I	61	★★★	$$+
WDW All-Star Resort	WDW	61	★★★	$$$−
Wynfield Inn Westwood	I	61	★★★	$$+
Hampton Inn International Drive	I	59	★★★	$$$−
Holiday Inn Universal Studios	I	57	★★★	$$$−
Courtyard Disney Village	WDW	56	★★★½	$$$
Days Inn Lake Buena Vista	2	56	★★★	$$+
Days Inn Lake Buena Vista Village	2	56	★★★	$$$−
Hilton Inn Gateway (garden rooms)	3	55	★★★½	$$$
Quality Suites Maingate East	3	54	★★★	$$$
Ramada Resort Maingate at the Parkway	3	54	★★★	$$$
Orlando Marriott	I	53	★★★½	$$$+
Holiday Inn International Resort	I	53	★★★	$$$
Travelodge Maingate East	3	53	★★★	$$$
Comfort Suites Orlando	2	51	★★★	$$$
Residence Inn Orlando	I	50	★★★½	$$$$
Delta Orlando Resort	I	50	★★★	$$$+
Clarion Plaza Hotel	I	49	★★★½	$$$$+

The Best Deals on Three-Star Rooms (continued)

Hotel	Location	Room Value Rating	Room Star Rating	Cost
Courtyard Maingate	3	46	★★★½	$$$
Radisson Twin Towers Hotel	I	46	★★★½	$$$$+
Days Suites Maingate East	3	36	★★★	$$$$
Embassy Suites Plaza International	I	35	★★★½	$$$$$$
Hilton Disney Village	WDW	33	★★★½	$$$$$$+

The Best Deals on Two-Star Rooms

Hotel	Location	Room Value Rating	Room Star Rating	Cost
International Gateway Inn	I	99	★★½	$+
Red Carpet Inn East	3	99	★★½	$
Sun Motel	3	98	★★½	$
Motel 6 International Drive	I	95	★★	$−
Choice Suites	3	93	★★½	$+
Buena Vista Motel	3	91	★★½	$+
Golden Link Motel	3	89	★★½	$+
Ho Jo Inn	3	89	★★½	$+
Knights Inn Maingate	3	87	★★½	$+
Inns of America International	I	86	★★½	$+
Knights Inn Maingate East	3	86	★★½	$+
Inns of America Maingate	3	84	★★½	$+
Howard Johnson Maingate	3	82	★★½	$$−
Ramada Limited	3	81	★★½	$+
Central Motel	3	80	★★	$
Best Western Eastgate	3	78	★★½	$+
Sleep Inn Maingate	3	78	★★½	$+
Key Motel	3	78	★★	$
Travelodge Orlando Flags	I	76	★★½	$$+
Motel 6 Maingate East	3	76	★★	$
Famous Host Inn	3	74	★★½	$+
Ramada Limited Universal Maingate	I	74	★★½	$+
Days Inn Orlando Lakeside	I	70	★★½	$$−
Comfort Inn Maingate	3	69	★★½	$$−

The Best Deals on Two-Star Rooms (continued)

Hotel	Location	Room Value Rating	Room Star Rating	Cost
Monte Carlo	3	68	★★	$+
Traveler's Inn	3	68	★★	$+
Howard Johnson Lodge	1	66	★★½	$$−
Riande Continental Plaza	1	66	★★½	$$−
Comfort Inn at Lake Buena Vista	2	65	★★½	$$−
Embassy Super 8 Motel	3	65	★★	$+
Best Western Maingate	3	62	★★½	$$−
Econo Lodge Maingate Central	3	62	★★½	$$−
Quality Inn Plaza	1	62	★★½	$$−
Crystal Tree Inn	1	61	★★½	$$−
Red Roof Inn Kissimmee	3	61	★★½	$$−
Economy Inns of America	3	59	★★	$+
Days Inn Maingate West	3	58	★★½	$$
Gateway Inn	1	58	★★½	$$
Rodeway Inn Eastgate	3	58	★★½	$+
Econo Lodge Maingate West	3	57	★★½	$$−
International Inn	1	57	★★½	$$−
King's Motel	3	56	★★	$+
Holiday Inn Maingate	3	55	★★½	$$
Travelodge Maingate West	3	55	★★½	$$
Howard Johnson South Int'l Drive	1	51	★★½	$$+
Quality Inn International	1	50	★★½	$$+
Wynfield Inn Maingate	3	50	★★½	$$+
Fairfield Inn International	1	48	★★½	$$+
Red Roof Inn Orlando	1	48	★★	$$−
Days Inn Universal Studios	1	46	★★½	$$+
Larson's Lodge Maingate	3	46	★★½	$$+
Park Inn International	3	46	★★½	$$+
Comfort Inn International	1	44	★★½	$$$−
Best Western Plaza International	1	43	★★½	$$$−
Days Inn International Drive	1	43	★★½	$$$−
Wilson World Maingate	3	42	★★½	$$$−
Ho Jo Inn Maingate	3	41	★★½	$$+
Econo Lodge Maingate Hawaiian	3	41	★★	$$−
Days Inn Civic Center	1	40	★★½	$$$−
Days Inn Maingate East	3	32	★★	$$+

— *When Only the Best Will Do*

The trouble with profiles, including ours, is that details and distinctions are sacrificed in the interest of brevity. For example, dozens of properties have swimming pools and though most are quite basic and ordinary, a few are pretty spectacular.

Because the World tends to be a family-oriented place, and because many of our young readers have let us know that their favorite activity while in Orlando was swimming in the hotel pool, we have included a pool ranking. The pools are evaluated on the basis of size, cleanliness, imagination, and general ambience. Consideration was also given to shade for the parents who will, of course, watch their children at all times.

All of the Disney-owned lodging properties, as well as the Walt Disney World Swan and Dolphin, have extraordinary swimming areas. Some, like the Grand Floridian, the Polynesian, the Beach Club, and the Yacht Club, feature a freshwater lake beach in addition to swimming pools. Because the Disney hotel swimming facilities are so uniformly outstanding, we have grouped them as follows.

The Best Hotel Swimming Facilities

1. Disney's Yacht & Beach Clubs
2. Disney's Port Orleans and Disney's Polynesian Resort
3. Disney's Caribbean Beach Resort
4. Disney's Wilderness Lodge Resort
5. WDW Dolphin & Swan and Disney's Grand Floridian
6. Ramada Resort Maingate at the Parkway
7. Hyatt Regency Grand Cypress
8. Other Disney properties*
9. Radisson Inn Lake Buena Vista
10. Radisson Inn Maingate
11. Grosvenor at Disney Village
12. Wynfield Inn
13. Sheraton Lakeside Inn
14. Hilton Inn Gateway
15. Quality Suites Maingate East
16. Holiday Inn Maingate
17. Hawthorn Suites
18. Summerfield Suites
19. Homewood Suites Maingate
20. The Hilton at Disney Village
21. Heritage Inn
22. Courtyard by Marriott
23. Wilson World Maingate
24. Hotel Royal Plaza
25. Holiday Inn Maingate East

*Includes the Contemporary, Port Orleans, Dixie Landings, Shades of Green, and Vacation Club resorts.

A few properties on US 192 are located on a lake. While their pool areas may not rank with those above, they do offer jet ski rentals, waterskiing, and other special activities. They are (listed in alphabetical order):

Embassy Motel	Park Inn International
Golden Link Motel	Quality Inn Lake Cecile
Key Motel	Residence Inn Lake Cecile
King's Motel	Traveler's Inn
Lakeview Motel	

PART FOUR: *Walt Disney World with Kids*

The Agony and the Ecstasy

· The national media and advertising presence of Disney is so over-whelming that any child who watches TV or shops with Mom is likely to get all revved up about going to Walt Disney World. Parents, if anything, are even more susceptible. Almost every parent has brightened with anticipation at the prospect of guiding their children through the wonders of this special place. "Imagine little Tammy's expression when she first sees Mickey Mouse. Think of her excitement and awe as she crosses the moat to Cinderella's Castle. Imagine her small arms around me when Dumbo takes off." Are these not the treasured moments we long to share with our children?

While dreams of visiting Disney World are tantamount to Nirvana for a three-year-old, and dear enough to melt the heart of any parent, the reality of actually taking that three-year-old (particularly during the summer) is usually a lot closer to "the agony" than to "the ecstasy."

A mother from Dayton, Ohio, describes taking her five-year-old to Walt Disney World in July:

> I felt so happy and excited before we went. I guess it was all worth it, but when I look back I think I should have had my head examined. The first day we went to Disney World [the Magic Kingdom] and it was packed. By 11 in the morning we had walked so far and stood in so many lines that we were all exhausted. Kristy cried about going on anything that looked or even sounded scary, and was frightened by all of the Disney characters (*they are so big!*) except Minnie and Snow White.
>
> We got hungry about the same time as everyone else but the lines for food were too long and my husband said we would have to wait. By one in the afternoon we were just plugging along, not seeing anything we were really interested in, but picking rides because the lines were short, or because whatever it was was air-conditioned. We rode Small World three times in a row and I'll never get that song out of my head (Ha!). At around 2:30 we

finally got something to eat, but by then we were so hot and tired that it felt like we had worked in the yard all day. Kristy insisted on being carried and we had fifty fights about not going on rides where the lines were too long. At the end, we were so P.O.'d and uncomfortable that we weren't having any fun. Mostly by this time we were just trying to get our money's worth.

Before you stiffen in denial, let me assure you that the Ohio family's experience is fairly typical. Most small children are as picky about the rides as they are about what they eat, and more than 50% of preschoolers are intimidated by the friendly Disney characters. Few humans (of any age), moreover, are mentally or physically equipped to march all day in a throng of 50,000 people, not to mention the unrelenting Florida sun. Finally, would you be surprised to learn that almost 60% of preschoolers said the thing they liked best about their Walt Disney World vacation was the hotel swimming pool?

Reality Testing—Whose Dream Is It?

Remember when you were little and you got that nifty electric train for Christmas, the one your Dad wouldn't let you play with? Did you ever wonder who that train was really for? Ask yourself the same question about your vacation to Walt Disney World. Whose dream are you trying to make come true, yours or your child's?

Small children are very adept at reading their parents' emotions. When you ask, "Honey, how would you like to go to Disney World?" your child will be responding more to your smile and excitement and the idea of doing something with Mom and Dad than to any notion of what Disney World is all about. The younger the child in question, the more this is true. For many preschoolers you could elicit the same enthusiastic response by asking, "Honey, how would you like to go to Cambodia on a dogsled?"

So, is your warm, fuzzy fantasy of introducing your child to the magic of Disney a pipe dream? Not necessarily, but you will have to be practical and open to a little reality testing. For instance, would you increase the probability of a happy, successful visit by holding off a couple of years? Is your child spunky and adventuresome enough to willingly sample the variety of Disney World? Will your child have sufficient endurance and patience to cope with long waits in line and large crowds?

—— Recommendations for Making the Dream Come True

When contemplating a Disney World vacation with small children, anticipation is the name of the game. Here are some of the things you need to consider:

Age. Although the color and festivity of Walt Disney World excite children of all ages, and while there are specific attractions that delight toddlers and preschoolers, the Disney entertainment mix is generally oriented to older kids and adults. We believe that children should be a fairly mature seven years old to *appreciate* the Magic Kingdom, and a year or two older to get much out of EPCOT Center or the Disney-MGM Studios.

Time of Year to Visit. If there is any way you can swing it, avoid the hot, crowded summer months. Try to go in October, November (except Thanksgiving), early December, January, February, and April (except Easter). If your kids are preschoolers, don't even think about going during the summer. If you have children of varying ages and your school-age kids are good students, take the older ones out of school so you can visit during the cooler, less congested off-season. Arrange special study assignments relating to the many educational aspects of Walt Disney World. If your school-age children are not great students and cannot afford to miss any school, take your vacation as soon as the school year ends in late May or early June. Nothing, repeat, nothing will enhance your Walt Disney World vacation as much as avoiding summer months and holiday periods.

Building Naps and Rest into Your Itinerary. The Disney theme parks are huge, so don't try to see everything in one day. Tour in the early morning and return to your hotel around 11:30 A.M. for lunch, a swim, and a nice nap. Even during the off-season when the crowds are smaller and the temperature more pleasant, the sheer size of the major theme parks will exhaust most children under eight by lunchtime. Go back to the park in the late afternoon or early evening and continue your touring. A family from Texas underlines the importance of naps and rest, writing:

> Despite not following any of your "tours," we did follow the
> theme of visiting a specific park in the morning, leaving mid-

afternoon for either a nap back at the room, or a trip to the Dixie Landings pool, and then a return trip to one of the parks in the evening. On the few occasions when we skipped your advice, I was muttering to myself by dinner. I can't tell you what I was muttering. . . .

Where to Stay. The time and hassle involved in commuting to and from the theme parks will be somewhat lessened if you can afford to stay in Walt Disney World. But even if, for financial or other reasons, you lodge outside of the World, it remains imperative that you get small children out of the parks each day for a few hours to rest and recuperate. Neglecting to relax and unwind is the best way we know to get the whole family in a snit and ruin the day (or the entire vacation).

With small children, there is simply no excuse for not planning ahead. Make sure you get a hotel, in or out of Walt Disney World, within a 20-minute one-way commute of the theme parks. Naps and relief from the frenetic pace of the theme parks, even during the off-season, are indispensable. While it's true that you can gain some measure of peace by retreating to one of the Disney resort hotels for lunch or by finding a quiet spot or restaurant in the theme parks, there is no substitute for returning to the familiarity and security of your own hotel. Regardless of what you have heard or read, children too large to sleep in a stroller will not relax and revive unless you get them back to your hotel.

Thousands of new rooms have been built in and around Walt Disney World, many of them very affordable. With sufficient lead time you should have no difficulty finding accommodations that fulfill your requirements.

Be in Touch with Your Feelings. While we acknowledge that a Walt Disney World vacation seems like a major capital investment, remember that having fun is not necessarily the same as seeing everything. When you or your children start getting tired and irritable, call time out and regroup. Trust your instincts. What would really feel best right now? Another ride, a rest break with some ice cream, going back to the room for a nap?

The way to protect your investment is to stay happy and have a good time, whatever that takes. You do not have to meet a quota for experiencing a certain number of attractions or watching parades or anything else. It's your vacation; you can do what you want.

Least Common Denominators.   Remember the old saying about a chain being only as strong as its weakest link? The same logic applies to a family touring the Disney theme parks. Somebody is going to run out of steam first; when they do the whole family will be affected. Sometimes a cold Coke and a rest break will get the flagging member back into gear. Sometimes, however, as Marshall Dillon would say, "You just need to get out of Dodge." Pushing the tired or discontented beyond their capacity is like driving on a flat tire: it may get you a few more miles down the road but you will further damage your car in the process. Accept that energy levels vary among individuals and be prepared to respond to small children or other members of your group who poop out. Hint: "We've driven a thousand miles to take you to Walt Disney World and now you're going to ruin everything!" is not an appropriate response.

Setting Limits and Making Plans.   The best way to avoid arguments and disappointment is to develop a game plan before you go. Establish some general guidelines for the day and get everybody committed in advance. Be sure to include:

1. Wake-up time and breakfast plans.
2. What time you need to depart for the park.
3. What you need to take with you.
4. A policy for splitting the group up or for staying together.
5. A plan for what to do if the group gets separated or someone is lost.
6. How long you intend to tour in the morning and what you want to see, including fall-back plans in the event an attraction is closed or too crowded.
7. A policy on what you can afford for snacks and refreshments.
8. A target time for returning to the hotel to rest.
9. What time you will return to the park and how late you will stay.
10. Plans for dinner.
11. A policy for shopping and buying souvenirs, including who pays: Mom and Dad or the kids.

Be Flexible.   Having a game plan does not mean forgoing spontaneity or sticking rigidly to the itinerary. Once again, listen to your intuition. Alter the plan if the situation warrants. Any day at Walt Disney World includes some surprises, so be prepared to roll with the punches.

About the **Unofficial Guide** ***Touring Plans.***   Parents who embark on one of our touring plans are often frustrated by the various interruptions and delays occasioned by their small children. In case you haven't given the subject much thought, here is what to expect:

1. Many small children will stop dead in their tracks whenever they see a Disney character. Our advice: live with it. An attempt to haul your child away before he has satisfied his curiosity is likely to precipitate anything from whining to a full-scale revolt.

2. The touring plans call for visiting attractions in a specified sequence, often skipping certain attractions along the way. Children do not like skipping *anything*! If they see something that attracts them they want to experience it that moment. Some children can be persuaded to skip attractions if parents explain things in advance. Other kids severely flip out at the threat of skipping something, particularly something in Fantasyland. A mom from Charleston, South Carolina, had this to say:

> We did not have too much trouble following the Touring Plans at [Disney-]MGM and at EPCOT. The Magic Kingdom plan, on the other hand, turned out to be a train wreck. The main problem with the plan is that it starts in Fantasyland. When we were on Dumbo, my five year old saw eight dozen other things in Fantasyland she wanted to see. The long and the short is that after Dumbo, there was no getting her out of there.

Also on the subject of Magic Kingdom touring plans, a Burlington, Vermont, mother of two made this observation:

> I found out that my kids were very curious about the castle because we had read *Cinderella* at home. Whenever I wanted to leave Fantasyland, I would just say 'Let's go to the castle and see if Cinderella is there.' Once we got as far as the front door to the castle it was no problem going out to the [central] hub and then to another land.

3. Children seem to have a genetic instinct when it comes to finding rest rooms. We have seen perfectly functioning adults equipped with all manner of maps search interminably for a rest room. Small children, on the other hand, including those who cannot read, will head for the nearest rest room with the certainty of a homing pigeon. While you may skip certain attractions, you can be sure that your children will ferret out (and want to use) every rest room in the theme park.

4. If you are using a stroller, you will not be able to take it into attractions or onto rides. This applies to rides such as the Walt Disney World Railroad that are included in the Touring Plans primarily as in-park transportation.

Overheating, Sunburn, and Dehydration. The most common problems of smaller children at Walt Disney World are overheating, sunburn, and dehydration. A small bottle of sunscreen carried in a pocket or fanny pack will help you take precautions against overexposure to the sun. Be sure to put some on children in strollers, even if the stroller has a canopy. Some of the worst cases of sunburn we have seen were on the exposed foreheads and feet of toddlers and infants in strollers. To avoid overheating, rest at regular intervals in the shade or in an air-conditioned restaurant or show.

Do not count on keeping small children properly hydrated with soft drinks and water fountain stops. Long lines often make buying refreshments problematic and water fountains are not always handy. What's more, excited children may not realize or inform you that they're thirsty or overheated. We recommend renting a stroller for children six years old and under and carrying plastic water bottles. If you forget to bring your own water containers, plastic squeeze bottles with caps are sold in all three parks for about three dollars.

Blisters and sore feet are common for visitors of all ages, so wear comfortable, well broken-in shoes and two pairs of thin socks (preferable to one pair of thick socks). If you or your children are unusually susceptible to blisters, carry some precut Moleskin bandages; they offer the best possible protection, stick great, and won't sweat off. When you feel a hot spot, stop, air out your foot, and place a Moleskin bandage over the area before a blister forms. Moleskin is available by name at all drugstores. Sometimes small children won't tell their parents about a developing blister until it's too late. We recommend inspecting the feet of preschoolers two or more times a day.

First Aid. There is a First Aid Center in each of the theme parks. In the Magic Kingdom it is next to the Crystal Palace at the end of Main Street near Adventureland. At EPCOT Center it is on the World Showcase side of the Odyssey Restaurant, and at Disney-MGM it is in the Guest Services Building just inside the main entrance. If you or your children have a medical problem, do not hesitate to use the First Aid Centers. The Disney First Aid Centers are warmer and friendlier than most doctor's offices and are accustomed to treating everything from paper cuts to allergic reactions.

Children on Medication. For various reasons, some parents of hyperactive children on medication elect to discontinue or decrease the child's normal dosage at the close of the school year. Be forewarned that Walt Disney World might stimulate such a child to the point of system overload. Consult your physician before altering your child's medication regimen.

Sunglasses.   If you want your smaller children to wear sunglasses, it's a good idea to affix a strap or string to the frames so the glasses will stay on during rides and can hang from the child's neck while indoors.

Things You Forgot or Things You Ran Out of.   Rain gear, diapers, diaper pins, formula, film, aspirin, topical sunburn treatments, and other sundries are available for sale at all the major theme parks and at Typhoon Lagoon, River Country, and Pleasure Island. For some reason rain gear is a bargain, but most other items are pretty high. Ask for goods you do not see displayed; some are stored behind the counter.

Caring for Infants at the Theme Parks.   The Magic Kingdom, EPCOT Center, and Disney-MGM Studios have special centralized facilities for the care of infants and toddlers. Everything necessary for changing diapers, preparing formulas, warming bottles and food, etc., is available in ample quantity. A broad selection of baby supplies is on hand for sale, and there are even rockers and special chairs for nursing mothers. In the Magic Kingdom the Baby Center is located next to the Crystal Palace at the end of Main Street. At EPCOT Center, Baby Services is located near the Odyssey Restaurant, to the right of the World of Motion in Future World. At Disney-MGM Studios, Baby Care is located in the Guest Services Building to the left of the entrance. Dads in charge of little ones are welcome at the centers and can avail themselves of most services offered. In addition, changing tables have been placed in several men's rooms in the major theme parks.

Strollers are available for a modest rental fee at all three major theme parks. The rental covers the entire day. If you rent a stroller at the Magic Kingdom and later decide to go to EPCOT Center or Disney-MGM Studios, turn in your Magic Kingdom stroller and hang on to your rental receipt. When you arrive at the next park present your receipt. You will be issued another stroller without additional charge.

Strollers at the Magic Kingdom and EPCOT Center are large, sturdy models with sun canopies and cargo baskets. We have seen families load as many as three children on one of these strollers at the same time. The strollers available at the Disney-MGM Studios are the light, collapsible type. Strollers can be obtained to the right of the entrance at the Magic Kingdom, on the left side of the Entrance Plaza at EPCOT Center, and at Oscar's Super Service just inside the entrance of the Disney-MGM Studios. The rental procedure at all parks is fast and efficient and returning the stroller is a breeze. Even at EPCOT Center, where up to 900 strollers are turned in following the evening fireworks show, there is almost no wait and/or hassle. If you don't mind forfeiting your dollar deposit, you can ditch your rental stroller anywhere in the park when you are ready to depart.

When you enter a show or board a ride, you will have to park your stroller, usually in an open, unprotected area. If it rains before you return, you will need a cloth, towel, or spare diaper to dry off the stroller.

For infants and toddlers the strollers are a must, but we have observed many sharp parents renting strollers for somewhat older children (up to five or six years old). The stroller prevents parents from having to carry children when they run out of steam and provides an easy, convenient way to carry water, snacks, diaper bags, etc.

If you elect to go to your hotel for lunch, a swim, or a nap, and intend to return to the park, do not turn in your rental stroller. Simply park it near an attraction located close to the entrance, marking the stroller with something personal like a bandanna. When you come back after your break, your stroller will be right there waiting for you.

If you would like to bring your own stroller from home, it is perfectly permissible to do so. You should not have to worry about your stroller being stolen, provided it is marked with your name. Be advised, however, that only collapsible strollers are permitted on the Disney monorails and buses.

A mother of two from Falls Church, Virginia, advocates taking your own stroller, commenting:

> I was glad I took my own stroller, because the rented strollers aren't appropriate for infants. (We had a five year old and a five month old in tow.) No one at the Magic Kingdom said anything about my using a bike lock to secure our brand-new Aprica stroller. However, at [Disney-]MGM, an attendent came over and told us not to lock it anywhere, because it's a fire hazard! (Outside?) When I politely asked the attendant if she wanted to be responsible for my $300 stroller, she told me to go ahead and lock it but not tell anyone! I observed the attendants at Magic Kingdom and [Disney-]MGM constantly moving the strollers. This seems

very confusing—no wonder people think their strollers are getting ripped off!

Stroller Wars. Sometimes strollers disappear while you are enjoying a ride or a show. Do not be alarmed. You won't have to buy the missing stroller and you will be issued a new stroller for your continued use. In the Magic Kingdom, replacement centers are located at Tinker Bell's Treasures in Fantasyland, and at Merchant of Venus in Tomorrowland, as well as at the main rental facility near the park entrance. At EPCOT Center, in addition to the Entrance Plaza rental headquarters, strollers can be replaced at the International Gateway (in the World Showcase between the United Kingdom and France). At present, strollers at Disney-MGM can only be replaced at Oscar's Super Service and at the Costume Shop near the Sci-Fi Dine-In Theater.

While replacing a ripped-off stroller is no big deal, it is an inconvenience. A family from Minnesota complained that their stroller had been taken six times in one day at EPCOT Center and five times in a single day at the Disney-MGM Studios. Even with free replacements, larceny on this scale represents a lot of wasted time. Through our own experiments, and suggestions from our readers, we have developed several techniques for hanging on to your rented stroller:

1. At EPCOT Center and the Magic Kingdom, write your name in magic marker on a 6 × 9 inch card, put the card in a transparent freezer bag, and secure the bag to the canopy of the stroller with masking or duct tape.

2. Affix something personal (but expendable) to the handle of the stroller. Evidently most strollers are pirated by mistake (since they all look the same) or because it's easier to swipe someone else's stroller (when yours disappears) than to troop off to the replacement center. Since most stroller theft is a function of confusion, laziness, or revenge, the average pram pincher will balk at hauling off a stroller bearing another person's property. After trying several items, we concluded that a bright, inexpensive scarf or bandanna tied to the handle works well, or a sock partially stuffed with rags or paper works even better (the weirder and more personal the object, the greater the deterrent). Best of all is a dead mackerel dangling from the handle, though in truth, the kid who rides in the stroller often prefers the other methods.

Bound and determined not to have her stroller ripped off, an Ann Arbor, Michigan, mother describes her stroller security plan as follows:

> We used a variation on your stroller identification theme. We tied a clear plastic bag with a diaper in it on the stroller. Jon even poured

a little root beer on the diaper for effect. Needless to say, no one took our stroller and it was easy to identify.

Finally, be aware that Disney cast members will often rearrange strollers parked outside of an attraction. Sometimes this is done simply to "tidy up." At other times the strollers are moved to make additional room along a walkway. In any event, do not assume your stroller has been stolen because it is not exactly where you left it. Check around. Chances are it will be "neatly arranged" just a few feet away.

——— Lost Children

Lost children do not usually pose much of a problem. All Disney employees are schooled in how to handle the situation should it be encountered. If you lose a child in the Magic Kingdom, report the situation to a Disney employee, and then check in at the Baby Center and at City Hall where lost-children "logs" are maintained. At EPCOT Center the procedure is the same; report the child lost and then check at Baby Services near the Odyssey Restaurant. At Disney-MGM Studios, report the child lost at the Guest Services Building at the entrance end of Hollywood Boulevard. Paging systems are not used in any of the parks, but in an emergency, an "all points bulletin" can be issued throughout the park(s) via internal communications.

It is amazingly easy to lose a child (or two) at the theme parks. We suggest that children under eight be color-coded by dressing them in purple T-shirts or equally distinctive attire. It is also a good idea to sew a label into each child's shirt that states his or her name, your name, and the name of your hotel. The same thing can be accomplished less elegantly by writing the information on a strip of masking tape: hotel security professionals suggest that the information be printed in small letters and that the tape be affixed to the outside of the child's shirt five inches or so below the armpit. Finally, special name tags can be obtained at all three major theme parks.

How Kids Get Lost. Children get separated from their parents every day at the Disney theme parks under circumstances that are remarkably similar (and predictable).

1. *Preoccupied Solo Parent.* In this scenario the only adult in the party is preoccupied with something like buying refreshments, loading the camera, or using the rest room. Junior is there one second and gone the next.

2. *The Hidden Exit.* Sometimes parents wait on the sidelines while allowing two or more young children to experience a ride together. As it usually happens, the parents expect the kids to exit the attraction in one place and, lo and behold, the young ones pop out somewhere else. The exits of some Disney attractions are consider-

ably distant from the entrances. Make sure you know exactly where your children will emerge before letting them ride by themselves.

3. *After the Show.* At the completion of many shows and rides, a Disney staffer will announce, "Check for personal belongings and take small children by the hand." When dozens, if not hundreds, of people leave an attraction at the same time it is easy for parents to temporarily lose contact with their children unless they have them directly in tow.

4. *Rest Room Problems.* Mom tells six-year-old Tommy, "I'll be sitting on this bench when you come out of the rest room." Three situations: One, Tommy exits through a different door and becomes disoriented (Mom may not know there *is* another door). Two, Mom decides belatedly that she will also use the rest room, and Tommy emerges to find her absent. Three, Mom pokes around in a shop while keeping an eye on the bench, but misses Tommy when he comes out.

If you cannot be with your child in the rest room, make sure there is only one exit. For disorienting visitors, the rest room situated along a passageway between Frontierland and Adventureland in the Magic Kingdom is the all-time champ. Children and adults alike have walked in from the Adventureland side and walked out on the Frontierland side (and vice versa). Adults making this mistake intuit pretty quickly that something is wrong. Young children, however, sometimes fail to get the message. Designate a meeting spot more distinctive than a bench, and be specific and thorough in your instructions: "I'll meet you by this flagpole. If you get out first, stay right here." Have your child repeat the directions back to you.

5. *Parades.* There are many special parades and shows at the theme parks during which the audience stands. Children, because they are small, tend to jockey around for a better view. By moving a little this way and a little that way, it is amazing how much distance kids can put between you and them before anyone notices.

6. *Mass Movements.* Another situation to guard against is when huge crowds disperse after fireworks, a parade, or at park closing. With 20,000 to 40,000 people suddenly moving at once, it is very easy to get separated from a small child or others in your party. Extra caution is recommended following the evening parade and fire-

works in the Magic Kingdom or IllumiNations at EPCOT Center. Families should develop specific plans for what to do and where to meet in the event they are separated.

7. *Character Greetings.*   A fair amount of activity and confusion is commonplace when the Disney characters are on the scene. See the section on meeting the Disney characters (pages 172–76).

Disney, Kids, and Scary Stuff

Disney rides and shows are adventures. They focus on the substance and themes of all adventure, and indeed of life itself: the quest, good and evil, death, beauty and the grotesque, fellowship and enmity. As you sample the variety of attractions at Walt Disney World, you transcend the mundane spinning and bouncing of midway rides to a more thought-provoking and emotionally powerful entertainment experience. Though the endings are all happy, the impact of the adventures, with Disney's gift for special effects, is often intimidating and occasionally frightening to small children.

There are rides with menacing witches, rides with burning towns, and rides with ghouls popping out of their graves, all done tongue-in-cheek and with a sense of humor, providing you are old enough to understand the joke. And bones, lots of bones: human bones, cattle bones, dinosaur bones, and whole skeletons, everywhere you look. There have to be more bones at Walt Disney World than at the Smithsonian Institution and Tulane Medical School combined. There is a stack of skulls at the headhunter's camp on the Jungle Cruise; a veritable platoon of skeletons sailing ghost ships in Pirates of the Caribbean; a haunting assemblage of skulls and skeletons in The Haunted Mansion; and more skulls, skeletons, and bones punctuate Snow White's Adventures, Peter Pan's Flight, and Big Thunder Mountain Railroad, to name a few.

It should be mentioned that the monsters and special effects at the Disney-MGM Studios are more real and sinister than those of the other theme parks. If your child is having difficulty coping with the witch in Snow White's Adventures, think twice about exposing him to machine-gun battles, earthquakes, and the creature from *Alien* at the Studios.

One reader wrote us the following after taking his preschool children on Star Tours:

> We took a four-year-old and a five-year-old and they had the shit scared out of them at Star Tours. We did this first thing in the morning and it took hours of Tom Sawyer Island and Small World to get back to normal.
>
> Our kids were the youngest by far in Star Tours. I assume that either other adults had more sense or were not such avid readers of your book.

Preschoolers should start with Dumbo and work up to the Jungle Cruise in the late morning, after being revved up and before getting hungry, thirsty, or tired. Pirates of the Caribbean is out for preschoolers. You get the idea.

The reaction of young children to the inevitable system overload of Walt Disney World should be anticipated. Be sensitive, alert, and prepared for almost anything, even behavior that is out of character for your child at home. Most small children take Disney's variety of macabre trappings in stride, and others are quickly comforted by an arm around the shoulder or a little squeeze of the hand. For parents who have observed in their kids a tendency to become upset, we recommend taking it slow and easy by sampling more benign adventures like the Jungle Cruise, gauging reactions, and discussing with the children how they felt about the things they saw.

Sometimes small children will rise above their anxiety in an effort to please their parents or siblings. This behavior, however, does not necessarily indicate a mastery of fear, much less enjoyment. If children come off a ride in ostensibly good shape, we recommend asking if they would like to go on the ride again (not necessarily right now, but sometime). The response to this question will usually give you a clue as to how much they actually enjoyed the experience. There is a lot of difference between having a good time and mustering the courage to get through something.

Evaluating a child's capacity to handle the visual and tactile effects of Walt Disney World requires patience, understanding, and experimentation. Each of us, after all, has our own demons. If a child balks at or is frightened by a ride, respond constructively. Let your children know that lots of people, adults as well as children, are scared by what they see and feel. Help them understand that it is okay with you if they get frightened, and that their fear does not lessen your love or respect. Take pains not to compound the discomfort by making a child feel inadequate; try not to undermine self-esteem, impugn courage, or subject a child to ridicule. Most of all, do not induce guilt, as if your child's trepidation might be ruining the family's fun. When older siblings are present, it is sometimes necessary to restrain their taunting and teasing.

A visit to Walt Disney World is more than an outing or an adventure for a small child. It is a testing experience, a sort of controlled rite of passage. If you help your little one work through the challenges, the time can be immeasurably rewarding, and a bonding experience for both of you.

The Fright Factor

While each youngster is different, there are essentially seven attraction elements that alone or combined punch a child's buttons:

1. *The name of the attraction.* Small children will naturally be apprehensive about something called "The Haunted Mansion" or "Mr. Toad's Wild Ride."

2. *The visual impact of the attraction from outside.* Splash Mountain and the Big Thunder Mountain Railroad look scary enough to give adults second thoughts. To many small children these rides are visually terrifying.

3. *The visual impact of the indoor queuing area.* Pirates of the Caribbean, with its caves and dungeons, and The Haunted Mansion, with its "stretch rooms," have the capability of frightening small children before they even board the ride.

4. *The intensity of the attraction.* Some attractions are so intense as to be overwhelming; they inundate the senses with sights, sounds, movement, and even smell. *Honey, I Shrunk the Audience* at EPCOT Center, for instance, combines loud music, laser effects, lights, and 3-D cinematography to create a total sensory experience. For some preschoolers, this is two or three senses too many.

5. *The visual impact of the attraction itself.* As discussed previously, the sights in various attractions range from falling boulders to lurking buzzards, from grazing dinosaurs to attacking white blood cells. What one child calmly absorbs may scare the bejabbers out of another child the same age.

6. *Dark.* Many Disney World attractions are "dark" rides, i.e., they operate indoors in the dark. For some children, this alone triggers a lot of apprehension. A child who is frightened on one dark ride, for example, Snow White's Adventures, may be unwilling to try other indoor rides.

7. *The ride itself; the tactile experience.* Some Disney rides are downright wild—wild enough to induce motion sickness, wrench backs, and generally discombobulate patrons of any age.

Small Child Fright Potential Chart

As a quick reference, we have provided a "Fright Potential Chart" to warn you which attractions to be wary of, and why. Remember that the chart represents a generalization and that all kids are different. The chart relates specifically to kids 3–7 years of age. On average, as you would expect, children at the younger end of the age range are more likely to be frightened than children in their sixth or seventh year.

MAGIC KINGDOM

Main Street, U.S.A.

Walt Disney World Railroad: Not frightening in any respect
Main Street Cinema: Not frightening in any respect.
Main Street Vehicles: Not frightening in any respect.

Adventureland

Swiss Family Treehouse: Not frightening in any respect.
Jungle Cruise: Moderately intense, some macabre sights; a good test attraction for little ones.
Tropical Serenade: A small thunderstorm momentarily surprises very small children.
Pirates of the Caribbean: Slightly intimidating queuing area; intense boat ride with gruesome (though humorously presented) sights, and a short, unexpected slide down a flume.

Frontierland

Splash Mountain: Visually intimidating from the outside with moderately intense visual effects. The ride itself is somewhat hair-raising for all ages, culminating in a 52-foot plunge down a steep chute. Switching-off option provided (see page 166–167).
Big Thunder Mountain Railroad: Visually intimidating from the outside with moderately intense visual effects. The roller coaster is wild enough to frighten many adults, particularly seniors. Switching-off option provided (see page 166–167).
Tom Sawyer Island: Some very small children are intimidated by dark, walk-through tunnels that can be easily avoided.
Country Bear Jamboree: Not frightening in any respect.
Frontierland Shootin' Gallery: Not frightening in any respect.

Liberty Square

The Hall of Presidents: Not frightening, but boring for small ones.
Liberty Square Riverboat: Not frightening in any respect.
Mike Fink Keelboats: Not frightening in any respect.
The Haunted Mansion: Name of attraction raises anxiety, as do the
    sounds and sights of waiting area. An intense attraction with
    humorously presented macabre sights.The ride itself is gentle.

Fantasyland

Mad Tea Party: Midway-type ride can induce motion sickness in all
    ages.
20,000 Leagues Under the Sea: Not frightening in any respect.
Mr. Toad's Wild Ride: Name of ride intimidates some. Moderately
    intense spook-house genre attraction with jerky ride. Only frightens
    a small percentage of preschoolers.
Snow White's Adventures: Moderately intense spook-house genre
    attraction with some grim characters. Absolutely terrifying to many
    preschoolers.
The Legend of the Lion King: Certain special effects frighten some
    small children.
Dumbo, the Flying Elephant: A tame midway ride; a great favorite of
    most small children.
Cinderella's Golden Carrousel: Not frightening in any respect.
It's a Small World: Not frightening in any respect.
Peter Pan's Flight: Not frightening in any respect.
Skyway to Tomorrowland: Not frightening except for those afraid of
    heights.

Mickey's Starland

Mickey's House and Starland Show: Not frightening in any respect.
Mickey's Hollywood Theater: Not frightening in any respect.
Grandma Duck's Petting Farm: Not frightening in any respect.

Tomorrowland

Alien Encounter: Extremely intense. Capable of frightening guests of
    all ages. Not for small children. Switching off option provided (see
    pages 166–167).
Transportarium: Realistic cinematic technique may frighten some
    small children.
Dreamflight: Not frightening in any respect.

Tomorrowland Transit Authority: Not frightening in any respect.

Skyway to Fantasyland: Not frightening in any respect.

Space Mountain: Very intense roller coaster in the dark; the Magic Kingdom's wildest ride and a scary roller coaster by anyone's standards; switching-off option provided (see page 166–167).

AstroOrbiter: Visually intimidating from the waiting area. The ride is relatively tame. See safety warning on page 169.

Carousel of Progress: Not frightening in any respect.

Grand Prix Raceway: Noise of waiting area slightly intimidating to preschoolers; otherwise, not frightening.

EPCOT CENTER

Future World

Spaceship Earth: Dark and imposing presentation intimidates a small percentage of preschoolers.

Innoventions East and West: Not frightening in any respect.

Universe of Energy: Dinosaur segment frightens some preschoolers; visually intense with intimidating effects in parts.

Wonders of Life – Body Wars: Very intense with frightening visual effects. Ride induces motion sickness in susceptible riders of all ages. Switching-off option provided (see page 166–167).

Wonders of Life – Cranium Command: Not frightening in any respect.

Wonders of Life – The Making of Me: Not frightening in any respect.

Horizons: Not frightening in any respect.

World of Motion – It's Fun to Be Free: Not frightening in any respect.

Journey into Imagination Ride: Contains a few sights that frighten an extremely small percentage of preschoolers.

Honey, I Shrunk the Audience: Extremely intense visual effects and loud volume frighten some children.

The Land – Living with the Land: Not frightening in any respect.

The Land – Harvest Theater: Not frightening in any respect.

The Land – Food Rocks: Not frightening in any respect.

World Showcase

Mexico – El Rio del Tiempo: Not frightening in any respect.

Norway – Maelstrom: Visually intense in parts. Ride ends with a plunge down a 20-foot flume. A few preschoolers are frightened.

China – Wonders of China: Not frightening in any respect, but audience must stand.

Germany: Not frightening in any respect.

Italy: Not frightening in any respect.

The American Adventure: Not frightening in any respect.

Japan: Not frightening in any respect.

Morocco: Not frightening in any respect.

France– Impressions de France: Not frightening in any respect.

United Kingdom: Not frightening in any respect.

Canada – O Canada!: Not frightening in any respect, but audience must stand.

DISNEY-MGM STUDIOS

The Twilight Zone Tower of Terror: Visually intimidating to small children; contains intense and realistic special effects. Be forewarned that plummeting elevator at end of ride frightens many adults.

The Great Movie Ride: Intense in parts with very realistic special effects and some visually intimidating sights.

SuperStar Television: Not frightening in any respect.

The Monster Sound Show: Name of show causes some apprehension; the actual production is not frightening.

Indiana Jones Epic Stunt Spectacular: An intense show with powerful special effects including explosions, but presented in an educational context that small children generally handle well.

Star Tours: Extremely intense visually for all ages; the ride itself is one of the wildest in the Disney repertoire. Not as likely to cause motion sickness as Body Wars at EPCOT Center. Switching-off option is provided (see page 166–167).

Backstage Shuttle Tour: Sedate and nonintimidating except for "Catastrophe Canyon," where an earthquake and a flash flood are simulated. Smaller children should be prepared for this part of the tour.

Backstage Walking Tour (Inside the Magic): Not frightening in any respect.

MuppetVision 4-D: Intense and loud, but not frightening.

Honey, I Shrunk the Kids Movie Set Adventure
   Playground: Everything is oversized, but nothing is scary.

The Voyage of the Little Mermaid: Not frightening in any respect.

Animation Tour: Not frightening in any respect.

A Bit of Preparation

We receive many tips from parents relating how they prepared their small children for the Walt Disney World experience. A common strategy is to acquaint children with the characters and the stories behind the attractions by reading Disney books and watching Disney videos at home. A more direct approach is to rent Walt Disney World travel videos that actually show the various attractions. Concerning the latter, a father from Arlington, Virginia, reported:

> My kids both loved the Haunted Mansion, with appropriate preparation. We rented a tape before going so they could see it, and then I told them it was all "Mickey Mouse Magic" and that Mickey was just "joking you," to put it in their terms, and that there weren't any real ghosts, and that Mickey wouldn't let anyone actually get hurt.

Along similar lines, a mother from Teaneck, New Jersey, reported the following:

> I rented movies to make my 5-year-old more comfortable with rides (*Star Wars, Indiana Jones, Honey I Shrunk the Kids*). We thought we might go to Universal so I rented *King Kong* and it is now my kid's favorite. If kids are afraid of rides in dark (like ours), buy a light-up toy and let them take it on the ride.

A mother from Gloucester, Massachussetts, handled her son's preparation a bit more extemporaneously, writing:

> The 3½ year old liked It's a Small World, [but] was afraid of the Haunted Mansion. We just pulled his hat over his face and quietly talked to him while we enjoyed [the ride].

—— Attractions That Eat Adults

You may spend so much energy worrying about Junior's welfare that you forget to take care of yourself. If the ride component of the attraction (i.e., the actual motion and movement of the conveyance itself) is potentially disturbing, persons of any age may be adversely affected. The attractions most likely to cause motion sickness or other problems for older children and adults are:

Magic Kingdom: Tomorrowland – Space Mountain
                        Tomorrowland – Alien Encounter
                        Fantasyland – Mad Tea Party
                        Frontierland – Big Thunder Mountain
                            Railroad
                        Frontierland – Splash Mountain

EPCOT Center: Future World – Body Wars

Disney-MGM Studios: Star Tours
                        Tower of Terror

Waiting Line Strategies for Adults with Small Children

Children hold up better through the day if you minimize the time they have to spend in lines. Arriving early and using the touring plans in this guide will reduce waiting time immensely. There are, however, additional measures you can employ to reduce stress on little ones.

1. Line Games. It is a smart parent who anticipates how restless children get waiting in line, and how a little structured activity can relieve the stress and boredom. In the morning kids handle the inactivity of waiting in line by discussing what they want to see and do during the course of the day. Later, however, as events wear on, they need a little help. Watching for, and counting, Disney characters is a good diversion. Simple guessing games like "20 Questions" also work well. Lines for rides move so continuously that games that require pen and paper are cumbersome and impractical. Waiting in the holding area of a theater attraction, however, is a different story. Here tic-tac-toe, hangman, drawing, and coloring can really make the time go by.

2. Last Minute Entry. If a ride or show can accommodate an unusually large number of people at one time, it is often unnecessary to stand in line. The Liberty Square Riverboat in the Magic Kingdom is a good example. The boat holds about 450 people, usually more than are waiting in line to ride. Instead of standing uncomfortably in a crowd with dozens of other guests, grab a snack and sit in the shade until the boat arrives and loading is well under way. After the line has all but disappeared, go ahead and board.

At large capacity theaters like that for *The American Adventure* in EPCOT Center, ask the entrance greeter how long it will be until guests are admitted to the theater for the next show. If the answer is fifteen minutes or more, use the time for a rest room break or to get a snack, returning to the attraction just a few minutes before the show starts. You will not be permitted to carry any food or drink into the attraction, so make sure you have time to finish your snack before entering.

The following is a list of attractions that you can usually enter at the last minute:

164

Magic Kingdom

Liberty Square	*The Hall of Presidents*
	Liberty Square Riverboat
Mickey's Starland	*Mickey's Starland Show*
Tomorrowland	*Transportarium*

EPCOT Center

Future World	*Circle of Life*
	Food Rocks
World Showcase	*Wonders of China*
	The American Adventure
	O Canada!

Disney-MGM Studios   SuperStar Television

3. The Hail-Mary Pass.   When waiting, certain lines are configured in such a way as to allow you and your smaller children to pass under the rail to join your partner just before actual boarding or entry. This technique allows the kids and one adult to rest, snack, cool off, or tinkle, while another adult or older sibling does the waiting. Other guests are very understanding when it comes to using this strategy to keep small children content. You are likely to meet hostile opposition, however, if you try to pass older children or more than one adult under the rail. Attractions where it is usually possible to complete a Hail-Mary Pass include:

Magic Kingdom

Adventureland	Swiss Family Treehouse
	Jungle Cruise
Frontierland	*Country Bear Jamboree*
Fantasyland	Mad Tea Party
	Mr. Toad's Wild Ride
	Snow White's Adventures
	Dumbo, the Flying Elephant
	Cinderella's Golden Carrousel
	Peter Pan's Flight
Tomorrowland	Grand Prix Raceway

EPCOT Center

Future World	Spaceship Earth
The Land	Living With The Land
World of Motion	It's Fun to Be Free

Disney-MGM Studios *The Monster Sound Show*
Indiana Jones

4. Switching Off (also known as The Baby Swap): Several attractions have minimum height and/or age requirements, usually 3'8" tall to ride with an adult, or seven years of age *and* 3'8" tall to ride alone. Some couples with children too small or too young forgo these attractions, while others split up and take turns riding separately. Missing out on some of Disney's best rides is an unnecessary sacrifice and waiting in line twice for the same ride is a tremendous waste of time.

A better way to approach the problem is to take advantage of an option known as "switching off" or "The Baby Swap." To switch off there must be at least two adults. Everybody waits in line together, both adults and children. When you reach a Disney attendant (known as a "greeter"), say you want to switch off. The greeter will allow everyone, including the small children, to enter the attraction. When you reach the loading area, one adult will ride while the other stays with the kids. The riding adult disembarks and takes responsibility for the children while the other adult rides. A third adult in the party can ride twice, once with each of the switching off adults, so they do not have to experience the attraction alone.

Most rides with minimum age and height requirements load and unload in the same area, thus facilitating switching off. An exception is Space Mountain where the first adult (at the conclusion of the ride) must inform the unloading attendant that he or she is engaged in switching off. The unloading attendant will admit the first adult to an internal stairway that goes back to the loading area.

Altogether, there are seven attractions where switching off is routinely practiced:

Magic Kingdom

Tomorrowland	Space Mountain
Tomorrowland	*Alien Encounter*
Frontierland	Splash Mountain
	Big Thunder Mountain Railroad

EPCOT Center

Future World	Wonders of Life pavilion: Body Wars

Disney-MGM Studios

	Star Tours
	Twilight Zone Tower of Terror

Switching Off

5. How to Ride Twice in a Row without Waiting. Many small children like to ride a favorite attraction two or more times in succession. Riding the second time often gives the child a feeling of mastery and accomplishment. Unfortunately, even in the early morning, repeat rides can be time consuming. If you ride Dumbo as soon as the Magic Kingdom opens, for instance, you will only have a minute or two wait for your first ride. When you come back for your second ride your wait will be about 12 minutes. If you want to ride a third time, count on a 20-minute or longer wait.

The best way for getting your child on the ride twice (or more) without blowing your whole morning is by using the "Chuck Bubba Relay" (named in honor of a reader from Kentucky):

a. Mom and little Bubba enter the waiting line.
b. Dad lets a certain number of people go in front of him (24 in the case of Dumbo) and then gets in line.
c. As soon as the ride stops, Mom exits with little Bubba and passes him to Dad to ride the second time.
d. If everybody is really getting into this, Mom can hop in line again, no less than 24 people behind Dad.

The Chuck Bubba Relay will not work on every ride because of differences in the way the waiting areas are configured (i.e., it is impossible in some cases to exit the ride and make the pass). For those rides (all in Fantasyland) where the Bubba Relay does work, however, here are the number of people to count off:

Mad Tea Party: 53 people
Mr. Toad's Wild Ride: 22 people
Snow White's Adventures: 52 people
Dumbo, the Flying Elephant: 24 people
Cinderella's Golden Carrousel: 75 people
Peter Pan's Flight: 64 people

If you are the second adult in line, you will reach a point in the waiting area that is obviously the easiest place to make the hand-off. Sometimes this point is where those exiting the ride pass closest to those waiting to board. In any event, you will know it when you see it. Once there, if the first parent has not arrived with little Bubba, just let those behind you slip past until they show up.

6. Last-Minute Cold Feet. If your small child gets cold feet at the last minute after waiting for a ride (where there is no age or height requirement), you can usually arrange with the loading attendant for a switch off. This situation arises frequently at Pirates of the Caribbean, where small children lose their courage while winding through the forbidding, dungeon-like waiting area.

There is no law that says you have to ride. If you get to the boarding area and someone is unhappy, just tell a Disney attendant you have changed your mind and you will be shown the way out.

7. Elevator Shoes for the Short and the Brave. If you have a child who is crazy to go on the rides with height requirements, but who is just a little too short, slip heel lifts into his Nikes before he gets to the measuring point. Be sure to leave the heel lifts in because he may get measured again at the boarding area.

8. Throw Yourself on the Grenade, Mildred! For by-the-book, do-the-right-thing parents determined to sacrifice themselves on behalf of their children, we provide a Magic Kingdom One-Day Touring Plan called the "Dumbo-or-Die-in-a-Day Touring Plan, for Parents with Small Children." This Touring Plan, detailed on pages 421–24, will ensure that you run yourself ragged. Designed to help you forfeit everything of personal interest for the sake of your children's pleasure, the plan is guaranteed to send you home battered and exhausted with extraordinary stories of devotion and heroic perseverance. By the way, the plan really works. Anyone under eight years old will love it.

9. Catch-22 at the Grand Prix Raceway. Though the Grand Prix Raceway is a great treat for small children, they are required to be 4' 4" tall in order to drive. In that very few children six and under top this height, the ride is essentially withheld from the very age group that would most enjoy it. To resolve this Catch-22, go on the ride with your small child. The attendants will assume that you will drive. After getting into the car, however, shift your child over behind the steering wheel. From your position you will still be able to easily control the foot pedals. Your child will feel like she is really driving. Because the car travels on a self-guiding track, there is no way your child can make a mistake while steering.

10. Tomorrowland AstroOrbiter—a Safety Warning. Sometimes parents get into the seat of the rocket prior to lifting their child on board from the loading platform. Because the attendant cannot see small children on the side of the ride opposite his control station, the ride can be activated before a child is safely placed in the cockpit. If you take a small child on this attraction, place the child in the rocket *first* and then get in.

11. 20,000 Leagues Under the Sea. This attraction is a lot better at night, but don't expect short lines unless you ride during the evening parade or fireworks.

The Disney Characters

For many years the costumed, walking versions of Mickey, Minnie, Donald, Goofy, and others have been a colorful supporting cast at Disneyland and Walt Disney World. Known unpretentiously as the "Disney characters," these large and friendly figures help provide a link between Disney animated films and the Disney theme parks.

Audiences, it has been observed, cry during the sad parts of Disney animated films and cheer when the villain is vanquished. To the emotionally invested, the characters in these features are as real as next-door neighbors, never mind that they are drawings on plastic. In recent years, the theme park personifications of Disney characters have likewise become real to us. For thousands of visitors, it is not just some person in a mouse costume they see, it is really Mickey. Similarly, running into Goofy or Snow White in Fantasyland is a memory to be treasured, an encounter with a real celebrity.

While there are literally hundreds of Disney animated-film characters, only about 250 have been brought to life in costume. Of these, a relatively small number (less than a fifth) are "greeters" (the Disney term for characters who mix with the patrons). The remaining characters are relegated exclusively to performing in shows or participating in parades. Originally confined to the Magic Kingdom, the characters can now be found in all three major theme parks and in the resort hotels.

Character Watching. Character watching has developed into a pastime. Where families were once content to stumble across a character occasionally, they now pursue them relentlessly, armed with autograph books and cameras. For those who pay attention, some characters are much more frequently encountered than others. Mickey, Minnie, and Goofy, for example, are seemingly everywhere, while Winnie the Pooh comes out only on rare occasions. Other characters are around regularly but limit themselves to a specific location. Cinderella, not unexpectedly, hangs out at Cinderella Castle in Fantasyland.

The very fact that some characters are seldom seen has turned character watching into character collecting. Mickey Mouse may be the best known and most loved character, but from a collector's perspective he is also the most common. To get an autograph from Mickey is no big

deal, but Daisy Duck's signature is a real coup. To commercially tap into the character collecting movement, Disney sells autograph books throughout Walt Disney World.

Preparing Your Children to Meet the Characters. Since most small children are not expecting Minnie Mouse to be the size of a forklift, it's best to discuss the characters with your kids before you go. Almost all of the characters are quite large, and several, like Brer Bear, are huge! All of them can be extremely intimidating to a preschooler.

On first encounter, it is important not to thrust your child on the character. Allow the little one to come to terms with this big thing from whatever distance the child feels safe. If there are two adults present, one should stay close to the youngster while the other approaches the character and demonstrates that the character is safe and friendly. Some kids warm to the characters immediately, while some never do. Most take a little time and often several different encounters.

The characters do not talk or make noises of any kind. Because the cast members could not possibly imitate the distinctive cinema voice of the character, the Disney folks have determined that it is more effective to keep them silent. Lack of speech notwithstanding, the characters are extremely warm and responsive and communicate very effectively with gestures. As with the characters' size, children need to be forewarned that the characters do not talk.

Parents need to understand that some of the character costumes are very cumbersome and that cast members often suffer from very poor visibility. You have to look close, but the eye holes are frequently in the mouth of the costume or even down on the neck. What this means in practical terms is that the characters are sort of clumsy and have a limited field of vision. Children who approach the character from the back or the side may not be noticed, even if the child is touching the character. It is perfectly possible in this situation for the character to accidently step on the child or knock him down. The best way for a child to approach a character is from the front, and occasionally not even this works. For example, the various duck characters (Donald, Daisy, Uncle Scrooge, etc.) have to peer around their bills. If it appears that the character is ignoring your child, pick your child up and hold her in front of the character until the character responds.

It is okay to touch, pat, or hug the character if your child is so inclined. Understanding the unpredictability of children, the character will keep his feet very still, particularly refraining from moving backwards or to the side. Most of the characters will sign autographs or pose for

pictures. Once again be sure to approach from the front so the character will understand your intentions. If your child collects autographs, it is a good idea to carry a big, fat pen the size of a magic marker. The costumes make it exceedingly difficult for the characters to wield a pen, so the bigger the better.

The Big Hurt. Many children expect to bump into Mickey the minute they enter the park and are disappointed when he is not around. If your children are unable to settle down and enjoy things until they see Mickey, simply ask a Disney cast member where to find him. If the cast member does not know Mickey's whereabouts, he or she can find out for you in short order.

"Then Some Confusion Happened." Be forewarned that character encounters give rise to a situation during which small children sometimes get lost. Usually there is a lot of activity around a character, with both adults and children touching the character or posing for pictures. In the most common scenario, Mom and Dad stay in the crowd while Junior marches up to get acquainted with the character. With the excitement of the encounter, all of the milling people, and the character moving around, Junior gets lost and heads off in the wrong direction looking for Mom and Dad. In the words of a Salt Lake City mom: "Milo was shaking hands with Dopey one minute, then some confusion happened and he [Milo] was gone." Families with several small children and parents who are busy fooling around with cameras can lose track of a youngster in a heartbeat. Our recommendation for parents of preschoolers is to stay with the kids when meeting the characters, stepping back only long enough to take a picture, if necessary.

Meeting Characters for Free. You can *see* the Disney characters in live shows at all three theme parks and in parades at the Magic Kingdom and the Disney-MGM Studios. For times consult your daily entertainment schedule. If you have the time and money, you can share a meal with the characters at the theme parks and at most of the resort hotels (more about this later). But if you want to *meet* the characters, get autographs, and take photos, it's helpful to know where the characters hang out.

At the Magic Kingdom. Characters are encountered more frequently at the Magic Kingdom than anywhere else in Walt Disney World. There will almost always be a character next to City Hall on Main Street, and usually one or more in Town Square or around the railroad station. If it's rainy, look for characters on the veranda of Tony's Restaurant. Characters make appearances in all the "lands," but are particularly thick in Fantasyland and Mickey's Starland. At Mickey's Hollywood Theater in Mickey's Starland, you can meet Mickey backstage in his dressing room. See pages 366–67 for touring tips. Cinderella regularly greets diners at King Stefan's Banquet Hall on the second floor of the Castle (reservation required). Also look for characters in the Central Hub and by Splash Mountain in Frontierland.

Characters are featured in the afternoon and evening parades and in *Mickey's Starland Show,* performed more than 20 times daily. Characters also play a major role in Castle Forecourt shows (at the entrance to the castle on the moat side) and at the Galaxy Palace Theater in Tomorrowland. Performance times for all shows and parades are listed in the Magic Kingdom daily entertainment schedule. Sometimes after the shows, characters will stick around to greet the audience.

At EPCOT Center. At first Disney management did not think that characters would be appropriate for the more serious, educational style of EPCOT Center. Later, however, in response to criticism that EPCOT lacked warmth and humor, the characters were imported. In an effort to integrate them thematically, new and often bizarre costumes were created. Goofy roams Future World in a metallic silver cape reminiscent of Buck Rogers. Mickey greets guests in front of *The American Adventure* decked out like Ben Franklin.

It is unclear whether there are fewer characters at EPCOT or if it just seems that way because the place is so big. In any event, don't expect to encounter either the number or variety of characters at EPCOT that you would in the Magic Kingdom. Characters appear several times a day at the Odyssey Restaurant, to the left of Mexico. At the Odyssey there is a short show after which the characters join the audience for photos and autographs. Show times are posted on the door of the restaurant. At the Odyssey, the arrangement is informal, and you do not have to buy anything. Two EPCOT original characters, Dreamfinder and Figment, lurk around the Journey to Imagination pavilion in Future World, and characters are commonly on hand at the American Adventure pavilion in the World Showcase. While characters are not featured in parades at EPCOT Center, character shows are performed daily at the American Gardens Theater in the World Showcase; check the park's daily entertainment schedule.

In the World Showcase, look for the following characters in these countries:

- Mexico: Donald Duck, Jose, Panchito, Baloo
- China: Chip 'n Dale
- Norway: Daisy Duck
- Germany: Pinocchio, Foulfellow, Gideon
- American Adventure: Mickey Mouse, Roger Rabbit
- Morocco: Pooh, Tigger, Eeyore
- France: Minnie Mouse, Pluto
- United Kingdom: Goofy

Characters may not be as plentiful at EPCOT Center, but they are often easier to meet. According to a father from Effingham, Illinois:

Trying to get autographs and pictures with Disney characters in the Magic Kingdom was a nightmare. Every character we saw was mobbed by kids *and adults*. Our kids had no chance. But at EPCOT and Disney-MGM things were much better. We got autographs, pictures, and more involvement. Our kids danced with several characters and received a lot of personal attention.

At the Disney-MGM Studios.   At the Studios, characters are likely to turn up anywhere but are most frequently found in front of the Animation Building, along Mickey Avenue (leading to the sound stages), and at the end of New York Street on the back lot. Characters figure prominently in shows, with *The Voyage of the Little Mermaid* running almost continuously, and the Teenage Mutant Ninja Turtles doing street shows about a dozen times daily. Each morning at the Soundstage Restaurant, next to the Animation Building, there is a breakfast buffet featuring characters from *Aladdin*.

—— *Character Dining*

Fraternizing with the characters has become so popular that the Disney folks offer character breakfasts, brunches, and dinners where families can eat a meal in the presence of Mickey, Minnie, Goofy, and the costumed versions of other animated celebrities. Besides grabbing some market share from Denny's and Hardees, the character meals provide a familiar, controlled setting in which small children can warm to the characters in an unhurried way. Though we mention only the featured character(s) in our descriptions, all meals are attended by several

"Casting? This is George at the character breakfast. There's been a mistake. We were supposed to get the Assorted *Character Package with 1 Mickey, 1 Goofy, 1 Donald, 1 Pluto . . ."*

different characters. Adult prices apply to anyone 10 or older, kids 3 to 9 are charged the children's price, and little ones under 3 eat free. Obtain additional information on character dining by calling (407) 939-3463.

Because character dining is very popular, we recommend that you make your reservations as far in advance as possible. Make reservations for dining up to 60 days prior to arrival by calling (407) WDW-DINE. If you forget to make advance reservations and all of the Disney resort and theme park character meals are sold out, try to book a character meal at the Swan or Dolphin. Because the Swan and Dolphin are not Disney-owned hotels, their character meals are not booked through the Disney central reservations number. Often, consequently, the Swan and Dolphin will have seating available when all the other character meals are completely booked.

Character Breakfasts

Though a number of character breakfasts are offered around Walt Disney World, attending them will usually prevent you from arriving at the theme parks in time for opening. If you want to try a character breakfast, go some morning when your touring objectives are pretty modest, such as the morning you check out or a day when you do not plan to go to the parks until late afternoon. If your kids are picky eaters, or simply do not like eggs, choose a breakfast that offers a buffet or general menu selection.

Disney-MGM Studios: Soundstage Restaurant. This cavernous eatery next to the Animation Building offers an excellent breakfast buffet daily from 8:30 until 10:15 A.M. While some characters circulate in the dining area, Pocahontas and Captain John Smith hang out upstairs and receive only visitors who "have cleaned their plate." Reservations are required, but can be made at the door of the restaurant. The buffet runs $13 for adults (over 10) and $8 for ages 3 to 9. Please note that the price of the character meal is in addition to your cost of admission to the theme park.

EPCOT Center: Coral Reef Restaurant. This breakfast is held daily from 8:30 to 10:30 A.M. The menu is fixed, but seconds are available. The cost is $15 for adults (10 and up) and $8 for children ages 3 to 9. Characters featured include Mickey (swimming in the fish tank), Minnie, Goofy, and Pluto. Please note that the price of the character meal is in addition to your cost of admission to the theme park.

Magic Kingdom: King Stefan's Restaurant in Cinderella's Castle. Served daily from 8 to 10 A.M., the breakfast features Cinderella as well as visiting character "friends." The menu is fixed and costs $15 for adults (10 or over) and $8 for children 3 to 9. Please note that the price of the character meal is in addition to your cost of admission to the theme park.

Disney Beach Club: Cape May Cafe. This breakfast is held daily from 7:30 to 11 A.M. The C.I.C. (Character in Charge) is Goofy. It costs $13 for adults (10 and over) and $8 for ages 3 to 9. No reservations are required.

Wilderness Lodge Resort: Artists Point. Chip 'n Dale hold court at this breakfast daily from 7:30 to 11:30 A.M. The cost is $13 for adults and $8 for children.

Contemporary Resort: Monorail Buffet. Goofy hosts this buffet daily from 7:30 to 11 A.M. The cost is $13 for adults and $8 for children. No reservations are required.

Polynesian Resort: Papeete Bay Verandah.   This breakfast is called Minnie's Menehune (difficult to pronounce at any time, much less first thing in the morning) and is served from 7:30 to 10:30 A.M., Monday through Saturday, 7:30 to 11 A.M. on Sundays. It costs $13 and $8 for adults and children respectively. Reservations are required; call (407) 824-1391. The C.I.C., obviously, is Minnie; the theme is tropical.

Grand Floridian Beach Resort: 1900 Park Fare.   This breakfast features a buffet hosted by Mary Poppins, and runs everyday from 8 to 11:30 A.M. The price is $15 for adults and $10 for children (3 to 11). Reservations can be made by calling (407) 824-2383.

Walt Disney World Village: Chef Mickey's Village Restaurant.   This character breakfast was moved to Chef Mickey's from the *Empress Lilly* riverboat at Pleasure Island. At press time it was undecided whether the breakfast would move back to the boat or remain at Chef Mickey's. Breakfast offers a set menu with eggs as the main dish. The C.I.C. is Mickey. There are 7:30 A.M., 9 A.M., and 10:30 A.M. seatings. The tab is $13 for adults and $8 for children. Reservations can be made by calling (407) 828-3900.

Walt Disney World Swan: Garden Grove Cafe.   Held only on Wednesdays and Saturdays from 8 to 11 A.M., the Garden Grove character breakfast offers you a choice of buffet or menu selection. Pluto and Goofy are usually the characters present. The cost is around $11 for adults and $7 for children. No reservations are required. For additional information, call (407) 934-3000, extension 1282.

Disney Vaction Club Resort: Olivia's Cafe.   This breakfast, held Sundays and Wednesdays from 7:30 to 10 A.M., features Winnie the Pooh and Tigger as hosts. The charge for adults is $11.50; children, $7.50. For reservations, call (407) 827-7700.

Character Brunches

Walt Disney World Dolphin: Harry's Safari Bar & Grill.   This brunch features Chip 'n Dale, Pluto, and Goofy, and offers a buffet at $16 for adults and $9 for kids (3 to 12). Available only on Sundays from 8:30 A.M. to 12:30 P.M. For reservations, call (407) 934-4889.

Character Dinners

Walt Disney World Swan: Garden Grove Cafe. Held only on Mondays and Fridays from 6 to 10 P.M., the dinner features Timon and Rafiki from *The Lion King.* Diners order from the regular dinner menu.

Grand Floridian Beach Resort: 1900 Park Fare. Mickey and Minnie host a dinner buffet daily from 5:30 to 9 P.M. It costs $19 for adults and $10 for children (3 to 11). For reservations, call (407) 824-2383.

Polynesian Resort: Mickey's Tropical Luau. This is actually a dinner show featuring Pacific Island dancing and the Disney characters. Staged outdoors at 4:30 P.M., the show is fun if: (1) you are hungry that early, and (2) you go during one of the cooler months of the year. Regardless of when you go, be prepared for the lackluster food. The cost is $29 for adults, $22 for juniors (12 to 20), and $13 for children (3 to 11).

Walt Disney World Village: Chef Mickey's Village Restaurant. Chef Mickey appears among the diners. Selection is from the menu and prices vary. Open for dinner from 5 to 10 P.M., daily. A decent restaurant, most folks go to Chef Mickey's for the food. Getting to meet Mickey is a nice extra. The restaurant, incidentally, also serves breakfast and lunch, but Mickey is not present except as noted above. For reservations, call (407) 828-3900.

Character Campfire

There is a campfire and sing-along each night at 7 or 8 P.M. (depending on the season) near the Meadow Trading Post and Bike Barn at the Fort Wilderness Campground. Chip 'n Dale lead the songs, and afterwards, a full-length Disney feature film is shown. The program is open to resort guests and is complimentary. For a campfire schedule, call (407) 824-2788.

—— Babysitting

Childcare Centers. Childcare services are not available within the theme parks, but each of the Magic Kingdom resorts (hotels connected by the monorail) and EPCOT resorts (Swan and Dolphin hotels, Yacht and Beach Club resorts) offer a childcare service for potty-trained children over three. Services vary somewhat, but in general children can be left between 4 P.M. and midnight. Milk and cookies are provided at all of the childcare centers, as are blankets and pillows. Play is supervised but not organized, and toys, videos, and games are on hand in quantity. Guests at any Walt Disney resort hotel (or campground) may use the childcare service.

The most elaborate of the childcare centers (variously called "clubs" or "camps") is the Neverland Club at the Polynesian Resort. This, and the Wilderness Lodge, are the only centers that include a buffet dinner at the club, though at the other locations you can arrange for hotel room service to bring your children's meals. At Camp Dolphin in the Walt Disney World Dolphin, there is the option of having children eat at the Coral Cafe or the Soda Shop next door.

We get a lot of mail from readers concerning the Neverland Club, invariably complimentary. A dad from Snohomish, Washington, wrote:

> A word about the Neverland Club. The boys loved it! They got a good choice of food to eat in buffet style. It was educational — someone from Discovery Island brought some animals in — and it was fun. There was something for every age — appropriate toys, games, and a game room with free video games. The boys also had a Polaroid picture taken with Goofy, and the boys' smiles showed how good a time they were having. The supervisors seemed very pleasant and caring. As you might expect, it was all very professional and well done, and the beepers they had us carry made us feel extra secure.

Along similar lines, a dad from Houston had this to say:

> There were two outstanding surprises during our visit. The first was the babysitting club at the Polynesian Hotel, the Neverland Club. I can tell you that our children enjoyed the Neverland Club as much as anything at WDW. It is somewhat expensive ($8 per child per hour, three hour minimum), but that includes dinner, free video games, Disney movies, group games and activities, and a visit by an expert from Discovery Island with several birds and animals. A woman registering her child told my wife that her daughter had stayed at the Neverland Club on a visit two years ago, and considered it her favorite attraction at WDW!

In addition to the above, a Disney character (usually Goofy) visits the children each night. What was the reader's second outstanding surprise? Pleasure Island.

The following childcare clubs operate afternoons and evenings. Reservations are required by all.

Hotel	Name of Program	Ages	Phone
Buena Vista Palace	All About Kids	All	(407) 827-2727
Contemporary Resort	Mouseketeer Clubhouse	4-12	(407) 824-1000, ext. 3038
Grand Floridian	Mouseketeer Club	4-12	(407) 824-3000, ext. 2985
The Hilton	Vacation Station	4-12	(407) 827-4000
Polynesian Resort	Neverland Club	4-12	(407) 824-2170
WDW Dolphin	Camp Dolphin	3-12	(407) 934-4241
WDW Swan	Camp Swan	3-12	(407) 934-1621
Wilderness Lodge Resort	Cub's Den	4-12	(407) 824-1083
Yacht and Beach Clubs	Sandcastle Club	4-12	(407) 934-7000

Kinder-Care Learning Centers also operate childcare facilities at Walt Disney World. Originally developed for the use of Disney employees, the Kinder-Care Centers will also take children of guests on a space available basis. Kinder-Care provides basically the same services as a hotel club, except that the daytime *Learning while Playing Development Program* is more structured and educational. For childcare service in the morning and early afternoon, Kinder-Care is the only game in town. They accept children from age 1 (provided they are walking and can eat table food) through age 12. Reservations can be made by calling (407) 827-5437.

In-Room Babysitting. For those staying in the World, in-room babysitting is available through Kinder-Care (407-827-5444) or through the Fairy Godmother service (no joke) described below.

Outside of Walt Disney World, childcare services and in-room sitting can be arranged through most of the larger hotels and motels, or by calling the Fairy Godmothers. On call 24 hours a day, you will never get an answering machine when you call the Fairy Godmothers. Though not cheap (the Godmothers can turn your billfold into a pumpkin), they offer the most flexible and diversified service in town. They will come to any hotel at any hour of the day or night. If you pay, they will take your children to the theme parks. No child is too young or too old for a Fairy Godmother (they also care for the elderly), and they will even take care of your pets. All sitters are female and non-smokers. Base rates are $7 an hour for up to three children (in the same family), with a four-hour minimum and a $5 travel fee. Godmothers will also sit a group of children from different families for $5 an hour per family. Wishing won't get it with these Fairy Godmothers; you've got to call them on the phone at (407) 277-3724 or 275-7326.

Walt Disney World Learning Programs for Children

Developed in coordination with leading educators, four special learning programs are available for persons 15 years and younger at Walt Disney World. The well-presented and enjoyable programs include admission to any theme park visited, classroom materials, and lunch. All of the courses are limited in class size, so make your reservation as soon as possible.

While the courses are expensive, they provide an interesting and educational glimpse of Walt Disney World behind the scenes. They also offer (as if you hadn't thought of it) some time for parents to be alone. If you are considering taking your children out of school to visit Walt Disney World, participation in one of the educational programs sometimes helps secure teacher approval for the absence.

Kidventure Program

This four-hour program held at the Discovery Island zoological park focuses on identifying plants and wildlife. Offered on Wednesdays and Sundays during the summer and only on Wednesdays during off-season months, the course costs $32 per person and is restricted to students 8 to 14 years old. Boat transportation to the island is included. For reservations call (407) 824-3784.

Wonders of Walt Disney World

Wildlife Adventure.   This program explores the interrelation of mankind and the natural environment. Students visit Discovery Island and the Disney World conservation area. Highlights include seeing several rare and endangered species. Six hours long, the course is limited to students 10 to 15 years old and costs $79. For reservations and information, call (407) 354-1855.

Art Magic: Bringing Illusion to Life.   In this program, students are offered an introduction to animation, as well as a look at how costuming, set design, and landscaping are used in movies, stage shows, and theme parks. Tuition for the six-hour program, open to students 10 to 15 years old, is $79. Reservations can be made by calling (407) 354-1855.

Show Biz Magic: The Walt Disney World of Entertainment takes a look at what goes into a Disney stage show. Students meet performers and technicians and observe how timing, music, lighting, and costumes combine to create a show. The six-hour course is for 10 to 15 year olds. Tuition is $79. For information, or to register, call (407) 354-1855.

PART FIVE: Special Tips for Special People

Walt Disney World for Singles

Most of the singles at Walt Disney World work there. If you are looking to hook up with someone new and exciting for a little romance, heaven knows there are better places than Walt Disney World. Even at Pleasure Island, the nighttime entertainment complex, you need to check your dancing partner's wristband to determine whether he or she is old enough to buy a drink.

A simple demographic truth is that single men, by and large, do not vacation at Walt Disney World while single women, including single parents, do. Generally speaking, therefore, for women there are precious few *qualified* prospects. There are men, of course, both single for real and single for the moment, attending meetings and conventions at the resort hotels, but these guys are rarely on a schedule that permits the development of anything meaningful. Filling the void, consequently, are local single (and married) men who realize all too well that single women on vacation (and looking for a little romance) are frequently vulnerable. As a rule, it's probably a good idea to avoid the locals.

For singles of both sexes, the rules at Walt Disney World are the same as at home. Take it slow and easy and make sure you know who you are dealing with. The easiest and safest way to meet anyone at Walt Disney World is at the theme parks, including the water theme parks. (Most locals "on the make" are not going to shell out the price of admission and hang around the park all day.) The theme parks give all guests something in common to talk about. There is no easier place on earth to strike up a conversation than waiting in line for an attraction. A more organized way to meet people at Walt Disney World is to take one of the several tours available especially for adults. These are listed and described on pages 396 and 496.

Walt Disney World for Couples

So many couples wed or honeymoon at Walt Disney World that Disney has organized an entire department to take care of their needs. *Disney's Fairy Tale Weddings & Honeymoons* department offers a full range of wedding venues and services, as well as honeymoon packages.

Weddings

The primary prerequisite for getting married at Walt Disney World is big bucks. A tiny wedding with all local guests (i.e., no hotel rooms) runs a minimum of $3,500 and does not include floral arrangements, decorations, entertainment, wedding officiant, or music. If you are willing to drop a bundle, however, you can arrive at your wedding in Cinderella's glass coach, have Goofy for an usher, Minnie as maid of honor, and drive off after the ceremony in a limo chauffeured by Mickey. If you don't have many friends, you can rent additional Disney characters by the half-hour to attend your wedding. Volume discounts are available; characters run: one for $395, two for $525, three for $775, and so on. If the character prices sound a little steep, be comforted that they don't eat or drink.

A number of indoor and outdoor locations are available for wedding ceremonies at the Grand Floridian, Yacht Club, Beach Club, Contemporary, Polynesian, and Disney Village resorts. You can have a nautical wedding aboard the Kingdom Queen stern wheeler on Bay Lake or the *Empress Lilly* Riverboat at the Walt Disney World Village. For the nocturnal, wedding sites are available at Pleasure Island nightclubs.

In 1995, Disney opened the Fairy Tale Wedding pavilion on a private island near the Grand Floridian Beach Resort. The glass-enclosed pavilion is non-denominational and will accommodate weddings with 250 guests as well as smaller, more intimate nuptials. The theme parks, incidentally, are supposedly not available for weddings, but, hey, this is *Walt Disney World.* . . . Money talks.

One of the most improbable services the wedding department offers is

arranging bachelor parties. I'm not sure what goes on at a Disney bachelor party. Maybe stag cartoons or a private showing of *The Making of Me*. Get down!

If you wish to be married at Walt Disney World, you can obtain a marriage license at any county courthouse in Florida. Currently blood tests are not required, but you must present proper identification in the form of a driver's license, passport, or birth certificate. If you were divorced within the last year, you must also produce a copy of your divorce decree. Marriage licenses cost about $89, statewide. Cash or money orders only, please. There is no waiting period in Florida; your license is issued at the time of application. The marriage license must be used within 60 days.

Honeymoons

The honeymoon packages are basically adaptations of the regular Disney Travel Company vacation packages. No special rooms or honeymoon suites are included in the packages unless you upgrade. In fact, the only specific honeymoon feature (in two of the packages) is room service.

If you are interested in either a Disney wedding or honeymoon, contact:

Disney's Fairy Tale Weddings & Honeymoons
P.O. Box 10,020
Lake Buena Vista, Florida 32830-0020
Phone (407) 363-6333

Romantic Getaways

Many people consider the utopian Disney environment very romantic. Consequently, Walt Disney World is a favorite getaway spot for honeymooners and other couples. Needless to say, you do not have to purchase a Disney honeymoon package to enjoy a romantic interlude at Walt Disney World.

Not all the Disney hotels are equally romantic. Some are too family oriented, others are aswarm with convention-goers. We recommend the following Disney lodgings for the romantically inclined:

1. Polynesian Resort
2. Disney's Wilderness Lodge Resort
3. Grand Floridian Beach Resort
4. Disney's Yacht and Beach Clubs

All of the properties listed are expensive. There are also some nice secluded villas at Disney's Village Resort. Possibly the most romantic of all Disney accommodations is the Moorea building at the Polynesian Resort. Couples at the Moorea with a waterfront-view room can watch the Magic Kingdom fireworks across the Seven Seas Lagoon.

Quiet, Romantic Places to Eat

If you are looking for a quiet, romantic setting and good food in the theme parks, your choices are extremely limited. Only the Coral Reef and the San Angel Inn at EPCOT Center satisfy both requirements. At the hotels, however, there is a wider selection. Victoria & Albert's at the Grand Floridian offers waterfront dining, as do the restaurants on the *Empress Lilly* Riverboat at the Walt Disney World Village, and Cap'n Jack's Oyster Bar at the Disney Village Marketplace. Ariel's at the Beach Club is a good spot for seafood and the Yachtsman Steakhouse at the Yacht Club serves a pretty decent steak. Sum Chows and Kimonos at the Swan and Dolphin resorts offer good food and a quiet atmosphere. Another good choice is 'Ohana at the Polynesian Resort.

Though eating later in the evening, as well as choosing from the restaurants mentioned above, will improve your chances for quiet, intimate dining, be forewarned that children are the rule, not the exception at Walt Disney World. Consider the comments of a honeymoon couple from Slidell, Louisiana:

> We made dinner reservations at some of the nicer Disney restaurants. When we made reservations we made sure they were past the dinner hours and we tried to stress that we were on our honeymoon. [In] every restaurant we went to, we were seated next to large families. The kids were usually tired and cranky. After a whole day in the parks, the kids were not excited about sitting through a long meal. It's very difficult to enjoy a romantic dinner when there are small children crawling around under your table. We looked around the restaurant and always noticed lots of non-children couples. Our suggestion is this: seat couples without children together and families with kids elsewhere. If Disney is such a popular honeymoon destination, then some attempt should be made to keep romantic restaurants romantic.

Along similar lines, a Woodbridge, Virginia, couple contributed this:

> We found it very difficult to find a quiet restaurant for dinner anywhere. We tried a restaurant which you recommended as quiet and pleasant. We even waited until 8:30 P.M. to eat and we were still surrounded by out-of-control children. The waiters were even singing the Barney the Dinosaur theme song. The food was very good but after a long day in the park, our nerves were shot.

For complete information about Disney restaurants, as well as some recommendations for off-World dining, see the chapter on "Dining In and Around Walt Disney World."

Romantic Stuff to Do

Couples, like everyone else, have their own agenda at Walt Disney World. That having been said, here are a few romantic diversions you might not have on your list:

1. There is a nice (albeit pricey) lounge on the top floor of the Contemporary Resort. This is a great place to watch a sunset or, later in the evening, view the fireworks at the nearby Magic Kingdom.

If you just want to go for the view (and not drink), you can access an outside promenade through a set of glass doors at the end of the lounge.

2. The Floating Electrical Pageant is one of Disney's most romantic entertainments. It consists of a train of barges, each with a spectacular light display depicting sea creatures. The show starts after dark to music by Handel played on synthesizers. All you can see are the lights. The best place to watch is from the pier or beach at the Polynesian Resort.

3. Take a launch to Fort Wilderness. At the Fort Wilderness dock you can rent various types of boats for exploring Bay Lake and the Seven Seas Lagoon. The Fort Wilderness Campground is honeycombed with footpaths and makes a lovely setting for an early morning or early evening walk. If you really enjoy hiking and boating, take a day and visit the Juniper Springs Recreation Area in the Ocala National Forest. About an hour and a half north of Walt Disney World, the forest is extraordinarily beautiful. Trails are well marked and canoes are available for rent (shuttle included). Paddling down Juniper Springs is like floating through a natural version of the Jungle Cruise.

4. During the more temperate months of the year, enjoy a picnic on the beaches of Bay Lake and the Seven Seas Lagoon. Room service at the resort hotels will prepare your lunch to order. Drinks, including wine and beer, are available at less cost from the hotel convenience shops. Fort Wilderness Campground is also a good place to picnic.

5. Small boats shuttle guests to and from the Grand Floridian, Polynesian Resort, Magic Kingdom, and Fort Wilderness Campground well into the night. On a summer night, cap your day with a tranquil cruise around Bay Lake and the Seven Seas Lagoon.

Some Things to Bring with You

Once ensconced in your Walt Disney World hideaway, it can be inconvenient to go out after something you've forgotten. Many couples have written us and listed things they wish they'd remembered to bring. Here are a few of the items most often mentioned.

1. Wine (wine can be purchased by the bottle at Walt Disney World, but the selection is pretty dismal)
2. Corkscrew (wine glasses are available from room service)
3. Liquor, apertifs, cordials
4. Mixers for fancy drinks like Margaritas, olives for Martinis, lemons and limes
5. Portable tape or disc player and your favorite music
6. Bicycles
7. Picnic basket and blanket or tablecloth
8. Candles and holders
9. Cooler
10. Special snacks such as caviar, chocolates, cheeses (with knife), fruit

Walt Disney World for Seniors

Most seniors' problems and concerns are common to Walt Disney World visitors of all ages. Even so, seniors often find themselves in predicaments attributable to touring with persons a few or many years their junior. Run ragged, and pressured by the grandchildren to endure a frantic pace, many seniors concentrate more on surviving their visit to Walt Disney World than enjoying it. The Disney parks have as much to offer the mature visitor as the youngster, and seniors must either insist on setting the pace or dispatch the young folks to tour on their own.

We received this letter from an older reader in Alabaster, Alabama:

> The main thing I want to say is that being a senior is not for wussies. At Disney World particularly, it requires courage and pluck. Things that used to be easy take a lot of effort, and sometimes your brain has to wait for your body to catch up. Half the time your grandchildren treat you like a crumbling ruin, and then turn around and trick you into getting on a roller coaster in the dark. What you need to tell seniors is that they have to be alert and not trust anyone. Not their children or even the Disney people, and especially not their grandchildren. When your grandchildren want you to go on a ride, don't follow along blindly like a lamb to the slaughter. Make sure you know what the ride is all about. Stand your ground and do not waffle. He who hesitates is launched!

Most seniors we interview enjoy Walt Disney World more (much more) when they tour with folks their own age, without any kids along. If you are contemplating a Walt Disney World visit with your grandchildren, however, we recommend a preliminary visit without them to get oriented. If you know first-hand what to expect, it is much easier to establish limits, maintain control, and set a comfortable pace when you visit with the youngsters.

If you are determined to bring the grandkids, we recommend that you read carefully those sections of this book that discuss family touring. (Hint: the Dumbo-or-Die-in-a-Day Touring Plan has been known to bring grown-ups of any age to their knees.)

In our experience, because seniors are a varied and willing lot, there are not any Walt Disney World attractions that we would categorically suggest they avoid. For seniors, as with other Walt Disney World patrons, personal taste is more important than age. We hate to see mature visitors pass up an exceptional attraction like Splash Mountain because some younger visitors classify it as a "thrill ride." Splash Mountain is a full-blown Disney adventure which derives its appeal more from its music and visual effects than from the thrill of the ride. As you must pick from many attractions those that might interest you, we have provided as much information as we can to help you make informed choices.

That having been said, we acknowledge that it's easy to get caught up in the spectacle and wonder of Walt Disney World—so much so that before you know it, you've followed the crowd onto something you haven't thought much about.

We believe that forewarned is forearmed, so below we discuss some of the rides offered in the name of "fun."

Magic Kingdom

Space Mountain.   If you thought the roller coaster at Coney Island was a thrill, this won't be far behind, with dips and pops that pull you through curves and over humps. This ride vibrates quite a bit, so take your glasses off and store them safely in your fanny pack. I can't guarantee they'll stay in your pocket.

Big Thunder Mountain Railroad.   Although rather sedate and constrained compared with Space Mountain, this ride is very jarring. The cars jerk back and forth along the track, and though there are a few drops, it is the side-to-side shaking that gets to most people.

Splash Mountain.   This ride combines the whimsy of Disney with the thrill of a log flume. There is one big drop near the end and a bit of a splash (engineered by spray guns and a water cannon, not the drop itself). The enchantment of the Brer Rabbit story makes it worth getting a little wet.

The Swiss Family Treehouse.   This is by no means a thrill ride, but it does involve a lot of stair climbing and a very unsteady pontoon bridge.

*Doris explains the importance of knowing
what you are getting in line for.*

Mad Tea Party. An adaptation of the standard carnival midway ride where you spin around in big tea cups until you are nauseated. If you approach this instrument of the devil while it is sitting still, your cunning grandchildren may try to pass it off as an *al fresco* dining patio.

EPCOT Center

Body Wars. This ride is more jolting than Star Tours (at the Disney-MGM Studios) and more prone to cause motion sickness than the Mad Hatter's tea cups. It combines the visual shock of a graphic anatomy lesson with the trauma of being chauffeured by a teenager driving his first stick-shift.

Disney-MGM Studios

Star Tours. Using the plot and characters from *Star Wars*, this flight-simulation ride is a real Disney masterpiece. If you are extremely prone to motion sickness, this ride will affect you. Otherwise, we suspect it might be the highlight of your Walt Disney World vacation.

Tower of Terror. Though most of the thrills are visual, the Tower of Terror features a gut-gripping simulation of an elevator in free-fall (after its cable has broken).

Getting Around

For many seniors, walking is a preferred form of exercise. Be advised, however, that you will normally walk between four and eight miles in the course of a seven-hour visit to one of the major theme parks. If you are not up for that much hiking, don't be reluctant to allow a more athletic member of your party to push you around in a rented wheelchair. EPCOT Center and the Magic Kingdom also offer electric carts (convenience vehicles), which, in addition to saving shoe leather, are fun to drive. The main thing is to not let your pride get in the way of having a good time. Sure, you could march ten miles if you had to, but the point is *you don't have to!* Pamper yourself; go for the good time instead of the Purple Heart.

A big advantage to renting a wheelchair is the special boarding privilege granted to guests (and their immediate parties) who use the special entrances for wheelchairs at most attractions. Waiting times at these special boarding areas will vary depending on the attraction and the crowd, but you will almost always get to ride sooner than if you had waited in the regular queue. You must check in with a host or hostess before you board.

Your wheelchair rental deposit slip is good for a replacement wheelchair in any park during the same day. So keep your ticket. You can rent a chair at the Magic Kingdom in the morning, turn it back in, go to EPCOT Center, present your deposit slip, and get another chair without paying twice.

Timing your Visit

Retired seniors are in an ideal position to take advantage of the "off-season" for visiting Walt Disney World. Make use of your flexible schedule — plan your trip for times when the weather is the nicest, and the crowds the thinnest, namely the fall and the spring, holiday weeks excluded. The crowds are also sparse from the end of January through the beginning of February, but the weather is unpredictable at this time of year. If you choose to see Walt Disney World in the winter, you will need to bring coats and sweaters as well as more moderate dress; be prepared for anything from near-freezing rain to afternoon temperatures in the 80's.

Visiting during the off-season also allows you more flexibility in choosing which days to go to the park. Normally Monday, Tuesday, and Wednesday are the most crowded days. The best possible option is to arrive on a Wednesday in order to start touring on a Thursday. However, the day of the week you choose to begin your touring is less crucial than it would be if you were visiting the park during peak season.

The Price of Admission

Walt Disney World offers senior discounts for admission to its theme parks (see page 46) to Florida residents only. For additional information, see the section in this guide on admission options.

Lodging

Like all sojourners to a strange place, seniors are concerned with their lodging options in the Orlando/Kissimmee area. Our first recommendation is to stay in Walt Disney World if economically feasible. If you are concerned about the quality of your accommodations or the availability of transportation, staying inside the Disney complex will do much to put your mind at ease. The rooms are some of the nicest in the area, always clean and well-kept. And transportation is always available, at no extra cost, to any destination in Walt Disney World.

At the Disney hotels, rooms closer to restaurants and transportation are kept available for guests of any age who cannot tolerate a lot of walking. The hotels provide fancy golf carts to pick up and deliver guests to and from their rooms. Pick-up times for the golf cart service can vary dramatically depending on the time of day and number of guests requesting service. For example, at check-in time (around 3 P.M.), the wait for a ride could be as long as 40 minutes.

While there are many quality hotels in the area that we could recommend, there are several reasons we think staying in Walt Disney World is a good idea for seniors:

1. The quality of the properties is consistently above average.
2. The transportation companies that operate buses for "outside" hotels run only every hour or so. Disney buses run continuously. By staying in Walt Disney World, you guarantee your ability to get transportation whenever you need it.
3. You will be able to make dinner reservations over the phone and in advance. Similarly, you can alert Disney restaurants in advance of any special dietary needs or restrictions.
4. You may be eligible for special discounts to shows and early entrance to the parks.
5. Boarding pets at the kennels overnight is available only to guests staying in Walt Disney World.
6. You are guaranteed admission to the theme parks during peak season.
7. You are eligible for free parking in the major theme parks' lots.
8. You are accorded preferential tee times on resort golf courses.

All of the Disney resort hotels are large and spread out. While it is easy to avoid most stairs, it is often a long hike to your guest room from the parking lot, bus stops, or public areas. Seniors intending to spend more time at EPCOT Center and the Disney-MGM Studios than at the Magic Kingdom, should consider the Yacht Club or Beach Club resorts.

The Contemporary Resort is a good choice for mobile seniors (wheelchairs cannot access the monorail platform) who want to be on the monorail system, as are the Grand Floridian and the Polynesian Resort, though both are spread over many acres and may entail a lot of walking. For a restful, outdoors feel, choose the new Wilderness Lodge. If you want a kitchen and all the comforts of home, the Disney Vacation Club is a good choice.

Finally, the RV crowd will find pleasant surroundings at Walt Disney World's Fort Wilderness Campground. In addition to Fort Wilderness, there are several KOA campgrounds within 20 minutes of Walt Disney World. None of the KOA sites, however, offer the wilderness setting or amenities of the Disney campground. On the other hand, they don't charge nearly as much either.

Elderhostels

Recently we were introduced to Elderhostel by friends active in the program. It is an educational travel and study program for seniors who are looking for something a little different. The one-week sessions are hosted, for the most part, by educational institutions, though some programs use private resort or hotel facilities.

The Elderhostel program offers classes on subjects ranging from anthropology to zoology, from French to cabinet making. These classes take about four-and-a-half hours each day. Most programs do not assign homework, so there is a lot of time left for visiting, making friends, or even taking an afternoon trip to Walt Disney World.

Elderhostel encourages its participants to be "students-in-residence," and advises them to arrange their sight-seeing before or after their stay with the Elderhostel system. However, several of the programs in the central Florida area advertise their proximity to Walt Disney World. These include:

- Camp Challenge in Sorrento, 20 miles north of Orlando
- Canterbury Retreat and Conference Center in Oviedo, 5 miles northeast of Orlando
- Thunderbird Outdoor Center at Wekiva Springs, 20 minutes northwest of Orlando
- Stetson University/Off Campus, in De Land, 35 miles north of Orlando
- Deerhaven Camp and Conference Center in the Ocala National Forest, 16 miles west of De Land and about an hour and 40 minutes from Orlando
- University of Florida/Cerveny Conference Center, two hours northwest of Orlando

For information on the Elderhostel program, do not contact the camps listed above. Instead, write or call Elderhostel:

Elderhostel
75 Federal Street
Boston, MA 02110
Phone: (617) 426-8056

Transportation

The roads throughout Walt Disney World can be daunting to the uninitiated. Armed with a moderate sense of direction and an above-average sense of humor, even the most timid driver can learn to get around in the World. If you are intimidated easily, pick a hotel on the monorail and stay off the road.

If you drive, or seek to limit your walking, parking is not a problem. Parking lots are serviced by a tram system that runs between the parking area and the front gate of the theme park. For guests who are marginally or wholly nonambulatory, parking spaces are reserved adjacent to the entrance complex at each park. The parking attendant at the pay booth will give you a special ticket for your dashboard, as well as direct you to the special lot. Though Walt Disney World stipulates that you be recognized as officially handicapped to utilize this parking, in practice the temporarily disabled or injured are also permitted access.

Senior Dining

Our advice is to either eat breakfast at your hotel restaurant or save money by having juice and rolls in your room. Although you are not allowed to bring any food into the parks, fruit, fruit juice, and soft drink vendors are located throughout Walt Disney World. We recommend you make your lunch reservations for early in the day, before noon, say, and avoid the lunch crowds altogether. This way, you'll be ready for an early dinner and will be out of the restaurants, rested and ready for evening touring and fireworks, long before the main crowd even begins to think about dinner.

Part of our senior touring plan is to fit dining and rest times into the day. Remember the Dad on the Dumbo-or-Die-in-a-Day Touring Plan? He will be scarfing down fast food as he hauls his toddlers around the park at breakneck speed. Reserve a window table for your early lunch, and wave to him as he goes by. Lunch is your break in the day, so sit back, relax, and enjoy. After lunch, return to your hotel for a nap.

Have a Plan

Our maxim for touring Walt Disney World ("Have a plan or get a frontal lobotomy") is easily adapted to senior touring. From planning the time of year to visit to the first rule of touring ("Arrive early! Arrive early! Arrive early!"), seniors are, in general, the perfect *Unofficial Guide* patrons. If you are a person who can get by on less sleep, enjoy the stress-free pleasure of touring the theme parks in the early morning. If you enjoy sleeping late, make sure you visit Walt Disney World during the less crowded, off-peak times of year.

Select the touring plan you want to follow. Pick what you want to see or skip ahead of time, so that you will be able to efficiently follow the plan. Check out the ride and show descriptions before you go. Arrive at the entrance gates at least a half hour before the official opening time. Move as fast as you can early in the day, so you will be able to slow down and relax after an hour or so, knowing the most strenuous part of the plan (as well as potential bottlenecks) is behind you.

Seniors who write to us asking whether the touring plans work for folks who want to take things a little slower will be encouraged by the following:

My mother (age 77) and myself (age 47) visited Disney for the first time. We followed your "Type A" schedule and really enjoyed the challenge of it. We were standing in line for Star Tours and the friendly attendant was advising us on the popular attractions to see. He suggested Tower of Terror, Indiana Jones, *Voyage of the Little Mermaid* and The Muppets. We said we had already seen them all. He said "It's only ten o'clock in the morning and you have seen all of those already?" We said "Yes," and held up your guide book. He couldn't believe it.

We think at least one of the behind-the-scenes tours should be part of any senior's visit. These tours, offering an in-depth look at the operations of Walt Disney World, are primarily at EPCOT Center. Especially worth seeing are Hidden Treasures and Gardens of the World. If you don't have the time for these lengthy tours, a "must-see" is the shorter Greenhouse Tour at The Land pavilion, also in EPCOT Center.

Finally, do not forget to include camper's quiet time in your itinerary.

We recommend Disney patrons of all ages return to the hotel during the hot, crowded part of the day for lunch, a nap, and even a swim.

When You Need to Contact the Outside World

Pay telephones are located throughout Walt Disney World. If your hearing is not what it used to be, special, amplified handsets are available in all three major theme parks. Handset locations are marked on each park's map, provided free when you enter. In addition, TDDs are available at City Hall in the Magic Kingdom, at Guest Relations at EPCOT Center, and Guest Services at the Disney-MGM Studios.

Telephones that guests in wheelchairs can reach are scattered all over the parks, except in the Magic Kingdom, where they are all under the Walt Disney World Railroad Station.

Walt Disney World for Disabled Guests

—— *Visitors with Special Needs*

Wholly or partially nonambulatory guests will find rental wheelchairs available if needed. Most rides, shows, attractions, rest rooms, and restaurants at the theme parks are designed to accommodate the nonambulatory disabled. For specific inquiries or problems, call (407) 824-4321. If you are in the Magic Kingdom and need some special assistance, go to City Hall on Main Street. At EPCOT Center, inquire at Guest Relations to the left of Spaceship Earth. At Disney-MGM Studios, assistance can be obtained at Guest Services to the left of the main entrance on Hollywood Boulevard.

In addition to ordinary wheelchairs, a limited number of self-propelled, electric "motorized convenience vehicles" are available for rent at the Magic Kingdom and EPCOT Center. Easy to operate and fun to drive, these vehicles afford nonambulatory guests a tremendous degree of freedom and mobility. For some unknown reason, the vehicles at the Magic Kingdom are much faster than those at EPCOT Center.

Close-in parking is available for disabled visitors at all Walt Disney World parking complexes. Simply request directions when you pay your parking fee upon entering. All monorails and most rides, shows, rest rooms, and restaurants can accommodate wheelchairs. One major exception is the Contemporary Resort monorail station, where passengers must enter or exit via escalators.

A special information booklet for disabled guests is available at wheelchair rental locations throughout Walt Disney World. Maps of the respective theme parks issued to each guest on admission are symbol-coded to inform nonambulatory guests which attractions accommodate wheelchairs. Peter Smith, a paraplegic, has authored an excellent book titled *Handicapped in Walt Disney World*. The three-hundred-page, indexed, $10.95 guide covers both trip planning and on-site touring. The book is sold at Walt Disney World, but can be ordered in advance by calling the publisher at (800) 669-5657.

Nonambulatory guests are welcome to ride almost all of the attractions at Walt Disney World. As mentioned above, many attractions are engineered to allow a guest to board the attraction in a wheelchair. For attractions that do not accommodate wheelchairs, nonambulatory guests may still ride if they can transfer from the wheelchair to the vehicle of the ride in question. Disney attraction staff, however, are not trained or permitted to assist nonambulatory guests in transferring from their wheelchair to the ride. Guests must be able to get on the ride alone or, alternatively, have a member of their own party assist them. In either case, members of the nonambulatory guest's party will be permitted to go along on the ride.

Because the queuing areas of most rides and shows will not accommodate wheelchairs, nonambulatory guests and their party should request special boarding instructions from a Disney attendant as soon as they arrive at an attraction. Almost always, the whole group will receive priority treatment and can board without a lengthy wait.

Telephones accessible to guests in wheelchairs are located throughout all three major theme parks.

Visitors with Dietary Restrictions. Visitors on special or restricted diets, including those requiring kosher meals, can make arrangements for assistance at the theme parks by going to City Hall in the Magic Kingdom, Guest Relations at EPCOT Center, or the Guest Services Building at the Disney-MGM Studios. For Walt Disney World restaurants located outside the theme parks, call the restaurant one day in advance for assistance.

Sight- and/or Hearing-Impaired Guests. The Magic Kingdom, EPCOT Center, and the Disney-MGM Studios each provide complimentary tape cassettes and portable tape players to assist sight-impaired guests. They are available at City Hall in the Magic Kingdom, Guest Relations at EPCOT Center, and the Guest Services Building at the Disney-MGM Studios. A deposit is required. At the same locations, a Telecommunication Device for the Deaf (TDD) is available for hearing-impaired guests.

In addition to TDDs, many of the pay phones in the major theme parks are equipped with amplified headsets. See your Disney map handout for phone locations.

Visitors from Other Countries

Visitors from outside the United States are warmly welcomed at Walt Disney World and represent a large percentage of its guests on any given day. Most Magic Kingdom attractions are straightforward and easily understood by visitors with limited English. Many attractions at EPCOT Center and the Disney-MGM Studios, however, depend heavily on narration. A Scandinavian visitor wrote suggesting that:

> You should write something about how interesting the attractions are to people who don't have English as their mother tongue. We are Norwegians, we all know English fairly well, but we still had problems understanding signficant parts of some attractions because the Disney people talk too fast. That goes especially for Body Wars, which we all thought was boring, but also for the Jungle Cruise, and the Backstage Tour.

Foreign language assistance is available throughout Walt Disney World. Inquire by calling (407) 824-4321; or by stopping at City Hall in the Magic Kingdom, Guest Relations at EPCOT Center, or at Hollywood Boulevard Guest Services at the Disney-MGM Studios.

It does not take most foreign guests long to notice the unabashedly patriotic atmosphere of the parks. There are flag-raising ceremonies, attractions that chronicle U.S. history, and whole themed areas, such as Frontierland and Liberty Square in the Magic Kingdom, that are inspired by events in America's past. While most of the patriotic fanfare is festive and enjoyable to anyone, two attractions, The Hall of Presidents in the Magic Kingdom, and *The American Adventure* at EPCOT Center, seem a bit of an overdose for many foreign visitors.

Along more practical lines, the currency of most countries can be exchanged for dollars before you enter the theme parks, at the Guest Services window of the Ticket and Transportation Center, the Guest Services window in the ticketing area of the Disney-MGM Studios, and at the Guest Services window to the right of the entrance turnstiles at EPCOT Center.

PART SIX: Arriving and Getting Around

Getting There

—— Directions

If you arrive by automobile you can reach any Walt Disney World attraction or destination via World Drive, off US 192, or via EPCOT Center Drive, off I-4 (see map, pages 214–15).

From I-10:   Take I-10 east across Florida to I-75 southbound. Exit I-75 onto the Florida Turnpike. Exit at Clermont and take US 27 south. Turn left onto US 192, and then follow the signs to Walt Disney World.

From I-75 southbound: Follow I-75 south to the Florida Turnpike. Exit at Clermont and take US 27 south. Turn left onto US 192, and then follow the signs to Walt Disney World.

From I-95 southbound: Follow I-95 south to I-4. Go west on I-4, passing through Orlando. Exit at EPCOT Center Drive and follow the signs.

From Daytona or Orlando: Go west on I-4 through Orlando. Exit at EPCOT Center Drive and follow the signs.

From the Orlando International Airport: Leaving the airport, take FL 528 (toll) west for approximately 12 miles to the intersection with I-4. Go west on I-4, exiting at EPCOT Center Drive.

From Miami, Fort Lauderdale, and southeastern Florida: Head north on the Florida Turnpike to I-4 westbound. Exit I-4 at EPCOT Center Drive.

From Tampa and southwestern Florida: Take I-75 northbound to I-4. Go east on I-4, exit on US 192 northbound, and then follow the signs.

Walt Disney World Village has its own entrance separate and distinct from entrances to the theme parks. To reach Walt Disney World Village take the FL 535 exit off I-4 and proceed north, following the signs.

—— *Getting to Walt Disney World from the Airport*

If you are flying, buy a package that includes transportation from the airport to your hotel if you do not intend to rent a car. If not on a package, try to find a hotel that offers shuttle service to the airport. Failing this, try to share transportation to the Disney World area. If you get stuck with a hired shuttle (where you ride with other Disney World bound passengers), expect to pay $22–35 per person round-trip. Mears Motor Transportation Service (407) 423-5566 charges $23 per adult round trip. Cabs run about $32–42 *one way*. One option, if there are at least two in your party, is to rent a compact car at a weekly rate (even if you will not need the car for an entire week). For only a few dollars more than the shuttle fee or the cab fare, you will take care of your airport transportation needs and have a car at your disposal to boot. Be advised, however, that many rental car companies require that you keep the car for a minimum of five 24-hour periods to get the weekly rate.

—— *Renting a Car*

Readers who plan to stay in Walt Disney World frequently ask if they will need a car. If your vacation plans do not include restaurants, attractions, or other destinations outside of Walt Disney World, the answer is a very qualified no. You will not need a car, but, after considering the thoughts of this Snohomish, Washington, reader, you might want one:

> We rented a car and were glad we did. It gave us more options, though we used the [Disney] bus transportation quite extensively. With a car we could drive to the grocery store to re-stock our snack supply. It also came in handy for our night out. I shudder at how long it might have taken us to get from the Caribbean Beach to the Polynesian to leave our kids [at the child care facility], then to Pleasure Island, then back to the Polynesian [to get the kids], and then back to the Caribbean Beach. At eight dollars an hour [for child care] you don't want to waste time! It was also nice to drive to Typhoon Lagoon with a car full of clothes, lunches, and other paraphernalia. It was also easier to drive to the other hotels for special meals. And, of course, if you plan to travel out of the World during your stay, a car is a must. I think you need to stress this more in your book.

Along similar lines, a dad from Avon Lake, Ohio, had this to say:

It was unbelievable how often we used our rental car. Although we stayed at the Grand Floridian, we found the monorail convenient only for the Magic Kingdom. Of the six nights we stayed, we used our car 5 days.

And from an Erie, Pennsylvania, family:

Bus travel at night was ridiculous — 1 hour and 15 minutes to get from Port Orleans to the Polynesian for the Luau by way of Pleasure Island. There must be a better way; we will rent a car next time.

If you rent a car, be forewarned that a 6% sales tax, an 8% airport tax, and $2.05 state surcharge will be heaped onto your rental fee. Finally, remember that you do not have to rent a car at the airport. If you want, you can wait until the day you actually need a car, and rent one at your hotel.

Getting Oriented

—— A Good Map Is Hard to Find

We frequently hear from readers complaining about the signs and maps provided by the Disney people. While it is not difficult to find the major theme parks, it can be quite an odyssey to strike out in search of other Walt Disney World destinations. Many maps supplied by the Disney organization are stylistically rendered and just plain hard to read, while others provide less than complete information. To make matters worse, the maps (all produced by various Disney divisions) do not always agree with each other.

A good map, modeled on the one originally produced by Disney Seminar Productions, can be obtained by calling (407) 824-4321. Ask for the Official Walt Disney World Resort Map that contains maps of the overall resort as well as the three major theme parks. This map is also referred to as the Walt Disney World Property Map. If you forget to get a map before you leave home, you can obtain one after you arrive from guest services at any of the theme parks or Disney hotels.

—— Finding Your Way Around

Going to Walt Disney World is like going to any big city. It's easy to get lost. The signs for the theme parks are excellent, but when it comes to finding a restaurant or hotel, even Disney World veterans get confused. The easiest way to orient yourself is to think in terms of five major areas, or clusters:

1. The first major cluster takes in all the hotels and theme parks around the Seven Seas Lagoon. This includes the Magic Kingdom, the hotels connected by the monorail, the Shades of Green resort, and three golf courses.

2. The second major cluster includes the developments on and around Bay Lake, specifically: Disney's Wilderness Lodge Resort, Fort Wilderness Campground, Discovery Island, River Country, and two golf courses.

3. EPCOT Center, the Disney-MGM Studios, the so-called EPCOT Center resort hotels, along with the Caribbean Beach resort, make up cluster number three.

4. The fourth cluster encompasses the Walt Disney World Village, the Disney Institute, the Disney Village Marketplace, Pleasure Island, Typhoon Lagoon, another golf course, the Disney World Village Hotels, and the Port Orleans, Dixie Landings, and Vacation Club resorts.

5. The fifth and newest cluster contains the Disney All-Star Resorts and Blizzard Beach.

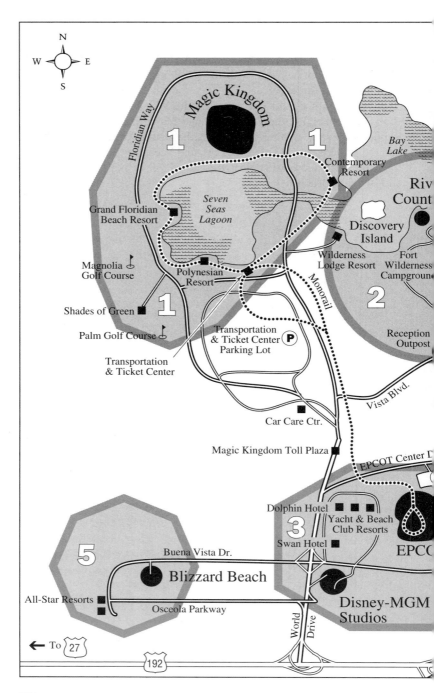

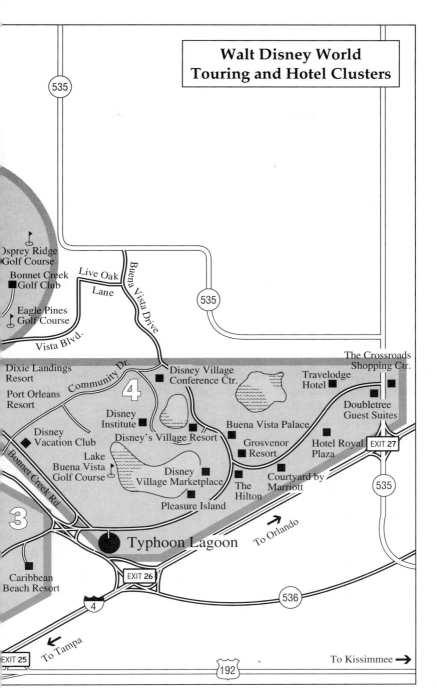

Walt Disney World
Touring and Hotel Clusters

535

535

Osprey Ridge
Golf Course

Bonnet Creek
Golf Club

Live Oak
Lane

Buena Vista Drive

Eagle Pines
Golf Course

Vista Blvd.

535

The Crossroads
Shopping Ctr.

Dixie Landings
Resort

Community Dr.

4

Disney Village
Conference Ctr.

Travelodge
Hotel

Port Orleans
Resort

Doubletree
Guest Suites

Disney
Institute

Buena Vista Palace

Disney's Village Resort

Hotel Royal
Plaza

EXIT 27

Disney
Vacation Club

Grosvenor
Resort

Lake
Buena Vista
Golf Course

Disney
Village Marketplace

Courtyard by
Marriott

535

Bonnet Creek Rd.

The
Hilton

Pleasure Island

3

Typhoon Lagoon

To Orlando

Caribbean
Beach Resort

EXIT 26

4

536

EXIT 25

To Tampa

To Kissimmee →

192

How to Travel Around the World
(or the Real Mr. Toad's Wild Ride)

Once, when asking directions to the town of Louisa in the eastern Kentucky mountains, I was told in so many words, "You can't get there from here." Sometimes trying to commute around Walt Disney World gives rise to a similar frustration. "What you can do is this," a Magic Kingdom street vendor proposed: "You can take the ferry or the monorail to the Transportation and Ticket Center. Then you can get another monorail, or you can catch the bus, or you can take a tram out to your car and drive over there yourself." What the vendor did not say was that any conceivable combination from this transportation smorgasbord would take longer than riding over to EPCOT Center on a mule. This must be what Toffler meant by "future shock."

Now having alerted you that there is no simple way to travel around Walt Disney World, we will endeavor to help you choose the *least* complicated way. Just don't wait until ten minutes before your seating at Alfredo's to get moving.

—— Transportation Trade-Offs for Guests Lodging Outside Walt Disney World

Walt Disney World day guests (those not staying in Walt Disney World) can use the monorail system, most of the bus system, and some of the boat system. If you go to the Disney-MGM Studios in the morning and decide to go over to EPCOT Center for lunch, for instance, you can take a bus directly there. The most important advice we can give to day guests is to make sure you end up with your car parked in the lot of the theme park (or other Walt Disney World destination) where you plan to finish your day. This is particularly critical if you stay at one of the parks until closing time.

Driving Your Car to the Magic Kingdom

Most Magic Kingdom day guests park in the Transportation and Ticket Center parking lot. As you will see when you arrive, the Magic Kingdom/Transportation and Ticket Center parking lot is about the size of Vermont. The various sections of the parking lot are named for Disney characters. When you pay your parking fee, you will be given a receipt with the aisle numbers and names of the parking sections listed on the reverse side. Mark where you have parked and jot down the aisle number in the space provided. Put the receipt in your billfold or some other safe place for referral when you return to your car. (Failure to take these precautions often results in a lengthy search for your car at a time when you are pretty tuckered out.) If you have a disabled person in your party, you will be directed to a special closed-in parking area.

After being directed to a parking space and marking its location on your receipt, you walk a short distance to a loading station where you can catch a tram to the Transportation and Ticket Center (TTC). Here you can buy passes to both the Magic Kingdom and EPCOT Center. If you wish to proceed to the Magic Kingdom you can either ride the ferryboat across Seven Seas Lagoon or catch the monorail. If the line for the monorail extends down the ramp from the loading platform, go with the ferry. Remember, one ferry holds almost as many passengers as three monorail trains. The trip takes the monorail about three-and-a-half to five minutes. Crossing time on the ferry is six-and-a-half minutes.

Going to EPCOT Center from the Magic Kingdom. If you are trying to get to EPCOT Center from the Magic Kingdom in the morning, take the monorail to the TTC and transfer to the EPCOT Center monorail. If you are commuting in the afternoon, take the ferry to the TTC. If you plan to spend the remainder of the day at EPCOT Center and your car is in the TTC lot, go ahead and drive your car over. But if you plan to return to the Magic Kingdom or you do not have a car at the TTC, catch the EPCOT Center monorail. Whenever you exit the Magic Kingdom and intend either to return or visit another park on the same day, you must have your hand stamped for reentry.

Going to the Disney-MGM Studios from the Magic Kingdom. To commute to the Disney-MGM Studios from the Magic Kingdom you can either take a Disney bus or drive. If you plan to conclude your day at the Studios, it is more convenient to drive. On the other hand, if you intend to return to the Magic Kingdom, take the bus. Incidentally, the loading area for the bus to the Studios is to your immediate left as you exit the Magic Kingdom. You do not, in other words, have to go all the way back to the TTC. Whenever you exit the Magic Kingdom and intend either to return or visit another park on the same day, you must have your hand stamped for reentry.

Leaving the Magic Kingdom at the End of the Day. If you close out the day at the Magic Kingdom and need to get back to the TTC, try the ferry first. If the ferry is mobbed (which usually happens only at closing), take either the "express" or "local" (also stops at hotels) monorail back to the TTC.

Sometimes when you reach the TTC, you will find a throng of people at the boarding area for the parking lot trams. Rather than wait with the crowd, walk to the closest section of the parking lot (Chip 'n Dale) and wait for a tram to come along. When the tram stops and a few people get off, hop on and ride to wherever your car is parked.

Driving Your Car to EPCOT Center

If you wish to visit EPCOT Center, you can park at the Magic Kingdom (Transportation and Ticket Center) parking lot and commute via monorail or park directly in the EPCOT Center parking lot. Parking at the EPCOT Center lot is your best bet unless you plan to visit the Magic Kingdom later and conclude your day there. Arrangements in the EPCOT Center lot are essentially the same as described for the Magic Kingdom; a tram will shuttle you from where you park to the EPCOT Center entrance, and you will be given a receipt on which you can mark your parking place for later reference. At EPCOT Center, the sections of the parking lot are named for pavilions in the Future World area of the park. There is close-in parking for disabled guests as at the TTC lot. The big difference between Magic Kingdom parking and EPCOT Center parking is that access to the park is direct from the tram at EPCOT Center, whereas to reach the Magic Kingdom you must transfer from the tram to the ferryboat or the monorail at the Transportation and Ticket Center.

Going to the Magic Kingdom from EPCOT Center. To go from EPCOT Center to the Magic Kingdom, take the monorail to the TTC and then transfer to the Magic Kingdom express monorail. If you do not plan to return to EPCOT Center and you have a car in the EPCOT Center lot, drive to the TTC and then take the ferry or monorail as crowd conditions allow. Whenever you exit EPCOT Center and intend either to return or to visit another park on the same day, you must have your hand stamped for reentry.

Going to the Disney-MGM Studios from EPCOT Center. If you are at EPCOT Center and want to go to the Studios, you have three choices. If you plan to finish the day at the Studios, drive your car. If you plan to return to EPCOT Center, you can either exit the park through the main entrance and catch a bus to the Studios, or you can exit through the International Gateway (in the World Showcase section of the park) and catch a boat from the dock of the nearby Beach Club resort. This last option is definitely best if you are returning to EPCOT Center for dinner at one of the World Showcase ethnic restaurants. Whenever you exit EPCOT Center and intend either to return or to visit another park on the same day, you must have your hand stamped for reentry.

Driving Your Car to the Disney-MGM Studios

The Disney-MGM Studios has its own pay lot, though the Disney planners seriously underestimated the number of cars the Disney-MGM parking lot would have to accommodate. During the summer of 1991, it was almost routine for the lot to fill by 10:30 or 11 A.M. Monday through Thursday, with thousands of late arriving guests being turned away. In 1992, however, the parking facility was greatly enlarged and it is more rare nowadays for the lot to fill to capacity. As at the other lots, trams transport you to the park entrance, and there is close-in parking for the disabled.

Going to the Magic Kingdom from the Disney-MGM Studios. Regardless of where you intend to conclude the day, it is probably easier to take the bus to the Magic Kingdom. Because the bus unloads at the entrance to the theme park as opposed to at the TTC, you by-pass all the hassle of reparking, taking the tram to the TTC, and then catching the monorail or ferry. With the bus, you get off and you are right there. It's the same story when you return to the Studios. Whenever you exit the Disney-MGM Studios and intend either to return or to visit another park on the same day, you must have your hand stamped for reentry.

Going to EPCOT Center from the Disney-MGM Studios. Drive your car to the EPCOT Center parking lot if you do not intend to return to the Studios. If you plan on coming back to the Studios, you can either take a bus or a boat to EPCOT Center. Take the bus if you want to initiate your EPCOT visit from the main entrance (Future World). If you are heading for the World Showcase, take the boat. Whenever you exit the Disney-MGM Studios and intend either to return or to visit another park on the same day, you must have your hand stamped for reentry.

Moving Your Car from Lot to Lot on the Same Day

Once you have paid to park in any of the major theme park lots, hang on to your receipt. If you decide to visit another theme park later in the same day, you will be admitted to that park's parking complex without additional charge upon showing your receipt. Walt Disney World lodging guests are not charged to park in any of the theme park lots.

Taking a Shuttle Bus from Your Out-of-the-World Hotel

Trams and shuttle buses are provided by many independent hotels and motels in the vicinity of Walt Disney World. They represent a fairly carefree alternative for getting to and from the theme parks, letting you off right at the entrance and saving you the cost of parking. The rub is that they might not get you there as early as you desire (a critical point if you take our touring advice) or be available at the time you wish to return to your lodging. Also, some shuttles go directly to Walt Disney World while others make stops at other motels and hotels in the vicinity. Each shuttle service is a little bit different so check out the particulars when you arrive at your hotel.

Be forewarned that most hotel shuttle services do not add additional vehicles at park opening or closing times. In the mornings, your biggest problem is you might not get a seat. However, at closing time or following a hard rain, you can expect a mass exodus from the park. The worst case scenario is that more people will be waiting for the shuttle to your hotel than the bus will hold and that some will be left behind. While most (but not all) hotel shuttles return for stranded guests, you may suffer a wait of 20 minutes to an hour or more. Our suggestion, if you are depending on hotel shuttles, is to leave the park at least 45 minutes before closing. If you stay in the park until closing and lack the energy to hassle with the shuttle, catch a bus or monorail to the nearest Disney hotel and take a cab from there.

If there is a hard rain during the day and you want to return to your hotel, we suggest taking a Disney bus or the monorail to the nearest resort hotel and catching a cab from there.

—— *Transportation Trade-Offs for Guests Lodging at Walt Disney World Resorts and Campground*

The most hotly debated topic among Disney resort guests is whether it is more efficient to use your own car or the Disney transportation system to get around Walt Disney World. The comments in the following letters are pretty representative:

From a single mom from Beaver Dam, Wisconsin:

> It was definitely worth staying in the park. In fact, if I had to do it over, we would not have left Dixie Landings for the entire nine nights of our Orlando stay. You do really feel a part of WDW, and the travel by bus, monorail, train, and boat is so convenient and fun. We had some wacky bus drivers and had the chance to meet and talk with other travellers on the buses.

From a New Orleans man:

> We found a car to be an absolute necessity. It added at least 2 hours each day to our schedule. The monorail system was a bit confusing and slow, not to mention very crowded. The bus stops were not particularly convenient to our room and there were always people waiting. On the other hand, with a car, parking was very easy, traffic was minimal, and once we had our basic orientation, it was easy to get around Disney World.

From a Germantown, Wisconsin, woman:

> The buses are great! So nice not to think about parking, hot car, where are the keys? Bus from All-Star [Resorts] to the Magic Kingdom took 11 minutes. Who can complain?

From a Madison, New Jersey, family:

> The second day we had a problem. We had taken the monorail from the Magic Kingdom to the Contemporary Hotel to eat dinner at the cafe, and after dinner we were unsure how to get back to

the All-Star Resorts. This was about 7 P.M. We asked two different hotel employees and were told to take the bus to the Disney Marketplace and then get another bus to the hotel. After we got on the bus and were on our way, it became obvious this could not have been the best way. It took 40 minutes to get to the Marketplace, then a 20-minute wait for the bus and another 40 minutes back to the All-Star Resorts. The whole time my husband and I held sleeping children in our arms.

From a father of two from Hillsboro, Oregon:

We originally thought that being in a monorail hotel would be convenient. It turned out that it still takes nearly an hour to go to places other than the Magic Kingdom or the TTC [Transportation & Ticket Center]. After one day of waiting for the Disney Transportation System, we decided to rent a car. The importance of having your own car in order to reduce the travel times cannot be said enough.

Finally, from a Minneapolis family:

Our group consisting of three adults and one seven-year-old child discovered that the [Wilderness Lodge] hotel also includes a new "ride" which we came to call the "Twilight Zone Bus Tour of Terror." The hotel is situated very near the transportation center, not far from the Contemporary Hotel. In fact, the "lodge" is within easy walking distance of the Transportation [and Ticket] Center. However the Disney folks insist that you ride their bus, which turns what could be a pleasant five-minute walk through the pines into a lurching, irritating 20–30 minute bus ride of uncertain destination. Of the two buses serving the hotel, one actually stops at a stop sign within fifty feet of the hotel's bus stop and proceeds then to turn right for a "milk-run" tour through Fort Wilderness. Disney clearly does not trust its visitors to cross the street. I suppose it is a legal thing or something, but after a week what started as a minor irritation became a major pain. In addition, to make things worse, in the middle of our vacation, Disney revamped the bus operation and began a practice of running the two routes in reverse based on the time of day. One way in the morning, the other in the afternoon.

Our real trial came, however, when we took a driver's advice on how to travel from the Disney Village Marketplace back to the "lodge." Here was born the name "Twilight Zone Bus Tour of Terror." We were treated to a two-bus, hour-and-fifteen-minute-long ride through the farthest-flung reaches of the Disney property, including some industrial areas that are not shown on any map available to the public. Consider this: an innocent family of four from Minnesota, lost forever, traveling endlessly in a frigidly air-conditioned bus, circling aimlessly through the unrecognizable reaches of Walt Disney World, no landmarks in sight, their "length of stay" passes trickling away, trapped in the "Twilight Zone Bus Tour of Terror." It made my blood curdle more than the [Tower of Terror] elevator drop.

While the Walt Disney World transportation system is large, diversified, and generally efficient, it is sometimes overwhelmed during peak traffic periods, most particularly at park opening and closing times. If you could be assured of getting on a bus or a launch or a monorail at these critical times, we would simply advise you to leave your car at home. The reality, however, is that when everyone wants to go somewhere at the same time, delays are unavoidable. In addition, while some destinations are served directly, many others require one or more transfers. Finally, it is rather difficult to figure out how the bus, boat, and monorail systems interconnect.

If a resort hotel offers boat or monorail service, its bus service will be limited. What this means, essentially, is you will have to transfer at the Transportation and Ticket Center (TTC) for many Walt Disney World destinations. If you are staying at one of the Magic Kingdom resort hotels serviced by monorail (Polynesian, Contemporary, Grand Floridian), you will be able to commute efficiently to the Magic Kingdom on the monorail. If, however, you want to visit EPCOT Center, you must take the monorail to the TTC and there transfer to the EPCOT loop monorail for EPCOT Center. (Guests at the Polynesian Resort can eliminate the need to transfer by walking [about 5 to 10 minutes] to the TTC and from there catching the direct monorail to EPCOT Center.)

If you are staying at one of the EPCOT resort hotels (Swan, Dolphin, Yacht and Beach Clubs) you can walk or commute via tram to the International Gateway (back door) entrance of EPCOT Center. Although bus service is available directly from the EPCOT resorts to the Magic Kingdom, there is no direct bus service to the main entrance of EPCOT Center or to the Disney-MGM Studios. To get to the Studios from the EPCOT resorts you must take a rather slow boat. Except in the case of commuting to the Magic Kingdom and EPCOT Center, you save time by driving your own car.

The Caribbean Beach, Dixie Landings, and Port Orleans resorts; the Disney Vacation Club; Disney's All-Star Resorts; and Disney's Village Resort offer the most efficient transportation with direct buses to all three theme parks. The rub here is that guests must sometimes walk a long way to the bus stops or sit through more than a half-dozen pick-up stops before actually getting under way to the park(s). Commuting to the parks in the mornings from these resorts is generally no sweat (though you may have to ride standing up). Returning in the evening, however, can be a different story.

As you may have gathered from our reader's experience on the "Twilight Zone Bus Tour of Terror," quoted above, the Wilderness Lodge resort has the most inefficient transportation service of any of the Disney lodging properties. The Wilderness Lodge is connected to the Magic Kingdom by boat and to all other Disney World destinations by bus. Bus routes are inexplicably long and convoluted with confusing schedules and transfers required to many places. Why the Wilderness Lodge alone is singled out for such fouled-up transportation service we don't know, but if Disney receives as many letters of complaint as we do, maybe someone will look into it. In the meantime, if you stay at the Wilderness Lodge, rent a car.

It should be noted that many of the Disney Village Hotels terminated their guest transportation contract with Disney Transportation Operations and initiated service with another carrier. The substitute service, which in our opinion does not measure up, constitutes a real problem for guests at these hotels. At the time of this revision, there were rumblings to the effect that other independently owned hotels in the Disney Village Hotels were considering scrapping the Disney bus service. Before booking a hotel in the Village, we suggest you check to determine the nature and frequency of the shuttle service.

Fort Wilderness guests must use the internal Fort Wilderness bus system to reach the boat landings or the Pioneer Hall bus stop. From these departure points, respectively, guests can travel directly by boat to the Magic Kingdom or by bus to the Disney-MGM Studios, or to other destinations via transfer at the TTC. With the exception of commuting to the Magic Kingdom, the best way for Fort Wilderness guests to get around Walt Disney World is to drive.

—— Using the Walt Disney World Transportation System vs. Driving Your Own Car

To allow you to assess your transportation options, we have developed a chart that compares the approximate commuting times from Disney resort hotels to various Walt Disney World destinations, by way of the Disney transportation system or in your own car.

Disney Transportation. The times listed on the chart in the Disney Transportation System (DTS) columns represent a range. For example, if you want to go from the Caribbean Resort to EPCOT Center, the chart indicates a range of 12 to 45 minutes. The first number, 12 minutes, is how long your commute will take if everything goes perfectly. In other words, your bus is at the bus stop when you walk up, departs for your destination as soon as you board, and no traffic jams or other delays are encountered en route. If you are staying at a resort where the bus makes numerous stops within the resort complex, the first number assumes that you board at the last embarkation point before the bus strikes out for the final destination.

The second number, 45 minutes, represents a sort of worst-case scenario. Here you arrive at the bus stop just as your bus is pulling away without you, and you must wait 20 minutes for the next bus. When you finally get on, the bus makes six more stops at the Caribbean Resort before getting underway to EPCOT Center. Once you are on your way you manage to hit every traffic light.

On busier days, buses run every 20 minutes all day. On less busy days, however, some buses run only once every 45 minutes between noon and 6 P.M. Our worst-case scenario assumes that buses run every 20 minutes. If buses are running every 45 minutes during your visit, you must add an additional 25 minutes to the second number to calculate the worst-case commuting scenario. If buses run from the Caribbean Resort to EPCOT every 45 minutes, for example, it is possible that it could take you as long as an hour and ten minutes (45 minutes + 25 minutes) to complete the commute. Be sure to ask guest information at your hotel about frequency of service during your stay.

If your bus makes intermediate stops *after leaving your resort complex*, the time spent making those stops is figured into both the best time and the worst time (because the stops are unavoidable either way). Finally, an asterisk indicates whether it is necessary to transfer to reach your destination.

Door-to-Door Commuting Times to and from the Disney Resorts and Parks: In Your Car versus the Disney Transportation System[†]

Time (in minutes) from	To Magic Kingdom		To EPCOT Center		To MGM Studios	
	Your Car	Disney System	Your Car	Disney System	Your Car	Disney System
Caribbean Beach	26–47	13–40	13–23	12–45	10–19	6–33
Village Resorts	27–48	15–45	13–23	10–37	15–24	8–35
Swan	24–45	21–41	10–20	10–15**	10–19	12–32
Dolphin	24–45	18–38	10–20	10–15**	10–19	12–32
Beach Club	25–46	14–34	11–21	5–8**	9–18	16–36
Yacht Club	25–46	11–31	11–21	5–8**	9–18	16–36
Vacation Club	25–46	12–40	13–23	7–35	13–22	9–36
Port Orleans	26–47	19–39	14–24	15–35	14–23	17–37
Dixie Landings	27–48	11–36	15–25	9–33	15–24	9–34
Fort Wilderness	26–47	13–33	13–23	14–60*	14–23	17–50*
Grand Floridian	NA	4–7	13–23	20–42*	15–24	9–29
Polynesian	NA	7–13	12–22	23–48*	14–23	12–32
Contemporary	NA	12–23	16–26	13–29*	18–27	22–42
All-Star Resorts	26–47	11–31	13–23	8–28	11–20	7–27
Wilderness Lodge	NA	11–41	15–25	18–47	17–26	21–51
Hotel Village Plaza	30–51	20–74*	16–26	12–50	15–24	9–49
Magic Kingdom			12–39	13–42*	13–29	14–34*
EPCOT	25–46	16–35			14–23	21–44*
MGM Studios	25–46	14–34	14–24	26–59*		
Typhoon Lagoon	26–47	18–51*	13–23	29–62*	10–19	38–75*
Pleasure Island/ Marketplace	27–49	24–58*	14–25	21–57*	12–22	30–69*
Blizzard Beach	25–46	17–37*	13–23	29–62*	13–22	30–50*

[†] Driving time vs. time on the Disney Transportation System (DTS). Driving times include time in your car, stops for toll payment, parking time, and transfers to Disney trams and monorails where applicable.

* This ride requires a transfer.

**This hotel is within walking distance of EPCOT Center; time given is for tram ride from International Gateway, if necessary.

To Typhoon Lagoon		To Pleasure Island/ Marketplace		To Blizzard Beach	
Your Car	Disney System	Your Car	Disney System	Your Car	Disney System
4–7	7–39	5–8	9–43	10–13	10–41
7–10	13–37	4–7	5–30	14–17	13–40
8–11	30–50	9–12	20–42	9–12	10–32
8–11	27–47	9–12	18–40	9–12	8–31
7–10	22–42	8–11	13–35	10–13	21–41
7–10	24–44	8–11	15–37	10–13	21–41
6–9	9–35	7–10	9–36	12–15	18–40
7–10	16–36	8–11	24–44	12–15	20–40
8–11	9–35	9–12	15–40	13–16	15–40
8–11	18–51*	9–12	27–60*	17–20	20–53
13–16	24–53*	14–17	37–64*	11–14	13–33
12–15	27–59*	13–16	40–70*	10–13	15–35
15–18	17–40*	15–17	28–51*	13–16	25–45
10–13	9–29	11–14	15–40	4–7	10–28
15–18	23–46*	16–19	27–67*	13–16	21–48
7–10	5–7	4–7	NA	14–17	NA
15–31	17–53*	17–36	30–64*	10–13	22–55*
10–13	22–43*	11–14	30–54*	9–12	23–45*
6–9	30–73*	7–10	41–74*	9–12	30–50*
		4–7	5–28	11–14	40–57*
4–7	5–28			12–16	30–50*
11–14	33–76*	12–15	44–77*		

Driving Your Own Car. This column ("by Car") on the chart indicates the best-case/worst-case situation for driving yourself. To make these times directly comparable to the Disney Transportion times, we have added the time spent getting from your parked car to the entrance of the theme park. While Disney buses and monorails drop guests off right at the front door, those who drive must sometimes take a tram from their car to the gate, or walk. In the case of the Magic Kingdom, you must take a tram from the parking lot to the TTC, and from there catch a monorail or ferry to the entrance of the park. As an aside, Walt Disney World resort guests do not have to pay to park in any of the theme park pay lots.

—— *Walt Disney World Transportation System for Teenagers*

If you are staying at Walt Disney World and there are teens in your party, familiarize yourself with the Walt Disney World bus system. Safe, clean, and operating until I A.M. on most nights, the buses are a great way for the young folks to get around the World. Buses from all over Walt Disney World stop at the TTC, from whence passengers can transfer to such destinations as Fort Wilderness/River Country, Disney-MGM Studios, Typhoon Lagoon, Blizzard Beach, Pleasure Island, Walt Disney World Village, EPCOT Center, and the golf courses.

—— *Walt Disney World Bus Service*

The Walt Disney World bus system has simplified its service, abandoning the color-coded pennants that formerly indicated the destination or route of the bus. As of 1994, each bus has an illuminated panel above the front windshield that flashes the bus's destination. Additionally, at the theme parks there are specially designated waiting areas for each Disney World destination. To catch the bus to the Caribbean Beach Resort from the Disney-MGM Studios, for example, simply go to the bus stop and wait in the area marked "To the Caribbean Beach Resort." At the resorts, simply go to any bus stop and wait for the bus with your destination displayed on the illuminated panel. Directions to various Disney World destinations are available for the asking when you check in, or can be obtained in your hotel at the guest services desk. The person at guest services can also answer any questions you may have about the Walt Disney World transportation system.

Service from the resorts to the major theme parks is fairly direct. You may have to sit through a number of intermediate stops en route, but you will not have to transfer. Service to the swimming theme parks, the Disney Village Marketplace, Pleasure Island, and other Walt Disney World hotels is more problematic, with transfers sometimes necessary. A Palo Alto, California, dad described his problems trying to get back to the Disney Inn (now Shades of Green) after dinner at the Beach Club:

> It took 1½ hours to get back to the Disney Inn by bus, a 10-minute drive by car. Crowds? Breakdowns? Hurricanes? Nope, just waits, connections and extra stops.

Buses initiate service to the theme parks at about 7 A.M. on days when the park's official opening time is 9 A.M. In general, the buses run once every 20 minutes. Buses to Disney-MGM or EPCOT deliver you to the entrance of the park. Buses to the Magic Kingdom, however, deliver you to the Transportation and Ticket Center (TTC) until one hour before the park opens, prior to 8 A.M. in this example. At the TTC you must transfer to the monorail or the ferry to complete your trip to the Magic Kingdom. Buses will take you directly to the Magic Kingdom upon the initiation of service on early-entry days, and starting one hour before the park's stated opening time on other days.

To be on hand for the *real* opening time (when the official opening time is 9 A.M.), catch direct buses to EPCOT Center and the Disney-MGM Studios between 7:30 and 8 A.M. Catch direct buses to the Magic Kingdom between 8 and 8:15 A.M. If you must transfer to reach the park of your choice, leave 15 to 20 minutes earlier. On days when the official opening time is 8 A.M., move up your departure time accordingly.

If you are commuting to a theme park on an early-entry morning, you can count on the park opening an hour to an hour and a half before the official opening time for the general public. Buses to whichever park is operating early-entry begin running about two hours before the stated opening time. Believe it or not, on an early-entry day when the Magic Kingdom's official opening time for the general public is 8 A.M., Disney lodging guests can catch a bus to the park as early as 6 A.M., and can enter the park by 6:30 A.M.

For your return bus trip in the evening, try to get out of the park 40 minutes to an hour before closing to avoid the rush. If you get caught in the mass exodus at closing, don't worry. You may be inconvenienced, but you will not be stranded. Buses, boats, and monorails continue to operate for two hours after the parks close.

—— *Walt Disney World Monorail Service*

When considering the much-vaunted monorail, picture three loops. Loop A is an express route that runs counterclockwise connecting the Magic Kingdom with the Transportation and Ticket Center (TTC). A second loop, B, runs clockwise alongside Loop A. Loop B makes all stops, with service to (in this order) the TTC, Polynesian Resort, Grand Floridian Beach Resort, Magic Kingdom, and Contemporary Resort (then around again). A third long loop, C, dips like a tail to the southeast connecting the TTC with EPCOT Center. The hub for all three loops is the TTC (where you usually park when visiting the Magic Kingdom).

The monorail system serving the Magic Kingdom resort hotels usually cranks up two hours before the official opening time on early entry days, and an hour and a half before official opening time on other days. If you are staying at a Magic Kingdom resort hotel and wish to be among the first in the Magic Kingdom on a non–early entry morning when the official opening time is 9 A.M., board the monorail at the times indicated below. On an early entry morning (when the official opening time is 9 A.M.), get moving 45–60 minutes earlier. If the official opening time is 8 A.M., bounce everything up yet another hour.

What's that? You don't possess the circadian rhythms of a farmer or a morning paper boy? Get with the program, Bubba, this is a *Disney* vacation. Haul your lazy behind out of bed and go have some fun!

From the Contemporary Resort	7:45–8 A.M.
From the Polynesian Resort	7:50–8:05 A.M.
From the Grand Floridian	8:00–8:10 A.M.

If you are a day guest (no early-entry privileges), you will be allowed on the monorail at the TTC between 8:15 and 8:30 A.M. on a day when the official opening time is 9 A.M. If you want to board earlier, take the walkway from the TTC to the Polynesian Resort and board there.

The monorail loop connecting EPCOT Center with the TTC opens at 7:30 A.M. on days when EPCOT Center's official opening time is 9 A.M. To be at EPCOT Center when the park opens, catch the EPCOT monorail (at the TTC) no later than 8:05 A.M.

While your multi-day pass suggests that you can flit from park to park at will, actually getting there is somewhat more complex. You cannot go directly from the Magic Kingdom to EPCOT Center, for example. You must catch the express monorail (Loop A) to the TTC and there transfer

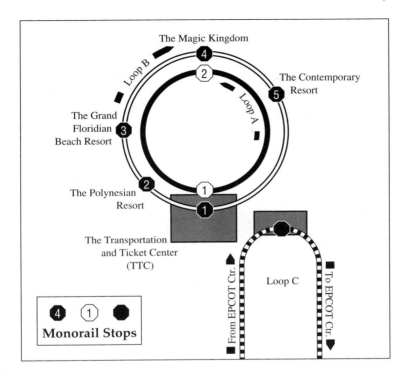

The Magic Kingdom

Loop B

The Contemporary
Resort

The Grand
Floridian
Beach Resort

Loop A

The Polynesian
Resort

The Transportation
and Ticket Center
(TTC)

From EPCOT Ctr.

Loop C

To EPCOT Ctr.

Monorail Stops

to the Loop C monorail over to EPCOT Center. If you do not have to wait in a long line to board either monorail, you can usually make it over to EPCOT Center in about 25 to 35 minutes. But should you want to go to EPCOT Center for dinner (as many people do) and you are departing the Magic Kingdom in the late afternoon, you might have to wait a half hour or more just to get on the Loop A monorail. Adding this wait pops your commuting time up to about 45 to 55 minutes.

The monorails usually run for two hours after closing to insure that everyone is accommodated. If the monorail is too crowded, or you need transportation after the monorails have stopped running, catch a bus.

It's great fun, incidentally, to ride in the front cab of the monorail with the conductor, and all you have to do is ask, according to a Richmond, Virginia, mom:

Speaking of the monorail — don't hesitate to ask about sitting up front — even if you aren't the first ones there. People are somewhat timid about asking, and the monorail attendants won't even suggest it, so ask! We got to ride up front three times during our stay.

PART SEVEN: *Bare Necessities*

Credit Cards and Money

—— Credit Cards

- MasterCard, VISA, and American Express are accepted for theme park admission.
- No credit cards are accepted in the theme parks at fast-food restaurants.
- Walt Disney World shops, sit-down restaurants, and theme resort hotels will accept MasterCard, VISA, and American Express credit cards only.

—— Financial Matters

Cash: Branches of the Sun Bank are located on Main Street in the Magic Kingdom and at 1675 Buena Vista Drive. Service at EPCOT Center and the Disney-MGM Studios is limited to an automatic teller machine. The Sun Bank at the Magic Kingdom and Buena Vista Drive locations will:

- *Provide cash advances* on MasterCard and VISA credit cards (no minimum with a maximum equaling the patron's credit limit). American Express Green Card holders can obtain a maximum of $200 in cash and $800 in traveler's checks. American Express Gold Card holders can obtain up to $500 in cash and $500 in traveler's checks.

- *Cash personal checks* of $25 or less drawn on U.S. banks upon presentation of a valid driver's license and a major credit card.

- *Cash and sell traveler's checks*. The bank cashes the first check without charge, but levies a $2 service fee for each additional check cashed.

- *Facilitate the wiring of money* from the visitor's bank to the Sun Bank.

- *Exchange foreign currency* for dollars.

Most Visa, MasterCard, and Discover cards are accepted at automatic teller machines at Walt Disney World. To use an American Express card, however, you must sign a specific agreement with American Express prior to your trip. Cash teller privileges are not automatic with American Express when you become a cardholder. If your credit card does not work in the automatic teller machines, a bank teller will be able to process your transaction at the teller window at any of Sun Bank's full-service locations.

—— A License to Print Money

One of Disney's more sublime ploys for separating you from your money is the printing and issuing of Disney Dollars. Available in denominations of $1 (Mickey Moolah), $5 (Goofy Greenbacks), and $10 (Minnie Money), the colorful cash can be used for purchases at Walt Disney World, Disneyland, and at Disney Stores nationwide. Disney Dollars can also be exchanged one-for-one for U.S. currency. Disney money can be acquired all over Walt Disney World and is sometimes included as a perk (for which you are charged dollar-for-dollar) in Walt Disney Travel Company packages.

While the idea of Disney Dollars sounds fun and innocent, it is one of the better moneymakers in the Disney bag of tricks. Some guests take the money home as souvenirs. Others forget to spend or exchange it before they leave Walt Disney World. Once home, it is rare that a tourist will go to the effort of finding a Disney Store or trying to get the money exchanged through the mail. Usually the weird dollars end up forgotten in a drawer, which is exactly what the Disney folks hoped would happen.

—— The P. T. Barnum Memorial Walkway

Oh, my stars and garters, Mildred, you won't believe what they're doing now! For only $96 you can buy a 10-inch hexagonal brick with your name on it. Of course, you're not allowed to take your brick home. Disney is going to use it to build a walkway around a big lake down there at Walt Disney World. They need that walkway real bad in case the monorails and the ferry boats all break down at the same time. Here's the really good news: it will only cost us and our friends who buy bricks about $9,600,000 to build the whole dadgum thing, and we can visit our brick anytime we want, . . . if we can find it. Maybe when they get our little sidewalk finished, they'll build another one from Walt Disney World out to Disneyland in California. Those interstate highways are about to give out, you know.

Problems and Unusual Situations

—— Attractions Closed for Repairs

It is always a good idea to check in advance with Walt Disney World to see which, if any, rides and attractions may be closed for maintenance or repair during your visit. If you are particularly interested in a certain attraction, this precaution could save you a lot of disappointment. A mother from Dover, Massachusetts, wrote, lamenting:

> We were disappointed to find Space Mountain, Swiss Family Treehouse, and the Liberty Square Riverboat closed for repairs. We felt that a large chunk of the Magic Kingdom was not working, yet the tickets were still full price and expensive!

—— Car Trouble

If you decide to lock your keys in your car to prevent losing them, or leave your headlights on to make the car easier to find at the end of the day, you may have a little problem leaving the theme park. Fortunately, with such simple problems, one of the security or tow truck patrols continually on duty can put you back in business. If your car seriously goes on the fritz, the closest repair centers are Felix's Exxon on US 192 east of I-4, (407) 396-2252, and Maingate Exxon, US 192 west of I-4, (407) 396-2721. Disney security will help you make contact with the service stations. Arrangements can be made for transportation to your Walt Disney World destination or for a lift to the nearest phone.

—— Lost and Found

If you lose (or find) something in the Magic Kingdom, City Hall (once again) is the place to go. At EPCOT Center the Lost and Found is located in the Entrance Plaza, and at Disney-MGM Studios it is located at Hollywood Boulevard Guest Services. If you do not discover your loss until you have left the park(s), call (407) 824-4245 (for all parks). See pages 27–28 for the number to call in each park if you *do* discover something is missing while still in the park(s).

—— *Medical Matters*

Relief for a Headache: Aspirin and various other sundries can be purchased on Main Street in the Magic Kingdom at the Emporium (they keep them behind the counter so you have to ask), at most retail outlets in EPCOT Center's Future World, and in many of the World Showcase shops. Likewise at the Disney-MGM Studios, aspirin is available at almost all retail shops.

If You Need a Doctor: If you require medical attention, Mediclinic provides 24-hour service. Doctors are available for house calls to all area hotels and campgrounds (Disney and non-Disney). House calls are $98 per visit, more after 10 P.M. If your problem does not require a house call, you can visit the clinic on a walk-in basis (no appointments taken) at 2901 Parkway Boulevard, Suite 3-A in Kissimmee. Minimum charge for a physician consultation at the clinic is $65. The clinic is open from 9 A.M. to 9 P.M. every day of the year. The Mediclinic main phone is (407) 396-1195.

If Kissimmee is inconvenient, consider the Buena Vista Walk-In Clinic located on FL 535 North near the entrance to the Walt Disney World Village. The Buena Vista Walk-In Clinic does not make house calls, but sees patients on a first-come, first-served basis for basic medical diagnostic and treatment services, 8 A.M. to 8 P.M. daily. Call (407) 828-3434 for fees and other information.

Prescription Medicine: The closest pharmacy is located in the Goodings Supermarket on FL 535 in Lake Buena Vista, (407) 827-1200. For a delivery fee of $5, Turner Drugs, (407) 828-8125, will deliver a filled prescription to the front desk of your hotel. The delivery fee is charged to your account at the hotel.

—— *Rain*

If it rains, go to the theme parks anyway; the bad weather will serve to diminish the crowds. Additionally, most of the rides and attractions are under cover. Likewise, all but a few of the waiting areas are protected from inclement weather. Most showers, particularly during the warmer months, are of short duration.

At the theme park shops, rain gear is available but not always displayed. As the Disney people say, it is sold "under the counter." In other words, you have to ask for it. If you are caught without protection on a rainy day, do not slog around dripping. Rain gear is one of the few shopping bargains at Walt Disney World. Ponchos can be had for less than $5 and umbrellas go for about $7.

—— *Visiting More Than One Park in a Single Day*

If you have a pass that allows you to visit the Magic Kingdom, EPCOT Center, and Disney-MGM Studios in the same day, the pass will be marked with the day's date when you enter your first park. Later if you decide to go to one of the other parks, you must get a reentry stamp on your hand before departing. If you start the day at the Magic Kingdom, for instance, and then want to go to EPCOT Center for dinner, you must get a reentry stamp when you leave the Magic Kingdom. When you arrive at EPCOT Center, use the entrance gate marked "Same Day Reentry" and show your hand stamp. The hand stamp, which is only visible under ultraviolet light, will not come off if you wash your hands or go swimming (usually).

A number of admission passes, including those purchased by Disney resort guests for the length of their stay, are authenticated by an electronic device at the park entrance turnstiles. If you use this type of pass at one park, and then decide to go to a second park on the same day, have your hand stamped as you leave the first park. At the second park, use the gates marked "Same Day Reentry" and show your hand stamp. Even though your pass is valid for the entire length of your stay, it will be rejected by the electronic authenticating device at the second park as "used and invalid" for the day in question if you try to enter though gates other than those marked "Same Day Reentry."

Services and Shopping

—— *Cameras and Film*

If you do not have a camera, Disney will rent you a 35mm Kodak Cameo. The rental fee is $5 per day, with a $70 deposit. Also available for rent are full-size VHS Sharp video camcorders at $40 for the first day, decreasing by $5 each succeeding day down to a minimum daily charge of $20. The deposit required on the camcorder is $600. You can use either cash or credit card to cover the deposit, and you must present a picture I.D. when you rent. Equipment is available at the Camera Centers of the Magic Kingdom, EPCOT Center, and Disney-MGM Studios. Equipment rented at one theme park can be returned to the Camera Center in another park. Film is available throughout Walt Disney World.

Film developing services are provided by most Disney hotel gift shops and the Camera Centers. For two-hour developing service look for the Photo Express sign at various locations around the theme parks. Simply drop your film in the container and pick up your pictures at the Camera Center as you leave the park. If you use the Express service and intend to stay in the park until closing, drop by and get your pictures sometime earlier in the evening to avoid the last-minute rush. The Magic Kingdom Camera Center almost always develops film within the advertised two hours. Camera Centers at EPCOT and at the Studios frequently run late.

Finally, photo tips as well as recommendations for settings and exposures are detailed in the respective theme park maps provided free when you enter the park.

—— *Shopping for Walt Disney World Resort Guests*

Walt Disney World resort guests who make purchases in any of the theme park shops can have their merchandise forwarded directly to their guest rooms.

—— *Disney Souvenirs*

Though Disney souvenirs can be found in any Walt Disney World structure large enough to hold a cash register, we get a lot of mail from readers asking where to find the greatest variety and the best deals. Starting with variety, these shops have the greatest selection of Disney trademark stuff (Mickey T-shirts, Goofy hats, etc.):

Magic Kingdom

Main Street	Emporium (largest selection at Magic Kingdom)
	Disneyana Collectibles
Fantasyland	The Mad Hatter
	The AristoCats
Tomorrowland	Mickey's Star Traders

EPCOT Center

Future World	Gateway Gifts
	Centorium (largest selection at EPCOT Center)
World Showcase	Disney Traders (on the left side of Showcase Plaza)

Disney-MGM Studios

Hollywood Boulevard	Mickey's of Hollywood
Studio Courtyard	Animation Gallery

There are stuffed toys of the Disney characters, Disney books and records, character hats, and a number of other items which are hard if not impossible to find outside the Disney shops. T-shirts, however, are another story. The most popular souvenir item of all, Disney T-shirts, can be found in stores all over the area.

The shirts sold at Walt Disney World are expensive ($15–32), but are high quality, 100% cotton. Shirts sold outside the world are usually of lesser quality, 50% cotton and 50% polyester, and sell for $7–18. Both inside and outside Walt Disney World, you can find many of the same designs of Mickey, Minnie, and Goofy. The only difference is that shirts sold in Disney shops will say "Walt Disney World" or, possibly, "EPCOT Center" or "Disney-MGM Studios." Shirts sold outside the world will usually say "Florida" next to the imprint of the character.

Mickey's Character Shop at the Disney Village Marketplace has the largest selection of Disney merchandise at Walt Disney World, and is decidedly less crowded and frenetic than the shops at the theme parks. In

a policy reversal, members of the Magic Kingdom Club are once again eligible for a 10% discount on merchandise purchased at Pleasure Island and the Disney Village Marketplace.

The only retailer that sells discounted items *from* Walt Disney World is the Character Warehouse, (407) 345-5285, located in Mall Two of the Belz Factory Outlet World at the north end of International Drive. Though the prices are good, the selection is generally limited to closeouts and remainders. In other words, do not expect to find the same merchandise that you saw in the parks. The store is open from 10 A.M. to 9 P.M. Monday through Saturday, and 10 A.M. to 6 P.M. on Sunday.

Bargain World, (407) 345-8772, with locations at 6454 International Drive (next to Shell World), 8520 International Drive, and 5781 and 7586 US 192, offers a good selection of the 50% cotton and 50% polyester shirts as well as Disney beach towels and other character merchandise.

—— *Messages*

Messages can be left at City Hall in the Magic Kingdom, Innoventions East Guest Relations at EPCOT Center, or at Hollywood Boulevard Guest Services at the Disney-MGM Studios.

—— *Pet Care*

Cooping up an animal in a hot car while you tour can lead to disastrous results. Additionally, pets are not allowed in the major or minor theme parks. Kennels and holding facilities are provided for the temporary care of your pets, and are located adjacent to the Transportation and Ticket Center, to the left of the EPCOT Center entrance plaza, and to the left of the Disney-MGM Studios entrance plaza. If you are adamant, the folks at the kennels will accept custody of just about any type of animal, though owners of exotic and/or potentially vicious pets must place their charges in the assigned cage. Small pets (mice, hamsters, birds, snakes, turtles, alligators, etc.) must arrive in their own escape-proof quarters.

In addition to the above, there are several other details that you may need to know:

- When traveling with your pet in Florida, bring your certificate of vaccination and immunization.

- It is against the law in the state of Florida to leave a pet in a closed vehicle.

- Advance reservations for animals are not accepted.

- Kennels are open 24 hours a day.

- Only Walt Disney World resort guests may board a pet overnight. Guests who board their pets should be advised that the kennels are not really set up for multiday boarding. You must feed and exercise your own pet.

- Guests leaving exotic pets should supply food for their pet.

—— *Religious Services*

Mass for Catholics is celebrated each Sunday at 8 and 10:15 A.M. at the Polynesian Resort. An interdenominational Protestant service is held at 9 A.M. each Sunday at the Polynesian Resort. For a schedule of services at churches and temples in the Walt Disney World area, inquire at the desk of your hotel.

—— *Excuse Me, but Where Can I Find . . .*

Someplace to Put All These Packages? Lockers are available on the ground floor of the Main Street railroad station in the Magic Kingdom, to the right of Spaceship Earth in EPCOT Center, and on both the east and west ends of the Ticket and Transportation Center. At Disney-MGM Studios, lockers are to the right of the entrance on Hollywood Boulevard at Oscar's Super Service.

A Package Pick-up service is available at EPCOT Center. Simply request the salesperson to send your purchases to Package Pick-up. When you leave the park they will be waiting for you at either the main entrance or the International Gateway. Be sure you specify the exit.

If you are a Disney resort guest, you can have your theme park purchase forwarded directly to your guest room.

A Mixed Drink or a Beer? If you are in the Magic Kingdom you are out of luck. You will have to exit the park and proceed to one of the resort hotels. In EPCOT Center you can have a drink, but you may need a reservation. Alcoholic beverages are served primarily in full-service eateries, although beer is available at the Cantina de San Angel opposite the Mexican pavilion; at Le Cellier, a cafeteria on the lower right side of the Canadian pavilion; and at the pub section of the Rose & Crown Pub & Dining Room in the United Kingdom complex. The latter is popular not only because of the beer, but because of its unparalleled view of the World Showcase Lagoon. Finally, beer is also available at Yakatori House, the fast-food eatery in the Japanese pavilion, and at Oktoberfest, the fast-food beer garden at the German pavilion. At Disney-MGM Studios, beer and wine are available at the Soundstage and Backlot restaurants, at the Catwalk Bar and the Tune-In Lounge, the full-service Hollywood Brown Derby, the 50's Prime Time Cafe, and at Mama Melrose's Ristorante Italiano.

Some Chewing Gum? Sorry, chewing gum is not sold in any of the theme parks. B.Y.O.

A Good Grocery Store? If you want to stock up on snacks or other edibles, try the Goodings Supermarket in the Crossroads Shopping Center on FL 535. The entrance to the shopping center is directly across FL 535 from the entrance to the Disney Village Marketplace and Village Hotels.

Suntan Lotion?   Suntan lotion and various other sundries can be purchased on Main Street in the Magic Kingdom at the Emporium (they keep them behind the counter so you have to ask), at most retail outlets in EPCOT Center's Future World, and in many of the World Showcase shops. At the Disney-MGM Studios, suntan lotion is sold at almost all retail shops.

A Smoke?   Cigarettes are readily available throughout the Magic Kingdom, EPCOT Center, and the Disney-MGM Studios. For the record, smoking is prohibited on all attractions, in all attraction waiting areas, and in all shops.

Feminine Hygiene Products?   Feminine hygiene products are available in women's rest rooms throughout Walt Disney World.

PART EIGHT: Dining In and Around Walt Disney World

Dining Outside of Walt Disney World

Unfortunately, we are not able to eat many meals outside of Walt Disney World, and a couple of our favorite off-World spots have dropped in quality lately. Restaurants we can recommend include Numero Uno for Cuban food (cheap), Siam Orchid for Thai food (expensive), and Ming Court for Chinese (moderate to expensive). Another great favorite of ours on International Drive is Passage to India, an outstanding and affordable Indian restaurant.

Scott Joseph, wine and food critic of the *Orlando Sentinel*, recommends the following restaurants:

American	Cafe Tu Tu Tango; 8625 International Drive, Orlando; Inexpensive to Moderate; 248–2222
	Chatham's Place; 7575 Dr. Phillips Blvd., Orlando; Moderate to expensive. (407) 345-2992
	Manuel's on the 28th; 390 North Orange Avenue, Orlando; Expensive; 246–6580
	Pebbles; 12551 FL 535, Crossroads Shopping Center, Lake Buena Vista; Moderate to expensive. (407) 827-1111
	Sam Snead's Tavern; 2461 South Hiawassee Road, Orlando; Inexpensive to moderate; 295–9999
	Wild Jack's; 7364 International Drive, Orlando; Moderate; 352–4407
Beef	Butcher Shop Steakhouse; 8445 International Drive, Mercado Mediterranean Village, Orlando; Moderate. (407) 363-9727
	Charlie's Steak House; 6107 South Orange Blossom Trail, Orlando; Moderate; 851–7130

Chinese	Ming Court; 9188 International Drive, Orlando; Expensive. (407) 351-9988
Cuban	Numero Uno; 2499 South Orange Avenue, Orlando; Inexpensive. (407) 841-3840.
French	Le Coq Au Vin; 4800 South Orange Avenue, Orlando; Moderate; 851–6980
	Le Provence; 50 East Pine Street, Orlando; Moderate; 843–1320
German	Old Munich; 5731 South Orange Blossom Trail, Orlando; Moderate; 438–8997
Indian	Passage to India; 5532 International Drive, Orlando; Moderate. (407) 351-3456
Italian	Capriccio; 9801 International Drive, Orlando; Moderate to expensive. (407) 342-4000
	Rosario's; 4838 W. Irlo Bronson, Kissimmee; Moderate. (407) 239-6118
	Tarantino's; 917 North Bermuda Avenue, Kissimmee; Inexpensive to moderate; 870–2622
Middle Eastern	Aladdin's Cafe; 1015 East Semoran Boulevard, Casselberry; Moderate; 331–0488
Seafood	Hemingway's; 1 Grand Cypress Blvd., Hyatt Regency Grand Cypress, Orlando; Expensive. (407) 239-1234
Thai	Siam Orchid; 7575 Republic Drive, Orlando; Moderate to expensive. (407) 351-0821

—— *Take Out Express*

If you are staying in a hotel or motel *outside* of Walt Disney World, Take Out Express, (407) 352-1170, will deliver a meal from your choice of five restaurants: T.G.I. Fridays, China Coast, Darryl's, Pacino's Italian Ristorante, or Havana's Cafe (Spanish/Cuban). There's a delivery charge of $3 per restaurant with a minimum $15 order. Gratuities are not included. Cash, travelers checks, MasterCard, Visa, and American Express are accepted for payment. Hours of operation are 5–11 P.M.

Dining in Walt Disney World

There are more than five dozen full-service restaurants to choose from at Walt Disney World, including 20 restaurants located inside the theme parks. Collectively, the restaurants of Walt Disney World offer exceptional variety, serving everything from Cajun to French, Moroccan to Texas barbeque. Most of the restaurants are expensive, and many serve less than distinguished fare, but in general the culinary scene at Walt Disney World is improving. Good deals can be had if you know where to look, and there are ethnic delights available that are rare outside of America's largest cities.

—— A Word about Fast Food in the Theme Parks

The purpose of this chapter is to help you find good food without going broke or tripping over one of Disney World's many culinary landmines. This chapter deals only with Walt Disney World full-service restaurants, both in the theme parks and at the hotels. Counter service and fast-food eateries are described in the sections on the respective theme parks (also included are suggestions for integrating meals into your touring itinerary). To give you some sense of comparison, however, here is what fast food and snacks in the parks will cost, tax included, rounded to the nearest nickel:

Soft drinks, Iced Tea, Lemonade: small: $1.55; large: $1.85
Coffee: small: 90¢   large: $1.15   Popcorn: $1.75
Potato Chips: 80¢   Ice Cream: $1.60   Churro: $1.55
Sandwiches: $3–6   Salads: $3–6   Fries: $1.25

—— Healthy Food in the Theme Parks

One of the most commendable developments in food service at Walt Disney World has been the introduction of healthier foods and snacks. Diabetics, vegetarians, weight watchers, and guests on restricted diets should have no trouble finding something to eat. Ditto for anyone

else who is simply seeking wholesome, nutritious food. Heathy food is available at all full-service restuarants, most fast-food counters, and even from vendors. All three of the major theme parks, for instance, sell a variety of fresh fruit from vendor stands.

—— *Tips for Saving Money on Food*

If you want to eat at full-service restaurants in the theme parks, consider having your main meal at lunch. The menus are largely the same, but the prices are lower. In 1995, special coupons were given to guests who had their midday meal at a theme park full-service restaurant. The coupons were good for 20% off the entire dinner tab (including alcoholic beverages) at 26 participating theme park and resort restaurants. The coupon had to be accompanied by your register receipt from lunch and had to be redeemed after 4 P.M. on the same day you purchased lunch. As an example of how much this coupon can save, our cartoonist had a $12 lunch at Akershus in Norway at EPCOT Center and was given a coupon. That night we used the coupon for 20% off our total bill, including wine, for a party of 6 at the Yachtsman Steakhouse (Disney's Yacht Club Resort).

Another 1995 initiative was discounted early bird meals at participating theme park restaurants. The special, which included choice of soup or salad, entree, and dessert, was good between 4:30 and 6 P.M. While there is no gaurantee that these dining specials will be continued into 1996, we recommend that you make inquiries at each theme park on arrival.

Because meals at the Walt Disney World theme parks and hotels are so expensive, cost-conscious families have invented a number of stategies for stretching their food dollar. Below are a number of cost-cutting strategies that *Unofficial Guide* readers have shared with us.

From a Lee's Summit, Missouri, family:

> Last year we requested a small refrigerator for our room and were given one for no charge. This year we were charged $5 a day for use of the fridge, but it was definitely worth it for us to be able to eat breakfast in the room to save time and money.

Another Missouri mom wrote, saying:

> I have shared our very successful meal plan with many families. We stayed six nights, and arrived at WDW after some days on the beach south of Sarasota. We shopped there, and arrived with our steel Coleman cooler well stocked with milk and sandwich fixings. I froze a block of ice in a milk bottle, and we replenished it daily with ice from the resort ice machine. I also froze small packages of deli-type meats for later in the week. We ate cereal, milk and fruit each morning, with boxed juices. I also had a hot pot to boil water for instant coffee, oatmeal and soup.
>
> Each child had a belt bag of his own, which he filled from a special box of "goodies" each day. I made a great mystery of filling that box in the weeks before the trip. Some things were actual food, like packages of crackers and cheese, packets of peanuts and raisins. Some were worthless junk, like candy and gum. They grazed from their belt bags at will throughout the day, with no interference from mom and dad. Each also had a small, rectangular plastic water bottle that could hang in the belt. We filled these at water fountains before getting into lines, and were the envy of many.
>
> We left the park before noon, ate sandwiches, chips and soda in the room, and napped. We purchased our evening meal in the park, at a counter service eatery. We budgeted for both morning and evening snacks from a vendor, but often did not need them. It

made the occasional treat all the more special. Our cooler had been pretty much emptied by the end of the week, but the block of ice was still there.

And finally, this from a Richland, Washington, man:

I think that you should in future editions promote the Cross Roads of Buena Vista [Shopping Center] a little stronger. There are plenty of non-WDW restaurants at non-WDW prices. The Cross Roads is nothing less than a small city that can service all of your needs.

The Cross Roads Shopping Center is located on FL 535 directly across from the entrance to the Walt Disney World Village and the Walt Disney World Hotel Plaza. As the reader suggests, you will find just about everything you need there. In the fast food department, there are McDonalds, Burger King, Taco Bell, and Johnny Rockets. Moving up a notch there are T.G.I. Fridays, Perkins, Jungle Jim's, Pizzeria Uno, and Red Lobster. For a really nice meal there's Pebbles, featuring fresh Florida seafood. You can fill your coolers and fridge at Goodings Supermarket. Goodings, open 24 hours, also has a deli, bakery, and full-service pharmacy. When you finish eating there are sportswear, swimwear, and athletic shoe retailers to check out. Finally, if you lose your *Unofficial Guide,* there is a bookstore where you can buy another.

—— *Reservations*

Almost all Walt Disney World full-service restaurants accept reservations, and for the better, more popular restaurants, reservations are a must. To make a reservation at a hotel, Disney Village Marketplace, or Pleasure Island restaurant, you can simply call the restaurant directly. Most hotel, Disney Village Marketplace, and Pleasure Island restaurants will accept reservations up to three days in advance.

Making a reservation at one of the theme park full-service restaurants is a bit more complicated. Variables affecting the difficulty of making reservations for a particular restaurant include its popularity, seating capacity, and the size of the crowd on the day of your visit. Each restaurant has seatings for both lunch and dinner. Lunch runs from 11 A.M. to 4 P.M. The dinner menu is served from 4 P.M. until one hour before the park closes.

Guests staying at a Walt Disney World hotel or campground may make reservations one to three days in advance by dialing 55 or 56 from their hotel room on the Disney World internal phone system. If you wish to make dining reservations prior to checking in at your Walt Disney World hotel (up to 60 days [with lodging confirmation number] in advance), call (407) 939-3463. For the record, guests at the seven hotels in the Disney Village Hotel Plaza are not eligible for making advance reservations. Even though these hotels are in Walt Disney World, they are not owned by Disney, hence no reservation privileges.

In a recent development, and without any stated change of official policy, Disney dining reservationists have begun accepting advance reservations from guests *not* staying in Disney resort hotels and campgrounds. Should this continue, it will go a long way toward redressing a long-standing practice of discriminating against "day guests." If on the other hand the new, more egalitarian reservations practice is abandoned, guests who are lodging out of the World will have to make their reservations at the theme park on the day of the meal. At all three parks, reservations can also be made at the door of the restaurant. While the theme park restaurants do not commence food service until 11 A.M., reservation desks are staffed from park opening time on at the entrance of each restaurant.

At EPCOT Center, there is also a central reservations service located at Innoventions East, to the left of the Spaceship Earth giant geodesic dome. Because EPCOT Center is such a large park, it is usually much more convenient to make dining reservations at the central reservations service than at the respective restaurants. At the Disney-MGM Studios, a reservations desk is operated on the corner of Hollywood and Sunset Boulevards. There is no central dining reservations service for Magic Kingdom restaurants.

—— *Dress*

Informal dress is the rule at all of the theme park restaurants. While theme park attire (shorts, T-shirts, sneakers, etc.) is tolerated at hotel restaurants, you would probably feel more comfortable if you dressed up just a bit. Restaurants requesting jackets for men are Victoria & Albert's at the Grand Floridian and the Empress Room on the *Empress Lilly* riverboat at the Disney Village Marketplace.

—— *A Few Caveats*

Before you commence eating your way through Walt Disney World there are a few things you need to know:

1. In many Walt Disney World restaurants, particularly full-service restaurants in the Magic Kingdom and the Disney-MGM Studios, the subtlety and creativity of the dishes described on the menu are often vastly beyond the kitchen's ability to deliver. Expressed differently, stay away from fancy food. Try to order dishes that would be really hard to screw up.

2. Do not order baked, broiled, poached, or grilled seafood unless the restaurant specializes in seafood or, alternatively, rates at least 3½ stars on our restaurant profile.

3. There seems to be a concerted effort in the theme park restaurants to rush you through your meal in order to clear the table for the next contingent of diners. This Mach 2 food ingestion may have appeal to a family with small, restless children; for anyone wanting to relax, it feels more like *Beat the Clock* than fine dining.

    If you want to relax and linger over your expensive meal, do not, repeat, do not, order your entire dinner at once. Place drink orders while you study the menu. If you would like a second drink, request it before you order. Order appetizers, but tell the waiter you need more time to choose your main course. Order your entree only after the appetizers have been served. Feel free to dawdle over coffee and dessert.

4. If you are dining in one of the theme parks, and expense is an issue, have your main meal at lunch. The entrees are much the same as on the dinner menu, but the prices are significantly lower.

—— Disney's Food 'N Fun Plan

Disney resort guests can sign up for a combination recreation and meal plan during their stay. The plan includes full-service breakfast and dinner daily, including tax and gratuities, at about 60 Walt Disney World participating restaurants. Alcoholic beverages, room service, and counter service fast food are excluded. The plan also includes daily use of all Walt Disney World recreational activities except golf. The plan must be booked for every person in your party, and there is a two-day minimum. The cost of the Food 'N Fun Plan is $58 per day for adults and juniors (10 years old and up), and $16.50 per day for children (ages 3 to 9). If you book the plan for your entire stay you are eligible for a 10% discount.

The value of the plan lies in its recreational features. If you do a lot of boating, water skiing, horseback riding, fishing, and tennis, as well as a lot of eating, the plan may be a good deal. Do not sign up, however, just for the food. First, while all of the full-service restaurants in the theme parks participate in the plan, the list of participating hotel restaurants is quite weak. In fact, the top dozen or so restaurants at Walt Disney World are excluded. Among those conspicuously absent are Ariel's, the Yachtsman Steakhouse, the Portobello Yacht Club, Narcoossee's, Victoria & Albert's, all of the restaurants at the Walt Disney World Swan and Dolphin hotels, and the restaurants on the *Empress Lilly* riverboat. Second, you will have to really pig out at both breakfast and dinner to eat your money's worth. We're talking appetizers, soup, salad, big main courses with extra side dishes, and lots of dessert. Third, if you take our touring advice, you don't want to be spending your mornings eating 9-course, full-service breakfasts.

—— *Where the Author and Research Team Eat*

Since we are very critical of the food served at Walt Disney World, it is only fair that we share our personal preferences for dining in the parks and hotels.

We try to avoid eating at the Magic Kingdom altogether. When we have no choice we usually go for fast food (the simpler the better) or eat at the Liberty Tree Tavern. The Liberty Tree is the best full-service restaurant in the Magic Kingdom, offering some excellent soups, sandwiches, and a pretty fair turkey dinner.

At EPCOT Center we enjoy chicken *mole* at the San Angel Inn Restaurante in Mexico, and the buffet and draft Ringnes beer at Restaurant Akershus in Norway. We also like most of the dishes at Restaurant Marrakesh in Morocco. The Biergarten is also pretty decent. Teppan dining at Japan is some of the best we have had anywhere, and the Bistro de Paris (France) and the Rose & Crown (United Kingdom) can always be counted on for a well-prepared meal. Finally, for good (albeit expensive) seafood in a knock-out underwater setting, you can't beat the Coral Reef at the Living Seas pavilion.

At the Disney-MGM Studios, the most fun restaurants (Sci-Fi Dine-In and 50's Prime Time Cafe) serve lackluster food. We eat at the Hollywood Brown Derby or Mama Melrose's and then go to the Sci-Fi or Prime Time for dessert.

The best deals in Walt Disney World are the Monorial Buffet in the Contemporary Resort and the clambake at the Cape May Cafe at Disney's Beach Club. The Contemporary dinner buffet includes such unlikely selections as pizza and peel-and-eat boiled shrimp. The clambake includes tasty (though extremely chewy) littleneck clams, mussels, superb New England clam chowder, barbequed pork ribs, corn on the cob, Caesar salad, and a great dessert selection.

Other restaurants we patronize when left to our own devices are Kimonos (Japanese) at the Swan, Ariel's at the Beach Club, and Planet Hollywood (loud) and the Portobello Yacht Club at Pleasure Island.

—— *The Full-Service Restaurants of Walt Disney World**

To assist you in your dining selection, we have developed profiles of the Walt Disney World full-service restaurants. Each profile allows you, in just a second, to check out the restaurant's cuisine, location, star rating, cost range, quality rating, and value rating. The restaurant profiles are listed alphabetically by the name of the restaurant, and follow the summary index below.

Star Rating.   The star rating represents the entire dining experience: style, service, and ambience in addition to taste, presentation, and quality of food. Five stars is the highest possible rating and indicates the restaurant offers the best of everything. Four-star restaurants are above average, and three-star restaurants offer good, though not memorable meals. Two-star restaurants serve essentially mediocre fare, and one-star restaurants are below average. Our star ratings do not correspond to ratings awarded by AAA, Mobil, Zagat, or other restaurant reviewers.

Cost.   The next rating gives a general description of how much a complete meal will cost. For our purposes, a complete meal consists of a main dish with vegetable or side dish and a choice of soup or salad. Appetizers, desserts, drinks, and tips are excluded. We've rated the cost as inexpensive, moderate, or expensive.

> Inexpensive = $14 or less per person
> Moderate = $15–25 per person
> Expensive = Over $25 per person

Quality Rating.   If you are a person who wants the best food available, and cost is not an issue, you need look no further than the quality ratings.

*For additional information on Disney character dining, see pages 178–180.

The quality rating is based on a scale of 0 to 100, with 100 as the best possible, and zero (0) as the worst. The quality rating is based solely on the preparation, presentation, taste, freshness of ingredients, and creativity of the food served. There is no consideration of price, service, or atmosphere — just the food.

Value Rating. If, on the other hand, you are looking for both quality and a good deal, then you should check the value rating. The value ratings range from A to F, as follows:

A = Exceptional value, a real bargain
B = Good value
C = Fair value, you get exactly what you pay for
D = Somewhat overpriced
F = Extremely overpriced

Readers' Restaurant Survey Response. For each Walt Disney World restaurant profiled, we include the results of last year's readers' response survey. Results are expressed as a percentage of responding readers who liked the restaurant well enough to eat there again (Thumbs Up) as opposed to the percentage of responding readers who had a bad experience and would not go back (Thumbs Down). (*Unofficial Guide* readers tend to be somewhat less critical than our *Unofficial Guide* restaurant critics.) If you would like to participate in the 1996 Walt Disney World Restaurant Survey, complete and return the restaurant survey form on the last page of this book.

Theme Park Full-Service Restaurants (in alphabetical order)

Name	Cuisine	Location	Star Rating	Cost Range	Quality Rating	Value Rating
Au Petit Cafe	French	EPCOT	★★★	Moderate	82	C
Biergarten	German	EPCOT	★★½	Moderate	75	D
Bistro de Paris	French	EPCOT	★★★½	Expensive	86	D
Chefs de France	French	EPCOT	★★★★	Moderate	91	B
Coral Reef	Seafood	EPCOT	★★★★	Expensive	89	D
50's Prime Time Cafe	American	Disney-MGM	★★	Moderate	69	D
The Garden Grill	American	EPCOT	★★½	Moderate	79	C
Hollywood & Vine Cafeteria	American	Disney-MGM	★★★	Inexpensive	84	B

Theme Park Full-Service Restaurants (in alphabetical order) (continued)

Name	Cuisine	Location	Star Rating	Cost Range	Quality Rating	Value Rating
The Hollywood Brown Derby	American	Disney-MGM	★★★	Expensive	84	C
King Stefan's Banquet Hall	American	Magic Kingdom	★½	Moderate	65	D
L'Originale Alfredo di Roma Ristorante	Italian	EPCOT	★★½	Expensive	74	D
Liberty Tree Tavern	American	Magic Kingdom	★★½	Moderate/Expensive	74	D
Mama Melrose's Ristorante Italiano	Italian	Disney-MGM	★★½	Expensive	74	D
Nine Dragons Restaurant	Chinese	EPCOT	★★½	Expensive	74	F
Restaurant Akershus	Norwegian	EPCOT	★★★½	Moderate	89	B
Restaurant Marrakesh	Moroccan	EPCOT	★★★	Moderate	81	C
Rose & Crown	English	EPCOT	★★★	Moderate	83	C
San Angel Inn	Mexican	EPCOT	★★★	Expensive	84	D
Sci-Fi Dine-In	American	Disney-MGM	★★	Moderate	67	D
Tempura Kiku	Japanese	EPCOT	★★★	Moderate	83	C
Teppanyaki	Japanese	EPCOT	★★★½	Expensive	86	C
Tony's Town Square	Italian	Magic Kingdom	★★½	Moderate	78	D

Walt Disney World Resort Restaurants (in alphabetical order)

Name	Cuisine	Location	Star Rating	Cost Range	Quality Rating	Value Rating
Ariel's	Seafood	Beach Club	★★★★	Expensive	91	C
Arthur's 27	Gourmet	Buena Vista Palace	★★★★	Expensive	90	C
Artist Point	Seafood	Wilderness Lodge	★★★½	Moderate	86	C
Baskervilles	American	Grosvenor Resort	★★★	Moderate	82	C
Benihana	Japanese	Hilton	★★½	Moderate	75	C

Walt Disney World Resort Restaurants *(in alphabetical order) (continued)*

Name	Cuisine	Location	Star Rating	Cost Range	Quality Rating	Value Rating
Boatwright's	American/ Cajun	Dixie Landings	★★½	Moderate	73	D
Bonfamille's	Seafood	Port Orleans	★★★	Moderate	80	C
California Grill	American	Contemporary	★★★★½	Moderate	96	C+
Cap'n Jack's	Seafood	Village Marketplace	★★★	Inexpensive	84	B
Cape May Cafe	Buffet	Beach Club	★★★	Moderate	84	B
Chef Mickey's	American	Village Marketplace	★★★	Moderate	84	B
Cinnamon's	American/ Polynesian	Polynesian	★★	Moderate	68	C
Concourse Steakhouse	Steak	Contemporary	★	Moderate	55	D
Crockett's Tavern	American	Fort Wilderness	★★	Moderate	66	C
Finn's Grill	Seafood	Hilton	★	Moderate	55	D
Fireworks Factory	Seafood and Barbecue	Pleasure Island	★★★½	Moderate	89	C
Flagler's	Italian	Grand Floridian	★★★	Moderate	79	D
Garden Grove Cafe	American	Swan	★★	Expensive	67	D
Grand Floridian Cafe	American	Grand Floridian	★★	Moderate	68	D
Harry's Safari	Steak/ Seafood	Dolphin	★★★	Expensive	81	D
Juan & Only's Bar and Jail	Tex-Mex	Dolphin	★★★	Moderate	80	B
Kimonos	Japanese	Swan	★★★★	Moderate	90	C
Monorail Buffet	American	Contemporary	★★★	Moderate	81	B
Narcoossee's	Steak/ Seafood	Grand Floridian	★★★★	Expensive	91	D
'Ohana	Polynesian	Polynesian	★★★	Moderate	79	C
Olivia's Cafe	American	Vacation Club	★★★	Moderate	81	C
Outback	Steak	Buena Vista Palace	★★	Expensive	67	D

Walt Disney World Resort Restaurants (in alphabetical order) (continued)

Name	Cuisine	Location	Star Rating	Cost Range	Quality Rating	Value Rating
Palio	Italian	Swan	★★★	Moderate	81	C
Planet Hollywood	American	Pleasure Island	★★★½	Moderate	87	C
Portobello Yacht Club	Italian	Pleasure Island	★★★½	Expensive	88	D
Sum Chows	Chinese	Dolphin	★★★★½	Expensive	95	C
Tangaroa Terrace	American	Polynesian	★★	Moderate	66	C
Victoria & Albert's	Gourmet	Grand Floridian	★★★★½	Expensive	96	D
Whispering Canyon Cafe	American	Wilderness Lodge	★★½	Moderate	79	B
Yacht Club Galley	American	Yacht Club	★★★	Moderate	81	C
Yachtsman Steakhouse	Steak	Yacht Club	★★★	Expensive	80	D

Walt Disney World Restaurants by Cuisine

Type of Restaurant	Overall Rating	Price	Quality Rating	Value Rating
American				
California Grill	★★★★½	Moderate	96	C+
Planet Hollywood	★★★½	Moderate	87	C
Chef Mickey's Village Restaurant	★★★	Moderate	84	B
Hollywood & Vine Cafeteria	★★★	Inexpensive	84	B
The Hollywood Brown Derby	★★★	Expensive	84	C
Baskervilles	★★★	Moderate	82	C
Olivia's Cafe	★★★	Moderate	81	C
Yacht Club Galley	★★★	Moderate	81	C
The Garden Grill Restaurant	★★½	Moderate	79	C
Whispering Canyon Cafe	★★½	Moderate	79	B
Liberty Tree Tavern	★★½	Moderate/Expensive	74	D

Walt Disney World Restaurants by Cuisine (continued)

Type of Restaurant	Overall Rating	Price	Quality Rating	Value Rating
Boatwright's Dining Hall	★★½	Moderate	73	D
50's Prime Time Cafe	★★	Moderate	69	D
Cinnamon's	★★	Moderate	68	C
Grand Floridian Cafe	★★	Moderate	68	D
Garden Grove Cafe	★★	Expensive	67	D
Sci-Fi Dine-In Theater Restaurant	★★	Moderate	67	D
Crockett's Tavern	★★	Moderate	66	C
Tangaroa Terrace	★★	Moderate	66	C
King Stefan's Banquet Hall	★½	Moderate	65	D
Barbecue				
Fireworks Factory	★★★½	Moderate	89	C
Buffet				
Cape May Cafe	★★★	Moderate	84	B
Monorail Buffet	★★★	Moderate	81	B
Chinese				
Sum Chows	★★★★½	Expensive	95	C
Nine Dragons Restaurant	★★½	Expensive	74	F
English				
Rose & Crown Dining Room	★★★	Moderate	83	C
French				
Chefs de France	★★★★	Moderate	91	B
Bistro de Paris	★★★½	Expensive	86	D
Au Petit Cafe	★★★	Moderate	82	C
German				
Biergarten Restaurant	★★½	Moderate	75	C
Gourmet				
Victoria & Albert's	★★★★½	Expensive	96	D
Arthur's 27	★★★★	Expensive	90	C
Italian				
Portobello Yacht Club	★★★½	Expensive	88	D
Palio	★★★	Moderate	81	C
Flagler's	★★★	Moderate	79	D
Tony's Town Square Restaurant	★★½	Moderate	78	D

Walt Disney World Restaurants by Cuisine (continued)

Type of Restaurant	Overall Rating	Price	Quality Rating	Value Rating
L'Originale Alfredo di Roma Ristorante	★★½	Expensive	74	D
Mama Melrose's Ristorante Italiano	★★½	Expensive	74	D
Japanese				
Kimonos	★★★★	Moderate	90	C
Teppanyaki	★★★½	Expensive	85	C
Tempura Kiku	★★★	Moderate	83	D
Benihana—The Japanese Steakhouse	★★½	Moderate	75	C
Mexican				
San Angel Inn Restaurant	★★★	Expensive	84	D
Moroccan				
Restaurant Marrakesh	★★★	Moderate	81	C
Norwegian				
Restaurant Akershus	★★★½	Moderate	89	B
Polynesian				
'Ohana	★★★	Moderate	79	C
Seafood				
Ariel's	★★★★	Expensive	91	C
Narcoossee's	★★★★	Expensive	91	B
Coral Reef	★★★★	Expensive	89	D
Fireworks Factory	★★★½	Moderate	89	C
Artist Point	★★★½	Moderate	86	B
Cap'n Jack's Oyster Bar	★★★½	Inexpensive	85	B
Harry's Safari Bar and Grill	★★★	Expensive	81	D
Bonfamille's Cafe	★★★	Moderate	80	C
Finn's Grill	★	Moderate	55	D
Steak				
Narcoossee's	★★★★	Expensive	91	D
Harry's Safari Bar and Grill	★★★	Expensive	81	D
Yachtsman Steakhouse	★★★	Expensive	80	D
The Outback	★★	Expensive	67	D
Concourse Steakhouse	★	Moderate	55	D
Tex-Mex				
Juan & Only's Bar and Jail	★★★	Moderate	80	B

Ariel's

Quality	Value
91	C

Seafood ★★★★ **Expensive**

Disney's Beach Club Resort
(407) 934-3357

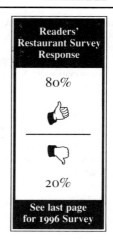

Readers'
Restaurant Survey
Response

80%

20%

See last page
for 1996 Survey

Customers: Hotel guests and locals
Reservations: Recommended
When to go: Anytime
Entree range: $18–30
Payment: VISA, MC, AMEX
Service rating: ★★★★
Friendliness rating: ★★★★
Parking: Valet or self-parking in the hotel lot
Bar: Full service
Wine selection: Excellent
Dress: Dressy; jackets not required
Disabled access: Yes

Dinner: Every day, 5:30–9:30 P.M.

Setting & atmosphere: The dining room is awash in deep greens and blues and a carpet with a Pisces fish pattern. Long green tablecloths are draped to the floor and tables are elegantly set. Mobiles of floating bubbles and colorful fish hang from the ceiling, and near the entrance there is a large saltwater aquarium. It's all meant to give an "under the sea" feel suitable for a mermaid, albeit a mermaid with plenty of sand dollars to her name. Diners enter past a show kitchen where the evening's desserts are displayed.

House specialties: Seafood strudel; Tuckernut gumbo; shellfish paella; and fresh fish selections.

Other recommendations: Lobster pasta; salmon Provençal. Instead of a full bottle of one wine, consider ordering one of the "flights" of wines by-the-glass for a variety of wines, each chosen to complement the meal. Glasses are arranged on a special placemat, on which you may write your tasting notes.

Summary & comments: Although it is named after the star of *The Little Mermaid,* this is not a restaurant for kids. It has a grown-up atmosphere with adult prices. The restaurant is entirely nonsmoking.

Arthur's 27

Gourmet ★★★★ **Expensive**

Quality	Value
90	C

Buena Vista Palace, Walt Disney World Village
(407) 827-2727

Customers: Hotel guests and locals
Reservations: Recommended
When to go: Sunset or during fireworks
  at any of the three parks
Entree range: $19–29
Payment: VISA, MC, AMEX, DC, D
Service rating: ★★
Friendliness rating: ★★
Parking: Complimentary valet parking
Bar: Full service
Wine selection: Excellent
Dress: Jackets preferred, tie optional
Disabled access: Yes

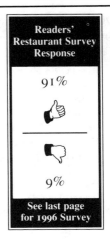

Readers'
Restaurant Survey
Response

91%

9%

See last page
for 1996 Survey

Dinner: Every day, 6–10 P.M.

Setting & atmosphere: From its perch on the 27th floor of the Buena Vista Palace, Arthur's gives a breathtaking view of the glittering lights of the Disney Village Marketplace and the twirling searchlights of Pleasure Island. Diners sit at large booths, all set apart from each other with their own windows.

House specialties: Florida Gulf shrimp; herb-crusted tuna; medallions of veal; breast of duckling.

Other recommendations: Loin of lamb; salmon in strudel leaves; chilled breast of chicken Alexandra.

Entertainment & amenities: Live entertainment in lounge.

Summary & comments: The best values at this overpriced restaurant are the four-, five-, and six-course table d'hôte offerings for $44, $49, and $55. If you're not looking for a lot of food, you'll pay too much for what you get. Still it is one of the most impressive views in the area, but only if you are facing the Disney side. Otherwise, you'll be looking at the taillights on Interstate 4 and you'll know what all the locals know: Florida is flat.

Honors & awards: DiRoNa winner.

Artist Point

Seafood   ★★★½   **Moderate**

Quality	Value
86	**C**

Disney's Wilderness Lodge Resort
(407) 824-3200

   Customers: Hotel guests, some locals
   Reservations: Recommended for dinner
     and character breakfasts
   When to go: Anytime
   Entree range: $14–21
   Payment: VISA, MC, AMEX
   Service rating: ★★★★
   Friendliness rating: ★★★★★
   Parking: Hotel lot
   Bar: Full service
   Wine selection: Features selections from
     wineries in America's Northwest
   Dress: Casual
   Disabled access: Yes

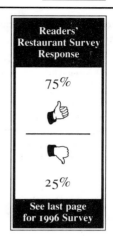

Readers'
Restaurant Survey
Response

75%

25%

See last page
for 1996 Survey

Breakfast: Every day, 7:30–11:30 A.M.
Dinner: Every day, 5–10:30 P.M.

Setting & atmosphere: Two-story-high paintings depicting the landscapes of the Pacific Northwest dominate the interior walls (and give the place its name) of this casually appointed restaurant. Tall windows offer guests a view of the lake or a waterfall that flows off high rocks and past wildflowers. Huge cast-iron chandeliers hold 12 lanterns with milk-glass panes. Tables are uncovered and each has a bust of an animal native to the Northwest engraved in it.

House specialties: Maple-glazed salmon fillet; grilled tuna loin steak; grilled halibut chop.

Other recommendations: Porterhouse steak; roasted duck chop; smoked prime rib; omelets; duck hash with egg.

Summary & comments: Unlike the other large hotels, Wilderness Lodge's top-of-the-line restaurant is not an elegant gourmet room. Still the beauty of the artwork and the room itself make dining here a pleasure. Breakfast is especially nice as the landscaping can be fully appreciated in the sunlight.

Au Petit Cafe

French   ★★★   **Moderate**

Quality	Value
82	C

France, World Showcase, EPCOT Center
(407) 824-2222

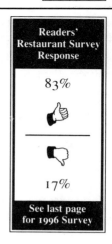

**Readers'
Restaurant Survey
Response**

83%

17%

**See last page
for 1996 Survey**

Customers: Theme park guests
Reservations: Not accepted
When to go: Late lunch
Entree range: $7.75–14.50
Payment: VISA, MC, AMEX
Service rating: ★★★★
Friendliness rating: ★★★★
Parking: EPCOT lot
Bar: Full service
Wine selection: Good
Dress: Casual
Disabled access: Yes

Lunch: Every day, 11 A.M.–4 P.M.
Dinner: Every day, 4–9 P.M.

Setting & atmosphere: One of three restaurants of the French pavilion, Au Petit is relegated to the outdoors (beware of hot Florida summers). It's a picture-perfect sidewalk cafe shielded from the elements by a huge awning. Diners face the World Showcase walkway, so it's a good place to people-watch. Female servers wear French maid uniforms, the men wear black vests, and they're all friendlier than any waiter on the Champs-Elysées.

House specialties: Several of the dishes are recreations of specialties featured at the restaurants of Paul Bocuse, Gaston LeNotre, and Roger Verge in France. Coq au vin (chicken in wine); brochette of prawns with rice in basil butter; beef Burgundy; quiche Lorraine.

Other recommendations: Seafood cream soup; salad Niçoise; escargot Burgundy.

Summary & comments: More a place for lunch or a quick sandwich. Not such a great place to view IllumiNations.

Baskervilles

Quality	Value
82	C

American   ★★★   **Moderate**

Grosvenor Resort, Walt Disney World Village
(407) 828-4444

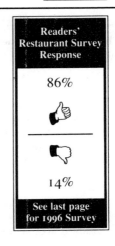

Readers'
Restaurant Survey
Response

86%

👍

👎

14%

See last page
for 1996 Survey

Customers: Hotel guests
Reservations: Not required
When to go: Anytime
Entree range: $8.50–19.50
Payment: VISA, MC, AMEX, DC, D
Service rating: ★★★
Friendliness rating: ★★
Parking: Hotel lot
Bar: Full service
Wine selection: Good
Dress: Casual
Disabled access: Yes

Breakfast: Every day, 7–11:30 A.M.
Lunch: Every day, 11:30 A.M.–1:30 P.M.
Dinner: Every day, 5–10 P.M.

Setting & atmosphere: This is a half-hearted attempt to create an English drawing room atmosphere. Unfortunately, it looks way too much like a cafeteria in a college dormitory.

House specialties: Prime rib; specialty buffets.

Other recommendations: Grilled grouper; stir-fried vegetables; Sherlock's breakfast.

Entertainment & amenities: Murder-mystery weekends where guests solve the crime. (Reservations required.)

Summary & comments: Elementary fare. If you're having trouble being entertained, try the murder-mystery dinner; it might help make the food a little more exciting. Otherwise the only reason to dine here is if you're just too tired to leave the hotel or you can't get a reservation anywhere else. Or if you really have your heart set on an average piece of prime rib.

Benihana—The Japanese Steakhouse

			Quality	Value
Japanese	★★½	**Moderate**	**75**	**C**

The Hilton, Walt Disney World Village
(407) 827-4865

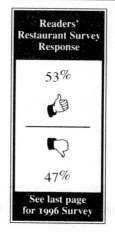

Readers' Restaurant Survey Response

53%

———

47%

See last page for 1996 Survey

Customers: Hotel guests and some locals
Reservations: Recommended
When to go: Anytime
Entree range: $15–25
Payment: VISA, MC, AMEX, DC
Service rating: ★★★★
Friendliness rating: ★★★★
Parking: Hotel lot
Bar: Full service
Wine selection: Good
Dress: Casual
Disabled access: Yes

Dinner: Every day, 5–10:30 P.M.

Setting & atmosphere: Large tables with built-in grills are crammed into small rooms decorated with rice paper panels and Japanese lanterns. Lighting is low and focused on the stage—the chef's grill.

House specialties: Teppanyaki service at large tables where the chef cooks dinner in front of you. Specialties include New York steak, lobster tail, and hibachi vegetables.

Other recommendations: Japanese onion soup.

Entertainment & amenities: Dinner is the show at this teppanyaki service restaurant where the chef does a lot of noisy chopping and grilling.

Summary & comments: If you're looking for a nice, quiet dinner be aware that diners sit at tables of eight and private conversation is almost impossible.

Biergarten Restaurant

German　　　　　★★½　　　　　**Moderate**

Quality	Value
75	C

Germany, World Showcase, EPCOT Center
(407) 939-3463

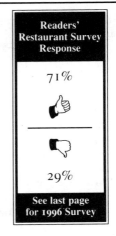

Readers'
Restaurant Survey
Response

71%

29%

See last page
for 1996 Survey

Customers: Theme park guests
Reservations: Recommended
When to go: After 6 P.M.
Entree range: $9.95, lunch; $14.50, dinner
Payment: VISA, MC, AMEX
Service rating: ★★★
Friendliness rating: ★★★
Parking: EPCOT lot
Bar: Beer and wine only
Wine selection: German
Dress: Casual
Disabled access: Yes

Lunch: Every day, 11:30 A.M.–3 P.M.
Dinner: Every day, 4–8:15 P.M.

Setting & atmosphere: Guests sit at long tables in a tiered dining area that surrounds a sort of town square of a German village, with the exteriors of shops and houses as the backdrop for the bandstand and dance floor. During the evening meal, an oom-pah-pah band plays on the stage and encourages diners to join them in singalongs and polka dancing. You may even find yourself swept up in a German version of a conga line.

House specialties: The Biergarten recently switched from an a la carte menu to an all-you-can-eat buffet concept. Even though it is all-you-can-eat, the pickings are rather meager. There are German potato salad, lentil salad, smallish sausages and wieners, spaetzle with gravy, and hot dogs in sauerkraut. There is also baked chicken, which looks and tastes like the baked chicken you would get at any other country in the World Showcase—or in the world, for that matter. The buffet is set up on wooden barrels and the food is served from vats, which is about as appealing as it sounds.

Other recommendations: Bratwurst; beer.

Entertainment & amenities: Oom-pah-pah band and German dancers perform after 6 P.M.

Summary & comments: This is not the greatest food at EPCOT, and even the service, which for a serve-yourself buffet is already minimal, doesn't meet usual Disney standards. Go if you can't get enough of polka music. Be aware that you may find yourself seated with other guests.

Bistro de Paris

French   ★★★½   **Expensive**

Quality	Value
96	D

France, World Showcase, EPCOT Center
(407) 939-3463

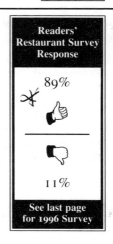

Readers'
Restaurant Survey
Response

89%

11%

See last page
for 1996 Survey

> **Customers:** Theme park guests
> **Reservations:** Required
> **When to go:** Anytime
> **Entree range:** $19.95–25
> **Payment:** VISA, MC, AMEX
> **Service rating:** ★★★★
> **Friendliness rating:** ★★★★
> **Parking:** EPCOT lot
> **Bar:** Full service
> **Wine selection:** Very good
> **Dress:** Casual
> **Disabled access:** Yes

Dinner: 5:30–8:45 P.M.

Setting & atmosphere: A beautiful spiral staircase leads to a bustling French bistro recreated on the second floor over the Chefs de France restaurant. Red burgundy banquettes, off-white tablecloths, wooden chairs, and a linen-like wallpaper set the tone. One of three restaurants at the France Pavilion, the bistro operates under the watchful eyes of three of France's most well-known chefs, Paul Bocuse, Roger Verge, and Gaston LeNotre.

House specialties: The famous triumvirate of chefs has contributed to the menu, but don't expect them to prepare your meal. Try the double consommé of chicken and beef with vegetables topped with puff pastry; real French onion soup gratinée; grilled tenderloin of beef with green peppercorn sauce; bouillabaisse Marsellaise.

Other recommendations: Cream of lobster bisque; sautéed veal tenderloin served with apple and calvados sauce; sautéed breast of duck.

Summary & comments: The food will make you feel as though you really are dining in a French bistro, but here the waiters are required to be friendly. Things can be a bit noisy here, and like all Disney restaurants, the numerous kids in highchairs detract from the illusion, but it's all part of the bustling authenticity of a French bistro.

Honors & awards: Ivy Award

Boatwright's Dining Hall

American/Cajun   ★★½   Moderate

Quality	Value
73	D

Disney's Dixie Landings Resort
(407) 934-6000

Customers: Hotel guests
Reservations: Recommended for dinner
When to go: Early evening
Entree range: $6.95–16.95
Payment: VISA, MC, AMEX
Service rating: ★★
Friendliness rating: ★★★★
Parking: Hotel lot
Bar: Full service
Wine selection: Fair; the beer selection is better.
Dress: Casual
Disabled access: Good

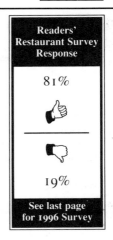

Readers'
Restaurant Survey
Response

81%

19%

See last page
for 1996 Survey

Breakfast: Every day, 7–11:30 A.M.
Dinner: Every day, 5–10 P.M.

Setting & atmosphere: Diners sit in a large, noisy room under the skeleton of a riverboat under construction that looks sort of like the carcass of a mastodon. Tables are set with a boatwright's tool kit that contains condiments instead of tools. The real tools—the two-handed saws, hatchets, chisels, and a few that are too foreign to identify—hang along the walls.

House specialties: Cajun étouffée; seafood jambalaya; steak; prime rib.

Other recommendations: Pirogue of pasta and seafood (pirogue means boat); bayou bouillabaisse with shrimp, mussels, crawfish, catfish fillets, blue crab, and chunks of new potatoes; grilled catfish served with a Cajun butter sauce.

Summary & comments: Servers can get a little caught up in the theme, a working riverboat-building operation, and forget the basics of good service. Long waits gain no apologies. Fans of true Cajun food may be disappointed with this version, which has been toned down to please the masses. There is, however, a fine selection of regional beers, including Dixie Beer, Blackened Voodoo Lager, and Abita Beer. You'll have a chance to decide which is your favorite while you're waiting for your table.

Bonfamille's Cafe

Quality	Value
80	C

Seafood   ★★★   **Moderate**

Disney's Port Orleans Resort
(407) 934-5000

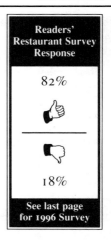

Readers' Restaurant Survey Response

82%

👍

👎

18%

See last page for 1996 Survey

Customers: Hotel guests
Reservations: Accepted for dinner only
When to go: Anytime
Entree range: $5.95–16.25
Payment: VISA, MC, AMEX
Service rating: ★★★★
Friendliness rating: ★★★★
Parking: Hotel lot
Bar: Full service
Wine selection: Fair
Dress: Casual
Disabled access: Yes

Breakfast: Every day, 7–11 A.M.
Dinner: Every day, 5–10 P.M.

Setting & atmosphere: A casual setting that recalls New Orlean's French Quarter, only cleaner. Paddle fans and exposed bricks set the mood for this family-oriented restaurant.

House specialties: Limited Creole recipes featuring shrimp, oysters, and crawfish, including jambalaya, chicken, and andouille sausage Creole in tomato sauce with onions and green peppers; blackened sea scallops.

Other recommendations: T-bone steak maître d'; roast prime rib of beef; center-cut pork chops; seafood kebab.

Summary & comments: The Creole creations aren't very authentic and most of the food is pretty tame. Even the andouille sausage, which should have some fire in it, just tasted like Polish sausage. The bayou crawfish pasta appetizer, though, is pretty tasty and at $4.95 is a real bargain, too. It is also available as an entree for $10.95, but the appetizer portion, along with a soup or salad, is plenty. The name Bonfamille means "good family" and the prices are fair enough for a family to eat pretty well. Don't expect anything out of the ordinary.

California Grill

American   ★★★★½   **Moderate**

Quality	Value
96	C+

Disney's Contemporary Resort
(407) 939-3463

Readers'
Restaurant Survey
Response

Not open
during
survey
period

See last page
for 1996 Survey

Customers: Locals and hotel guests
Reservations: Recommended
When to go: During evening fireworks
Entree range: $14.75–23.75
Payment: AMEX, MC, VISA
Service rating: ★★★★
Friendliness rating: ★★★★
Parking: Complimentary valet
Bar: Full service
Wine selection: California wines
Dress: Casual
Disabled access: Yes

Dinner: Every day, 5:30–10 P.M.

Setting & atmosphere: From the 15th floor of the Contemporary Resort, Disney's newest restaurant commands one of the most impressive panoramas in central Florida. The dining room is inspired by Wolfgang Puck's Spago restaurant and the Rainbow Room in New York. A show kitchen where the chefs prepare all foods is the centerpiece of the dining room.

House specialties: The catchword for the menu is "market inspired," which means the menu changes regularly to take advantage of the freshest produce and available meats and fish. The menu is creative, with Pacific Rim accents. The pork tenderloin is quickly becoming a house favorite and is likely to be kept on most menu rotations.

Other recommendations: Spicy rock shrimp and lemongrass soup, similar to the Thai tom ka gai; goat cheese ravioli; California designer pizzas; pan-seared tuna; chocolate quake dessert.

Entertainment & amenities: The lights are dimmed during the Magic Kingdom fireworks and the accompanying music is piped in. You can also step outside onto the 15th floor deck for a closer look. Other entertainment includes watching the chefs; instead of begging for a window seat, sit at the counter. The chefs love to slip samples to the people sitting there.

Summary & comments: This restaurant was designed to be adult-oriented and medium-priced. It is operated under a recent policy that allows the chef and manager to run the restaurant as if it were their own. The result is a classy, well-operated restaurant that is attracting even Disney-reluctant locals.

Cap'n Jack's Oyster Bar

Seafood   ★★★   **Inexpensive**

Quality	Value
84	**B**

Disney Village Marketplace
(407) 828-3870

Customers: Tourists
Reservations: Not accepted
When to go: Anytime
Entree range: $5.95–19.95
Payment: VISA, MC, AMEX
Service rating: ★★★★
Friendliness rating: ★★★★
Parking: Marketplace lot
Bar: Beer and wine only
Wine selection: Not a specialty
Dress: Casual
Disabled access: Yes

Lunch & dinner: Every day, 11:30 A.M.–10 P.M.

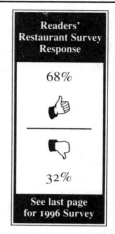

Readers'
Restaurant Survey
Response

68%

32%

See last page
for 1996 Survey

Setting & atmosphere: An upscale pierhouse on the edge of the Buena Vista Lagoon.

House specialties: Cap'n Jack's has a limited menu, but what it does it does well. New England clam chowder, spicy conch chowder with tomatoes, carrots, and onions, and crabcakes made with lump crabmeat mixed with onions are a few of the cooked items, but peel-and-eat shrimp, oysters and clams on the half-shell are really this restaurant's forte. You can also get a fresh fish dinner, usually mahi mahi, tuna, or grouper, at a fair price, and a stuffed Maine lobster that is more than twice the cost of anything else on the menu, but stick with the oyster bar items. A bucket of steamers and a cold beer are hard to beat.

Entertainment & amenities: The lagoonside setting offers views of amateur boaters, and sunsets are pretty here.

Summary & comments: Most entrees are under $10 — only the stuffed lobster climbs higher. But this is really a place for some shrimp or steamed clams and cold beer.

Cape May Cafe

Buffet ★★★ **Moderate**

Quality	Value
84	B

Disney's Beach Club Resort
(407) 934-3358

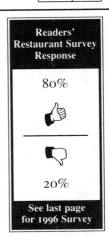

Readers'
Restaurant Survey
Response

80%

20%

See last page
for 1996 Survey

Customers: Theme park and hotel guests
Reservations: Accepted and recommended
When to go: Anytime
Entree range: Breakfast: $13 adults, $8 children;
dinner: $17 adults, $9 children
Payment: VISA, MC, AMEX
Service rating: ★★★★
Friendliness rating: ★★★★
Parking: Hotel lot
Bar: Full service
Wine selection: Limited
Dress: Casual
Disabled access: Yes

Breakfast: Every day, 7:30–11 A.M.
Dinner: Every day, 5:30–9:30 P.M.

Setting & atmosphere: The natural-finish wood furniture and padded booths are in a clean, nautical New England style—bright, airy, and informal.

House specialties: The buffet features peel-and-eat shrimp, tasty (albeit chewy) clams, mussels, baked fish, barbecued ribs, corn-on-the-cob, Caesar salad, and a good dessert bar.

Other recommendations: Lobster can be ordered as a supplement to the buffet.

Summary & comments: This buffet consistently serves some of the best food available at Walt Disney World. While the restaurant is large and tables turn over rapidly, reservations are recommended. Because the Cape May is within easy walking distance of the World Showcase entrance to EPCOT Center, it is a perfect and affordable place to dine before IllumiNations.

Chef Mickey's
Village Restaurant

American ★★★ **Moderate**

Quality	Value
84	B

Disney Village Marketplace
(407) 828-3900

Customers: Theme park guests
Reservations: Recommended
When to go: Early evening
Entree range: $12.95–19.95
Payment: VISA, MC, AMEX
Service rating: ★★★★
Friendliness rating: ★★★★
Parking: Marketplace lot
Bar: Full service
Wine selection: Good
Dress: Casual
Disabled access: Yes

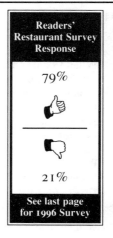

Readers'
Restaurant Survey
Response

79%

21%

See last page
for 1996 Survey

Breakfast & lunch: Every day, 9 A.M.–2 P.M.
Dinner: Every day, 5–10 P.M.

Setting & atmosphere: Chef Mickey's has a large, open dining room with tiered seating that overlooks the Buena Vista Lagoon. The building is showing its age despite regularly scheduled upgrading. Still it is a bright and cheery place to dine.

House specialties: For breakfast the chef prepares classic Eggs Benedict, three-egg omelets, and Goofy's corned beef hash with fried eggs. A crabcake appetizer and a bowl of conch chowder would make a good light lunch. For dinner there's smoked spare ribs dipped in honey barbecue sauce, prime rib, country meatloaf with mushroom gravy, and salmon lasagna.

Other recommendations: Old-fashioned beef stew; salmon lasagna; chicken and scampi combo.

Entertainment & amenities: It is likely that Chef Mickey himself will make an appearance to greet the kids. Many of the recipes are available to take home.

Summary & comments: Mickey is a better cook than you might imagine. The food is good and is one of the better values in the Marketplace.

Chefs de France

Quality	Value
91	B

French ★★★★ **Moderate**

France, World Showcase, EPCOT Center
(407) 939-3463

Customers: Theme park guests
Reservations: Recommended
When to go: Anytime
Entree range: $15.25–22.75
Payment: VISA, MC, AMEX
Service rating: ★★★★
Friendliness rating: ★★★★
Parking: EPCOT lot
Bar: Full service
Wine selection: Very good
Dress: Casual
Disabled access: Yes

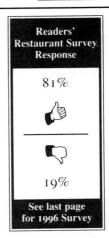

Readers'
Restaurant Survey
Response

81%

19%

See last page
for 1996 Survey

Lunch: Every day, noon–4 P.M.
Dinner: Every day, 4:30–8:45 P.M.

Setting & atmosphere: The smell of buttery croissants is as much a part of the decor here as the gilded chandeliers and framed oil paintings. White tablecloths and padded banquettes accentuate the classy French decor of the main dining room. Another room sits off to the side, this one a more casual sun room with a better view of what's going on outside, but you're there for the illusion—insist on a seat in the main room.

House specialties: One of three restaurants with similar menus at the French pavilion, Chefs de France features some of the dishes served at the real restaurants of the three chefs for whom this restaurant is named: Paul Bocuse, Roger Verge, and Gaston LeNotre. You may sample Verge's brochette of prawns from Moulin de Mougins, LeNotre's filet of orange roughy in a hazlenut butter from Pre Catelan, or Bocuse's beef braised in Burgundy from his Lyon restaurant.

Other recommendations: Roasted red snapper; salmon tartare; strip steak bordelaise.

Summary & comments: Here is your chance to eat in a restaurant supervised by three of France's best chefs. Paul Bocuse, Roger Verge, and Gaston LeNotre take turns visiting from France and supervising the staff in the preparation of their creations, so you just might get a chance to meet a culinary legend. But don't expect them to actually prepare your meal.

Cinnamon's

American/Polynesian ★★ **Moderate**

Quality	Value
68	C

Disney's Polynesian Resort
(407) 824-2170

**Readers'
Restaurant Survey
Response**

**Not open
during
survey
period**

**See last page
for 1996 Survey**

Customers: Hotel guests
Reservations: Recommended
When to go: Breakfast or lunch
Entree range: $9.75–19.95
Payment: VISA, MC, AMEX
Service rating: ★★★
Friendliness rating: ★★★
Parking: Hotel lot; Magic Kingdom lot
Bar: Full service
Wine selection: Fair
Dress: Casual
Disabled access: Yes

Breakfast: Monday–Saturday, 7–11:30 A.M.; Sunday, 7 A.M.–noon
Lunch: Every day, 11:30 A.M.–5 P.M.
Dinner: Every day, 5–11 P.M.

Setting & atmosphere: Coffee shop goes Polynesian; bare tabletops and bamboo chairs. Open to the hotel's atrium lobby with views of the rain-forest foliage and the sounds of waterfalls, the restaurant is in the Great Ceremonial House on the second floor.

House specialties: Banana-stuffed French toast; Aloha platter with tempura shrimp; lemon chicken; barbecued pork ribs.

Other recommendations: Broiled lemon chicken; Neptune tempura; traditional beef stew.

Summary & comments: Have the French toast at breakfast or a sandwich for lunch; save the big bucks for someplace else.

Concourse Steakhouse

Quality	Value
55	**D**

Steak   ★   **Moderate**

Contemporary Resort

(407) 939-3463

   Customers: Hotel guests
   Reservations: Recommended
   When to go: Anytime
   Entree range: $8.95–21.95
   Payment: VISA, MC, AMEX
   Service rating: ★
   Friendliness rating: ★★
   Parking: Hotel lot
   Bar: Full service
   Wine selection: Limited
   Dress: Casual
   Disabled access: Yes

Dinner: Every day, 5:30–10 P.M.

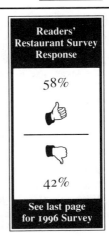

Readers'
Restaurant Survey
Response

58%

42%

See last page
for 1996 Survey

Setting & atmosphere: The decor is a cross between Art Deco and *2001: A Space Odyssey.* Large booths sit in the "open air" of the Contemporary's Concourse, with the monorails gliding by overhead on either side.

House specialties: As the name would suggest, steak is the specialty, but it isn't treated specially. The menu says that all the steaks are prime cuts, but that doesn't help when the kitchen staff doesn't know how to cook it. New York strip, filet, T-bone, and top sirloin are some of the cuts.

Other recommendations: Besides meat, roasted double breast of chicken, grilled chicken kebabs, grilled shrimp tossed with pasta, garlic and fresh herbs, roasted salmon coated with maple syrup and black peppercorns, and Caesar salad are also offered.

Summary & comments: One of the newer restaurants at Disney, Concourse Steakhouse does not represent the best the company has to offer. Servers are aloof and unconcerned with the needs of the diners. It takes a lot to screw up steaks, but the cooks manage it. An appetizer of homemade potato chips with melted cheese was an unpleasant glop of grease and goo, and when that was pointed out to the server there was no apology or response. This restaurant cannot be recommended for any occasion.

Coral Reef

Quality	Value
89	D

Seafood   ★★★★   **Expensive**

The Living Seas, Future World, EPCOT Center
(407) 939-3463

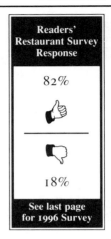

Readers' Restaurant Survey Response

82%

18%

See last page for 1996 Survey

   Customers: Theme park guests
   Reservations: Required
   When to go: Anytime
   Entree range: $11.50–36.75, lunch;
     $18.25–39.25, dinner
   Payment: VISA, MC, AMEX
   Service rating: ★★★★
   Friendliness rating: ★★★★
   Parking: EPCOT lot
   Bar: Full service
   Wine selection: Adequate
   Dress: Theme park casual
   Disabled access: Yes

Lunch: Every day, 11:30 A.M.–2:45 P.M.
Dinner: Every day, 4:30–9 P.M.

Setting & atmosphere: Plush deep greens and blues complement the linen table service. Tiered rows of tables face the floor-to-ceiling windows that look into the main marine life tank of The Living Seas. Lighting is subdued, which enhances the deep-sea atmosphere.

House specialties: Pan-seared swordfish with Thai curry lobster sauce; mixed seafood grill with tuna, salmon, and shrimp; seafood Provençal.

Other recommendations: Caribbean tuna grilled with Jamaican jerk spices; fried calamari or stone crab appetizer.

Entertainment & amenities: Viewing live marine life.

Summary & comments: Though it has taken awhile for the Coral Reef to live up to its potential, the restaurant now serves food worthy of its elegant venue. Fresh seafood, competently prepared, beautifully presented, and enhanced by delicate (and sometimes exotic) sauces, makes the Coral Reef a standout among seafood restaurants. Because of its atmosphere and creative menu, the Coral Reef is one of the first EPCOT Center restaurants to fill its reservations. Lunch and dinner menus are pretty much the same.

Crockett's Tavern

American ★★ **Moderate**

Quality	Value
66	**C**

Disney's Fort Wilderness Resort and Campground
(407) 824-2900

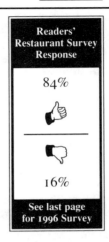

Readers'
Restaurant Survey
Response

84%

👍

👎

16%

See last page
for 1996 Survey

Customers: Campground guests
Reservations: Not required
When to go: Early evening
Entree range: $9–16
Payment: VISA, MC, AMEX
Service rating: ★★★
Friendliness rating: ★★★★
Parking: Must park in main lot and take shuttle bus to Pioneer Hall
Bar: Full service
Wine selection: Limited
Dress: Casual
Disabled access: Yes

Dinner: Sunday to Thursday, 5–10 P.M.; Friday and Saturday, 5–10:30 P.M.

Setting & atmosphere: A rustic setting stocked with Davy Crockett stuff, including Davy's rifle, Ol' Betsy, Jim Bowie's knife, and a birch bark canoe.

House specialties: Appetizers include Crockett's chili cheese chips (nachos to the rest of the world), homemade sausage, cheese and fruit platter, and smoked spare ribs. For the main course there are hickory smoked prime rib, charbroiled T- bone steak, and filet of beef tenderloin marinated in bourbon (after all, Davy was a Kentucky man). Jim Bowie gets into the act with his jumbo smoked pork chops, and there is a Mexican fiesta platter for two with chargrilled shrimp, beef and chicken burritos, Mexican rice, and refried beans, in remembrance of the Alamo.

Other recommendations: Homeplace rib and chicken dinner; Santa Ana's chicken and beef fajitas; Berry Patch shortcake.

Entertainment & amenities: Folk singing nightly.

Summary & comments: The food is secondary to the surroundings, which will thrill fans of the old Crockett series. For an extra treat order the chardonnay from Parker Winery. That's Fess Parker Winery.

50's Prime Time Cafe

American   ★★   **Moderate**

Quality	Value
69	**D**

Disney-MGM Studios
(407) 939-3463

Customers: Theme park guests
Reservations: Suggested
When to go: Anytime
Entree range: $7–16, lunch; $11–20, dinner
Payment: VISA, MC, AMEX
Service rating: ★★★★
Friendliness rating: ★★★★
Parking: Disney-MGM lot
Bar: Full service
Wine selection: Limited
Dress: Theme park casual
Disabled access: Yes

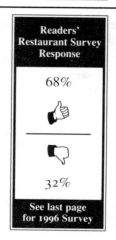

Readers'
Restaurant Survey
Response

68%

32%

See last page
for 1996 Survey

Lunch: Every day, 11 A.M.–3:45 P.M.
Dinner: Every day, 4 P.M. until park closing

Setting & atmosphere: A meal at the 50's Prime Time Cafe is like eating a meal in your own kitchen, 50's style. Pastel formica, gooseneck lamps, and black-and-white televisions, which run vintage sit-coms, are the rule.

House specialties: Meatloaf, pot roast, chicken, and other homey fare are featured. We get a lot of mail from readers who like the 50's Prime Time Cafe. Most say the food is good, the portions large, and that it is easy to find something the kids like. We, unfortunately, cannot concur in that opinion. By our evaluation the food is bland, more resembling the meals served in an elementary school cafeteria than in someone's home. The pot roast, for instance, is cooked by itself without the usual onions, potatoes, and carrots—it is served with mashed potatoes.

Entertainment & amenities: 50's sit-com clips on television.

Summary & comments: While we enjoy the ambience of the 50's Prime Time Cafe, and particularly like watching the old sit-coms, we cannot recommend having a meal there. Our suggestion for making the scene is to get late afternoon or evening reservations and order only dessert.

Finn's Grill

Seafood ★ **Moderate**

Quality	Value
55	D

The Hilton, Walt Disney World Village
(407) 827-4000

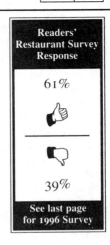

Readers'
Restaurant Survey
Response

61%

39%

See last page
for 1996 Survey

   Customers: Unsuspecting hotel guests
   Reservations: Not necessary
   When to go: Anytime
   Entree range: $10.95–21.95
   Payment: VISA, MC, AMEX, DC, D
   Service rating: ★
   Friendliness rating: ★★
   Parking: Valet or hotel lot
   Bar: Full service
   Wine selection: Fair
   Dress: Casual
   Disabled access: Yes

Dinner: Every day, 5:30–11 P.M.

Setting & atmosphere: Walls are painted with the bright colors of the sea and are decorated with stylized fish fins, sort of abstract abalone. The oyster bar area is decorated with crab and lobster traps. Staff members wear silly fish hats that seem to denote some staffing hierarchy. The menu is fraught with puns on the word Finn, such as finn-omenal, finn-icky, and finn-tastic.

House specialties: Fresh fish, including snapper, salmon, and swordfish depending on availability, prepared blackened or grilled. Other items include shrimp scampi served with herb butter over yellow rice; Finn's gumbo, with shrimp, crabmeat, chicken and sausage; and a number of pasta dishes.

Other recommendations: Alaskan king crab legs, steamed Maine lobster, fresh oysters, stone crab claws, or shrimp.

Summary & comments: Someone spent an awful lot of time coming up with pleasing decor and a nice collection of dishes that accompany some of Florida's finest seafood. Unfortunately, the rest of the time was spent on clever puns, leaving no time to train the staff on even the most rudimentary service skills. Most of the food is acceptable, but only acceptable; service this poor at a hotel this large is not. Might not be bad for a bucket of steamers and a few cold beers.

Fireworks Factory

Quality	Value
89	**C**

Seafood and Barbecue   ★★★½   **Moderate**

Pleasure Island
(407) 934-8989

Customers: Theme park guests
Reservations: Not necessary
When to go: Anytime
Entree range: $13.95–23.95
Payment: VISA, MC, AMEX
Service rating: ★★★
Friendliness rating: ★★★★
Parking: Valet parking or self-park
Bar: Full bar
Wine selection: Fair
Dress: Casual
Disabled access: Yes

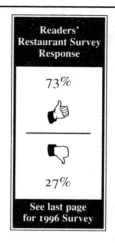

Readers'
Restaurant Survey
Response

73%

27%

See last page
for 1996 Survey

Lunch & dinner: Every day, 11:30 A.M.–11 P.M.;
open for snacks and light dinner, 11 P.M.–3 A.M.

Setting & atmosphere: Part of the legend of Merriweather Pleasure and his Pleasure Island, this restaurant is a huge fireworks warehouse where a terrible accident occurred after Pleasure got too close with a cigar, hence the crumbled brick walls and scorch marks. The brick and the high ceilings make this a pretty noisy restaurant. And even after the accident a smoking section is available.

House specialties: Executive chef Ron Pollack recently introduced a new menu that gets away from a rather bland barbecue style yet still sticks to the theme. You'll find such things as mesquite smoked chicken, smoked chicken pasta, seared sea scallops, and a "firecracker platter" featuring a half-pound of Dungeness crab clusters, a slab of babyback ribs, and a quarter chicken, served with sweet corn and baked potato. Seafood is given special attention here. The oak-roasted salmon, served with tomato-corn relish, is a good bet.

Other recommendations: Fire-roasted duck skewer appetizer, rock shrimp quesadilla.

Entertainment & amenities: Lots of loud music; good people-watching.

Summary & comments: It may be a fireworks factory but the food doesn't get a lot of "oohs" and "ahs," although the chef has a special flair for seafood. The beer list is commendable—and the view from the men's room is a hoot (you'd have to be there). This restaurant is owned and operated by the Levy Restaurants of Chicago.

Flagler's

Italian ★★★ **Moderate**

Quality	Value
79	D

Disney's Grand Floridian Beach Resort
(407) 824-1696

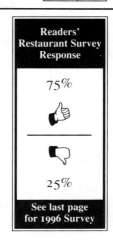

Readers' Restaurant Survey Response

75%

———

25%

See last page for 1996 Survey

    Customers: Hotel guests
    Reservations: Recommended
    When to go: Early or late evening
    Entree range: $19–44
    Payment: VISA, MC, AMEX
    Service rating: ★★★
    Friendliness rating: ★★★
    Parking: Valet (self-parking is
      deceptively far away)
    Bar: Full service
    Wine selection: Heavy on Italian selections
    Dress: Casual
    Disabled access: Yes

Dinner: Every day, 5:30–10 P.M.

Setting & atmosphere: The elegant decor reflects the hotel's turn-of-the-century flavor. Windows offer a view of the Grand Floridian's marina.

House specialties: Even though the hotel is decorated as a turn-of-the-century Florida resort, Flagler's is a not-so-thinly disguised Italian restaurant. Hot and cold antipasti include thinly sliced raw beef carpaccio, fresh mozzarella with sliced tomatoes and basil, deep-fried squid served with marinara sauce, and baked clams. Entrees include osso buco Milanese, breaded veal scallopine, sautéed snapper with sun-dried tomatoes and lobster sauce, and veal saltimbocca with fresh basil, mozzarella cheese, and prosciutto.

Other recommendations: Pasta dishes include penne with pancetta, onion, and basil, spaghetti with meatballs and marinara sauce, and lasagna alla Bolognese.

Entertainment & amenities: Singing waiters.

Summary & comments: The food is good, but be prepared to pay dearly for it. The restaurant is named for Henry Flagler, who helped Rockefeller found Standard Oil Co. He is sometimes referred to as a "robber baron." With $18.50 for a plate of spaghetti with meatballs are you surprised?

The Garden Grill
Restaurant

Quality	Value
79	**C**

American   ★★½   **Moderate**

The Land, Future World, EPCOT Center
(407) 939-3463

   Customers: Theme park guests
   Reservations: Recommended
   When to go: Anytime
   Entree range: $9.95–15.50
   Payment: VISA, MC, AMEX
   Service rating: ★★★
   Friendliness rating: ★★★★
   Parking: EPCOT lot
   Bar: Full service
   Wine selection: Fair
   Dress: Casual
   Disabled access: Yes

Lunch & dinner: 11:30 A.M. until park closing

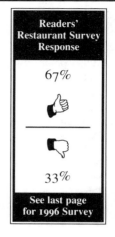

Readers'
Restaurant Survey
Response

67%

33%

See last page
for 1996 Survey

Setting & atmosphere: The Garden Grill is a revolving restaurant, but unlike the ones found at the top of high-rise hotels in large cities, this one is found at ground level and it doesn't even have windows. Instead the booths rotate past the various scenes of the Living with the Land boat ride. Although diners can't see the boats, they can see a rain forest and a prairie, among others. When you're not looking at the scenes of the rain forest, you'll see brightly painted murals of sunflower fields.

House specialties: The restaurant recently switched from an a la carte menu to a rather limited all-you-can-eat concept of fried chicken and barbecued ribs, which are brought to the table on large platters and served "family style." Accoutrements include salad, bread, and potatoes.

Entertainment & amenities: The view.

Summary & comments: You can bet the vegetables are fresh—many of them are grown in the EPCOT experimental farms seen on the pavilion's boat ride. And the lettuce is hydroponically grown. But most of the food is pretty mediocre—not a good thing in a restaurant that moves.

Garden Grove Cafe

American ★★ **Expensive**

Quality	Value
67	**D**

Walt Disney World Swan
(407) 934-3000

    Customers: Hotel guests
    Reservations: Recommended
    When to go: Lunch
    Entree range: lunch, $5.95–11.95;
      dinner, $13–25
    Payment: VISA, MC, AMEX, DC, D
    Service rating: ★★
    Friendliness rating: ★★
    Parking: Hotel lot
    Bar: Full service
    Wine selection: Good
    Dress: Casual
    Disabled access: Yes

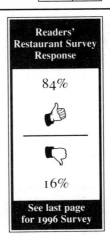

Readers'
Restaurant Survey
Response

84%

16%

See last page
for 1996 Survey

Breakfast & lunch: Every day, 8 A.M.–2 P.M.
Dinner: Every day, 6–10 P.M.

Setting & atmosphere: A large greenhouse-like rotunda with tall palm trees and parrot figures attached to street lamps. Faux stone tabletops are set with peach placemats and napkins.

House specialties: Lunch sandwiches include Italian sub, chicken salad, French dip, and grilled salmon BLT. Evening appetizers are uninspired. Entrees include steaks, such as New York strip, filet mignon with béarnaise sauce, and 18-ounce porterhouse. Prime rib, swordfish, salmon, and snapper are also available. Dinners include Caesar salad tossed tableside, Italian bread with herb butter and rice, steak fries, or baked potato. Vegetables are extra.

Entertainment & amenities: Character breakfasts Wednesdays and Saturdays

Summary & comments: There is only one item on the evening menu under $21 (yep, you guessed it, the chicken breast), and none of the food is worth the inflated pricing. Eat here in a pinch, or take advantage of the late hours; otherwise there is better food and friendlier service nearby.

Grand Floridian Cafe

American   ★★   **Moderate**

Quality	Value
68	D

Disney's Grand Floridian Beach Resort
(407) 824-2496

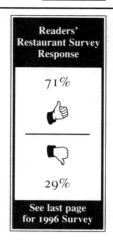

Readers'
Restaurant Survey
Response

71%

29%

**See last page
for 1996 Survey**

Customers: Hotel guests
Reservations: Not required
When to go: Breakfast or late evening
Entree range: $10.45–23.15
Payment: VISA, MC, AMEX
Service rating: ★★
Friendliness rating: ★★★
Parking: Valet; self-parking is deceptively
far away
Bar: Full service
Wine selection: Very good
Dress: Casual
Disabled access: Yes

Breakfast: Every day, 7–11 A.M.
Lunch & dinner: Every day, noon–11 P.M.

Setting & atmosphere: The large dining room, with high ceilings and decorative windows, looks out on the hotel's pool and center courtyard.

House specialties: Breakfasts include eggs prepared just about every way known to mankind, including omelets, fritatas, and huevos rancheros. Dinnertime appetizers are fairly pedestrian, including fried mozzarella cheese and chicken wings. Entrees have a Southern accent with items such as fried chicken (battered and deep-fried) served with mashed potatoes and gravy (of course), roast prime rib of beef with garlic and pan drippings, deep-fried cornmeal-battered catfish, seafood "waterzooi" stew with fresh fish, scallops, shrimp, and rice.

Other recommendations: If fried Southern cooking and beef with pan drippings aren't on your diet this decade, GFC offers a good selection of nutritional lighter meals, including fruit plate, vegetable lasagna, turkey burger, and smoked fish platter.

Summary & comments: The impersonal service detracts from the overall quality. Try it for breakfast or for a burger after the parks close.

Harry's Safari Bar and Grill

Steak/Seafood ★★★ **Expensive**

Quality	Value
81	D

Walt Disney World Dolphin
(407) 934-4000, ext. 6155

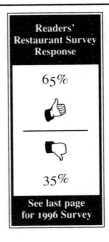

Readers'
Restaurant Survey
Response

65%

35%

See last page
for 1996 Survey

Customers: Hotel guests
Reservations: Recommended
When to go: Early dinner
Entree range: $21–35
Payment: VISA, MC, AMEX, DC, D
Service rating: ★★
Friendliness rating: ★
Parking: Hotel lot
Bar: Full service
Wine selection: Good
Dress: Casual
Disabled access: Yes

Dinner: Every day, 6–11 P.M.

Setting & atmosphere: A jungle atmosphere with huge stuffed animals sitting around on the floor. Waiters will often plop a hairy gorilla into an empty seat to fill up a table.

House specialties: The food here is extraordinarily expensive but the quality doesn't warrant the high price. Appetizers include crab cakes, tiger shrimp, spring rolls stuffed with a mixture of alligator and kangaroo meat, and escargot. Entrees feature broiled South American lobster tail and filet mignon, roast duck, and prime rib.

Other recommendations: Mahi mahi, salmon, tuna, or swordfish prepared to request, either plank-roasted; pan-grilled with pistachios, pecans, and citrus; or jerk-blackened.

Summary & comments: The staff spends more time making the stuffed animals comfortable than making the guests comfortable. The food, though good, is terribly expensive. The prices are given in U.S. dollars and English pounds, ostensibly to fit in with Harry's "legend" (you can't have a restaurant here without a legend), which claims Harry grew up in Great Britain before heading to Africa to become an explorer. Oh, please.

Hollywood & Vine
Cafeteria

Quality	Value
84	B

American ★★★ **Inexpensive**

Disney-MGM Studios
(407) 939-3463

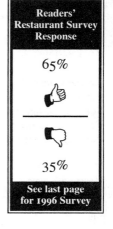

Readers' Restaurant Survey Response

65% 👍

35% 👎

See last page for 1996 Survey

    Customers: Theme park guests
    Reservations: Not accepted
    When to go: Lunch
    Entree range: lunch, $5.50–11.75; dinner buffet:
      $9.95 adults; $4.95 ages 3 to 9
    Payment: AMEX, MC, VISA
    Service rating: ★★★
    Friendliness rating: ★★★★
    Parking: Theme park lot
    Bar: Full service
    Wine selection: Limited
    Dress: Theme park casual
    Disabled access: Yes

Breakfast: Every day, 8:30–11 A.M.
Lunch: Every day, 11 A.M.–4 P.M.
Dinner: Every day (during peak seasons), 4 P.M. until park closes

Setting & atmosphere: Large Art Deco-style cafeteria with tile floors and lots of chrome. The opposing walls are decorated with huge murals that resemble old postcards with vintage scenes of old Hollywood and other California landmarks.

House specialties: Grilled chicken, barbecued ribs, pasta stuffed with cheese and a tomato herb sauce, Cahuenga chicken (rotisserie chicken with rice), spaghetti with meatballs, beef tips served over rice with a mushroom gravy.

Other recommendations: Chef salad.

Summary & comments: If you feel the need to stuff yourself after walking around the park all day, try the all-you-can-eat buffet for dinner. Otherwise a piece of chicken for lunch is plenty. Be prepared for lots of noise—with all the glass, tile, and chrome, the noise echoes for days.

The Hollywood Brown Derby

American   ★★★   **Expensive**

Quality	Value
84	C

Disney-MGM Studios, Hollywood Boulevard
(407) 939-3463

Customers: Theme park guests
Reservations: Recommended
When to go: Early evening
Entree range: $15.25–29.95
Payment: VISA, MC, AMEX
Service rating: ★★★★
Friendliness rating: ★★★★
Parking: Park lot
Bar: Full service
Wine selection: Very good
Dress: Casual
Disabled access: Yes

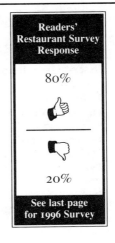

Readers'
Restaurant Survey
Response

80%

20%

See last page
for 1996 Survey

Lunch: Every day, 11 A.M.–3:15 P.M.
Dinner: Every day, 4:30 P.M. until park closes

Setting & atmosphere: A replica of the original Brown Derby restaurant (not the one shaped like a derby) in California, including duplicates of the celebrity caricatures that cover the paneled walls. An elegant sunken dining room with curved booths, tables draped with yards of white linen, and romantic shaded candles. Tall palm trees in huge pots stand in the center of the room and reach for the high ceiling. Waiters wear white jackets and are better dressed than most of the park guests.

House specialties: Cobb salad (a Brown Derby creation named for Bob Cobb, not Lee J.), baked grouper (battered and topped with meuniere butter and served over pasta), sautéed veal.

Other recommendations: Fettucine Derby (pasta with parmesan sauce with a choice of shrimp or chicken), grilled steaks, rack of lamb, beef stroganoff, mixed grill.

Summary & comments: The decor is so perfect you'll feel as though you're in 1930s Hollywood. In fact it is so elegant that it is a shame it is located in a theme park full of T-shirted guests. Everyone should really dress in white ties and long chiffon gowns and do their best Fred Astaire and Ginger Rogers impersonations. Don't expect to see any real stars dining in the next booth, however. There is outdoor dining available, but it is much better to sit inside here.

Juan & Only's
Bar and Jail

Tex-Mex ★★★ **Moderate**

Quality	Value
80	**B**

Walt Disney World Dolphin
(407) 934-4000

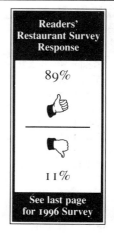

Readers'
Restaurant Survey
Response

89%

11%

See last page
for 1996 Survey

    Customers: Hotel guests
    Reservations: Recommended
    When to go: Anytime
    Entree range: $7.50–19.50
    Payment: VISA, MC, AMEX
    Service rating: ★★
    Friendliness rating: ★★★
    Parking: Complimentary valet
    Bar: Full service
    Wine selection: Fair
    Dress: Casual
    Disabled access: Yes

Dinner: Monday–Saturday, 5–11 p.m.

Setting & atmosphere: An upscale jail setting with iron bars and the usual stereotypical bric-a-brac that decorates most Tex-Mex restaurants. However, the designer wisely decided not to trash the interior, much of which is left over from the previous Italian tenant.

House specialties: Fajitas; chili rellenos; grilled chicken Yucatan; tortilla soup.

Other recommendations: Juan & Only's sampler, including poblano chili stuffed with chicken, beef taco, and cheese enchilada.

Summary & comments: This restaurant tries a little too hard to theme itself. The menu contains a lengthy description of Juan and his sidekick Only. Still the food is good, and if you like it hot and spicy, you won't be disappointed.

Kimonos

Quality	Value
90	**C**

Japanese   ★★★★   **Moderate**

Walt Disney World Swan
(407) 934-1621

   Customers: Hotel guests, locals
   Reservations: Accepted
   When to go: Anytime
   Payment: VISA, MC, AMEX, DC, Discover
   Service rating: ★★★★
   Friendliness rating: ★★★★
   Parking: Hotel lot
   Bar: Full service
   Wine selection: Very good
   Dress: Dressy casual
   Disabled access: Yes

Dinner: Every day, 5:30–11:45 P.M.

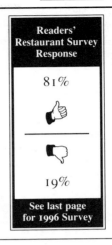

Readers'
Restaurant Survey
Response

81%

👍

👎

19%

See last page
for 1996 Survey

Setting & atmosphere: The decor consists of black lacquered tabletops and counters, tall pillars rising to bamboo rafters with rice-paper lanterns, and elegant kimonos that hang outstretched on the walls and between the dining sections. The chefs will greet you with a friendly welcome and you'll be offered a hot towel to clean your hands. Even if you're not in the mood for sushi, this is a delightful place to just sit and sip sake.

House specialties: Although sushi and sashimi are the focus, Kimonos also serves a number of hot appetizers, including tempura battered shrimp, fish, and vegetables; skewered chicken yakitori; beef teriyaki and gyoza; and steamed dumplings stuffed with a pork mixture. The crispy soft shell crab is wonderful.

Other recommendations: Yakitori, gyoza, beef teriyaki, tempura.

Summary & comments: The skill of the sushi artists is as much a joy to watch as is eating the wonderfully fresh creations. There are no full entrees here, just good sushi and appetizers. The Walt Disney World Swan is host to many Japanese tourists and you'll find many of them here on any given night. Enough said.

King Stefan's Banquet Hall

American　　　★½　　　**Moderate**

Quality	Value
65	D

Cinderella's Castle, Fantasyland, Magic Kingdom
(407) 939-3463

Customers: Theme park guests
Reservations: Required
When to go: Early
Entree range: $15–20
Payment: VISA, MC, AMEX
Service rating: ★★★
Friendliness rating: ★★★
Parking: Magic Kingdom lot
Bar: None
Wine selection: None
Dress: Casual
Disabled access: Limited

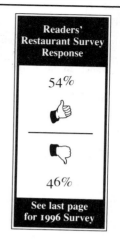

Readers'
Restaurant Survey
Response

54%

46%

See last page
for 1996 Survey

Lunch: Every day, 11:30 A.M.–3:30 P.M.
Dinner: Every day, 4:30 P.M. until park closes

Setting & atmosphere: A medieval banquet hall, appointed with the requisite banners and Round Table-like regalia, located on the second floor of Cinderella's Castle—windows look out over the park.

House specialties: Prime rib; steak; seafood.

Other recommendations: Grilled chicken; sandwiches; salads.

Entertainment & amenities: Cinderella makes appearances in the lobby.

Summary & comments: Although it has a fun decor and is one of the few full-service restaurants in the Magic Kingdom, the food in this banquet hall is not fit for a king. Many of the locals, including the folks who work in the theme park, have a number of pet names for this place, none of which are kind. Still this place fills up fast, so if you have your heart set on dining here, make the reservations desk one of your first stops when you arrive. One assumes that because this is Cinderella's Castle she must dine here herself. That may explain why she is so thin.

L'Originale Alfredo di
Roma Ristorante

Quality	Value
74	D

Italian ★★½ **Expensive**

Italy, World Showcase, EPCOT Center
(407) 939-3463

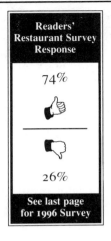

Readers'
Restaurant Survey
Response

74%

26%

See last page
for 1996 Survey

    Customers: Theme park guests
    Reservations: Required
    When to go: Midafternoon
    Entree range: $8.95–24.75
    Payment: VISA, MC, AMEX
    Service rating: ★★★★
    Friendliness rating: ★★★★
    Parking: EPCOT lot
    Bar: Beer and wine only
    Wine selection: All Italian
    Dress: Casual
    Disabled access: Yes

Lunch: Every day, noon–4 P.M.
Dinner: Every day, 4 P.M. until park closes

Setting & atmosphere: The elegant—some would say garish—Roman decor features huge murals of an Italian piazza along the wall behind the upholstered banquettes. Dark woods and latticework on the high ceilings add to a sumptuous atmosphere. It is, however, a noisy dining room, one that is nearly always filled. This is yet another location for the so-called famous restaurant of the inventor of fettucine Alfredo, the favorite dining spot of Mary Pickford and Douglas Fairbanks.

House specialties: Fettucine Alfredo (what else?); pasta e fagioli; linguine al pesto; vitello alla Milanese.

Other recommendations: Pollo alla Milanese; pollo alla parmigiana; roasted lamb chop.

Entertainment & amenities: Strolling opera singers at dinner.

Summary & comments: Although the word "original" appears in the name, the food is a little worn and old. (So what did Mary Pickford and Douglas Fairbanks know about restaurants?) Most of the entrees are heavy and will have you plodding the rest of the way through the park.

Liberty Tree Tavern

American ★★½ **Moderate/Expensive**

Quality	Value
74	**D**

Liberty Square, Magic Kingdom
(407) 939-3463

Customers: Theme park guests
Reservations: Suggested
When to go: Anytime
Entree range: $9–14, lunch; $10–20, dinner
Payment: VISA, MC, AMEX
Service rating: ★★★½
Friendliness rating: ★★★★
Parking: Magic Kingdom lot
Bar: None
Wine selection: None
Dress: Theme park casual
Disabled access: Yes

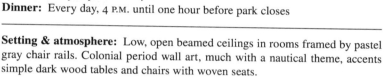

Readers'
Restaurant Survey
Response

77%

👍

👎

23%

See last page
for 1996 Survey

Lunch: Every day, 11 A.M.–4 P.M.
Dinner: Every day, 4 P.M. until one hour before park closes

Setting & atmosphere: Low, open beamed ceilings in rooms framed by pastel gray chair rails. Colonial period wall art, much with a nautical theme, accents simple dark wood tables and chairs with woven seats.

House specialties: Prime rib; roast turkey; chicken breast with Virginia ham; shrimp with spinach linguini; braised beef in Burgundy wine.

Other recommendations: Sandwiches and salads are good here.

Summary & comments: Though the Liberty Tree is the best of the Magic Kingdom's full-service resturants, it is often overlooked at lunch. A good plan is to make a reservation at the Liberty Tree about an hour or so before parade time. After you eat, you can walk right out and watch the parade.

Mama Melrose's Ristorante Italiano

Italian ★★½ **Expensive**

Quality	Value
74	D

Disney-MGM Studios
(407) 939-3463

Customers: Theme park guests
Reservations: Suggested
When to go: Anytime
Entree range: $8–16, lunch; $10–25, dinner
Payment: VISA, MC, AMEX
Service rating: ★★★★
Friendliness rating: ★★★★
Parking: Disney-MGM lot
Bar: Full service
Wine selection: Limited
Dress: Theme park casual
Disabled access: Yes

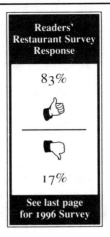

Readers'
Restaurant Survey
Response

83%

17%

See last page
for 1996 Survey

Lunch: Every day, 11 A.M.–3:45 P.M.
Dinner: Every day, 4 P.M. until one hour before park closes

Setting & atmosphere: Mama Melrose's looks like a big-city neighborhood restaurant of the 30s, with bare wooden floors, red- and-white checkered table-cloths, red vinyl booths, and grape vines hanging from the rafters. By far the most relaxing restaurant at the Disney-MGM Studios, Mama Melrose's sports a worn, ethnic look that is as comfortable as an old sweatshirt.

House specialties: Pasta and seafood combos are excellent, as are salads and some of the designer pizzas. Bread is served in the traditional style with olive oil.

Other recommendations: Veal parmesan served with pasta, vegetable lasagna, chicken marsala.

Summary & comments: Because of its out-of-the-way location, you can some-times just walk into Mama Melrose's, especially in the evening.

Monorail Buffet

American   ★★★

Quality	Value
	B

Disney's Contemporary Resort

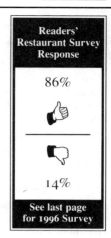

Readers'
Restaurant Survey
Response

86%

14%

See last page
for 1996 Survey

   Customers: Hotel guests
   Reservations: Not required
   When to go: Anytime
   Entree range: Breakfast, $12.95; dinner, $14.95
   Payment: VISA, MC, AMEX
   Service rating: ★★★★
   Friendliness rating: ★★★★
   Parking: Complimentary valet
   Bar: Full service
   Wine selection: Limited
   Dress: Casual
   Disabled access: Yes

Breakfast: Every day, 7:30–11:30 A.M.
Dinner: Every day, 5–10 P.M.

Setting & atmosphere: Monorail Buffet replaces Contemporary Cafe, the last of the resort's restaurants to undergo contemporizing. It is designed to highlight what has always been the hotel's greatest claim to fame: the monorails that pass through the grand atrium. The decor has a Tomorrowland feel with futuristic canopies over the buffet and modernistic mouse ear designs. The buffet is a state-of-the-art granite serving line. The children's buffet is set lower so kids can help themselves.

House specialties: While a buffet isn't much of an update in design, the way it is presented will be. The new design promises no chafing dishes. All hot foods will be presented in special casseroles and the line will feature cooking stations so chefs may prepare food to order. The menu will change according to the season, but may include such items as chicken pot pie, meat loaf, and carving stations featuring turkey, ham, or roast beef. There will also be a salad station and circular dessert table with a five-tier pie stand.

Summary & comments: The Monorail Buffet is tentatively scheduled to open in late 1995 or early 1996. Ratings are based on the Contemporary Cafe buffet, the Monorail Buffet's immediate predecessor in the same facility.

Narcoossee's

Steak/Seafood   ★★★★   **Expensive**

Quality	Value
91	**D**

Disney's Grand Floridian Beach Resort
(407) 939-3463

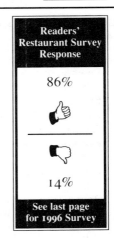

Readers'
Restaurant Survey
Response

86%

14%

See last page
for 1996 Survey

Customers: Hotel guests, locals
Reservations: Recommended
When to go: Early evening
Entree range: $14.95–49.95
Payment: VISA, MC, AMEX
Service rating: ★★★★
Friendliness rating: ★★★★
Parking: Valet; self-parking is
deceptively far away.
Bar: Full service
Wine selection: Good
Dress: Casual
Disabled access: Yes

Lunch: Every day, 11:30 A.M.–3 P.M.
Dinner: Every day, 5–10 P.M.

Setting & atmosphere: Part of the Grand Floridian Beach Resort complex, Narcoossee's is a free-standing octagonal building at the edge of Seven Seas Lagoon. It offers a great view of the Magic Kingdom and the boats that dock nearby to pick guests up and drop them off after a day at the park. The lack of carpeting and tablecloths, and the high noise level, belie the fine dining aspect.

House specialties: The food is surprisingly good, with such items as lamb chops served on an eggplant crouton; fresh fish, such as grouper with brown butter; swordfish marinated in hazelnut oil.

Other recommendations: Farm-raised gator steak (if you really must), grilled swordfish, lamb chops.

Summary & comments: Although it is expensive, Narcoossee's is one of Disney's best kept dining secrets. Many locals make the trip out here just to have dinner, but not unless they have reservations. Waits of up to two hours are not unusual. When the kitchen is hitting its mark the food is exceptionally good, but the atmosphere, which often features children running freely about, can spoil a forty-dollar steak. Do not under any circumstances order the gator steak. There is a reason those animals have survived millions of years—they are not worth eating.

Nine Dragons Restaurant

Quality	Value
74	F

Chinese   ★★½   **Expensive**

China, World Showcase, EPCOT Center
(407) 939-3463

Customers: Theme park guests
Reservations: Suggested
When to go: Anytime
Entree range: $9–18, lunch; $10–23, dinner
Payment: VISA, MC, AMEX
Service rating: ★★½
Friendliness rating: ★★★½
Parking: EPCOT lot
Bar: Full service
Wine selection: Limited
Dress: Theme park casual
Disabled access: Yes

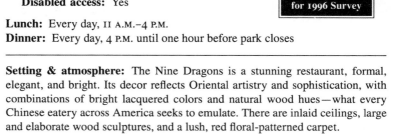

Readers'
Restaurant Survey
Response

50%

50%

See last page
for 1996 Survey

Lunch: Every day, 11 A.M.–4 P.M.
Dinner: Every day, 4 P.M. until one hour before park closes

Setting & atmosphere: The Nine Dragons is a stunning restaurant, formal, elegant, and bright. Its decor reflects Oriental artistry and sophistication, with combinations of bright lacquered colors and natural wood hues—what every Chinese eatery across America seeks to emulate. There are inlaid ceilings, large and elaborate wood sculptures, and a lush, red floral-patterned carpet.

House specialties: The Nine Dragons fare, unfortunately, does not live up to its decor. The limited menu features the same tired sweet and sour pork, beef with broccoli, and moo goo gai pan that you can buy for one-third the price at your own neighborhood Chinese restaurant.

Summary & comments: This should be one of the best Chinese restaurants in the United States, but it's not. The lack of a creative menu, along with assembly-line preparation and service, makes Nine Dragons a lost opportunity at best, and an overpriced tourist trap at worst. For better Chinese food at Walt Disney World, try Sum Chows at the Walt Disney World Dolphin.

'Ohana

	Quality	Value
	79	C

Polynesian ★★★ **Moderate**

Polynesian Resort Hotel
(407) 824-2000

Customers: Resort guests
Reservations: Recommended
When to go: Anytime
Entree range: $19.50, adults; $13,
  juniors; $8, children
Payment: VISA, MC, AMEX
Service rating: ★★★
Friendliness rating: ★★★★
Parking: Hotel lot
Bar: Full service
Wine selection: Limited
Dress: Casual
Disabled access: Yes

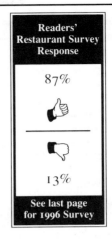

Readers'
Restaurant Survey
Response

87%

13%

See last page
for 1996 Survey

Breakfast: Every day, 7:30–11 A.M.
Dinner: Every day, 4:30–10 P.M.

Setting & atmosphere: This restaurant replaces the Papeete Bay Verandah. A large open pit is the centerpiece of the room. Here the grilled foods are prepared with a flare—literally. From time to time the chef will pour some liquid on the fire, causing huge flames to shoot up. This is usually in response to something one of the strolling entertainers has said, evoking a sign from the fire gods. At any given moment there may be a hula hoop contest or a coconut race, where the children in the dining room are invited to push coconuts around the dining room with broomsticks.

House specialties: Skewer service is the specialty here. There is no menu. As soon as you are seated, your server will begin to deliver food. First a couple of sausages, which are portioned off from long skewers right onto the diner's plate. These are followed by smoked turkey, beef and spareribs, then huge shrimp. These are accompanied by assorted salads, placed on a lazy susan in the center of the table, along with pot sticker dumplings and teriyaki noodles.

Entertainment & amenities: Strolling singers; games.

Summary & comments: 'Ohana, which means family, is a fun place. The food is good, but not superior. The method of service and the fact that it just keeps coming make it all taste a little better. Insist on being seated in the main dining room, where the fire pit is located. There are tables around the back, but you can't see what's going on from back there.

Olivia's Cafe

Quality	Value
81	C

American   ★★★   **Moderate**

Disney's Vacation Club
(407) 827-7700

**Readers'
Restaurant Survey
Response**

69%

👍

👎

31%

**See last page
for 1996 Survey**

    Customers: Resort guests
    Reservations: Not required
    When to go: Lunch
    Entree range: $8.95–14.95
    Payment: VISA, MC, AMEX
    Service rating: ★★★★
    Friendliness rating: ★★★★
    Parking: Hotel lot
    Bar: Full service
    Wine selection: Limited
    Dress: Casual
    Disabled access: Yes

Breakfast: Every day, 7:30–10:30 A.M.
Lunch: Every day, 11 A.M.–2 P.M.
Dinner: Every day, 5–10 P.M.

Setting & atmosphere: This is Disney's idea of Key West, with lots of pastels and rough wood siding on the walls, mosaic tile floors, potted palms and tropical trees in the center of the room and plenty of nautical gewgaws, including vintage photos of Key West and its inhabitants of long ago. (Key West is nothing like this.) There is some outside seating, which looks out over the waterway. Tile, wood siding, and no tablecloths add up to a very noisy dining room.

House specialties: Appetizers include conch fritters, seafood nachos, and guacamole and chips. Entrees feature prime rib, breaded and deep-fried Gulf shrimp, fresh fish grilled with fresh spices, and fried chicken with mashed potatoes and gravy. Many of the dishes are accompanied by what is referred to as real Cuban-style black beans and rice, but these beans would look pretty Americanized to anyone from Havana.

Other recommendations: Turkey pot pie; fried chicken; country-fried steak.

Summary & comments: Though perhaps not Key West, the charming atmosphere and low-key pace make the food taste even better than it already is. Not wonderful, just nice. The servers are upbeat and move with alarming speed, though food tends to come out of the kitchen at a more Key Westerly pace (slowly).

The Outback

Steak ★★ **Expensive**

Quality	Value
67	D

Buena Vista Palace, Walt Disney World Village
(407) 827-2727

Customers: Tourists, locals
Reservations: Recommended
When to go: Very early lunch or dinner
Entree range: $12.95–32.95
Payment: VISA, MC, AMEX
Service rating: ★
Friendliness rating: ★
Parking: Complimentary valet parking
  at the rear of the hotel
Bar: Full service
Wine selection: Excellent
Dress: Casual
Disabled access: Yes

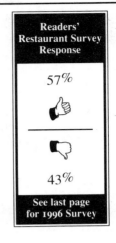

Readers'
Restaurant Survey
Response

57%

43%

See last page
for 1996 Survey

Dinner: 5:30–11 P.M.

Setting & atmosphere: A large open room with two-story ceiling and a cascading waterfall. Servers are in Australian bush outfits. That and the menu printed on a boomerang are supposed to make it an Australian restaurant, though the bulk of the menu is what you'd find in just about any American restaurant.

House specialties: There aren't many places where you can get kangaroo steak and rattlesnake salad, but you can here if you really want it. Otherwise there is filet mignon with béarnaise sauce, rack of spring lamb, grilled tuna, prime rib.

Other recommendations: Six-pound live Maine lobster.

Summary & comments: For some reason that no one bothers to explain, dinner rolls are delivered to the table at the end of long poles. Staff members tend to treat guests as though they'll never be back. The food isn't good enough to put up with rude service. This is not part of the Outback Steakhouse national chain.

Palio

Italian ★★★ **Moderate**

Quality	Value
81	**C**

Walt Disney World Swan
(407) 934-3000

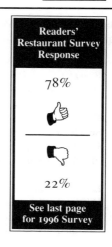

Readers' Restaurant Survey Response

78%

22%

See last page for 1996 Survey

Customers: Hotel guests
Reservations: Recommended
When to go: Anytime
Entree range: $9.95–25.50
Payment: VISA, MC, AMEX, DC, D
Service rating: ★★★
Friendliness rating: ★★★
Parking: Hotel lot
Bar: Full service
Wine selection: Very good
Dress: Casual
Disabled access: Yes

Dinner: Every day, 6–11 P.M.

Setting & atmosphere: The name means banner, and they're hanging all over this upscale Italian trattoria and are even draped over the tables. It is a pretty place and bustles with excitement and the sounds of happy diners. Like just about everything else in the hotel, designer Michael Graves had a hand in the decor and design of the restaurant, and it shows. It is a beautiful place.

House specialties: Veal alla lemone, a scallopine served with lemon butter and linguine; saltimbocca alla Romana, veal medallions topped with prosciutto and sage, served with risotto; and osso buco alla Milanese, veal shank braised in white wine and vegetable stock, served with saffron risotto.

Other recommendations: Veal picante alla marsala; sautéed chicken breast with tomato; red snapper with sautéed fennel.

Summary & comments: The food isn't bad and the experience is satisfying overall, but there are more exciting dining options available. The roasted garlic spread served with the hot bread is nice. Fill up on that and then order one of the reasonably priced pizzas.

Planet Hollywood

American ★★★½ **Moderate**

Quality	Value
87	C

Pleasure Island
(407) 827-7827

Customers: Tourists, locals
Reservations: Not accepted
When to go: Late lunch
Entree range: $7.50–16.95
Payment: VISA, MC, AMEX
Service rating: ★★★★
Friendliness rating: ★★
Parking: Pleasure Island lot
Bar: Full service
Wine selection: Limited
Dress: Casual
Disabled access: Yes

Lunch & dinner:

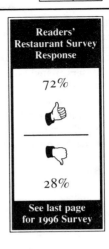

Readers'
Restaurant Survey
Response

72%

28%

See last page
for 1996 Survey

Setting & atmosphere: A large planet-shaped structure "floating" in the lagoon next to Pleasure Island. Planet Hollywood's decor is something of a movie museum with memorabilia from famous movies. These items are easy to come by since Sylvester Stallone, Arnold Schwarzenegger, Bruce Willis, and other actors are partners in the restaurant. Orlando is world headquarters for the chain and the hometown restaurant is really a special structure. Still, the artifacts leave something to be desired. New York's Planet has Judy Garland's ruby slippers; Orlando's has the gilded potty seat from "The Last Emperor."

House specialties: The menu is all over the place with pasta dishes, fajitas, burgers, dinner salads, and pizzas. The burgers are huge (the bleu cheese burger is wonderful), and the creole pizza—with mustard and red sauce topped with blackened shrimp, andouille sausage, and chicken—is delicious. Desserts are incredible, especially the white chocolate bread pudding.

Other recommendations: Chicken fajitas; linguini and sausage pasta; grilled swordfish.

Summary & comments: Because of its star power, Planet Hollywood attracts a lot of people. But even with the never-ending stream of guests, the kitchen doesn't slack off. The food is good and well thought out. And while $7.50 may seem like a lot of money for a burger, you'll get a thick, juicy patty, cooked the way you want it, with fries. And to give you an idea of the restaurant's attention to details, the potatoes for the fries are stored on the premises until the proper amount of sweetness from aging is achieved.

Portobello Yacht Club

Italian ★★★½ **Expensive**

Quality	Value
88	**D**

Pleasure Island
(407) 934-8888

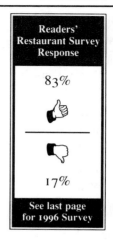

Customers: Tourists, locals
Reservations: Recommended
When to go: Anytime
Entree range: $12.95–22.95
Payment: VISA, MC, AMEX
Service rating: ★★★★
Friendliness rating: ★★★★
Parking: Pleasure Island lot
Bar: Full service
Wine selection: Very good; heavy on Italian selections
Dress: Casual
Disabled access: Yes

Readers'
Restaurant Survey
Response

83%

17%

See last page
for 1996 Survey

Lunch: Every day, 11:30 A.M.–4 P.M.
Dinner: Every day, 4 P.M.–midnight

Setting & atmosphere: This restaurant sports an upscale nautical theme with lots of polished brass, dark woods, and canvas window coverings. There is a patio overlooking the lagoon for those days with low humidity.

House specialties: Northern Italian cuisine; breaded veal ribeye; charcoal-grilled shrimp on a rosemary skewer; boneless half chicken marinated in olive oil, garlic, and fresh rosemary.

Other recommendations: Crispy thin-crust pizza appetizers, including a vegetarian pizza with eggplant, zucchini, and mushrooms and a four-cheese pizza with sun-dried tomatoes. The butterfly pasta with fresh asparagus and snow peas is a good inexpensive selection.

Summary & comments: Tends to be overpriced, but one can make a meal of a pizza and pasta selection for under $20. Ask for the patio if it's a cool evening.

Restaurant Akershus

Quality	Value
89	**B**

Norwegian buffet   ★★★½   **Moderate**

Norway, World Showcase, EPCOT Center
(407) 939-3463

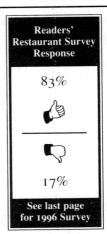

Readers'
Restaurant Survey
Response

83%

17%

See last page
for 1996 Survey

Customers: Theme park guests
Reservations: Required
When to go: Anytime
Entree range: Lunch: $12 adults, $5 kids;
    dinner: $17 adults, $8 kids
Payment: VISA, MC, AMEX
Service rating: ★★★
Friendliness rating: ★★★★
Parking: EPCOT lot
Bar: Full service
Wine selection: Limited
Dress: Theme park casual
Disabled access: Yes

Lunch: Every day, 11 A.M.–4 P.M.
Dinner: Every day, 4 P.M. until one hour before park closing

Setting & atmosphere: Modeled on a 14th-century fortress, Akershus entertains its guests in a great banquet hall under high A-framed ceilings and massive iron chandeliers. Stone arches divide the dining rooms. A red carpet alternates with patterned hardwood floors.

House specialties: A bountiful hot and cold buffet features salmon, herring, various Norwegian salads and cheeses, hearty stews, and a variety of hot fish and meats. Be sure to try the mashed rutabagas.

Other recommendations: Cold Rignes beer on tap.

Summary & comments: Akershus offers a unique introduction to delightful Scandinavian cuisines. The dishes may not be familiar, but the quality is superb, and the overall experience is a real adventure in dining. Akershus's popularity grows every year as word of its quality spreads. We think it's one of the better restaurants at Walt Disney World.

Restaurant Marrakesh

Quality	Value
81	C

Moroccan   ★★★   **Moderate**

Morocco, World Showcase, EPCOT Center
(407) 939-3463

Customers: Theme park guests
Reservations: Suggested
When to go: Anytime
Entree range: $12–26, lunch; $14–50, dinner
Payment: VISA, MC, AMEX
Service rating: ★★★
Friendliness rating: ★★★★
Parking: EPCOT lot
Bar: Full service
Wine selection: Limited
Dress: Theme park casual
Disabled access: Yes

Readers'
Restaurant Survey
Response

82%

👍

👎

18%

See last page
for 1996 Survey

Lunch: Every day, 11 A.M.–4 P.M.
Dinner: Every day, 4 P.M. until one hour before park closes

Setting & atmosphere: One of the more exotic World Showcase restaurants, Marrakesh re-creates a Moroccan palace with gleaming tile mosaics, high inlaid wood ceilings with open beams and brass chandeliers, and red Bukhara carpets.

House specialties: Start with bastilla (a minced chicken pie sprinkled with confectionary sugar), followed by cornish hen, tangine chicken, or roast lamb. Split an order of couscous. For some reason, beef kebabs are available, but the more traditional lamb kebabs are not.

Other recommendations: If you are hungry, curious, or both, go for one of the combination platters for two persons.

Entertainment & amenities: Moroccan band and belly dancing.

Summary & comments: Interesting fare that is almost impossible to find except in the largest U.S. cities. Unlike diners at most Moroccan restaurants, those at Marrakesh sit at tables (instead of on the floor) and eat with utensils rather than with their hands. Because Moroccan food is unfamiliar to most visitors, Marrakesh often has tables available for walk-ins.

Rose & Crown
Dining Room

Quality	Value
83	C

English ★★★ **Moderate**

United Kingdom, World Showcase, EPCOT Center
(407) 939-3463

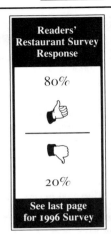

Readers' Restaurant Survey Response

80%

20%

See last page for 1996 Survey

Customers: Theme park guests
Reservations: Required
When to go: Anytime
Entree range: $8–12, lunch; $14–20, dinner
Payment: VISA, MC, AMEX
Service rating: ★★★★
Friendliness rating: ★★★★
Parking: EPCOT lot
Bar: Full bar with Bass ale and Guinness-Harp beer on tap
Wine selection: Limited
Dress: Theme park casual
Disabled access: Yes

Lunch: Every day, 11 A.M.–4 P.M.
Dinner: Every day, 4 P.M. until one hour before park closes

Setting & atmosphere: The Rose & Crown is both a pub and dining establishment. The traditional English pub has a large cozy bar with rich wood appointments and trim, beamed ceilings, and hardwood floor. The adjoining English country dining room is rustic and simple. Meals are served outdoors overlooking the Seven Seas Lagoon when the weather is nice.

House specialties: Hearty, but simple food; try fish and chips or the Welsh chicken and leek pie, washed down with Bass ale.

Other recommendations: Steak and kidney pie; cottage pie; sautéed Irish chicken; grilled lamb chop.

Summary & comments: You do not need reservations to stop and refresh yourself on a hot (or cold) afternoon at the friendly bar. The waitresses and barmaids are saucy in the best English tradition and add immeasurably to the experience. Unfortunately, the number of selections on the menu has been cut significantly since our last visit. The Rose & Crown is usually more popular at lunch than dinner. It is about the fifth EPCOT restaurant to book its seatings, owing more to its small size than its popularity.

San Angel Inn Restaurante

Mexican   ★★★   **Expensive**

Quality	Value
84	**D**

Mexico, World Showcase, EPCOT Center
(407) 939-3463

Customers: Theme park guests
Reservations: Required
When to go: Anytime
Entree range: $8–15, lunch; $13–26, dinner
Payment: VISA, MC, AMEX
Service rating: ★★★½
Friendliness rating: ★★★★
Parking: EPCOT lot
Bar: Full service
Wine selection: Limited
Dress: Theme park casual
Disabled access: Yes

Readers'
Restaurant Survey
Response

76%

👍

👎

24%

See last page
for 1996 Survey

Lunch: Every day, 11 A.M.–4 P.M.
Dinner: Every day, 4 P.M. until one hour before park closing

Setting & atmosphere: The San Angel Inn is inside the great Aztec pyramid of the Mexican pavilion. A romantically crafted open-air cantina, the restaurant overlooks both El Rio del Tiempo (the River of Time) and the bustling plaza of a small Mexican village.

House specialties: In addition to enchiladas, tacos, quesadillas, and other routine Mexican fare, San Angel Inn features mole poblano (chicken with an exotic sauce made from several kinds of peppers and unsweetened Mexican chocolate) and some interesting regional fish preparations.

Other recommendations: Blackened mahi mahi or poached red snapper.

Entertainment & amenities: Mariachi or marimba bands in the adjacent courtyard.

Summary & comments: The San Angel Inn serves good, sometimes excellent, Mexican food at prices much higher than you would find at most Mexican restaurants. The shrimp grilled with pepper sauce, for example, is five medium-sized shrip for the outrageous sum of $22 ($4.50 per shrimp!). The menu goes beyond normal Mexican selections, offering special and regional dishes that are difficult to find in the United States. If you go, we recommend you skip the tacos and try one of these more unique dishes.

Sci-Fi Dine-In Theater
Restaurant

Quality	Value
67	D

American   ★★   **Moderate**

Disney-MGM Studios
407) 939-3483

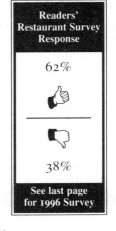

Readers'
Restaurant Survey
Response

62%

38%

See last page
for 1996 Survey

    Customers: Theme park guests
    Reservations: Required
    When to go: Anytime
    Entree range: $7–13, lunch; $11–20, dinner
    Payment: VISA, MC, AMEX
    Service rating: ★★★★★
    Friendliness rating: ★★★★★
    Parking: Disney-MGM park lot
    Bar: Beer and wine
    Wine selection: Limited
    Dress: Theme park casual
    Disabled access: Yes

Lunch: Every day, 11 A.M.–4 P.M.
Dinner: Every day, 4 P.M. until one hour before park closes

Setting & atmosphere: You sit in little cars in a large building where it is always night and watch vintage film clips on a drive-in movie screen as you eat. Free popcorn is served before your meal by waiters on roller skates.

House specialties: The fare consists of sandwiches, burgers, salads, and shakes, as well as fancier stuff like barbecued ribs, baked chicken, roast turkey, fried shrimp, and linguini with either veggies or seafood. While we think the food quality is way out of line with the cost, you can have an adequate meal at the Sci-Fi if you stick with simple fare.

Entertainment & amenities: Cartoons and clips of vintage horror and sci-fi movies are shown, such as *The Attack of the Fifty-foot Woman, Robot Monster,* and *Son of the Blob.* Also shown are lurid previews, proclaiming "See a sultry beauty in the clutches of a half-crazed monster!

Summary & comments: We recommend making a late afternoon or late evening reservation and ordering only dessert. In other words, think of the Sci-Fi as an attraction (which it is) as opposed to a good dining opportunity (which it is not). If you want to try the Sci-Fi Dine-In and do not have reservations, try walking in at 11 A.M. or around 3 P.M.

Sum Chows

Chinese ★★★★½ **Expensive**

Quality	Value
97	C

Walt Disney World Dolphin
(407) 934-4000 ext. 6150

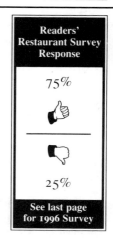

Readers' Restaurant Survey Response

75%

25%

See last page for 1996 Survey

Customers: Hotel guests, locals
Reservations: Recommended
When to go: Anytime
Entree range: $25–34
Payment: VISA, MC, AMEX, DC, D
Service rating: ★★★★
Friendliness rating: ★★★
Parking: Complimentary valet
Bar: Full service
Wine selection: Very good
Dress: Dressy, jackets not required
Disabled access: Yes

Dinner: Wednesday–Sunday, 6–10 P.M.

Setting & atmosphere: The restaurant's interior (as well as the plates and many of the utensils) was designed by Michael Graves, who also designed the Dolphin hotel. The decor has traditional Chinese influences but is modern and elegant. It is a dark room with lighting provided by high-intensity spotlights that focus on the Chinese artwork and stark flower arrangements. Tables are set with wooden chopsticks.

House specialties: Seared center loin of swordfish; medallions of beef with ginger shoots; rack of lamb with sesame crust.

Other recommendations: Honeycomb red snapper; shrimp with vegetables; pork tenderloin with sweet and sour sauce.

Summary & comments: This is not your typical Chinese restaurant; dinners are not served with a bowl of white rice and fortune cookies are not offered at the end of the meal. This is a fine-dining restaurant with the emphasis on *fine*. With advance reservations, your party can dine in the kitchen at the chef's table, where you can watch your meal—and everyone else's in the main dining room—being prepared in front of you. But for sheer elegance, stick to the dining room.

Tangaroa Terrace

American ★★ **Moderate**

Quality	Value
66	C

Disney's Polynesian Resort
(407) 824-1360

    Customers: Hotel guests
    Reservations: Recommended
    When to go: Breakfast
    Entree range: $12.95–20.95
    Payment: VISA, MC, AMEX
    Service rating: ★★
    Friendliness rating: ★★★
    Parking: Hotel lot; Magic Kingdom lot
    Bar: Full service
    Wine selection: Fair
    Dress: Casual
    Disabled access: Yes

> **Readers' Restaurant Survey Response**
>
> 33% 👍
>
> ———
>
> 👎 67%
>
> **See last page for 1996 Survey**

Breakfast: Every day, 7:30–11 A.M.
Dinner: Every day, 5–10 P.M.

Setting & atmosphere: Picture a Denny's done over in floral prints.

House specialties: Breakfast includes King Kamehameha's feast, with fresh salmon, three eggs cooked to order, pancakes, and choice of bacon, sausage, or ham. In the evening there is Queen Liliuokalani's buffet, with all-you-can-eat pasta, chicken, and salad. A la carte selections include surf and turf and snow crab legs.

Other recommendations: Roast prime rib of beef; shrimp and pasta fra diavolo; pizza. Steak and eggs and stuffed french toast for breakfast.

Summary & comments: O.K. for starting the day off, but there is much better food just a monorail ride away. And closer if you count 'Ohana in the resort's main building.

Tempura Kiku

Japanese   ★★★   Moderate

Quality	Value
83	C

Japan, World Showcase, EPCOT Center
(407) 939-3463

    Customers: Theme park guests
    Reservations: Not required
    When to go: Lunch
    Entree range: $14.50–21.95
    Payment: VISA, MC, AMEX
    Service rating: ★★★★
    Friendliness rating: ★★★
    Parking: EPCOT lot
    Bar: Full service
    Wine selection: Limited
    Dress: Theme park casual
    Disabled access: Yes

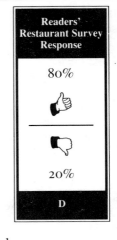

Readers'
Restaurant Survey
Response

80%

20%

D

Lunch: Every day, 11 A.M.–4 P.M.
Dinner: Every day, 4 P.M. until one hour before park closes

Setting & atmosphere: Tempura Kiku is a small (25-person) tempura bar where most patrons sit around the outside of a square counter. The setting is intimate, almost cramped, and very communal. There's a good view of the World Showcase lagoon.

House specialties: Tempura—battered deep-fried foods featuring chicken, shrimp, and vegetables. The menu tells the story of tempura, which apparently came about when some Portuguese sailors were shipwrecked on a Japanese shore. The Catholic Portuguese did not eat meat on the holy days, which came four times a year and were called *quattuor tempora*. On these days the sailors ate fried shrimp. The Japanese adapted the word tempura to mean fried shrimp, and the rest of the world adapted it to mean all kinds of fried food.

Other recommendations: Kabuki beef, sushi, and sashimi.

Summary & comments: Not the most appealing restaurant at Epcot, but the tempura is arguably the best in the Japan pavilion. The sushi and sashimi are not heavily marketed, but you can bet the sanitation—important in any restaurant but crucial where sushi is served—is impeccable.

Teppanyaki Dining Rooms

Japanese   ★★★½   **Expensive**

Quality	Value
85	C

Japan, World Showcase, EPCOT Center
(407) 939-3463

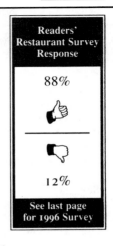

Readers'
Restaurant Survey
Response

88%

12%

See last page
for 1996 Survey

Customers: Theme park guests
Reservations: Required
When to go: Anytime
Entree range: $9–19, lunch; $15–29, dinner
Payment: VISA, MC, AMEX
Service rating: ★★★★
Friendliness rating: ★★★★
Parking: EPCOT lot
Bar: Full service
Wine selection: Limited
Dress: Theme park casual
Disabled access: Yes, via elevator

Lunch: Every day, 11 A.M.–4 P.M.
Dinner: Every day, 4 P.M. until one hour before park closes

Setting & atmosphere: The decor is upscale Japanese, only roomier, with light wood-beam ceilings, grass-cloth walls, and lacquered-finish oak chairs. Overall very clean and spare.

House specialties: Chicken, shrimp, beef, scallops, and oriental vegetables stir-fried on a teppan grill by a knife-juggling chef. Teppanyaki is a fancy version of the Benihana restaurant chain.

Entertainment & amenities: Watching the teppan chefs.

Summary & comments: While this restaurant offers some of the best teppan dining you will find in the United States, it has missed a wonderful opportunity to introduce the diversity and beauty of authentic Japanese cuisine to the American public. Be aware that diners at the teppan tables (large tables with a grill in the middle) are seated with other parties. Finally, if you would like to try more traditional Japanese fare, consider Tempura Kiku, a small restaurant in the same building.

Tony's Town Square Restaurant

Italian   ★★½   **Moderate**

Quality	Value
78	**D**

Main Street, U.S.A., Magic Kingdom
(407) 939-3463

> **Customers:** Theme park guests
> **Reservations:** Recommended
> **When to go:** Late lunch or early dinner
> **Entree range:** $15–22
> **Payment:** VISA, MC, AMEX
> **Service rating:** ★★★
> **Friendliness rating:** ★★★★
> **Parking:** Magic Kingdom lot
> **Bar:** None
> **Wine selection:** None
> **Dress:** Casual
> **Disabled access:** Yes

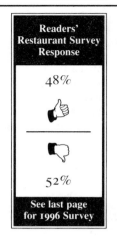

Readers' Restaurant Survey Response

48% 👍

52% 👎

See last page for 1996 Survey

Breakfast: Every day, 8:30–11:30 A.M.
Lunch: Every day, noon–3:30 P.M.
Dinner: Every day, 3:30 P.M. until park closes

Setting & atmosphere: Decorated like a New York Italian eatery, with tile floors, tablecloths, dark woods, and lots of plants. The walls are filled with memorabilia from *Lady and the Tramp*. It is a bright and open place, but it somehow always has a trampled and unkempt appearance.

House specialties: Spaghetti (long noodles for those who want to try that *Lady and the Tramp* kiss technique); lasagna primavera (the kiss technique doesn't work with this one); Joe's fettucini.

Other recommendations: Lady and the Tramp waffles; shrimp scampi.

Summary & comments: Perhaps the most pleasant place to dine in the Magic Kingdom, but the choices are few. The pace can be hectic, but the atmosphere is light and airy and the pictures and other knickknacks from *Lady and the Tramp* are a lot of fun. Go ahead, share a plate of overpriced spaghetti with someone you love.

Victoria & Albert's

Gourmet   ★★★★½   **Expensive**

Quality	Value
96	**D**

Disney's Grand Floridian Beach Resort
(407) 824-2383

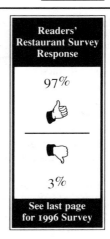

Readers'
Restaurant Survey
Response

97%

3%

See last page
for 1996 Survey

Customers: Hotel guests, locals
Reservations: Mandatory; must be confirmed
by noon the day of your reservation
When to go: Anytime
Entree range: Fixed price, $80 per person;
$105 with wine pairings
Payment: VISA, MC, AMEX
Service rating: ★★★★
Friendliness rating: ★★★
Parking: Valet parking; self-parking is
deceptively far away
Bar: Full service
Wine selection: Excellent
Dress: Jacket required
Disabled access: Yes

Dinner: Two seatings nightly at 6 P.M. and 9 P.M.

Setting & atmosphere: Victoria & Albert's is a small, intimate room under a domed ceiling; elegantly appointed with large floral displays, fine china, crystal, and silver.

House specialties: The menu changes daily but always features selections of fresh game, poultry, fish, and beef.

Entertainment & amenities: A harpist or violinist entertains from the foyer. Guests receive souvenir menus personalized with gold lettering.

Summary & comments: Except for one bit of kitsch—instead of waiters each table is attended by a maid and butler named Victoria and Albert—this is Disney's most elegant restaurant. It also features some of the finest culinary talent in the southeastern United States. Victoria & Albert's dining room is entirely nonsmoking.

Honors & awards: AAA 4-Diamond Award

Whispering Canyon Cafe

American ★★½ **Moderate**

Quality	Value
79	**B**

Disney's Wilderness Lodge
(407) 824-3200

> **Customers:** Hotel guests
> **Reservations:** Not accepted
> **When to go:** Anytime
> **Entree range:** Fixed price, $15.75 for adults; $6.50 for children
> **Payment:** VISA, MC, AMEX
> **Service rating:** ★★
> **Friendliness rating:** ★★★
> **Parking:** Hotel lot
> **Bar:** Full service
> **Wine selection:** Limited
> **Dress:** Casual
> **Disabled access:** Yes

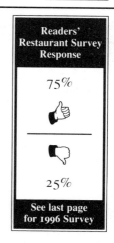

Readers' Restaurant Survey Response

75% 👍

25% 👎

See last page for 1996 Survey

Breakfast: Every day, 7–11 A.M.
Lunch: Every day, 11:30 A.M.–3 P.M.
Dinner: Every day, 4:30–10 P.M.

Setting & atmosphere: Located just off the hotel's atrium lobby, the restaurant looks out on the lobby on one side and a mountain prairie, created by the Disney landscapers, on the other. Tables have a barrel-top lazy Susan where the food is placed; diners dish out their own helpings from the platters.

House specialties: Apple-rosemary rotisserie chicken; maple-garlic pork spareribs; braised lamb shank.

Other recommendations: Smoked barbecue beef brisket; smoked barbecue veal ribs.

Summary & comments: The food is served "family style," meaning it is brought to the table on platters or in crocks and you dish out however much you'd like. The food is pretty good and if you're looking to stuff yourself silly, this is the place to be. Although reservations are not accepted, the host will give you a beeper so you can roam about the facility until your table is ready.

Yacht Club Galley

Quality	Value
81	C

American   ★★★   **Moderate**

Disney's Yacht Club Resort
(407) 934-7000

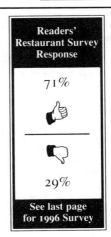

**Readers'
Restaurant Survey
Response**

71%

29%

**See last page
for 1996 Survey**

Customers: Hotel guests
Reservations: Not necessary
When to go: Breakfast or lunch
Entree range: $9.95–16.95
Payment: VISA, MC, AMEX
Service rating: ★★★★
Friendliness rating: ★★★★
Parking: Hotel lot
Bar: Full service
Wine selection: Good
Dress: Casual
Disabled access: Yes

Breakfast: Every day, 7–11 A.M.
Lunch: Every day, 11:30 A.M.-4 P.M.
Dinner: Every day, 5–10 P.M.

Setting & atmosphere: The Yacht Club Galley features a bright nautical theme with colorful pastels, blue striped wallpaper, and tablecloths. A moving seascape mural is the focal point of the large and somewhat noisy dining room.

House specialties: Daily fresh fish specials; barbecued pork ribs; seafood stir-fry with shrimp, scallops, and fish. Breakfast features a buffet or a la carte menu, with such selections as "the catamaran," a flour tortilla filled with scrambled eggs, onions, and peppers, and topped with salsa, sour cream, and shredded cheddar cheese.

Other recommendations: Chicken commodore, a breast of chicken with prosciutto ham, fontina cheese sauce, and linguini, tossed with green peppers, garlic, and olive oil; roast prime rib with burgundy horseradish sauce; breaded clam strips.

Entertainment & amenities: Strolling band in the evening.

Summary & comments: Stop here for breakfast or lunch; it's a short walk from EPCOT and a good escape if you just need to get out of the park and relax for a while.

Yachtsman Steakhouse

Steak ★★★ **Expensive**

Quality	Value
80	**D**

Disney's Yacht Club Resort
(407) 934-7000

Customers: Hotel guests, locals
Reservations: Recommended
When to go: Anytime
Entree range: $16.95–25.50
Payment: VISA, MC, AMEX
Service rating: ★★★
Friendliness rating: ★★★★
Parking: Hotel lot
Bar: Full service
Wine selection: Very good
Dress: Casual
Disabled access: Yes

Dinner: Every day, 6–10 P.M.

Readers'
Restaurant Survey
Response

91%

9%

See last page
for 1996 Survey

Setting & atmosphere: This restaurant is decorated country style—lots of knotty pine and chintz tablecloths. A refrigerated display case with big slabs of beef in various stages of the aging process allows you to get acquainted with your steak before you're seated. You can watch it being cooked at the show kitchen, if you wish, and the staff encourages you to ask questions about your meal's preparation. (How about, "Is it ready yet?")

House specialties: All steaks are cut and trimmed on the premises daily. Yacht Club porterhouse, Kansas City strip, prime rib of beef au jus are just some of the cuts. Mixed grill includes filet, lamb chops, and chicken breast served with three sauces. All entrees include baked potato and bread board assortment. Béarnaise and bordelaise sauces are available to complement your meat selection.

Other recommendations: Whole Maine lobster stuffed with crabmeat; full rack of lamb; grilled pork chops.

Entertainment & amenities: Strolling musicians (the same ones who stroll through the Yacht Club Galley).

Summary & comments: For die-hard meat lovers who don't mind paying a lot for a good steak. The chintz tablecloths keep it from being a male domain, but women should be offended by the "yachtress" cut of meat. Besides a good wine list, the Yachtsman also has an impressive beer list.

PART NINE:
The Magic Kingdom

—— *Arriving*

Three days each week (usually on Monday, Thursday, and Saturday) Walt Disney World hotel and campground guests (excluding guests at the Walt Disney World Village Hotels) are invited to enter the Magic Kingdom one hour before the general public is admitted. During this hour, the early entrants can enjoy all of the attractions in Fantasyland, as well as Space Mountain and the Grand Prix Raceway in Tomorrowland.

If you stay at a Walt Disney World hotel or campground and want to tour the Magic Kingdom on a morning when the program is in effect, plan to arrive a half hour before the early-entry opening time. If the official opening time is 9 A.M., for example, then the official early-entry time for Disney hotel guests is 8 A.M. You should arrive at the park 30 to 40 minutes before that, at about 7:30 A.M.

One year, during our revision research, the official opening time was 8 A.M. Testing the system, we were stationed at the bus stop at the Dixie Landings Resort by a little after 6 A.M. Sure enough, the bus rolled up a few minutes later, full of sleepy parents and excited children. We were admitted to the Magic Kingdom at 6:30 A.M., about a half hour before sunrise. Though Main Street was lighted, Disney cast members kept us moving past the closed shops to Fantasyland. There, dads huddled over coffee and bran muffins in the Village Haus restaurant while moms and children soared aloft on Dumbo to greet the rising sun.

In the summer and over holiday periods, increases in crowd levels (a result of Disney resort guests exercising their early-entry option at the Magic Kingdom) create near unmanageable congestion by around 10 A.M. Even if you are eligible for early entry, you will be better off touring one of the other parks where early entry is not in effect. An alternate strategy is to take advantage of early entry for an hour or two first thing in the morning at the Magic Kingdom and then head to another park for the rest of the day.

Because the Disney people are always changing things, we suggest you call Walt Disney World Information at (407) 824-4321 before you leave home to verify which days of the week will be early-entry days during your stay. As an aside, those not eligible for early entry should not attempt sneaking in with the early-entry guests. All Disney hotel and campground guests, including children, are issued dated identification cards on check-in at their hotel. These Disney I.D.'s must be presented along with a valid admission pass in order to enter a park on an early-entry morning.

If you drive, the Magic Kingdom/Transportation and Ticket Center parking lot opens about two hours before the park's official opening time for the general public. After paying a parking fee, you are directed to parking space and then transported to the Transportation and Ticket Center (TTC) on a tram. From the TTC, you can take either a monorail or a ferry to the entrance of the Magic Kingdom. If you are a guest at a Disney hotel or campground, you can take a monorail or bus directly to the entrance of the park, bypassing the TTC.

—— *Getting Oriented*

The ferryboat, monorail, and Walt Disney World buses discharge passengers at the entrance to the Magic Kingdom—the train station at the foot of Main Street. Stroller and wheelchair rentals are to the right, lockers for your use are on the ground floor of the train station. Entering Main Street, City Hall is to your left, serving as the center for information, lost and found, some reservations, and entertainment.

If you haven't been given a guide to the Magic Kingdom by now, City Hall is the place to pick one up. The guide contains maps; gives tips for good photos; lists all the attractions, shops, and eating places; and provides helpful information about first aid, baby care, assistance for the handicapped, and more.

While at City Hall inquire about special events, live entertainment, Disney character parades, concerts, and other activities scheduled for that day. Usually City Hall will have a printed schedule of the day's events.

Notice on your map that Main Street ends at a central hub, from which branch the entrances to five other sections of the Magic Kingdom: Adventureland, Frontierland, Liberty Square, Fantasyland, and Tomorrowland. Mickey's Starland is wedged like a dimple between the cheeks of Fantasyland and Tomorrowland and does not connect to the central hub.

Cinderella Castle serves as the entrance to Fantasyland and is the focal landmark and visual center of the Magic Kingdom. If you start in Adventureland and go clockwise around the Magic Kingdom, the castle spires will always be roughly on your right; if you start in Tomorrowland and go counterclockwise through the park, the spires will always be roughly on your left. Cinderella Castle is a great place to meet if your group decides to split up for any reason during the day, or as an emergency meeting place if you are accidentally separated.

—— *Starting the Tour*

Everyone soon finds their own favorite and not-so-favorite attractions in the Magic Kingdom. Be open-minded and adventuresome. Don't dismiss a particular ride or show as not being for you until **after** you have tried it. Our personal experience, as well as our research, indicates that each visitor is different in terms of which Disney offerings are most enjoyed. So don't miss seeing an attraction because a friend from home didn't like it; that attraction may turn out to be your favorite.

We do recommend that you take advantage of what Disney does best — the fantasy adventures like the Jungle Cruise and The Haunted Mansion, and the AudioAnimatronics (talking robots, so to speak) attractions such as *The Hall of Presidents* and Pirates of the Caribbean. Unless you have almost unlimited time, don't burn a lot of daylight browsing through the shops. Except for some special Disney souvenirs, you can find most of the same merchandise elsewhere. Try to minimize the time you spend on carnival-type rides; you've probably got an amusement park, carnival, or state fair close to your hometown. (Don't, however, mistake rides like Space Mountain and the Big Thunder Mountain Railroad as amusement park rides. They may be of the roller coaster genre, but they represent pure Disney genius.) Similarly, do not devote a lot of time to waiting in lines for meals. Food at most Magic Kingdom eateries is mediocre and uninspiring at best. Eat a good early breakfast before you come and snack on vendor-sold foods during the touring day.

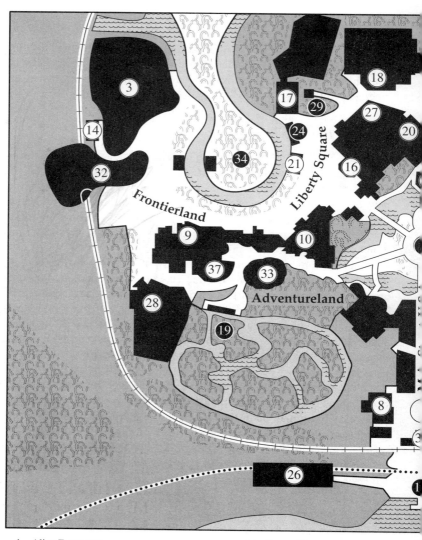

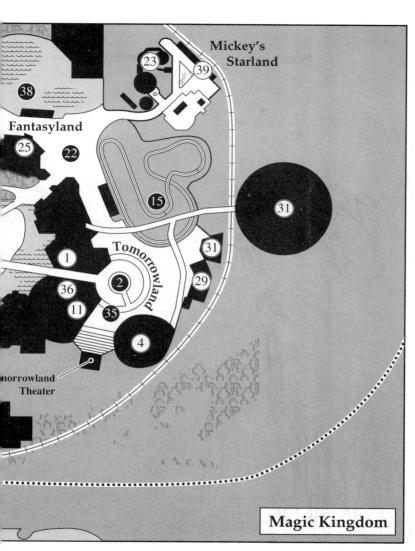

Magic Kingdom

Main Street, U.S.A.

Main Street opens a half hour to an hour before, and closes a half hour to an hour after, the rest of the park. This is where you'll begin and end your visit to the Magic Kingdom. We have already mentioned that assistance and information are available at City Hall. The Walt Disney World Railroad stops at the Main Street Station: you can board here for a grand tour of the Magic Kingdom, or you can get off the train in Frontierland or Mickey's Starland.

Main Street is a re-creation of a turn-of-the-century American small town street. Many visitors are surprised to discover that all the buildings are real and not elaborate props. Attention to detail here is exceptional— all the interiors, furnishings, and fixtures are true to the period. As with any Main Street, the Disney version is a collection of shops and eating places, a city hall, and a fire station, with an old-time cinema thrown in for good measure. Horse-drawn trolleys, double-decker buses, fire engines, and horseless carriages offer rides along Main Street and transport visitors to the central hub.

Main Street Services

Most of the park's service facilities are centered in the Main Street section, including the following:

Wheelchair & Stroller Rental	To the right of the main entrance before passing under the railroad station
Banking Services/ Currency Exchange	To the left of City Hall at the railroad station end of Main Street
Storage Lockers	On the ground floor of the railroad station at the end of Main Street. All lockers are cleaned out each night.
Lost & Found	City Hall at the railroad station end of Main Street

Live Entertainment and Parade Information	City Hall at the railroad station end of Main Street
Lost Persons	City Hall
Walt Disney World & Local Attraction Information	City Hall
First Aid	Next to the Crystal Palace around the central hub to the left (toward Adventureland)
Baby Center/Baby Care Needs	Next to the Crystal Palace around the central hub to the left (toward Adventureland)

Walt Disney World Railroad

Type of Attraction: Scenic railroad ride around perimeter of the Magic Kingdom; also transportation to Frontierland and Mickey's Starland.

When to Go: Anytime

Special Comments: Main Street is usually the least-congested station

Author's Rating: Plenty to see; ★★★½ [Critical ratings are based on a scale of zero to five stars. Five stars is the best possible rating.]

Overall Appeal by Age Group:

Pre-school	Grade School	Teens	Young Adults	Over 30	Senior Citizens
★★★★	★★★	★★½	★★★	★★★½	★★★½

Duration of Ride: About 19 minutes for a complete circuit

Average Wait in Line per 100 People Ahead of You: 8 minutes

Assumes: 2 or more trains operating

Loading Speed: Fast

DESCRIPTION AND COMMENTS   A transportation ride that blends an unusual variety of sights and experiences with an energy-saving way of getting around the park. The train provides a glimpse of all the lands except Adventureland.

TOURING TIPS   Save the train ride until after you have seen the featured attractions, or use when you need transportation. On busy days, lines form at the Frontierland Station, but rarely at the Main Street and Mickey's Starland stations. Strollers are not allowed on the train.

Main Street Cinema

Type of Attraction: Old-time movies and vintage Disney cartoons
When to Go: Whenever you want
Author's Rating: Wonderful selection of flicks; ★★★
Overall Appeal by Age Group:

Pre-school	Grade School	Teens	Young Adults	Over 30	Senior Citizens
★★½	★★★	★★½	★★★	★★★	★★★

Duration of Presentation: Runs continuously
Preshow Entertainment: None
Probable Waiting Time: No waiting

DESCRIPTION AND COMMENTS   Excellent old-time movies including some vintage Disney cartoons. Since the movies are silent, six are shown simultaneously. No seats; viewers stand. A new Mickey Mouse flick, with sound, was added in 1995 and alternates with the vintage stuff.

TOURING TIPS   Good place to get out of the sun or rain, or to kill time while others in your group shop on Main Street. Not something you can't afford to miss.

Transportation Rides

DESCRIPTION AND COMMENTS   Trolleys, buses, etc., which add color to Main Street.

TOURING TIPS   Will save you a walk to the central hub. Not worth waiting in line.

Main Street Eateries and Shops

DESCRIPTION AND COMMENTS   Some of the Magic Kingdom's better food and specialty/souvenir shopping in a nostalgic, happy setting. The Emporium offers the best selection of Disney trademark souvenir items in the Magic Kingdom.

TOURING TIPS   The shops are fun but the merchandise can be had elsewhere (except for certain Disney trademark souvenirs). If seeing the park attractions is your objective, save the Main Street eateries and shops until the end of the day. If shopping is your objective, you will find the shops most crowded during the noon hour and near closing time. Remember, Main Street opens at least a half hour earlier, and closes a half hour to an hour later than the rest of the Magic Kingdom.

The Crystal Palace, at the central hub end of Main Street (towards Adventureland) provides good cafeteria service and is often overlooked by the lunch-hour (but not dinner-hour) masses. Give it a try if you are nearby at noon.

Adventureland

Adventureland is the first land to the left of Main Street and combines an African safari theme with an old New Orleans/Caribbean atmosphere.

Swiss Family Treehouse

Type of Attraction: Walk-through exhibit
When to Go: Before 11:30 A.M. and after 5 P.M.
Special Comments: Requires climbing a lot of stairs
Author's Rating: A very creative exhibit; ★★★½
Overall Appeal by Age Group:

Pre-school	Grade School	Teens	Young Adults	Over 30	Senior Citizens
★★★★	★★★★	★★★★	★★★★	★★★★	★★★★

Duration of Tour: 10–15 minutes
Average Wait in Line per 100 People Ahead of You: 7 minutes
Assumes: Normal staffing
Loading Speed: Does not apply

DESCRIPTION AND COMMENTS   A fantastic replication of the shipwrecked family's home will fire the imagination of the inventive and the adventurous.

TOURING TIPS   A self-guided walk-through tour involves a lot of climbing up and down stairs, but no ropes or ladders or anything fancy. People who stop during the walk-through to look extra long or to rest sometimes create bottlenecks that slow crowd flow. We recommend visiting this attraction in the late afternoon or early evening if you are on a one-day tour schedule, or first thing in the morning of your second day.

Jungle Cruise

Type of Ride: A Disney boat ride adventure
When to Go: Before 11 A.M. or two hours before closing
Author's Rating: A long-enduring Disney masterpiece; ★★★★
Overall Appeal by Age Group:

Pre-school	Grade School	Teens	Young Adults	Over 30	Senior Citizens
★★★★½	★★★★½	★★★★	★★★★	★★★★	★★★★

Duration of Ride: 8–9 minutes
Average Wait in Line per 100 People Ahead of You: 3½ minutes
Assumes: 10 boats operating
Loading Speed: Moderate to fast

DESCRIPTION AND COMMENTS   A boat ride through jungle waterways. Passengers encounter elephants, lions, hostile natives, and a menacing hippo. A long-enduring Disney favorite; the boatman's spiel adds measurably to the fun.

TOURING TIPS   One of the park's "not to be missed" attractions. A good staff and an improved management plan have speeded up the lines for this ride. On the negative side, it is very difficult to estimate the length of the wait for the Jungle Cruise. A mother from the Bronx, New York, wrote complaining:

> The line for this ride is extremely deceiving. We got on line towards the early evening; it was long but we really wanted to take this ride. Every time the winding line brought us near the loading dock and we thought we were going to get on, we'd discover a whole new section of winding lanes to go through. It was extremely frustrating. We must have waited a good 20–30 minutes before the two of us finally gave up and got out.

Pirates of the Caribbean

Type of Ride: A Disney adventure boat ride
When to Go: Before noon or after 5 P.M.
Special Comments: Frightens some small children
Author's Rating: Disney AudioAnimatronics at its best; ★★★★★

Overall Appeal by Age Group:

Pre-school	Grade School	Teens	Young Adults	Over 30	Senior Citizens
★★★	★★★★★	★★★★★	★★★★★	★★★★★	★★★★★

Duration of Ride: Approximately 7½ minutes

Average Wait in Line per 100 People Ahead of You: 1½ minutes

Assumes: Both waiting lines operating

Loading Speed: Fast

DESCRIPTION AND COMMENTS   Another boat ride, this time indoors, through a series of sets depicting a pirate raid on an island settlement, from the bombardment of the fortress to the debauchery that follows the victory. Speaking of debauchery, Pirates of the Caribbean is one of several Walt Disney World attractions that have been administered a strong dose of political correctness. See if you can spot the changes.

TOURING TIPS   Another "not to be missed" attraction. Undoubtedly one of the most elaborate and imaginative attractions in the Magic Kingdom. Engineered to move large crowds in a hurry, Pirates is a good attraction to see during the later part of the afternoon. It has two waiting lines, both under cover.

Tropical Serenade (Enchanted Tiki Birds)

Type of Attraction: AudioAnimatronic Pacific Island musical show

When to Go: Before 11 A.M. and after 3:30 P.M.

Author's Rating: Very, very unusual; ★★★

Overall Appeal by Age Group:

Pre-school	Grade School	Teens	Young Adults	Over 30	Senior Citizens
★★½	★★★	★★	★★★	★★★	★★★

Duration of Presentation: 15½ minutes

Preshow Entertainment: Talking birds

Probable Waiting Time: 15 minutes

DESCRIPTION AND COMMENTS   An unusual sit-down theater performance where more than two hundred birds, flowers, and Tiki-god statues sing and whistle through a musical program.

TOURING TIPS   One of the more bizarre of the Magic Kingdom's entertainments, but usually not too crowded. We like it in the late afternoon, when we can especially appreciate sitting for a bit in an air-conditioned theater.

A reader from Cookeville, Tennessee, took exception to our rating for preschoolers, writing:

> I know that visitor reactions vary widely, but the Tropical Serenade was our toddler's favorite Magic Kingdom attraction (we nearly omitted it because of the rating for preschoolers).

And a Bethesda, Maryland, dad contributed this:

> Our kids love nature and ANYTHING to do with animals, so one of the biggest hits for our kids was the Enchanted Tiki Birds, which per your guide, has rapidly lost its drawing power over the past several years. I can concur with your observations as almost one-fourth of the audience got up and left the "show" while it was still in progress. How sad that our society has become so jaded that anything that doesn't "sizzle" with excitement is treated with disrespect. Had I not even liked the show, I would have been embar-

The 357th Stroller Squadron: the Mowin' Mamas

rassed to walk out midway through a 15 minute show. My daughter bought a stuffed tiki bird at the conclusion of the show and it never left her side for the remainder of the trip.

Adventureland Eateries and Shops

DESCRIPTION AND COMMENTS You will find more specialty shopping a la Banana Republic in Adventureland. There are also several restaurants, which tend to be less crowded during lunch than other Magic Kingdom eateries.

TOURING TIPS El Pirata Y el Perico, featuring Mexican fast food, is often overlooked.

Frontierland

Frontierland adjoins Adventureland as you move clockwise around the Magic Kingdom. The focus here is on the Old West with stockade-type structures and pioneer trappings.

Splash Mountain

Type of Ride: Water-flume ride

When to Go: As soon as the park opens

Special Comments: Children must be 3'8" tall to ride; those under 7 years must ride with an adult. Switching-off option provided (see page 166).

Author's Rating: A wet winner, not to be missed; ★★★★★

Overall Appeal by Age Group:

Pre-school	Grade School	Teens	Young Adults	Over 30	Senior Citizens
†	★★★★★	★★★★★	★★★★★	★★★★★	★★★½

† Many preschoolers are too short to meet the height requirement and others are visually intimidated by watching the ride from standing in line. Of those preschoolers who actually ride, most give the attraction high marks (3–5 stars).

Duration of Ride: About 10 minutes

Average Wait in Line per 100 People Ahead of You: 3½ minutes

Assumes: Operation at full capacity

Loading Speed: Moderate

DESCRIPTION AND COMMENTS   Splash Mountain is an amusement park flume ride Disney style, bigger than life and more imaginative than anyone thought possible. The ride combines steep chutes with a variety of Disney's best special effects. Covering over half a mile, the ride splashes through swamps, caves, and backwood bayous before climaxing in a five-story plunge and Brer Rabbit's triumphant return home. The entire ride

is populated by more than 100 AudioAnimatronic characters, including Brer Rabbit, Brer Bear, and Brer Fox, all regaling riders with songs, including "Zip-a-Dee-Doo-Dah."

TOURING TIPS   This ride, happy, exciting, and adventuresome all at once, vies with Space Mountain as the most popular ride in the Magic Kingdom. Even as the park opens, hundreds are poised to move as rapidly as their feet will carry them to Splash Mountain. Crowds will build fast in the morning, and waits of more than two hours can be expected once the Magic Kingdom fills on a busy day. Get in line first thing, and certainly no later than 45 minutes after the park opens. Long lines will persist throughout the day. If you miss Splash Mountain in the morning, your best shot at a shorter wait is to ride during the afternoon or evening parade(s), or just before the Magic Kingdom closes.

As with Space Mountain in Tomorrowland, literally hundreds crowd the starting gate to race to Splash Mountain when the park opens. The best strategy for this sprint (which we call the Rapid Rampage) is to go to the end of Main Street and turn left to the Crystal Palace restaurant. In front of the Crystal Palace you will find a bridge that provides a shortcut to Adventureland. Stake out a position at the barrier rope, and wait until the park opens and the rope is dropped. While we do not advocate running, we will tell you candidly that all the folks around you aren't down in a four-point stance to inspect the pavement.

When the rope drops, move as fast as feels comfortable (understanding the pandemonium just unleashed behind you is comparable to a buffalo stampede) and cross the bridge to Adventureland. Okay, now pay attention, here's another shortcut. Just past the first group of buildings on your right, roughly across from the Swiss Family Treehouse, there is a small passageway where rest rooms and phones are located. This passageway, which is easy to overlook, connects Adventureland to Frontierland. Go through the passageway into Frontierland and take a hard left. As you emerge along the waterfront you will see Splash Mountain ahead. If you miss the passageway and the shortcut, don't fool around looking for it. You can also reach Splash Mountain by continuing straight on through Adventureland.

A less exhausting way to reach Splash Mountain first thing in the morning is to board the Walt Disney World Railroad as soon as you enter the park. Take a seat on the train at Main Street Station and wait for the rest of the park to open. The train will pull out of the station at the same time the rope drops at the central hub end of Main Street. Ride to the Frontierland Station (the first stop) and disembark. As you come down the stairs at the station, the entrance to Splash Mountain will be on your right. Because of the time required to unload at the station, train passengers will not arrive at Splash Mountain ahead of those who sprint from the central hub. You will, however, arrive well in advance of most other guests.

If you ride in the front seat, it is almost a certainty that you will get wet. Riders in other seats get splashed a bit, but usually not doused. Since there is no way of knowing which seat you will be assigned, it is best to be prepared. If you visit on a cool day, you may want to carry a plastic garbage bag. By tearing holes in the bottom and sides, you can fashion a sack dress of sorts to keep you dry (oops, make that drier). Be sure to tuck the bag in under your bottom. If you have a camera, either leave it with a nonriding member of your party or wrap it in a plastic bag.

One final word: This is not just a fancy flume ride, it is a full-blown Disney adventure. The scariest part, by far, is the steep chute you see when standing in line, and even this drop looks worse than it really is. Despite reassurances, however, many children wig out after watching the big drop from their place in line. A mom from Grand Rapids, Michigan, recalls her kids' rather unique reaction:

> We discovered after the fact that our children thought they would *go underwater* after the five-story drop, and tried to hold their breath throughout the ride in preparation. They were really too preoccupied to enjoy the clever Brer Rabbit story.

Big Thunder Mountain Railroad

Type of Ride: Tame roller coaster with exciting special effects
When to Go: Before 11 A.M. or after 5:30 P.M.
Special Comments: Children must be 3'4" tall to ride. Those under 7 years must ride with an adult. Switching-off option provided (see page 166).

Author's Rating: Great effects, relatively tame ride; ★★★★½
Overall Appeal by Age Group:

Pre-school	Grade School	Teens	Young Adults	Over 30	Senior Citizens
★★★	★★★★	★★★★	★★★★	★★★★	★★★

Duration of Ride: Almost 3½ minutes
Average Wait in Line per 100 People Ahead of You: 2½ minutes
Assumes: 5 trains operating
Loading Speed: Moderate to fast

WARNING!
For Bouffants, Rug Wearers, and Elvis Impersonators
This Ride Will Muss Your 'Do

DESCRIPTION AND COMMENTS   A roller coaster ride through and around a Disney "mountain." The time is Gold Rush days, and the idea is that you are on a runaway mine train. Along with the usual thrills of a roller coaster ride (about a 5 on a "scary scale" of 10), the ride showcases some first-rate examples of Disney creativity; lifelike scenes depicting a mining town, falling rocks, and an earthquake, all humorously animated.

TOURING TIPS   A superb Disney experience, but not too wild of a roller coaster. The emphasis here is much more on the sights than on the thrill of the ride itself. Regardless, it's a "not to be missed" attraction. The best bet for riding Big Thunder without a long wait in line is to ride early in the morning or between 10:00 and 11:00 when the ride has been brought up to peak carrying capacity.

The opening of nearby Splash Mountain in the fall of 1992 has changed forever the traffic patterns to Big Thunder Mountain Railroad. More adventuresome guests ride Splash Mountain first and then go next door to ride Big Thunder. This means much larger crowds in Frontierland all day and longer waits for Big Thunder Mountain. The best way to experience the Magic Kingdom's "mountains" is to ride Space Mountain first thing when the park opens and then go directly to Big Thunder Mountain, and from there to Splash Mountain. If you miss Big Thunder in the morning, try again during one of the parades or just before the park closes.

As an example of how differently guests experience Disney attractions, consider this letter we received from a lady in Brookline, Massachusetts:

> Being in the senior citizens' category and having limited time, my friend and I confined our activities to those attractions rated as four or five stars for seniors.
>
> Because of your recommendation and because you listed it as "not to be missed," we waited for one hour to board the Big Thunder Mountain Railroad, (which you) rated a "5" on a scary scale of "10." After living through three-and-a-half minutes of pure terror, I will rate that attraction a "15" on a scary scale of "10." We were so busy holding on and screaming and even praying for our safety that we did not see any falling rocks, a mining town, or an earthquake. In our opinion the Big Thunder Mountain Railroad should not be recommended for seniors or preschool children.

Along similar lines, another woman from New England writes,

> My husband, who is 41, found Big Thunder Mountain too intense for his enjoyment, and feels that anyone who does not like roller coasters would not enjoy this ride.

Country Bear Jamboree

Type of Attraction: AudioAnimatronic country hoedown stage show
When to Go: Before 11:30 A.M. and during the two hours before closing
Special Comments: Changes shows at Christmas and during the summer
Author's Rating: A Disney classic, not to be missed; ★★★★
Overall Appeal by Age Group:

Pre-school	Grade School	Teens	Young Adults	Over 30	Senior Citizens
★★★★	★★★★	★★★	★★★½	★★★★	★★★★

Duration of Presentation: 15 minutes
Preshow Entertainment: None
Probable Waiting Time: This is a very popular attraction with a comparatively small seating capacity. An average waiting time on a busy day between the hours of noon and 5:30 P.M. would be from 30–50 minutes.

DESCRIPTION AND COMMENTS A cast of charming AudioAnimatronic (robotic) bears sing and stomp their way through a Western-style hoedown. Though one of the Magic Kingdom's most humorous and upbeat shows, *Country Bear Jamboree* has not been revised for many moons, much to the consternation of repeat visitors.

TOURING TIPS   Yet another "not to be missed" attraction, the *Jamboree* is extremely popular and draws large crowds even early in the day. We recommend seeing this one before 11:30 A.M. Another good time to visit is right before a parade.

Tom Sawyer Island and Fort Sam Clemens

Type of Attraction: Walk-through exhibit/rustic playground
When to Go: Mid-morning through late afternoon
Special Comments: Closes at dusk
Author's Rating: The place for rambunctious kids; ★★★★
Overall Appeal by Age Group:

Pre-school	Grade School	Teens	Young Adults	Over 30	Senior Citizens
★★★★★	★★★★★	★★★½	★★★	★★★	★★★

DESCRIPTION AND COMMENTS   Tom Sawyer Island manages to impart something of a sense of isolation from the rest of the park. It has hills to climb, a cave and a windmill to explore, a tipsy barrel bridge to cross, and paths to follow. It's a delight for adults and a godsend for children who have been in tow all day. They love the freedom of the exploration and the excitement of firing air guns from the walls of Ft. Sam Clemens. There's even a "secret" escape tunnel.

TOURING TIPS   Tom Sawyer Island is not one of the Magic Kingdom's more celebrated attractions, but it's certainly one of its better conceived. Attention to detail is excellent and kids particularly revel in its adventuresome frontier atmosphere. We think it's a must for families with children 5 through 15. If your party is all adults, visit the island on your second day or stop by on your first day if you have seen the attractions you most wanted to see.

We like Tom Sawyer Island from about noon until the island closes at dusk. Access is by raft from Frontierland and you may have to stand in line to board both coming and going. Two rafts operate simultaneously, however, and the round-trip is usually pretty efficient. Tom Sawyer Island takes about 25 minutes or so to see; many children could spend a whole day visiting. As an aside, our favorite Magic Kingdom restaurant for lunch, Aunt Polly's Landing, is located on Tom Sawyer Island. Be forewarned, however, that the menu at Aunt Polly's is quite limited.

For a Duncan, South Carolina, mother, Tom Sawyer Island was as much a refuge as an attraction:

> I do have one tip for parents. In the afternoon when the crowds were at their peak, the weather [at] its hottest, and the kids started lagging behind, our organization began to suffer. We then retreated over to Tom Sawyer's Island, which proved to be a true haven. My husband and I found a secluded bench and re-grouped while sipping iced tea and eating delicious soft ice cream. Meanwhile, the kids were able to run freely in the shade. Afterwards we were ready to tackle the park again refreshed and with direction once more. (Admittedly, I got this tip from another guidebook.)

Davy Crockett's Explorer Canoes

Type of Ride: Scenic canoe ride

When to Go: Before noon or after 5 P.M.

Special Comments: Skip if the lines are long; closes at dusk

Author's Rating: The most fun way of seeing the Rivers of America;
★★★½

Overall Appeal by Age Group:

Pre-school	Grade School	Teens	Young Adults	Over 30	Senior Citizens
★★★★	★★★★	★★★★	★★★★	★★★★	★★★★

Duration of Ride: 9–15 minutes depending on how fast you paddle

Average Wait in Line per 100 People Ahead of You: 28 minutes

Assumes: 3 canoes operating

Loading Speed: Slow

DESCRIPTION AND COMMENTS Paddle-powered ride around Tom Sawyer Island and Ft. Sam Clemens. Runs the same route with the same sights as the Liberty Square Riverboat and the Mike Fink Keelboats. The canoes only operate during the busy times of the year. The sights are fun and the ride is a little different in that the tourists paddle the canoe.

TOURING TIPS The canoes represent one of three ways to see the same territory. Since the canoes and keelboats are slower loading, we usually opt for the large riverboat. If you are not up for a boat ride, a different view of the same sights can be had hoofing around Tom Sawyer Island and Ft. Sam Clemens.

Frontierland Shootin' Gallery

Type of Attraction: Electronic shooting gallery
When to Go: Whenever convenient
Special Comments: Costs 25¢ per play
Author's Rating: A very nifty shooting gallery; ★★½
Overall Appeal by Age Group:

Pre-school	Grade School	Teens	Young Adults	Over 30	Senior Citizens
★★★½	★★★½	★★★½	★★★	★★½	★★★

DESCRIPTION AND COMMENTS   A very elaborate shooting gallery, this is one of the few attractions not included in the Magic Kingdom admission.

TOURING TIPS   Good fun for them "what likes to shoot," but definitely not a place to be blowing your time if you are on a tight schedule. Try it on your second day if time allows.

Walt Disney World Railroad

DESCRIPTION AND COMMENTS   The Walt Disney World Railroad stops in Frontierland on its circle-tour around the park. See the description of the Walt Disney World Railroad under Main Street for additional details regarding the sights along the route.

TOURING TIPS   A pleasant and feet-saving way to commute to Main Street and Mickey's Starland. Be advised, however, that the Frontierland Station is usually more congested than its two counterparts. Strollers are not allowed on the train.

Frontierland Eateries and Shops

DESCRIPTION AND COMMENTS   Coonskin caps and western-theme specialty shopping, along with fast-food eateries that are usually very crowded between 11:30 A.M. and 2 P.M. An exception is Aunt Polly's Landing, on Tom Sawyer Island. Under cover, but outdoors, Aunt Polly's is a great place to escape the jostling crowds on a busy day. You can sit on the veranda and watch riverboats and canoes drift past on the waterway below. Fare is pretty much limited to cold fried chicken, served with potato salad and a biscuit; ham and swiss cheese sandwiches and peanut butter and jelly sandwiches. Prices (for Disney) are reasonable and the food is good.

TOURING TIPS Don't waste time browsing in shops unless you have a very relaxed schedule or came specifically to shop. If the wait to board the raft to Tom Sawyer Island is not prohibitive, try Aunt Polly's Landing for lunch.

Disney World Problem 204: Too Short to Ride

Liberty Square

Liberty Square re-creates the atmosphere of colonial America at the time of the American Revolution. Architecture is federal or colonial, with a real 130-year-old live oak (dubbed the "Liberty Tree") lending dignity and grace to the setting.

The Hall of Presidents

Type of Show: AudioAnimatronic historical presentation

When to Go: Anytime

Author's Rating: Impressive and moving; ★★★½

Overall Appeal by Age Group:

Pre-school	Grade School	Teens	Young Adults	Over 30	Senior Citizens
★	★★½	★★★	★★★½	★★★★	★★★★

Duration of Presentation: Almost 23 minutes

Preshow Entertainment: None

Probable Waiting Time: Lines for this attraction LOOK awesome but are usually swallowed up as the theater turns over. Your wait will probably be the remaining time of the show that's in progress when you arrive. Even during the busiest times of the day, waits rarely exceed 40 minutes.

DESCRIPTION AND COMMENTS   A 20-minute, strongly inspirational and patriotic program highlighting milestones in American history. The performance climaxes with a roll call of presidents from Washington through the present, with a few words of encouragement from Presidents Lincoln and Clinton. A very moving show coupled with one of Disney's best and most ambitious AudioAnimatronics (robotic) efforts. The production was updated in 1994. Narration is by Maya Angelou.

Our high opinion notwithstanding, we have received a lot of mail from readers who get more than entertainment from *The Hall of Presidents*. A lady in St. Louis wrote: "We always go to the Hall of Presidents when my husband gets cranky so he can take a nice nap." And, from a young mother in Marion, Ohio: "The Hall of Presidents is a great place to breast feed."

With an election year coming up, *The Hall of Presidents* is being singled out for political comment. A woman from St. Charles, Missouri, observed that *"The Hall of Presidents* has added Clinton: they let him talk too much." From the other side of the aisle, a Lincoln, Nebraska, visitor complained that *"The Hall of Presidents* lacks realism. President Reagan was able to stay awake through the entire show."

TOURING TIPS   The thorough detail and costumes of the chief executives is incredible, and if your children tend to fidget during the show, take notice of the fact that the presidents do, too. This attraction is one of the most popular, particularly among older visitors, and draws large crowds from 11 A.M. through about 5 P.M. Do not be dismayed by the lines, however. The theater holds more than 700 people, thus swallowing up large lines at a single gulp when visitors are admitted. One show is always in progress while the lobby is being filled for the next show. At less than busy times you will probably be admitted directly to the lobby without waiting in line. When the waiting lobby fills, those remaining in line outside are held in place until those in the lobby move into the theater just prior to the next show, at which time another 700 people from the outside line are admitted to the lobby.

Liberty Square Riverboat

Type of Ride: Scenic boat ride
When to Go: Anytime
Author's Rating: Provides an excellent vantage point; ★★★
Overall Appeal by Age Group:

Pre-school	Grade School	Teens	Young Adults	Over 30	Senior Citizens
★★★	★★★	★★½	★★★	★★★	★★★

Duration of Ride: About 16 minutes
Average Wait to Board: 10–14 minutes
Assumes: Normal operations

DESCRIPTION AND COMMENTS   Large-capacity paddle wheel riverboat that navigates the waters around Tom Sawyer Island and Ft. Sam Clemens.

A beautiful craft, the riverboat provides a lofty perspective of Frontierland and Liberty Square.

TOURING TIPS   One of three boat rides that survey the same real estate. Since Davy Crockett's Explorer Canoes and the Mike Fink Keelboats are slower loading, we think the riverboat is the best bet. If you are not in the mood for a boat ride, much of the same sights can be seen by hiking around the island.

The Haunted Mansion

Type of Ride: A Disney one-of-its-kind

When to Go: Before 11:30 A.M. or after 8 P.M.

Special Comments: Frightens some very small children

Author's Rating: Some of Walt Disney World's best special effects;
   ★★★★★

Overall Appeal by Age Group:

Pre-school	Grade School	Teens	Young Adults	Over 30	Senior Citizens
Varies	★★★★★	★★★★½	★★★★½	★★★★½	★★★★½

Duration of Ride: 7-minute ride plus a 1½-minute preshow

Average Wait in Line per 100 People Ahead of You: 2½ minutes

Assumes: Both "stretch rooms" operating

Loading Speed: Fast

DESCRIPTION AND COMMENTS   A fun attraction more than a scary one with some of the best special effects in the Magic Kingdom. In their guidebook the Disney people say, "Come face to face with 999 happy ghosts, ghouls, and goblins in a 'frightfully funny' adventure." That pretty well sums it up. Be warned that some youngsters become overly anxious concerning what they think they will see. The actual attraction scares almost nobody.

TOURING TIPS   This attraction would be more at home in Fantasyland, but no matter, it's Disney at its best; another "not to be missed" feature. Lines at The Haunted Mansion ebb and flow more than do the lines of most other Magic Kingdom high spots. This is due to the Mansion's proximity to *The Hall of Presidents* and the Liberty Square Riverboat. These two attractions disgorge 750 and 450 people respectively at the completion of each show or ride. Many of these folks head right over and hop in line at The Haunted Mansion. Try this attraction before noon and after 4:30 P.M. and make an effort to slip in between crowds.

Mike Fink Keelboats

Type of Ride: Scenic boat ride
When to Go: Before 11:30 A.M. or after 5 P.M.
Special Comments: Don't ride if the lines are long; closes at dusk
Author's Rating: ★★★
Overall Appeal by Age Group:

Pre-school	Grade School	Teens	Young Adults	Over 30	Senior Citizens
★★★½	★★★	★★★	★★★	★★★	★★★

Duration of Ride: 9½ minutes
Average Wait in Line per 100 People Ahead of You: 15 minutes
Assumes: 2 boats operating
Loading Speed: Slow

DESCRIPTION AND COMMENTS Small river keelboats that circle Tom Sawyer Island and Ft. Sam Clemens, taking the same route as Davy Crockett's Explorer Canoes and the Liberty Square Riverboat. The top deck of the keelboat is exposed to the elements.

TOURING TIPS This trip covers the same circle traveled by Davy Crockett's Explorer Canoes and the Liberty Square Riverboat. Since the keelboats and the canoes load slowly we prefer the riverboat. Another way to see much of the area covered by the respective boat tours is to explore Tom Sawyer Island and Ft. Sam Clemens on foot.

Liberty Square Eateries and Shops

DESCRIPTION AND COMMENTS American crafts and souvenir shopping, along with one restaurant, the Liberty Tree Tavern, which is often overlooked by the crowds at lunch.

TOURING TIPS Even though the Liberty Tree Tavern is the most improved restaurant in the Magic Kingdom, our suggestion is to stick with sandwiches. Reservations are recommended.

Fantasyland

Truly an enchanting place, spread gracefully like a miniature Alpine village beneath the lofty towers of Cinderella Castle, Fantasyland is the heart of the Magic Kingdom.

It's a Small World

Type of Ride: Scenic boat ride

When to Go: Anytime

Author's Rating: A pleasant change of pace; ★★★½

Overall Appeal by Age Group:

Pre-school	Grade School	Teens	Young Adults	Over 30	Senior Citizens
★★★★	★★★½	★★½	★★★	★★★	★★★½

Duration of Ride: Approximately 11 minutes

Average Wait in Line per 100 People Ahead of You: 1¾ minutes

Assumes: Busy conditions with 30 or more boats operating

Loading Speed: Fast

DESCRIPTION AND COMMENTS   A happy, upbeat attraction with a world brotherhood theme and a catchy tune that will roll around in your head for weeks. Small boats convey visitors on a tour around the world, with singing and dancing dolls showcasing the dress and culture of each nation. Almost everyone enjoys It's a Small World, but it stands, along with the *Enchanted Tiki Birds*, as an attraction that some could take or leave, while others think it is one of the real masterpieces of the Magic Kingdom. A Holbrook, New York, woman, who is apparently in the "leave it" camp, wrote suggesting that "Small World" would be much better "if each person got 3 to 4 softballs on the way in!"

TOURING TIPS   A good place to cool off during the heat of the day, It's a Small World is a fast-loading ride with two waiting lines and is usually a good bet between 11 A.M. and 5 P.M.

Skyway to Tomorrowland

Type of Ride: Scenic transportation to Tomorrowland

When to Go: Before noon or during special events

Special Comments: If there's a line, it will probably be quicker to walk

Author's Rating: Nice view; ★★★

Overall Appeal by Age Group:

Pre-school	Grade School	Teens	Young Adults	Over 30	Senior Citizens
★★★★	★★★★	★★★½	★★★½	★★★½	★★★½

Duration of Ride: Approximately 5 minutes one way

Average Wait in Line per 100 People Ahead of You: 10 minutes

Assumes: 45 or more cars operating

Loading Speed: Moderate to slow

DESCRIPTION AND COMMENTS Part of the Magic Kingdom internal transportation system, the Skyway is a chairlift that conveys tourists high above the park to Tomorrowland. The view is great, and sometimes the

Skyway can even save a little shoe leather. Usually, however, you could arrive in Tomorrowland much faster by walking.

TOURING TIPS   We enjoy this scenic trip in the morning, during the afternoon character parade, during an evening parade, or just before closing (this ride opens later and closes earlier than other rides in Fantasyland). In short, before the crowds fill the park, when they are otherwise occupied, or when they are on the decline. These times also provide the most dramatic and beautiful vistas. Note to parents with small children: you cannot take strollers on the Skyway.

Peter Pan's Flight

Type of Ride: A Disney fantasy adventure
When to Go: Before 10 A.M. or after 6 P.M.
Author's Rating: Happy, mellow, and well done; ★★★★
Overall Appeal by Age Group:

Pre-school	Grade School	Teens	Young Adults	Over 30	Senior Citizens
★★★★	★★★★	★★★½	★★★★	★★★★	★★★★

Duration of Ride: A little over 3 minutes
Average Wait in Line per 100 People Ahead of You: 5½ minutes
Assumes: Normal operation
Loading Speed: Moderate to slow

DESCRIPTION AND COMMENTS   Though not considered one of the major attractions, Peter Pan's Flight is superbly designed and absolutely delightful with a happy theme, a reunion with some unforgettable Disney characters, beautiful effects, and charming music. Because Peter Pan is so well done, it invites comparison with the other Fantasyland attractions of similar design. A man from Maryland wrote, saying:

> We agree with the statement that of the three similar rides in Fantasyland (Peter Pan, Snow White and Mr. Toad), Peter Pan is by far the best. We were able to ride all three in a row due to no lines, and feel that Mr. Toad and possibly Snow White can be plowed to make room for new attractions.

TOURING TIPS   Though not a major feature of the Magic Kingdom, we nevertheless classify it as "not to be missed." Because Peter Pan's Flight is extremely popular, you can count on long lines all day. Try to ride before 10 A.M., during a parade, or just before the park closes.

Legend of the Lion King

Type of Show: Live mixed-media and puppet show
When to Go: Before 11 A.M. and during parades
Special Comments: The most recent addition to Fantasyland
Author's Rating: Uplifting and fun; ★★★½
Overall Appeal by Age Group:

Pre-school	Grade School	Teens	Young Adults	Over 30	Senior Citizens
★★★★	★★★★	★★★½	★★★★	★★★★	★★★★

Duration of Presentation: Approximately 16 minutes
Preshow Entertainment: 7-minute preshow
Probable Waiting Time: 12 minutes

DESCRIPTION AND COMMENTS In an unprecedented move, the Magic Kingdom opened an attraction based on an animated feature while the film was in its first run. A good example of Disney's hallmark integrated marketing strategy, the attraction serves to stimulate demand for the *Legend of the Lion King* movie. In its production and script, the attraction is a close cousin to *Voyage of the Little Mermaid* at the Disney-MGM Studios. The storyline is poignant and engaging with some dark moments, but ends on a happy and triumphant note. Imaginative puppet work combines with animation and special effects in an effective mixed-media collage.

TOURING TIPS The popularity of *Legend of the Lion King* has grown as guests have become more familiar with its characters and their story. We recommend seeing this show early in the morning or during parades or other special live events. The theater holds about 500 persons, so most of the outside line disappears each time guests are admitted. Even so, you'd be smart to budget a 40-minute wait for this attraction after about 10 A.M.

Cinderella's Golden Carrousel

Type of Ride: Merry-go-round
When to Go: Before 11 A.M. or after 8 P.M.
Special Comments: Adults enjoy the beauty and nostalgia of this ride
Author's Rating: A beautiful children's ride; ★★★
Overall Appeal by Age Group:

Pre-school	Grade School	Teens	Young Adults	Over 30	Senior Citizens
★★★★	★★½	★	★★½	★★★	★★★

Duration of Ride: Approximately 2 minutes
Average Wait in Line per 100 People Ahead of You: 5 minutes
Assumes: Normal staffing
Loading Speed: Slow

DESCRIPTION AND COMMENTS   A merry-go-round to be sure, but certainly one of the most elaborate and beautiful you will ever see, especially when the lights are on.

TOURING TIPS   Unless there are small children in your party we suggest you appreciate this ride from the sidelines. If your children insist on riding, try to get on before 11 A.M. or after 8 P.M. While nice to look at, the Carrousel loads and unloads very slowly.

Mr. Toad's Wild Ride

Type of Ride: Disney version of a spook-house track ride
When to Go: Before 11 A.M. or after 6 P.M.
Author's Rating: Just O.K.; ★★½
Overall Appeal by Age Group:

Pre-school	Grade School	Teens	Young Adults	Over 30	Senior Citizens
★★★½	★★★½	★★★	★★½	★★½	★★½

Duration of Ride: About 2 ¼ minutes
Average Wait in Line per 100 People Ahead of You: 5½ minutes
Assumes: Both tracks operating
Loading Speed: Slow

DESCRIPTION AND COMMENTS   This is an amusement park spook house that does not live up to many visitors' expectations or to the Disney reputation for high quality. The facade is intriguing; the size of the building that houses the attraction suggests an elaborate ride. As it happens, the building is cut in half with similar, though not identical, versions of the same ride in both halves. There is, of course, a separate line for each half.

TOURING TIPS   We receive a lot of mail disagreeing with our critical appraisal of this ride. Clearly, Mr. Toad has his advocates. If you are on a tight schedule, we do not suggest waiting very long for Mr. Toad. If you have two days allotted for the Magic Kingdom, or just want to add your opinion to the controversy, go ahead and ride. If you want to be a supertoad, be sure to try both sides.

Snow White's Adventures

Type of Ride: Disney version of a spook-house track ride
When to Go: Before 11 A.M. and after 6 P.M.
Special Comments: Terrifying to many small children
Author's Rating: Worth seeing if the wait is not long; ★★★
Overall Appeal by Age Group:

Pre-school	Grade School	Teens	Young Adults	Over 30	Senior Citizens
★★★	★★★	★★½	★★★	★★★	★★★

Duration of Ride: Almost 2½ minutes
Average Wait in Line per 100 People Ahead of You: 6¼ minutes
Assumes: Normal operation
Loading Speed: Moderate to slow

DESCRIPTION AND COMMENTS   You ride in a mining car through a spook house featuring Snow White as she narrowly escapes harm at the hands of the wicked witch. The action and effects are a cut above Mr. Toad's Wild Ride, but not as good as Peter Pan's Flight.

TOURING TIPS   We get more mail from our readers about this ride than any other Disney attraction. In short, it terrifies a lot of kids six and under. Though Snow White plays more of a role in the attraction story following a 1995 upgrade, the witch (who is both relentless and ubiquitous) continues to be the focal character. Many readers inform us that their small children will not ride *any* attraction that operates in the dark after experiencing Snow White's Adventures. A mother from Knoxville, Tennessee, commented:

> The outside looks cute and fluffy, but inside, the evil witch just keeps coming at you. My five-year-old, who rode Space Mountain three times and took the Great Movie Ride's monster from *Alien* right in stride, was near panic when our car stopped unexpectedly twice during Snow White. [After Snow White] my six-year-old niece spent a lot of time asking "if a witch will jump out at you" before other rides. So I suggest that you explain a little more what this ride is about. It's tough on preschoolers who are expecting forest animals and dwarfs.

A mom from Long Island, New York, commented similarly, though more succinctly:

> My daughter screamed the whole time and was shot for the day. Grampa kept asking, "Where in the hell is Snow White?"

Experience Snow White if the lines are not too long or on a second day at the park. Ride before 11 A.M. or after 6 P.M., if possible.

20,000 Leagues Under the Sea

Type of Ride: Adventure/scenic boat ride
When to Go: Before 9:30 A.M., during parades, or just before closing
Special Comments: This ride is better if experienced after dark
Author's Rating: Interesting and fun; ★★★
Overall Appeal by Age Group:

Pre-school	Grade School	Teens	Young Adults	Over 30	Senior Citizens
★★★★	★★★	★★★	★★★	★★★	★★★½

Duration of Ride: Approximately 8½ minutes
Average Wait in Line per 100 People Ahead of You: 8 minutes
Assumes: 9 submarines operating
Loading Speed: Slow

DESCRIPTION AND COMMENTS This attraction is based on the Disney movie of the same title. One of several rides that have been successful at both Disneyland (California) and the Magic Kingdom, the ride consists of a submarine voyage that encounters ocean-floor farming, various marine life (robotic), sunken ships, giant squid attacks, and other sights and adventures. Though scheduled for renovation and upgrade, the ride in its present version struggles to maintain its appeal alongside such marvels as Pirates of the Caribbean or Splash Mountain. A reader from Hawthorne Woods, Illinois, writes:

> The only ride that I would not rate as highly as you was 20,000 Leagues Under the Sea. The lines were really slow moving and the ride was not nearly as imaginative as some of the others. I almost felt like we were riding through a concrete ditch with plastic fish on strings and coral stuck around the ditch for effect.

Another reader from Pittsburgh made this comment:

> At 20,000 Leagues Under the Sea, lines were long all day, and Grandma (who loves Disney World) said it was stupid.

TOURING TIPS   This ride could be renamed "20,000 Bottlenecks Under the Sun." It is the traffic-engineering nightmare of the Magic Kingdom. Even 15 minutes after opening, there are long lines and 20- to 30-minute waits. The problem is mainly due to the fact that this slow-loading boat ride is brought up to maximum carrying capacity (nine subs) very tardily. Ride operators fall behind almost as soon as the park opens and never seem to clear the backlog. If you do not want to ride Splash Mountain or Space Mountain, ride 20,000 Leagues first thing in the morning when the park opens.

Dumbo, the Flying Elephant

Type of Ride: Disneyfied midway ride
When to Go: Before 10 A.M. and after 9 P.M.
Author's Rating: An attractive children's ride; ★★★
Overall Appeal by Age Group:

Pre-school	Grade School	Teens	Young Adults	Over 30	Senior Citizens
★★★★★	★★★★	★★	★½	★½	★½

Duration of Ride: 1½ minutes
Average Wait in Line per 100 People Ahead of You: 20 minutes
Assumes: Normal staffing
Loading Speed: Slow

DESCRIPTION AND COMMENTS   A nice, tame, happy children's ride based on the lovable Disney flying elephant, Dumbo. An upgraded rendition of a ride that can be found at state fairs and amusement parks across the country. This notwithstanding, Dumbo is the favorite Magic Kingdom attraction of many younger children.

A lot of readers take us to task for lumping Dumbo in with carnival midway rides. These comments from a reader in Armdale, Nova Scotia, are representative:

> I think you have acquired a jaded attitude. I know [Dumbo] is not for everybody, but when we took our oldest child (then just four), the sign at the end of the line said there would be a ninety-minute wait. He knew and he didn't care, and he and I stood in the hot afternoon sun for 90 blissful minutes waiting for his 90-second flight. Anything that a four-year-old would wait for that long and that patiently must be pretty special.

TOURING TIPS   This is a slow-loading ride that we recommend you bypass unless you are on a very relaxed touring schedule. If your kids are excited about Dumbo, try to get them on the ride before 10 A.M. or just before the park closes.

Mad Tea Party

Type of Ride: Midway-type spinning ride
When to Go: Before 11 A.M. and after 5 P.M.
Special Comments: You can make the tea cups spin
    faster by turning the wheel in the center of the cup.
Author's Rating: Fun, but not worth the wait; ★★½

Motion Sickness WARNING!

Overall Appeal by Age Group:

Pre-school	Grade School	Teens	Young Adults	Over 30	Senior Citizens
★★★★	★★★★	★★★★	★★★	★★	★★

Duration of Ride: 1½ minutes
Average Wait in Line per 100 People Ahead of You: 7½ minutes
Assumes: Normal staffing
Loading Speed: Slow

DESCRIPTION AND COMMENTS   An amusement park ride, though well done in the Disney style. *Alice in Wonderland*'s Mad Hatter provides the theme, and riders whirl around feverishly in big tea cups. A rendition of this ride, sans Disney characters, can be found at every local carnival and fair.

TOURING TIPS   This ride, aside from not being particularly unique, is notoriously slow to load. Skip it on a busy schedule if the kids will let you. Ride in the morning of your second day if your schedule is more relaxed. A warning for parents who have not given this ride much thought: Teenagers like nothing better than to lure an adult onto the tea cups and then turn the wheel in the middle (which makes the cup spin faster) until the adults are plastered against the side of the cup and are on the verge of throwing up. Unless your life's ambition is to be the test subject in a human centrifuge, do not even consider getting on this ride with anyone younger than 21.

Fantasyland Eateries and Shops

DESCRIPTION AND COMMENTS   If you prefer atmosphere with your dining, you can (with reservations) eat at King Stefan's Banquet Hall in Cinderella Castle. Many of the Magic Kingdom visitors we surveyed wanted to know "What is in the castle?" or "Can we go up into the castle?" Well, Virginia, you can't see the whole thing, but if you eat at King Stefan's you can inspect a fair-sized chunk. Be forewarned, however, that our dining experiences at King Stefan's have been unqualified disasters. We eat there at least once each year and anticipate it with dread. If your kids are really hot to see the inside of the castle, we recommend making a reservation at King Stefan's for a time convenient to you. However, order only dessert. Eat your main meal someplace else.

Our opinion of King Stefan's sometimes puts parents at loggerheads with their children, who are hell-bent to see Cinderella. Happily a Stone Mountain, Georgia, mother wrote reporting that "Cinderella greets diners in the waiting area of King Stefan's at Cinderella's Castle. You can meet her there without the torture of eating at the restaurant. Just enter the area through the left door by the hostess stand."

Shops in Fantasyland present more specialty and souvenir shopping opportunities. Mickey's Christmas Carol offers an exceptional selection of Christmas decorations and ornaments.

TOURING TIPS   To eat at King Stefan's in the castle you must have reservations. If you are lodging in Walt Disney World, you can call 55 or 56 one to three days in advance to make reservations. Otherwise, make reservations first thing in the morning at the door of the restaurant. We do not recommend a meal at King Stefan's if you are on a tight schedule or if you are sensitive about paying fancy prices for ho-hum (or worse) food. If you plan to spend two days in the Magic Kingdom and are curious about the inside of the castle, you might give it a try on your second day. If there are small children in your party, ask when Cinderella will be present before making your reservation. Sometimes, as mentioned, Cinderella also makes appearances in the lower lobby and outside the door of the restaurant.

Other Fantasyland lunch options include Lumière's Kitchen (formerly Gurgi's Munchies & Crunchies), where parents can obtain special lunches for children, and the Pinocchio Village Haus, which serves up a good albeit expensive bratwurst. If you find yourself somehow transported to Fantasyland at the crack of dawn on an early-entry morning, the Pinocchio Village Haus also serves good coffee and a wide assortment of breakfast rolls and pastries. As for shopping, don't waste time in the shops unless you have a relaxed schedule or shopping is a big priority.

Mickey's Starland

Mickey's Starland is the first new "land" to be added to the Magic Kingdom since its opening, and the only land that does not connect to the central hub. Attractions include a live musical stage show featuring the Disney characters, a chance to meet Mickey Mouse, Mickey Mouse's house, a town of miniature buildings (Duckburg), a petting farm, and a young children's play area.

All in all, as Whoopi Goldberg might say, Mickey's Starland is a strange piece of work. To begin with, it is sandwiched between Fantasyland and Tomorrowland, like an afterthought, on about three acres that were formerly part of the Grand Prix Raceway. It is by far the smallest of the "lands" and seems more like an attraction than a section of the park. Though you can wander in on a somewhat obscure path from Fantasyland, Mickey's Starland is basically set up to receive guests arriving by the Walt Disney World Railroad.

Once you arrive at Mickey's Starland (which is located in the town of Duckburg), there is no indication of where or when the character show takes place. What you see as you leave the train station is a children's play area on your left, and a street of miniature buildings on your right. There is one normally sized house (Mickey's) among the little buildings, with a cluster of what looks like circus tents puffing up colorfully behind. To see the show, go through Mickey's house and watch cartoons in the waiting area until show time.

Mickey's House and Mickey's Starland Show

Type of Show: Live musical comedy featuring the Disney characters
When to Go: Anytime
Special Comments: After the show, guests can meet Mickey backstage at Mickey's Hollywood Theater
Author's Rating: Warm, happy, funny, and all Disney; ★★★

Overall Appeal by Age Group:

Pre-school	Grade School	Teens	Young Adults	Over 30	Senior Citizens
★★★★½	★★★★	★★★½	★★★	★★★½	★★★½

Duration of Presentation: Approximately 14 minutes
Preshow Entertainment: Mickey Mouse cartoons
Probable Waiting Time: About 10 minutes

DESCRIPTION AND COMMENTS   *Mickey's Starland Show*, the feature attraction of Mickey's Starland, is reached by walking through Mickey's House (which is full of Mickey Mouse and Walt Disney memorabilia), through Mickey's backyard, and into an air-conditioned, pre-show tent where Mickey Mouse cartoons are viewed on TV monitors. Many patrons who find their way this far have no idea that there is anything more to see. They watch cartoons for a few minutes and then turn around and walk out. Had they stayed, they would have been treated to a funny, happy, and energetic live stage show featuring the Disney characters.

After the show, guests pass through a gift shop and photo opportunity area. As you exit outside, Mickey's Hollywood Theater is on the right. Here Mickey receives visitors in his dressing room to pose for photographs. This is a nice touch, but as with the stage show, this business of meeting Mickey in person backstage is never made very clear. For the most part, folks just walk into Mickey's Hollywood Theater and line up, not knowing what the line is for.

TOURING TIPS   There is no problem catching a performance of *Mickey's Starland Show* once you know it's there and how to get to it. We recommend seeing the show during the hot, early afternoon hours when a few minutes in a nice, air-conditioned theater is relaxing. Be aware that performances are often suspended immediately before and during parades. Consult the daily entertainment schedule for show times. If you want to meet Mickey backstage without a lot of waiting, try one of the following:

1. In the waiting area for the character show (a tentlike structure with Mickey Mouse cartoons on T.V.), position yourself in front of the farthest left of several doors leading to the theater. When admitted you will proceed down a long passageway to another set of doors. Again try to be in front and on the left. When finally admitted to the actual theater, you will enter a row of seats and move all the way to the far end. At this point you should be positioned perfectly

to duck out of the theater as soon as the curtain falls. When the time comes, hustle out the door to your immediate left, pass quickly through the postshow area, and go outside. Mickey's Hollywood Theater will be on your right and several hundred other guests will be 30 steps behind you and headed for the same place. Or;

2. Enjoy the petting farm or walk around Duckburg for about 15 minutes after exiting the show. Line up to see Mickey just before the show following yours concludes; this is when the line will be shortest. A lady from Pittsburgh wrote, suggesting:

You might want to mention that only a few people are let into Mickey's dressing room at a time—maybe four small family groups. When they are done, the next batch comes in. So it's more intimate than, say, seeing Santa at the mall. By the way, Mickey autographed our *Unofficial Guide*, shaking his head sadly, and underlining "unofficial" several times, both on the cover and on the frontispiece.

An Atlanta, Georgia, mother reported that "you can meet Mickey anytime at Mickey's [Hollywood] Theater, not just after the Starland Show. We went just before park closing and had Mickey all to ourselves."

—— *Other Mickey's Starland Attractions*

Grandma Duck's Petting Farm

Type of Attraction: Walk-through petting farm
When to Go: Anytime
Special Comments: Animals are real
Author's Rating: Improved; ★★½
Overall Appeal by Age Group:

Pre-school	Grade School	Teens	Young Adults	Over 30	Senior Citizens
★★★	★★★	★½	★½	★½	★½

DESCRIPTION AND COMMENTS   This attraction was improved and up-graded in 1994. There are now more animals, and the gravel paths have been replaced by a nice boardwalk that is easily negotiated by persons in wheelchairs. Unlike most petting farms, this one does not let you walk among the animals (goats, pigs, ducks, chickens, calves, etc.). You must pet them when possible over or through fences.

TOURING TIPS   Visit the animals anytime. You will not encounter large crowds here, as a rule.

Small Children's Play Area

DESCRIPTION AND COMMENTS   This area is designed for small children and features an interconnected system of slides, tunnels, and ladders. Children enjoy the chance to let off steam while adults enjoy the tour intermission. From our perspective, the major shortcoming is the lack of shade; attending adults must swelter in the hot Florida sun. A dad from Arlington, Virginia, however, voiced a more expanded perspective:

> WDW people [need to] move, eliminate, or change this thing. It needs shade and parents need to be told there is a back exit (or better yet, make all the exits come out in the same place). Too many parents running around trying to find their kids. Too many kids come out crying when they can't find their parents, who are patiently waiting on the other side. Little kids can get run over or overwhelmed easily [children up to nine years are allowed in the play area], and out of the view of parents.

TOURING TIPS   If you are on a tight schedule, or it is a particularly hot day, skip this attraction. Preschoolers should take a potty break before hitting the playground.

Tomorrowland

Tomorrowland is a futuristic mix of rides and experiences that relate to the technological development of man and what life will be like in the years to come. If this sounds a little bit like the EPCOT Center theme, it's because Tomorrowland was very much a breeding ground for the ideas that resulted in EPCOT Center. Yet Tomorrowland and EPCOT Center are very different. Aside from differences in scale, Tomorrowland is more "just for fun." While EPCOT Center educates in its own style, Tomorrowland allows you to experience the future as described in science fiction.

An exhaustive renovation of Tomorrowland was completed in 1995. Prior to the renovation, Tomorrowland's 24-year-old buildings more resembled 70s motel architecture than anyone's vision of the future. Tomorrowland's renovated design is ageless, reflecting a nostalgic vision of the future as imagined by dreamers and scientists in the 1920s and 30s. Now frozen in time, Tomorrowland conjures up visions of Buck Rogers, fanciful mechanical rockets, and metallic cities spread beneath towering obelisks. Disney calls the renovated Tomorrowland the "Future That Never Was," while Spencer Reise of *Newsweek* dubbed it "retro-future."

In the new Tomorrowland, *Alien Encounter* replaces *Mission to Mars* (formerly *Spaceflight to the Moon*). The *Carousel of Progress* has been jazzed up and moved forward in time, and *American Journeys*, with the addition of AudioAnimatronic characters and a plot, has been recast as *Transportarium*. The Starjets ride, now sporting a campy Jules Verne look, is a bit higher off the ground, but still goes around in circles. Its new name is the AstroOrbiter. The WEDway PeopleMover has become the Tomorrowland Transit Authority. Venerable Space Mountain continues to hold its own, but the Grand Prix Raceway and the Skyway to Fantasyland seem incongruous.

Space Mountain

Motion
Sickness

WARNING!

Type of Ride: Roller coaster in the dark
When to Go: First thing when the park opens or during
the hour before closing or between 6 and 7 P.M.
Special Comments: Great fun and action, much wilder
than Big Thunder Mountain. Children must be
3'8" tall to ride, and if under seven years old,
must be accompanied by an adult. Switching-off
option provided (see page 166).
Author's Rating: A great roller coaster with excellent special effects;
★★★★★

Overall Appeal by Age Group:

Pre-school	Grade School	Teens	Young Adults	Over 30	Senior Citizens
†	★★★★★	★★★★★	★★★★½	★★★★	†

† Some preschoolers loved Space Mountain, others were frightened. The
sample size of senior citizens who experienced this ride was too small to
develop an accurate rating.

Duration of Ride: Almost 3 minutes
Average Wait in Line per 100 People Ahead of You: 3 minutes
Assumes: Two tracks operating at 21-second dispatch intervals
Loading Speed: Moderate to fast

WARNING!
For Bouffants, Rug Wearers, and Elvis Impersonators
This Ride Will Muss Your 'Do

DESCRIPTION AND COMMENTS   Space Mountain is a roller coaster in the
dark. Totally enclosed in a mammoth futuristic structure, the attraction is
a marvel of creativity and engineering. The theme of the ride is a space-
flight through the dark recesses of the galaxy. The effects are superb and
the ride is the fastest and wildest in the Disney repertoire. As a roller

coaster, Space Mountain is a lulu, much zippier than the Big Thunder Mountain ride.

TOURING TIPS   Space Mountain is a "not to be missed" feature (if you can handle a fairly wild roller coaster ride). People who are not timid about going on roller coasters will take Space Mountain in stride. What has always set Space Mountain apart is that the cars plummet through the dark with only occasional lighting effects piercing the gloom. During our revision research in 1994 and 1995, however, we noticed that Space Mountain had been lightened up a bit. We could see the track in front of the car and much of the roller coaster superstructure. Subsequently, a number of readers wrote confirming this observation. We hope that the additional lighting is a temporary experiment. Half the fun of Space Mountain is not knowing where the car will go next.

Space Mountain is the favorite attraction of many Magic Kingdom visitors between 7 and 50 years of age. Each morning prior to opening, particularly during the summer and holiday periods, several hundred S.M. "junkies" crowd the rope barriers at the central hub awaiting the signal to sprint (literally) the 250 yards to the ride's entrance. The "Space Mountain Morning Mini Marathon," as our research team called it, pits tubby, out-of-shape dads and moms against their svelte, speedy offspring, brother against sister, blossoming coeds against truck drivers, nuns against beauticians. If you want to ride Space Mountain without a long wait, you had better do well in the "Mini Marathon," because at five minutes after opening, Space Mountain has more guests in line waiting to ride than any other attraction in the Magic Kingdom.

There was a time when Disney personnel tried to keep guests from running (they still tell you not to run) to Space Mountain, but even in the Magic Kingdom reality is a force to be reckoned with. The reality in this case is that a dozen Disney security personnel cannot control several hundred stampeding, flipped-out, early-morning space cadets. So here you are, a nice normal dental hygienist from Toledo, and you are thinking you'd like to ride Space Mountain. Well, Virginia, you're in the big league now; tie up them Reeboks and get ready to run.

But first, a word from the coach. There are a couple of things you can do to get a leg up on the competition. First, arrive early; be one of the first in the park. Proceed to the end of Main Street and cut right past the Plaza Restaurant, and stop under an archway that says:

The Plaza Pavilion Terrace Dining

where a Disney worker will be standing behind a rope barrier. From this point, you are approximately 100 yards closer to Space Mountain, on a route through the Plaza Pavilion, than your competition waiting to take off from the central hub. From this point of departure, middle-aged folks walking fast can beat most of the teens sprinting from the central hub. And if you are up to some modest jogging, well . . . . Another advantage of starting from the Plaza Pavilion entrance is that your wait until opening will be cool, comfortable, and in the shade.

Couples touring with children too small to ride Space Mountain can both ride without waiting in line twice by taking advantage of a procedure called "switching off." Here is how it works. When you enter the Space Mountain line alert the first Disney attendant (known as Greeter One) that you want to switch off. The attendant will allow you, your spouse, and your small child (or children) to continue together, phoning ahead to Greeter Two to expect you. When you reach Greeter Two (at the turnstile near the boarding area), you will be given specific directions. One of you will go ahead and ride while the other stays with the kids. Whoever rides will be admitted by the unloading attendant to stairs leading back up to the boarding area. Here you switch off; the second parent rides, and the first parent takes the kids down the stairs to the unloading area where everybody joins up and exits. Switching off is also available as an option on the Big Thunder Mountain Railroad and on Splash Mountain.

For parents whose children meet the minimum height and age requirements to ride Space Mountain, be advised that all riders have their own seat. You cannot sit next to your child.

If you do not catch Space Mountain early in the morning, try again during the hour before closing. Often at this time of day, Space Mountain visitors are held in line outside the entrance until all those previously in line have ridden, thus emptying the attraction inside. The appearance from the outside is that the waiting line is enormous when, in reality, the only people waiting are those visible in front of the entrance. This crowd-control technique, known as "stacking," has the effect of discouraging visitors from riding because they perceive the wait to be too long. Stacking is used in several Walt Disney World rides and attractions during the hour before closing to ensure that the ride will be able to close on schedule. It is also used to keep the number of people waiting inside from overwhelming the air conditioning. For those who do not let the seemingly long line run them off, the waiting period is usually no longer than if you had been allowed to queue up inside.

Splash Mountain, which opened in 1992, siphons off a number of guests who previously would have made Space Mountain their first stop. Even so, you can still depend on a mob rushing to Space Mountain as soon as the park opens. If you especially like the thrill rides, ride Space Mountain first thing in the morning, followed by *Alien Encounter,* Big Thunder Mountain Railroad, and then Splash Mountain.

If you are a Disney resort hotel or campground guest and are eligible for early admission, you can enjoy Space Mountain to your heart's content for an hour before the general public is admitted on Mondays, Thursdays, and Saturdays. Though Disney staff may insist that only Fantasyland is "officially" open for early entrants, Space Mountain and, sometimes, the Grand Prix Raceway (both in Tomorrowland) are often open as well. To determine whether Space Mountain is open early, simply head for Tomorrowland. If you are permitted to enter Tomorrowland, Space Mountain will be operating (Disney security will not allow early-entry guests into any part of the park not yet open). If you are not allowed to enter Tomorrowland from its main entrance at the central hub, try again about 20 minutes later using the walkway between Fantasyland and Tomorrowland.

If you are an early entrant and Big Thunder Mountain and Splash Mountain are also high on your priority list, ride Space Mountain (as well as Fantasyland attractions) until about 10 to 15 minutes before the hour the general public is admitted. At this time, return to Fantasyland and continue to the boundary of Fantasyland and Liberty Square and wait for the rest of the park to open. When it does, enter Liberty Square and move quickly along the Liberty Square and Frontierland waterfronts to Big Thunder Mountain and Splash Mountain.

If you are not eligible for early entry, try to visit the Magic Kingdom on a Tuesday, Wednesday, Friday, or Sunday and make Space Mountain your first attraction of the day. If you are not eligible for early entry, but your schedule requires that you visit on an early entry day, ride Splash Mountain and Big Thunder Railroad first, then head to Space Mountain.

Grand Prix Raceway

Type of Ride: Drive-'em-yourself miniature cars
When to Go: Before 11 A.M. and after 5 P.M.
Special Comments: Must be 4'4" tall to drive
Author's Rating: Boring for adults (★); great for preschoolers

Overall Appeal by Age Group:

Pre-school	Grade School	Teens	Young Adults	Over 30	Senior Citizens
★★★½	★★★	★	½	½	½

Duration of Ride: Approximately 4¼ minutes

Average Wait in Line per 100 People Ahead of You: 4½ minutes

Assumes: 285-car turnover every 20 minutes

Loading Speed: Slow

DESCRIPTION AND COMMENTS An elaborate miniature raceway with gasoline-powered cars that will travel at speeds of up to seven miles an hour. The raceway design, with its sleek cars, racing noises, and Grand Prix billboards, is quite alluring. Unfortunately, however, the cars poke along on a track leaving the driver with little to do. Pretty ho-hum for most adults and teenagers. Small children, who would enjoy the ride, are often excluded by the height requirement.

TOURING TIPS This ride is appealing to the eye but definitely expendable to the schedule of adults. Preschoolers, however, love it. If your preschooler is too short to drive, ride along and allow your child to steer (the car runs on a guide rail) while you work the foot pedal.

A mom from North Billerica, Massachusetts, writes:

> I was truly amazed by the number of adults in the line. Please emphasize to your readers that these cars travel on a guided path and are not a whole lot of fun. The only reason I could think of for adults to be in the line would be an insane desire to go on absolutely every ride at Disney World. The other feature about the cars is that they tend to pile up at the end, so it takes almost as long to get off as it did to get on. Parents riding with their preschoolers should keep the car going as slow as [possible] without stalling. This prolongs the preschooler's joy and decreases the time you will have to wait at the end.

Skyway to Fantasyland

Type of Ride: Scenic transportation to Fantasyland

When to Go: Before noon and during special events

Special Comments: If a line, probably quicker to walk

Author's Rating: Nice view; ★★★

Overall Appeal by Age Group:

Pre-school	Grade School	Teens	Young Adults	Over 30	Senior Citizens
★★★★	★★★★	★★★½	★★★½	★★★½	★★★½

Duration of Ride: Approximately 5 minutes one way

Average Wait in Line per 100 People Ahead of You: 10 minutes

Assumes: 45 or more cars operating

Loading Speed: Moderate

DESCRIPTION AND COMMENTS   A skylift that transports you from Tomorrowland to the far corner of Fantasyland near the border it shares with Liberty Square. The view is one of the best in the Magic Kingdom, but walking is usually faster if you just want to get there.

TOURING TIPS   Unless the lines are short, the Skyway will not save you any time as a mode of transportation. As a ride, however, it affords some incredible views. Ride in the morning, during the two hours before the park closes, or during one of the daily parades (this ride sometimes opens later and closes earlier than other rides in Tomorrowland). Parents with small children should be advised that strollers are not allowed on the Skyway.

AstroOrbiter

Motion Sickness

WARNING!

Type of Ride: Buck Rogers–style rockets revolving around a central axis

When to Go: Before 11 A.M. or after 5 P.M.

Special Comments: This attraction, formerly known as StarJets, is not as innocuous as it appears.

Author's Rating: Not worth the wait; ★★

Overall Appeal by Age Group:

Pre-school	Grade School	Teens	Young Adults	Over 30	Senior Citizens
★★★★	★★★	★★½	★½	★	★

Duration of Ride: 1½ minutes

Average Wait in Line per 100 People Ahead of You: 13½ minutes

Assumes: Normal staffing

Loading Speed: Slow

DESCRIPTION AND COMMENTS   Though recently upgraded and quite appealing visually, AstroOrbiter is still pretty much a carnival midway ride. Simply put, the fat little rocketships fly around in circles. The best thing about AstroOrbiter is the nice view when you are aloft.

TOURING TIPS   Slow loading and expendable on any schedule. If you take preschoolers on this ride, place them in the seat first, then situate yourself. Be aware that the AstroOrbiter flies higher and faster than Dumbo and that it frightens some small children. It also apparently messes with certain adults, as a mother from Lev Has Homron, Israel, attests:

> I think your assessment of [AstroOrbiter] as "very mild" is way off. I was able to sit through all the "Mountains," the "Tours" and the "Wars" without my stomach reacting even a little, but after [AstroOrbiter] I thought I would be finished for the rest of the day. Very quickly I realized that my only chance for survival was to pick a point on the toe of my shoe and stare at it (and certainly not lift my eyes out of the "jet") until the ride was over. My 4-year-old was my co-pilot and she loved the ride (go figure) and she had us up high the whole time. It was a nightmare—people should be forewarned.

Tomorrowland Transit Authority

Type of Ride: Scenic

When to Go: During the hot, crowded period of the day (11:30 A.M.–4:30 P.M.)

Special Comments: A good way to check out the crowd at Space Mountain

Author's Rating: Scenic, relaxing, informative; ★★★

Overall Appeal by Age Group:

Pre-school	Grade School	Teens	Young Adults	Over 30	Senior Citizens
★★★	★★★	★★½	★★½	★★★	★★★

Duration of Ride: 10 minutes

Average Wait in Line per 100 People Ahead of You: 1½ minutes

Assumes: 39 trains operating

Loading Speed: Fast

DESCRIPTION AND COMMENTS   A once unique prototype of a linear induction-powered system of mass transportation. Tram-like cars take you on a leisurely tour of Tomorrowland, including a peek at the inside of Space Mountain. The Tomorrowland Transit Authority was formerly known as the WEDway PeopleMover.

TOURING TIPS   A nice, pleasant, relaxing ride where the lines move quickly and you seldom have to wait. A good ride to take during the busier times of the day, the Transit Authority, according to a Texas mom, can also double as a nursery:

> The [Transit Authority] is an excellent ride for getting a tired infant to fall asleep. You can stay on for several times around. It is also a moderately private and comfortable place for nursing an infant.

Carousel of Progress

Type of Show: AudioAnimatronic theater production
When to Go: Anytime
Author's Rating: Nostalgic, warm, and happy; ★★★½
Overall Appeal by Age Group:

Pre-school	Grade School	Teens	Young Adults	Over 30	Senior Citizens
★★★	★★★½	★★★½	★★★½	★★★★	★★★★½

Duration of Presentation: 18 minutes
Preshow Entertainment: Documentary on the attraction's long history
Probable Waiting Time: Less than 10 minutes

DESCRIPTION AND COMMENTS   Updated and improved during the 1993–94 Tomorrowland renovation, the *Carousel of Progress* is a warm and nostalgic look at the way technology and electricity have changed the lives of an AudioAnimatronics family over several generations. Though not rated "not to be missed," *Carousel of Progress* is thoroughly delightful. The family depicted is easy to identify with, and a happy, sentimental tune serves to bridge the gap between generations.

TOURING TIPS   While not on our "not to be missed" list, this attraction is a great favorite of Magic Kingdom repeat visitors. A great favorite of ours as well, it is included on all of our one-day touring plans. *Carousel of*

Progress handles big crowds effectively and is a good choice for touring during the busier times of the day.

Dreamflight

Type of Ride: Special-effects travel ride
When to go: Anytime
Author's Rating: Pleasant; ★★★
Projected Overall Appeal by Age Group:

Pre-school	Grade School	Teens	Young Adults	Over 30	Senior Citizens
★★★½	★★★½	★★★½	★★★½	★★★½	★★★½

Duration of Ride: About 6 minutes
Average Wait in Line per 100 People Ahead of You: 3 minutes
Assumes: Normal operation
Loading Speed: Fast

DESCRIPTION AND COMMENTS: Presented by Delta Airlines, Dreamflight is a somewhat fanciful depiction of the history of flight. Pleasant but not particularly compelling, this new addition to the Tomorrowland lineup could have been a lot more interesting. A bit like Peter Pan's Flight, with an EPCOT Center–style presentation, Dreamflight is best characterized as "nice."

TOURING TIPS Very seldom is there a line at Dreamflight. See it during the heat of the day or whenever the mood strikes.

Transportarium

Type of Attraction: Time travel movie adventure
When to Go: Anytime
Special Comments: Audience must stand throughout presentation
Author's Rating: Outstanding; ★★★★½
Overall Appeal by Age Group:

Pre-school	Grade School	Teens	Young Adults	Over 30	Senior Citizens
★★★	★★★½	★★★½	★★★½	★★★★	★★★★

Duration of Presentation: About 20 minutes

Preshow Entertainment: Robots, lasers, and movies
Probable Waiting Time: 8–15 minutes

DESCRIPTION AND COMMENTS   Originally developed as *Le Visionarium* for Euro Disneyland, *Transportarium* adds AudioAnimatronic characters and a storyline to the long successful 360° Circle-Vision technology. Guests first view a preshow introducing Timekeeper (a humanoid) and 9-Eye (a time-traveling robot so named because she has nine cameras that serve as eyes). Following the preshow, the audience is ushered into the main theater, where the AudioAnimatronic (robotic) Timekeeper places 9-Eye into a time machine and dispatches her on a crazed journey into the past and then into the future. What 9-Eye sees on her odyssey (through her nine camera eyes) is projected onto huge screens that completely surround the audience, providing a 360° perspective of all the action. The robot's travels take her back to prehistoric Europe and then forward to meet French author and visionary Jules Verne, who hitches a ride with 9-Eye into the future. Circle-Vision film technology, Disney AudioAnimatronics, and high-tech special effects combine to establish *Transportarium* as one of Tomorrowland's premier attractions. We rate it as "not to be missed."

TOURING TIPS   *Transportarium* promises to be extremely popular, drawing large crowds from midmorning on. The theater is huge, however, accommodating more than 1,000 guests per showing. If you try *Transportarium* before noon, your wait should be in the 5- to 15-minute range. During the crowded middle of the day, expect a longer wait.

Alien Encounter

Type of Show: Theater-in-the-round science fiction drama
When to Go: Before 10:30 A.M. or after 5 P.M.
Special Comments: Frightening to children
Author's Rating: ★★★★
Overall Appeal by Age Group:

Pre-school	Grade School	Teens	Young Adults	Over 30	Senior Citizens
★★★	★★★★½	★★★★	★★★★	★★★★	★★★

Duration of Presentation: About 12 minutes
Preshow Entertainment: About 6 minutes
Probable Waiting Time: 12–40 minutes

DESCRIPTION AND COMMENTS   Heralded as the showpiece of the "new" Tomorrowland, *Alien Encounter* is a theater production situated in the building that previously housed the *Mission to Mars*. Guests are invited to witness a demonstration of "interplanetary teleportation," a technique that breaks travelers down into electrons for transmission to distant locations. In this case the demonstration goes awry, of course, and an extremely unsavory alien (with pronounced asocial tendencies) arrives in the theater. Mayhem ensues, but everything is tidied up in plenty of time for the next audience to be admitted.

TOURING TIPS   One of Disney's most intense and frightening attractions, *Alien Encounter* was initially rejected by Walt Disney Company Chairman Michael Eisner for not being scary enough. *Alien Encounter* stays busy throughout the day. Try to go early in the morning, during the afternoon or evening parades, or during the last hour the park is open.

Tomorrowland Eateries and Shops

DESCRIPTION AND COMMENTS   Cosmic Ray's Starlight Cafe (formerly the Tomorrowland Terrace) is the largest and most efficient of the Magic Kingdom's numerous fast-food restaurants. The Plaza Pavilion, however, serves better food. Several shops provide yet additional opportunities for buying souvenirs and curiosities.

TOURING TIPS   Forget browsing the shops until your second day unless shopping is your top priority.

Not to Be Missed at the Magic Kingdom

Adventureland	Jungle Cruise
	Pirates of the Caribbean
Frontierland	Big Thunder Mountain Railroad
	Country Bear Jamboree
	Splash Mountain
Liberty Square	The Haunted Mansion
Fantasyland	Peter Pan's Flight
Tomorrowland	Space Mountain
	Transportarium
	Alien Encounter
Special events	Evening Parade

Live Entertainment in the Magic Kingdom

Live entertainment in the form of bands, Disney character appearances, parades, singing and dancing, and ceremonies further enliven and add color to the Magic Kingdom on a daily basis. For specific information about what's happening on the day you visit, stop by City Hall as you enter the park. Be forewarned, however, that if you are on a tight schedule, it is impossible to see both the Magic Kingdom's featured attractions **and** take in the numerous and varied live performances offered. In our one-day touring plans we exclude the live performances in favor of seeing as much of the park as time permits. This is a considered, tactical decision based on the fact that some of the parades and other performances siphon crowds away from the more popular rides, thus shortening waiting lines.

But the color and pageantry of live happenings around the park are an integral part of the Magic Kingdom entertainment mix and a persuasive argument for second-day touring. The following is an incomplete list and description of those performances and events that are scheduled with some regularity and for which no reservations are required.

Fantasy Faire Stage	Site of various concerts in Fantasyland.
Steel Drum Bands	Steel drum bands perform daily at the Caribbean Plaza in Adventureland.
Frontierland Stuntmen	Stuntmen stage shootouts in Frontierland according to the daily live entertainment schedule.
Kids of the Kingdom	A youthful song and dance group that performs popular music daily in the Castle Forecourt. Disney characters usually join in the fun.
Flag Retreat	Daily at 5 P.M. at Town Square (the railroad station end of Main Street). Sometimes done with great fanfare and college marching bands, sometimes with a smaller Disney band.

Sword in the Stone Ceremony	A ceremony with audience participation based on the Disney animated feature of the same name. Merlin the Magician selects youngsters from among the guests to test their courage and strength by removing the sword, Excalibur, from the stone. Staged several times each day behind Cinderella Castle; check the daily entertainment schedule.
Bay Lake and Seven Seas Lagoon Floating Electrical Pageant	This is one of our favorites of all the Disney extras, but you have to leave the Magic Kingdom to see it. The Floating Electrical Pageant is a stunning electric light show afloat on small barges and set to nifty electronic music. The Pageant is performed at nightfall on the Seven Seas Lagoon and on Bay Lake. Exit the Magic Kingdom and take the monorail to the Polynesian Resort. Get yourself a drink and walk out to the end of the pier. The show will begin shortly (about 9 P.M. during the summer).
Fantasy in the Sky	A stellar fireworks display unleashed after dark on those nights the park is open late.
Cosmic Ray's Starlight Cafe Theater	These stages in Tomorrowland feature top-40 rock music, rap, and jazz, as well as Disney characters and the Kids of the Kingdom.
Disney Character Shows & Appearances	On most days, a character *du jour* is on duty for photo posing from 9 A.M. until 10 P.M. next to City Hall. Disney character shows run according to the daily entertainment schedule at Mickey's Starland. Shows at the Castle Forecourt Stage (front of the castle) feature the Disney characters several times a day according to the daily entertainment schedule, as do shows in the Tomorrowland Galaxy Palace Theater. Finally, characters roam the park throughout the day, but can almost always be found in Fantasyland and Mickey's Starland.
Magic Kingdom Bands	Various banjo, dixieland, steel drum, marching, and fife and drum bands roam the Magic Kingdom daily.

Tinker Bell's Flight
A nice special effect in the sky above Cinderella Castle at 10 P.M. to herald the beginning of Fantasy in the Sky fireworks (when the park is open late).

———— Parades

Parades are a big deal at the Magic Kingdom, full-fledged spectaculars with dozens of Disney characters and some amazing special effects. In late 1991, the beloved Main Street Electrical Parade was unplugged and sent abroad, and the afternoon parade was replaced by an eye-popping celebration of carnivals around the world. The new parades are larger, more colorful, and more elaborate than any Disney street production to date. We rate the afternoon parade as outstanding and the evening parade as "not to be missed."

In addition to providing great entertainment, the parades also serve to lure guests away from the attractions. If getting on rides is more appealing than watching a parade, you will find the wait for all attractions substantially diminished just before and during parades. Because the parade route does not pass through Adventureland, Tomorrowland, or Fantasyland, attractions in these lands are particularly good bets. Be forewarned that parades disrupt traffic in the Magic Kingdom. It is near impossible, for example, to get to Adventureland from Tomorrowland, or vice versa, during a parade.

Afternoon Parade

Usually staged at 3 P.M., the parade features bands, floats, and marching Disney characters, as well as huge, inflated Disney characters towering 55 feet above Main Street. The latest edition of the afternoon parade is called *Mickey Mania.*

Evening Parade(s)

The evening parade goes high-tech with a whole new production featuring giant holographs, electro-luminescent and fiber-optic technologies, light-spreading thermoplastics (do not try this at home), and clouds of underlit liquid nitrogen smoke. In spite of how appealing this sounds, don't worry. You won't need a gas mask or an asbestos suit, nor will your hair fall out in three weeks. For those who flunked chemistry and physics, the parade also features music, Mickey Mouse, and twinkling lights. Depending on closing time, the evening parade is staged once at 9 P.M.; or twice when the park is open late, at 9 and 11 P.M.

During less busy times of year, the evening parade is held only on weekends, and sometimes not even then. If the evening parade figures prominently in your vacation plans, call (407) 824-4321 before you go to ascertain the parade's status during your visit.

Parade Route and Vantage Points

Magic Kingdom parades circle Town Square, head down Main Street, go around the central hub, and then cross over the bridge to Liberty Square. In Liberty Square the parade progresses along the waterfront and ends in Frontierland. Sometimes parades begin in Frontierland and run the same route in the opposite direction, terminating in Town Square.

Most guests tend to watch from the central hub or from Main Street. One of the best vantage points, and certainly one of the most popular, is the upper platform of the Walt Disney World Railroad Station at the Town Square end of Main Street. This is also a particularly good place for watching the Fantasy in the Sky fireworks. A big problem with the train platform, however, is that you literally have to stake out your position 30 to 45 minutes before the parade begins.

Because the majority of spectators pack Main Street and the central hub, we recommend watching the parades from Liberty Square or Frontierland. There are several great vantage points frequently overlooked:

1. The Sleepy Hollow sandwich shop, on your immediate right as you cross the bridge into Liberty Square, is a good spot. If you arrive early you can buy refreshments and get a table by the rail. You will have a perfect view of the parade as it passes over the Liberty Square bridge.

2. A pathway runs along the Liberty Square side of the moat from the Sleepy Hollow sandwich shop to Cinderella's Castle. Any point along this path offers a clear and unobstructed view of the parade as it passes over the Liberty Square bridge.

3. There is a covered walkway connecting the Liberty Tree Tavern and the Diamond Horseshoe Saloon. This elevated vantage point is perfect for watching parades (particularly on rainy days) and usually goes unnoticed until just before the parade starts.

4. There are elevated wooden platforms in front of the Frontierland Shootin' Gallery, the Frontier Trading Post, and in front of

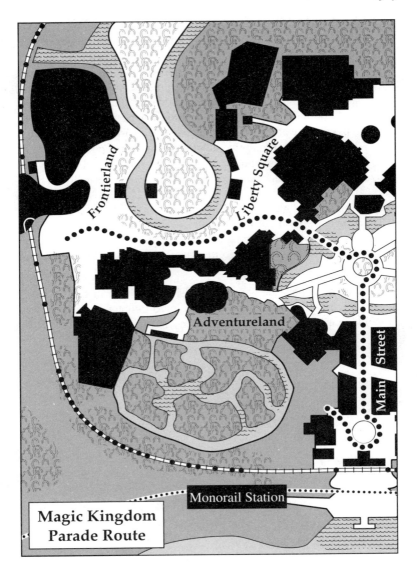

Magic Kingdom
Parade Route

the building with the sign reading "Frontier Merchandise." These select spots usually get picked off 10 to 12 minutes before parade time.

5. Along the outside perimeter of the central hub, between the entrances to Liberty Square and Adventureland, are several benches. Usually not occupied until after the parade begins, the benches offer a comfortable resting place and an unobstructed (though somewhat removed) view of the parade as it crosses the Liberty Square bridge. What you lose in proximity, however, you make up in comfort.

6. There are also some good viewing places along the Liberty Square and Frontierland dockside areas, but these spots are usually grabbed early.

7. If you want to watch the parade in air-conditioned comfort, enter the preshow lobby of the *Country Bear Jamboree*. From the lobby you can view the whole parade through the window. Don't let the Disney folks shoo you into the theater until after the parade has passed.

If you elect to view the parade from Liberty Square or Frontierland, be advised that it will take the parade 16 to 20 minutes to work its way around to you (assuming the parade begins on Main Street).

Eating in the Magic Kingdom

The Magic Kingdom is a wonder and a marvel, a testimony to the creative genius of man. But for all of the beauty, imagination, and wholesomeness of this incredible place, it is almost impossible to get a really good meal. Simply put, what is available is that same computerized, homogenized fare that languishes beneath the heat lamps of every fast-food chain restaurant in America. We are sympathetic; it is overwhelming to contemplate preparing and serving 130,000-or-so meals each day. But our understanding, unfortunately, does not make the food any more palatable. Do not misunderstand, the food at the Magic Kingdom is not awful. It is merely mediocre in a place that has set the standard in virtually every other area for quality in tourism and entertainment. Given the challenge of feeding so many people each day, we might be more accepting of the bland fare if (1) we didn't believe the Disney people could do better, and if (2) obtaining food didn't require such an investment of time and effort. The variety found on the numerous menus indicates that somebody once had the right idea.

Most of the following deals with avoiding the Magic Kingdom's full-service, reservations-required restaurants. If you are interested in the Magic Kingdom's version of fine dining, all of its full-service restaurants are profiled in detail and rated in *Dining In and Around Walt Disney World*, pages 265–322.

—— Alternatives and Suggestions for Eating in the Magic Kingdom

Remember, this discussion is about the Magic Kingdom. EPCOT Center and the Disney-MGM Studios are treated separately under a similar heading beginning on pages 488 and 554. All Walt Disney World full-service restaurants, both in the theme parks and at the hotels, are rated and described in *Dining In and Around Walt Disney World*.

1. Eat a good breakfast before arriving at the Magic Kingdom. You do not want to waste touring time eating breakfast at the park.

389

Besides, there are some truly outstanding breakfast specials at restaurants outside of Walt Disney World.

2. Having eaten a good breakfast, keep your tummy happy as you tour by purchasing snacks from the many vendors stationed throughout the Magic Kingdom. This is especially important if you have a tight schedule; you cannot afford to spend a lot of time waiting in line for food.

3. Correctly assuming that we don't take off for Orlando every time we get hungry, readers frequently ask where we eat when working in the Magic Kingdom. Fair enough; here's where:

Adventureland	*El Pirata Y el Perico*. We eat here sometimes, as it is frequently overlooked. Nothing fancy. We usually have tacos.
Frontierland	*Aunt Polly's Landing*. Located on Tom Sawyer Island, this is our overall favorite lunch spot in the Magic Kingdom. Aunt Polly's serves cold fried chicken, as well as ham and swiss cheese sandwiches and PB&J's. Not always convenient, you have to take a raft to the island to enjoy Aunt Polly's. Also, Aunt Polly's is al fresco dining—not air conditioned.
Liberty Square	*Sleepy Hollow*. If we get hungry between 2 and 3 P.M., we head for Sleepy Hollow. The food is decent, but more importantly, we can settle comfortably at a table along the rail to watch the 3 P.M. parade.
	Liberty Tree Tavern. Our favorite full-service restaurant in the Magic Kingdom, particularly for sandwiches.
Fantasyland	*Pinocchio Village Haus*. The grilled brats are good for lunch. Also a great place for breakfast rolls and muffins in the morning.
Contemporary Resort	*Monorail Buffet*. Our absolute favorite, if we have the time, is this buffet on the main level of the Contemporary Resort. Always good for breakfast or dinner. Usually closed at lunch.

| Favorite Snacks | We love churros, a Mexican pastry sold by vendor wagons. Magic Kingdom popcorn is also good. In a move we heartily applaud, all the Walt Disney World theme parks began selling fresh fruit from streetside stands in 1994. |

4. If you are on a tight schedule and the park closes early, stay until closing and eat dinner outside of Walt Disney World before returning to your hotel. If the Magic Kingdom stays open late, eat an early dinner at about 4 P.M. or 4:30 P.M. in the Magic Kingdom eatery of your choice. You should have missed the last wave of lunch diners and sneaked in just ahead of the dinner crowd.

5. Take the monorail to one of the resort hotels for lunch. The trip over and back takes very little time, and because most guests have left the hotels for the parks, the resort hotels' restaurants are often slack. The food is better than in the Magic Kingdom, the service is faster, the atmosphere more relaxed, and beer, wine, and mixed drinks are available. Of the resort hotels connected directly to the Magic Kingdom by monorail, we prefer the fare at the Contemporary Resort. The restaurants at the Grand Floridian are good, but pricey.

6. If you decide to eat in the Magic Kingdom during the midday rush (11 A.M. to 2 P.M.) or the evening rush (5 P.M. to 8 P.M.), try the Crystal Palace toward Adventureland at the central hub end of Main Street; El Pirata Y el Perico in Adventureland, around the corner from Frontierland's Pecos Bill Cafe; or Aunt Polly's Landing on Tom Sawyer Island. All of these eateries serve passable food and usually are not crowded.

7. Many of the Magic Kingdom restaurants serve a cold sandwich of one sort or another. It is possible to buy a cold lunch (except for the drinks) before 11 A.M. and then carry your food until you are ready to eat. We met a family that does this routinely, with Mom always remembering to bring several small plastic bags in which to pack the food. Drinks are purchased at an appropriate time from any convenient drink vendor.

8. Most fast-food eateries in the Magic Kingdom have more than one service window. Regardless of time of day, check out the lines at *all* of the windows before queuing. Sometimes a manned, but out

of the way, window will have a much shorter line or no line at all. Be aware, however, that some serving windows may offer different fare than others. At Cosmic Ray's Starlight Cafe (formerly the Tomorrowland Terrace), for example, some windows serve only soup and salad, while others serve sandwiches.

9. Restaurants that accept reservations for lunch and/or dinner fill their respective meal seatings quickly. To obtain reservations you must hot-foot it over to the restaurant in question (King Stefan's Banquet Hall, etc.) as soon as you enter the park, or blow your most effective touring time waiting in line to make your meal reservation. Often you are asked to return well in advance of your seating time, and even then, on many occasions, will have to wait well past your scheduled time for a table. Guests staying at one of the Walt Disney World lodging properties can avoid some of this hassle by making reservations by phone up to 60 days in advance of their visit. All of the Magic Kingdom full-service restaurants are profiled in detail in the chapter titled "Eating In and Around Walt Disney World."

10. Of the three Magic Kingdom full-service restaurants, the Liberty Tree Tavern in Liberty Square is the best. Tony's Town Square Restaurant on Main Street serves consistently nice salads, but is otherwise hit or miss. We don't recommend King Stefan's Banquet Hall in Cinderella Castle for anything except dessert. A good rule of thumb at any Magic Kingdom full-service eatery is to keep it simple. Go for sandwiches and other basic dishes (roast turkey and mashed potatoes, etc.) that are hard to mess up. Stay away from roast beef or steak, whether offered as a main dish or in sandwich form.

11. Just so you know, the Disney people have a rule against bringing your own food and drink into the park. We interviewed one woman who, ignoring the rule, brought a huge picnic lunch for her family of five packed in a large diaper/baby paraphernalia bag. She secured the bag in a locker under the Main Street Station and retrieved it later when the family was hungry. A Texas family returned to their camper in the parking lot for lunch, where they had a cooler, lawn chairs, and plenty of food in the college-football tailgating tradition.

We receive many letters from readers relating how they approached eating at the Magic Kingdom. Here is one from a family in Pennsylvania:

Despite the warning against bringing food into the park, we packed a double picnic lunch in a backpack and a small shoulder bag. Even with a small discount, it cost $195 for the seven of us to tour the park for a day, and I felt that spending another $150 or so on two meals was not in the cards. We froze juice boxes to keep the meat sandwiches cool (it worked fine), and had an extra round of juice boxes and peanut butter sandwiches for a late afternoon snack. We took raisins and a pack of fig bars for sweets, but didn't carry any other cookies or candy to avoid a "sugar-low" during the day. Fruit would have been nice, but it would have been squashed.

——— The Cost of Fast Food and Snacks in the Magic Kingdom

Sandwiches, hot dogs, burgers, tacos, and the like sell within the range of $3–7. Two tacos and a coke at El Pirata Y el Perico in Adventureland, for example, run about $6. The quality of the tacos is consistent with what you'd expect at a Taco Bell. A ham and cheese sandwich and coffee at Lumière's Kitchen in Fantasyland costs around $5.60. A seafood salad and a coke at Cosmic Ray's Starlight Cafe (formerly the Tomorrowland Terrace) costs approximately $7.50. Snack and drink prices are as follows, tax included and rounded to the nearest nickel:

Cokes, Iced Tea, and Lemonade: small $1.55; large $1.85
Coffee: small 90¢; large $1.15
Popcorn: $1.75
Potato chips: 80¢
Ice cream: $1.60 and up
Churros: $1.55
Cookies: $1.25

Shopping in the Magic Kingdom

Shops in the Magic Kingdom add realism and atmosphere to the various theme settings and make available an extensive inventory of souvenirs, clothing, novelties, decorator items, and more. Much of the merchandise displayed (with the exception of Disney trademark souvenir items) is available back home and elsewhere at a lower price. In our opinion, shopping is not one of the main reasons for visiting the Magic Kingdom. We recommend bypassing the shops on a one-day visit. If you have two or more days to spend in the Magic Kingdom, browse the shops during the early afternoon when many of the attractions are crowded. Remember that Main Street, with its multitude of shops, opens earlier and closes later than the rest of the park. Lockers in the Main Street Station allow you to stash your purchases safely, as opposed to dragging them around the park with you. Although the Parcel Pick-up service has been discontinued, Disney resort guests can have their purchases delivered to their hotel rooms.

Our recommendations notwithstanding, we realize that for many guests Disney souvenirs and memorabilia are irresistible. If you have decided that you would look good in a Goofy hat with shoulder-length floppy ears, you are in the right place. What's more, you have plenty of company. Writes one of our readers,

> I've discovered that people have a compelling need to buy Disney stuff when they are at WDW. When you get home you wonder why you ever got a cashmere sweater with Mickey Mouse embroidered on the breast, or a tie with tiny Goofys all over it. Maybe it's something they put in the food.

Disney trademark merchandise tends to be more expensive at the Disney shops than in independent stores out of the World. Quality, however, is better at the Disney shops. The best place for quality and value is the Character Warehouse in Mall 2 of the Belz Factory Outlet World on International Drive off I-4. Unfortunately, the selection at the outlet store is rather limited.

If you remember on your flight home that you forgot to buy mouse ears for your nephew, you can order most of the Disney trademark merchadise sold at Walt Disney World by calling the Walt Disney Attractions Mail Order Department at (407) 363-6200 or (800) 272-6201.

Behind the Scenes in the Magic Kingdom

Innovations in Action provides an opportunity for groups of no fewer than 15 adults (16 years and over) to tour the Magic Kingdom behind the scenes. This fascinating guided program provides an informative and detailed look at the logistical, technical, and operational side of the Magic Kingdom, including the tree farm, the waste treatment plant, and the tunnel system (under the theme park). For additional information, call (407) 824-7997. The program, which costs $60 per person, runs for about three-and-a-half hours, and is available only to Walt Disney World resort guests. Groups must be formed and arrangements made prior to arrival.

Traffic Patterns in the Magic Kingdom

When we began our research on the Magic Kingdom, we were very interested in traffic patterns throughout the park, specifically:

1. *Which sections of the park and what attractions do visitors head for when they first arrive?* When visitors are admitted to the various lands on non-early-entry days during the summer and holiday periods, traffic to Tomorrowland and Frontierland is heaviest, followed by Fantasyland, Adventureland, Liberty Square, and Mickey's Starland. On early-entry days during busier times of the year, Disney hotel and campground guests fairly well inundate Fantasyland and Space Mountain in Tomorrowland before the "general public" is admitted. The early-morning presence of large numbers of Disney resort guests serves to accelerate the filling of the park by about an hour.

During the school year, when there are fewer young people in the park, early-morning traffic is more evenly distributed, but is still heaviest in Tomorrowland, Frontierland, and Fantasyland. In our research we tested the claim, often heard, that most people turn right into Tomorrowland and tour the Magic Kingdom in an orderly counterclockwise fashion. We found it without basis. As the park fills, visitors seem to head for the top attractions, which they wish to ride before the lines get long. This more than any other factor determines traffic patterns in the morning. Attractions that receive considerable patronage in the early morning are:

Tomorrowland:	Space Mountain
	Alien Encounter
Frontierland:	Splash Mountain
	Big Thunder Mountain Railroad
Fantasyland:	Dumbo, the Flying Elephant
	20,000 Leagues Under the Sea
Adventureland:	Jungle Cruise

2. *How long does it take for the park to reach peak capacity for a given day? How are the visitors dispersed throughout the park?* On non-early-entry days, there is a surge of "early birds" who arrive before or around opening time, but are quickly dispersed throughout the empty park. After the initial onslaught is absorbed, there is a lull that lasts roughly an hour after opening. Then the park is inundated with arriving guests for about two hours, peaking between 10 and 11 A.M. Guests continue to arrive in a steady, but diminishing stream until around 2 P.M. The lines we sampled were longest between 1 and 2 P.M., indicating more arrivals than departures into the early afternoon. For general touring purposes, most attractions develop long lines between 10:30 and 11:30 A.M.

On early-entry days, Fantasyland fills with early-entry guests who later spill over into Tomorrowland, Frontierland, Liberty Square, and Adventureland. The presence of these resort guests naturally slows the touring progress of the day guests who are admitted later (at the official opening time). During the summer season and holidays, the result of two successive waves of arriving guests (first the early-entrant resort guests, and later the day guests), is to overwhelm many popular attractions by midmorning. On early-entry days, many rides develop long lines as early as 9:10 A.M. Guests continue to stream into the park through the morning and into the afternoon. Though many early-entry guests leave the park between noon and 2 P.M., the overall effect of early entry is to markedly increase the daily attendance. Thus, on early-entry days during busier times of the year, the Magic Kingdom stays packed most of the day.

From late morning through the early hours of the afternoon, on both early-entry and non-early-entry days, attendance is equally distributed through all of the lands. In late afternoon, however, we noted a concentration of visitors in Fantasyland, Liberty Square, and Frontierland, with a decrease of visitors in Adventureland and Tomorrowland. While the Jungle Cruise in Adventureland, along with *Alien Encounter* and Space Mountain in Tomorrowland, continue to be crowded, most other attractions in these lands are readily accessible in the late afternoon.

3. *How do most visitors go about touring the park? Is there a difference in the touring behavior of first-time visitors versus repeat visitors?* Many first-time visitors are accompanied by friends or relatives familiar with the Magic Kingdom, who guide their tour. The tours sometimes do and sometimes do not proceed in an orderly touring sequence. First-time visitors without personal touring guides tend to be more orderly in

their touring. Many first-time visitors, however, are drawn to Cinderella Castle upon entering the park and thus commence their rotation from Fantasyland. Repeat visitors usually proceed directly to their favorite attractions. In 1996, expect veteran and first-time guests alike to head directly for Tomorrowland to check out the recent renovation and the new attractions.

Early-entry guests go directly to Fantasyland and to specific rides in Tomorrowland. Later, when the remainder of the Magic Kingdom opens, most either continue touring Tomorrowland or alternatively head for Frontierland and Splash Mountain.

4. *What effect do special events, such as the parades and live shows, have on traffic patterns?*   The parades pull huge numbers of guests away from attraction lines and provide a window of opportunity for experiencing the more popular attractions with less of a wait. Castle Forecourt shows also attract a lot of people but have only a slight effect on lines.

5. *What are the traffic patterns near to and at closing time?*   On our sample days, in season and out of season, park departures outnumbered arrivals beginning midafternoon. Many visitors left during the late afternoon as the dinner hour approached. When the park closed early, there were steady departures during the two hours before closing, with a huge exodus of remaining visitors at closing time. When the park closed late, the exodus immediately followed the evening parade and fireworks. Mass departures at closing time mainly affect conditions on Main Street and at the monorail and ferry stops, because Main Street and the transportation services remain open after the other six lands close. In the hour before closing, the other six lands are normally uncrowded.

6. *I have heard that when there are two or more lines, the shortest wait is always the left line. Is this true?*   We do not recommend the "left-line strategy" because, with the occasional exception of food lines, it simply does not hold up. The Disney people have a number of techniques for both internal and external crowd control that distribute line traffic nearly equally. Placing research team members at the same time in each available line, we could discern no consistent pattern as to who was served first. Further, staffers entering the same attraction via different lines would almost always exit the attraction within 30 to 90 seconds of each other.

What does occasionally occur, however, is that guests will ignore a second line that has just been opened and persist in standing in the established line. As a rule, if you encounter a waiting area with two lines and no barrier to entry for either, and one line is empty or conspicuously less populated than the other, get in it.

Magic Kingdom
Touring Plans

The Magic Kingdom touring plans are field-tested, step-by-step plans for seeing as much as possible in one day with a minimum of time wasted standing in line. They are designed to assist you in avoiding crowds and bottlenecks on days of moderate to heavy attendance. On days of lighter attendance (see "Selecting the Time of Year for Your Visit," page 30), the plans will still save you time, but will not be as critical to successful touring as on busier days. Do not be concerned that other people will be following the same touring strategy, thus rendering it useless. Fewer than 1 in every 500 people in the park will have been exposed to this information.

Choosing the Right Touring Plan

We present these six different Magic Kingdom touring plans:

- Magic Kingdom One-Day Touring Plan for Adults

- Author's Selective Magic Kingdom One-Day Touring Plan for Adults

- Magic Kingdom One-Day Touring Plan for Parents with Small Children

- Magic Kingdom Dumbo-or-Die-in-a-Day Touring Plan for Parents with Small Children

- Magic Kingdom Two-Day Touring Plan A for When the Park Is Open Late

- Magic Kingdom Two-Day Touring Plan B for Morning Touring and for When the Park Closes Early

If you have two days to spend at the Magic Kingdom, the two-day touring plans are by far the most relaxed and efficient. Two-Day Touring

Plan B takes advantage of early-morning touring when lines are short and the park has not yet filled with guests. This plan works well year-round, and is particularly recommended for days when the Magic Kingdom closes before 9 P.M. On the other hand, Two-Day Touring Plan A combines the efficiency of early-morning touring on the first day with the splendor of the Magic Kingdom at night on the second day. The plan is perfect for guests who wish to sample both the attractions and the special atmosphere of the Magic Kingdom after dark, including parades and fireworks.

If you only have one day, but wish to see as much as possible, use the One-Day Touring Plan for Adults. This plan packs as much into a single day as is humanly possible, but is pretty exhausting. If you prefer a more relaxed visit, try the Author's Selective One-Day Touring Plan. This plan features the best the Magic Kingdom has to offer (in the author's opinion), eliminating some of the less impressive attractions.

If you have children under eight years of age, you may want to use the One-Day Touring Plan for Adults with Small Children. This plan represents a compromise, integrating the preferences of smaller children with those of older siblings and adults. The plan includes many of the children's rides in Fantasyland, but omits roller coaster rides and other attractions that are frightening, or that little ones cannot ride because of Disney height requirements. An alternative would be to use the One-Day Touring Plan for Adults or the Author's Selective One-Day Touring Plan, and take advantage of switching off, a technique where children accompany adults to the loading area of a ride with age and height requirements but do not actually ride (see page 166). Switching off allows adults to enjoy the more adventuresome attractions while keeping the whole group together.

Finally, there is the Dumbo-or-Die-in-a-Day Touring Plan for Parents with Small Children. This plan is designed for the peace of mind of parents who want to insure that no effort and sacrifice has been spared on behalf of the children. On the Dumbo-or-Die plan, adults pretty much just stand around, sweat, wipe noses, pay for stuff, and watch the children enjoy themselves. It's great.

Touring Plan Clip-out Pocket Outlines

For your convenience, we have prepared outline versions of all the touring plans presented in this guide. The pocket outline versions present the same touring itineraries as the detailed touring plans, but with vastly abbreviated directions. First, select the touring plan which is most appropriate for your party, then familiarize yourself with the detailed version of the touring plan. Once you understand how the touring plan works, clip out the pocket outline version of your selected touring plan from the back of this guide, and carry it with you as a quick reference when you visit the theme park.

The Single-Day Touring Conundrum

Touring the Magic Kingdom in a single day is complicated by the fact that the Magic Kingdom's premier attractions, Splash Mountain and Big Thunder Mountain in Frontierland, and Space Mountain and *Alien Encounter* in Tomorrowland, are almost at opposite ends of the park, making it virtually impossible to ride all four without encountering a line at one or another. If you ride Space Mountain and see *Alien Encounter* right after the park opens, you will ride without much, if any, wait. By the time you exit Tomorrowland and hustle over to Frontierland, however, the line for Splash Mountain will have grown to substantial proportions. The same situation prevails if you ride the Frontierland duo first: Splash Mountain and Big Thunder Mountain, no problem; Space Mountain and *Alien Encounter,* fair-sized lines. From ten minutes after opening until just before closing, you can expect long waits at these headliner attractions.

The only effective way to ride all four without a lot of waiting is to tour the Magic Kingdom in two days: ride Space Mountain and see *Alien Encounter* first thing one morning and ride Splash Moutain and Big Thunder Mountain first thing on the other. If you have only one day and are basically unwilling to suffer a lengthy wait (45 minutes to 2 hours) for these rides, you can do one of two things. Your first option is to ride one set when the park opens and the others just before closing. Many guests who attempt this strategy fail, because they become too worn out to stay until near closing time.

The second option, which we recommend in the one-day touring plans, requires a lot of hustle and still involves some waiting. It is sort of a "bite the bullet" strategy, but all things considered, probably works best. Make sure you arrive early and rush straight to Space Mountain and ride. After Space Mountain, experience *Alien Encounter* and then speed over to Frontierland and ride Big Thunder Mountain Railroad. When you leave Big Thunder, exit to your right and ride Splash Mountain, next door. If your group travels fast, your wait should be less than 5 minutes at

Space Mountain, about 10 minutes at *Alien Encounter*, 10 to 15 minutes at Big Thunder Mountain, and about 15 to 30 minutes at Splash Mountain. After riding Splash Mountain, you can be comforted by the knowledge that you have the most popular attractions and longest lines behind you.

This strategy takes advantage of what we call the morning lull, a period of about 30 to 45 minutes after the park opens, when those on hand at opening have been absorbed and new arrivals are comparatively few. While you are riding Space Mountain and visiting *Alien Encounter*, Big Thunder Mountain and Splash Mountain are accommodating the crowd of early birds who rushed directly to Frontierland as soon as the Magic Kingdom opened. By the time you finish Space Mountain and *Alien Encounter*, most of this first wave will have finished riding Big Thunder and Splash Mountains. Because of the morning lull, the lines at Big Thunder Mountain and Splash Mountain will not have built up again and your wait will be tolerable.

Bear in mind that early entry at the Magic Kingdom totally eliminates any morning lull. If you plan to incorporate the morning lull into your touring strategy, make sure you visit the Magic Kingdom on a day when early entry is not scheduled.

Magic Kingdom Early Entry for
Walt Disney World Resort Guests

Walt Disney World hotel and campground guests have the opportunity to enter the Magic Kingdom one hour before the general public on selected days of the week. Early-entry guests can enjoy all of the attractions in Fantasyland (except *Legend of the Lion King*), as well as Space Mountain and, sometimes, the Grand Prix Raceway in Tomorrowland.

Early entry at the Magic Kingdom, unfortunately, is a mixed blessing during the busier times of year. The opportunity to get a jump on the general public lures so many Disney resort guests to the Magic Kingdom on early-entry days that the park fills much earlier than usual. In the hour or so before the general public is admitted, you have a great advantage, particularly if you are among the first early entrants to arrive on the scene. You can get most of the attractions in Fantasyland, plus Space Mountain in Tomorrowland under your belt, and be poised to head for *Alien Encounter*, Splash Mountain, and Big Thunder Mountain when the remainder of the park opens. But by about 10 A.M., following the admission of the general public, the park will be packed. If you remain in the Magic Kingdom, you will have to fight incredible crowds the rest of the day.

By our observation, the earlier the official opening time of the Magic Kingdom, the better early entry works. During major holiday periods, for example, the Magic Kingdom opens to the general public at 8 A.M., with early entrants admitted to the park at 6:30 A.M. Because comparatively few people are willing to haul themselves out of bed and off to a theme park at 6 in the morning, those who do make the effort are substantially rewarded. On days when the official opening time is 9 or 10 A.M., however, literally thousands of Disney resort guests are up and at 'em and waiting at the turnstiles to take advantage of their early-entry privileges.

If you are eligible for early entry and visit the Magic Kingdom during the off-season, by all means take advantage of your privileges. You will get a jump on the general public and add an extra hour to what, in the off-season, is already a short touring day. During busier times of year, you are probably better off avoiding the Magic Kingdom altogether on early-entry days. If you are really hot to participate in early entry at the Magic Kingdom during the summer or holiday periods, we recommend arriving at the park 1½ hours before the official opening time (when the general public is admitted) and seeing everything you can before the park fills up. At that point, leave the Magic Kingdom and spend the rest of the day at one of the other parks.

If you are not eligible for early entry, avoid the Magic Kingdom on early-entry days regardless of the time of year.

Preliminary Instructions for All Magic Kingdom Touring Plans

On days of moderate to heavy attendance follow the touring plan of your choice exactly, deviating only:

1. *When you are not interested in an attraction called for on the touring plan.* For instance, the touring plan may indicate that you go next to Tomorrowland and ride Space Mountain, a roller coaster ride. If you do not enjoy roller coasters, simply skip this step of the plan and proceed to the next step.

2. *When you encounter a very long line at an attraction called for by the touring plan.* Crowds ebb and flow at the Magic Kingdom, and by chance an unusually large line may have gathered at an attraction to which you are directed. For example, upon arrival at The Haunted Mansion, you find the waiting lines to be extremely long. It is possible that this is a temporary situation occasioned by several hundred people arriving en masse from a recently concluded performance of *The Hall of Presidents* nearby. If this is the case, simply skip The Haunted Mansion and move to the next step, returning later in the day to try The Haunted Mansion once again.

What To Do If You Get Off Track

If you experience an unexpected interruption or problem that throws the Touring Plan off, refer to the "Magic Kingdom: Best Time to Visit Attractions" chart on page 661. This chart lists the better times of day to visit each attraction.

Park Opening Procedures

Your success during your first hour of touring will be affected somewhat by the particular opening procedure the Disney people use that day.

A. Sometimes all guests are held at the turnstiles until the entire park opens (which may or may not be at the official opening time). If this is the case on the day you visit, blow right past Main Street and head for the first attraction on whatever touring plan you are following.

B. Sometimes guests are admitted to Main Street a half hour to an hour before the remaining lands open. Access to the other lands will be blocked by a rope barrier at the central hub end of Main Street. Once admitted, move to the rope barrier and stake out a position as follows:

If you are going to Frontierland first (Splash Mountain and Big Thunder Mountain), take up a position in front of the Crystal Palace restaurant, on the left at the central hub end of Main Street. Wait next to the rope barrier blocking the walkway to Adventureland. When the rope is dropped, move quickly to Frontierland by way of Adventureland. This is also, of course, the place to line up if your first stop is Adventureland.

If you are going to Space Mountain and *Alien Encounter* first, turn right at the end of Main Street and wait at the entrance of the Plaza Pavilion restaurant. When the rope drops at opening time, run *through* the Plaza Pavilion into Tomorrowland and then bear right to Space Mountain. After riding Space Mountain, backtrack to *Alien Encounter*.

If you are going to Fantasyland or Liberty Square, proceed to the end of Main Street and line up left of center at the rope.

If you are going to Mickey's Starland first, go to the Main Street Station of the Walt Disney World Railroad and board the first train of the day. Get off at the second stop. The train pulls out of the Main Street Station at the same time the rope is dropped at the central hub end of Main Street.

C. If you are admitted on the early-entry program for Disney hotel and campground guests, you will encounter little to no congestion at the entrance turnstiles. Be prepared to show your Disney guest I.D. as well as a valid admission pass. Once inside the park, you will be directed down Main Street (everything on Main Street will be closed) to the central hub, and from there to Fantasyland. With early entry, you will rarely experience the crush associated with opening the park to the general public. Proceed leisurely to Fantasyland and from there (if you want to ride Space Mountain) to Tomorrowland. If Space Mountain is high on your priority list, head there first. Sometimes Disney opens only one of the two available Space Mountain tracks for early-entry guests. When this occurs, long lines form at Space Mountain, even during the early-entry period.

Try to time your early entry rides so that you're finished about 10–15 minutes before the day guests are admitted. You will need this time to position yourself for the sprint to Big Thunder and Splash Mountain.

Before You Go

1. Call (407) 824-4321 the day before you go for the official opening time. At the same time, determine whether the early-entry program for Walt Disney World resort guests will be in effect the day you plan to visit.
2. Purchase admission prior to your arrival. You can either order tickets through the mail before you leave home or buy them at the Disney Store in your local mall, the Walt Disney World Information Center off I-75 near Ocala (north of Orlando), the Disney Store in the Orlando airport, or at Walt Disney World lodging properties.
3. Become familiar with the park opening procedures (described above) and read over the touring plan you've chosen so that you will have an understanding of what you are likely to encounter.

—— Magic Kingdom One-Day Touring Plan for Adults

FOR: **Adults without small children.**

ASSUMES: Willingness to experience all major rides (including roller coasters) and shows.

Be forewarned that this plan requires a lot of walking and some backtracking; this is necessary to avoid some long waits in line. A little extra walking coupled with some hustle in the morning will save you from two to three hours of standing in line. Note also that you might not complete the tour. How far you get will depend on how quickly you move from ride to ride, how many times you pause for rest or food, how quickly the park fills, and what time the park closes. With a little zip and some luck, it is possible to complete the touring plan even on a busy day when the park closes early.

1. Arrive at the Magic Kingdom's parking lot 50 minutes before the park's stated opening time. This will give you time to park and catch the tram to the Transportation and Ticket Center (TTC). Arrive an hour earlier than opening time if it is a holiday period or you must purchase your admission.

2. If the line for the monorail is short, take the monorail; otherwise catch the ferry.

3. When you arrive at the Magic Kingdom, proceed through the entry turnstiles and have one person go to City Hall for park maps and a copy of the daily entertainment schedule.

4. Regroup and move as fast as you can down Main Street to the central hub. Because the Magic Kingdom uses two basic procedures when opening the park to the general public, you will probably encounter one of the following:

   a. The entire park will be open. If this is the case, proceed quickly to Space Mountain in Tomorrowland.

   b. Only Main Street will be open. In this case, turn right at the end of Main Street (before you reach the central hub), past the

Plaza Ice Cream Parlor and the Plaza Restaurant, and stake out a place for your group at the entrance of the Plaza Pavilion. When the rope barrier is dropped at opening time, jog through the Plaza Pavilion and on to Space Mountain. Starting at the entrance to the Plaza Pavilion will give you about a 100-yard head start over anyone coming from the central hub. Ride Space Mountain.

Warning: Because it is new, *Alien Encounter* develops large lines as soon as the park opens. If you are a Magic Kingdom veteran, you may want to experience *Alien Encounter* first and then proceed to Space Mountain. If you go to Space Mountain first, be prepared for a 30-minute plus wait at *Alien Encounter* unless you really hustle.

NOTE: If you are a Walt Disney World resort guest and enter the park on an early-entry day, ride Space Mountain and see as much of Fantasyland and Tomorrowland as possible. As the time approaches for the park to open to the public, go to Fantasyland and position yourself at the boundary of Fantasyland and Liberty Square. When the other lands open, head for Frontierland via the Liberty Square waterfront. Pick up the touring plan at Big Thunder Mountain, skipping past any steps that direct you to attractions experienced during your early-entry hour.

5. After Space Mountain, backtrack toward the central hub and the main entrance to Tomorrowland. Experience the *Alien Encounter*.
6. Leave Tomorrowland via the central hub and enter Liberty Square. Turn left and proceed along the waterfront to Big Thunder Mountain. Ride.
7. Exit Big Thunder to the right and go next door to Splash Mountain.
8. Exit Splash Mountain to the right and enter Adventureland. Ride the Jungle Cruise.
9. Go to Fantasyland, ride Peter Pan's Flight.
10. Exit Peter Pan to the right and see *Legend of the Lion King* next door.
11. Exit left and return to Liberty Square. Bear right at the waterfront and experience The Haunted Mansion.
12. Leave The Haunted Mansion and follow the waterfront back around to Frontierland. While in Frontierland, see *Country Bear Jamboree*.
13. Head in the direction of Splash Mountain and return to Adventureland to ride Pirates of the Caribbean.

NOTE: This is about as far as you can go on a busy day before the crowds catch up with you, but you will have experienced ten of the more popular rides and shows and cleared almost all of the Magic Kingdom's traffic bottlenecks. Note also that you are doing a considerable amount of walking and some backtracking. Do not be dismayed; the extra walking will save you as much as two hours of standing in line. Remember, during the morning (through Step 13) keep moving. In the afternoon, adjust the pace to your liking.

14. If you have not had lunch, go ahead and eat. Fast-food eateries that are generally less crowded include Aunt Polly's Landing in Frontierland, El Pirata Y el Perico in Adventureland, and the Crystal Palace at the central hub end of Main Street.

15. After lunch, check out *The Hall of Presidents* and the Liberty Square Riverboat. If either is within ten minutes of getting underway, choose the one with the shortest wait. When you have experienced both of these attractions, proceed to Step 16.

16. Leave Liberty Square and return to Frontierland. Pass into Adventureland using the passage that runs between the Frontierland Shootin' Gallery and the wood carving shop. See *Tropical Serenade (Enchanted Tiki Birds)*.

17. While in Adventureland, explore the Swiss Family Treehouse.

18. Turn left upon exiting the Treehouse, pass by the Pirates of the Caribbean, and head for the Frontierland Station of the Walt Disney World Railroad. Take the train one stop to Mickey's Starland.

19. In Mickey's Starland, walk through Mickey's House to see a performance of *Mickey's Starland Show*. Check your daily entertainment schedule for show times. Note that the shows generally begin on the half hour, except that sometimes there isn't a 3 or 3:30 P.M. show (presumably so the characters can participate in the parade). If it works out that this step directs you to Mickey's Starland during the show hiatus, postpone Mickey's Starland until later in the day.

20. After the show, go to Mickey's Hollywood Theater to meet and photograph Mickey. If this is something you want to do, read the Touring Tips for *Mickey's Starland Show* to help you avoid a long wait.

21. Exit Mickey's Starland following the path to Fantasyland.

22. While in Fantasyland, ride It's a Small World.

23. Go to Tomorrowland via the Skyway from Fantasyland (if the line

is not long) or on foot. In Tomorrowland, ride the Tomorrowland Transit Authority.

24. While in Tomorrowland, see the *Carousel of Progress*.

25. Try Dreamflight, also in Tomorrowland.

26. Proceed toward the central hub entrance to Tomorrowland and experience *Alien Encounter*, if you missed it earlier. If the wait for this attraction is excessive, consider trying it again after 6 P.M.

27. Walk across the street and see the *Transportarium*.

28. If you have some time left before closing, backtrack to pick up attractions you may have missed or bypassed because the lines were too long. Check out any parades, fireworks, or live performances that interest you. Grab a bite to eat. Save Main Street until last since it remains open after the rest of the park closes.

29. Continue to tour until everything closes except Main Street. Finish your day by browsing along Main Street.

30. If you leave the park at closing time, the express monorail to the TTC will be mobbed. Either take the ferry or board the monorail that stops at the resort hotels. Exit at the TTC.

Author's Selective Magic Kingdom
One-Day Touring Plan for Adults

FOR: **Adults touring without small children.**

ASSUMES: Willingness to experience all major rides (including roller coasters) and shows.

This touring plan is selective and includes only those attractions which, in the author's opinion, represent the best the Magic Kingdom has to offer. Be forewarned that this plan requires a lot of walking and some backtracking; this is necessary to avoid some long waits in line. A little extra walking coupled with some hustle in the morning will save you from two to three hours of standing in line. Note also that you might not complete the tour. How far you get will depend on how quickly you move from ride to ride, how many times you pause for rest or food, how quickly the park fills, and what time the park closes. With a little zip and some luck, it is possible to complete the touring plan even on a busy day when the park closes early.

1. Arrive at the Magic Kingdom's parking lot 50 minutes before the park's stated opening time. This will give you time to park and catch the tram to the Transportation and Ticket Center (TTC). Arrive an hour earlier than opening time if it is a holiday period or you must purchase your admission.

2. If the line for the monorail is short, take the monorail; otherwise catch the ferry.

3. When you arrive at the Magic Kingdom, proceed through the entry turnstiles and have one person go to City Hall for park maps and a copy of the daily entertainment schedule.

4. Regroup and move as fast as you can down Main Street to the central hub. Because the Magic Kingdom uses two basic procedures when opening the park to the general public, you will probably encounter one of the following:

   a. The entire park will be open. If this is the case, proceed quickly to Space Mountain in Tomorrowland.

   b. Only Main Street will be open. In this case, turn right at the end of Main Street (before you reach the central hub), past the

413

Plaza Ice Cream Parlor and the Plaza Restaurant, and stake out a place for your group at the entrance of the Plaza Pavilion. When the rope barrier is dropped at opening time, jog through the Plaza Pavilion and on to Space Mountain. Starting at the entrance to the Plaza Pavilion will give you about a 100-yard head start and an advantage over anyone coming from the central hub. Ride Space Mountain.

Warning: Because it is new, *Alien Encounter* develops large lines as soon as the park opens. If you are a Magic Kingdom veteran, you may want to experience *Alien Encounter* first and then proceed to Space Mountain. If you go to Space Mountain first, be prepared for a 30-minute plus wait at *Alien Encounter* unless you really hustle.

NOTE: If you are a Walt Disney World resort guest and enter the park on an early-entry day, ride Space Mountain and see as much of Fantasyland and Tomorrowland as possible. As the time approaches for the park to open to the public, go to Fantasyland and position yourself at the boundary of Fantasyland and Liberty Square. When the other lands open, head for Frontierland via the Liberty Square waterfront. Pick up the touring plan at Big Thunder Mountain, skipping steps that direct you to attractions experienced during your early-entry hour.

5. After Space Mountain, backtrack toward the central hub and the main entrance to Tomorrowland. Experience the *Alien Encounter.*
6. Leave Tomorrowland via the central hub and enter Liberty Square. Turn left and proceed along the waterfront to Big Thunder Mountain. Ride.
7. Exit Big Thunder to the right and go next door to Splash Mountain.
8. Exit Splash Mountain to the right and enter Adventureland. Ride the Jungle Cruise.
9. Leave Adventureland and go to Fantasyland via the central hub. Ride Peter Pan's Flight.
10. Exit Peter Pan to the right and see *Legend of the Lion King,* next door.
11. Exit *The Lion King* to the left and return to Liberty Square. Bear right at the waterfront and experience The Haunted Mansion.
12. Leave The Haunted Mansion and follow the waterfront back around to Frontierland. While in Frontierland, see *Country Bear Jamboree.*

13. Head in the direction of Splash Mountain and return to Adventureland to ride Pirates of the Caribbean.

    NOTE: This is about as far as you can go on a busy day before the crowds catch up with you, but you will have experienced eight of the more popular rides and shows and cleared almost all of the Magic Kingdom's traffic bottlenecks. Note also that you are doing a considerable amount of walking and some backtracking. Do not be dismayed; the extra walking will save you as much as two hours of standing in line. Remember, during the morning (through Step 13), keep moving. In the afternoon, adjust the pace to your liking.

14. If you have not had lunch, go ahead and eat. Fast-food eateries that are generally less crowded include Aunt Polly's Landing in Frontierland, El Pirata Y el Perico in Adventureland, and the Crystal Palace at the central hub end of Main Street.

15. After lunch, go to Liberty Square and check out *The Hall of Presidents* and the Liberty Square Riverboat. If either is within ten minutes of getting underway, choose the one with the shortest wait. When you have experienced both of these attractions, proceed to Step 16.

16. Return to Frontierland. Take the Walt Disney Railroad to Mickey's Starland.

17. In Mickey's Starland, walk through Mickey's House to see a performance of *Mickey's Starland Show*. Be advised that on certain days, no shows are scheduled at 3 or 3:30 P.M. If it works out that the touring plan directs you to Mickey's Starland during this time, postpone your visit until later in the day. Show times are listed in the daily entertainment schedule.

18. Exit Mickey's Starland along the path to Fantasyland. In Fantasyland, ride It's a Small World.

19. Go to Tomorrowland via the Skyway from Fantasyland (if the line is not long) or on foot.

20. While in Tomorrowland, see the *Carousel of Progress*.

21. Ride Dreamflight, also in Tomorrowland.

22. Go next door and see the *Transportarium*.

23. Leave Tomorrowland via the central hub and proceed to Adventureland. See *Tropical Serenade (Enchanted Tiki Birds)*.

24. Turn left after *Tropical Serenade* and proceed to the Swiss Family Treehouse.

25. If you have some time left before closing, backtrack to pick up at-

tractions you may have missed or bypassed because the lines were too long. Check out any parades, fireworks, or live performances that interest you. Grab a bite to eat. Save Main Street until last since it remains open after the rest of the park closes.

26. Continue to tour until everything closes except Main Street. Finish your day by browsing along Main Street.

27. If you leave the park at closing time, the express monorail to the TTC will be mobbed. Either take the ferry or board the resort hotel monorail, getting off at the TTC.

—— Magic Kingdom One-Day Touring Plan for Parents with Small Children

FOR: **Parents with children under 8 years of age.**

ASSUMES: Periodic stops for rest, rest rooms, and refreshment.

This touring plan represents a compromise between the observed tastes of adults and the observed tastes of younger children. Included in this touring plan are many amusement park rides that children may have the opportunity to experience (although in less exotic surroundings) at local fairs and amusement parks. Though these rides are included in the touring plan, we suggest, nevertheless, that they be omitted if possible. The following cycle-loading rides often require long waits in line, consuming valuable touring time:

Mad Tea Party	Dumbo, the Flying Elephant
Cinderella's Golden Carrousel	AstroOrbiter

This time could be better spent experiencing the many attractions that best demonstrate the Disney creative genius and are only found in the Magic Kingdom. As an alternative to this touring plan, we suggest trying either of the one-day plans for adults and taking advantage of "switching off." This allows parents and small children to enter the ride together. At the boarding area, the parents take turns watching the children while the other rides.

The big decision you need to make before going to the Magic Kingdom is whether you will come back to your hotel for a rest in the middle of the day. We strongly recommend that you break off your tour and return to your hotel for a swim and a nap (even if you are not lodging in Walt Disney World). True, you will not see as much, but what's more important: keeping everyone relaxed, fresh, and happy, or trying to see everything?

Be forewarned that this touring plan requires a lot of walking and some backtracking; this is necessary to avoid long waits in line. A little extra walking will save you from two to three hours of standing in line. Note also that you may not complete the tour. How far you get will depend on how quickly you move from ride to ride, how many times you pause for rest or food, how quickly the park fills, and what time the park closes. With a little hustle and some luck, it is possible to complete the touring plan even on a busy day when the park closes early.

1. Arrive at the Magic Kingdom's parking lot at least 50 minutes before the stated opening time. Arrive an hour earlier than opening time if it is a holiday period or you must purchase your admission.
2. Take the monorail to the Magic Kingdom. When the gates open, enter the park.
3. Rent strollers (if necessary); pick up a daily entertainment schedule; and proceed to Step 4 of this touring plan.
4. Move quickly to the end of Main Street. If the entire park is open, proceed quickly to Fantasyland. Otherwise, take a position by the rope barrier at the central hub. When the barrier is dropped, go through the main door of the castle and ride Dumbo, the Flying Elephant.

    NOTE: If you are a Walt Disney World resort guest and are admitted to the park early, ride Dumbo; Peter Pan's Flight; 20,000 Leagues Under the Sea; Cinderella's Golden Carrousel; Mr. Toad's Wild Ride; the Mad Tea Party; and, if it's operating, the Grand Prix Raceway in Tomorrowland. As the time approaches for the park to open to the public, go to Fantasyland and get in line for *Legend of the Lion King*. Pick up the touring plan at (step 8), skipping past steps that direct you to attractions you experienced during your early-entry hour.

5. While in Fantasyland, ride 20,000 Leagues Under the Sea.
6. While in Fantasyland, ride Mr. Toad's Wild Ride.
7. While in Fantasyland, also ride Peter Pan's Flight.
8. While in Fantasyland, see *Legend of the Lion King*.
9. Exit left from *Lion King* and head toward Liberty Square. In Liberty Square, turn right at the waterfront and go to The Haunted Mansion.
10. Leave Liberty Square and enter Frontierland. Move on to Adventureland via the passageway between the Frontierland Shootin' Gallery and Frontier Wood Carving. In Adventureland, ride the Jungle Cruise.
11. Exit left from the Jungle Cruise and ride Pirates of the Caribbean.
12. Turn left out of Pirates of the Caribbean and then turn right into Frontierland.
13. In Frontierland, see the *Country Bear Jamboree*.

14. After the show, return to Main Street (you can walk or take the railroad) and leave the park for lunch and an afternoon rest break at your hotel. Be sure to have your hand stamped for reentry as you leave. Also hang on to your parking receipt so you won't have to pay for parking again when you come back. Return refreshed to the Magic Kingdom at about 3:30 or 4 P.M.; once inside the park, walk or take the train to Frontierland and proceed to Step 15.

15. In Frontierland, take the raft to Tom Sawyer Island. Children will play here all day, so set some limits based on the park's closing time, your energy level, and how many more attractions you wish to experience. If you elected to stay in the park instead of going back to the hotel for rest, you may want to consider having lunch at Aunt Polly's Landing on Tom Sawyer Island. The food is good, and there is usually less of a crowd during lunch hours.

16. Return via the raft from Tom Sawyer Island and check the daily entertainment schedule for show times at Mickey's Starland. On certain days, no shows are scheduled for 3 or 3:30 P.M. If it works out that you coincidently hit that time period after returning from Tom Sawyer Island, postpone visiting Mickey's Starland until later in the day. Otherwise, go to the Frontierland Railroad Station and catch the Walt Disney World Railroad to Mickey's Starland. If you have a stroller, leave it at the Frontierland train station for the time being.

17. Get off the train at Mickey's Starland. Go see *Mickey's Starland Show* (enter through Mickey's House). After the show, visit Mickey in his dressing room at Mickey's Hollywood Theater (see pages 366–67 for instructions on avoiding a long wait). Next enjoy the playground and Grandma Duck's Petting Farm.

18. From Mickey's Starland take the train back to Frontierland. Reclaim your stroller.

19. Return to Fantasyland, ride It's a Small World.

20. Exit Fantasyland via the Skyway (if not too crowded) or on foot by way of the castle and central hub and go to Tomorrowland. Be advised that you are not allowed to take strollers on the Skyway. Once in Tomorrowland, ride Dreamflight.

21. While in Tomorrowland, ride the Tommorrowland Transit Authority.

22. Enjoy *Carousel of Progress*, also in Tomorrowland.

23. Head back toward the entrance of Tomorrowland and try the *Transportarium*.

24. If you have any time or energy left, catch a live performance, grab a bite, or try any attractions you might have missed using the touring plan.

25. Save touring Main Street until last, since it stays open later than the rest of the park.

26. If you are parked at the Transportation and Ticket Center (a.k.a. the main parking lot), catch the ferry or ride the express monorail. If the express monorail and the ferry are mobbed, catch the resort monorail and get off at the TTC.

—— Magic Kingdom Dumbo-or-Die-in-a-Day Touring Plan for Parents with Small Children

FOR: Adults who feel compelled to devote every waking moment to the pleasure and entertainment of their small children, or rich people who are paying someone else to take their children to the theme park.

PREREQUISITE: This touring plan is designed for days when the Magic Kingdom does not close until 9 P.M. or later.

ASSUMES: Frequent stops for rest, rest rooms, and refreshment.

NOTE: The name of the touring plan notwithstanding, this itinerary is not a joke. Regardless of whether you are loving, guilty, masochistic, truly selfless, insane, or saintly, this touring plan will provide a small child with about as perfect a day as is possible at the Magic Kingdom.

This touring plan is a concession to those adults who are determined, even if it kills them, to give their small children the ultimate Magic Kingdom experience. The touring plan addresses the preferences, needs, and desires of small children to the virtual exclusion of those of adults or older siblings. If you left the kids with a sitter yesterday or wouldn't let little Marvin eat barbeque for breakfast, this is the perfect plan for expiating your guilt. This is also a wonderful touring plan if you are paying a sitter, nanny, or chauffeur to take your children to the Magic Kingdom.

1. Arrive at the Magic Kingdom's parking lot at least 50 minutes before the park's stated opening time. Arrive an hour earlier than opening time if you must purchase your ticket.
2. Take the monorail to the Magic Kingdom.
3. Enter the park and rent a stroller, if needed.
4. Move quickly to the end of Main Street. If the entire park is open, proceed quickly to Fantasyland. Otherwise, take a position by the rope barrier at the central hub. When the barrier is dropped, go through the main door of the castle to King Stefan's Banquet Hall (see Step 5).

NOTE: If you are a Walt Disney World resort guest and are admitted to the park early, ride Dumbo; Peter Pan's Flight; 20,000 Leagues Under the Sea; Cinderella's Golden Carrousel; Mr. Toad's

Wild Ride; the Mad Tea Party; and make lunch or dinner reservations at King Stefan's. Then, if it is operating, ride the Grand Prix Raceway in Tomorrowland. Before the other lands open, return to Fantasyland and get in line for *Legend of the Lion King*. After seeing *Lion King*, pick up the touring plan at Step 13. Skip any subsequent steps that direct you to attractions experienced during your early-entry hour.

5. At King Stefan's (on your right as you enter Cinderella Castle), make dinner reservations for 7 P.M. This will give your kids a chance to see the inside of the castle and to meet Cinderella. If you are a guest at a Walt Disney World hotel or campground, you can make your reservation one to three days in advance by dialing 55 or 56.
6. Go next to Dumbo, the Flying Elephant and ride.
7. Hey, you're on vacation! Ride again (using the Bubba Relay if there are two adults in your party; see page 168).
8. While in Fantasyland, ride 20,000 Leagues Under the Sea.
9. Next, ride Mr. Toad's Wild Ride, also in Fantasyland (back toward Dumbo).
10. Ride Peter Pan's Flight, also in Fantasyland.
11. Ride Cinderella's Golden Carrousel, also in Fantasyland.
12. In Fantasyland, see *Legend of the Lion King*.
13. Bearing left, go to the Skyway. Ride to Tomorrowland. Be advised that strollers are not allowed on the Skyway. If you have a stroller, hoof it over to Tomorrowland.
14. In Tomorrowland, ride the Grand Prix Raceway. Let your child control the steering wheel (cars run on a guide rail) while you work the foot pedal.
15. In Tomorrowland, ride the AstroOrbiter. Safety note: Seat your children in the plane before you get in. Also note that the Astro-Orbiter goes higher and is faster than Dumbo, and may frighten some children.
16. While in Tomorrowland, ride Dreamflight (near the Astro-Orbiter).
17. Exit Tomorrowland via the central hub and return to Main Street. Leave the park and return to your hotel for lunch, a nice nap, and even a swim. Have your hand stamped for reentry when you leave the Magic Kingdom, and make sure (if you have a car) that you hang on to your parking receipt so you will not be charged for parking when you return.

If you elect not to take a rest break out of the park, skip ahead to Step 19.

18. Return to the Magic Kingdom refreshed at about 4 or 4:30 P.M. Take the Walt Disney World Railroad to Frontierland.

19. In Frontierland, take the raft to Tom Sawyer Island. Stay as long as the kids want. If you are hungry, Aunt Polly's Landing on Tom Sawyer Island is a winner for both kids and adults.

20. After you return from the island, see the *Country Bear Jamboree,* also in Frontierland.

21. Return to Frontierland Station. Take the train to Mickey's Starland. Be aware that on certain days, no shows are scheduled at Mickey's Starland at 3 or 3:30 P.M. If it happens that you will arrive during this hiatus, postpone touring Mickey's Starland until later in the day. Show times are listed in the daily entertainment schedule. Note that you will have to leave your stroller in Frontierland for the time being.

22. Walk through Mickey's House and see *Mickey's Starland Show.* If you want to meet Mickey after the show, follow the Touring Tips for *Mickey's Starland Show* on pages 366–67.

23. After you see the show and meet Mickey, go pet some animals at Grandma Duck's Petting Farm, also in Mickey's Starland.

24. Right next to the farm is a nice playground. Try it out.

25. Check your watch. You should be within an hour or less of your dinner reservations at King Stefan's. If you left your stroller in Frontierland, take the train back to retrieve it and then head on foot to Fantasyland. If you do not have a stroller, take the direct path from Mickey's Starland to Fantasyland. In Fantasyland, if you have 20 minutes or more before your King Stefan seating, ride It's a Small World (don't forget to sing).

NOTE: In our opinion the main dishes at King Stefan's are average at best, totally unappetizing at worst, and expensive regardless. Try to get by with a salad for yourself and a hot dog and alphabet fries for the kids. Or better yet, just order dessert. If you plan to make an early night of it, let the kids eat while you have coffee. Later, back at your hotel, you can order a pizza.

26. Leave Fantasyland and go to Liberty Square. If your children are up to it, try The Haunted Mansion. If not, skip to the next step.

27. The evening parade is quite worthwhile. If you are interested, adjust the remainder of the touring plan to allow you to take

up a viewing position about ten minutes before the parade starts (usually 9 P.M.). See our recommendations for good vantage points on pages 386–88. If the parade doesn't excite you, enjoy the attractions in Adventureland while the parade is in progress. The lines will be vastly diminished.

28. Go by way of Liberty Square, Frontierland, or the central hub to Adventureland. Take the Jungle Cruise if the wait is not prohibitive. If the line for the Jungle Cruise is too intimidating, try the *Tropical Serenade* and/or the Swiss Family Treehouse. If you think your children can stand a few skeletons, Pirates of the Caribbean is also in Adventureland.

29. If you have time or energy left, repeat any attractions the kids especially liked or try ones you might have missed using the touring plan. Buy some Goofy hats if that cranks your tractor.

30. This concludes the touring plan. If you are parked at the Transportation and Ticket Center (a.k.a. the main parking lot) catch the ferry or the express monorail. If the line for the express monorail is intimidating, catch the resort monorail and get off at the TTC.

── *Magic Kingdom Two-Day Touring Plan A for When the Park Is Open Late*

FOR: **Parties who want to enjoy the Magic Kingdom at different times of day,** including evenings and early mornings.

ASSUMES: Willingness to experience all major rides (including roller coasters) and shows.

TIMING: This two-day touring plan is for those visiting the Magic Kingdom on days when the park is open late (after 8 P.M.). The plan offers morning touring on one day and late afternoon and evening touring on the other day. If the park closes early, or if you prefer to do all your touring during the morning and early afternoon, use the Magic Kingdom Two-Day Touring Plan B on pages 430–34. If you do not have early-entry privileges, schedule Day One of this touring plan for a day when early entry is *not* in effect.

Day One

1. Arrive at the Magic Kingdom's parking lot 50 minutes before the park's stated opening time. This will give you time to park and catch the tram to the Transportation and Ticket Center (TTC). Arrive an hour earlier than opening time if it is a holiday period or you must purchase your admission.

2. If the line for the monorail is short, take the monorail; otherwise catch the ferry.

3. When you arrive at the Magic Kingdom, proceed through the entry turnstiles. Go to City Hall for park maps and a copy of the daily entertainment schedule.

4. Move as fast as you can down Main Street to the central hub. Because the Magic Kingdom uses two basic procedures when opening the park to the general public, you will probably encounter one of the following:

   a. The entire park will be open. If this is the case, proceed quickly to Space Mountain in Tomorrowland.

   b. Only Main Street will be open. In this case, turn right at the end of Main Street (before you reach the central hub), past the Plaza Ice Cream Parlor and the Plaza Restaurant, and stake out a place for your group at the entrance of the Plaza Pavilion. When the rope barrier is dropped at opening time, jog through the Plaza Pavilion and on to Space Mountain. Starting at the entrance to the Plaza Pavilion will give you about a 100-yard head start and an advantage over anyone coming from the central hub. Ride Space Mountain.

NOTE: If you are a Walt Disney World resort guest and enter the park on an early-entry day, ride Space Mountain and see as much of Fantasyland and Tomorrowland as possible. As the time approaches for the park to open to the public, position yourself in Fantasyland at the boundary of Fantasyland and Liberty Square. When the other lands open, head for Frontierland via the Liberty Square waterfront. Pick up the touring plan at Big Thunder Mountain (Step 6), skipping steps that direct you to attractions experienced during your early-entry hour.

5. Backtrack toward the main entrance of Tomorrowland. Experience *Alien Encounter*.
6. Leave Tomorrowland via the central hub and enter Liberty Square. Turn left and proceed along the waterfront to Big Thunder Mountain. Ride.
7. Exit Big Thunder to the right and ride Splash Mountain, next door.
8. Exit Splash Mountain to the right and enter Adventureland. Ride the Jungle Cruise.
9. Leave Adventureland and go to Fantasyland via the central hub. Ride Peter Pan's Flight.
10. Exit Peter Pan to the right and see *Legend of the Lion King*.
11. Exit *Lion King* to the left and return to Liberty Square. Bear right at the waterfront and go to The Haunted Mansion.
12. Leave The Haunted Mansion and follow the waterfront back around to Frontierland. While in Frontierland, see *Country Bear Jamboree*.
13. Head in the direction of Splash Mountain; return to Adventureland to ride Pirates of the Caribbean.

NOTE: This is about as far as you can go on a busy day before the crowds catch up with you, but you will have experienced ten of the more popular rides and shows and cleared almost all of the Magic Kingdom's traffic bottlenecks. Note also that you are doing a considerable amount of walking and some backtracking. Do not be dismayed; the extra walking will save you as much as two hours of standing in line. Remember, during the morning (through Step 13), keep moving. In the afternoon, adjust the pace to your liking.

14. If you have not had lunch, go ahead and eat. Fast-food eateries that are generally less crowded include Aunt Polly's Landing in Frontierland, El Pirata Y el Perico in Adventureland, and the Crystal Palace at the central hub end of Main Street.

15. After lunch, go to Liberty Square and check out *The Hall of Presidents* and the Liberty Square Riverboat. If either is within ten minutes of getting underway, choose the one with the shortest wait. When you have experienced both of these attractions, proceed to Step 16.

16. At the Frontierland waterfront, take a raft to Tom Sawyer Island.

17. After exploring the island, return to the mainland and check your daily entertainment schedule for show times at Mickey's Starland. On certain days, no shows are scheduled at 3 or 3:30 P.M. If it works out that this step of the touring plan is coincidental with that time period, postpone visiting Mickey's Starland until later in the day. Otherwise, proceed to Frontierland Station and take the train to Mickey's Starland.

18. In Mickey's Starland, walk through Mickey's House to see a performance of *Mickey's Starland Show*.

19. After the show you can visit Mickey's Hollywood Theater to meet and photograph Mickey. If this is something you want to do, read the Touring Tips for *Mickey's Starland Show* to help you avoid a long wait (pages 000–00).

20. Return to the Mickey's Starland Station and ride the train to Main Street.

21. Before you leave the Magic Kingdom, browse along Main Street.

22. If for some reason (shopping, eating, parades, etc.) you think you might return to the Magic Kingdom that evening or you plan to visit EPCOT Center or the Disney-MGM Studios, have your hand stamped as you exit.

Day Two

1. If you want to see the afternoon parade, arrive at the TTC at about 2 P.M. If the afternoon parade does not interest you, arrive at the TTC at about 4:30 P.M. and skip Step 3.

2. Take the ferry to the Magic Kingdom if it is in port, otherwise catch the monorail.

3. Enter the Magic Kingdom and pick a good spot to watch the afternoon parade. The earlier you arrive, the better your vantage point will be (see parade suggestions on pages 386–88).

4. After the parade, make dinner reservations at the Liberty Tree Tavern in Liberty Square if you want to have a full-service dinner in the park. For other dining options, see Step 13.

5. Go to Fantasyland and ride It's a Small World.

6. Turn right after exiting, proceed to the Skyway, and ride to Tomorrowland. If the wait for the Skyway is too long, walk to Tomorrowland. Note that strollers are not allowed on the Skyway.

7. While in Tomorrowland, ride the Tomorrowland Transit Authority.

8. Try the *Carousel of Progress*, also in Tomorrowland.

9. In Tomorrowland, also ride Dreamflight.

10. Proceed toward the central hub entrance to Tomorrowland and experience *Alien Encounter* if you missed it on Day One.

11. Walk across the street and view the *Transportarium*.

12. If you are hungry, leave Tomorrowland and proceed via the central hub to the Crystal Palace on Main Street for dinner. The best choice for a full-service meal in the park is the Liberty Tree Tavern in Liberty Square. For a more leisurely meal, leave the park (get your hand stamped for reentry) and take the monorail to one of the Magic Kingdom resort hotels for dinner. If you wish to limit your time outside the park to a minimum, try the buffet at the Contemporary Resort.

    NOTE: At this point check your daily entertainment schedule to see if there are any parades, fireworks, or live performances that interest you. Make note of the times and alter the touring plan accordingly. Since you have already seen all the attractions that cause bottlenecks and have big lines, an interruption of the touring plan here will not cause you any problems. Simply pick up where you left off before the parade or show. The evening parade and the Fantasy in the Sky fireworks are particularly worthwhile.

13. After dinner, proceed to Adventureland and tour the Swiss Family Treehouse.

14. While in Adventureland, see the *Tropical Serenade (Enchanted Tiki Birds)*.

15. If you have some time left before closing, backtrack to any attractions you may have missed, such as 20,000 Leagues Under the

Sea in Fantasyland, or bypassed because the lines were too long. Explore the shops, but save Main Street until last since it remains open after the rest of the park closes.

16. In the hour just before closing, lines range from short to nonexistent for almost all attractions. If you have a favorite ride you would enjoy experiencing one more time, try it now.

17. Continue touring until everything closes except Main Street. Finish your day by browsing along Main Street.

18. If you leave the park at closing time, the express monorail to the TTC will be mobbed. Either take the ferry or board the resort monorail to the TTC.

Magic Kingdom Two-Day Touring Plan B for Morning Touring and for When the Park Closes Early

FOR: **Parties wishing to spread their Magic Kingdom visit over two days and parties preferring to tour in the morning.**

ASSUMES: Willingness to experience all major rides (including roller coasters) and shows.

TIMING: The following two-day touring plan takes advantage of early morning touring. On each day you should complete the structured part of the plan by about 3 P.M. or so. If you are visiting the Magic Kingdom during a period of the year when the park is open late (after 8 P.M.), you might prefer our alternate two-day touring plan, which offers morning touring on one day and late afternoon and evening touring on the other day. If you are not a Walt Disney World resort or campground guest, schedule both days of this touring plan for mornings when the early-entry program (for resort guests) in not in effect.

Day One

1. Arrive at the Magic Kingdom's parking lot 50 minutes before the park's stated opening time. This will give you time to park and catch the tram to the Transportation and Ticket Center (TTC). Arrive an hour earlier than opening time if it is a holiday period or you must purchase your admission.
2. If the line for the monorail is short, take the monorail; otherwise catch the ferry.
3. When you arrive at the Magic Kingdom, proceed through the entry turnstiles and stop at City Hall for park maps and a copy of the daily entertainment schedule.
4. Next, move as fast as you can down Main Street to the central hub. Because the Magic Kingdom uses two basic procedures when opening the park to the general public, you will probably encounter one of the following:

    a. The entire park will be open. If this is the case, proceed quickly to Space Mountain in Tomorrowland.

b. Only Main Street will be open. In this case, turn right at the end of Main Street (before you reach the central hub), past the Plaza Ice Cream Parlor and the Plaza Restaurant, and stake out a place for your group at the entrance of the Plaza Pavilion. When the rope barrier is dropped at opening time, jog through the Plaza Pavilion and on to Space Mountain. Starting at the entrance to the Plaza Pavilion will give you about a 100-yard head start and an advantage over anyone coming from the central hub. Ride Space Mountain.

Warning: Because it is new, *Alien Encounter* develops large lines as soon as the park opens. If you are a Magic Kingdom veteran, you may want to experience *Alien Encounter* first and then proceed to Space Mountain. If you go to Space Mountain first, be prepared for a 30-minute plus wait at *Alien Encounter* unless you really hustle.

NOTE: If you are a Walt Disney World resort guest and enter the park on an early-entry day, ride Space Mountain and see as much of Fantasyland and Tomorrowland as possible. As the time approaches for the park to open to the public, position yourself in line for *Legend of the Lion King* in Fantasyland. After *Lion King*, pick up the touring plan at The Haunted Mansion (Step 11), skipping steps that direct you to attractions experienced during your early-entry hour.

5. Backtrack toward the main entrance of Tomorrowland. Experience *Alien Encounter*.
6. Exiting *Alien Encounter* to the left, bear left around the corner and head for Fantasyland, keeping the Grand Prix Raceway on your right. In Fantasyland, ride 20,000 Leagues Under the Sea.
7. Exit 20,000 Leagues to the right and proceed to the courtyard of the castle. If you have small children in your party, let them ride Dumbo, the Flying Elephant.
8. Ride Peter Pan's Flight, also in Fantasyland.
9. In Fantasyland, see *Legend of the Lion King.*
10. Exiting *Lion King* to the left, cross the courtyard and ride It's a Small World.
11. Proceed to Liberty Square and experience The Haunted Mansion.
12. While in Liberty Square, visit *The Hall of Presidents.*
13. If you are hungry, go ahead and eat lunch. Fast-food eateries that are generally less crowded include Aunt Polly's Landing in

Frontierland, El Pirata Y el Perico in Adventureland, and the Crystal Palace at the central hub end of Main Street.

14. After lunch, see *The Hall of Presidents* and the Liberty Square Riverboat. If either is within ten minutes of getting underway, choose the one with the shortest wait. When you have experienced both of these attractions, proceed to Step 15.

   NOTE: At this point check your daily entertainment schedule to see if there are any parades or live performances that interest you. Make note of the times and alter the touring plan accordingly. Since you have already seen all the attractions that cause bottle-necks and have big lines, an interruption of the touring plan here will not cause you any problems. Simply pick up where you left off before the parade or show.

15. In Frontierland, take a raft to Tom Sawyer Island and explore.
16. After you leave Tom Sawyer Island, go to Adventureland and see the *Tropical Serenade (Enchanted Tiki Birds)*.
17. While in Adventureland, walk through the Swiss Family Tree-house.
18. This concludes the touring plan for the day. Enjoy the shops, see some of the live entertainment offerings, or revisit your favorite attractions until you are ready to leave.
19. If you leave the park at closing time, the express monorail to the TTC will be mobbed. Either take the ferry or board the resort monorail to the TTC.

Day Two

1. Call (407) 824-4321 the day before you go for the official opening time.
2. Arrive at the Magic Kingdom's parking lot 50 minutes before the park's stated opening time. This will give you time to park and catch the tram to the TTC. Arrive an hour earlier than opening time if it is a holiday period.
3. If the line for the monorail is short, take it; otherwise catch the ferry.
4. When you arrive at the Magic Kingdom, proceed through the entry turnstiles. Stop at City Hall for park maps and a copy of the daily entertainment schedule.

NOTE: If you are a Walt Disney World resort guest and enter the park on an early-entry day, revisit Space Mountain and enjoy your favorite Fantasyland attractions. As the time approaches for the park to open to the public, position yourself in Fantasyland at the boundary of Fantasyland and Liberty Square. When the other lands open, head for the Liberty Square waterfront and from there to Splash Mountain. After Splash Mountain, pick up the touring plan at Big Thunder Mountain Railroad (Step 6), skipping steps that direct you to attractions experienced during your early-entry hour.

5. Proceed to the end of Main Street. If the entire park is open, head immediately for Frontierland and Splash Mountain. Otherwise, turn left past Refreshment Corner and position yourself in front of the Crystal Palace facing the walkway bridge to Adventureland. When the rope barrier is dropped, cross the bridge and turn left into Adventureland. Cut through Adventureland into Frontierland. Head straight for Splash Mountain and ride.

6. While in Frontierland, ride the Big Thunder Mountain Railroad, next door.

7. Return to Adventureland and ride the Jungle Cruise.

8. Exit the Jungle Cruise to the left. While in Adventureland, enjoy Pirates of the Caribbean.

9. Return to Frontierland and turn right to the *Country Bear Jamboree*.

10. After the show, exit left and catch the Walt Disney World Railroad to Mickey's Starland (the first stop).

11. Tour Mickey's House and proceed through Mickey's backdoor to *Mickey's Starland Show*, a live show featuring the Disney characters. After the show, you can exit the theater and visit Mickey in his dressing room, where he will pose with your group for photographs. If this interests you, see the Touring Tips for *Mickey's Starland Show* on pages 366–67.

NOTE: At this point check your daily entertainment schedule to see if there are any parades or live performances that interest you. Make note of the times and alter the touring plan accordingly. Since you have already seen all the attractions that cause bottlenecks and have big lines, an interruption of the touring plan here will not cause you any problems. Simply pick up where you left off before the parade or show.

12. Exiting Mickey's Starland via the path to Fantasyland, turn left at the Grand Prix and go to Tomorrowland.

13. In Tomorrowland, if you are hungry, eat lunch at Cosmic Ray's Starlight Cafe (okay) or the Plaza Pavilion (better).

14. While in Tomorrowland, ride the Tomorrowland Transit Authority.

15. Try the *Carousel of Progress*, also in Tomorrowland.

16. In Tomorrowland, also ride Dreamflight.

17. Proceed toward the central hub entrance to Tomorrowland and experience *Alien Encounter* if you missed it on Day One.

18. Walk across the street and see the *Transportarium*.

19. This concludes the touring plan. Enjoy the shops, see some of the live entertainment offerings, or revisit your favorite attractions until you are ready to leave.

21. If you leave the park at closing time, the express monorail to the TTC will be mobbed. Either take the ferry or board the resort monorail to the TTC.

PART TEN: EPCOT Center

—— Overview

EPCOT Center is more than twice the physical size of the Magic Kingdom or the Disney-MGM Studios, and it has lines every bit as long as those waiting for the Jungle Cruise or Space Mountain. Obviously, visitors must come prepared to do a considerable amount of walking from attraction to attraction within EPCOT Center and a comparable amount of standing in line.

The size and scope of EPCOT Center also means that one can't really see the whole place in one day without skipping an attraction or two and giving other areas a cursory glance. A major difference between the Magic Kingdom and EPCOT Center, however, is that some of the EPCOT attractions can be either lingered over or skimmed, depending on one's personal interest. A good example is the General Motors' World of Motion pavilion, which consists of two sections. The first section is a 15-minute ride, while the second section is a collection of educational walk-through exhibits and mini-theaters. Nearly all visitors opt to take the ride, but many people, due to time constraints or lack of interest, bypass the exhibits.

Generally speaking, the rides at the Magic Kingdom are designed to create an experience of adventure or fantasy; while at EPCOT, attractions are oriented toward education or inspiration.

Some people will find that the attempts at education are superficial; others will want more entertainment and less education. Most visitors are somewhere in between, finding plenty of entertainment **and** education.

In any event, EPCOT Center is more of an adult place than the Magic Kingdom. What it gains in taking a futuristic, visionary, and technological look at the world, it loses, just a bit, in warmth, happiness, and charm.

As in the Magic Kingdom and the Disney-MGM Studios, we have identified several attractions in EPCOT Center as "not to be missed." But part of the enjoyment of a place like EPCOT Center is that there is something for everyone. If you go in a group, no doubt there will be quite a variety of opinions as to which attraction is "best."

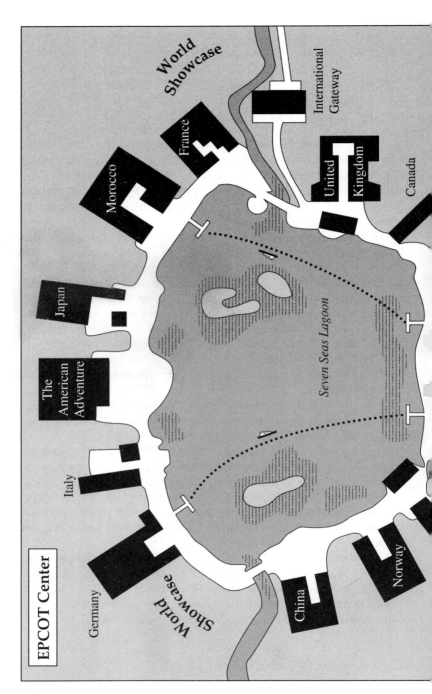

EPCOT Center

World Showcase

World Showcase

International Gateway

Morocco

France

United Kingdom

Canada

Japan

The American Adventure

Italy

Germany

Seven Seas Lagoon

China

Norway

438

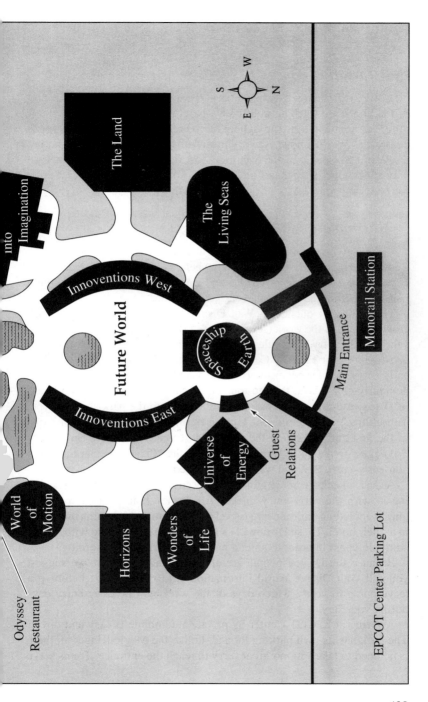

—— *Operating Hours*

EPCOT Center's two primary theme areas, Future World and World Showcase, each have different operating hours. Though schedules differ from time to time throughout the year, Future World always opens before the World Showcase in the morning and usually closes before the World Showcase in the evening. Most of the year, World Showcase opens two hours later than Future World. For exact opening and closing times during your visit, call (407) 824-4321.

—— *Arriving*

Disney hotel and campground guests are invited to enter EPCOT Center one hour early two days each week, usually Tuesday and Friday. If you have early-entry privileges and want to use them, arrive about a half hour before the designated early-entry time.

Those lodging outside of Walt Disney World must balance the least crowded days of the week (see pages 34–37) with an estimation of the impact of early entry. As a rule of thumb, we recommend that off-property patrons not tour EPCOT Center on the days when it is scheduled for early entry. It is far better to arrive early and stay ahead of the crowd on non-early-entry days, than to tour on an early-entry day when a hoard of Disney lodging guests have been allowed into the park ahead of you. The ultimate key to efficient touring in any of the parks is to be one of the first guests through the turnstiles. If you do not have early-entry privileges, arrive 40 to 50 minutes before the official opening time on a non-early-entry day, and wait to be admitted.

As an aside, those not eligible for early entry should not attempt sneaking in with the early-entry guests. All Disney hotel and campground guests, including children, are issued dated identification cards on check-in at their hotel. These Disney I.D.'s must be presented along with a valid admission pass in order to enter a park on an early-entry morning.

Because the Disney people are always changing things, we suggest you call Walt Disney World Information at (407) 824-4321 before you leave home to verify which days of the week will be early-entry days during your stay.

Arriving at EPCOT Center by private automobile is easy and direct. The park has its own parking lot and, unlike the Magic Kingdom, there is no need to take a monorail or ferry to reach the entrance. Trams serve the entire EPCOT Center lot, or if you wish, you can walk to the front gate. Monorail service connects EPCOT Center with the Transportation and Ticket Center, the Magic Kingdom (transfer required), and with the Magic Kingdom resort hotels (transfer also required).

— *Getting Oriented*

Like the Magic Kingdom, EPCOT Center has sections based on a theme, but only two: Future World and World Showcase. The technological resources of major corporations and the creative talent of Disney combine in Future World, which presents a look at where man has come from and where he is going. World Showcase, featuring the distinctive landmarks, cuisine, and culture of a number of nations, is meant to be a sort of permanent world's fair.

From the standpoint of finding your way around, however, EPCOT Center is not at all like the Magic Kingdom. The Magic Kingdom is designed so that at nearly any location in the park you feel a part of a very specific environment—Liberty Square, let's say, or Main Street, U.S.A. Each of these environments is visually closed off from other parts of the park to preserve the desired atmosphere. It wouldn't do for the Jungle Cruise to pass the roaring blacktop of the Grand Prix Raceway, for example.

EPCOT Center, by contrast, is visually open. And while it seems strange to see a Japanese pagoda on the same horizon with the Eiffel Tower, in-park navigation is fairly simple. A possible exception is in Future World, where the enormous east and west Innoventions buildings effectively hide everything on the opposite side.

While Cinderella Castle is the focal landmark of the Magic Kingdom, Spaceship Earth is the architectural symbol of EPCOT Center. This shiny, 180-foot "geosphere" is visible from almost every point. Like Cinderella Castle, it can help you keep track of where you are in the park. But because it's in a high-traffic location, and because it's not centrally located, it does not make a very good meeting place.

Any of the distinctively designed national pavilions make good meeting places, but be more specific than, "Hey, let's meet in Japan!" That may sound fun and catchy, but remember that the national pavilions are mini-towns with buildings, monuments, gardens, and plazas. You could wander around quite awhile "in Japan" without making connection with your group. Pick out a specific place in Japan, the sidewalk side of the pagoda, for example.

—— *The New EPCOT*

Correctly assessing that EPCOT Center was getting a little stale, Disney undertook a number of improvements in 1994 to make the park more current. The Land Pavilion, along with its attractions, were renovated and updated. Communicore, at the heart of Future World, was replaced by Innoventions, a sort of ongoing trade show featuring products and technologies of the near future. Spaceship Earth, the attraction situated inside the huge dome, was partially redesigned and enhanced, and a new 3-D movie premiered at the Journey into Imagination Pavilion. Additional street vendors and entertainers were introduced in the World Showcase to impart a sense of liveliness and community, and two new shows were integrated into the park's live entertainment schedule.

The EPCOT Acronym

It has become somewhat of a pastime among Walt Disney World employees and guests to create new and amusing definitions for the letters E.P.C.O.T. The official translation, of course, is:

Experimental **P**rototype **C**ommunity **O**f **T**omorrow

Readers and Disney employees have shared these *un*official versions:

Every **P**erson **C**omes **O**ut **T**ired

Every **P**arent **C**arries **O**ut a **T**oddler

Every **P**ocketbook **C**omes **O**ut **T**rashed

Economic **P**rivation **C**ity of **O**rlando **T**axbase

More Information and Help Galore —
WorldKey Information Service

Whether you need more information or assistance or not, you should know about the innovative WorldKey Information Service. It not only may be useful as you visit EPCOT Center, it will also give you some experience dealing with what may be one of the common video systems of the future.

WorldKey is a network of interactive video display terminals—televisions that react when you touch certain parts of the screen.

The WorldKey system, developed by the Bell System and the Walt

Disney Company, Inc., will provide you with up to 40 minutes of information about EPCOT Center, showing maps and pictures, and describing attractions, restaurants, entertainment, guest services, and shops.

Be patient with the WorldKey and it will guide you, step by step, through an explanation of how to use the system—in English or in Spanish (French and German are to be added later). Stick with the program through at least a few steps and you can use the WorldKey to contact an attendant. Via two-way television and hands-free two-way speakers, the WorldKey attendant can answer your questions, make hotel or restaurant reservations, and help find lost children, among other things.

Because the WorldKey system is so novel, a lot of visitors "play" with it as though it were just another video game. For most people this play is actually an educational experience. They are using what could become one of the data retrieval systems of tomorrow. They are learning about touch-sensitive screens. (You don't need to press, by the way; sometimes the system reacts even before your finger touches the screen.)

But whether people play with the WorldKey or put it to work, they usually end up walking away from the screen without completing the WorldKey program and setting it up for the next user. If people get frustrated with the WorldKey it's usually because they walked up to it while it was in the middle of showing the last user what he asked to see.

If, as opposed to finding a program in progress left from a previous user, you initiate the program, the WorldKey will quickly show you, step by step, how to use the system.

If you wish to speak to an attendant, work through the program until a prompt for an attendant is displayed on the screen. Touch the screen as indicated and soon one of the WorldKey attendants will come "live" onto the screen, ready to communicate with you.

Future World

Gleaming, futuristic structures of immense proportions leave little in doubt concerning the orientation of this, the first theme area you encounter at EPCOT Center. The thoroughfares are broad and punctuated with billowing fountains—all reflected in the shining facades of the space-age architecture. Everything, including the bountiful landscaping, is clean and sparkling to the point of asepsis and seemingly bigger than life. Pavilions dedicated to man's past, present, and future technological accomplishments form the perimeter of the Future World area, with Spaceship Earth and its flanking Innoventions East and West standing preeminent front and center.

Most of EPCOT Center services are concentrated in Future World's Entrance Plaza, near the main gate. Guest Relations, directly to the left of the geodesic sphere, is the EPCOT Center equivalent of City Hall in the Magic Kingdom

—— *Future World Services*

EPCOT Center's service facilities in Future World include the following:

Wheelchair & Stroller Rental	Inside the main entrance and to the left toward the rear of the Entrance Plaza
Banking Services	There is an ATM outside the main entrance near the kennels
Currency Exchange	Limited services available at the American Express Travel Service located outside of the main entrance and to the right.
Storage Lockers	Turn right at Spaceship Earth (lockers are cleaned out every night)
Lost & Found	Outside the main entrance and to the far right

Live Entertainment and Parade Information	At Guest Relations to the left of Spaceship Earth
Lost Persons	At Guest Relations and at the Baby Center on the World Showcase side of the Odyssey Restaurant
Dining Reservations	At Guest Relations
Walt Disney World & Local Attraction Information	At Guest Relations
First Aid	Next to the Baby Center on the World Showcase side of the Odyssey Restaurant
Baby Center/Baby Care Needs	On the World Showcase side of the Odyssey Restaurant

—— *Guest Relations*

DESCRIPTION AND COMMENTS   Not an attraction as such, Guest Relations is situated to the left of the geosphere and serves as the park headquarters. It also serves as EPCOT Center's primary information center. Attendants staff information booths and a number of WorldKey terminals are available just outside. If you have spent any time in the Magic Kingdom, Guest Relations is EPCOT Center's version of City Hall.

TOURING TIPS   If you wish to eat in one of the EPCOT Center sit-down restaurants, you can make your reservations at Guest Relations through a WorldKey Information Service attendant (instead of running to the restaurant itself and standing in line for reservations, which is another alternative). In the morning, all of the WorldKey screens outside Guest Relations are tuned to restaurant reservationists. All you have to do is march up to the terminal and tell the reservationist where you want to eat. See the description of the WorldKey system, pages 442–43, and the section dealing with eating in EPCOT Center, pages 488–94.

Spaceship Earth

Type of Ride: Educational journey through past, present, and future
When to Go: Before 10 A.M. or after 4 P.M.
Special Comments: If lines are long when you arrive, try again after 4 P.M.

Author's Rating: One of EPCOT's best; ★★★★½

Overall Appeal by Age Group:

Pre-school	Grade School	Teens	Young Adults	Over 30	Senior Citizens
★★★★	★★★★½	★★★★½	★★★★½	★★★★½	★★★ ★½

Duration of Ride: About 16 minutes

Average Wait in Line per 100 People Ahead of You: 3 minutes

Assumes: Normal operation

Loading Speed: Fast

DESCRIPTION AND COMMENTS   This Bell System ride spirals through the 17-story interior of EPCOT Center's premier landmark, taking visitors past AudioAnimatronic scenes depicting man's developments in communications, from cave painting to printing to television to space communications and computer networks. The ride, which was updated and improved in 1994, is compelling and well done. We rate Spaceship Earth a "not to be missed" attraction.

TOURING TIPS   Because of its location near EPCOT Center's main entrance, Spaceship Earth is literally inundated with arriving guests throughout the morning. If you are among the first guests in the park, go ahead and ride. Otherwise, it might be better to postpone Spaceship Earth until later in the day, say, after 4 P.M.

As you face the entrance to Spaceship Earth, you will notice that the direct walkway to the entrance runs between two labyrinthine queuing areas under the cover of the sphere. If these queuing areas are in use, bypass Spaceship Earth for the time being. If, on the other hand, these areas are nearly empty, feel free to hop in line. Spaceship Earth loads continuously and expeditiously. Therefore, if the line runs only along the right side of the sphere you will board in less than 15 minutes.

Global Neighborhood

Type of Attraction: Interactive Communications Playground

When to Go: After riding Spaceship Earth

Special Comments: Spaceship Earth disembarks passengers directly into the Global Neighborhood

Author's Rating: High-tech fun; ★★★

Overall Appeal by Age Group:

Pre-school	Grade School	Teens	Young Adults	Over 30	Senior Citizens
★★	★★★½	★★★½	★★★½	★★★	★★★½

Duration of Attraction: Not limited

Average Wait in Line per 100 People Ahead of You: No wait

DESCRIPTION AND COMMENTS The Spaceship Earth ride discharges passengers into the Global Neighborhood at the base of the geosphere. Presented by AT&T, Global Neighborhood is a walk-through playground of futuristic, interactive communications devices. Platform simulator rides take 2–6 guests at a time on a tour of the AT&T Network. A *Storyteller* touch screen allows guests to embellish a story setting by accessing computer-programmed visual and sound effects. The best of the interactive devices is *Communications Breakthrough,* which combines word cues and teamwork with an electronic shooting gallery. Least compelling of the Global Neighborhood's offerings is *Interactive Wonderland,* a plodding interactive video game involving characters from *Alice In Wonderland.*

TOURING TIPS If Spaceship Earth is busy, the Global Neighborhood will be, too. If you want to spend some time enjoying the interactive games, try to stop in during the late afternoon or evening. Incidentally, you do not have to ride Spaceship Earth to enter the Global Neighborhood. You can walk directly in from the plaza on the far side of the geosphere.

—— *Innoventions*

Type of Attraction: Multifaceted attraction featuring static and "hands-on" exhibits relating to products and technologies of the near future

When to Go: On your second day at EPCOT or after you have seen all the major attractions

Special Comments: Most exhibits demand time and participation to be rewarding; not much gained here by a quick walk-through

Author's Rating: Vastly improved; ★★★½

Overall Appeal by Age Group:

Pre-school	Grade School	Teens	Young Adults	Over 30	Senior Citizens
★½	★★★½	★★★★	★★★½	★★★	★★★

DESCRIPTION AND COMMENTS   Innoventions consists of two huge, crescent-shaped, glass-walled structures separated by a central plaza. Formerly known as CommuniCore, the two-building complex was originally designed to be the communications and community hub of EPCOT. In execution, however, something was lost. For most guests during EPCOT's first twelve years, CommuniCore was, at best, a rather staid museum of science and industry, and at worst, a huge obstacle to circumnavigate every time you wanted to cross from one side of Future World to the other.

In 1994, Disney attempted to return to the original concept, only this time with more of a marketplace than a communications orientation. The result is Innoventions, a huge, busy collection of industry-sponsored walk-through and "hands-on" exhibits. Dynamic, interactive, and forward looking, Innoventions most closely resembles a high-tech trade show. Featured products provide guests with a preview of consumer and industrial goods of the near future. Electronics, communications, and entertainment technology, as you would expect, play a prominent role. Exhibits, many of which are scheduled to be changed each year, demonstrate such products as virtual-reality games, high-definition TV, voice-activated appliances, and various CD-ROM applications, among others. In all, there are about 15 major exhibit areas, each sponsored by a different manufacturer or research lab. The emphasis in the respective exhibits is on the effect of the product or technology on daily living. The most popular Innoventions attraction (as you might expect) is an arcade of video and simulator games. A well-done but frequently overlooked attraction is a tour of a Disney Imagineering studio, where guests are exposed to motion picture and theme park applications of virtual reality. The Innoventions buildings also house restaurants, gift shops, and the EPCOT Discovery Center, described below.

As the following comments suggest, *Unofficial* reader response to Innoventions is mixed. First, a letter from a Port Chester, New York, family:

> The more unstructured "interactive" parts were incredibly noisy and confusing—rather like a crowded video arcade with games that didn't work very well. Crowd control was poor. The setup leads to pushing and shoving to get to control boards. My kids, being small girls, didn't stand a chance of getting near anything. The display portions of the attraction "Home of the Future," etc., most clearly resembled a trade show at the Javits Center or the

fixture displays at Home Depot. Such treats as a booth devoted entirely to faucets hardly suggested the fun and magic one usually associates with WDW. This whole pavilion seemed far more commercial than magical.

A man from Detroit chimed in with this:

I had to laugh at the big "self-cleaning" toilet so prominently displayed between the Innoventions buildings. I kept waiting for a street person to climb up on the pot and have a good constitutional — but then I remembered this wasn't Detroit.

And from a Tulsa, Oklahoma, father of three:

The best things at EPCOT for my kids were the hands-on exhibits at Innoventions. We bumped into the computer games there as we were passing through en route to something else (I don't remember what because we never got there).

TOURING TIPS   Innoventions East and West (two buildings) provide visitors an opportunity to preview the products of tomorrow in a fun, "hands-on" manner. Some of the exhibits are quite intriguing, while others are less compelling. We observed a wide range of reactions by visitors to the many Innoventions exhibits and can only suggest that you form your own opinion. In terms of touring strategy, we suggest you spend time at Innoventions on your second day at EPCOT Center. If you only have one day, visit sometime during the evening if you have the time and endurance. Be warned, however, that many Innoventions exhibits are technical in nature and may not be compatible with your mood or level of energy toward the end of a long day of touring. Also be advised that you cannot get much of anything out of a quick walk-through of Innoventions; you have to invest a little time to understand what is going on.

EPCOT Discovery Center

DESCRIPTION AND COMMENTS   The EPCOT Discovery Center consists of static displays illustrating various EPCOT projects and developments, and a library service that provides information on demand concerning any topic presented in either Future World or World Showcase. If you have used these services in the past, note that their location in Innoventions West has been moved.

TOURING TIPS   This is where someone will try to answer that question you have been kicking around all day. If you are an educator with a group, special tour-enhancing handouts can be obtained here.

The Living Seas

Type of Attraction: Multifaceted attraction consisting of an underwater ride beneath a huge saltwater aquarium and a number of exhibits and displays dealing with oceanography, ocean ecology, and sea life

When to Go: Before 10 A.M. or after 3 P.M.

Special Comments: The ride is only a small component of this attraction. See description and touring tips below for information on the rest of the attraction.

Author's Rating: An excellent marine exhibit; ★★★½

Overall Appeal by Age Group:

Pre-school	Grade School	Teens	Young Adults	Over 30	Senior Citizens
★★★	★★★½	★★★½	★★★★	★★★★	★★★★

Duration of Ride: 3 minutes

Average Wait in Line per 100 People Ahead of You: 3½ minutes

Assumes: All elevators in operation

Loading Speed: Fast

DESCRIPTION AND COMMENTS   The Living Seas is one of the most ambitious Future World offerings. The focus is a huge, 200-foot diameter, 27-foot-deep main tank containing fish, mammals, and crustaceans in a simulation of a real ocean ecosystem. Scientists and divers conduct actual marine experiments underwater in view of EPCOT Center guests. Visitors can view the undersea activity through eight-inch-thick windows below the surface (including viewing windows in the Coral Reef restaurant), and via a three-part adventure ride that is the featured attraction of The Living Seas. It consists of a movie dramatizing the link between the ocean and man's survival, followed by a simulated elevator descent to the bottom of the tank. Here guests board gondolas for a three-minute voyage through an underwater viewing tunnel.

The fish population of The Living Seas has grown substantially, but the underwater ride is over before you have gotten comfortably situated in the gondola. No matter, the strength of this attraction lies in the dozen or so exhibits offered after the ride. Visitors can view aquaculture fish-breeding experiments, watch short films about various forms of sea life, and much more. The main aquarium, which the ride passes through, can be additionally viewed through huge viewing windows (after the ride is completed). You can stay as long as you wish in the exhibit areas.

The Living Seas is a high-quality marine/aquarium exhibit, but is no substitute for visiting Sea World, an enormous marine theme park, every bit on a par in terms of quality, appeal, educational value, and entertainment with the Magic Kingdom, EPCOT Center, or Disney-MGM Studios.

TOURING TIPS   The exhibits at the end of the ride are the best part of The Living Seas. In the morning, these are often bypassed by guests trying to rush or stay ahead of the crowd. The Living Seas needs to be lingered over at a time when you are not in a hurry. We recommend seeing The Living Seas in the late afternoon or evening, or on your second day at EPCOT Center.

—— *The Land Pavilion*

DESCRIPTION AND COMMENTS   The Land is in fact a huge pavilion sponsored by Nestle which contains three attractions (discussed next) and a number of restaurants. The Land underwent an extensive renovation in 1994, including updating and improving its three resident attractions. Where the pavilion's original emphasis was on farming, its current message deals more with environmental concerns.

TOURING TIPS   The Land is a good place for a fast-food lunch; if you are there to see the attractions, however, don't go during meal times.

Living with the Land

Type of Ride: A boat ride adventure through the past, present, and future of U.S. farming and agriculture

When to Go: Before 10:30 A.M. or after 7:30 P.M.

Special Comments: Take this ride early in the morning but save the other Land attractions for later in the day; located on the lower level of The Land pavilion

Author's Rating: Interesting and fun; ★★★★

Overall Appeal by Age Group:

Pre-school	Grade School	Teens	Young Adults	Over 30	Senior Citizens
★★★	★★★	★★★½	★★★★	★★★★★	★★★★★

Duration of Ride: About 12 minutes

Average Wait in Line per 100 People Ahead of You: 3 minutes

Assumes: 15 boats operating

Loading Speed: Moderate

DESCRIPTION AND COMMENTS A boat ride that takes visitors through tropic swamps, past various inhospitable environments man has faced as a farmer, and through a futuristic, innovative greenhouse where real crops are being grown using the latest agricultural technologies. Inspiring and educational, with excellent effects and a good narrative, this attraction rates "not to be missed."

TOURING TIPS This attraction should be seen before the lunch crowd hits The Land restaurants, i.e., before 10:30 A.M., or in the evening after 7:30 P.M.

If you really enjoy this ride, or if you have a special interest in the agricultural techniques demonstrated, consider taking the Greenhouse Tour. At $5 for adults and $3 for children ages 3–9, this 45-minute guided tour takes guests behind the scenes for an in-depth examination of advanced and experimental growing methods. Reservations for the Greenhouse Tour are made on a space-available basis at the guided tour waiting area (to the far right of the restaurants on the lower level).

Food Rocks

Type of Show: AudioAnimatronic variety show about food and nutrition

When to Go: Before 11 A.M. or after 2 P.M.

Special Comments: Located on the lower level of The Land pavilion

Author's Rating: Lively and amusing; ★★★

Overall Appeal by Age Group:

Pre-school	Grade School	Teens	Young Adults	Over 30	Senior Citizens
★★★½	★★★½	★★★	★★★	★★★	★★★

Duration of Presentation: Approximately 13 minutes

Preshow Entertainment: None
Probable Waiting Time: Less than 10 minutes

DESCRIPTION AND COMMENTS   Disney AudioAnimatronic characters in the forms of various foods and cooking utensils take the stage in a marginally educational (and highly improbable) rock concert. Featured artists include the Peach Boys, Chubby Cheddar, Neil Moussaka, and Pita Gabriel. Little Richard, belting out Tutti Frutti, provides the sound track for a singing pineapple. Fast-paced and imaginative, *Food Rocks* is better entertainment than its predecessor, *Kitchen Kaberet*, and delivers the proper-diet-and-balanced-nutrition message about as well.

TOURING TIPS   One of the few light entertainment offerings at EPCOT Center. Slightly reminiscent of *Country Bear Jamboree* in the Magic Kingdom (but not quite as humorous or endearing in our opinion). Though the theater is not large, we have never encountered any long waits at *Food Rocks* (even during meal times). Nevertheless, we recommend you go before 11 A.M. or after 2 P.M.

Harvest Theater

Type of Show: Film exploring man's relationship with his environment
When to Go: Before 11 A.M. and after 2 P.M.
Author's Rating: Extremely interesting and enlightening; ★★★½
Overall Appeal by Age Group:

Pre-school	Grade School	Teens	Young Adults	Over 30	Senior Citizens
★★★½	★★★★	★★★½	★★★½	★★★★	★★★½

Duration of Presentation: Approximately 12½ minutes
Preshow Entertainment: None
Probable Waiting Time: 10–15 minutes

DESCRIPTION AND COMMENTS   This attraction features a film called *The Circle of Life* starring Simba, Timon, and Pumbaa from Disney's *Legend of the Lion King*. The subject is the environmental interdependency of all the creatures that share the earth, demonstrating how easily ecological balance can be upset. The film is superb in its production and not too heavy-handed in its sobering message.

TOURING TIPS   This extremely worthwhile film should be part of every visitor's touring day. If you are trying to stay ahead of the crowd, postpone seeing the film until late afternoon. Long waits are almost never a problem at the Harvest Theater.

—— *Journey into Imagination Pavilion*

DESCRIPTION AND COMMENTS   Another multi-attraction pavilion, located on the west side of Innoventions West and down the walk from The Land. Outside is an "upside-down waterfall" and one of our favorite Future World landmarks, the so-called "jumping water," a leapfrogging fountain that seems to hop over the heads of unsuspecting passersby.

TOURING TIPS   We recommend early morning or late evening touring. See the individual attractions for specifics.

Journey into Imagination

Type of Ride: Fantasy adventure

When to Go: Before 10:30 A.M. or after 6 P.M.

Author's Rating: Colorful but dull; ★★½

Overall Appeal by Age Group:

Pre-school	Grade School	Teens	Young Adults	Over 30	Senior Citizens
★★★★	★★★★	★★★	★★★	★★★	★★★

Duration of Ride: Approximately 13 minutes

Average Wait in Line per 100 People Ahead of You: 3 minutes

Assumes: 20 trains operating

Loading Speed: Moderate to fast

DESCRIPTION AND COMMENTS   This ride features two Disney characters —Figment, an impish purple dragon, and Dreamfinder, a red-bearded adventurer who pilots a contraption designed to search out and capture ideas. This ride, with its happy, humorous orientation, is one of the lighter and more fanciful offerings in the park. It is the favorite ride of some, while others find it dull and vacuous.

The Journey into Imagination ride stimulates varied responses (mostly polar) among our readers. A mother from Springfield, Missouri, who toured with her husband and children (ages four, seven, and ten), tells us:

> Keep telling people that Journey into Imagination is boring. It is not worth a five minute wait. We voted it the most boring ride at WDW.

While a reader from Montreal, Quebec, says:

> I don't agree with your rating for Journey into Imagination. You claimed it to be dull, but I find it warm, happy, and a great ride. I feel this should be on the "not to be missed" list.

TOURING TIPS This ride, combined with the 3-D movie in the same building, draws large crowds, beginning about 10:45 A.M. We recommend riding before 10:30 A.M. or after 6 P.M.

The Image Works

Type of Attraction: Hands-on creative playground employing color, music, touch-sensation, and electronic devices

When to Go: Anytime you please

Special Comments: You do not have to wait in the long line for the ride in this pavilion to gain access to The Image Works. Simply go through the open door just to the left of where the line for the ride is entering. You will not have a wait.

Author's Rating: A fun change of pace; be sure to see the Dreamfinder's School of Drama; ★★★

Overall Appeal by Age Group:

Pre-school	Grade School	Teens	Young Adults	Over 30	Senior Citizens
★★★	★★★½	★★★	★★★	★★★	★★★

Probable Waiting Time: No waiting required

DESCRIPTION AND COMMENTS This is a playground for the imagination utilizing light, color, sound, and electronic devices that can be manipulated by visitors. There's the Magic Palette, with a video-screen canvas and an electronic paintbrush. Especially fun is the Electronic Philharmonic, which enables visitors to conduct the brass, woodwind, percussion, and string sections of an orchestra by movements of the hand. (The secret is raising and lowering your hands over the labeled discs on the console. Don't try pressing the discs as if they were buttons. Pretend you're a conductor—raise a hand away from the disc labeled brass, for example, and you will get louder brass. Lower your hand toward the disc labeled woodwinds and you'll get less volume from the woodwinds section.)

Dreamfinder's School of Drama is the best of The Image Works' offerings. Children volunteer to act in a short play augmented by video effects. A couple touring with their three-year-old writes:

> Another favorite of his [the child] and mine [Mom] was the chance to perform in a Dreamfinder short story at the Image Works. In these stories the players stand in front of a large blue screen and watch themselves get inserted [by video] into a simple story. The process is the same as is used by a local [TV] weatherman, and the acting instructions are clear and easy: "run in place" or "duck down." Video-taping the large [video] screen makes a great souvenir—just don't dress in blue.

TOURING TIPS   There are quite a number of interesting things to do and play with here, far more than the representative examples we listed. If you have more than one day at EPCOT Center, save The Image Works for the second day. If you are on a one-day schedule, try to work it in during the evening or late afternoon.

Magic Eye Theater: "Honey, I Shrunk the Audience"

Type of Show: 3-D film

When to Go: Before 10 A.M.or just before Future World closes

Special Comments: Adults should not be put off by the sci-fi theme; loud, intense show with tactile effects frightens some small children

Author's Rating: An absolute hoot! Not to be missed; ★★★★

Overall Appeal by Age Group:

Pre-school	Grade School	Teens	Young Adults	Over 30	Senior Citizens
★★★½	★★★★½	★★★★½	★★★★	★★★★	★★★½

Duration of Presentation: Approximately 17 minutes

Preshow Entertainment: 8 minutes

Probable Waiting Time: 12 minutes (at suggested times)

DESCRIPTION AND COMMENTS   *Honey, I Shrunk the Audience* is a 3-D off-shoot of Disney's feature film, *Honey, I Shrunk the Kids*. Replacing the long-running *Captain EO* (starring Michael Jackson) in the fall of 1994, *Honey, I Shrunk the Audience* features a similar array of special effects, including simulated explosions, smoke, fiberoptics, lights, water spray, and even moving seats. Where *Captain EO* had a brotherly love message, *Honey, I Shrunk the Audience* is played strictly for laughs, a commodity in short supply in the EPCOT entertainment mix.

TOURING TIPS   The audio level is earsplitting for productions in this theater. Small children are sometimes frightened by the sound volume, and many adults report that the loud soundtrack is distracting and even uncomfortable. While *Honey, I Shrunk the Audience* is a huge hit, it can be a bit overwhelming for preschoolers. A Lexington, South Carolina, dad wrote that *Honey, I Shrunk the Audience* is too intense for kids. Our 4-year-old took off his glasses 5 minutes into the movie. Because of this experience he would not wear glasses in the muppet movie at MGM." A New York City dad agreed, writing:

> One note about *Honey, I Shrunk the Audience:* we all loved it except our four-year-old. He's a brave kid, but this film definitely scared him: specifically the snake and lion 3-D effects. He refused to see it again although everyone else in the family wanted to. He loved the Muppet movie at MGM.

Because *Honey, I Shrunk the Audience* is new, expect larger-than-average crowds through the fall of 1995 and throughout 1996. Try to work the production into your touring schedule before 10 A.M. The Magic Eye Theater is located to the left of the Journey into Imagination ride, but it is not necessary to go on the ride in order to access *Honey, I Shrunk the Audience.* Finally, try to avoid seats in the first several rows. If you are too close to the screen, the 3-D images do not focus properly.

—— *World of Motion Pavilion*

DESCRIPTION AND COMMENTS   Presented by General Motors, this pavilion is to the left of Spaceship Earth when you enter and down toward the World Showcase from the Universe of Energy pavilion. The pavilion is home to It's Fun to Be Free, a ride, and to TransCenter, an assembly of stationary exhibits and mini-theater productions on the theme of transportation.

We receive a considerable volume of mail from readers who maintain that the World of Motion "is one big commercial" for General Motors. While we agree that the promotional hype is a little more heavy-handed than in most of the other business-sponsored attractions, we maintain that the World of Motion is one of the most creatively conceived and executed attractions in Walt Disney World.

It's Fun to Be Free

Type of Ride: AudioAnimatronic survey of the history of transportation
When to Go: Before noon and after 4 P.M.
Author's Rating: Not to be missed; ★★★★½
Overall Appeal by Age Group:

Pre-school	Grade School	Teens	Young Adults	Over 30	Senior Citizens
★★★½	★★★★	★★★★	★★★★	★★★★	★★★★

Duration of Ride: Approximately 14½ minutes
Average Wait in Line per 100 People Ahead of You: 2¾ minutes
Assumes: Normal operation
Loading Speed: Moderate to fast

DESCRIPTION AND COMMENTS   A "not-to-be-missed" attraction, this ride conducts visitors through a continuum of twenty-four AudioAnimatronic scenes depicting where and how man has traveled, and what the future has in store for travel. The detail in individual scenes is amazing and the tongue-in-cheek, humorous tone of the ride makes the history lesson more than tolerable.

TOURING TIPS   This ride has a large carrying capacity and an efficient loading system, keeping lines generally manageable. Many days you can hop on this ride anytime you want. Its largest crowds build between noon and 4 P.M.

TransCenter

Type of Attraction: Exhibits and mini-theater productions concerning the evolution and future of transportation, particularly as relates to the automobile
When to Go: On your second day or after you've seen the major attractions
Special Comments: World of Motion has a separate entrance to the exhibit area, making visitation possible even if you don't take the It's Fun to Be Free ride.
Author's Rating: Informative with a healthy dose of humor; ★★★

Overall Appeal by Age Group:

Pre-school	Grade School	Teens	Young Adults	Over 30	Senior Citizens
★★½	★★★	★★★	★★★	★★★	★★★

Probable Waiting Time: No waiting required if you enter through the rear entrance

DESCRIPTION AND COMMENTS   Most visitors enter TransCenter when they disembark from the ride described above, but there are separate doors on the east side of the pavilion for those who wish to visit the various exhibits without taking the ride. TransCenter's walk-through attraction takes up 33,000 square feet and deals with a wide range of topics relating to transportation. One major display demonstrates the importance of aerodynamics to fuel economy, while others evaluate the prospects of future power systems and explain why the industry is turning to robotic production techniques. Yet another display shows some advanced designs for the possible land, sea, and air conveyances of tomorrow.

TOURING TIPS   There's a lot to see here. How much you take in will be determined by your interest in the subject and the flexibility of your schedule. We like TransCenter on the second day of a two-day visit, or during the midafternoon if you enjoy this sort of display more than the offerings of the World Showcase. Late evening, after you have finished your "must list," is also a good time.

—— *Horizons Pavilion*

Type of Ride: A look at man's evolving perception of the future
When to Go: Before 11 A.M. or after 3:30 P.M.
Author's Rating: Not to be missed; ★★★★
Overall Appeal by Age Group:

Pre-school	Grade School	Teens	Young Adults	Over 30	Senior Citizens
★★★★	★★★★	★★★★	★★★★½	★★★★½	★★★★½

Duration of Ride: Approximately 15 minutes
Average Wait in Line per 100 People Ahead of You: 4 minutes
Assumes: Normal operation
Loading Speed: Moderate to fast

DESCRIPTION AND COMMENTS   This pavilion takes a look back at yesterday's visions of the future, including Jules Verne's concept of a moon rocket and a 1930s preview of a neon city. Elsewhere guests visit Future-Port and ride through a family habitat of the next century, with scenes depicting apartment, farm, underwater, and space communities.

Horizons was closed in 1994 when its corporate sponsor withdrew and it is rarely open these days. In the spring and summer of 1995, the attraction was not even listed on the official park map.

TOURING TIPS   The entire Horizons pavilion is devoted to a single, continuously loading ride, which has a large carrying capacity. If open, this "not to be missed" attraction can be enjoyed almost any time of day without long waits in line. One exception occurs immediately following the conclusion of a Universe of Energy performance, when up to 580 patrons can troop over and queue up for Horizons en masse. If by chance you encounter this deluge or its aftermath, take a 15-minute break. Chances are when you return to Horizons, you will be able to walk right in.

—— Wonders of Life Pavilion

DESCRIPTION AND COMMENTS   Presented by the Metropolitan Life Insurance Company, this newest addition to the Future World family is a multifaceted pavilion dealing with the human body, health, and medicine. Housed in a 100,000-square-foot, gold-domed structure, Wonders of Life houses a variety of attractions focusing on the capabilities of the human body and the importance of keeping it fit.

Body Wars

Motion Sickness

WARNING!

Type of Ride: Flight-simulator ride through the human body

When to Go: As soon as possible after the park opens

Special Comments: Not recommended for pregnant women or those prone to motion sickness

Author's Rating: Absolutely mind-blowing, not to be missed; ★★★★½

Overall Appeal by Age Group:

Pre-school	Grade School	Teens	Young Adults	Over 30	Senior Citizens
★★★	★★★★½	★★★★★	★★★★	★★★★	★★★

Duration of Ride: 5 minutes
Average Wait in Line per 100 People Ahead of You: 4 minutes
Assumes: All simulators operating
Loading Speed: Moderate to fast

DESCRIPTION AND COMMENTS   This is a thrill ride through the human body, developed along the same lines as the Star Tours space-simulation ride. The idea is that you are a passenger in a sort of miniature space capsule that is injected into a human body. Once inside the body your mission is to pick up a scientist who has been inspecting a splinter in the patient's finger. Before retrieval, however, the scientist gets sucked into the circulatory system and you end up chasing her all over the body in an attempt to rescue her. The simulator creates a vividly realistic experience as guests seem to hurtle at fantastic speeds through anatomical images. The sights are as mind-boggling as the ride is breathtaking in this "not to be missed" attraction.

TOURING TIPS   This is EPCOT Center's first and only thrill ride and is popular with all age groups. Ride first thing after the park opens or just before closing time. Be advised that Body Wars makes a lot of people motion sick and that it is not at all unusual for a simulator to be taken off-line to clean up some previous rider's mess. If you are at all susceptible to motion sickness we suggest you reconsider riding Body Wars. If you are on the ride and begin to get nauseated, fix your gaze on something other than the screen as far away as possible, i.e., the ceiling or the side and back walls. Without the visual effects, the ride itself is not rough enough to disturb most guests. If you do get queasy, there are rest rooms nearby as you get off the ride. As an aside, Star Tours, another simulator ride at the Disney-MGM Studios, is just as wild but makes very few people sick. If you successfully rode Star Tours, that does not necessarily mean Body Wars will not upset you. Conversely, if Body Wars made you ill, you cannot assume Star Tours will do the same.

While reader comments on Body Wars cover the spectrum, the following quotes are fairly representative:

> The only thing we won't do on this next trip is go on Body Wars in EPCOT. The line is so deceptive. We waited almost two hours and then it was only to get motion sickness and feel awful!

and:

> I made the mistake of riding Body Wars first thing in the morning, on an empty stomach, and with a hangover. I thought I was going

to throw up. It was very close. Strangely enough, I rode Body Wars again a week later, feeling fine. Guess what? I thought I was going to throw up. It was very close.

and:

Body Wars did not measure up to all the hype and warnings. We expected Space Mountain with visual effects, and it wasn't even close. You Weenies!

and:

The ride felt more like the involuntary movements of a hammock.

and finally:

Body Wars at EPCOT was great fun. We rode it twice and loved it. A little scary but exciting. Some of the other things seemed kind of boring after our ride here.

Motion sickness aside, Body Wars is incredibly intense, too intense for some, especially preschoolers and seniors. As one elderly gentleman confided, "Feeling sick at my stomach took my mind off being terrified."

Cranium Command

Type of Show: AudioAnimatronic character show about the brain
When to Go: Before 11 A.M. or after 3 P.M.
Author's Rating: Funny, outrageous, and educational. Not to be missed;
★★★★★
Overall Appeal by Age Group:

Pre-school	Grade School	Teens	Young Adults	Over 30	Senior Citizens
★★★	★★★★★	★★★★★	★★★★★	★★★★★	★★★★★

Duration of Presentation: About 20 minutes
Preshow Entertainment: Explanatory lead-in to feature presentation
Probable Waiting Time: Less than 10 minutes at touring times suggested

DESCRIPTION AND COMMENTS *Cranium Command* is EPCOT Center's great sleeper attraction. Stuck on the backside of the Wonders of Life pavilion and far less promoted than Body Wars, many guests elect to bypass this most humorous of all EPCOT Center offerings. Disney characters called "Brain Pilots" are trained to operate human brains. The show consists of a day in the life of one of these Cranium Commanders as he tries to pilot his assigned brain (that of an adolescent boy). We do not know who designed this attraction, but EPCOT Center in particular, and Walt Disney World in general, could use a lot more of this type of humor.

TOURING TIPS   The presentation kicks off with a preshow cartoon that is essential to understanding the rest of the show. If you arrive in the waiting area while the cartoon is in progress, make sure you see enough to get a sense of the story line before going into the main theater. Another comment: while most preschoolers enjoy *Cranium Command*, many of them do not really understand it.

The Making of Me

Type of Show: Humorous movie about human conception and birth
When to Go: Early in the morning or after 4:30 P.M.
Author's Rating: Well done; ★★★½
Overall Appeal by Age Group:

Pre-school	Grade School	Teens	Young Adults	Over 30	Senior Citizens
★★★	★★★	★★★½	★★★½	★★★	★★★

Duration of Presentation: 14 minutes
Preshow Entertainment: None
Probable Waiting Time: About 25 minutes (or more), unless you go early in the morning or after 4:30 P.M.

DESCRIPTION AND COMMENTS   This funny, lighthearted, and very sensitive movie about human conception, gestation, and birth was considered a controversial addition to the Wonders of Life pavilion. In point of fact, Disney audiences have received it well, with most guests agreeing that the material is tastefully and creatively presented. The plot is in the *Back to the Future* genre and has the main character going back in time to watch his parents date, fall in love, marry and, yes, conceive and give birth to him. By the way, there is a biological error in the film. If you spot it, write and tell us what it is. We will put all correct answers into a box and draw a winner at the end of the year. The prize? A free salpingoplasty.

Errors aside, the sexual material is well handled, with loving relationships given much more emphasis than plumbing. Parents of children under seven tell us that the sexual information presented went over their children's heads for the most part. For children a little older, however, the film seems to precipitate quite a few questions. You be the judge.

A gentleman from Cheshire, England, who believes (correctly, in our view) that Americans are sexually repressed, had this to say:

> By the standards of sex education programmes shown to English children of ages 8–9, *The Making of Me* seemed almost Mary Poppinsish in tone. Certainly other Brits found your warnings over content quite puzzling.

The reader quoted above would have a great time living in my city (Birmingham, Alabama), where some of the local clergy harangued the city council for months to have Bermuda shorts welded onto the bare buttocks of a large statue depicting Vulcan at his forge.

TOURING TIPS   *The Making of Me* is an excellent film shown in a theater not much larger than a phone booth. It is our fervent hope that the Disney people will soon relocate this show to a larger, more suitable theater. At present, however, the diminutive size of the theater ensures that there will be a long wait unless you go just after the park opens or during the very late afternoon or evening.

Fitness Fairgrounds

DESCRIPTION AND COMMENTS   Much of the pavilion's interior is devoted to an assortment of visitor participation exhibits, where guests can test their senses in a fun house, receive computer-generated health analyses of their personal lifestyles, work out on electronically sophisticated exercise equipment, and watch a video presentation called "Goofy About Health" (starring who else?).

TOURING TIPS   We recommend you save the Fitness Fair exhibits for your second day, or the end of your first day at EPCOT Center.

—— Universe of Energy Pavilion

Type of Attraction: Combination ride/theater presentation about energy
When to Go: Before 10:30 A.M. or after 4:30 P.M.
Special Comments: Don't be dismayed by large lines; 580 people
disappear into the pavilion each time the theater turns over
Author's Rating: A creative combination of theater and ride; ★★★½

Overall Appeal by Age Group:

Pre-school	Grade School	Teens	Young Adults	Over 30	Senior Citizens
★★★	★★★	★★★½	★★★½	★★★½	★★★½

Duration of Presentation: Approximately 26½ minutes
Preshow Entertainment: 8 minutes
Probable Waiting Time: 20–40 minutes

DESCRIPTION AND COMMENTS The AudioAnimatronic dinosaurs and the unique traveling theater make this Exxon pavilion one of the most popular in Future World. Since this is a theater with a ride component, the line does not move at all while the show is in progress. When the theater empties, however, a large chunk of the line will disappear as people are admitted for the next show. At this "not to be missed" attraction, visitors are seated in what appears to be a fairly ordinary theater while they watch an animated film on fossil fuels. Then, the theater seats divide into six 97-passenger traveling cars, which glide among the swamps and reptiles of a prehistoric forest. The special effects include the feel of warm, clammy air from the swamp, the smell of sulphur from an erupting volcano, and the sight of red lava hissing and bubbling toward the passengers. The remainder of the performance utilizes some nifty cinematic techniques to bring you back to the leading edge of energy research and development.

The Universe of Energy is a real toss-up for kids. Preschoolers are sometimes frightened by the dinosaurs, and almost all kids (as well as many adults) are bored by the educational segments. Guest ratings for this attraction (per our surveys) have been dropping slowly, but steadily, over the past two years. The comments of a man from Greely, Colorado, are typical:

> The Universe of Energy was the most boring ride in all of WDW. The preshow is interesting and the dinosaurs were great, but to have to go through the extremely long presentation on energy just to see the dinosaurs is far from worth it. I actually fell asleep (and I love WDW).

TOURING TIPS This attraction draws large crowds beginning early in the morning. Either catch the show before 10:30 A.M. or wait until after 4:30 P.M. Waits for the Universe of Energy are normally within tolerable limits, however, since the Universe of Energy can operate more than one presentation at a time. If you decide to write off the Universe of Energy show, make an effort to cruise past the Energy pavilion and see the great dinosaur topiaries.

—— *The "Mom, I Can't Believe It's Disney!" Fountain*

Type of Attraction: Combination fountain and shower
When to Go: When it's hot
Special Comments: Secretly installed by Martians during IllumiNations
Author's Rating: Yes!! ★★★★
Overall Appeal by Age Group:

Pre-school	Grade School	Teens	Young Adults	Over 30	Senior Citizens
★★★★★	★★★★★	★★★★	★★★★	★★★★	★★★★★

Duration of Experience: Indefinite
Probable Waiting Time: None

DESCRIPTION AND COMMENTS   On the walkway linking Future World to the World Showcase is a fountain. Quite simple and not much to look at, the fountain consists of spouts of water that erupt randomly out of the sidewalk. What makes this fountain so extraordinary is that it affords the opportunity for what may be the only truly spontaneous (legal) experience at Walt Disney World.

In an environment where everything is controlled, from the snow peas in your stir-fry to how frequently the crocodile yawns in the Jungle Cruise, this modest fountain is an anomaly of the first order. Why? Because you can swim in it, or more accurately, let it cascade down on you or blow up your britches. If, on a broiling Florida day you think you might suddenly combust, you can fling yourself into the fountain. Once there, you can do such decidedly un-Disney things as dance, skip, sing, jump, splash, cavort, roll around, stick your toes down the spouts, or catch the water in your mouth as it decends. You can do all of this with your clothes on, or, depending on your age, with your clothes off. It's hard to imagine so much personal freedom at Walt Disney World, almost unthinkable to contemplate soggy people slogging and squishing around the park, but there you have it. Hurrah!

TOURING TIPS   We don't know how long the fountain will last before its creator is hauled before the Disney Tribunal of People-Who-Sit-on-Sticks, but we hope it's around for a long time. What we do know is that your kids will be right in the middle of this thing before the alert buzzer sounds in your brain. Our advice is to pack a pair of dry shorts and let them have at it. You might even want to bring a pair dry shorts for yourself. Or maybe not . . . so much advanced planning would stifle the spontaneity.

World Showcase

The second theme area of EPCOT Center is World Showcase. Situated around picturesque World Showcase Lagoon, it is an ongoing world's fair, with the cuisine, culture, history, and architecture of almost a dozen countries permanently on display in individual national pavilions. The so-called pavilions, which generally consist of familiar landmarks and typically representative street scenes from the host countries, are spaced along a 1.2-mile promenade that circles the impressive forty-acre lagoon.

While most adults enjoy the World Showcase, many children find it boring. To make the World Showcase more interesting to children, the Camera Center in Future World sells Passport Kits for about $9. Each kit contains a blank passport and stamps for all of the World Showcase countries. As the kids accompany their folks to each country, they tear out the appropriate stamp and stick it in the passport. The kit also contains some basic information on the respective countries, as well as a Mickey Mouse button. As I'm in the publishing business myself, I can tell you that Disney has built a lot of profit margin into this little product, but I guess that's not the salient issue. More importantly, parents tell us the passport kit helps get the kids through the World Showcase with a minimum of impatience, whining, and fits.

For the footsore and weary, there are double-decker omnibuses to carry visitors around the promenade and boats to ferry guests across the lagoon (the lines at the bus stops tend to be pushy, however, and it's almost always quicker to walk than use the buses or the boats). Moving clockwise around the promenade, the nations represented are:

—— *Mexico Pavilion*

DESCRIPTION AND COMMENTS   Two pre-Columbian pyramids dominate the architecture of this exhibit. The first makes up the facade of the pavilion and the second overlooks the restaurant and plaza alongside the boat ride, El Rio del Tiempo, inside the pavilion.

TOURING TIPS   A romantic and exciting testimony to the charms of Mexico, this pavilion probably contains more authentic and valuable artifacts and objets d'art than any other national pavilion. Many people zip right past these treasures, unfortunately, without even stopping to look. The village scene inside the pavilion is both beautiful and exquisitely detailed. We recommend seeing this pavilion before 11 A.M. or after 6 P.M.

El Rio del Tiempo

Type of Ride: Boat ride
When to Go: Before 11 A.M. or after 3 P.M.
Author's Rating: Light and relaxing; ★★½
Overall Appeal by Age Group:

Pre-school	Grade School	Teens	Young Adults	Over 30	Senior Citizens
★★★	★★★	★★★	★★★	★★★	★★★

Duration of Ride: Approximately 7 minutes (plus 1½-minute wait to disembark)
Average Wait in Line per 100 People Ahead of You: 4½ minutes
Assumes: 16 boats in operation
Loading Speed: Moderate

DESCRIPTION AND COMMENTS   El Rio del Tiempo, the River of Time, is a boat trip that winds among AudioAnimatronic and cinematic scenes depicting the history of Mexico from the ancient cultures of the Maya, Toltec, and Aztec civilizations to modern times. Special effects include fiber-optic projections that provide a simulated fireworks display near the end of the ride.

While the volcano at the entrance suggests great things to come, the ride is disappointing to many guests. Pleasant and relaxing, but not particularly interesting or compelling, El Rio del Tiempo is definitely not worth a long wait.

TOURING TIPS   El Rio del Tiempo tends to get crowded during the early afternoon. Try it in the morning or early evening.

—— Norway Pavilion

DESCRIPTION AND COMMENTS   A very different addition to the World Showcase international pavilions, the Norwegian pavilion is complex, beautiful, and architecturally diverse. There is a courtyard surrounded by an assortment of traditional Scandinavian buildings, including a replica of the 14th-century Akershus Castle, a wooden stave church, red-tiled cottages, and replicas of historic buildings representing the traditional designs of Bergen, Ålesund, and Oslo. Attractions in Norway include an adventure boat ride in the mold of Pirates of the Caribbean, a movie about Norway, and, in the stave church, a gallery of art and artifacts. Located between China and Mexico, the Norway pavilion houses the Restaurant Akershus, a sit-down eatery (requiring reservations) that features koldtboard (cold buffet) plus a variety of hot Norwegian fare. For those on the run there is an open-air cafe and a bakery. For shoppers there is an abundance of native handicrafts.

Maelstrom

Type of Ride: Disney adventure boat ride

When to Go: Before noon or after 4:30 P.M.

Author's Rating: One of EPCOT Center's most exciting rides, also one of its shortest; ★★★½

Overall Appeal by Age Group:

Pre-school	Grade School	Teens	Young Adults	Over 30	Senior Citizens
★★★★	★★★★	★★★★	★★★★	★★★★	★★★★

Duration of Ride: 4½ minutes, followed by a five-minute film with a short wait in between; about 14 minutes for the whole show

Average Wait in Line per 100 People Ahead of You: 4 minutes

Assumes: 12 or 13 boats operating

Loading Speed: Fast

DESCRIPTION AND COMMENTS Guests board dragon-headed ships for an adventure voyage through the fabled rivers and seas of Viking history and legend. In one of Disney's shorter water rides, guests brave trolls, rocky gorges, waterfalls, and a storm at sea. A new-generation Disney water ride, the Viking voyage assembles an impressive array of special effects, combining visual, tactile, and auditory stimuli in a fast-paced and often humorous odyssey. After the ride guests are shown a short (five-minute) film on Norway. While we do not have any major problems with Maelstrom, a vocal minority of our readers consider the ride altogether too brief and resent having to sit through what they characterize as a travelogue after they disembark.

TOURING TIPS   Ride Maelstrom before noon or in the late afternoon. Sometimes several hundred guests from a recently concluded performance of the *Wonders of China* arrive at Maelstrom en masse. Should you encounter this horde, bypass Maelstrom for the time being.

— *People's Republic of China Pavilion*

DESCRIPTION AND COMMENTS   A half-sized replica of the Temple of Heaven in Beijing (Peking) identifies this pavilion. Gardens and reflecting ponds simulate those found in Suzhou, and an art gallery features a "Lotus Blossom" gate and formal saddle roof line.

Pass through the Hall of Prayer for Good Harvest to see the Circle-Vision 360 motion picture, *Wonders of China*. Warm and appealing, the film serves as a brilliant introduction to the people and natural beauty of this little-known nation. Two restaurants have been added to the China pavilion since its opening, a fast-food eatery and a lovely, reservations-only, full-service establishment.

TOURING TIPS   A truly beautiful pavilion, serene yet exciting. The movie, *Wonders of China*, plays in a theater where guests must stand, but can usually be enjoyed at any time during the day without much waiting. If you are touring the World Showcase in a counterclockwise rotation and plan to go next to Norway and ride Maelstrom, take up a viewing position on the far left of the theater (as you face the attendant's podium). After the show, make sure you are one of the first to exit the theater. Hustle over to Maelstrom as fast as you can to arrive ahead of the several hundred other *Wonders of China* patrons who will be right behind you.

Wonders of China

Type of Show: Film essay on the Chinese people and country
When to Go: Anytime
Special Comments: Audience stands throughout performance
Author's Rating: Well produced, though film glosses over recent events in Tibet; ★★★½
Overall Appeal by Age Group:

Pre-school	Grade School	Teens	Young Adults	Over 30	Senior Citizens
★★★	★★★½	★★★½	★★★★½	★★★★½	★★★★

Duration of Presentation: Approximately 19 minutes

Preshow Entertainment: None
Probable Waiting Time: 10 minutes

Germany Pavilion

DESCRIPTION AND COMMENTS   A clock tower, adorned with boy and girl figures, rises above the platz, or plaza, that marks the German pavilion. Dominated by a fountain depicting St. George's victory over the dragon, the platz is encircled by buildings reflecting traditional German architecture. The focal attraction is the Biergarten, a full-service (reservations only) restaurant featuring German food and beer. Yodeling, German folk dancing, and oompah band music accompany the fare during the evening meal.

TOURING TIPS   The pavilion is pleasant and festive. Germany is recommended for touring at any time of the day.

Italy Pavilion

DESCRIPTION AND COMMENTS   The entrance to the Italian pavilion is marked by a 105-foot campanile, or bell tower, said to be a mirror image of the tower in St. Mark's Square in Venice. To the left of the campanile is a replica of the 14th-century Doge's Palace, also a Venetian landmark. Other buildings are composites of architecture found throughout Italy. For example, L'Originale Alfredo di Roma Ristorante is Florentine. Visitors can watch pasta being made in this popular restaurant, which specializes in Fettuccine all'Alfredo. The Italian pavilion even has a waterfront with gondolas tied to striped moorings at the edge of the World Showcase Lagoon.

TOURING TIPS   The streets and courtyards in the Italian pavilion are among the most realistic in the World Showcase — you really feel as if you have been transplanted to Italy. Since there is no attraction (film, ride, etc.) at the Italian pavilion, touring is recommended at all hours.

The American Adventure

Type of Show: Patriotic mixed-media and AudioAnimatronic presentation on U.S. history
When to Go: Anytime

Author's Rating: Possibly the best attraction at EPCOT Center (for Americans); not to be missed; ★★★★★

Overall Appeal by Age Group:

Pre-school	Grade School	Teens	Young Adults	Over 30	Senior Citizens
★★★	★★★★	★★★★	★★★★½	★★★★★	★★★★★

Duration of Presentation: Approximately 29 minutes

Preshow Entertainment: Voices of Liberty choral singing

Probable Waiting Time: 16 minutes

DESCRIPTION AND COMMENTS   The United States pavilion, generally referred to as the American Adventure for the historical production performed there, consists (typically) of a fast-food restaurant and a patriotic, AudioAnimatronic show.

The American Adventure is a composite of everything the Disney people do best. Located in an imposing brick structure reminiscent of colonial Philadelphia, the production is a stirring, 29-minute rendition of American history narrated by Mark Twain (who carries a smoking cigar) and Ben Franklin (who climbs a set of stairs to visit Thomas Jefferson). Behind a stage that's almost half the size of a football field is a 28 × 155–foot rear projection screen (the largest ever used) on which appropriate motion picture images are interwoven with the action occurring on stage. Updated and re-engineered in 1992, the American Adventure is "not to be missed."

TOURING TIPS   Though large and patriotic, *The American Adventure* is not as interesting externally as most of the other pavilions. But *The American Adventure* is, in the opinion of our research team, the very best attraction at EPCOT Center. It usually plays to capacity audiences from around noon to 3:30 P.M., but it is not hard to get into. Because of the theater's large capacity, waiting during the busy times of the day hardly ever approaches an hour, and will probably average 25 to 40 minutes. Finally, because of its patriotic theme, *The American Adventure* is decidedly less compelling to non-Americans.

The Liberty Inn restaurant is a good place to obtain a quick nonethnic, fast-food meal.

"I'm sorry, Mister. He thinks you're a Disney character."

—— *Japan Pavilion*

DESCRIPTION AND COMMENTS   The five-story, blue-roofed pagoda, inspired by a shrine built in Nara in the seventh century, sets this pavilion apart from its neighbors. A hill garden rises behind it with arrangements of waterfalls, rocks, flowers, lanterns, paths, and rustic bridges. The building on the right (as one faces the entrance) was inspired by the ceremonial and coronation hall on the Imperial Palace grounds at Kyoto. It contains restaurants and a large retail store.

TOURING TIPS   A tasteful and elaborate pavilion that creatively blends simplicity, architectural grandeur, and natural beauty, Japan can be toured at any time of day.

—— *Morocco Pavilion*

DESCRIPTION AND COMMENTS   The bustle of the market; narrow, winding streets; lofty minarets; and stuccoed archways re-create the romance and intrigue of Tangiers and Casablanca. Attention to detail makes Morocco one of the most exciting of the World Showcase pavilions. In addition to the bazaar, Morocco also features a museum of Moorish art and the Restaurant Marrakesh, which serves some unusual and difficult-to-find North African ethnic specialities.

TOURING TIPS   Since there is no ride or theater attraction in Morocco, it can be toured any time at your convenience.

—— *France Pavilion*

DESCRIPTION AND COMMENTS   Naturally there is a replica of the Eiffel Tower (and a big one at that), but the rest of the pavilion is meant to reflect the ambience of France in the period from 1870 to 1910, a period known as La Belle Epoque (the beautiful time). The sidewalk cafe and the restaurant are both very popular here, but so is the pastry shop. You won't be the first visitor to get the idea of buying a croissant to tide you over until your next real meal.

Impressions de France is the name of an 18-minute movie that is projected over 200° onto five screens. They let you sit down in France (compared to the standing-only theaters in China and Canada) to view this well-made film introduction to the people, cities, and natural wonders of France.

TOURING TIPS   This pavilion is rich in atmosphere because of its detailed street scenes and evocation of a bygone era.

The streets of the French pavilion are diminutive and become quite congested when visitors line up for the film. Waits in line can be substantial here, so we recommend viewing before 11 A.M. and after 6 P.M.

Impressions de France

Type of Show: Film essay on the French people and country

When to Go: Before noon and after 4 P.M.

Author's Rating: An exceedingly beautiful film; not to be missed;
★★★★

Overall Appeal by Age Group:

Pre-school	Grade School	Teens	Young Adults	Over 30	Senior Citizens
★★½	★★★½	★★★½	★★★★½	★★★★½	★★★★½

Duration of Presentation: Approximately 18 minutes
Preshow Entertainment: None
Probable Waiting Time: 12 minutes (at suggested times)

—— *United Kingdom Pavilion*

DESCRIPTION AND COMMENTS   This pavilion, which is mostly shops, uses a variety of period architectural styles in an attempt to capture Britain's city, town, and rural atmospheres. One street has a thatched-roof cottage, a four-story timber and plaster building, a pre-Georgian plaster building, a formal Palladian exterior of dressed stone, and a city square with a Hyde Park bandstand (whew!). The Rose & Crown Pub and Dining Room is the only World Showcase full-service restaurant with dining on the water side of the promenade.

TOURING TIPS   There are no attractions here to create congestion, so tour at any time you wish. Reservations are not needed to enjoy the Pub section of the Rose & Crown pub, making it a nice place to stop for a beer along about midafternoon.

—— *Canada Pavilion*

DESCRIPTION AND COMMENTS   The cultural, natural, and architectural diversity of the United States' neighbor to the north is reflected in this large and impressive pavilion. Thirty-foot totem poles embellish an Indian village at the foot of a magnificent château-style hotel. Near the hotel is a rugged stone building said to be modeled after a famous landmark near Niagara Falls, reflective of Canada's British influence. Canada also has a fine film extolling its many virtues. *O Canada!* is very enlightening, and demonstrates the immense pride Canadians have in their beautiful country. Visitors leave the theater through Victoria Gardens, inspired by the famed Butchart Gardens of British Columbia.

TOURING TIPS   *O Canada!*, a large-capacity theater attraction (guests must stand), sees fairly heavy late-morning attendance since Canada is the first pavilion encountered as one travels counterclockwise around World Showcase Lagoon. We recommend late afternoon or early evening as the best time for viewing the film. Le Cellier, a cafeteria-style restaurant on the lower level of the Canadian pavilion, is the only non-fast-food restaurant in the World Showcase that does not require reservations.

O Canada!

Type of Show: Film essay on the Canadian people and country
When to Go: Anytime
Special Comments: Audience stands during performance
Author's Rating: Makes you want to catch the first plane
to Canada! ★★★½
Overall Appeal by Age Group:

Pre-school	Grade School	Teens	Young Adults	Over 30	Senior Citizens
★★½	★★★	★★★½	★★★★	★★★★½	★★★★½

Duration of Presentation: Approximately 18 minutes
Preshow Entertainment: None
Probable Waiting Time: 10 minutes

Not to Be Missed at EPCOT Center

World Showcase	*The American Adventure* IllumiNations
Future World	Spaceship Earth Living with the Land *Honey, I Shrunk the Audience* It's Fun to Be Free Body Wars *Cranium Command* Horizons

Live Entertainment in EPCOT Center

Live entertainment in EPCOT Center is somewhat more diversified, as might be expected, than that of the Magic Kingdom. World Showcase provides almost unlimited potential for representative entertainment from the respective nations, and Future World allows for a new wave of creativity in live entertainment offerings. Information concerning the live entertainment on the day of your visit can be obtained from the information desk at Guest Relations.

Listed below are some of the performers and performances you are likely to encounter.

Future World Brass

A roving brass band that marches and plays according to a more or less extemporaneous schedule near Spaceship Earth and at other Future World locations.

Disney Characters

The Disney characters, once believed to be inconsistent with the image of EPCOT Center, have now been imported in number. The Disney characters appear for breakfast at the Coral Reef Restaurant at The Living Seas pavilion. This breakfast is held daily from 8:30 to 10:30 A.M. The menu is fixed, but seconds are available. The cost is $15 for adults (10 and up) and $8 for children ages 3 to 9. Characters featured include Mickey (swimming in the fish tank), Minnie, Goofy, and Pluto. Please note that the price of the character meal is in addition to your cost of admission to the theme park.

Characters additionally appear at the Odyssey Restaurant several times each day according to the daily live entertainment schedule available at Guest Relations. The Disney characters are also featured in live shows on the American Gardens Stage and at the Showcase Plaza between Mexico and Canada.

American Gardens Stage

The site of EPCOT Center's premier live performances is near *The American Adventure*, facing World Showcase Lagoon, in a large amphitheater. Top talent imported from all over the world plays the American Gardens Stage on a limited engagement basis. Many shows highlight the music, dance, and costumes of the performer's home country. In 1994, Disney introduced a stage show based on the popular doll, Barbie. In this improbable production, Barbie and her boyfriend, Ken, tour the world with their friends. The show is very popular with children, but another audience might be adult males who are super keen to take a peek at a real-life Barbie. Other shows include the Disney characters.

IllumiNations

An after-dark show, consisting of music, fireworks, erupting fountains, special lighting, and laser technology, performed on the World Showcase Lagoon when the park is open late. Not to be missed.

Around World Showcase

A variety of unscheduled, impromptu performances take place in and around the various pavilions of World Showcase. You may encounter a strolling mariachi group in Mexico, street actors in Italy, a fife-and-drum corps or a singing group (The Voices of Liberty) at *The American Adventure*, traditional songs and dances in Japan, comical street drama in the United Kingdom, white-faced mimes in France, and bagpipes in Canada. There are street entertainment performances at most of the World Showcase pavilions about every half hour (though not scheduled *on* the hour or half hour).

Dinner & Lunch Shows

The restaurants in World Showcase serve up healthy portions of live entertainment to accompany the victuals. Examples of restaurant floorshow fare include folk dancing and a baskapelle band in Germany (dinner only), singing waiters in Italy and Germany, and belly dancers in Morocco. Restaurant shows are performed only at dinner in Italy, but at both lunch and dinner in Morocco. Reservations are required (see "Eating in EPCOT Center," pages 488–94).

World Showcase Lagoon

The World Showcase Lagoon provides the stage for a number of shows during the course of the day featuring boats, kites, hang gliders, music, and a variety of other strange combinations. Check the daily entertainment schedule for times and details.

—— IllumiNations

IllumiNations is EPCOT Center's great outdoor spectacle, integrating fireworks, laser lights, neon, and music in a stirring tribute to the nations represented at the World Showcase. The climax of every EPCOT Center day, we rate IllumiNations as "not to be missed."

Getting Out of EPCOT after IllumiNations (Read This before Selecting a Viewing Spot)

A major consideration in picking your vantage point is how anxious you are to leave the park at the conclusion of the show. IllumiNations essentially ends the day at EPCOT Center. After IllumiNations, you will find nothing open except a couple of gift shops in Future World. Because there is nothing to do, everyone left in the park leaves at the same time. Needless to say, this creates a great snarl at Package Pick-up, the EPCOT monorail station, and the Disney bus stop. It also pushes the tram system to the limit, hauling guests to their cars in the EPCOT Center parking lot. Stroller return, however, is extraordinarily efficient and does not occasion any delay.

If you are staying at one of the EPCOT Resorts (Swan and Dolphin hotels, Yacht and Beach Clubs), we recommend watching IllumiNations from somewhere in the southern (American Adventure) half of the World Showcase Lagoon, and then exiting through the International Gateway (between France and the United Kingdom). You can walk or take a tram back to your hotel from the International Gateway. If you have a car and are visiting EPCOT Center in the evening for dinner and IllumiNations, park at the Yacht or Beach Club. After the show, you can duck out the International Gateway and be on the road to your hotel in 15 minutes. If you are staying at any other Walt Disney World hotel, and do not have a car, the fastest way home is to join the mass exodus through the main gate following IllumiNations and then catch a bus or the monorail.

For those who have a car in the EPCOT lot, the situation is more problematic. If you want to beat the crowd, your only option is to find a viewing spot at the end of the World Showcase Lagoon nearest Future World (and the exits). Take off as soon as IllumiNations concludes, and try to get out ahead of the crowd. Be forewarned, however, that thousands of people will be doing exactly the same thing. To get a good vantage point anywhere between Mexico and Canada on the southern end of the lagoon, you will have to stake out your spot a good 45 to 55 minutes before the show. Quite conceivably, you may squander more time holding down your spot before IllumiNations than you would if you watched from the less congested southern end of the lagoon, and then took your chances with the crowd on departure.

More groups get separated, and more children lost, following IllumiNations than at any other time. In the summer, you literally will be walking among a throng of up to 30,000 people. If you are heading for the parking lot, you need to anticipate this congestion and preselect a meeting spot in the EPCOT Center entrance area. You can hook back up there in the event that someone gets separated from the group. The place we recommend is the fountain just inside the main entrance. Everyone in your party should be told not to exit through the turnstiles until it has been verified that your group is together. It can be a real nightmare if the group gets split up and you don't know whether the others are inside or outside the park.

For those with a car, the main problem is just getting to it. Once there, traffic flows out of the parking lot pretty well. If you paid close attention to where you parked, you might consider blowing off the tram and walking. Be aware, however, that the parking lot is a pretty wild place this time of night. If you have children and decide to walk, hang on to them for all you're worth.

Good Locations for Viewing IllumiNations and Other World Showcase Lagoon Performances

The best place to be for any World Showcase Lagoon presentation is seated comfortably on the lakeside veranda of the Cantina de San Angel in Mexico. Come early (*at least* 70 minutes for IllumiNations) and relax with a cold drink or a snack while you wait for the show. There is also outdoor lagoonside seating at the Rose & Crown Pub in the United Kingdom. Because of a small wall, the view is not quite as good as from the Cantina. On the bright side, however, you can often get a table on the Rose & Crown beer terrace within 30 to 40 minutes of show time.

If you would like to combine dinner on the Rose & Crown's veranda with IllumiNations, make a dinner reservation for about an hour and 15 minutes before show time. Later in the day, as you are touring the World

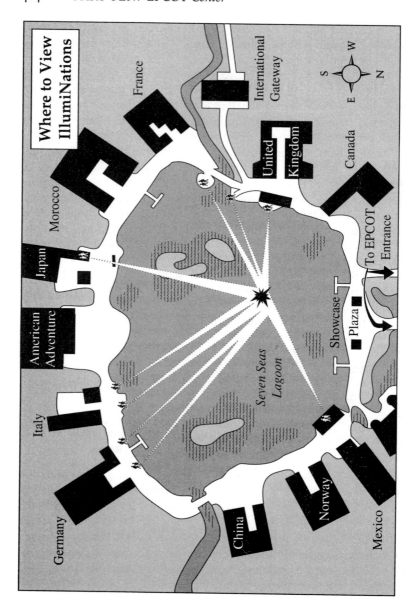

Where to View
IllumiNations

France

International
Gateway

S
E · W
N

United
Kingdom

Canada

Morocco

Japan

To EPCOT
Entrance

American
Adventure

Showcase

Plaza

Italy

Seven Seas
Lagoon

Germany

China

Norway

Mexico

Showcase, stop by the restaurant and inform the Rose & Crown host that you want a table outside where you can view IllumiNations during or after dinner. Our experience is that the Rose & Crown folks will bend over backwards to accommodate you.

Because most guests are hot to run for the exits following a presentation, and because islands in the southern (American Adventure) half of the lagoon block the view from some places, the most popular spectator positions are along the northern waterfront from Norway and Mexico on around to Canada and the United Kingdom. Although the northern end of the lagoon unquestionably offers excellent viewing positions, it is usually necessary to claim a spot 35 to 60 minutes before IllumiNations begins. For those who are late finishing dinner, or anyone else who does not want to invest 45 minutes standing by a rail, here are some good viewing spots along the southern perimeter (moving counterclockwise from the United Kingdom to Germany) that often go unnoticed until 10 to 20 minutes before show time:

1. *The Once-Secret Park.* There is a wonderful waterside park, accessible from the United Kingdom, which is unknown to all but a few. To reach the park, walk toward France from the Rose & Crown Pub in the United Kingdom. As you pass near the end of the pub, stay on the sidewalk and bear left. You will shortly find yourself in an almost private park, complete with benches and a perfect view of IllumiNations. En route to the park, you will see a roped-off back entrance to the terrace of the pub. This is another good viewing spot (don't be shy about ducking under the rope). Following an earlier edition, as sometimes happens, the "secret park" became somewhat less secret. A reader from Demotte, Indiana, wrote describing this improbable scene:

> We watched the Illuminations show from the "Secret Park" behind the British pub. It was a very good location and allowed us an easy exit after the show. On a humorous note, about ten minutes before the show was to begin, a lady came hiking down the path to the park with a copy of your guide in her hand. She became quite agitated when she saw that the area was full and exclaimed quite loudly, "I thought this place was a secret!" About half the people in place for the show held up copies of your book.

A Texas man was somewhat more pointed in his comment:

> Which brings us, finally, to the justly renowned IllumiNations at EPCOT. Since we did not stake out our turf until thirty minutes

before the show, we got the vantage point we deserved. Still, by now you should probably concede to your readers that the cover has been thoroughly blown from the so-called "Secret Park" — due, we suspect, to the wide circulation of your guide.

In addition to the park not being very secret, you should also know that the Disney people frequently close it for private parties.

2. *International Gateway Island.* The pedestrian bridge across the canal near the International Gateway spans an island that offers great viewing spots. This island is much more obvious to passersby than the secret park and normally fills up 20 minutes before show time.

3. *Second-floor (Restaurant Level) Deck of the Mitsukoshi Building in Japan.* Though an oriental arch slightly blocks your line of sight, this second-floor covered deck offers a great vantage point. If the weather is iffy, it is the most protected viewing area in the World Showcase, except for the Cantina de San Angel in Mexico.

4. *Gondola Landing at Italy.* An elaborate waterfront promenade offers excellent viewing positions for IllumiNations. Claim your spot at least 20 minutes before show time.

5. *The Boat Dock opposite Germany.* Another good vantage point, the dock generally fills up 20 minutes before IllumiNations begins.

6. *Waterfront Promenade by Germany.* A good view is possible from the lagoonside walkway, about 90-feet long, from Germany toward China.

7. *The Magic Johnson Hedge.* Near the boat dock in Germany and next to the WorldKey Information kiosk is a tall, thick hedge. Viewing positions behind the hedge offer a great perspective for people over six feet tall or children on their parents' shoulders.

Do these suggestions work every time? No. A dad from San Ramon, California, had this to say:

> Your recommendations for IllumiNations didn't work out in the time frame you mentioned. People had the area staked out *two hours* ahead of time.

It should be noted that none of the above viewing locations are reserved for *Unofficial Guide* readers and, on busier nights, good spots are claimed early. Personally, we think it's a drag to hold down a slab of concrete for two hours in advance of IllumiNations. Most nights you can find an acceptable vantage point 15 to 30 minutes prior to the show. Because most of the action is significantly above ground level, you do not need to be right on the rail or have an unobstructed view of the water. It is important, however, not to position yourself under a tree, awning, or anything else that blocks your overhead perspective. If IllumiNations is a top priority for you, and you want to be absolutely certain of nailing down a good viewing position, claim your place an hour or more before show time. A New Yorker who staked out his turf well in advance made this suggestion for staying comfortable until showtime:

> Your excellent guidebook also served as seat cushion while waiting seated on the ground. Make future editions thicker for greater comfort.

The Smith family from East Wimple stakes out their viewing spot for IllumiNations.

Eating in EPCOT Center

There are 13 full-service restaurants at EPCOT Center, 2 in Future World, and 11 in the World Showcase. With a couple of exceptions, these restaurants rank among the best at Walt Disney World, in or out of the theme parks.

Future World Full-Service Restaurants

Coral Reef	The Living Seas
The Garden Grill Restaurant	The Land

World Showcase Full-Service Restaurants

Biergarten	Germany
Bistro de Paris	France
Chefs de France	France
L'Originale Alfredo di Roma Ristorante	Italy
Restaurant Akershus	Norway
Restaurant Marrakesh	Morocco
Tempura Kiku	Japan
Teppanyaki Dining Room	Japan
Nine Dragons Restaurant	China
Rose & Crown Dining Room	United Kingdom
San Angel Inn Restaurante	Mexico

For ratings and detailed profiles of EPCOT Center full-service restaurants, refer to Dining In and Around Walt Disney World, pages 265–322. Restaurants are listed by name in alphabetical order.

Fourteen Years and Counting

We've been reviewing EPCOT Center's food service since the park opened in 1982 and have seen a lot of changes, most of them for the better. There is more variety now than ever before, and more choices for folks who do not want to take the time for a full-service, sit-down meal. The fast food is quite good, better than in the Magic Kingdom or the

Disney-MGM Studios, and more of the full-service ethnic restaurants are now offering sampler platters to showcase the variety of their cuisine.

Where certain World Showcase restaurants were once timid about delivering an honest representation of the host nation's cuisine, we are now seeing bold ethnic menus—*mole* in Mexico, sushi in Japan, and couscous and bastila in Morocco. Some restaurants, however, still sacrifice ethnic authenticity to please the tastes of picky Americans, who, more than anyone, need their palates challenged (or do not need to be eating in ethnic restaurants).

In our opinion there is no logical correlation between price, quality, and popularity of the World Showcase restaurants. Our researchers, for example, found L'Originale Alfredo di Roma Ristorante (Italy) sometimes disappointing despite the fact it is almost always one of the first two restaurants to fill its seatings.

Many EPCOT Center restaurants are overpriced, most conspicuously Nine Dragons (China) and the Coral Reef (The Living Seas pavilion). Chefs de France and Bistro de Paris (France), Restaurant Akershus (Norway), Biergarten (Germany), and Restaurant Marrakesh (Morocco) represent a relatively good value through a combination of well-prepared food, ambience, and in the case of Germany, entertainment. If expense is an issue, have your main meal at lunch. The entrees are much the same as on the dinner menu, but the prices are significantly lower.

Making reservations for full-service restaurants still involves standing in line in the morning when you would rather be doing something else, and in most cases, abandoning your touring itinerary to hustle (usually from the opposite side of the park) to the restaurant to be seated. The restaurants are such an integral part of EPCOT Center, however, that we think it would be a mistake not to have a meal in at least one of them.

Getting a Reservation at an EPCOT Center Full-Service Restaurant

Getting a reservation for a particular restaurant depends on its popularity and seating capacity and, of course, the size of the crowd on the day of your visit. Each restaurant has seatings for both lunch and dinner.

Guests staying at Walt Disney World lodgings may make reservations one to three days in advance by dialing 55 or 56. If you wish to make dining reservations prior to arriving at Walt Disney World (up to 60 days in advance), call (407) 939-3463. Reservations can likewise be made for restaurants at the Disney-MGM Studios and at the Magic Kingdom.

According to official policy, those guests who are lodging outside of the World must make their reservations at EPCOT Center on the day of the meal. In 1995, however, without any announcement, Disney reservationists began accepting reservations from guests who were not staying at Disney hotels. While this courtesy may be changed or terminated at any time, we recommend that you call (407) 939-3463 and try to make dining reservations in advance.

For those who are making same-day reservations on site (during the busier times of the year), arrive at the entrance turnstiles, passport in hand, 45 minutes before EPCOT Center opens. On admission go quickly to the Guest Relations reservations service (to the left of the dome). Both lunch and dinner reservations can be made at the same time. Be prepared with alternatives for both restaurants and seatings in case your first choices are filled.

If you don't follow this plan, you might have a long wait in line to make reservations, with no guarantee that anything will be available. On many days the World Showcase restaurants and the Coral Reef (in Future World) book solid for preferred seating times within an hour to an hour and a half of the park opening. Even if you get a reservation, you will have spent your most productive, crowd-free touring time in the process.

If you visit EPCOT Center during a quieter time of year, you do not need to be so compulsive about making dining reservations first thing in the morning. During slower periods, most restaurants have plenty of seats available. One notable exception is the San Angel Inn in Mexico, which fills quickly because of its relatively small size.

If you follow one of our touring plans, you will be near the United States (American Adventure) pavilion at noon. We suggest, therefore, a lunch reservation for 12:30 P.M. or 1 P.M. at nearby Germany, or for a lighter meal, Tempura Kiku in Japan. For dinner, we recommend reservations at the San Angel Inn in Mexico or Akershus in Norway. If you plan to eat your evening meal at the Coral Reef (in Future World), you may want to wait until after dinner to see the attraction itself.

If you blow it and arrive late but still want to eat in one of the World Showcase restaurants, here are some strategies that often pay off:

1. Go to the restaurant of your choice and apply at the door for a reservation. Sometimes only lunch reservations are taken at the door, but lunch and dinner menus are comparable if not the same. Just have your main meal at lunch.

2. If the first option does not work, go to the restaurant of your choice and ask the hostess to call you if she gets a cancellation. A reservation is held about 15 to 20 minutes before the vacancy is filled with "standby" diners. Very early and very late seatings have more "no shows."

3. If you want to try an EPCOT Center full-service restaurant, but do not have reservations, try walking in at about 11 A.M. or from 3 to 4 P.M.

4. If the options mentioned above do not pan out, you can often get a table just by showing up at Restaurant Marrakesh (reservations often go unfilled because of American unfamiliarity with the cuisine).

Avoiding the Bum's Rush

One of the most persistent problems for many exhausted EPCOT Center diners is Disney's stopwatch efficiency. Unless you know how to slow down the service, you will literally be processed through your "fine dining" experience before you have a chance to catch your breath. This can be advantageous, of course, if you have small, fussy children in your party. If, however, you have spent an entire day hoofing all over the Isle of Walt, the last thing you need is the bum's rush.

If you want to relax and linger over your expensive meal, do not, repeat, do not, order your entire dinner at once. Place drink orders while you study the menu. If you would like a second drink, ask for it before you order. Next, order appetizers but tell the waiter you need more time to choose your main course. Order your entree only after the appetizers have been served. Feel free to dawdle over coffee and dessert.

EPCOT Center Dining for Families with Small Children

EPCOT Center's restaurants offer an excellent (though not inexpensive) opportunity to introduce small children to the variety and excitement of ethnic food. No matter how fancy or formal an EPCOT restaurant looks or sounds, rest assured that the staff is well accustomed to wiggling, impatient, and often boisterous small children. Chefs de France, for example, may be the only French restaurant in the country where a majority of the clientele is clad in shorts and T-shirts, and where you can count on finding at least two dozen small diners formally attired in basic-black mouse ears. Bottom line: small children are the rule,

not the exception, at EPCOT restaurants. All EPCOT restaurants offer children's menus.

The restaurants that preschoolers enjoy most are the Biergarten in Germany, the San Angel Inn Restaurante in Mexico, and the Coral Reef in The Living Seas pavilion in Future World. The Biergarten combines a rollicking and noisy atmosphere with good basic fare like roast chicken. A German oompah band provides entertainment (dinner only). Children often have the opportunity to participate in native Bavarian dances.

The San Angel Inn Restaurante is located in the Mexican village marketplace. From the table, children can watch boats from El Rio del Tiempo drift beneath a smoking volcano. Between chips, tacos, and other familiar items, there is usually no difficulty finding something picky children will eat. The Coral Reef, with tables set alongside viewing windows of The Living Seas aquarium, offers a satisfying mealtime diversion for children and adults alike. If your kids do not eat fish, the Coral Reef also serves chicken. The Biergarten and the San Angel Inn offer reasonable value, as well as good food. The Coral Reef, though overpriced, also serves very good food.

EPCOT Center restaurants understand how itchy children get when they have to sit for an extended period. Your server will keep the small ones supplied with crackers and rolls, and will get your dinner on the table much faster than in comparable restaurants elsewhere. Letters from readers suggest that being served too quickly (i.e., not having enough time to relax) is a much more frequent occurrence than having to wait a long time. Finally, most EPCOT Center restaurants have special children's menus, and all have booster seats and highchairs.

If you are on hand when the park opens, and intend to rent a stroller, the best strategy is for one parent to run ahead to Guest Relations (just to the left of the big dome) and make dining reservations while the other obtains the stroller.

Carpe Diem

While eating at EPCOT Center can be the consummate hassle, it is likewise true that an afternoon in the World Showcase section of EPCOT Center without a dinner reservation is something like not having a date on the day of the prom. Each pavilion has a beautifully seductive ethnic eatery, offering the hungry tourist the gastronomic delights of the world. To tour these exotic foreign settings and not partake is almost beyond the limits of willpower.

In all honesty, the food in some of the World Showcase restaurants is not very compelling, but the overall experience is exhilarating. And if you fail to dine in the World Showcase, you will miss out on one of EPCOT Center's more delightful features.

Alternatives for Guests on the Go or on a Tight Budget

Listed below are some suggestions for any epicurean who wants to sample EPCOT Center's ethnic fare, but does not have either the time or the bucks for a fancy, sit-down meal:

1. For fast-food meals, EPCOT Center is like the Magic Kingdom; eat before 11 A.M. or after 2 P.M. The Odyssey Restaurant and the Liberty Inn at the American Adventure pavilion move people through pretty speedily, and sometimes you can get served in a reasonable time in The Land pavilion (the latter being a bit more iffy). The Land is a cut above the average, as are many of the counter-service restaurants in the World Showcase.

2. If you want to sample the ethnic diversity of the World Showcase without eating in the reservations-only restaurants, we recommend:

Norway	Kringla Bakeri og Kafé for pastries, open-face sandwiches, and Ringnes beer (our favorite)
Germany	Sommerfest, for bratwurst and Becks beer
Japan	Matsu No Ma Lounge, for sushi and sashimi
France	Boulangerie Pâtisserie, for French pastries
United Kingdom	Rose & Crown Pub for Guinness-Harp and Bass beers and ales

While many readers concur in our counter service recommendations, a Laurel, Maryland, man took exception:

I disagree with one recommendation your book makes. In the section for cheap eating in EPCOT, we ate at most of the locations suggested and were displeased with the Kringla Bakeri and Kafe[*sic*]. For five dollars we each received half a roast beef sandwich. Though a good sandwich, five dollars for this was quite extreme. I recommend you remove this restaurant from your listing. We were very pleased with the other suggestions on this list, especially the sausages in the German pavilion. One restaurant I believe could be added to this list is the Yakitori House in the Japanese pavilion. We received an excellent and filling meal here for about five or six dollars.

3. Review the "Alternatives and Suggestions for Eating in the Magic Kingdom," pages 389–93. Many tips for the Magic Kingdom also apply to EPCOT Center.

Shopping in EPCOT Center

The shops in Future World seem a little out of place, the atmosphere too visionary and grandiose to accommodate the pettiness of the bargain table. Similarly, it obviously has been difficult to find merchandise consistent with the surroundings. Expressed differently, what is available for purchase in Future World is generally available at a lot of other places. Exceptions include EPCOT and Disney trademark souvenirs.

The World Showcase shops add a lot of realism and atmosphere to the street scenes of which they are part. Much of the merchandise is overpriced and is readily available elsewhere. On the other hand, some of the shops in the World Showcase really are special. In the United Kingdom, visit the Queen's Table (fine china); in China, Yong Feng Shangdian (crafts, rugs, carvings, furniture); in Japan, Mitsukoshi Department Store (porcelain, bonsai trees, pearls straight from a live oyster).

If you do not want to haul your purchases around, have the salesperson forward them to Package Pick-up where they can be collected when you leave the park. Be sure to specify whether you will be departing through the main entrance or through the International Gateway. Allow three hours from time of purchase for your goods to reach the pick-up facility. If you are Walt Disney World resort guests, you can arrange to have your purchases delivered directly to your guest room.

Behind-the-Scenes Tours in EPCOT Center

Interested adults (16 and over) can book guided walking tours that explore, respectively, the architecture of the international pavilions of EPCOT Center (Hidden Treasures of World Showcase), and/or Walt Disney World's gardens (Gardens of the World), horticulture, and landscaping. Each tour lasts about four hours. Many of our readers rave about the behind-the-scenes tours. A couple from Los Angeles had this to say:

> The best kept secret is the adult tour, *Hidden Treasures of the World Showcase* in EPCOT. The description is misleading and sounds like a real bore, but we got a behind the scenes tour with lots of information on everything we ever wanted to know or were curious about. Definitely the best part of our trip. (This is a walking tour and is mostly outside in the heat.)

And from a gentleman who resides in Houston, Texas:

> Keep telling people about the *Hidden Treasures of the World Showcase* tour; we finally got to take it and it was a real highlight. The cast member who took us on the tour (there were only four of us) told us about a new tour of the Magic Kingdom, called *Keys to the Kingdom*, which we took the very next day. It was similar, with backstage touring and a look at the utilidor system, although it also included going on several rides. Tell people about this one, too.

Cost for the tours is about $20, plus an EPCOT Center admission ticket. For reservations, call (407) 560-6150.

A shorter tour is the Greenhouse Tour, which takes guests behind the scenes to tour the vegetable gardens in The Land pavilion of EPCOT Center. The tour requires same-day reservations made on the lower level of The Land (to the far right of the fast-food windows). The charge for the Harvest Tour, which lasts an hour, is $5 for adults and $3 for children ages 3–9.

Traffic Patterns in EPCOT Center

After admiring the way traffic is engineered at the Magic Kingdom for many years, we were somewhat amazed at the way EPCOT Center was laid out. At the Magic Kingdom, Main Street, U.S.A., with its many shops and eateries, serves as a huge gathering place when the park opens and subsequently funnels visitors to the central hub; from there, equally accessible entrances branch off to the various lands. Thus the crowds are first welcomed and entertained (on Main Street) and then distributed almost equally to the respective lands.

At EPCOT Center, by contrast, Spaceship Earth, the park's premier architectural landmark and one of its featured attractions, is situated just inside the main entrance. When visitors enter the park they invariably and almost irresistibly head right for it. Hence crowds tend to bottleneck as soon as the park opens less than 75 yards from the admission turnstiles. For those in the know, however, the congestion at Spaceship Earth provides some excellent opportunities for escaping waits at other rides and shows in the Future World section of EPCOT Center.

Early-morning crowds are contained in the Future World half of EPCOT Center for the simple reason that most of the rides and shows are located in Future World. Except for Spaceship Earth, Body Wars in the Wonders of Life pavilion, and *Honey, I Shrunk the Audience* in the Imagination pavilion, distribution of visitors to the various Future World attractions is fairly equal. Before the opening of the Wonders of Life pavilion, attractions on the west side of Future World (The Living Seas, The Land, Journey into Imagination) drew larger crowds. With the addition of Body Wars and the other Wonders of Life attractions, traffic is now more evenly distributed.

Between 9 A.M. and 11 A.M. crowds build in Future World. Even when the World Showcase opens (usually at 11 A.M.), there are more people entering Future World than departing it for World Showcase. Attendance continues building in Future World until sometime between noon and 2 P.M. World Showcase attendance builds rapidly with the approach of the midday meal. Exhibits at the far end of World Showcase Lagoon report playing to full-capacity audiences from about noon through 6:30 to 7:30 P.M.

The central focus of World Showcase in the eyes of most visitors is its atmosphere, featuring international landmarks, romantic street scenes, quaint shops, and ethnic restaurants. Unlike the Magic Kingdom with its premier rides and attractions situated along the far perimeters of its respective lands, World Showcase has only two major entertainment draws (Maelstrom in Norway and *The American Adventure*). So where the Magic Kingdom uses its super attractions to draw and distribute the crowds rather evenly, EPCOT Center's cluster of premier attractions in Future World serves to hold the greater part of the crowd in the smaller part of the park. There is no compelling reason to rush to the World Showcase. The bottom line in Future World is that the crowd builds all morning and into the early afternoon. The two main sections of EPCOT Center do not approach having equal attendance until close to the evening meal. It should be stated, however, that evening crowds in World Showcase do not compare with the size of morning and midday crowds in Future World. Attendance throughout EPCOT Center is normally lighter in the evening.

An interesting observation at EPCOT Center from a crowd-distribution perspective is the indifference of repeat visitors for one attraction over another. At the Magic Kingdom repeat visitors make a mad dash for their favorite ride, and preferences are strong and well defined. At EPCOT Center, by contrast, many returning tourists indicate that (with the possible exceptions of Body Wars and *Honey, I Shrunk the Audience*) they enjoy the major rides and features "about the same." The conclusion suggested here is that touring patterns at EPCOT Center will be more systematic and predictable (i.e., by the numbers, clockwise, counterclockwise, etc.) than at the Magic Kingdom.

While some guests leave EPCOT Center in the early evening, the vast majority troop out en masse following IllumiNations. Upwards of 30,000 people head for the parking lot and monorail station at the same time.

Closing time at EPCOT Center does not precipitate congestion like that observed when the Magic Kingdom closes. One primary reason for the easier departure from EPCOT Center is that its parking lot is adjacent to the park, not separated from it by a lake as at the Magic Kingdom. At the Magic Kingdom, departing visitors form bottlenecks at the monorail to the Transportation and Ticket Center and main parking lot. At EPCOT Center you can proceed directly to your car.

EPCOT Center Touring Plans

The EPCOT Center touring plans are field-tested, step-by-step itineraries for seeing all of the major attractions at EPCOT Center with a minimum of waiting in line. They are designed to keep you ahead of the crowds while the park is filling in the morning and to place you at the less crowded attractions during EPCOT Center's busier hours of the day. They assume that you would be happier doing a *little* extra walking rather than a lot of extra standing in line.

Touring EPCOT Center is much more strenuous and demanding than touring the Magic Kingdom. To begin with, EPCOT Center is about twice as large as the Magic Kingdom. Secondly, unlike the Magic Kingdom, EPCOT Center has no effective in-park transportation system; wherever you want to go, it's always quicker and easier to walk. Visitors arriving at the Magic Kingdom disperse rather evenly, while visitors arriving at EPCOT Center tend to cluster. Spaceship Earth forms immense lines ten minutes after opening, while the rest of the park is virtually empty. The touring plans will assist you in avoiding crowds and bottlenecks on days of moderate to heavy attendance, but cannot lessen the distance you will have to walk. Wear comfortable shoes and be prepared for a lot of hiking. On days of lighter attendance, when crowd conditions are not a critical factor, the touring plans will serve primarily to help you organize your tour.

Touring plans provided for EPCOT Center include the following:

- EPCOT Center One-Day Touring Plan
- Author's Selective EPCOT Center One-Day Touring Plan
- EPCOT Center Two-Day Touring Plan

Touring Plan Clip-out Pocket Outlines. For your convenience, we have prepared outline versions of all the touring plans presented in this guide. The pocket outline versions present the same touring itineraries as the detailed touring plans, but with vastly abbreviated directions. First, select the touring plan that is most appropriate for your party, then familiarize yourself with the detailed version of the touring plan. Once you understand how the touring plan works, clip out the pocket outline version of your selected touring plan from the back of this guide, and carry it with you as a quick reference when you visit the theme park.

—— EPCOT Center Touring Plans and Small Children

EPCOT Center is educationally oriented and considerably more adult in tone and presentation than the Magic Kingdom. Most younger children enjoy EPCOT Center if their visit is seven hours or less in duration, and if their tour emphasizes the Future World section of the park. Younger children, especially grade-school children, find the international atmosphere of the World Showcase exciting but do not have the patience for much more than a quick walk-through. While we found touring objectives of adults and younger children basically compatible in Future World, we noted that children tired quickly of World Showcase movies and shows, and tried to hurry their adult companions.

If possible, we recommend that adults touring with children eight years old and younger use the Two-Day Touring Plan (pages 515–19) or the Author's Selective One-Day Touring Plan (pages 511–14). The Two-Day Touring Plan is comprehensive but divides the tour into two less arduous visits. The Author's Selective One-Day Touring Plan includes only EPCOT Center's very best attractions (according to the author) and is, therefore, shorter and less physically demanding. Adults with small children following the One-Day Touring Plan should consider bypassing movies in Canada and China where the audience must stand. Also, be sure to review EPCOT Center attractions in the Small Child Fright Potential Chart on pages 160–61.

At EPCOT Center, sometimes less is more. Our bet is that you and your small children will better enjoy the day if you leave the park after lunch for a swim and a nap. We consider this rest break critical to having a happy and successful day, and recommend it even for families lodging outside of Walt Disney World. If you are following one of our touring plans, simply break it off right after lunch and go back to your hotel. Resist the temptation to rest in the park unless your children are small enough to take a good long nap in a stroller. When you return refreshed to EPCOT Center in the late afternoon, visit any attractions in Future World that you missed while following the touring plan in the morning.

—— *A Word about the International Gateway*

The International Gateway is a secondary entrance to EPCOT Center between the United Kingdom and France in the World Showcase section of the park. The purpose of the International Gateway is to provide easy access by tram or foot to guests lodging at the Walt Disney World Swan and Dolphin hotels, Disney's Boardwalk, and Disney's Yacht and Beach Club resorts. As at the main entrance, stroller and wheelchair rentals are available. If you enter through the International Gateway in the morning before World Showcase opens (around 10 or 11 A.M.), you will be transported to Future World on Disney double-decker buses.

On days of moderate to heavy attendance follow the touring plans exactly; do not deviate from them except:

1. When you do not want to experience an attraction called for on the touring plans—simply skip that step and proceed to the next.

2. When you encounter an extremely long line at an attraction called for by the touring plans—the central idea is to avoid crowds, not join them. Crowds build and dissipate throughout the day for a variety of reasons. The touring plans anticipate recurring crowd patterns but cannot predict spontaneously arising situations (Spaceship Earth breaking down, for instance, with the hundreds of people standing in line suddenly descending on the nearby Universe of Energy). If a line is ridiculously long, simply skip that step and move on to the next; you can always come back later and give it another try.

Park Opening Procedures

Your success during your first hour of touring will be affected somewhat by the particular opening procedure the Disney people use that day.

EPCOT Center almost always opens a half hour before the official opening time, using one of two basic opening procedures:

1. Some days, usually when attendance is expected to be heavy, all of EPCOT Center opens at once. If this is the case, go directly to Guest Relations (to the left of the dome) and make your restaurant reservations for lunch and/or dinner. After making reservations, set out on the touring plan of your choice.

2. On other days, only Spaceship Earth (the ride in the sphere) and Guest Relations (where you make restaurant reservations) will be open when guests are admitted to the park. If this is the case, ride Spaceship Earth after you make your dining reservations, then line up as follows:

a. If you are going to Body Wars in the Wonders of Life pavilion first, proceed to Innoventions East (to the left of Earth Station as you exit

Spaceship Earth). When the rest of the park opens, pass through Innoventions East, taking the first exit to the left, and proceed directly to the Wonders of Life pavilion.

b. If you are going to Living with the Land boat ride in The Land pavilion first, proceed to Innoventions West (to the right of Earth Station as you exit Spaceship Earth). When the rest of the park opens, pass through Innoventions West, taking the second exit to the right, and walk directly to The Land pavilion.

Early Entry at EPCOT Center

On two days each week (usually Tuesday and Friday), Disney resort and campground guests are invited to enter EPCOT Center before the park is opened to the general public. On these days, Disney resort and campground guests are admitted 90 minutes before the published opening time. If the park's stated hours are 9 A.M. to 10 P.M., for example, Disney resort and campground guests are admitted at 7:30 A.M., while the general public is admitted at 8:30 A.M. Attractions in The Living Seas, The Land, and Journey Into Imagination pavilions, as well as Spaceship Earth, are usually open for early-entry touring at 7:30 A.M. Innoventions usually opens at 8:30 A.M. when the general public is admitted.

In the summer and over holiday periods, increases in crowd levels (a result of Disney resort guests exercising their early-entry option at EPCOT Center) create considerable congestion in Future World by around 10:30 A.M. Even if you are eligible for early entry, you will be better off touring one of the other parks where early entry is not in effect. An alternate strategy, if you are eligible, is to take advantage of early entry for an hour or two first thing in the morning at EPCOT Center and then head to another park for the rest of the day. During less busy times of the year, early entry works more to the resort guest's advantage, adding an extra hour to an otherwise short touring day. Those not eligible for early entry should avoid EPCOT Center on days when early entry is scheduled, regardless of the time of year.

If you participate in early entry, tour The Living Seas, and then proceed to The Land pavilion. At The Land, take the boat ride, saving other attractions for later. After the boat ride, head for Spaceship Earth and ride. By the time you complete Spaceship Earth, it should be about time for the rest of EPCOT Center to open. At this time go ahead and launch into the touring plan of your choice, skipping steps that call for you to visit attractions you have already seen.

If you reserved a room at the Beach Club, Yacht Club, Swan, or Dolphin hotels, or Disney's Boardwalk, in order to be close to EPCOT Center, you may use the nearby International Gateway for early entry. Disney double-decker buses will transport you from the International Gateway to Future World.

Making Your EPCOT Center Restaurant Reservations

If you are a Walt Disney World resort hotel or campground guest, you can make EPCOT Center restaurant reservations from one to three days in advance. Dial 55 for same-day reservations and 56 for advance reservations. You can also make reservations up to 60 days in advance from home (or en route) by calling (407) 939-3463.

If you are not a Walt Disney World lodging or campground guest, or did not make reservations in advance, you can make same-day reservations for EPCOT Center restaurants when you arrive at the park. When admitted at the main entrance, proceed to Guest Relations, to the left of the giant sphere on the far side. Here an attendant will direct you to one of many two-way television monitors to make your reservations for lunch and dinner. Simply look into the monitor and state your preference, for instance, "I would like reservations for four persons for lunch at 12:30 in Germany." If you want to eat a meal in France, which has more than one restaurant, you will be asked to specify the restaurant by name. Though France is not on our list of top recommendations, we prefer Chefs de France over Bistro de Paris for most entrees.

Lunch Situation A. If your group is small (four persons or less) and you follow one of our touring plans walking at a moderately fast pace throughout the morning, this is approximately where you will be during the lunch hours:

If You Want to Eat at	*You Will Be Near*
11:00–11:30 A.M.	Mexico, Norway, China
11:30–12:00 noon	Norway, China, Germany
12:00–12:30 P.M.	China, Germany, Italy
12:30–1:00 P.M.	Germany, Italy, Japan
1:00–1:30 P.M.	Italy, Japan, Morocco, France
1:30–2:00 P.M.	Morocco, France, United Kingdom
2:00–2:30 P.M.	France, United Kingdom, Canada (no reservations required)

Lunch Situation B. If your group is large (five or more persons), **or** you follow one of our touring plans walking at a leisurely pace throughout the morning, this is approximately where you will be during the lunch hours:

If You Want to Eat at	You Will Be Near
11:00–11:30 A.M.	Mexico, Norway
11:30–12:00 noon	Mexico, Norway, China
12:00–12:30 P.M.	Norway, China, Germany
12:30–1:00 P.M.	China, Germany, Italy
1:00–1:30 P.M.	Germany, Italy, Japan
1:30–2:00 P.M.	Italy, Japan, Morocco
2:00–2:30 P.M.	Japan, Morocco, France

Author's Recommendation for Lunch: Regardless of whether you are moving fast or slow, we recommend lunch in Mexico or Norway.

Author's Recommendation for Dinner: You can eat your evening meal in any of EPCOT Center's restaurants without interrupting the sequence and efficiency of the touring plans. We recommend a 7 P.M. reservation when it gets dark early and an 8 P.M. reservation during the late spring, summer, and early fall. The timing of the reservation is important if you want to see IllumiNations, EPCOT Center's nightly grand laser and fireworks spectacular, held over the World Showcase Lagoon shortly after dark.

Our suggestions for dinner include the premier restaurants in Norway, Mexico, Germany, Morocco, and the Bistro de Paris in France. We also like sashimi at the Matsu No Ma Lounge in Japan followed by dinner in the Tempura Kiku Restaurant. If you are hot for some good seafood, make reservations at the Coral Reef in Future World. Finally, if you are a picky eater, or simply prefer American cuisine, try the Garden Grill (Land pavilion), also in Future World.

Before You Go

1. Call (407) 824-4321 the day before you go for the official opening time.

2. Purchase admission prior to your arrival. You can either order tickets through the mail before you leave home or buy them at the Disney Store in your local mall, the Walt Disney World Information

Center off I-75 near Ocala (north of Orlando), the Disney Store in the Orlando airport, or at Walt Disney World lodging properties.

3. Make lunch and dinner reservations before arriving at EPCOT Center. If you are staying in Walt Disney World, dial 55 or 56. If you want to make reservations before checking into your hotel, call (407) 939-3463.

4. Become familiar with the park opening procedures (described above) and read over the touring plan you've chosen so you have an understanding of what you are likely to encounter.

FOR: **Adults and children eight years or older.**

ASSUMES: Willingness to experience all major rides and shows.

Be forewarned that this plan requires a lot of walking and some back-tracking; this is necessary to avoid long waits in line. A little extra walking and some early morning hustle will save you from two to three hours of standing in line. Note also that you might not complete the tour. How far you get will depend on how quickly you move from attraction to attraction, how many times you pause for rest and food, how quickly the park fills, and what time the park closes.

This touring plan is not recommended for families with children under eight years of age. If you are touring with young children and have only one day, use the Author's Selective EPCOT Center One-Day Touring Plan. Break off after lunch to go to your hotel for a swim and a nap, and then return to the park in the late afternoon. If you can allocate two days to EPCOT Center, use the EPCOT Center Two-Day Touring Plan.

1. Arrive 45 to 50 minutes prior to the park's official opening time. Wait to be admitted.
2. When admitted to the park, move quickly (jog if you are up to it—but do not run) around the left side of Spaceship Earth to Guest Relations (across the walkway from the big sphere) to make lunch and dinner reservations. If you do not wish to make lunch or dinner reservations, or have made them already by phone, skip ahead to Step 3.
3. **If only Spaceship Earth and Guest Relations are open** when you are admitted to the park, go ahead and ride Spaceship Earth after making your restaurant reservations. When you exit Space-ship Earth, turn left and proceed to Innoventions East. When the rest of the park opens, pass through Innoventions East, bearing left through the first exit; go on to the Wonders of Life pavilion.

    If the entire park is open, make your restaurant reservations, ride Spaceship Earth, and then head directly to the Wonders of Life pavilion by way of Innoventions East.

If you want to eliminate some backtracking in the touring plan, you can go straight from making restaurant reservations and riding Spaceship Earth to The Land (Step 5), skipping the Body Wars ride in the Wonders of Life pavilion for the moment. If you are not that keen on Body Wars, or do not mind risking a long wait (30 to 55 minutes) for Body Wars later in the day, jumping ahead to Step 5 will save about ten minutes of crisscrossing the park. If Body Wars is really important to you, stick with the touring plan.

4. In the Wonders of Life pavilion, ride Body Wars. Body Wars, incidentally, has quite a track record for making people sick. Be sure to check our Touring Tips on pages 461–62 before riding. Save the other attractions at the Wonders of Life pavilion for later. If you do not want to ride Body Wars, skip ahead to Step 5.

5. Go next to The Land pavilion and ride Living with the Land. Save other attractions in The Land for later and move directly to Step 6.

6. Leave The Land pavilion and bear right. Proceed to the left side of the Journey into Imagination pavilion; see the 3-D movie, *Honey, I Shrunk the Audience*.

7. Exit the movie and bear left. Experience the Journey into Imagination ride.

8. After the ride, leave the Journey into Imagination pavilion and take the first available path to Innoventions West. Cut through Innoventions West, proceed across the plaza, and pass through Innoventions East. Exiting Innoventions East on the far side, proceed to the World of Motion pavilion.

9. Experience the World of Motion ride. Do not linger too long in the exhibit area at the end of the ride.

10. Bear left after exiting the World of Motion exhibit area, and bear left again on the path that leads to the Odyssey Restaurant. Cut through the Odyssey Restaurant to the World Showcase.

11. Turn left and proceed around the World Showcase Lagoon clockwise. Stop at Mexico and experience El Rio del Tiempo boat ride. The ride is located in the far left corner of the interior courtyard and is not very well marked. If you make any purchases, consign them to Package Pick-up for collection when you leave the park.

12. As you leave the Mexican pavilion continue left to Norway. Ride Maelstrom.

NOTE: Be aware of the time with respect to your lunch reservations. Simply break off the touring plan and go to the restaurant when the time comes. After lunch pick up the touring plan where you left off.

13. Continue left around the World Showcase Lagoon to China. See *Wonders of China*.

14. Continue on to Germany and Italy. There are no attractions at either pavilion. If you do not have a restaurant reservation, Sommerfest (fast food) at Germany serves tasty bratwurst, soft pretzels, desserts, and Beck's beer on draft.

15. Continue your clockwise circuit to the American Adventure pavilion. See the show. Once again, if you do not have restaurant reservations, the Liberty Inn (on the left side of the American Adventure) offers fast food: hamburgers, hot dogs, chicken breast sandwiches.

16. Resuming your stroll, visit Japan and Morocco. If you make any purchases, consign them to Package Pick-up for collection when you leave the park.

17. Go left from Morocco to France. See the film *Impressions de France*.

18. Go next to the United Kingdom.

19. Turn left as you leave the United Kingdom and visit Canada. See the film *O Canada!*

20. Return to Future World via the central plaza and cut through Innoventions East to Horizons. Ride.

21. Following Horizons, bear right and return to the Wonders of Life pavilion. See *Cranium Command*. Note that the preshow is essential in understanding the main attraction.

22. If you missed Body Wars earlier, ride now. If the wait is prohibitive try again after Step 26.

23. Exit the Wonders of Life and go right to the Universe of Energy. Do not be dismayed if the line looks long. This production swallows up almost 600 people every 15 minutes.

NOTE: Be aware of the time in respect to your dinner reservations. Simply break off the touring plan and go to the restaurant when the time comes. After dinner, check your daily entertainment schedule for the show time of IllumiNations, EPCOT Center's superb laser and fireworks spectacular. This is not to be missed; give yourself at least a half hour after dinner to find a good viewing spot along the perimeter of the World Showcase Lagoon.

For additional information on the best viewing spots, see pages 483–87.

24. Departing the Universe of Energy, cross Future World, passing through Innoventions East and West to The Living Seas. For maximum efficiency, try to be one of the last people to enter the theater (where you sit), from the preshow area (where you stand). Take a seat as close to the end of a middle row as possible. This will put you in position to be first on the ride that follows the theater presentation. After the ride, enjoy the various exhibits of Sea Base Alpha.

25. Leave The Living Seas, exiting right, and return to The Land. See *Food Rocks* and/or the film shown in the Harvest Theater.

26. If there is still time before closing and you have some energy left, stroll the streets of the World Showcase nations or check out the exhibits in Innoventions East and West. Another fun exhibit is The Image Works upstairs in the Journey into Imagination pavilion.

27. Unless a special holiday schedule is in effect, everything at EPCOT Center (except for a few shops) closes after IllumiNations. Thirty thousand people bolt for the exits at the same time. Suggestions for coping with this mass exodus can be found on pages 482–83.

—— Author's Selective EPCOT Center One-Day Touring Plan

FOR: **All parties.**

ASSUMES: A willingness to experience major rides and shows.

This touring plan is selective and includes only the very best EPCOT Center has to offer according to the author. The absence of a particular attraction in the itinerary should not be construed as negative relative to the attraction's worth.

Families with children under eight using this touring plan are encouraged to review EPCOT Center attractions in the Small Child Fright Potential Chart on pages 158–61. We recommend that you rent a stroller for any child small enough to fit in one, and that you take your small children back to the hotel for a nap after lunch. If you can allocate two days to see EPCOT Center, we suggest trying the EPCOT Center Two-Day Touring Plan.

1. Arrive 45 to 50 minutes prior to the park's official opening time. Wait to be admitted.

2. When admitted to the park, move quickly (jog if you are up to it—but do not run) around the left side of Spaceship Earth to Guest Relations (across the walkway from the big sphere) to make lunch and dinner reservations. If you do not wish to make lunch or dinner reservations, or have made them already by phone, skip ahead to Step 3.

3. **If only Spaceship Earth and Guest Relations are open** when you are admitted to the park, go ahead and ride Spaceship Earth after making your restaurant reservations. When you exit Spaceship Earth, turn left and proceed to Innoventions East. When the rest of the park opens, pass through Innoventions East and bear left through the first exit; go on to the Wonders of Life pavilion and Body Wars.

   If the entire park is open, make your restaurant reservations, ride Spaceship Earth, and then head directly to Body Wars in the Wonders of Life pavilion by way of Innoventions East.

If you want to eliminate some backtracking in the touring plan, you can go straight from making restaurant reservations and riding Spaceship Earth to The Land (Step 5), skipping the Body Wars ride in the Wonders of Life pavilion for the moment. If you are not that keen on Body Wars, or do not mind risking a long wait (30 to 55 minutes) for Body Wars later in the day, bouncing ahead to Step 5 will save about ten minutes of crisscrossing the park. If Body Wars is really important to you, stick with the touring plan.

4. In the Wonders of Life pavilion, ride Body Wars. Body Wars, incidentally, has quite a track record for making people sick. Be sure to check our Touring Tips on pages 461–62 before riding. Save the other attractions at the Wonders of Life pavilion for later. If you do not want to ride Body Wars, skip ahead to Step 5.

5. Go next to The Land pavilion and ride Living with the Land. Skip the other attractions in The Land for later and move directly to Step 6.

6. Leave The Land and turn right to Journey into Imagination. Enter via the doors on the upper left side of the building. Follow the corridor to the Magic Eye Theater and see the 3-D movie, *Honey, I Shrunk the Audience*.

7. After the 3-D movie, leave the Journey into Imagination pavilion and take the first available path to Innoventions West. Cut through Innoventions West, proceed across the plaza, and pass through Innoventions East. Exiting Innoventions East on the far side, proceed to the World of Motion pavilion.

8. Experience the World of Motion ride. Do not linger too long in the exhibit area at the end of the ride.

9. Bear left after exiting the World of Motion exhibit area, and bear left again on the path that leads to the Odyssey Restaurant. Cut through the Odyssey Restaurant to the World Showcase.

10. Turn left and proceed around the World Showcase Lagoon clockwise. Visit the interior courtyard at Mexico, but skip the boat ride. If you make any purchases, consign them to Package Pick-up for collection when you leave the park.

11. Continue left to Norway. Ride Maelstrom.

12. Continue left around the World Showcase Lagoon to China. See *Wonders of China*.

NOTE: Be aware of the time with respect to your lunch reservations. Simply break off the touring plan and go to the restaurant when the time comes. After lunch pick up the touring plan where you left off.

13. Walking clockwise around the World Showcase Lagoon, visit Germany and Italy. There are no attractions at either pavilion. If you do not have a restaurant reservation, Sommerfest (fast food) at Germany serves tasty bratwurst, soft pretzels, desserts, and Beck's beer on draft.

14. Continue your clockwise circuit to the American Adventure pavilion. See the show. Once again, if you do not have restaurant reservations, the Liberty Inn (on the left side of the American Adventure) offers fast food: hamburgers, hot dogs, chicken breast sandwiches.

15. Resuming your stroll, visit Japan and Morocco. If you make any purchases, consign them to Package Pick-up for collection when you leave the park.

16. Leave Morocco and go to France. See the film *Impressions de France*.

17. Go next to the United Kingdom.

18. Turn left as you leave the United Kingdom and visit Canada. The film *O Canada!* is quite good, but the audience must stand. Optional.

19. Return to Future World via the central plaza and cut through Innoventions East to Horizons. Ride.

20. Following Horizons, bear right and return to the Wonders of Life pavilion. See *Cranium Command*. Note that the preshow is essential in understanding the main attraction.

21. While at the Wonders of Life pavilion, ride Body Wars if you missed it earlier.

22. Exit the Wonders of Life and go right to the Universe of Energy. Do not be dismayed if the line looks long. This production swallows up almost 600 people every 15 minutes.

NOTE: Be aware of the time in respect to your dinner reservations. Simply break off the touring plan and go to the restaurant when the time comes. After dinner, check your daily entertainment schedule for the show time of IllumiNations, EPCOT Center's superb laser and fireworks spectacular. This is not to be missed; give yourself at least a half hour after dinner to find a good viewing spot along the perimeter of the World Showcase Lagoon.

For additional information on the best viewing spots, see pages 483–87.

23. Exiting the Universe of Energy, cross Future World passing through Innoventions East and West to The Living Seas. For maximum efficiency at The Living Seas, try to be one of the last people to enter the theater (where you sit) from the preshow area (where you stand). Take a seat as close to the end of a middle row as possible. This will put you in position to be first on the ride that follows the theater presentation. After the ride, enjoy the various exhibits of Sea Base Alpha.

24. This concludes the touring plan. If you have any time or energy left, visit attractions you missed or shop until time for IllumiNations. Unless a special holiday schedule is in effect, everything at EPCOT Center (except for a few shops) closes after IllumiNations. Thirty thousand people bolt for the exits at the same time. Suggestions for coping with this mass exodus can be found on pages 482–83.

—— EPCOT Center Two-Day Touring Plan

FOR: **All parties.**

This touring plan is for EPCOT Center visitors who wish to tour EPCOT Center comprehensively over a two-day period. Day One takes advantage of early morning touring opportunities, while Day Two begins in the late afternoon and continues until the park closes.

Many readers who spend part of their Walt Disney World arrival day traveling, checking into their hotels, and unpacking are not free to head for the theme parks until sometime in the afternoon. The second day of the EPCOT Center Two-Day Touring Plan is ideal for people who want to commence their EPCOT Center visit later in the day.

Families with children under eight using this touring plan are encouraged to review EPCOT Center attractions in the Small Child Fright Potential Chart on pages 158–61. We recommend that you rent a stroller for any child small enough to fit in one. We also suggest that you break off Day One no later than 2:30 P.M. in order to return to your hotel for rest. If you missed attractions called for in Day One of the Plan, add them to your itinerary on Day Two.

Day One

1. Arrive 45 to 50 minutes prior to the park's official opening time. Wait to be admitted.

2. When admitted to the park, move quickly (jog if you are up to it—but do not run) around the left side of Spaceship Earth to Guest Relations (across the walkway from the big sphere) to make lunch and dinner reservations. If you do not wish to make lunch or dinner reservations, or have made them already by phone, skip ahead to Step 3.

3. **If only Spaceship Earth and Guest Relations are open** when you are admitted to the park, go ahead and ride Spaceship Earth after making your restaurant reservations. When you exit Spaceship Earth, turn left and proceed to Innoventions East. When the rest of the park opens, pass through Innoventions East and bear

left through the first exit; go on to the Wonders of Life pavilion and Body Wars.

If the entire park is open, make your restaurant reservations, ride Spaceship Earth, and then head directly to Body Wars in the Wonders of Life pavilion by way of Innoventions East.

If you want to eliminate some backtracking in the touring plan, you can go straight from making restaurant reservations and riding Spaceship Earth to The Land (Step 7), skipping the Body Wars ride and the *Making of Me* in the Wonders of Life pavilion for the moment. If you are not that keen on Body Wars, or do not mind risking longer waits (30 to 55 minutes) later in the day, bouncing ahead to Step 5 will save about ten minutes of criss-crossing the park. If Body Wars or *The Making of Me* is really important to you, stick with the touring plan.

4. In the Wonders of Life pavilion, ride Body Wars. Body Wars, incidentally, has quite a track record for making people sick. Be sure to check our Touring Tips on pages 461–62 before riding. If you do not want to ride Body Wars, skip ahead to Step 5.

5. While at the Wonders of Life, see *The Making of Me*.

6. Departing the Wonders of Life, go next to The Land pavilion, passing through both Innoventions buildings. Ride Living with the Land. Save other attractions in The Land for later and move directly to Step 7.

7. Leave The Land pavilion and bear right. Proceed to the left side of the Journey into Imagination pavilion and see the 3-D movie, *Honey, I Shrunk the Audience*.

8. Exit the movie and bear left. Experience the Journey into Imagination ride.

9. After the ride, leave the Journey into Imagination pavilion and take the first available path to Innoventions West. Cut through Innoventions West, proceed across the plaza, and pass through Innoventions East. Exiting Innoventions East on the far side, proceed to the World of Motion pavilion.

10. Experience the World of Motion ride. Do not linger too long in the exhibit area at the end of the ride.

11. Bear left after exiting the World of Motion exhibit area, and bear left again on the path that leads to the Odyssey Restaurant. Cut through the Odyssey Restaurant to the World Showcase.

12. Turn left and proceed around the World Showcase Lagoon clockwise. Stop at Mexico and experience El Rio del Tiempo boat ride.

The ride is located in the far left corner of the interior courtyard and is not very well marked. If you make any purchases, consign them to Package Pick-up for collection when you leave the park.

13. Upon exiting the Mexican pavilion, continue left to Norway. Ride Maelstrom.

    NOTE: Be aware of the time with respect to your lunch reservations. Simply break off the touring plan and go to the restaurant when the time comes. After lunch pick up the touring plan where you left off.

14. Continue left around the Lagoon to China. See *Wonders of China*.

15. Walking clockwise around the World Showcase Lagoon, visit Germany and Italy. There are no attractions at either pavilion. If you do not have a restaurant reservation, Sommerfest (fast food) at Germany serves tasty bratwurst, soft pretzels, desserts, and Beck's beer on draft.

16. Continue your clockwise circuit to the American Adventure pavilion. See the show. Once again, if you do not have restaurant reservations, the Liberty Inn (on the left side of the American Adventure) offers fast food: hamburgers, hot dogs, chicken breast sandwiches.

17. Resuming your stroll, visit Japan and Morocco. If you make any purchases, consign them to Package Pick-up for collection when you leave the park.

18. Go left from Morocco to France. See the film *Impressions de France*.

19. This concludes the touring plan for Day One. Attractions and pavilions not included today will be experienced tomorrow. If you are full of energy and wish to continue touring, follow the EPCOT Center One-Day Touring Plan, starting at Step 18. If you've had enough, you can either exit through the International Gateway or head out through the main entrance. To reach the main entrance without hoofing around the World Showcase Lagoon, catch a boat at the dock near Morocco.

Day Two

1. Enter EPCOT Center at about 2 P.M. Pick up a daily entertainment schedule and a park map at Guest Relations.

2. While at Guest Relations make dinner reservations, if you have

not done so by phone. Since it will be well past the usual time for making reservations, you may have to summon a reservationist by using the WorldKey Information Service terminals (see page 445).

You can eat your evening meal in any of EPCOT Center's restaurants without interrupting the sequence and efficiency of the touring plan. We recommend a 7 P.M. reservation when it gets dark early and an 8 P.M. reservation during the late spring, summer, and early fall. The timing of the reservation is important if you want to see IllumiNations, EPCOT Center's nightly grand laser and fireworks spectacular, held over the World Showcase Lagoon shortly after dark.

If your preferred restaurants and seatings are filled, try for a reservation at Morocco or Norway. Because the delightful ethnic dishes of these countries are not well known to most Americans, it is often possible to get a reservation late in the day.

3. Go to The Living Seas. For maximum efficiency, try to be one of the last people to enter the theater (where you sit) from the preshow area (where you stand). Take a seat as close to the end of a middle row as possible. This will put you in position to be first on the ride that follows the theater presentation. After the ride, enjoy the various exhibits of Sea Base Alpha.

4. Exit The Living Seas to the right and return to The Land. See *Food Rocks*. Also see the film at the Harvest Theater featuring characters from *The Lion King*.

5. Cross the park, passing through Innoventions East and West, and proceed to the Universe of Energy. See the show.

6. Exit to the left and proceed to the Wonders of Life pavilion. See *Cranium Command*. Be sure to catch the preshow.

7. Ride Body Wars and see *The Making of Me* if you missed them on Day One.

8. Exit Wonders of Life to the left and proceed next door to Horizons. Ride.

NOTE: Be aware of the time with respect to your dinner reservations. Simply break off the touring plan and go to the restaurant when the time comes. After dinner, check your daily entertainment schedule for the show time of IllumiNations, EPCOT Center's superb laser and fireworks spectacular. This is not to be missed; give yourself at least a half hour after dinner to find a good viewing spot along the perimeter of the World Showcase Lagoon. For additional information on the best viewing spots, see pages 483–87.

9. Leave Future World and walk counterclockwise around the World Showcase Lagoon to Canada. See *O Canada!*
10. Turn right as you leave Canada and visit the United Kingdom.
11. This concludes the touring plan. Enjoy your dinner and IllumiNations. If you have time, shop or revisit your favorite attractions.
12. Unless a special holiday schedule is in effect, everything at EPCOT Center (except for a few shops) closes after IllumiNations. Thirty thousand people bolt for the exits at the same time. Suggestions for coping with this mass exodus can be found on pages 482–83.

PART ELEVEN: The Disney-MGM Studios, Universal Studios Florida, and Sea World

Disney-MGM Studios

Several years ago, the Disney folks decided they wanted to make movies for adults. Figuring that Snow White wouldn't share the set with Bette Midler mouthing four-letter words, they cranked up a brand new production company to handle the adult stuff. Results have been impressive; a complete rejuvenation of their movies, with new faces and tremendous creativeness, and an amazing resurgence at the box office.

So, as a new era of Disney film and television success began to crest, what better way to showcase and promote their product than with an all-new motion-picture and television entertainment park at Walt Disney World?

—— The MGM Connection

To broaden the appeal and to lend additional historic impact, Disney obtained the rights to use the MGM (Metro-Goldwyn-Mayer) name, the MGM film library, MGM motion picture and television titles, excerpts, costumes, music, sets, and even Leo, the MGM logo lion. Probably the two most readily recognized names in the motion picture industry, Disney and MGM in combination showcase more than 65 years of movie history.

—— Comparing Disney-MGM Studios to the Magic Kingdom and EPCOT Center

Such a comparison appears to be an "apples and oranges" proposition at first glance. The Magic Kingdom has modeled most of its attractions on Disney movie and TV themes; EPCOT Center has pioneered attractions and rides as vehicles for learning. Looking more closely, however, there are numerous similarities. Like EPCOT Center, the Disney-MGM Studios is at once fun and educational, and as in the Magic Kingdom, the themes for the various rides and shows are drawn from movies and television. All three parks rely heavily on Disney special effects and AudioAnimatronics (robotics) in their entertainment mix.

The Disney-MGM Studios is about the same size as the Magic Kingdom and about one-half as large as the sprawling EPCOT Center. Unlike the other parks, however, Disney-MGM Studios is a working motion picture and television production facility. This means, among other things, that about half of the entire Studios area is controlled access, with guests permitted only on tours accompanied by guides or restricted to observation walkways.

When EPCOT Center opened in 1982, Disney patrons expected a futuristic version of the Magic Kingdom. What they got was humanistic inspiration and a creative educational experience. Since then, the Disney folks have tried to inject a little more magic, excitement, and surprise into EPCOT Center. But remembering the occasional disappointment of those early EPCOT Center guests, Disney planners fortified the Disney-MGM Studios with megadoses of action, suspense, surprise, and, of course, special effects. If you are interested in the history and technology of the motion picture and television industries, there is plenty of education to be had. However, if you feel lazy and just want to be entertained, the Disney-MGM Studios is a pretty good place to be.

—— How Much Time to Allocate

A guest really has to scurry to see all of EPCOT Center or the Magic Kingdom (some say it can't be done) in one day. The Disney-MGM Studios are more manageable. There is much less ground to cover by foot. Trams transport guests throughout much of the back lot and working areas, and the attractions in the open-access parts are concentrated in an area about the size of Main Street, Tomorrowland, and Mickey's Starland put together. There will be a day, no doubt, as the Disney-MGM Studios develop and grow, when you will need more than a day to see everything without hurrying. For the time being, however, the Studios are a nice one-day outing.

Because it is smaller, however, the Disney-MGM Studios is more affected by large crowds. Likewise, being the newest Disney theme park, large crowds can be considered the norm for the foreseeable future. To help you avoid the crowds we have developed touring plans for the Disney-MGM Studios that will keep you a step ahead of the mob and minimize any waits in line. Even when the park is heavily attended, however, you can see most everything in a day.

—— The Disney-MGM Studios in the Evening

Because the Disney-MGM Studios can be seen in two-thirds of a day, most guests who arrive in the morning run out of things to do by 3:30 or 4 P.M., and leave the park. Their departure greatly diminishes the crowd and makes the Studios an ideal park for evening touring. Lines for most attractions are short and manageable, and the park is cooler and more comfortable. Productions at the *Indiana Jones Stunt Spectacular* and other outdoor theaters are infinitely more enjoyable during the evening than in the sweltering heat of the day. And, finally, there is Sorcery in the Sky, thought by many of our readers to be the most spectacular fireworks show at Walt Disney World. A drawback to touring the Studios at night is there will not be much activity on the production soundstages or in the Animation Building. Another problem is you might get stuck eating dinner at the Studios. If you've got to eat, try Mama Melrose's or the Hollywood Brown Derby for full-service dining, or the Hollywood & Vine cafeteria.

—— Arriving

Two days each week, usually on Wednesday and Sunday, Disney resort and campground guests are invited to enter the Disney-MGM Studios 90 minutes before the official opening time. During the early-entry hour, guests can usually enjoy The Great Movie Ride, *MuppetVision 4-D,* Star Tours, and the Twilight Zone Tower of Terror. These attractions, however, are subject to change, as are the days of the week that early entry is scheduled. If the official opening time is 9 A.M., and you are eligible for early entry, plan to arrive at the park by 7:30 A.M. If you are not eligible for early entry, arrive at the Studios 40 minutes before the official opening time on a day when early entry is not in effect.

The Disney-MGM Studios has its own pay parking lot and is also serviced by shuttle bus from the Transportation and Ticket Center, from EPCOT Center, and from Walt Disney World hotels. In addition, many of the larger "out-of-the-World" hotels shuttle guests to the Studios. If you drive, Walt Disney World's ubiquitous trams will arrive to transport you to the ticketing area and entrance gate.

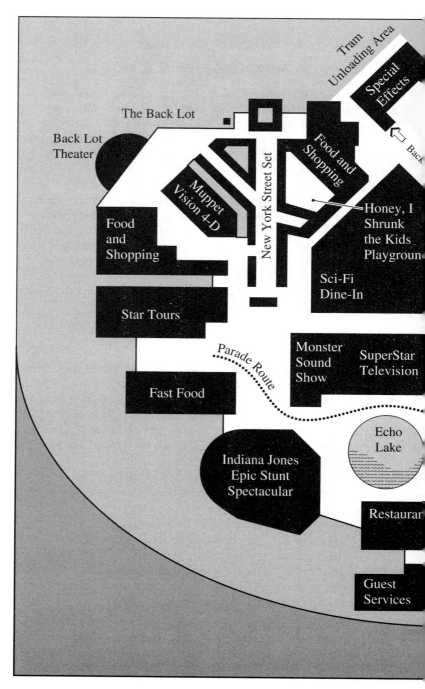

Tram Unloading Area

Special Effects

The Back Lot

Back Lot Theater

Food and Shopping

Back

Muppet Vision 4-D

New York Street Set

Honey, I Shrunk the Kids Playground

Food and Shopping

Sci-Fi Dine-In

Star Tours

Parade Route

Monster Sound Show

SuperStar Television

Fast Food

Echo Lake

Indiana Jones Epic Stunt Spectacular

Restaurant

Guest Services

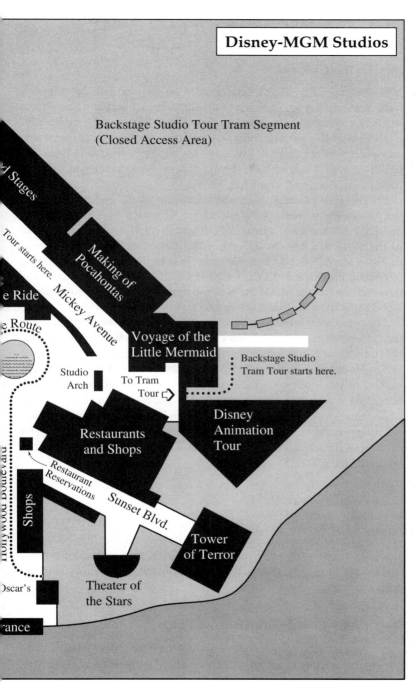

Disney-MGM Studios

Backstage Studio Tour Tram Segment
(Closed Access Area)

d Stages

Tour starts here.

Making of
Pocahontas

e Ride

Mickey Avenue

e Route

Voyage of the
Little Mermaid

Backstage Studio
Tram Tour starts here.

Studio
Arch

To Tram
Tour

Disney
Animation
Tour

Restaurants
and Shops

Restaurant
Reservations

Sunset Blvd.

Shops

Tower
of Terror

Oscar's

Theater of
the Stars

ance

— *Getting Oriented*

As you enter, Guest Services will be on your left, serving as a park headquarters and information center similar to City Hall in the Magic Kingdom and Guest Relations at EPCOT Center. Check here for a schedule of live performances, lost persons, lost objects, emergencies, and general information. If you have not been provided with a map of the Studios, pick one up here. To the right of the entrance you will find lockers, strollers, and wheelchair rentals.

For the sake of orientation, about one-half of the entire complex is set up as a theme park. As at the Magic Kingdom, you enter the park and pass down a main street; only this time it's Hollywood Boulevard of the 1920s and 30s. At the end of Hollywood Boulevard is a replica of Hollywood's long-famous Chinese Theater. While not as imposing as Cinderella Castle or EPCOT Center's Spaceship Earth, the theater is nevertheless Disney-MGM Studios' most central landmark and serves as a good spot to meet if your group gets separated.

The open-access (theme park) areas of the Studios complex are at the theater end of Hollywood Boulevard, off Sunset Boulevard (branching off Hollywood Boulevard to the right), and around Echo Lake, off to the left of Hollywood Boulevard as you face the theater. Attractions in this section of the Studios are rides and shows, which you can experience according to your own tastes and timetable. The remainder of the Disney-MGM Studios consists of the working sound stages, technical facilities, wardrobe shops, administrative offices, animation studios, and back lot sets; these are accessible to visitors by foot or by a combination tram and walking Studio Tour.

— *What to See*

As in our coverage of the Magic Kingdom and EPCOT Center, we have identified certain attractions as "not to be missed." We suggest, however, that you try everything. Usually exceeding your expectations, and always surprising, Disney rides and shows are rarely what you would anticipate.

— *Chalk Board with Waiting Times*

As a courtesy, Disney-MGM provides a large chalk board that lists the current waiting times for all Disney-MGM attractions. Updated continuously throughout the day, the chalk board is situated on Hollywood Boulevard at its intersection with Sunset Boulevard. It is our experience that the waiting times listed on the chalkboard are slightly conservative. If the chalkboard indicates that the wait for Star Tours is 45 minutes, for example, you will probably have to wait about 35 to 40 minutes.

In the early morning, well-meaning Disney employees will try to direct you to the *Indiana Jones Stunt Spectacular,* saying, "Go now or you will have a long wait." Simply ignore them and stick to the touring plan. A Detroit woman reported the following:

> My older sister and family went to [Disney-]MGM. They got there and were encouraged by Disney people to go to a different show other than your plan. They did and ended up waiting in line for everything.

"It's my husband. He refuses to get up early when he's on vacation."

Open-Access Movie Theme Park

Hollywood Boulevard

Hollywood Boulevard is a palm-lined re-creation of Hollywood's main drag during the city's golden age. Architecture is streamlined *moderne* with art deco embellishments. Most of the theme park's service facilities are located here, interspersed with numerous shops and eateries. Shoppers can select from among Hollywood and movie-related souvenir items to one-of-a-kind collectibles obtained from studio auctions and estate sales. Disney trademark items are, of course, also available.

In addition to the services and commercial ventures, characters from Hollywood's heyday, as well as roving performers, entertain passersby. The Boulevard also serves as the site for daily parades and other happenings.

Hollywood Boulevard Services

Most of the park's service facilities are housed along Hollywood Boulevard, including the following:

Wheelchair & Stroller Rental	To the right of the entrance at Oscar's Super Service
Banking Services	An automated bank teller can be found to the right of the entrance turnstiles (outside the park).
Storage Lockers	Rental lockers are located to the right of the main entrance on Hollywood Boulevard, on the left side of Oscar's.
Lost & Found	Lost & Found is in Guest Services, to the left of the entrance on Hollywood Boulevard.
Live Entertainment/ Parade Information	Available at Guest Services
Lost Persons	Lost persons can be reported at Guest Services.

Walt Disney World & Local Attraction Information	At Guest Services
First Aid	At Guest Services
Baby Center/Baby Care Needs	At Guest Services. Oscar's sells baby food and other necessities.
Film	At The Darkroom on the right side of Hollywood Boulevard, just beyond Oscar's

Sunset Boulevard

Sunset Boulevard is a major new addition to the Disney-MGM Studios. Intersecting Hollywood Boulevard near the Brown Derby restaurant, Sunset Boulevard provides another venue for dining, shopping, and street entertainment. The new thoroughfare is evocative of 1940s Hollywood in theme and architecture.

"The Twilight Zone" Tower of Terror

Type of Attraction: Disney mixed-media adventure ride

When to Go: Before 10 A.M. and after 5 P.M.

Special Comments: Not to be missed

Author's Rating: ★★★★★

Overall Appeal by Age Group:

Pre-school	Grade School	Teens	Young Adults	Over 30	Senior Citizens
★★★★	★★★★★	★★★★★	★★★★★	★★★★½	★★★★½

Duration of Ride: About 4 minutes plus preshow

Average Wait in Line per 100 People Ahead of You: 4 minutes

Assumes: All elevators operating

Loading Speed: Moderate

DESCRIPTION AND COMMENTS   The Tower of Terror is a new species of thrill ride in the Disney repertoire, though it borrows elements from The Haunted Mansion at the Magic Kingdom. The idea is that you are touring a once-famous Hollywood hotel gone to ruin. As at Star Tours, the queuing area serves to integrate the guests into the adventure as they pass through the hotel's once-opulent public rooms and lobby. From the lobby, guests are escorted into the hotel's library where Rod Serling, speaking on an old black-and-white television, greets the guests and introduces the plot.

If bigger is indeed better, The Tower of Terror should be the hottest attraction at the Disney-MGM Studios. The Tower of Terror is a whopper, thirteen-plus-stories high. Breaking tradition in terms of isolating theme areas within the park, you can see the entire Studios from the top of the tower, but you have to look quick.

The ride vehicle, one of the hotel's service elevators, takes the guests for a tour of the haunted hostelry. The tour begins innocuously enough, but by about the fifth floor things get pretty weird. You have just entered the Twilight Zone. Guests are subjected to the full range of Disney special effects as they encounter various unexpected horrors and optical illusions. The climax of the adventure occurs when the elevator reaches the top floor (the thirteenth, of course) and the elevator cable snaps.

The Tower of Terror is an experience to savor. Though the sensation of the final plunge is calculated to give thrill-seekers something to sink their teeth into, the attraction is really about its extraordinary visual and audio effects. There is richness and subtlety here: enough to keep the ride fresh and stimulating after many repetitions.

Finer points aside, the Tower of Terror has great potential for terrifying small children and rattling the dentures of more mature visitors. If you have teenagers in your party, use them as experimental probes. If they report back that they really, really liked the Tower of Terror, run in the opposite direction as fast as you can.

TOURING TIPS   Because of its height, the tower is visible even before you enter the Disney-MGM Studios. It is a veritable beacon, luring curious guests as soon as they pass through the turnstiles. Because of its popularity with school kids, teens, and young adults, you can count on a footrace to the attraction when the park opens. For the foreseeable future, plan on the Tower of Terror being mobbed most of the day. Experience the tower either first thing in the morning or in the last hour before the park closes.

To save some time, when you enter the library waiting area, position yourself in the far back corner at the opposite end of the long wall from the television set. When the doors to the loading area open, you will be one of the first of those admitted. Finally, if you have small children (or anyone else) who are apprehensive about this attraction, ask the attendant about switching off (see page 166).

The Great Movie Ride

Type of Attraction: Disney mixed-media adventure ride
When to Go: Before 10 A.M. and after 5 P.M.
Special Comments: Elaborate, with several surprises; not to be missed
Author's Rating: ★★★★
Overall Appeal by Age Group:

Pre-school	Grade School	Teens	Young Adults	Over 30	Senior Citizens
★★★★	★★★★	★★★★	★★★★½	★★★★½	★★★★½

Duration of Ride: About 19 minutes
Average Wait in Line per 100 People Ahead of You: 2 minutes
Assumes: All trains operating
Loading Speed: Fast

DESCRIPTION AND COMMENTS   Entering through a re-creation of Hollywood's Chinese Theater, guests board vehicles for a fast-paced tour through soundstage sets from such classic films as *Casablanca*, *The Wizard of Oz*, *Aliens*, *Raiders of the Lost Ark*, and many more. Each set is populated with new-generation Disney AudioAnimatronics (robots), as well as an occasional human, all assisted by a variety of dazzling special effects. Disney's largest and most ambitious ride-through attraction, The Great Movie Ride encompasses 95,000 square feet and showcases some of the most famous scenes in filmmaking history. Life-sized Audio-Animatronic sculptures of such stars as Gene Kelly, John Wayne, James Cagney, Julie Andrews, and Harrison Ford inhabit the largest sets ever constructed for a Disney ride.

TOURING TIPS   The Great Movie Ride is a Disney-MGM feature attraction that draws large crowds (and lines) from the moment the park opens. An interval-loading, high-capacity ride, lines disappear quickly. Even so, waits can exceed an hour after midmorning (as an aside, actual waits usually run about one-third shorter than the time posted on the "Waiting Sign." If the sign indicates an hour wait, your actual wait will probably be around 40 minutes).

SuperStar Television

Type of Attraction: Audience participation television production
When to Go: After 10 A.M.

Author's Rating: Well-conceived; ★★★½
Overall Appeal by Age Group:

Pre-school	Grade School	Teens	Young Adults	Over 30	Senior Citizens
★★★½	★★★★★	★★★★★	★★★★½	★★★★½	★★★★½

Duration of Presentation: 30 minutes
Preshow Entertainment: Participants selected from guests waiting in the preshow area
Probable Waiting Time: 10–20 minutes

DESCRIPTION AND COMMENTS   Audience volunteers (conscriptees) participate in a television production that uses special effects to integrate the actions of the amateurs with footage of well-known stars of past and current TV shows. The combined result, a sort of video collage where the volunteers miraculously end up in the footage with the stars, is broadcast on large-screen monitors above the set. The outcome, always rated in laughs, depends on how the volunteers respond in their dramatic debut.

TOURING TIPS   The theater seats 1,000 people, so it is not usually difficult to get in. If you want to be in the production, however, it is essential that you enter the preshow holding area at least 15 minutes before the next performance. Participants for the show are more or less drafted by a casting director from guests of both genders and from all age groups. Those who stand near the director and those who are distinctively (outlandishly?) attired seem to be selected most often. A woman from New York patted herself on the back, writing: "We were selected to be in *SuperStar Television* when I raised our hands and screamed 'Honeymooners!' "

Star Tours

Motion Sickness

WARNING!

Type of Attraction: Space-flight simulation ride
When to Go: First hour and a half the park is open
Special Comments: Expectant mothers or anyone prone to motion sickness are advised against riding.
   The ride is too intense for many children under 8.
Author's Rating: Disney's absolute best, anytime, anyplace; not to be missed; ★★★★★

Overall Appeal by Age Group:

Pre-school	Grade School	Teens	Young Adults	Over 30	Senior Citizens
★★★★	★★★★★	★★★★★	★★★★★	★★★★★	★★★★

Duration of Ride: Approximately 7 minutes

Average Wait in Line per 100 People Ahead of You: 5 minutes

Assumes: All simulators operating

Loading Speed: Moderate to fast

DESCRIPTION AND COMMENTS   This attraction is so amazing, so real, and so much fun that it just makes you grin and giggle. The attraction consists of a ride in a flight simulator modeled after those used in the training of pilots and astronauts. Guests, supposedly on a little vacation outing in space, are piloted by a droid (android, a.k.a. humanoid, a.k.a. robot) on his first flight with real passengers. Mayhem ensues almost immediately, the scenery flashes by at supersonic speed, and the simulator bucks and pitches. You could swear you were moving at light speed. After several minutes of this, the droid somehow gets the spacecraft landed and you discover you are about ten times happier than you were before you boarded. Speaking strictly for the research team, we would like to see a whole new generation of Disney rides on the order of Star Tours.

TOURING TIPS   This one ride is worth your admission to Disney-MGM Studios. Interestingly, Star Tours has not been as popular at Disney-MGM Studios as at Disneyland in California. Except on unusually busy days, waits rarely exceed 30 to 40 minutes. For the first couple of hours the park is open, you can anticipate a wait of 20 minutes or less. Even so, we recommend seeing Star Tours before 11 A.M. If you have small children (or anyone else) who are apprehensive about this attraction, ask the attendant about switching off (see page 166).

Monster Sound Show

Type of Attraction: Audience-participation show demonstrating sound effects

When to Go: Before 11 A.M. or after 5 P.M.

Author's Rating: Funny and informative; ★★★½

Overall Appeal by Age Group:

Pre-school	Grade School	Teens	Young Adults	Over 30	Senior Citizens
★★★½	★★★★½	★★★★½	★★★★½	★★★★½	★★★★½

Duration of Presentation: 12 minutes

Preshow Entertainment: David Letterman and Jimmy McDonald video

Probable Waiting Time: 15–30 minutes, except during the first half hour the park is open

DESCRIPTION AND COMMENTS   A live show where guests are invited on stage for a crash course in becoming sound-effects technicians. If the participating guests are duds the show really tends to suffer. Most of the time, luckily, guests rise to the occasion and the audience is well entertained. First, a short feature is shown to demonstrate what the sound effects are supposed to sound like. Next the guest volunteers make a stab at providing the sound effects. The result of their efforts are played back at the end of the show for the audience to enjoy.

TOURING TIPS   Because the theater is relatively small, long waits (partially in the hot sun) are common here. Another thing: the *Monster Sound Show* is periodically inundated by guests coming from a just-concluded performance of SuperStar Television or the *Indiana Jones Stunt Spectacular*. This is not the time to get in line. Wait at least 20 minutes and try again.

A reader from Israel suggests that a good time to catch the Sound Show is just before the Aladdin Royal Caravan parade. If the parade starts on Hollywood Boulevard, it takes about 15 to 18 minutes to wind over to the Sound Show; just long enough to catch the show and pop out right in time for the parade.

Being chosen for participation in the *Monster Sound Show* is pretty much a function of luck. There is not much beyond being in the right place at the right time to enhance your chances for getting picked.

Indiana Jones Stunt Spectacular

Type of Attraction: Movie stunt demonstration and action show

When to Go: First three morning shows or last evening show

Special Comments: Performance times posted on a sign at the entrance to the theater

Author's Rating: Done on a grand scale; ★★★★

Overall Appeal by Age Group:

Pre-school	Grade School	Teens	Young Adults	Over 30	Senior Citizens
★★★★½	★★★★★	★★★★★	★★★★½	★★★★½	★★★★½

Duration of Presentation: 30 minutes
Preshow Entertainment: Selection of "extras" from audience
Probable Waiting Time: None

DESCRIPTION AND COMMENTS   Coherent and educational, though somewhat unevenly paced, the production showcases professional stunt men and women who demonstrate various dangerous stunts with a behind-the-scenes look at how it's all done. The sets, props, and special effects are extremely elaborate.

TOURING TIPS   The Stunt Theater holds 2,000 people but, owing to the popularity of the presentation, generally plays to capacity audiences. On busy days, you can walk into the first performance, even if you arrive 5 minutes late. For the second performance you will need to show up about 25–30 minutes ahead of time. For the third show of the day and subsequent shows, arrive 35–45 minutes early. If you plan to tour during the late afternoon and evening, try attending the last scheduled performance of the day. If you want to beat the crowd out of the stadium, select seats on the far right (as you face the staging area) and near the top.

A number of guests are selected from the audience to be "extras" in the stunt show. To be chosen arrive early, sit down front, and display unmitigated enthusiasm. A Richmond, Virginia, woman explains one of the many possible variations on the theme:

Indiana Jones was far and away the best show—we saw it twice on two different days. After the first performance, I realized the best way to get picked was to stand up, wave my arms, and shout when the "casting director" called for volunteers—sheer enthusiasm wins every time, and sitting towards the front helps, too. We stayed afterwards for autographs of the performers in the obligatory Mickey Mouse autograph book.

Theater of the Stars

Type of Attraction: Live Hollywood-style musical, usually featuring the Disney characters; performed in an open-air theater
When to Go: In the evening
Special Comments: Performance times are listed in the daily entertainment schedule
Author's Rating: Excellent; ★★★★

Overall Appeal by Age Group:

Pre-school	Grade School	Teens	Young Adults	Over 30	Senior Citizens
★★★★½	★★★★	★★★	★★★★	★★★★	★★★½

Duration of Presentation: 25 minutes
Preshow Entertainment: None
Probable Waiting Time: 20–30 minutes

DESCRIPTION AND COMMENTS   The Theater of the Stars combines Disney characters with singers and dancers in upbeat and humorous Hollywood musical productions. The *Beauty and the Beast* show, in particular, is outstanding. The theater, which has been situated in three different park locations over the years, seems finally to have found a permanent home in the Sunset Boulevard section of the Disney-MGM Studios. Vastly improved, there is now a clear field of vision from most every seat. Best of all, the audience is protected from the Florida sun (or rain) by a canopy. The open-air theater still gets mighty hot in the summer, but you can make it through a performance now without succumbing to heat stroke.

TOURING TIPS   Unless you visit during a cooler time of year, try to see this show in the evening. The production is sometimes so popular that you might have to show up 20 to 50 minutes in advance to get a seat. To get to the theater, follow Sunset Boulevard, off Hollywood Boulevard.

Voyage of the Little Mermaid

Type of Attraction: Musical stage show featuring characters from the Disney movie *The Little Mermaid*
When to Go: Before 9:30 A.M., or just before closing
Author's Rating: Romantic, lovable, and humorous in the best Disney tradition; ★★★★

Overall Appeal by Age Group:

Pre-school	Grade School	Teens	Young Adults	Over 30	Senior Citizens
★★★★	★★★★	★★★½	★★★★	★★★★	★★★★

Duration of Presentation: 15 minutes
Preshow Entertainment: Taped ramblings about the decor in the preshow holding area

Probable Waiting Time: Before 9:30 A.M., 30 minutes; after 9:30 A.M., 50–90 minutes

DESCRIPTION AND COMMENTS *Voyage of the Little Mermaid* is a real winner, appealing to every age group. Cute without being silly or saccharine, as well as infinitely lovable, the *Little Mermaid* show is the most tender and romantic entertainment offered in any Disney theme park. A simple and engaging story, an impressive mix of special effects, and some memorable Disney characters make *Voyage of the Little Mermaid* a "not-to-be-missed" attraction.

TOURING TIPS Because it is well done and situated at a busy pedestrian intersection, *Voyage of the Little Mermaid* plays to capacity crowds all day. Unless you make the first or second show of the day, you will probably have to wait an hour or more. If you plan to spend an evening (as well as a morning) at the Disney-MGM Studios, see the first *Little Mermaid* show and save the *Indiana Jones Stunt Spectacular* for evening viewing.

When you enter the preshow lobby for the *Little Mermaid*, position yourself near the doors to the theater. When the doors open, go into the theater, pick a row of seats, and let about six to ten people enter the row ahead of you. The strategy here is twofold: to obtain a good seat and be close to the exit doors.

The Making of Pocahontas

Type of Attraction: Movie about the making of Disney's animated feature, *Pocahontas*

When to Go: Before noon and after 4 P.M.

Author's Rating: Educational and enlightening; ★★★½

Overall Appeal by Age Group:

Pre-school	Grade School	Teens	Young Adults	Over 30	Senior Citizens
★★½	★★★	★★★½	★★★½	★★★½	★★★½

Duration of Presentation: 17 minutes

Preshow Entertainment: Tour of post-production facilities

Probable Waiting Time: 20 minutes

DESCRIPTION AND COMMENTS Located down Mickey Avenue from *The Voyage of the Little Mermaid*, the attraction features a short documentary describing the casting, art, music, and production of the Disney animated feature *Pocahontas*. Before the documentary, guests are guided through the Disney-MGM post-production studios where the process of combining sound with film animation is explained.

TOURING TIPS   *The Making of Pocahontas* is entertaining, but primarily educational. Children who have seen *Voyage of the Little Mermaid* and are expecting a similar show based on the characters from *Pocahontas* will probably be disappointed. We expect *The Making of Pocahontas* to be quite popular, particularly while the *Pocahontas* feature film is in its first run at theaters. Try to see the show before noon or during the late afternoon.

Jim Henson's MuppetVision 4-D

Type of Attraction: 4-D movie starring the Muppets
When to Go: Before 11 A.M. and after 4 P.M.
Author's Rating: Uproarious, not to be missed; ★★★★½
Overall Appeal by Age Group:

Pre-school	Grade School	Teens	Young Adults	Over 30	Senior Citizens
★★★★½	★★★★★	★★★★½	★★★★½	★★★★½	★★★★½

Duration of Presentation: 17 minutes
Preshow Entertainment: Muppets on television
Probable Waiting Time: 12 minutes

DESCRIPTION AND COMMENTS   *MuppetVision 4-D* provides a total sensory experience, with the wild 3-D action augmented by auditory, visual, and even tactile special effects in the theater. If you are tired and hot, this presentation will make you feel brand new. Not to be missed.

TOURING TIPS   This production has been rising in popularity since its introduction. Usually you will not have more than a 20-minute wait if you line up before noon. During the hot, busy, middle of the day, however, until about 4 P.M. or so, expect long lines. Also, watch out for huge throngs of people arriving en masse from just concluded performances of the *Indiana Jones Stunt Spectacular*. If you encounter a long line, chalk it up to bad timing and try again later.

Honey, I Shrunk the Kids Movie Set Adventure Playground

Type of Attraction: Small, but elaborate, playground
When to Go: Before 10 A.M. or after dark
Author's Rating: Great for small children, expendable for adults; ★★½
Overall Appeal by Age Group:

Pre-school	Grade School	Teens	Young Adults	Over 30	Senior Citizens
★★★★½	★★★★	★★	★★½	★★★	★★½

Duration of Presentation: Varies
Average Wait in Line per 100 People Ahead of You: 20 minutes

DESCRIPTION AND COMMENTS   This attraction is an elaborate playground, particularly appealing to kids 11 and younger. The idea is that you have been "miniaturized" and have to make your way through a yard full of 20-foot-tall blades of grass, giant ants, lawn sprinklers, and other oversized wonders.

TOURING TIPS   Honey, I Shrunk the Kids is strictly a playground for children. It is imaginative and has tunnels, slides, rope ladders, and a variety of oversized props. All surface areas are padded, and Disney personnel are on hand to help keep children in some semblance of control. While this Movie Set Adventure undoubtedly looked good on paper, the actual attraction has problems that are hard to "miniaturize." First, it's not nearly large enough to accommodate the number of kids who would like to play. Only 240 people are allowed "on the set" at any one time, and many of these are supervising parents or other curious adults who hopped in line for the attraction without knowing what they were waiting for. By 10:30 or 11 A.M., the play area is full to capacity with seven to ten dozen waiting outside (none too patiently) to be admitted.

This brings us to the second major flaw: the absence of any provision for getting people to leave. Once inside, kids can play as long as their parents allow. This results in an uneven flow of traffic through the playground, and extremely long waits for those outside in line. If it were not for the third flaw, that the attraction is poorly ventilated, and is as hot and sticky as an Everglades swamp, there is no telling when anyone would leave.

A Shawnee Mission, Kansas, mom, however, wrote disagreeing with our assessment:

Some of the things your book said to skip were our favorites (at least for the kids). We all thought the playground from *Honey, I Shrunk the Kids* was great—definitely worth seeing.

If you want your children to experience Honey, I Shrunk the Kids, get them in and out before 11 A.M. (preferably before 10:30 A.M.). By late morning this attraction is way too hot and crowded for anyone to enjoy. You can access the playground via the New York back lot set, or through the Backstage Plaza fast-food and retail area. As a time-saving measure, a Grand Rapids, Michigan, couple offered the following:

> We staked out a seat at the Back Stage Plaza near the exit of [Honey, I Shrunk the Kids] with our children. They then went in to play while I got their snacks and beverages. Meanwhile, we had an opportunity to rest and determine our next game plan. When they emerged they were parched and tired, so the refreshment break was well timed.

Teenage Mutant Ninja Turtles

Type of Attraction: Short stage show and autograph session

When to Go: At your convenience (check the daily entertainment schedule)

Author's Rating: Great for small children, totally expendable for adults; ★½

Overall Appeal by Age Group:

Pre-school	Grade School	Teens	Young Adults	Over 30	Senior Citizens
★★★★½	★★★★	★★	★½	★	★½

Duration of Presentation: 2½ minute show followed by 10 minutes of autographing

Average Wait in Line per 100 People Ahead of You: Street theater; no waiting, except for autographs.

DESCRIPTION AND COMMENTS   Located at the far end of the New York Street area, the *Teenage Mutant Ninja Turtles* show is performed about 12 times each day. Show times are listed in the daily entertainment schedule. There is no shade. The audience must endure the sweltering sun throughout. Fortunately for everyone, however, the production is mercifully short; so short, in fact, that if you arrive three minutes late you will have missed it! Essentially, the Turtles drive up in their customized van, prance around, and do a few choreographed ninja moves on stage. Apparently this short burst of activity so exhausts the Turtles that a longer or more elaborate performance is out of the question. After the show, each Turtle works his way along a police barricade shaking hands, high-fiving, and stamping (that's right—stamping) the autograph books of waiting children. While to adults the Turtles look exactly alike, most kids are able to identify them.

TOURING TIPS   What can I say? None of this Turtle stuff makes sense unless you are under 12 or a Samurai herpetologist. Because the audience stands, small children can't see a thing unless they are right up front. The real event seems to be the autograph (stamping) party. Savvy kids, ignoring the show altogether, take up positions in advance along the police barricade to get their favorite Turtle's stamp. The only people not arrayed along the barricade are uninitiated kids and totally confused adults. And so it goes.

If your children desire to participate in this ritual, get them situated along the barricade about 10–15 minutes before show time. If they complain that they can't see the show from where they are, just remind them that Disney is weird and nothing here is *supposed* to make sense. After about ten minutes of stamping, a nonterrapin cast member herds the Turtles back to their van. Kids left without autographs are admonished to arrive earlier next time.

Though we have our doubts about the Turtles, they are the highlight of the day for many children. One mother of two voiced this opinion:

Although you give a low rating to the *Ninja Turtle* show, it should be mentioned that it gives a great opportunity to take beautiful and colorful pictures of your kids afterwards. Since no one is absolutely guaranteed to run into Disney characters in any of the parks, this is a perfect chance to be seen with the next best thing. They may not have big, black ears, but they are very green and they photograph beautifully.

New York Street Back Lot

Type of Attraction: Walk-through back lot movie set
When to Go: Anytime
Author's Rating: Interesting with great detail; ★★★★

Overall Appeal by Age Group:

Pre-school	Grade School	Teens	Young Adults	Over 30	Senior Citizens
★★★	★★★★	★★★★	★★★★	★★★★	★★★★

Duration of Presentation: Varies

Average Wait in Line per 100 People Ahead of You: No waiting

DESCRIPTION AND COMMENTS   This part of the Studios' back lot was previously accessible to tourists only on the tram segment of the Backstage Tour. Now guests can walk around the elaborate New York Street set and appreciate its rich detail at their leisure. A second benefit of opening this part of the Studios to pedestrian traffic is that it creates a little more elbow room, relieving some of the congestion in the Hollywood Boulevard and Echo Lake areas.

TOURING TIPS   Because there is never a wait to enjoy the New York back lot set, save it until you have seen those attractions that develop long lines. As an aside, Mickey Mouse signs autographs and poses for photos on the steps of the hotel in the middle of the block. The hotel, which has no sign or visible name, can be identified by the flags above the entrance. Consult the daily entertainment schedule for session times.

Studio Tours

Disney-MGM Studios Animation Tour

Type of Attraction: Walking tour of the Disney Animation Studio
When to Go: Before 11 A.M. and after 5 P.M.
Author's Rating: A masterpiece; not to be missed; ★★★★½
Overall Appeal by Age Group:

Pre-school	Grade School	Teens	Young Adults	Over 30	Senior Citizens
★★★★	★★★★	★★★★	★★★★★	★★★★★	★★★★★

Duration of Presentation: 36 minutes
Preshow Entertainment: Gallery of animation art in waiting area
Average Wait in Line per 100 People Ahead of You: 7 minutes

DESCRIPTION AND COMMENTS Disney-MGM Studios Animation Tour gives the public, for the first time, the opportunity to watch Disney artists at work. Since Disneyland opened in 1955, Walt Disney Productions has been petitioned by its fans to operate an animation studio tour. Finally, after a brief three-and-a-half decade wait, an admiring public can watch artists create beloved Disney characters.

The Animation Tour more than exceeds expectations. Much more than watching a few artists at work, the tour is dynamic, fast-paced, educational, and most of all, fun. After entering the Animation Building, most guests spend a few minutes waiting in a gallery of Disney animation art. Use your waiting time to enjoy this combination of art and animation history. From the gallery, guests enter a theater where an eight-and-a-half minute introductory film on animation is shown. Starring Walter Cronkite and Robin Williams as your tour hosts, the film is an absolute delight.

After the film, guests enter the working studio, where they view artists and technicians at work through large plate glass viewing windows. Arranged according to the sequence of creation for an animated production, each work station and task is explained by hosts Walter and Robin via video monitors mounted in each area. Starting with story and character development, guests work sequentially through animation (where the characters are brought to life in rough art), to clean up (where the rough art is refined to finished line drawings), to effects and backgrounds (where backgrounds for the characters are developed), to photocopying, where drawings are transferred from paper to plastic sheets, called cels, prior to being finished with ink and paint. Finally the cels are photographed, put together, and edited.

Having completed the walk-through of the working studio, guests gather in another holding area and view a multimonitor video presentation in which the Disney animators share their personal perspectives on the creative process. While it serves the purpose of keeping guests occupied and entertained while awaiting the conclusion of the tour, the presentation is especially warm and endearing, and worthwhile in its own right.

Finally, guests are seated in a commodious theater to enjoy a concluding film. Pulling together all the elements of animation production, the film features clips from many Disney animation classics.

TOURING TIPS   On some days the Animation Tour does not open until II A.M., by which time the park is pretty full. Check the daily entertainment schedule to determine the Animation Tour's hours, and try to go before noon. The Animation Tour is a relatively small-volume attraction, and lines begin to build on busy days by mid- to late morning.

After the introductory film, when you enter the working part of the studio, feel free to stay and watch as long as you like. The Cronkite and Williams narrative (on video monitors in each work area) rolls along in sequence at a fairly brisk pace and most guests try to keep up. Since at each work station the video repeats about every two to three minutes, you can let the better part of your 160-person tour group work past you while you hang out at the first station. Then take your time, watching the artists and technicians as long as you wish. You will most likely catch up with your group. If you don't, no big deal; enjoy the conclusion of the tour with the next group.

Backstage Studio Tour

Type of Attraction: Combination tram and walking tour of modern film and video production

When to Go: Anytime

Author's Rating: One of Disney's better efforts; efficient, compelling, informative, fun; not to be missed; ★★★★

Overall Appeal by Age Group:

Pre-school	Grade School	Teens	Young Adults	Over 30	Senior Citizens
★★★★½	★★★★½	★★★★	★★★★½	★★★★	★★★★

Duration of Presentation: About 1 hour overall; 15 minutes for the tram segment, and 40 minutes for the walking segment called *Inside the Magic*

Special Comments: You can discontinue the tour, if you wish, following the tram segment

Preshow Entertainment: Musicians in the entrance plaza and a video in the tram boarding area

Average Wait in Line per 100 People Ahead of You: 2 minutes

Assumes: 16 tour departures per hour

Loading Speed: Fast

DESCRIPTION AND COMMENTS Approximately two-thirds of the Disney-MGM Studios is occupied by a working film and television facility, where throughout the year actors, artists, and technicians work on various productions. Everything from TV commercials, specials, and game shows to feature motion pictures are produced here. Visitors to the Disney-MGM Studios can avail themselves of a veritable "behind-the-scenes" education in the methods and technologies of motion picture and television production. The vehicle for this learning experience is a comprehensive tour of the working studios.

At the end of Hollywood Boulevard, to the right of the Chinese Theater (The Great Movie Ride), guests enter the limited-access area through an ornate studio gate (a sort of art deco version of the Arc de Triomphe) into a large plaza. In the plaza, lines form for the Backstage Studio Tour on the left and for the Animation Tour (described earlier) on the right.

The Tram Segment

As the anchor (though perhaps not the most popular) attraction at Disney-MGM, the Backstage Studio Tour is fast-paced, informative, and well designed. Divided into riding and walking segments, the tour begins aboard the ever-faithful tram. Departing (on busy days) about once every four minutes, the tour winds among various production and shop buildings and on to the elaborate back lot sets.

The Backstage Studio Tour stops first at the wardrobe and crafts shops. Here costumes are designed, created, and stored, as are sets and props. From the tram, guests watch craftsmen at work through large picture windows in the shops.

The tour proceeds to the winding streets of the back lot where western desert canyons and New York City brownstones exist side by side with suburban residential streets. The highlight of the back lot tour for many is going through Catastrophe Canyon, a special-effects adventure that includes a thunderstorm, an earthquake, an oil-field fire, and a flash flood.

The tram portion of the tour terminates at the Backstage Plaza, where guests can avail themselves of rest rooms, food, and shopping (if they desire) before commencing the walking part of the tour. To reach the starting point of the walking segment, follow the large, pink rabbit footprints out of the tram unloading area.

The Walking Segment: Inside the Magic

Taking the walking segment of the Backstage Studio Tour immediately following the tram segment is not mandatory. You can take a break after getting off the tram and return to finish the walking tour anytime you wish. However, there is something to be said for the educational continuity of experiencing the segments back-to-back, not to mention the convenience. If you do elect to go directly from the tram segment to the walking segment, however, we recommend using the rest room in between. The walking segment lasts over a half-hour with no opportunity for pit stops. Also be aware that you will be walking and standing the entire time.

The first stop is a special-effects water tank where technicians explain the mechanical and optical tricks that "turn the seemingly impossible into on-screen reality." Included here are rain effects, a naval battle, and a storm at sea. The waiting area for this part of the tour features a display of miniature navy vessels used in the filming of famous war movies.

Next, guests enter the special effects workshop, where the arts of enlargement, miniaturization, stop-frame photographic animation, and other technical mysteries are demonstrated and explained.

After special effects it's on to the soundstages, where specially designed and soundproofed observation platforms allow unobtrusive viewing of ongoing productions. After the guide explains the basics of whatever productions are in progress (if any), guests view a video that explores the technical and artistic aspects of soundstage work.

Finally, guests enjoy a four-minute movie, *The Lottery*, starring Bette Midler, that was produced in its entirety at the Disney-MGM Studios. In addition to being amusing, *The Lottery* provides an example of a finished production. At the next stop guests inspect the sets and props used in *The Lottery* and watch a video explaining how the film was produced. After all of the behind-the-scenes secrets are revealed, guests walk among the sets, props, and special-effects equipment for a closer inspection. The tour exits on Mickey Avenue near the entrance to *The Making of Pocahontas*.

TOURING TIPS   Do not be discouraged if the line for the tram segment appears long when you arrive. Trams depart (on busy days) about every 4 minutes and each tram can hold as many as 200 guests. During warm weather months, the most comfortable time of day to take the tram portion of the Backstage Studio Tour is in the evening. A drawback to this is most of the behind-the-scenes workers have gone home. Their absence, however, only affects a small part of the tour.

You will almost never have to wait longer than 15 minutes to join the tour for the walking segment.

Not to Be Missed at the Disney-MGM Studios

Star Tours
Backstage Studios Tour
Animation Tour
Indiana Jones Stunt Spectacular
The Great Movie Ride
MuppetVision 4-D
Voyage of the Little Mermaid
"The Twilight Zone" Tower of Terror

Live Entertainment at the Disney-MGM Studios

Until 1993, live entertainment, parades, and special events were not as fully developed or as elaborate at the Disney-MGM Studios as at the Magic Kingdom or EPCOT Center. With the introduction of Aladdin's Royal Caravan parade and the *Beauty and the Beast* stage show, the Disney-MGM Studios joined the big leagues. These outstanding performances, coupled with the Sorcery in the Sky fireworks spectacular, give the Studios a live entertainment repertoire every bit as compelling as that offered by the other parks.

Aladdin's Royal Caravan

A daytime parade that begins near the park's main entrance, continues down Hollywood Boulevard, and circles in front of The Great Movie Ride. From there it passes in front of Superstar Television and *Monster Sound* and eventually winds up by Star Tours. An alternate route begins at the far end of Sunset Boulevard and turns right onto Hollywood Boulevard. The parade features huge, inflated versions of the characters from Disney's animated feature *Aladdin*, as well as stilt walkers, floats, bands, and acrobats. Colorful, creative, and totally upbeat, Aladdin's Royal Caravan may be Disney's most entertaining daytime parade. Because the *Aladdin* parade will begin its fourth season in 1996, there is some speculation that it will be replaced by a parade based on *Legend of the Lion King*. Stay tuned.

Staged one to three times a day, the parade brings pedestrian traffic to a standstill along its route and makes moving from one part of the park to another problematic. If you are anywhere along the parade route when the Caravan gets underway, your best bet is to stay put and enjoy it. Unlike Magic Kingdom parades, there are no unusually good or frequently overlooked vantage points for *Aladdin*.

Theater of the Stars

This covered amphitheater on Sunset Boulevard is the stage for a variety of production reviews, usually featuring music from Disney movies and starring Disney characters. Performance times are posted in front of the theater and are listed in the daily entertainment schedule.

Disney Characters

In addition to appearing at the Theater of the Stars and in parades, Disney characters, particularly Mickey, Minnie, and Roger Rabbit, can be found in the Studio Courtyard. They're usually in front of the Animation Building, in the Backstage Plaza, or along Mickey Avenue (which runs next to the soundstages). Mickey and the Teenage Mutant Ninja Turtles appear for autographs and photos (though not together) on New York Street at times listed in the daily entertainment schedule. Finally, a character breakfast featuring characters from *Aladdin* is offered most mornings at the Soundstage restaurants from 8:30 until 10:15 A.M.

Mickey Mouse Club

The Mickey Mouse Club is taped on one of the Studios' soundstages. Inquire at the Production Information Window, just inside the main entrance and to the right, if you would like to join the audience. In addition to the taping, cast members participate in casual conversation on the stage of the Backlot Theater. Conversation time is listed in the daily entertainment schedule.

Star Today

Some days there is a visiting celebrity at the Studios. In addition to riding in a motorcade on Hollywood Boulevard, the star appears at various locations and sits for interviews, etc. To find out if a star is visiting, inquire at Guest Services at the entrance end of Hollywood Boulevard.

Sorcery in the Sky Fireworks	An excellent fireworks show based on Mickey Mouse's exploits in his role as the Sorcerer's apprentice in *Fantasia*. Held daily at closing time, when the park stays open after dark. Watch the show from anywhere along Hollywood Boulevard.
Street Entertainment	Street entertainment is provided along Hollywood and Sunset boulevards in the form of jugglers and other roving performers. The Studios has its own modest marching band and a tuba quartet, both of which play in the Hollywood Boulevard, Sunset Boulevard, Studio Courtyard, and Echo Lake areas. While not exactly street entertainment, a piano player performs daily at the Brown Derby.

Eating at Disney-MGM Studios

Dining in the Disney-MGM Studios is more interesting than in the Magic Kingdom and less ethnic than at EPCOT Center. Disney-MGM has four reservations-recommended restaurants, the Hollywood Brown Derby, the '50s Prime Time Cafe, the Sci-Fi Dine-In Theater Restaurant, and Mama Melrose's Ristorante Italiano. We receive a fair amount of mail from readers who tell us about their Disney-MGM dining experiences. The following comments are typical:

From a Sumter, South Carolina, man:

> We had lunch at the Sci-Fi Dine-In. In the guide you gave it a terrible review, but I have always felt you guys are too hard on the Disney restaurants, so we went ahead and ate there. Well, on this one you were right on target! While the atmosphere was fun, and the clips were a hoot, the food was lousy . . . and expensive!

From a Maryland reader:

> Prime Time Cafe was a fun experience, but again, the food quality was, at best, mediocre. If my mom really did cook that way, I would have many times run away from home. Our poor reaction to the food quality pushed us quickly into the car and out of WDW. I never thought I would get down on my knees and kiss the sidewalk outside of a Perkins Pancake House.

And finally:

> The Brown Derby was a special treat. Sitting in one of the wall booths enveloped by the wood paneling [listening to] the piano player, dressed in the style of a by-gone era, was a real experience. One word I think you should mention is about the Cobb salad. The lettuce was PULVERIZED—not what I expected. I am used to having a salad with lettuce I could recognize. I would not order it again. The oyster-brie soup on the other hand was fabulous! I asked for

the recipe and they very generously brought me a pre-printed copy.

For ratings and detailed profiles of the Disney-MGM Studios' full-service restaurants, refer to Dining In and Around Walt Disney World, pages 265–322. Restaurants are listed by name in alphabetical order.

Reservations. Make reservations at the door of the restaurant; at the Restaurant Reservations Desk on the corner of Hollywood and Sunset Boulevards; or, for Walt Disney World lodging and campground guests, by dialing 55 or 56 at least one day, but no more than three days, in advance. If you want to try a Disney-MGM Studios full-service restaurant, but do not have reservations, try walking in at about 11 A.M. or from 3 to 4 P.M. Note that in 1995, Disney quietly began accepting advance dining reservations (at the (407) 939-3463 number) from guests lodging *outside* of Walt Disney World. Because this practice contradicts Disney's stated policy, there's no telling how long it will last.

Other Disney-MGM Studios Restaurants

A cut below the headliner restaurants is Hollywood and Vine, featuring baby-back ribs, steaks, prime rib, rotisserie chicken, and a variety of salads. Lunch entrees run $6–11; dinners run $8–15. Beer and wine are available.

For the masses, the Studios has several bulk loaders: the 560-seat Soundstage Restaurant, the 600-seat Backlot Express, and a number of small sandwich and pastry vendors. Menu offerings are varied and interesting, running the gamut from down-home cooking to California *nouvelle cuisine*. Beer and wine can be purchased at the Soundstage Restaurant and Backlot Express.

The Disney-MGM Studios has three bars, the large Catwalk Bar, upstairs over the Soundstage Restaurant; the Tune-In Lounge (part of the '50s Prime Time Cafe); and the pleasant, old neighborhood bar at Mama Melrose's Ristorante Italiano.

Shopping at Disney-MGM Studios

Shops throughout the park carry movie-oriented merchandise and, of course, lots of Disney trademark souvenir items. Most of the shopping is concentrated on Hollywood Boulevard and features movie nostalgia goodies ranging from JuJubes (if you are over 40, you still probably have some stuck in your teeth) to black-and-white postcards of the stars.

Unusual shops include the Animation Gallery, which is located in the Animation Building and markets reproductions of "cels" from animated features and other animation art. Sid Cahuenga's near the main entrance sells vintage movie posters and celebrity autographs. Mickey's of Hollywood on Hollywood Boulevard is the place to buy Disney trademark merchandise.

Disney-MGM Studios One-Day Touring Plan for Visitors of All Ages

Because it offers a smaller number of attractions, touring Disney-MGM Studios is not as complicated as touring the Magic Kingdom or EPCOT Center. In addition, most Disney-MGM rides and shows are oriented to the entire family, thus eliminating differences of opinion regarding how to spend the day. Where in the Magic Kingdom Mom and Dad want to see *The Hall of Presidents*, Big Sis is revved up to ride Space Mountain, and the preschool twins are clamoring for Dumbo, the Flying Elephant, at Disney-MGM Studios the whole family can pretty much see and enjoy everything together.

Since there are fewer attractions at Disney-MGM than at the other parks, the crowds are more concentrated. If a line seems unusually long, ask a Disney-MGM attendant what the estimated wait is. If you find the wait is too long, try the same attraction again while *Indiana Jones* is in progress or while a parade or some special event is going on. All of these activities serve to draw people away from the lines.

The Disney-MGM Studios One-Day Touring Plan assumes a willingness to experience all major rides and shows. Be forewarned that Star Tours, The Great Movie Ride, the Tower of Terror, and the Catastrophe Canyon segment of the Backstage Studios Tram Tour are sometimes frightening to children under eight years old. Star Tours, additionally, can be upsetting to anyone prone to motion sickness.

When following the touring plan, simply skip any attraction you do not wish to experience. Likewise, if you are a Disney resort or campground guest, and take part in the early-entry program, simply skip any step in the touring plan that calls for you to visit attractions you have already seen. Try to time your early-entry touring so that you arrive at *The Voyage of the Little Mermaid* ten minutes before the first scheduled show. If you are not eligible for early entry, or visit during the summer or a holiday period, plan to visit the Disney-MGM Studios on one of the days when early entry is not scheduled.

Before You Go

1. Call (407) 824-4321 the day before you go for the official opening times.
2. Purchase your admission prior to arrival. You can either order tickets through the mail or buy them at a local Disney Store before you leave home. You can also buy them at the Walt Disney World Information Center off I-75 near Ocala, if you are driving. If you arrive by plane, purchase your admission at the Disney Store in the Orlando airport or at a Walt Disney World resort hotel.
3. If you are lodging at a Walt Disney World hotel or campground, make lunch and dinner reservations (if desired) before your arrival. Dial 55 or 56 to make Disney-MGM lunch and dinner reservations. You can make your restaurant reservations from home or en route by calling (407) 939-3463. As an aside, Disney reservationists at this number have been known to accept advance dining reservations from guests not staying in Disney hotels.
4. Because the performance schedule for live entertainment changes from month to month and even from day to day, you will have some variables with which to contend. Carefully review the first six steps in the touring plan so that you will know what your options are.

At the Disney-MGM Studios

1. Arrive at the park 40 minutes before the official opening time. Obtain a daily entertainment schedule. Wait at the entrance turnstiles to be admitted.

    On your daily entertainment schedule, check out the time for the first performance of *Voyage of the Little Mermaid*.
2. When you are admitted to the park (which may be at the official opening time or 30 minutes early), blow down Hollywood Boulevard and turn right at Sunset Boulevard. Proceed to the Tower of Terror and ride. If you have small children or terrified adults in your party, take advantage of switching off (see page 166). If the Tower of Terror does not sound appealing first thing in the morning, skip ahead to Step 3.

3. Having (hopefully) survived the Tower of Terror, backtrack to Hollywood Boulevard and bear right. Disney cast members may try to direct you to *Indiana Jones* as you proceed down Hollywood Boulevard. Though they are well meaning, stick to the plan. At the far end of Hollywood Boulevard, turn right through the large arch (on your right beyond the Brown Derby restaurant), and then take a hard left to the *Voyage of the Little Mermaid*. Get in line.

Once you are admitted indoors to the preshow area at the *Little Mermaid*, position yourself next to the doors leading to the theater. When these doors open, enter the theater and pick a row of seats, allowing about six folks to enter the row ahead of you. Your objective is to score seats near the exit doors on the far side, but not to get stuck with the four or five seats closest to the exits. This strategy will ensure a good view of the stage and will also put you in a perfect position to be one of the first to exit at the conclusion of the show.

NOTE: On days when the official opening time is 9 A.M., the gates almost always open at 8:30 A.M., with the first performance of the *Little Mermaid* at 9 A.M. If you are one of the first through the turnstiles at 8:30 A.M., and if your whole party is capable of pretty good speed, you should be able to experience the Tower of Terror before going to *Voyage of the Little Mermaid*. It depends on the crowd, but you've usually got about 26 minutes to hustle to the Tower of Terror, ride, and get to *Little Mermaid* before the 9 A.M. show fills up. It can be done, but you can't fool around. If all this sounds too Type A to suit your vacation mentality, blow off the Tower of Terror and head straight for the *Little Mermaid*, or vice versa.

Incidentally, on days when guests are admitted on the hour (instead of on the half hour), the first showing of *Voyage of the Little Mermaid* is usually 15 minutes after the hour. When this schedule is in operation, don't even think about the Tower of Terror if you want to see the *Little Mermaid* without a 45-minute-plus wait.

4. At the conclusion of the *Little Mermaid*, the exit doors to your left will open automatically. Bear right on exiting the theater and backtrack to Hollywood Boulevard. Experience the Great Movie Ride.

5. After The Great Movie Ride head for Star Tours. Pass in front of SuperStar Television and then bear right on the far side of the *Monster Sound Show*. Ride Star Tours.

6. After Star Tours, exit to the left and enter the square with the Muppet fountain. See *Muppet Vision 4-D*.

7. After the Muppets, check your daily entertainment schedule for the next performance of *Indiana Jones*. If you are within 45 minutes of the next performance, head for the Stunt Spectacular Theater and line up. If there are less than 25 minutes until showtime, that performance may possibly be sold out. If this is the case, ask an *Indiana Jones* attendant how early you should arrive to be assured of a seat at the next scheduled performance. Make plans accordingly.

8. Next, backtrack through the studios arch (past the *Little Mermaid*) and continue across the square to the Animation Building on the far right. Take the Animation Tour. If you are in need of a rest room, you will find them at the *left* rear of the same square.

9. We do not include a restaurant meal as part of this touring plan. If you want to try one of Disney-MGM's full-service restaurants, make your reservations now. Reservations can be made at the door of the restaurant of your choice or at the Restaurant Reservations Desk at the intersection of Hollywood and Sunset Boulevards. Walt Disney World lodging and campground guests can make advance reservations by dialing 55 or 56. The Studios' full-service restaurants are reviewed and rated in Part Eight: Dining In and Around Walt Disney World, pages 265–322.

10. Passing through the archway to the left of the Animation Building, proceed to the tram loading area of the Backstage Studio Tour. Board a tram and enjoy. The tram tour takes about 15 minutes.

11. When you get off the tram, follow the pink rabbit footprints to the entrance of the walking segment of the tour (described in Disney handouts as *Inside the Magic*). If you need a rest room, refreshment, or lunch break before beginning the walking segment, go ahead. When you are ready for the tour, just follow the pink footprints to the starting point. The walking segment, once underway, takes about a half-hour.

12. After the walking tour, see *The Making of Pocahontas* located on Mickey Avenue between the soundstages and *Voyage of the Little Mermaid*.

13. At this point the park's greatest potential bottlenecks are behind you. Review the daily entertainment schedule to see if there are any parades, live shows, or special events that interest you. Work them into your itinerary.

14. By now you will have seen all the major attractions except Super-Star Television, the *Monster Sound Show*, and possibly *Indiana Jones*. If you have not seen *Indiana Jones*, make it your top priority, ideally arriving at the Stunt Spectacular Theater 40–45 minutes before the next scheduled showtime. If you have already seen *Indiana Jones*, check the daily entertainment scheduled for Super-Star Television performance times. If a performance is scheduled within the next 20 to 30 minutes, go ahead and enjoy SuperStar Television. Otherwise, see the *Monster Sound Show* first. When you check out the line at the *Monster Sound Show*, be aware that this attraction is often inundated following a performance of *Indiana Jones* nearby. If the *Monster Sound Show* has a long line when you arrive, chalk it up to bad timing and try again later.

15. After the *Monster Sound Show* and SuperStar Television, bear right and explore the New York street set.

16. Tour Hollywood and Sunset boulevards. Consult your daily entertainment schedule for parades, special events, and theater performances. Musicals performed at the Theater of the Stars are particularly worthy of your attention.

17. This concludes the touring plan. Eat, shop, enjoy live entertainment, or revisit your favorite Disney-MGM attraction as desired. When you're ready to leave the park, walk (the Disney-MGM parking lot is not all that big) or take a tram to your car.

Universal Studios Florida

Universal City Studios, Inc., has been running a studios tour and movie-theme tourist attraction for more than 25 years, predating all of the Disney parks except Disneyland. In the early 1980s, Universal announced plans to build a studios/theme park complex in Florida. While Universal labored over its new project, however, the Disney organization jumped into high gear and rushed its own studios/theme park onto the market, beating out Universal by a year and a half.

Universal Studios Florida opened its doors to the public in June of 1990. At that time it was almost four times the size of the Disney-MGM Studios (Disney-MGM having expanded somewhat subsequently), with much more of the total facility accessible to the visiting public. Like its sister facility in Hollywood, Universal Studios Florida is spacious, beautifully landscaped, meticulously clean, and delightfully varied in its entertainment offerings. Yet, in certain important, almost critical ways, the Florida complex is quite different from Universal Studios Hollywood.

Universal Studios Hollywood is one of the most well-conceived and well-executed tourist attractions in the world. It accommodates large numbers of guests with practically no waiting in line. While Disneyland, several miles away, was testing new techniques in queuing management (how to keep guests happy standing in a line for 45 minutes), Universal Studios was operating a park where lines were the exception, not the rule.

After buying admission to Universal Studios Hollywood, each guest is assigned a reservation for the Tram Tour, a well-paced, multisegmented tour of Universal's famed film and television studios. Educational, dramatic, and exciting, the tour is a clinic in television and motion picture art and is the feature attraction of the park. Guests are relieved of the drudgery of waiting in line for the tour by simply showing up at the embarkation point at their appointed reservation time. Many surprises are built into the tour, including an attack by "Jaws," an earthquake, and an encounter with King Kong. In addition to being a wonderful experience, the Tram Tour is also easy on the feet.

All other attractions at Universal Studios Hollywood are extra-large theaters featuring various movie- and TV-theme presentations that are performed according to a show schedule (provided to each guest on admission). Once again there are no lines. As show time approaches, guests simply enter the empty theater and take a seat, first-come-first-serve. No lines, no standing, no bother, plus you get to wait for the show sitting down in the theater.

As Universal Studios Hollywood has engineered one of the most guest-considerate and stress-free theme attractions in the world, it is only logical to expect that Universal Studios would build on these same proven, successful techniques when designing a second-generation, mega-attraction in Florida. Right? Think again.

Incredibly, at Universal Studios Florida, the Universal planners and designers trashed most of the formats and techniques that made the Hollywood park so exceptional, electing instead to develop an attraction in the Disney style, with hours of waiting and miles of walking. In Hollywood, Universal created a superior product by going in a different direction, marching to their own beat. In Florida, unfortunately, Universal has tried to "out Disney" Disney, and the results have been mixed.

Gone in Florida is the all-encompassing tram tour, and the much appreciated reservation system. Gone, also, is any sort of integrated educational presentation on movie and television production. True, there are individual shows on costuming and make-up, set construction, special effects, film making, and post production, but it is unlikely that each patron will see them all or that the presentations will be viewed in any sort of logical sequence. Worst, in California a guest gets all the above during the Tram Tour with no wait; in Florida a guest must wait in line for each different show.

Then, there are the rides. In Hollywood, there is one ride, the Tram Tour. Everything, from earthquakes to avalanches to an attack by "Jaws," happens while you ride the tram. At Universal Studios Florida, the rides are more in the Disney mold, i.e., totally separate ride/adventure experiences. On the bright side, the Universal Florida rides are exciting and innovative, and as with many Disney rides, focus on familiar and/or beloved motion picture characters or situations.

On Universal Studios Florida's E.T. ride, you escape the authorities on a flying bike and leave the earth for a visit to E.T.'s home planet. In Kongfrontation, King Kong tears up a city with you in it. In Jaws, the persistent great white makes heart-stopping assaults on your small boat, and in Earthquake — The Big One, special effects create the most realistic

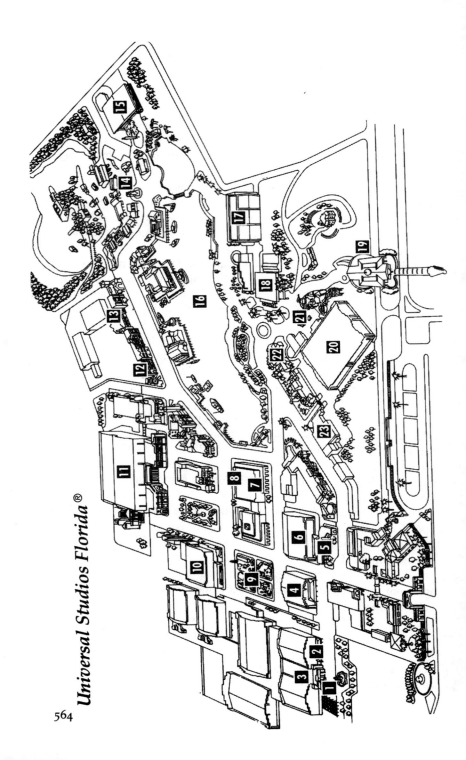

Universal Studios Florida ®

For daily operating hours and other information call (407) 363-8000.

1 Production Studio Tram Tour

2 Nickelodeon Tour

3 Nickelodeon® Studios®

4 The Funtastic World of Hanna-Barbera™

5 Lucy: A Tribute℠

6 Hitchcock's 3-D Theatre

7 "Murder, She Wrote"® Mystery Theatre

8 The Adventures of Rocky and Bullwinkle™

9 The Boneyard

10 Ghostbusters® Spooktacular

11 Kongfrontation®

12 Beetlejuice's™ Graveyard Revue

13 Earthquake®--The Big One

14 JAWS®

15 The Wild, Wild, Wild West Stunt Show℠

Selected Rides and Shows presented on a weather permitting or seasonal basis.

16 Dynamite Nights Stunt Spectacular®

17 Back To The Future® ...The Ride℠

18 Animal Actors Stage®

19 Hard Rock Café®

20 E.T. Adventure®

21 Fievel's Playland®

22 AT&T at the Movies

23 The Gory Gruesome & Grotesque Horror Make-Up Show

earthquake simulation ever produced. The Funtastic World of Hanna-Barbera places you in a bucking rocket simulator for a high-speed chase with Yogi Bear and the Flintstones. Finally, guests ride in a Delorean-cum-time machine in yet another chase, this one based on the film *Back to the Future*.

While many of these rides represent prototypical state-of-the-art technology and live up to their advance billing in terms of excitement, creativity, uniqueness, and special effects, they unfortunately lack the capacity to handle the number of guests who frequent major Florida tourist destinations. If a ride has great appeal, but can accommodate only a small number of guests per ride or per hour, long lines will form. It is not unusual for the wait to exceed an hour and a quarter for the E.T. ride, and 50 minutes for the Hanna-Barbera ride.

Happily, most of the shows and theater performances at Universal Studios Florida are in good-sized theaters, which accommodate large numbers of people. Since most performances run continuously, waits usually do not exceed twice the performance time of the show (40 to 50 minutes). Many shows are multisegmented, with the audience moving to three or more staging areas during the course of the presentation.

—— *Growth Spurt*

Universal Studios Florida announced plans in 1994 for a second theme park based on Steven Spielberg's motion picture *Jurassic Park*. In addition to the theme park, the multibillion dollar expansion will also include a nighttime entertainment complex, five hotels, a convention facility, a golf course, and a tennis center. Construction is scheduled to begin in late 1995 or in 1996, and will continue in phases until the project, to be called Universal City Florida, is complete.

—— *Arriving and Getting Oriented*

Today's Universal Studios Florida is located on Kirkman Road, accessible from I-4 via exits 29 or 30B. The parking lot holds about 7,000 cars and is filled each day starting with those areas closest to the gate. Parking costs $5 for cars and $7 for RV's and trailers. A tram transports guests to the ticket booths and entrance. One-Day and Two-Day Tickets are available (including tax) at about $37 and $55, respectively, for adults; $30 and $44 for children (3 to 9). Annual Passes cost about $94 for adults and $75 for children.

Universal Studios Florida is laid out in an upside down "L" configuration. Beyond the main entrance, a wide boulevard stretches past a number of rides and shows down to a New York City back lot set. Branching off this major pedestrian thoroughfare to the right are five streets that access other areas of the studios and ultimately intersect a promenade circling a large lake.

The park is divided into six sections: the Front Lot, Production Central, New York, Hollywood, San Francisco/Amity, and Expo Center. Where one section begins and another ends is a little blurry, but no matter. Guests orient themselves by the major rides, sets, and landmarks, and will refer, for instance, to "New York," "the waterfront," "over by E.T.," or "by Mel's Diner." Overall, the area of Universal Studios Florida open to guest visitation is about the same size as EPCOT Center.

Universal Studios Florida offers all the services and amenities you would expect from a major theme park including: stroller and wheelchair rental, lockers, diaper-changing and infant-nursing facilities, car assistance, and foreign language assistance. Most of the studios are accessible to disabled guests and TDD's are available to the hearing impaired. Almost all of the Universal Studios Florida services are located in the Front Lot, just inside the main entrance.

In an earlier edition of the *Unofficial Guide* we listed the Universal Studios Florida information number as (407) 636-8000. In revising the guide we routinely called to verify the number and reached the following recorded message: "Hello, you have reached the Universal Studios Florida dyslexic hot line. If you dialed '636-' instead of '363-' 8000, you have reached the right number."

Sorry to contribute to the confusion, guys. The correct number for information is (407) 363-8000.

Universal Studios Florida Attractions

The Funtastic World of Hanna-Barbera

Type of Attraction: Flight-simulation ride

When to Go: Before 11 A.M.

Special Comments: Very intense for some
  preschoolers

Author's Rating: A delight for all ages; ★★★½

Motion
Sickness

WARNING!

Overall Appeal by Age Group:

Pre-school	Grade School	Teens	Young Adults	Over 30	Senior Citizens
★★★★	★★★★½	★★★★	★★★★	★★★★	★★★★

Duration of Ride: 4½ minutes with a 3½ minute preshow
Loading Speed: Moderate to slow

DESCRIPTION AND COMMENTS A flight-simulation ride in the same family as Disney's Star Tours and Body Wars, except that all the visuals are cartoons. Guests accompany Yogi Bear in a high-speed chase to rescue a child snatched by kidnappers.

TOURING TIPS This wild, funny, and thoroughly delightful ride is also unfortunately a cycle ride (the whole ride must shut down during loading and unloading). Consequently large lines build early in the day and move very slowly. Ride during the first two hours the park is open.

"Alfred Hitchcock: The Art of Making Movies"

Type of Attraction: Mini-course on filming action sequences and a testimonial to the talents of Alfred Hitchcock
When to Go: After you have experienced all the rides
Special Comments: May frighten small children
Author's Rating: A little slow moving, but well done; ★★★½
Overall Appeal by Age Group:

Pre-school	Grade School	Teens	Young Adults	Over 30	Senior Citizens
★★½	★★★	★★★½	★★★½	★★★½	★★★½

Duration of Presentation: 40 minutes
Probable Waiting Time: 22 minutes

DESCRIPTION Guests view a film collage featuring famous scenes from Hitchcock films (including some unreleased 3-D footage), and then exit to an adjoining soundstage, where the stabbing scene from *Psycho* is recreated using professional actors and audience volunteers. Finally guests move to a third area, where the technology of filming action scenes on a soundstage is explained. The Hitchcock "greatest hits" film is disjointed and pretty confusing, unless you have a good recollection of the movies and scenes highlighted. The soundstage reenactment of the shower scene from *Psycho* is both informative and entertaining, as are the special sets and film techniques demonstrated in the third staging area.

TOURING TIPS   Because of its location just beyond the main entrance, the lines for the Hitchcock attraction appear long, but usually disappear quickly. In any event, we recommend you let the morning crowds clear, and postpone seeing this attraction until just before you leave the park in the evening.

Nickelodeon Studios Walking Tour

Type of Attraction: Behind-the-scenes guided tour
When to Go: When Nickelodeon shows are in production (usually weekdays)
Author's Rating: ★★★
Overall Appeal by Age Group:

Pre-school	Grade School	Teens	Young Adults	Over 30	Senior Citizens
★★½	★★★	★★★	★★★	★★★	★★★

Duration of Tour: 36 minutes
Probable Waiting Time: 30–45 minutes

DESCRIPTION AND COMMENTS   This walking tour of the Nickelodeon studio examines set construction, soundstages, wardrobe, props, lighting, video production, and special effects. While a lot of the same information is presented more creatively in the "Alfred Hitchcock," "Murder, She Wrote," and Horror Make-up Show productions, the Nickelodeon Tour is specifically tailored to kids. Not only are they made to feel supremely important on this tour, their opinions are used to shape future Nickelodeon programming.

A new addition to the tour, which adds some much needed zip, is "Game Lab," where guests preview strange games being tested for possible inclusion on Nickelodeon. The Game Lab segment ends with a lucky child getting "slimed." If this ritual is unknown to you, consult your children.

TOURING TIPS   While grade schoolers, in particular, enjoy this tour, it is pretty expendable for everyone else. Go on a second day at the Studios, or a second visit. If Nickelodeon is not in production, forget it entirely.

Production Tram Tour

Type of Attraction: Guided tram tour of the various outdoor sets

When to Go: Late in the afternoon

Special Comments: Not comparable to the Disney-MGM Studios tram tour

Author's Rating: Interesting; ★★½

Overall Appeal by Age Group:

Pre-school	Grade School	Teens	Young Adults	Over 30	Senior Citizens
★★	★★	★★	★★½	★★½	★★½

Duration of Tour: 20 minutes

Probable Waiting Time: Varies widely, but usually less than 12 minutes

DESCRIPTION AND COMMENTS   The tram tour offers guests an informative, effortless way to see the various sets on the back lot. Though you see essentially the same sights when you tour the park on foot, the background provided by the tram tour guide enhances your understanding and appreciation of the sets and props.

TOURING TIPS   We like the tram tour, if the wait to board is short. The tram tour offers a good general orientation to the studios, but is not the best way to use your time early in the morning. Try it late in the afternoon if you are interested in learning more about the sets.

"Ghostbusters"

Type of Attraction: Theater presentation featuring special effects from *Ghostbusters*

When to Go: Should be your first show after experiencing all of the rides

Special Comments: A limited potential for frightening young children

Author's Rating: Upbeat and fun with great special effects; ★★★★

Overall Appeal by Age Group:

Pre-school	Grade School	Teens	Young Adults	Over 30	Senior Citizens
★★★★	★★★★½	★★★★½	★★★★½	★★★★	★★★★

Duration of Presentation: 15 minutes

Probable Waiting Time: 26 minutes

DESCRIPTION AND COMMENTS   An elaborate set from *Ghostbusters* is used to demonstrate a variety of incredible special effects. Fast-paced with lots of humor, *Ghostbusters* has been improved with the addition of a new story line and an excellent preshow. The whole production is punctuated by the catchy rock theme from the movie.

TOURING TIPS   This is a fun show that draws big crowds. Enjoy "Ghostbusters" in the morning, after you've experienced the rides. Note that the entrance to "Ghostbusters" is not very well marked. Look for the "Ghostbusters" sign hanging over the sidewalk, and duck into the first open door to its right.

Kongfrontation

Type of Attraction: Adventure ride
When to Go: Before 11 A.M.
Special Comments: May frighten small children
Author's Rating: Not to be missed; ★★★★★
Overall Appeal by Age Group:

Pre-school	Grade School	Teens	Young Adults	Over 30	Senior Citizens
★★★½	★★★★★	★★★★★	★★★★	★★★★	★★★★

Duration of Ride: 4½ minutes
Loading Speed: Moderate

DESCRIPTION AND COMMENTS   At one of Universal Studios Florida's headliner attractions, guests board an aerial tram for a ride from Manhattan to Roosevelt Island. En route news reaches the group that the giant ape has escaped. The tram passes evidence of Kong's path of destruction and finally encounters the monster himself. In the course of the journey, King Kong demolishes buildings, uproots utility poles, swats helicopters, and hurls your tram car to the ground.

TOURING TIPS   A truly amazing piece of work; not to be missed. Ride in the morning following Back to the Future, E.T. Adventure, and Jaws.

The Gory Gruesome & Grotesque Horror Make-up Show

Type of Attraction: Theater presentation on the art of make-up
When to Go: After you have experienced all the rides
Special Comments: May frighten small children
Author's Rating: A gory knee-slapper; ★★★★
Overall Appeal by Age Group:

Pre-school	Grade School	Teens	Young Adults	Over 30	Senior Citizens
★★★	★★★★	★★★★	★★★½	★★★½	★★★½

Duration of Presentation: 25 minutes
Probable Waiting Time: 20 minutes

DESCRIPTION AND COMMENTS   A lively, well-paced look at how make-up artists create film monsters, realistic wounds, severed limbs, and other unmentionables. In addition to being one of the funnier and more up-beat presentations at Universal Studios, the *Horror Make-up Show* also presents a wealth of fascinating information. Overall, it is an excellent and enlightening, if somewhat gory, introduction to the blood-and-guts art of cinema monster-making.

TOURING TIPS   Exceeding most guest's expectations, the *Horror Make-up Show* is the "sleeper" attraction of Universal Studios. Presented in a tongue-in-cheek style, humor transcends the gruesome effects, and most folks (including preschoolers) take all the blood and guts in stride. It's usually not too hard to get into, so enjoy the *Horror Make-up Show* after you've had your fill of rides. The lobby of the theater that houses the *Make-up Show*, incidentally, has been turned into a *Jurassic Park* exhibit. We mention this because some guests have a hard time finding the new *Make-up Show* entrance situated off to the left.

"Murder, She Wrote" Mystery Theater

Type of Attraction: A multisequence mini-course on the post-production techniques of sound effects, editing, background music, and dubbing.
When to Go: After you have experienced all the rides
Special Comments: A nice air-conditioned break during the hottest part of the day

Author's Rating: Well presented; ★★★½
Overall Appeal by Age Group:

Pre-school	Grade School	Teens	Young Adults	Over 30	Senior Citizens
★★	★★½	★★★	★★★½	★★★★	★★★½

Duration of Presentation: 40 minutes
Probable Waiting Time: 20 minutes

DESCRIPTION AND COMMENTS   Guests move from theater to theater in this multisequence introduction to post-production technology. The presentation consists of editing, dubbing, and adding sound effects to a climactic scene from "Murder, She Wrote." Members of the audience are recruited to assist with the sound effects and voice-overs.

TOURING TIPS   Informative, worthwhile, and often hilarious, "Murder, She Wrote" does a good job of making fairly technical information understandable. In spite of the name, there is nothing here that will intimidate small children. We recommend enjoying the show during the heat of the day.

Earthquake — The Big One

Type of Attraction: Combination theater presentation and adventure ride
When to Go: In the morning, after Kongfrontation
Special Comments: May frighten small children
Author's Rating: Not to be missed; ★★★★½
Overall Appeal by Age Group:

Pre-school	Grade School	Teens	Young Adults	Over 30	Senior Citizens
★★★	★★★★★	★★★★★	★★★★½	★★★★½	★★★★½

Duration of Presentation: 20 minutes
Loading Speed: Moderate

DESCRIPTION AND COMMENTS   Guests view a film on how miniatures are used to create special effects in earthquake movies, followed by a demonstration of how miniatures, blue screen, and matte painting are integrated with live-action stunt sequences (starring audience volunteers) to achieve a realistic final product. Next, guests board a subway from Oakland to San Francisco, and experience an earthquake — the big one. Special effects range from fires and runaway trains to exploding tanker trucks and tidal waves. This ride is one of Universal's more compelling efforts. Not to be missed.

TOURING TIPS   Experience Earthquake in the morning, after you've gone on Back to the Future, E.T., Jaws, and Kongfrontation.

Jaws

Type of Attraction: Adventure boat ride
When to Go: Before II A.M.
Special Comments: Will frighten small children
Author's Rating: Not to be missed; ★★★★★
Overall Appeal by Age Group:

Pre-school	Grade School	Teens	Young Adults	Over 30	Senior Citizens
★★★★	★★★★★	★★★★★	★★★★★	★★★★★	★★★★½

Duration of Ride: 5 minutes
Loading Speed: Fast

DESCRIPTION AND COMMENTS   The original Jaws ride never operated dependably, and was ultimately closed and dismantled. A new ride, in which guests on an excursion boat encounter and do battle with the great white shark, was opened in the summer of 1993. This version, while also mechanically temperamental, manages to stay up and running most of the time. Rated as "not to be missed," the current version delivers five minutes of nonstop action, with the huge shark attacking again and again. A West Virginia woman, fresh from the Magic Kingdom, told us the shark is "about as pesky as that witch in Snow White." While the storyline is entirely predictable, the shark is quite realistic and about twice the size of Rush Limbaugh. What makes the ride truly unique is that there is a sense of journey. Far from floating into the middle of a pond and being interminably assaulted by a fat rubber fish, Jaws builds an amazing degree of suspense and anticipation into the brief five-minute ride. Add inventive sets and some powerful special effects, and you've got a first-rate attraction.

A variable in the Jaws experience is the enthusiasm and acting ability of your boat guide. Throughout the ride, the guide is called on to set the proper tone, elaborate the plot, drive the boat, and fight the shark. Most of the guides are quite good. They may overact a bit, but you can't fault them for lack of enthusiasm. Consider also that each guide goes through this wrenching ordeal once every eight minutes.

TOURING TIPS   Jaws is as well designed to handle crowds as any theme park attraction in Florida. By our calculation, you should have only a three-minute wait for every 100 guests ahead of you (if all 8 of Jaws' boats are up and running). People on the left side of the boat tend to get splashed more. Skip Jaws if your children are not particularly stalwart, or use the Switching Off option (see page 166). Try to ride before 11 A.M.

Back to the Future

Type of Attraction: Flight simulator thrill ride
When to Go: First thing in the morning
Special Comments: Very rough ride; may induce
    motion sickness. Must be 3'4" tall to ride.
    Switching off option available (see page 166).
Author's Rating: Not to be missed, if you have a strong stomach;
    ★★★★★
Overall Appeal by Age Group:

Pre-school	Grade School	Teens	Young Adults	Over 30	Senior Citizens
†	★★★★★	★★★★★	★★★★★	★★★★	★★½

† Sample size too small for an accurate rating
Duration of Ride: 4½ minutes
Loading Speed: Moderate

DESCRIPTION AND COMMENTS   This attraction is to Universal Studios Florida what Space Mountain is to the Magic Kingdom: the most popular thrill ride in the park. Guests in Doc Brown's lab get caught up in a high-speed chase through time that spans a million years. An extremely intense simulator ride, Back to the Future is similar to Star Tours and Body Wars at Walt Disney World, but is a whole lot rougher and more jerky. Though the storyline doesn't make much sense, the visual effects are wild and powerful. The guest vehicles (Delorean time machines) in the Back to the Future ride are much smaller than those of Star Wars and Body Wars, so the ride feels more like a personal adventure (and less like a group experience).

In a survey of 84 tourists who had experienced simulator rides in both

Universal Studios and Disney World, riders under 35 preferred Back to the Future to the Disney attractions by a seven-to-four margin. Older riders, however, stated a two-to-one preference for Star Tours over either Back to the Future or Body Wars. The remarks of a Mount Holly, New Jersey, woman are typical: "Our favorite [overall] attraction was Back to the Future at Universal. Comparing it to Star Tours and Body Wars, it was more realistic because the screen surrounds you." Most guests also find Back to the Future a bit wilder than its Disney cousins. A Michigan woman wrote that "Back to the Future was off the charts on the scary-o-meter. It made Splash and Big Thunder Mountains seem like carnival kiddie rides. Even Busch Gardens' Kumba was tame by comparison."

Because the height requirement on Back to the Future has been lowered from 46 inches to 40 inches, younger children are riding. Many of these kids require some preparation like that administered by a Virginia mother:

> The five year old was apprehensive about the ride, but he liked it a lot. We assured him ahead of time that (1) it's only a movie; and (2) the car doesn't actually go anywhere, just shakes around. This seemed to increase his ability to enjoy that ride (rather than taking all the fun out of it).

TOURING TIPS   As soon as guests are allowed into the park, there is a veritable stampede in the direction of Back to the Future. Our recommendation is to be on hand when the park opens and zip over to Back to the Future first thing. If you do not ride before 10 A.M., expect exceptionally long waits. One final note: sitting in the rear seat of the car makes the ride more realistic.

E.T. Adventure

Type of Attraction: Adventure ride

When to Go: Before 10 A.M.

Special Comments: This ride was renovated and greatly improved in 1992

Author's Rating: ★★★★

Overall Appeal by Age Group:

Pre-school	Grade School	Teens	Young Adults	Over 30	Senior Citizens
★★★★½	★★★★½	★★★★	★★★★	★★★★	★★★★

Duration of Ride: 4½ minutes
Load Speed: Moderate

DESCRIPTION AND COMMENTS   Guests board a bicycle-like conveyance
to escape with E.T. from earthly law enforcement officials, and then journey to E.T.'s home planet. An attraction similar to Peter Pan's Flight in
the Magic Kingdom, only longer with more elaborate special effects and
a wilder ride.

TOURING TIPS   Most preschoolers and grade-school children love E.T.
We thought it worth a 20 to 30 minute wait, but nothing longer. Lines
build quickly for this attraction after 9:45 A.M., and waits can extend
to more than two hours on busy days. Ride in the morning, right after
Back to the Future. Guests who balk at the idea of sitting on the bicycle
can ride in a comfortable gondola. A Columbus, Ohio, mother wrote
this about horrendous lines at E.T.: "The line for E.T. took two hours!
The rest of the family waiting outside thought that we had gone to E.T.'s
planet for real." Along similar lines, a Richmond woman objected to the
way Universal represented the waiting time to ride, commenting:

> We got into E.T. without much wait, but the line is very deceptive.
> When you see a lot of people waiting outside and the sign says "10
> minute wait from this point," it means 10 minutes until you are
> inside the building. But there's a very long wait inside [before] you
> get to the moving vehicles.

Animal Actors Stage

Type of Attraction: Trained animals stadium performance
When to Go: After you have experienced all the rides
Author's Rating: Warm and delightful; ★★★½
Overall Appeal by Age Group:

Pre-school	Grade School	Teens	Young Adults	Over 30	Senior Citizens
★★★★	★★★★	★★★★	★★★★	★★★★	★★★★

Duration of Presentation: 20 minutes
Probable Waiting Time: 25 minutes

DESCRIPTION AND COMMENTS   A humorous presentation demonstrating
how animals are trained for film work. Well-paced and informative, the

show features cats, dogs, monkeys, birds, and other creatures. Sometimes the animals do not behave as expected, but that's half the fun.

TOURING TIPS   We would like this show better if guests were simply allowed to enter the theater at their leisure and sit down. As it is, everyone must stand in line waiting to be admitted. Presented about 6 to 10 times daily, the *Animal Actors Stage* schedule is listed in the daily entertainment guide. See the show whenever it is convenient; get in line about 15 minutes before show time.

Dynamite Nights Stunt Spectacular

Type of Attraction: Simulated stunt scene filming

When to Go: At your convenience; check the daily entertainment schedule

Special Comments: Viewing is more comfortable at the night show

Author's Rating: Well done; ★★★★

Overall Appeal by Age Group:

Pre-school	Grade School	Teens	Young Adults	Over 30	Senior Citizens
★★★	★★★★½	★★★★½	★★★★½	★★★★	★★★★

Duration of Presentation: 20 minutes

Probable Waiting Time: None

DESCRIPTION AND COMMENTS   In this show, performed each evening on the Lagoon, stunt men demonstrate a variety of spectacular stunts and special effects. The plot involves lawmen trying to intercept and apprehend drug smugglers. Our main problem with this presentation is that the Lagoon is so large it is somewhat difficult to follow the action. The production was upgraded and improved in 1994.

TOURING TIPS   On a par with Disney-MGM's stunt show, the Universal Studios version is staged on the Lagoon, with the audience taking up positions along the encircling rail. There is no waiting in line, but if you want to nail down a really good vantage point, you need to stake out your position about 25 minutes before show time. The best viewing spots are along the docks at Lombard's Landing and adjacent areas on the Embarcadero waterfront, across the street from Earthquake. The park map, incidentally, has primo viewing spots identified with a little "PV" icon.

Wild, Wild, Wild West Stunt Show

Type of Attraction: Stunt show with a western theme
When to Go: After you've experienced all the rides, go at your convenience
Author's Rating: Solid and exciting; ★★★★
Overall Appeal by Age Group:

Pre-school	Grade School	Teens	Young Adults	Over 30	Senior Citizens
★★★★½	★★★★★	★★★★½	★★★★	★★★★	★★★★

Duration of Presentation: 16 minutes
Probable Waiting Time: None

DESCRIPTION AND COMMENTS   A Wild West stunt show with shootouts, fist fights, horse tricks, and high falls, staged about 10 times daily in a 2,000-seat, covered stadium. The pace is quick, the stunts are exciting and well executed, and unlike the stunt show performed on the Lagoon, the action is easy to follow.

TOURING TIPS   Go whenever convenient. Show times are listed in the daily entertainment guide. During the summer, the stadium is more comfortable after dusk.

Fievel's Playland

Type of Attraction: Children's play area with water slide and stage show
When to Go: Anytime
Author's Rating: A much needed attraction for preschoolers; ★★★★
Overall Appeal by Age Group:

Pre-school	Grade School	Teens	Young Adults	Over 30	Senior Citizens
★★★★	★★★★	★★★	★★★	★★★	★★★

Probable Waiting Time: 20–30 minutes for the water slide; otherwise, no waiting at all.

DESCRIPTION AND COMMENTS   Fievel's Playland is an imaginative children's play area where ordinary household items are reproduced on a giant scale, as a mouse would experience them. Preschoolers and grade-schoolers can climb nets, walk through a huge boot, splash in a sardine-can fountain, seesaw on huge spoons, or climb onto a cow skull. Though most of Fievel's Playland is reserved for preschoolers, a water slide/raft ride is open to guests of all ages.

TOURING TIPS   You can walk right into Fievel's Playland without having to wait in line, and you can stay as long as you want. Younger children love the oversized household items, and there is enough to keep teens and adults busy while the little ones let off steam. The water slide is open to all ages, but is extremely slow in loading and accommodates only 300 riders per hour. With an average wait in line of 20 to 30 minutes, we do not think the 16-second raft ride is worth the trouble. In addition, your chances of getting soaked are high. A major shortcoming of the entire attraction is its lack of shade. Visiting the play area during the heat of the day is not advised.

Beetlejuice's Rock 'N Roll Graveyard Revue

Type of Attraction: Rock-and-roll stage show
When to Go: At your convenience
Author's Rating: Outrageous; ★★★★
Overall Appeal by Age Group:

Pre-school	Grade School	Teens	Young Adults	Over 30	Senior Citizens
★★★★	★★★★½	★★★★½	★★★★	★★★★	★★★½

Duration of Presentation: 16 minutes
Probable Waiting Time: None

DESCRIPTION AND COMMENTS   The *Graveyard Revue* is a high-powered rock-and-roll stage show starring Beetlejuice, Frankenstein, the Bride of Frankenstein, the Wolfman, Dracula, and the Phantom of the Opera. In addition to some fine vintage rock, the show features some of the most exuberant choreography to be found on any stage, and some impressive sets and special effects.

TOURING TIPS   Mercifully, this attraction has been moved under cover. See the show at your convenience.

The Adventures of Rocky and Bullwinkle

Type of Attraction: Live character stage show
When to Go: Early evening, or at night when it is cooler

Author's Rating: A reunion with old friends; ★★★½

Overall Appeal by Age Group:

Pre-school	Grade School	Teens	Young Adults	Over 30	Senior Citizens
★★★★	★★★★	★★★½	★★★	★★★★	★★★½

Duration of Presentation: 15 minutes

Probable Waiting Time: None

DESCRIPTION AND COMMENTS   This show reminds you how funny cartoons used to be. If you are a Rocky (the Flying Squirrel) and Bullwinkle (the Moose) fan, it's the same old stuff; you know, bad guys Boris and Natasha present bombs disguised as food, trophies, and the like to Rocky and Bullwinkle. The show is a little unevenly paced, but funny with good special effects. As with the cartoon, the humor operates on one level for children and on another, with its puns and double entendres, for adults.

TOURING TIPS   Universal has a habit of surrounding new live productions with temporary bleachers exposed to the sun. *Rocky and Bullwinkle*, unfortunately, is no exception. Try to see the show when the weather is cooler, or after sunset.

Lucy, a Tribute

Type of Attraction: Walk-through exhibit

When to Go: Anytime

Author's Rating: A touching remembrance; ★★★

Overall Appeal by Age Group:

Pre-school	Grade School	Teens	Young Adults	Over 30	Senior Citizens
★	★	★★	★★★	★★★	★★★

Probable Waiting Time: None

DESCRIPTION AND COMMENTS   This exhibit depicts the life and career of comedienne Lucille Ball, with emphasis on her role as Lucy Ricardo in the long-running television series "I Love Lucy." Well-designed and informative, the attraction succeeds admirably in recalling the talent and temperament of the beloved redhead.

TOURING TIPS   See the Lucy exhibit during the hot, crowded midafternoon, or alternatively, on your way out of the park. An adult could easily spend 15 to 30 minutes here. Children, on the other hand, tend to get restless after a couple of minutes.

Street Scenes

Type of Attraction: Elaborate outdoor sets for making films
When to Go: Anytime
Special Comments: You will see most sets without special effort as you tour the park
Author's Rating: One of the park's great assets; ★★★★★
Overall Appeal by Age Group:

Pre-school	Grade School	Teens	Young Adults	Over 30	Senior Citizens
★★★	★★★★½	★★★★½	★★★★½	★★★★★	★★★★★

Probable Waiting Time: No waiting

DESCRIPTION AND COMMENTS   Unlike the Disney-MGM Studios, all of Universal Studios Florida's back lot sets are open to guest inspection. Sets include New York City streets, San Francisco's waterfront, a New England coastal town, the house from *Psycho*, Rodeo Drive and Hollywood Boulevard, and a Louisiana bayou, among others.

TOURING TIPS   You will see most of the sets as you walk through the park. If you want to learn more about them, however, take the Production Tram Tour that loads in the Production Central area outside the Nickelodeon soundstage.

"Jurassic Park" Exhibit

Type of Attraction: Props and costumes from the film *Jurassic Park*
When to Go: Anytime
Author's Rating: Limited, but interesting; ★★★
Overall Appeal by Age Group:

Pre-school	Grade School	Teens	Young Adults	Over 30	Senior Citizens
★★	★★★★	★★★	★★★	★★	★★

Probable Waiting Time: No waiting

DESCRIPTION AND COMMENTS   The lobby of the Pantages Theatre across from Mel's Diner has been converted into an exhibit showcasing props, vehicles, costumes, and film clips from Steven Spielberg's film *Jurassic Park*. The film clips, which show how some of the special effects were created, are particularly interesting. The centerpiece of the exhibit is a life-size model dinosaur from the movie. While I don't know what kind of dinosaur it is, I'm pretty sure your children will be able to tell you.

One-Day Touring Plan for Universal Studios Florida

This plan is for all visitors. If there is a ride or show listed that you prefer not to experience, simply skip that step in the plan and proceed to the next. Try to move from attraction to attraction quickly and, if possible, not stop for lunch until after Step 10.

The Hard Rock Cafe is a fun place for lunch or dinner if you enjoy rock 'n' roll. The food is good (though they sometimes overcook their burgers) and the service, once you are seated, is usually efficient. If you go, get your hand stamped for reentry (the restaurant is technically located outside of the park), and be prepared for a wait. We arrived at the Hard Rock at 3 P.M. on a Wednesday and had to wait in 4 different lines for a total of 35 minutes before being seated. On another occasion, at 8 P.M. on a Thursday, we waited in 11 different lines (no kidding! and all in the same restaurant) for a total of an hour and a half before getting a table.

A Word about Buying Admission to Universal Studios Florida

One of our big gripes about Universal Studios is that there are never enough ticket windows open in the morning to accommodate the crowd arriving early. You can arrive 45 minutes before the official opening time and still be standing in line to buy your admission when the park opens. We strongly recommend, therefore, that you buy your admission before you arrive at the park. Passes are available by mail from Ticket-Master at (800) 745-5000 and at the concierge desk or attractions box office of many Orlando area hotels. If your hotel does not have a ticket sales operation, try Guest Services at the Radisson Twin Towers (407) 351-1000, located at the intersection of Major Boulevard and Kirkman Avenue, directly across from the main entrance of Universal Studios.

Many of the hotels that sell Universal admissions do not issue actual passes. Instead the purchaser is given a voucher that can be redeemed for a pass at the theme park. Fortunately, the voucher redemption window at Universal Studios is totally separate from the ticket sales operation. You can quickly exchange your voucher for a pass and be on your way with little or no waiting in line.

Touring Plan

1. Call (407) 363-8000 the day before your visit for the official opening time.
2. On the day of your visit, eat breakfast and arrive at Universal Studios Florida 50 minutes before opening time with your admission pass or an admissions voucher in hand. If you have a voucher, exchange it for a pass at the special voucher redemption window.
3. At the front gate, line up at the turnstile. Be sure to pick up a map and the daily entertainment schedule. Ask the ticket seller, or any other attendant, whether any rides or shows are closed that day. Adjust the Touring Plan accordingly.
4. When the park opens, take a right on Hollywood Boulevard, first passing Mel's Diner (on your left) and then keeping the lagoon on your left. Head directly to Back to the Future and ride.
5. After Back to the Future, exit left and pass the International Food Bazaar. Continue bearing left past the Animal Actors Stage and proceed to E.T. Adventure. Ride.
6. Following E.T., retrace your steps back toward Back to the Future. Keeping the lagoon on your left, cross over the bridge to Amity. Ride Jaws.
7. Exit Jaws and turn left down the Embarcadero. Skip Earthquake for the moment and head directly to Kongfrontation in the New York set. Go ape.
8. After Kongfrontation, go back to San Francisco and ride Earthquake.
9. Following Eathquake, work your way back toward the main entrance and ride The Funtastic World of Hanna Barbera. Expect a wait of 25–40 minutes. If you have had enough simulator rides for a while, skip ahead to Step 10.
10. If you are still in one piece after the Flintstones, a bike ride to another galaxy, a shark attack, an earthquake, and an encounter with King Kong, you may as well take on some ghosts. Return to the New York set and see "Ghostbusters." The line will appear long, but should move quickly as guests are admitted inside.
11. This is a good time for lunch, if you have not already eaten. Cafe La Bamba in the Hollywood area offers tacos and burgers, and

Mel's Diner nearby has good, machine-made milkshakes. The International Food Bazaar next to Back to the Future serves gyros, bratwurst, pizza, and other ethnic goodies. A good, but often overlooked eatery is the Studio Stars Restaurant across the street from the prop "Boneyard" and down a block from "Alfred Hitchcock." This restaurant alternatively features California and Italian cuisine and also serves a buffet. In the New York area we like Louie's Italian Restaurant for pizza, calzone, and salads; and the outrageous sandwiches and pastries that are the specialty of the Beverly Hills Boulangerie near the park's main entrance. If you are in the mood for a more relaxed, upscale dining experience, the nicest restaurant in the park is Lombard's Landing on the waterfront (across the street from Earthquake). In addition to prime rib and creative seafood entrees, Lombard's also serves a truly exceptional hamburger at a fair price. Finally, there is the Hard Rock Cafe. Serving good food to the accompaniment of vintage rock music, the Hard Rock is a cultural institution.

12. At this point you have seven major attractions or shows left to see:

    (1) *The Gory Gruesome & Grotesque Horror Make-up Show*
    (2) "Murder, She Wrote" Mystery Theater
    (3) *Animal Actors Stage*
    (4) *Dynamite Nights Stunt Spectacular*
    (5) *Wild, Wild, Wild West Stunt Show*
    (6) "Alfred Hitchcock: The Art of Making Movies"
    (7) *Beetlejuice's Rock 'N Roll Graveyard Revue*

    Animal Actors Stage, the *Beetlejuice* show, and the stunt shows are performed several times each day, as listed in the daily entertainment schedule. Plan the remainder of your itinerary according to the next listed show times for these presentations. The *Horror Make-up Show* and "Murder, She Wrote" Mystery Theater (situated on opposite sides of Mel's Diner) run continuously, and can be worked into your itinerary as time permits. Save "Alfred Hitchcock" for your last attraction as you leave the park.

13. We have not included the Nickelodeon Studios Tour or the Production Tram Tour in the Touring Plan. If you have school age children in your party, you might consider taking the Nickelodeon tour late in the afternoon or on a second day at the park. Ride the tram tour second to last before "Alfred Hitchcock."

14. This concludes the touring plan. Spend the remainder of your

day at Universal Studios Florida revisiting your favorite rides and shows, or inspecting any of the sets and street scenes you may have missed earlier. Also check your daily entertainment schedule for any live performances. Street entertainment at Universal Studios includes the Blues Brothers and *The Adventures of Rocky and Bullwinkle*, performed in the New York and San Francisco areas.

Constructive Criticism

A teen from Rockton, Illinois, who had a tough time with the *Unofficial Guide's* Universal Studios Touring Plan, wrote offering the following constructive criticism:

Dear Mr. Sehlinger,

My family and I went to Florida in March, we used your book, it worked like clockwork at Disney. But for your Universal Studios Plan, let me offer you some constructive criticism: It was Horrible! We had only planned to go there one day, and we used your plan. It screwed up the whole day! The Universal staff gave us free admission the next day. I stayed up till 11 P.M. writing a plan and it worked perfect. It went like this:

1. Literally run to Back to the Future. 2. You can walk over to Earthquake while the line is still at Back to the Future. 3. Get over to New York and ride Kongfrontation. 4. Get over to the lake and ride Jaws (don't leave because of a long line, the entertainment while waiting in line is great). 5. Ride E.T. 6. Ride Funtastic World of Hanna Barbera. 7. Slap on your proton pack and see "Ghostbusters." 8. Take a Production Tram Tour. 9. See *Beetlejuice's Graveyard Revue*. 10. See *Wild, Wild, Wild West Stunt Show*. 11. Have a big lunch at Hard Rock Cafe. 12. Like animals? If so, go see *Animal Actors Stage*. 13. Now's a good time for the *Adventures of Rocky and Bullwinkle*. 14. Take a break from the lines and go to Fievel's Playland (if you're burning up from the Florida sun, go down the water slide). 15. Go to the "Murder, She Wrote!" Mystery Theater. 16. Test your stomach at the *Gory Gruesome & Grotesque Make-Up Show*. 17. If you see short lines, go to Nickelodeon Studios (but don't be heartbroken if you miss it). 18. Are you a Lucy lover? If so, take a walking tour through "Lucy, A Tribute." 19. Alfred Hitchcock's 3-D Theater should not be missed (see it in good health). 20. Walk through the park and see the

street scenes (my favorite was the Psycho house and Bates Motel). 21. Now's a good time for dinner at Lombard's Landing. 22. Be sure to stay for the *Dynamite Stunt Show*. 23. Be sure to shop, shop, shop! (preferably at Bates Motel Shop).

I hope to see my letter in future editions.

Your Friend,
Eric Lewin

For your information, Eric, we tried your plan and it worked pretty well. Maybe some of our readers will enjoy it, too.

Disney-MGM Studios vs. Universal Studios Florida

Nearly half of Disney-MGM Studios is off-limits to guests except by guided tour, while virtually all of Universal Studios Florida is open to patron exploration. Unlike Disney-MGM, Universal Florida's open area includes the entire back lot, where guests can walk at their leisure among the many and varied sets.

Universal hammers on the point that it is a working motion picture and television studio first, and only incidentally a tourist attraction. Whether this assertion is a point of pride with Universal or an apology to the tourist is unclear. It is true, however, that guests are more likely to see movie or television production in progress at Universal Florida than at Disney-MGM. On any given day, several production crews will be shooting on the Universal back lot sets in full view of any guests who care to watch.

Universal Studios Florida is so large, and because almost all of it is open to the public, most of the crowding and congestion so familiar in the streets and plazas of Disney-MGM is eliminated. At Universal Studios Florida there is plenty of elbow room.

The quality of the attractions is excellent at both parks, though the Disney-MGM rides and attractions are generally engineered to move people more efficiently. This disadvantage at Universal is somewhat offset, however, by the fact that there are more rides and shows there.

Though Universal Studios must be given credit for pioneering a number of innovative and technologically advanced rides, it must also be pointed out that Universal Studios' attractions break down more often than Disney-MGM's attractions. Jaws and Kongfrontation in particular are notorious for frequent breakdowns. A woman from Detroit, who visited Universal Studios on a particularly bad day, had this to say:

> Kongfrontation was broken, Earthquake was broken (with us in it for 30 minutes), and E.T. was broken (with us in line for 20 minutes). We got VIP passes for Earthquake, to come later without waiting. It was finally on line at about 6:45, and when we were just about to get on, it broke again. The rides at this park are really

589

stupendous—very different from WDW, but I think they've bit off more than they can chew.

A Wisconsin family encountered a similar situation, writing:

What happened!??! We arrived at opening, and tried to follow the [Touring] plan, but the lines were horrendous, and we left at 2:30 after having a *baaad day*. Kongfrontation was closed down and E.T. broke down several times. I don't think it was the fault of the plan, and I will probably skip Universal when I go back to Orlando.

Amazingly, and to the visitor's advantage, each of these parks offers a completely different product mix, so there is little or no redundancy for a person who visits both. Disney-MGM and Universal Florida each offer a good exposure to the cinematic arts, though Disney-MGM's presentations are crisper, better integrated, and more coherent.

Stunt shows are similar at both parks. The Disney version and the *Wild, Wild, Wild West Stunt Show* are both staged in 2,000-seat stadiums that allow a good view of the action. The *Dynamite Nights Stunt Spectacular* at Universal Studios is staged in the large Lagoon, with patrons simply taking up viewing positions along the railing. The Lagoon provides a realistic setting, but is so large that sometimes the action is hard to see or follow. All three shows have their moments, and the two stadium shows are fairly informative. In the final analysis, Disney-MGM wins for drama and intensity, while Universal Studios gets the call for variety.

Our recommendation is to try one of the studios. If you enjoy one, you will probably enjoy the other. If you have to choose between the studios, consider the following:

1. ***Touring Time.*** If you tour efficiently, it takes about seven to eight hours to see the Disney-MGM Studios (including a lunch break). Because Universal Studios Florida is larger, and contains more (and often less efficiently engineered) rides and shows, touring time, including one meal, runs about eight to eleven hours. One reader wrote, lamenting that:

... there is a lot more "standing" at Universal Studios, and it isn't as organized as [Disney-MGM]. Many of the attractions don't open until 10 A.M., and many shows seem to be going at the same time. We were not able to see nearly as many attractions at Universal as we were at [Disney-MGM] during the same amount of time. The one plus here is that there seems to be more property, and things are spaced out better so you have more elbow room.

2. ***Convenience.*** If you are lodging along International Drive, I-4's northeast corridor, the Orange Blossom Trail (US 441), or in Orlando, Universal Studios Florida will be closer. If you are lodging along US 27, FL 192, or in Kissimmee or Walt Disney World, the Disney-MGM Studios will be more convenient.

3. ***Endurance.*** Universal Studios Florida is larger and requires more walking than Disney-MGM, but it is also much less congested so the walking is easier. Wheelchairs are available, as is handicapped access, at both parks.

4. ***Cost.*** Both parks cost about the same for admission, food, and incidentals. All attractions are included in the price of admission.

5. ***Best Days to Go.*** (In order) Tuesdays, Mondays, Thursdays, and Fridays (except on holiday weekends) are the best days to visit Universal Studios Florida. Saturdays, Fridays, and Mondays are the best days for visiting the Disney-MGM Studios during the busier times of the year. During the off-season, visit the Disney-MGM Studios on Fridays, Tuesdays, Mondays, and Thursdays.

6. ***When to Arrive.*** For Disney-MGM, arrive with your ticket in hand 40 minutes before the official opening time. For Universal Studios, arrive with your admission already purchased about 45 minutes before the official opening time.

7. ***Small Children.*** Both Disney-MGM Studios and Universal Studios Florida are relatively adult entertainment offerings. By our reckoning, half the rides and shows at Disney-MGM, and about two-thirds of the rides and shows at Universal Studios Florida, have a significant potential for frightening small children.

8. ***Food.*** For the most part, the food is much better at Universal Studios.

A Word about Sea World

Many dozens of readers have written requesting that we provide some coverage of Sea World. This letter from a lady in Alberta, Canada, is representative of most:

> We chose Sea World as our 5th day at "The World." What a pleasant surprise. It was every bit as good (and in some ways better) than WDW itself. Well worth the admission, an excellent entertainment value, educational, well run, and better value for the dollar in food services. Perhaps expand your coverage to give them their due!

O.K. In brief, here's what you need to know (for any additional information, call (407) 363-2613):

Sea World is a world-class marine life theme park located near the intersection of I-4 and the Bee Line Expressway. Open daily from 8:30 A.M. to 10 P.M., Sea World charges about $36 admission (including tax) for adults and $31 for children (3 to 9). Parking is $5 per car, $7 per RV or camper. Discount coupons for Sea World admission are available in the free visitor magazine found in most hotel lobbies. It takes about six to nine hours to see everything, but you can see the big deal stuff in five hours or so.

Sea World is approximately the size of the Magic Kingdom, and requires about the same amount of walking. Most attractions are accessible to nonambulatory disabled persons.

In terms of size, quality, and creativity, Sea World is unequivocally on a par with the three major theme parks in Walt Disney World. Unlike Walt Disney World, however, Sea World primarily features stadium shows or walk-through exhibits. This means that you will spend about 90% less time waiting in line during eight hours at Sea World than you would for the same length visit at a Disney park.

Because lines, with one or two exceptions, are not much of a problem at Sea World, you can tour at almost any time of day. We recommend that you start your tour at about 3:30 or 4 P.M. (when the park is open until

9 P.M. or later). Many of the day's early guests will have departed by this hour, and you will be able to enjoy the various outdoor attractions in the relative cool of late afternoon and evening. If you visit in the morning, either arrive early or late. Midmorning arrivals tend to create long waits at the ticket windows. If you eat at Sea World, try the Smokehouse for barbecue.

Most of Sea World's shows operate according to a daily entertainment schedule that is printed conveniently on a placemat-sized map of the park. The four featured shows are:

The Shamu Killer Whale Show

The Sea Lion and Otter Show

The Water Ski Show

The Whale and Dolphin Discovery Show

When you arrive, develop your touring itinerary around these four shows. One of the first things you will notice as you check out the performance times is that the shows are scheduled in a way that make it almost impossible to see the productions back-to-back in sequence. The Shamu show, for instance, might run from 5 to 5:25 P.M. Ideally, you would like to bop over to the Sea Lion and Otter Show which begins at 5:30 P.M. Unfortunately, however, five minutes is not enough time to exit Shamu Stadium and walk all the way across the park to the Sea Lion & Otter Stadium. Sea World, of course, planned it this way so you would spend more time in the park.

It is possible to catch the Shamu show and the Sea Lion and Otter Show in succession by sitting near an exit at Shamu Stadium and leaving just a minute or two early (while the performers are taking their bows). Getting a couple of minutes head start on the crowd and hustling directly to the Sea Lion & Otter Stadium will get you seated just as the show is beginning.

If you are going to a show in Shamu Stadium or at the Atlantis Water Ski Stadium, don't worry about arriving late. Both of these stadiums are huge, so you will almost certainly get a seat. Plus, there is not much in the first few minutes of either show that you can't afford to miss. Same with the Whale and Dolphin Discovery Show. For the Sea Lion and Otter Show, however, the beginning is really good, so try to be on time.

Below is a list rating Sea World attractions:

★★★★½   Terrors of the Deep (shark and eel exhibit)

★★★★½   Penguin Encounter (penguin and puffin exhibit)

★★★★	Manatees: The Last Generation (manatee exhibit)
★★★★	Wild Arctic (simulation ride and Arctic wildlife including polar bears)
★★★★	Shamu Killer Whale Show
★★★★	Sea Lion and Otter Show
★★★★	Mission: Bermuda Triangle (simulation ride)
★★★★	Atlantis Water Ski Show
★★★★	Pacific Point Preserve (sea lion exhibit)
★★★★	Shamu's Happy Harbor (children's play area)
★★★½	Tropical Reef (reef fish aquarium exhibit)
★★★	Hawaiian Rhythms (Polynesian dance and music)
★★★	Monster Marsh (walk-through dinosaur exhibit)
★★½	Mermaids, Myths, & Monsters (fireworks and lasers: nights only)
★★½	Sea World Theater (Sea World propaganda and dancing fountains)
★½	Nautilus Theatre (musical revue)

There are also stand-alone exhibits featuring, respectively, dolphins, sting rays, pelicans, spoonbills, flamingos, and the Anheuser-Busch Clydesdale horses, as well as a tidal pool and tropical rain forest.

PART TWELVE:
The Water Theme Parks
and Discovery Island

Captain Nemo surfaces by mistake at Blizzard Beach.

The Water Theme Parks

There are three swimming theme parks to chose from at Walt Disney World, plus two more independent water parks in the immediate area. In Walt Disney World, River Country is the oldest and smallest park. Typhoon Lagoon, about five years old, is the most diversified of the Disney splash pads, while brand new Blizzard Beach takes the prize for the most slides, as well as for the most bizarre theme.

—— *Blizzard Beach*

Blizzard Beach is Walt Disney World's third and most exotic water adventure park, and like Typhoon Lagoon, it arrived with its own legend. This time, as the story goes, an optimistic entrepreneur tried to open a ski resort in Florida during a particularly savage winter. But alas, the snow melted, the palm trees grew back, and all that remained of the ski resort was its Alpine lodge, the ski lifts, and of course, the mountain. Plunging off the mountain are ski slopes and bobsled runs transformed into water slides. Visitors to Blizzard Beach catch the thaw in midcycle — with dripping icicles and patches of snow here and there. The melting snow has formed a large lagoon (the wave pool), fed by gushing mountain streams.

Like Typhoon Lagoon, Blizzard Beach is distinguished by its landscaping and by the attention paid to detailing its theme. As you enter Blizzard Beach, you face the mountain. Coming off the highest peak, and bisecting the area at the base of the mountain, are two long slides. To the left of the slides is the wave pool. To the right of the slides are the children's swimming area and the ski lift. Surrounding the whole shooting match like a moat, is a tranquil stream for floating in tubes. Picnicking areas are scattered around the park, as are pleasant areas for sunbathing.

On either side of the highest peak are a variety of tube, raft, and body slides. Including the two slides coming off the peak, there are seventeen slides in all. Among them is the Summit Plummet, the World's longest speed slide, which begins with a 120-foot free fall, and the Teamboat Springs bobsled run, 1,200-feet long.

For our money, the most exciting and interesting slides are the Slush Gusher and Teamboat Springs on the front right of the mountain, and the Runoff Rapids on the back side of the mountain. The Slush Gusher is an undulating speed slide that we think is as exciting as the more vertical Summit Plummet without being as bone-jarring. For the Teamboat Springs slide, you ride in a raft that looks like a round, children's blow-up wading pool (without the urine). The more people you load into the raft, the faster it goes. If you only have a couple of folks in the raft the slide is kind of a snore.

The Runoff Rapids are accessible from a path that winds around the far left bottom of the mountain. The Rapids consist of three corkscrew tube slides, one of which is totally enclosed and dark. As at Teamboat Springs, you'll go much faster on a two- or three-person tube than on a one-person tube. If you lean your bodies so that you enter the curves high and come out low, you will really fly. Because we like to steer the tube and go fast, we preferred the open slides (where we could see) much better than the dark, totally enclosed tube. We thought crashing through the pitch dark tube felt disturbingly like being flushed down a toilet.

The Snow Stormer mat slides on the front of the mountain are fun, but not as fast or interesting as Runoff Rapids. The Toboggan Racers at front and center on the mountain consists of eight parallel slides where sliders are dispatched in heats to race to the bottom. The ride itself is no big deal, and trying to get everybody lined up ensures that you will wait extra long to ride. When we were visiting, as an added annoyance, you had to line up once to get a mat and a second time to actually ride.

A ski lift carries guests to the top of the mountain where they can choose from the Summit Plummet, the Slush Gusher, or Teamboat Springs. For all other slides at Blizzard Beach, the only way to the top is by foot. If you are among the first in the park and you do not have to wait to ride, the ski lift is fun and provides a good bird's-eye view of the park. After riding once to satisfy your curiosity, however, you are better off taking the stairs to the top of the mountain.

There is a wave pool called Melt Away Bay, with waves of the gentle bobbing variety, and Cross Country Creek, a float creek that circles the park, passing through the mountain in the process. The children's areas, Tike's Peak and Ski Patrol Training Camp, are creatively designed, nicely isolated and, like the rest of the park, visually interesting.

Like Typhoon Lagoon, Blizzard Beach is a bit convoluted in its layout. With slides on both the front and back of the mountain, it is not always easy to locate a path that leads where you want to go.

Shops, counter-service food, rest rooms, as well as tube, towel, and locker rentals are located in the ski resort's now-converted base area. There are no lodging accommodations at Blizzard Beach, though the Disney All-Star Resorts are almost within walking distance. Blizzard Beach has its own pay parking lot. Disney resort and campground guests can commute to and from the park via the Walt Disney World bus system.

Because it is new, and because of its popular slides, Blizzard Beach fills up early during the hotter months of the year. In order to stake out a nice sunning spot, and to enjoy the slides without long waits, arrive at Blizzard Beach at least 15 minutes before opening. Admission to Blizzard Beach is about $24 a day for adults and $18 a day for children ages three to nine. Children under three are admitted free. If you are going primarily for the slides, you will have about two hours in the early morning to enjoy them before the waiting becomes completely intolerable.

——— *Typhoon Lagoon*

Typhoon Lagoon is somewhat smaller than Blizzard Beach and about four times the size of River Country, Walt Disney World's first splash-and-sun attraction. Nine water slides and streams, some as long as 400 feet, drop from the top of a 100-foot-high man-made mountain. Landscaping and an "aftermath of a typhoon" theme impart an added adventurous touch to the wet rides.

Beautifully landscaped, Typhoon Lagoon is entered through a misty rain forest that emerges in a ramshackle tropical town, where concessions and services are situated. Disney special effects make every ride an odyssey as swimmers encounter bat caves, lagoons and pools, spinning rocks, dinosaur bone formations, and countless other imponderables.

Typhoon Lagoon has its own 1,000-car pay parking lot. Disney resort and campground guests can commute to and from the park via the Disney bus system. There are no lodging accommodations at Typhoon Lagoon.

Like Blizzard Beach, Typhoon Lagoon is expensive, about $24 a day for adults and $18 a day for children ages three to nine. Children under three are admitted free. If you enjoy all the features of Typhoon Lagoon, the admission cost is a fair value. If, however, you are going primarily for the slides, you will have only two early-morning hours to enjoy the slides before the waiting lines become prohibitive.

Typhoon Lagoon provides water adventure for all age groups. Activity pools for young children and families feature geysers, tame slides, bubble jets, and fountains. For the older and more adventurous there are two speed slides, three corkscrew body slides, and three tube rapids rides (plus one children's rapids ride) plopping off Mount Mayday. For slower metabolisms there is a scenic, relaxed, meandering, 2,100-foot-long stream that floats tubers through a hidden grotto and a rain forest. And, of course, for the sedentary, there is usually plenty of sun to sleep in. Two of Typhoon Lagoon's attractions, the surf pool and Shark Reef, are truly unique. The wave pool is the world's largest inland surf facility, with waves up to six feet in height in a lagoon large enough to "encompass an oceanliner." Shark Reef is a saltwater snorkeling pool, where guests can swim around with a multitude of real fish.

Shark Reef

At Shark Reef, fins, mask, snorkel, and wetsuit vest are provided at no charge in the wooden building flanking the diving pool. Having obtained proper equipment (no forms or money involved), you are directed to take a shower and then to report to a snorkeling instructor. After a few minutes of instruction, you swim approximately 60 feet to the other side of the pool. You are not allowed to paddle about aimlessly, but must traverse the pool more or less directly.

The reef is fun early in the morning. Equipment collection, shower, instruction, and, finally, the quick swim can be accomplished without too much hassle. Also, owing to the small number of guests present, the attendants are more flexible about your lingering in the pool or minor departures in your charted course.

Later, as crowds build, it becomes increasingly difficult and time-consuming to provide the necessary instruction. The result: platoons of would-be frogmen, zippily attired in their diving regalia, all restlessly awaiting their snorkeling lesson. Guests are grouped into impromptu classes with the entire class briefed, and subsequently launched, together. What takes four or five minutes shortly after opening can take over an hour by 11 A.M.

By far the most prevalent and exotic species to be viewed in the pool are the dual-finned *homo sapiens*. Other denizens of the deep include small, colorful tropical fish, some diminutive rays, and a few very small leopard and hammerhead sharks. In terms of numbers, it would be unusual to swim the length of the pool and not see some fish. On the other hand, you are not exactly bumping into them either.

It is very important to fit your diving mask on your face so that it seals around the edges. Brush hair away from your forehead and take a couple of sniffs with your nose, once the mask is in place, to create a vacuum. Be advised that mustaches often prevent the mask from sealing properly. The first indication that your mask is not correctly fitted will be saltwater in your nose.

If you do not want to swim around with fish early in the morning, or fight crowds later in the day, you can avail yourself of an underwater viewing chamber, accessible anytime without waiting, special equipment, showers, instruction, or water in your nose.

Surf Pool

While Blizzard Beach, Wet 'n Wild, and Water Mania each have wave pools, Typhoon Lagoon has a *surf* pool. You will experience larger waves in the Typhoon Lagoon surf pool than most folks have ever encountered in the ocean. The surf machine puts out a wave about every 90 seconds (just about how long it takes to get back in position if you caught the previous wave). Perfectly formed and ideal for riding, each wave is about five- to six-feet tall from trough to crest. Before you throw yourself into the fray, watch two or three waves from shore. Since each wave breaks in almost the same spot, you can get a feel for position and timing. Observing the technique of other surfers will help also.

The best way to ride the waves is to swim out about three-fourths of the way to the wall at the wave machine end of the surf pool. When the wave comes (you will both feel and hear it), swim vigorously toward the beach, attempting to position yourself one-half to three-fourths of a body length below the breaking crest. The waves are so perfectly engineered that they will either carry you forward or bypass you (unlike an ocean wave, they will not slam you down).

As a teenaged girl from Urbana, Illinois, noted, the primary hazard in the surf pool is collision with other surfers and swimmers.

The surf pool was nice except that I kept landing on really hairy fat guys whenever the big waves came.

If you are surfing, the best way to avoid collision is to paddle out pretty far so that you will be at the top of the wave as it breaks. This tactic eliminates the possibility of anyone landing on you from above, while assuring maximum forward visibility. A corollary to all this: the worst place to swim is in the area where the wave actually breaks. As you look up you

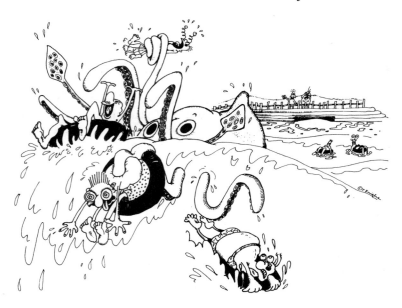

will see a six-foot wall of water carrying eight-dozen screaming surfers bearing down on you at 90 miles an hour. This is the time to remember every submarine movie you've ever seen . . . Dive! Dive! Dive!

Finally, an additional warning: Typhoon Lagoon surf has an uncanny knack for loosening watchbands, stripping jewelry, and sucking stuff out of your pockets. Don't take anything out there except your swimsuit (and hold on to it).

—— *River Country*

River Country is among the most aesthetically pleasing of the water theme parks—it is beautifully landscaped and immaculately manicured, with rocky canyons and waterfalls skillfully blending in with white sand beaches. The park is even situated to take advantage of the breeze blowing in from Bay Lake. For pure and simple swimming and splashing, River Country gets high marks. For its slides, however, River Country does not begin to compete with its big brothers, or with its nearby competitors. Where Blizzard Beach and Wet 'n Wild (on International Drive) feature in excess of 16 major slides and tube rides, River Country has 1 tube ride and 2 corkscrew-style slides. Few slides and many swimmers add up to long lines. If slides are your thing, you will be happier elsewhere.

Sunbathers will enjoy River Country, particularly if they position themselves near the lakefront to take advantage of the cooling breezes. Be forewarned, however, that most chaise lounges are basically flat, with the head slightly elevated, and do not have adjustable backs. For a comfortable reading position or for lying on your stomach, they leave a great deal to be desired.

Access to River Country by car is a hassle. First you are directed to a parking lot, where you leave your car, gather your personal belongings and wait for a Disney bus to transport you to the water park. The ride is rather lengthy, and pity the poor soul who left his bathing suit in the car (a round-trip to retrieve it will take about a half hour). In the morning, because the bus from the parking lot to River Country is very crowded, we suggest catching the bus to Pioneer Hall (which loads at the same place in the parking lot) and then walking over to River Country from there.

There are no lodging accommodations at River Country. Food is available, or you can pack in a picnic lunch to enjoy in River Country's picturesque, shaded lakeside picnic area. Access is by bus from the Transportation and Ticket Center (junction and transfer point for the EPCOT Center and Magic Kingdom monorails) or from the River Country parking lot at the entrance of Fort Wilderness Campground. River Country can also be reached by boat from the Magic Kingdom and any of the Bay Lake or Seven Seas Lagoon resort hotels.

—— *Disney vs. Wet 'n Wild and Water Mania Theme Parks*

Wet 'n Wild, on International Drive in Orlando, is on a par with Blizzard Beach, and has Typhoon Lagoon, River Country, and Water Mania beat in the slide department. The headliners at Wet 'n Wild are the Black Hole and the Surge. At the Black Hole, guests descend on a two-person tube down a totally enclosed corkscrew slide, sort of a wet version of Space Mountain—only much darker. Our research team thinks this is the single most exciting slide offered at any Florida swimming theme park (Water Mania and Blizzard Beach have similar slides). The Surge launches groups of five down a 580 feet twisting, turning course. Another Wet 'n Wild thrill slide is the Bomb Bay, where guests are dropped from a compartment resembling a bomb bay down a 79°-angle chute.

Water Mania, on US 192 south of I-4, edges out Typhoon Lagoon in the slide department and is less crowded than its local competitors. In addition, Water Mania is the only water park to offer a *surfing wave*.

What sets the Disney water parks apart is not so much their various slides and individual attractions, but the Disney attention to detail in creating an integrated adventure environment. The eye (as well as the body) is deluged with the strange, the exotic, the humorous, and the beautiful. In point of fact, wilder slides and rapid rides can be found elsewhere. But other water parks cannot compete with Disney in terms of diversity, variety, adventure, and total impact. Water Mania is nicely landscaped, but does not have a theme; while Wet 'n Wild, though attractive and clean, is cluttered and not especially appealing to the eye.

In the surf and wave pool department Typhoon Lagoon wins hands down, with Wet 'n Wild taking second place. All of the parks have an outstanding water activity area for small children and all, except River Country, feature unique attractions. Wet 'n Wild has a ride in which guests kneel on water skis, and Blizzard Beach has its 1,200-foot water bobsled. At Typhoon Lagoon, guests can snorkel among live fish, and Water Mania has its surfing wave.

Prices for one-day admission are about the same at Wet 'n Wild, Blizzard Beach, and Typhoon Lagoon, and a little cheaper at Water Mania. Discount coupons, however, are often available in local visitor magazines for Water Mania and Wet 'n Wild.

Wet 'n Wild stays open until 11 P.M. during the summer; the Disney swimming parks and Water Mania generally close between 5 and 8 P.M. We think the late closing time is a great plus for Wet 'n Wild. Warm Florida nights are a great time to enjoy a water theme park. There is less waiting for slides and the pavement is cooler on your feet. Not only that, Wet 'n Wild features live music in the evenings at its Wave Pool Stage. To top it off, admission prices at Wet 'n Wild are discounted 50% after 5 P.M. on days when the park is open late.

If your primary interest is sunning and swimming, you cannot beat River Country. It is beautifully landscaped and usually has a nice breeze blowing off Bay Lake. If you are into slides, Blizzard Beach is the better of the Disney water parks, with Wet 'n Wild leading the independents. Typhoon Lagoon offers enough slides to keep most folks happy, has the largest wave pool, and provides the most variety. If you are interested in the slides, but seek a less crowded venue, and are willing to sacrifice exotic surroundings for more elbow room, Water Mania (on US 192 south of I-4) is a good choice. Water Mania is cheaper, too. For late evening and nighttime swimming fun, Wet 'n Wild is the only game in town.

—— When to Go

The best way to avoid standing in lines is to visit the water parks on a day when they are less crowded. Because of the parks' popularity among Florida locals, weekends can be tough. We recommend going on a Monday or Tuesday, when most other tourists will be visiting the Magic Kingdom, EPCOT Center, or the Disney-MGM Studios and the locals will be at work. Fridays are also a good bet since people traveling by car commonly use this day to get a start on their trip home. Sunday morning is also a good time to go. Be forewarned, however, that during the summer and holiday periods, Typhoon Lagoon and Blizzard Beach fill to capacity and close their gates before 11 A.M. To give you an idea of what "crowded" means, we quote a reader from Newbury Park, California:

> The only disappointment we had at WDW was Typhoon Lagoon. While WDW was quite uncrowded, Typhoon Lagoon seemed choked with people. I'd hate to see it on a really crowded day. Even the small slides had lines greater than thirty minutes. They weren't worth half the wait. Castaway Creek might have been relaxing, but I found it to be a continuous traffic jam. I [also] would have enjoyed the snorkeling area except we were forced to go through at warp speed. After half a day we returned to the Yacht Club where Stormalong Bay provided much more pleasant water recreation.

And from a Manlius, New York, mom:

> Because we had the 5-day Park-Hopper, we also visited Typhoon Lagoon, arriving before opening so we could stake out a shady spot. The kids loved it until the lines got long (11:00-12:00), but I hated it. It made Coney Island seem like a deserted island in the Bahamas. Floating on Castaway Creek was really unpleasant. Whirling around in a chlorinated, concrete ditch with some stranger's feet in my face, periodically getting squirted by water-guns, passing under cascades of cold water, and getting hung up by the crowd is not at all relaxing for me. My husband and I then decided to "bob" in the surf pool. After about 10 minutes of being tossed around like corks in boiling water, he turned a little green

around the gills and we sought the peace of our shady little territory which, in our absence, had become much, much smaller. We sat and read our books, elbow to elbow with other pleasure seekers until the kids had their fill. They, however, loved the body slides and the surf waves, commenting on how useful your "coach's tip" was.

Another New Yorker, this time from Middletown, had a somewhat better experience:

On our second trip [to Typhoon Lagoon], we dispensed with the locker rental (having planned to stay for only the morning when it was least crowded), and at park's opening just took right off for the Storm Slides before the masses arrived—it was perfect! We must have ridden the slides at least 5 times before any kind of line built up, and then we were also able to ride the tube and raft rides (Keelhaul and Mayday Falls) in a similar uncrowded, quick fashion because everyone else was busy getting their lockers! We also experienced the Shark Reef snorkeling three times with minimal crowds that day, because, I think, most people overlook this attraction. Shark reef is lots of fun and a great way to cool off since their water temp is well below the wave pool's.

If your schedule is flexible, the best time of all to enjoy the swimming parks is from mid-afternoon to late in the day when the weather has cleared after a storm. The swimming parks usually close during bad weather. If the storm is prolonged, most guests in the park go back to their hotels. When Typhoon Lagoon, Blizzard Beach, or River Country reopen after the inclement weather has passed, you can almost have a whole park to yourself.

—— *Planning Your Day*

The Disney swimming theme parks are almost as large and elaborate as the Magic Kingdom, EPCOT Center, and the Disney-MGM Studios. Thus to have a great day and beat the crowd, we recommend the following:

1. ***Getting Information.*** Call (407) 824-4321 the night before you go to inquire when the park of your choice opens.

2. ***To Picnic or Not to Picnic.*** Decide whether or not you want to bring a picnic lunch. Guests are permitted to bring lunches and

beverage coolers to the parks. No alcoholic beverages are allowed. Glass containers of all kinds (including mayonnaise, mustard, peanut butter, and pickle jars) are likewise forbidden.

3. ***Getting Started.*** If you are going to Blizzard Beach or Typhoon Lagoon, get up early, have breakfast, and arrive at the park a half hour before opening time. If you have a car, we recommend driving instead of taking a Walt Disney World bus. If you are going to River Country, you do not have to be quite so compulsive about getting there early.

4. ***Attire.*** We suggest that you wear your bathing suit under shorts and a T-shirt so you do not need to use lockers or dressing rooms. Be sure to wear shoes. The footpaths are relatively easy on bare feet, but there is a lot of ground to cover. If you have tender feet, we recommend you wear your shoes as you move around the park, taking them off whenever you raft, slide, or go into the water. Along similar lines, shops in the Disney water parks sell various types of sandals, "Reef Runners," and other protective footwear that can be worn in and out of the water.

5. ***What to Bring.*** Things you will need include a towel, suntan lotion, and of course, money. Since wallets and purses just get in the way, lock them safely in your trunk or leave them in your hotel room. Carry enough money for the day along with your Disney resort I.D. (if you have one) in a plastic bag or a Tupperware container. Though no place is completely safe, our folks felt very comfortable hiding our plastic money bags in our cooler. Nobody disturbed our stuff and our cash was much easier to access than if we had had to run across the park to a locker. If you are really carrying a wad or you tend to worry about money anyway, get the locker.

6. ***What Not to Bring.*** Personal swim gear (fins, masks, rafts, etc.) are not allowed. Everything you will need is either provided or available to rent. If you forget your towel, you can rent one (cheap!). If you forget your swimsuit or lotion, these can be purchased. Personal flotation devices (life jackets) are available free of charge. To obtain a PFD you must leave a credit card number or a driver's license as a deposit (held until the equipment is returned).

7. ***Admissions.*** Purchase your admission about a half hour before opening time. If you are staying at a Walt Disney World lodging property, you may be entitled to an admission discount, so bring your hotel or campground I.D. Combination passes, which include both River Country and Discovery Island, are available and represent the best buy for anyone interested in these two minor Disney theme parks. For guests staying at Walt Disney World for five or more days, the 5-Day World-Hopper Pass includes unlimited admission to all three Disney swimming parks.

   In 1995, Disney experimented with a Water Park Hopper pass that allowed guests to visit more than one water park on the same day. Theoretically, you could enjoy the slides at Blizzard Beach until things got crowded and then head for the wave pool at Typhoon Lagoon. The flaw in the plan is that Typhoon Lagoon and Blizzard Beach sell out and close their doors on most days by 10:30 or 11 A.M. Thus by the time you wear yourself out on the slides at Blizzard Beach, Typhoon will have stopped admitting guests.

8. ***Lockers.*** Lockers are available and come in small and large sizes for a $5 or $7 per day rental fee, respectively, of which $2 is refundable when you return your key. The lockers are roomy enough for one person or a couple, but are a bit of a stretch when it comes to accommodating an entire family. Though you can access your locker freely all day, it should be noted that not all lockers are conveniently located.

   Getting a locker at Blizzard Beach or Typhoon Lagoon is truly competitive. When the gates open, guests literally race to the locker rental desk. Once there, the rental procedure is somewhat slow and cumbersome. If you are not among the first in line you can burn some daylight waiting to be served. Our recommendation for a less stressful beginning to your day is to pass on the locker. Carry only as much cash as you will need for the day in a water-tight container that you can stash in the bottom of your cooler. Ditto for personal stuff like watches, eyeglasses, and the like. With a little planning you can get along nicely without the locker, and save time and hassle in the bargain.

9. ***Tubes.*** Tubes for bobbing on the waves, floating in the creeks, and riding the tube slides are available for free.

10. ***Getting Settled In.*** Establish your base for the day. There are many beautiful sunning and lounging spots scattered through all three Disney swimming parks. The breeze is best along the beaches of the surf pools at Blizzard Bay and Typhoon Lagoon. At River Country, pick a spot that fronts on Bay Lake. At Typhoon Lagoon, if there are children under six in your party, you might choose an area to the left of Mount Mayday (with the ship on top) near the children's swimming area.

Arriving early, you can just about have your pick. There are flat lounges (unadjustable) and chairs (better for reading). There are shelters for those who prefer shade and even a few hammocks. There are also picnic tables.

The best spectator sport at Typhoon Lagoon is the bodysurfing action in the surf pool. The second-best thing to being out there yourself is watching the zany antics of the other guests. With this in mind, you might choose a nesting spot with a good unobstructed view of the waves.

11. ***A Word about the Slides.*** Water slides come in various shapes and sizes. Some are steep and vertical, some long and undulating. Some resemble corkscrews, while still others imitate the pool-and-drop nature of whitewater streams. Depending on the particlar slide, swimmers ride mats, inner tubes, or rafts. On body slides, as the name implies, swimmers slosh to the bottom on the seat of their pants.

When it comes to water slides, unfortunately, modern traffic engineering bows to old-fashioned queuing theory. It's one person, one raft, or one tube at a time, and the swimmer "on deck" cannot go until the person preceding him is safely out of the way. Thus the hourly carrying capacity of a slide is nominal compared to the continuously loading rides of EPCOT Center, the Disney-MGM Studios, and the Magic Kingdom. Since a certain interval between swimmers is required for safety, the only way to increase capacity is to increase the number of slides and rapids rides.

Though Typhoon Lagoon and Blizzard Beach are huge parks with lots of slides, they are overwhelmed almost daily by armies of guests. If your main reason for going to Typhoon Lagoon or Blizzard Beach is the slides (and you hate to wait in long lines), be among the first guests to enter the park. Go directly to the slides and ride as many times as you can before the park fills up. When

the lines for the slides become intolerable, head for the surf or wave pool or the mellow tube-floating streams.

To go as fast as possible on a body slide, cross your legs at the ankles and cross your arms over your chest. When you take off, arch your back so that almost all your weight is on your shoulder blades and heels (the less contact with the surface, the less resistance). You can steer by shifting most of your upper body weight onto one shoulder blade. For maximum speed, weight the shoulder blade on the outside of each curve. If you want to go slow (what's the point?), distribute your weight equally as if you were lying on your back in bed. For all curving slides, regardless of whether you are body sliding or using a mat or tube, you can maximize speed by hitting the entrance to each curve high and exiting the curve low.

Be aware that some of the slides and rapids stipulate a minimum height requirement. Riders for Humunga Kowabunga at Typhoon Lagoon, and for Slush Gusher and Summit Plummet at Blizzard Beach, for example, must be four-feet tall. Pregnant women and those with back problems and various other health deficits are warned against riding.

12. ***Floating Streams.***   Both Blizzard Beach and Typhoon Lagoon (as well as Water Mania and Wet 'n Wild) offer mellow floating streams. A great idea, the floating streams are long, long tranquil inner-tube rides that give you the illusion you are doing something while you are being sedentary. For wimps, wussies, and exhausted people of all ages, floating streams are the answer to a prayer. Flowing ever so slowly around the whole park, through caves and beneath waterfalls, past gardens, and under bridges, the floating streams offer a relaxing, foot-saving alternative for touring a park.

The floating streams can be reached from a number of put-in and take-out points. There are never any lines; just wade out into the creek and plop into one of the inner tubes floating by. Ride the gentle current all the way around or get out at any exit. If you lay back and go with the flow, it will take from 30 to 35 minutes to float the full circuit.

As you might anticipate, there will be other guests on whom the subtlety of the floating streams is lost. They will be the ones racing, screaming, and splashing. Let them pass, stopping in place for a few moments, if necessary, to put some distance between yourself and them.

13. ***Lunch.***   If you did not bring a picnic lunch, you can, of course, purchase food. Portions are adequate to generous, quality is comparable to chain fast-food restaurants, and prices are (as you would expect) a bit high.

14. ***More Options.***   If you are really a water puppy, you might consider returning to your hotel for a little heat-of-the-day siesta and returning to the water park for some early evening swimming.

Special lighting after dusk makes Typhoon Lagoon and Blizzard Beach enchanting places to be. Crowds also tend to be lighter in the evening. If you leave the park and want to return, be sure to hang on to your admission ticket and have your hand stamped. If you are staying in a hotel serviced by Walt Disney World buses, older kids can return on their own to the water parks, giving Mom and Dad a little private quiet time.

15. *A Word about Bad Weather.*   Thunder storms are quite common in Florida. During summer afternoons such storms are often a predictable, daily occurrence. Most storms, fortunately, are short-lived, allowing the swimming park to resume normal operations. If a storm is severe and prolonged, however, it can occasion a great deal of inconvenience. In addition to the swimming park shutting down, guests will find themselves competing aggressively for available cover; many Disney resort guests may also find themselves competing for space on a bus back to the hotel.

Our advice is to monitor the local weather forecast the day before you go, checking it again in the morning before heading off to the swimming park. Scattered thundershowers are to be expected, but moving stormfronts are to be avoided. Because Florida is so flat, you can see the weather coming from atop the slide platforms at the swimming parks. Particularly if you are dependent on Disney bus transportation, leave the park earlier rather than later when you see bad weather moving in.

Discovery Island

Situated in Bay Lake close to the Magic Kingdom, Discovery Island is a tropically landscaped, small zoological park primarily featuring birdlife. Small, intimate trails wind through the exotic foliage, in contrast to the broad thoroughfares of the major theme parks. Plants and trees are marked for easy identification and the island features an absolutely enormous walk-through aviary, so cleverly engineered that you are essentially unaware of the confining netting.

In the best traditions of Florida, small-attraction tourism, Discovery Island offers three shows called "Animal Encounters." *Feathered Friends* features cockatoos and macaws in a variety of natural and not-so-natural behaviors. *Birds of Prey* showcases owls, hawks, vultures, and the like (mostly disabled birds that are convalescing at Discovery Island). The third show, curiously called *Reptile Relations*, introduces guests to alligators, snakes, and other scaly species indigenous to Florida. Informative, interesting, and well presented, all of the "Animal Encounters" are staged in natural surroundings with few props. Seating is in the round on benches, not unlike what you might expect at camp. Show times, four for each of the encounters, are normally scheduled between 11 A.M. and 4 P.M., thus insuring that guests will be in the company of "mad dogs and Englishmen" as they sit through presentations during the hottest time of day.

A trip to Discovery Island is fairly pricey (about $12 for adults and $7 for kids) for three shows, a few birds and animals, and a short stroll through the woods. As for children, they enjoy Discovery Island if allowed to explore on their own, but become bored and restless touring under the thumb of their elders. Probably the best deal for those spending four days or more at Walt Disney World is the 5-Day World-Hopper Pass that in addition to providing admission to the three major parks also provides unlimited admission to Typhoon Lagoon, River Country, Blizzard Beach, Pleasure Island, and Discovery Island. Do not spring for the 5-Day World-Hopper Pass, however, unless you intend to take advantage of its features.

There are no lodging accommodations on Discovery Island, but food is available. For anyone on a World-Hopper pass, it's fun to take a break from touring the Magic Kingdom and boat over to Discovery Island for lunch. The boat ride is pleasant, the island setting tranquil and serene. Best of all, there are no crowds to fight. Lunch fare is simple, but on the whole pretty good.

Access to Discovery Island is exclusively by boat from the main Bay Lake docks (Magic Kingdom dock, Fort Wilderness Landing, resort hotel docks). Boats run about every 15 to 20 minutes. Dock to dock, it takes about 12 minutes to cover the distance from the Magic Kingdom to Discovery Island. The last boat of the day departs the Magic Kingdom dock at 3:34 P.M. While you could spend up to three hours on Discovery Island, most folks are ready to split in an hour or so.

As the following comments suggest, reader reaction to Discovery Island is most decidedly mixed. First, from a dad of two, who lives in Manning, South Carolina:

> The bad news is that you overestimated Discovery Island. Although you made it sound dreary and a bit dull, that is giving it too much credit. You would have to be a bird fanatic to really enjoy Discovery Island, in our opinion. It was a complete waste of time, and we spent more time waiting on boats than on seeing the island.

Another father, this time from Bethesda, Maryland, disagrees:

> It's probably their love of animals that caused our kids to flip out over Discovery Island. Despite our repeated earlier trips to WDW, I had personally always escaped going to this attraction. My kids enjoyed every moment of our excursion one sunny afternoon, and it really served to take the edge off an otherwise hectic day.

PART THIRTEEN: *Night Life In and Out of Walt Disney World*

Walt Disney World at Night

The Disney folks contrive so cleverly to exhaust you during the day that the mere thought of night activity sends most visitors into anaphylactic shock. For the hearty and the nocturnal, however, there is a lot to do in the evenings at Walt Disney World.

In the Parks

At EPCOT Center the major evening event is IllumiNations, a mixed-media laser and fireworks show at the World Showcase Lagoon. Show time is listed on the daily entertainment and special events schedule.

In the Magic Kingdom there are the ever-popular evening parade(s) and Fantasy in the Sky fireworks. Consult the daily entertainment schedule for performance times.

The Disney-MGM Studios feature a laser and fireworks spectacular called Sorcery in the Sky on nights when the park is open late. Consult the daily entertainment schedule for show times.

At the Hotels

The Floating Electrical Pageant is sort of a Main Street Electrical Parade on barges. Starring King Neptune and various creatures of the sea, the pageant (which floats by to the accompaniment of Handel on a doozy of a synthesizer), is one of our favorite Disney productions. The short, but captivating show is staged nightly. The first performance takes place at 9 P.M. off the Polynesian Resort docks. From there it circles around and repeats at the Grand Floridian at 9:15 P.M., it then heads to Fort Wilderness, the Wilderness Lodge, and the Contemporary Resort.

For something more elaborate, consider one of the dinner theaters described on the next page. Finally, if you want to go honky-tonkin', many of the hotels at the Disney Village have lively bars with rock bands and other entertainment.

At Fort Wilderness Campground

A campfire program is conducted each night at the Fort Wilderness Campground. Open only to Walt Disney World resort guests, the event begins with a sing-along led by Disney characters Chip and Dale and progresses to cartoons and a Disney feature movie. There is no charge.

At Pleasure Island

Pleasure Island, Walt Disney World's nighttime entertainment complex, features seven nightclubs for one admission price. Dance to rock or country, or take in a bar show, or see a movie. Pleasure Island is located in Walt Disney World Village and is accessible from the theme parks and the Transportation and Ticket Center by shuttle bus. For a detailed description of Pleasure Island, plus touring plan, see pages 622–25.

—— Walt Disney World Dinner Theaters

There are several dinner theater shows each night at Walt Disney World. Reservations can be made on the day of the show at any of the resort hotels or by calling (407) 824-8000. Visitors with reservations for a Walt Disney World lodging property can make reservations up to 60 days before they arrive by calling (407) 939-3463. Getting reservations for the *Polynesian Revue* is not too tough. Getting a reservation to the *Hoop-Dee-Doo Musical Revue* is a trick of the first order.

The Polynesian Revue

Presented nightly at the Polynesian Resort, the evening consists of a "Polynesian-style" all-you-can-eat meal followed by South Sea island native dancing. The dancing is interesting and largely authentic, and the dancers are comely, but definitely PG in the Disney tradition. We think that the show has its moments and the meal is adequate, but that neither is particularly special. Cost per adult is about $33 and $17 for kids ages 3–11. If you really enjoy this type of entertainment, and experience a problem getting a reservation for the *Polynesian Revue,* Sea World presents a similar dinner show each evening.

A well-traveled, married couple from Fond du Lac, Wisconsin, described the *Polynesian Revue* this way: "The Polynesian Revue was a beautiful presentation, better than some shows we have seen in Hawaii! The food, however, lacked in all areas."

Also at the Polynesian Resort's Luau Cove is *Mickey's Tropical Revue*, where Disney characters are added to the regular entertainment show. This show starts at 4:30 P.M. when it is too early to be hungry and too hot to be sitting around outdoors. Cost is about $29 for adults, $23 for juniors (12 to 20), and $14 for children (3 to 11).

Hoop-Dee-Doo Musical Revue

This show, presented nightly at Pioneer Hall at Fort Wilderness Campgrounds, is by far the most popular of the Disney dinner shows. The meal, served family style, consists of barbequed ribs, fried chicken, corn on the cob, and baked beans, along with chips, bread, salad, and dessert. Though the quality has slipped a bit, most of the fare is satisfactory (albeit greasy). Portions are generous and service is excellent.

The show consists of western dance hall song, dance, and humor. The cast is talented, energetic, and lovable, each one a memorable character. Between the food, the show, and the happy, appreciative audience, the *Hoop-Dee-Doo Revue* is a delightful way to spend an evening. It costs about $35 for adults, $26 for juniors, and $18 for children. Showtimes are 5:00, 7:15, and 9:30 p.m.

Now for the bad news. The *Hoop-Dee-Doo Revue* is sold out months in advance to guests who hold lodging reservations at Walt Disney World properties. If you plan to stay at one of the Walt Disney World hotels, try making your *Hoop-Dee-Doo* reservations when you book your room. If you have already booked your room, call (407) 939-3463 as far in advance as possible. For those with accommodations outside of Walt Disney World:

1. Call (407) 939-3463 four to seven months in advance of your visit and try to make a reservation. While technically this is the dining reservations line for Disney resort guests, reservationists will sometimes take your reservation without asking if you are staying in a Disney hotel.
2. Call (407) 824-2748 30 days before your visit. If that doesn't work:
3. Call (407) 824-2748 at 9 A.M. each morning while you are at Walt Disney World to make a same-day reservation. There are three performances each night, and for all three combined only 3 to 24 people, total, will be admitted with same-day reservations. If no reservations are available:
4. Show up at Pioneer Hall (no easy task in itself unless you are staying in the campgrounds) 45 minutes before show time (early and

late shows are your best bets) and put your name on the standby list. If someone with reservations fails to show, you may be admitted.

If you go to the *Hoop-Dee-Doo Revue*, with or without reservations, give yourself plenty of time to get there. The experience of a Houston, Texas, reader makes the point well:

> We had 7:30 P.M. reservations for the *Hoop Dee Doo Revue*, so we left [Disney-]MGM just before 7:00 and drove directly to Fort Wilderness. Two important things to note: First, the road direction signs at WDW are terrible. I would recommend a daylight orientation drive upon arrival, except that there are so many ways to get confused that one might be lulled into a false sense of security. Second, when we got to Fort Wilderness, we had great difficulty determining where Pioneer Hall was and how to get there. I accosted several people and found a man who could tell us where we were on the map, and that a bus was the only way to get to Pioneer Hall. I would recommend leaving for Pioneer Hall one hour before your show reservations. Boredom is not nearly so painful as anxiety (reservations are held until fifteen minutes after the stated time).

A California dad had this tip to offer:

> To go to the *Hoop Dee Doo* at Fort Wilderness, take the boat from the Magic Kingdom rather than any bus. This [is] contrary to the "official" directions. The boat dock is a short walk from Pioneer Hall [in Fort Wilderness], while the bus goes to the [main] Fort Wilderness parking lot where one has to transfer to another bus to Pioneer Hall.

Transportation problems aside, most, but not all of our readers, enjoy the *Hoop Dee Doo Revue*. The thoughts of a Texas family are typical of those who remain unimpressed:

> What is all the hoop-dee-doo with the *Hoop Dee Doo Revue*? The food was okay, if "gut-busting" fare is your idea of a fine night out, and the entertainment was pleasant. As a dinner theatre, however, our family of three found it unexceptional in every respect but its cost. Had your review of the "Revue" tempered its enthusiasm (much as you present its Polynesian counterpart), we probably would have cancelled our reservation, pocketed the $100, and spent the evening joyously stunned by another glorious light-and-fireworks spectacle.

An alternative to the *Hoop Dee Doo Revue* is the *Fort Liberty* show, a non-Disney attraction on FL 192. Call (407) 351-5151 for reservations.

—— *Other Area Dinner Theaters*

There are more than a dozen dinner theaters within 20 minutes of Walt Disney World. Of these, *Fort Liberty* is a good substitute for the *Hoop-Dee-Doo Musical Revue*. *Medieval Times*, featuring mounted knights in combat, is fun and most assuredly different, and *King Henry's Feast* is a fun variety show about King Henry's birthday celebration. The food at all three of these dinner theaters is both good and plentiful, and all three shows are highly recommended. Cost per adult is around $30–34, but discount coupons are readily available at brochure racks and in local tourism periodicals found in motel lobbies. *Fort Liberty* and *King Henry* reservations can be made by calling (407) 351-5151. Call (407) 239-0214 for *Medieval Times*.

A relative newcomer among dinner shows is *Arabian Nights*, located on US 192 east of I-4 on the way to Kissimmee. A prime-rib dinner is featured here, along with a show that could be called "Everything You Ever Wanted to Know about Horses." The tab for adults is about $36. The phone number for information and reservations is (407) 239-9223.

Pleasure Island

Pleasure Island, which opened in 1989, is a six-acre nighttime entertainment complex situated on a man-made island in Walt Disney World Village. The complex consists of seven nightclubs, a ten-theater movie complex, restaurants, and shops. While some of the restaurants and shops are open during the day, Pleasure Island does not really come alive until after 7 P.M., when the nightclubs open.

Admission Options.   One admission (about $18) entitles a guest to enjoy all seven nightclubs (the Baton Rouge Lounge on the *Empress Lilly* riverboat is not part of Pleasure Island per se, but is so close that we include it in our discussion and Touring Plan as an eighth club). Guests younger than 18 years old must be accompanied by a parent after 7 P.M. Unlimited seven-day admission to Pleasure Island is also included in the 5-Day World-Hopper Pass.

Alcoholic Beverages.   Guests not recognizably older than 21 are required to provide proof of their age if they wish to purchase alcoholic beverages. To avoid repeated checking as the patron moves from club to club, a color-coded wristband indicating eligibility status is provided. All the nightclubs on Pleasure Island serve alcohol. Those under 21, while allowed in all of the clubs except Mannequins, are not allowed to purchase alcoholic beverages. Finally, and gratefully, you do not have to order any drinks at all. You can go into any club, enjoy the entertainment, and never buy that first beer. You won't be hassled a bit.

Dress Code.   Casual is in. Shirts and shoes are required.

New Variations on an Old Theme.   The single-admission nightclub complex was originated in Florida at Orlando's Church Street Station, still very much alive and well in historic downtown Orlando. Starting fresh, the Disney folks have been able to eliminate some of the problems that have haunted Church Street Station and a lot of other nightspots over the years.

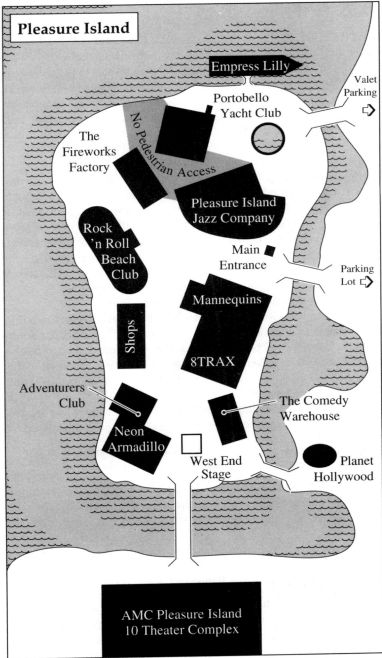

Pleasure Island

Empress Lilly

Valet Parking ⇨

Portobello Yacht Club

No Pedestrian Access

The Fireworks Factory

Pleasure Island Jazz Company

Rock 'n Roll Beach Club

Main Entrance

Parking Lot ⇨

Mannequins

Shops

8TRAX

Adventurers Club

The Comedy Warehouse

Neon Armadillo

West End Stage

Planet Hollywood

AMC Pleasure Island 10 Theater Complex

Good News for the Early to Bed Crowd.   If you are not nocturnal by nature, or if you are tired from a long day in the theme parks, you do not have to wait until 11 or 12 P.M. for the Disney nightspots to get revved up. There is no waiting till the wee hours for Pleasure Island to hit its stride. All bands, dancers, comedians, and showmen come on like gangbusters from the very beginning of the evening. For *real* night people, it feels weird to be dancing to "Shout" at 8:15 P.M. But that's the way it is at Pleasure Island; there are no "best sets" or grand finales.

It's Possible to Visit All the Clubs in One Night.   Where a performance in most nightclubs might be an hour or more in duration, at Pleasure Island (with the exception of the Comedy Warehouse) the performances are shorter but staged more frequently. This allows a guest to move around from club to club without missing much. Since you can experience the essence of a given club pretty quickly, there is no need to hang around for two or three drinks just to see what is going on. This format enables a guest to have a complete and satisfying experience in a brief time and then, if desired, to move on to another club.

The music clubs (Rock & Roll Beach Club, 8TRAX, Neon Armadillo, Baton Rouge Lounge, Mannequins, and Jazz Club) go nonstop. Sometimes there are special performances within the context of ongoing club entertainment. The Adventurers Club and the Comedy Warehouse offer scheduled shows. All shows are of short duration, leaving plenty of time to sample other Pleasure Island offerings.

A reader wrote reminding us that "sampling" the clubs, as we suggest, is not the same as spending some time and really appreciating them:

> Pleasure Island clubs take much more time to appreciate than you allow. We spent two evenings and only got to 4 places.

We are very high on Pleasure Island. The cover is a little pricey and the drinks are not cheap, but the entertainment is absolutely top-notch. And if you arrive before 9 P.M., you will have time to sample all of the clubs.

We get a lot of mail from couples in their thirties and forties arguing Pleasure Island's merits (or lack thereof). The following quotes are representative. A reader from Bettendorf, Iowa, states:

> I would not spend the money to go to Pleasure Island again. It is quite obvious that Disney is interested in the 21–30-year-old crowd here. There were many people our age (38) and older looking for something to do and not finding it. The Adventurers Club is the

only real Disney creation on the island. Walt Disney World crosses all age brackets and I expected the same from Pleasure Island. What a disappointment! I think you need to go back to the drawing board on your evaluation of Pleasure Island (and so does Disney).

A central Texas couple, however, had this to say:

Your description, even with the statement that you are high on Pleasure Island, didn't prepare my wife and me for what a great place it is. Perhaps our expectations were moderate, but we thought it was an absolute blast, and we are neither under 40 nor club hounds.

Sorry, Invited Guests Only. From time to time, particularly during the early evening (before 9 P.M.), certain Pleasure Island clubs are reserved for private parties and declared temporarily off-limits to paying guests.

Parking Is a Hassle. Though Pleasure Island has its own parking lot, it often fills up. Additionally, the lot is confusing, unnecessarily convoluted, and not well-marked. If you drive, study all landmarks and other identifying objects near your parking space so you will be able to locate your car when you are ready to leave. A good parking strategy is to park in the lot adjacent to the movie theaters and enter via the bridge that connects the movie complex to Pleasure Island. Because there is an admissions booth at the bridge, there is no need to enter through the main gate.

—— Pleasure Island First Timers' Touring Plan

This itinerary is for first-time visitors to Pleasure Island who want to check out all of the clubs in one night. The idea here is to give you a taste of each of Pleasure Island's distinct venues. If you settle in someplace that you really enjoy, that's fine, but you will probably not be able to complete the circuit.

1. Arrive by 6:30 or 7 P.M., if you intend on eating at a Pleasure Island restaurant. If you eat before you go, try to arrive about 8 P.M.

2. Purchase your admission or enter using your 5-Day World-Hopper Pass.

3. *Comedy Warehouse.* Bearing left from the admission windows at the main entrance, proceed to the Comedy Warehouse. This is Pleasure Island's toughest ticket. There are usually five shows each night, with the two earlier shows (usually 7:30 and 8:25 P.M.) easiest to get in. If a show is scheduled to begin within 30 minutes, go ahead and hop in line. If show time is more than 30 minutes off, check out the country and bluegrass music at the Neon Armadillo, located across the street from the Comedy Warehouse. Use your own judgment about whether you have time to buy a drink. Return to the Comedy Warehouse 30 minutes before show time. If you do not arrive at Pleasure Island in time to catch either of the first two shows, plan to line up at least 35 minutes before show time for subsequent shows.

4. *Adventurers Club.* After the show at the Comedy Warehouse, cross the street to the Adventurers Club. Patterned after a rather stuffy English gentlemen's club, the Adventurers Club is a two-story, turn-of-the-century affair with big armchairs, walls covered with animal heads (some of which talk), and other artifacts.

Many guests will stroll through the Adventurers Club, inspect the ridiculous decor, and then leave, not realizing that they missed anything. The main attraction at the Adventurers Club is a show in the club's private library. About once every 30 or 40 minutes all the guests present will be ushered into the library for a show. Nobody informs the guests that a show is upcoming; they either must hang around long enough to be invited in or, alternatively, intuit that with Disney what you see isn't what you get.

When you arrive at the Adventurers Club, ask an attendant when the next show in the library will be starting. If show time is 20 minutes or less away, go on in and have a drink. If it's a long while until the next show, the Neon Armadillo is right next door.

5. *Neon Armadillo Music Saloon.* Located next door to the Adventurers Club, what you see here is definitely what you get: first-class country and bluegrass music. If you have not been counting down to show time for one of the comedy presentations, go ahead and visit the Neon Armadillo now.

6. *8TRAX.* When Pleasure Island opened in 1989, this club was an under-21 club called Videopolis East. For various reasons (fights and teenage gang conflicts), it was closed and reopened as Cage. Cage was targeted to older (over 21) rockers, but never really achieved much of an identity. Now enters 8TRAX, a so-called '70s club featuring the music of Iron Butterfly, Led Zeppelin, the Doors, and Grand Funk Railroad, any one of which would have sent Walt Disney into anaphylactic shock. Though the decor during our last visit was the same steel beams, catwalks, and metal mesh that imbued the previous incarnations with such charm, it was clear that the '70s concept had taken root. Expressed succinctly, the place was rocking.

7. *Mannequins Dance Palace.* Backtrack toward Pleasure Island's front entrance to Mannequins. Mannequins is a ritzy, techno-pop, rock dance club with a revolving dance floor, incredible lighting, and some wild special effects. Music for dancing is recorded but the sound system is superb (and very, very loud). There is often a waiting line to enter Mannequins. This has less to do with the club's popularity than with the fact that the Disney folks prefer guests to enter via an elevator to the second floor. Though the elevator helps distribute guests throughout the club, there is a perfectly good entrance on the first floor. For some reason, cast members manning the entrance will often invite 40-something (and up) guests to enter directly, without being subjected to the hoopla of the elevator. Patrons under 21 are not permitted in Mannequins through either entrance.

8. *Jazz Club.* Located across the walkway from the entrance of Mannequins, this is the next nightspot on the Touring Plan. The Jazz Club is the newest of the Pleasure Island clubs and occupies a space previously used as a food court and a private party room. The club features live jazz and blues and hosts jam sessions with local musicians. The crowd, more diverse in age and appearance than at the other clubs, sits at tables that surround the stage on three sides.

9. *Rock & Roll Beach Club.* The next stop is the Beach Club, featuring oldies and current rock. The bands here are always first-rate and they raise the roof beginning early in the evening. A variety of electronic games and pool are available for those who do not wish to dance.

10. *West End Stage.* The West End Stage, while not a club, is the most happening place on Pleasure Island. Live rock bands play under the stars in the plaza, with the Neon Armadillo and the Adventurers Club on one side and the Comedy Warehouse on the other. The bands are, without exception, super, as are the lighting and sound systems. The high stage provides excellent visibility. Performances at the West End Stage usually run four times each night, with a grand finale at 11:45 accompanied by fireworks, showers of confetti, and blazing searchlights. Drinks are available from street vendors.

11. *Pleasure Island Restaurants.* The Pleasure Island dining scene has improved over the past year or so. Though still noisy, crowded, and pricey, Pleasure Island restaurants feature creative menus offering a wide variety of well-prepared dishes. For detailed profiles of Pleasure Island restaurants, see Part Eight: Dining In and Around Walt Disney World.

Across from the *Empress Lilly* riverboat is the Portobello Yacht Club, which serves seafood, pasta, and pizza. Casual yet stylish, the Portobello does a credible job with its varied Italian fare. On the down side, we get mixed messages from our readers on this restaurant—most complain it is overpriced.

The Fireworks Factory specializes in barbeque, with several types of ribs available. Slaw and cornbread are some of the best we have had anywhere. Appetizers (catfish, buffalo wings, barbequed shrimp) are disappointing. If you stick to ribs and chicken and skip the appetizers, you can have a good meal here.

The big new player on the Pleasure Island dining scene is Planet Hollywood, located down by the AMC movie theater complex. While the food is pretty good and the servings large, the main draw here is all of the Hollywood memorabilia that serve as the restaurant's decor. Expect long waits for a table unless you eat at strange times.

If you want to eat dinner at a Pleasure Island full-service restaurant, we recommend arriving by 6:30 P.M. and eating early or waiting until after 10:00 P.M. An alternative, of course, is to eat sandwiches and munchies in the clubs. It is not necessary to buy any sort of club admission to eat at Pleasure Island restaurants. Most of the restaurants are open during the day as well as in the evening.

13. ***Pleasure Island Shopping.*** Pleasure Island features some shops that are entertainment attractions in themselves. At Cover Story, guests dress up prior to being photographed for the mock cover of a major magazine. Want to see yourself on the cover of *Cosmo*? Here's the place. In a similar vein, Superstar Studio provides the opportunity to star in your own music video. Props, including keyboard, drums, and guitar are available. Video technicians record your lip syncing (or you can actually sing); varying camera angles make you look good. Post production adds background to your tape for added realism. Work alone or make up a whole group with your friends. If you do not want your own magazine cover or rock video made, drop in and watch others; it's a hoot!

It is not necessary to pay any sort of admission to shop at Pleasure Island during the day. In the evening, however, all of Pleasure Island except the restaurants is gated.

—— *Pleasure Island vs. Church Street Station*

Both Pleasure Island and Church Street Station are worthwhile attractions. Pleasure Island has a plastic, trendy, brand-new (translate Disney) feel. Church Street Station is situated in a restored city block of historic old Orlando adjacent to the railroad tracks. Both sites have their strong points, but architecturally Church Street is much more interesting. In addition to the gated (admission required) entertainment at Church Street Station, a huge nighttime shopping and independent club scene has sprung up in the two blocks on the opposite side of the tracks from the attraction. These pubs and clubs have a personality and feel all their own and provide a vastly expanded selection of entertainment.

Parking, previously a problem at Church Street, is now plentiful. Parking at Pleasure Island can be a pain in the butt.

Performances are longer and fewer at Church Street, making it much more difficult to see all the shows covered in your admission than at Pleasure Island. Also, the timing of performances (starting and ending times) at Church Street mitigates against getting from one show to another or getting a good seat. Pleasure Island's comedy clubs feature shorter shows performed more frequently, and the music clubs run pretty much continuously, so that making the rounds is no particular problem.

Rock music and dancing is more diversified at Pleasure Island with the addition of 8TRAX. Guests can now enjoy classic rock at the Beach Club and on the West End Stage, '70s rock at 8TRAX, and techno-pop at Mannequins. Church Street Station offers only two rock venues, but both are outstanding. The Orchid Garden Ballroom features some of the best live oldies rock in the area, while Phineas Phogg's (no admission required) offers Top-40 music and dancing.

When it comes to country music and dancing, as good as the Neon Armadillo is, it cannot compare to Church Street's rollicking Cheyenne Saloon & Opera House. Comedy is good at both places, although different.

Church Street is a more adult night complex. The humor is bawdier, the crowd older, and you don't have to check out the wristband of the girl by the bar to know she's over 21.

Food is a toss-up. Both places serve good, if undistinguished, fare at

The regular crowd settles in at Pleasure Island.

an upscale price. You just have to ask the right questions and pick your way carefully through the menus.

Church Street admission is about $17 per adult (including sales tax). Discount coupons for both Church Street and Pleasure Island can be found in local visitor magazines, available free in most hotels outside Walt Disney World.

For additional information, call:

Church Street Station: (407) 422-2434
Pleasure Island: (407) 934-7781

Readers' Questions to the Author

Q: When you do your research, are you admitted to the parks free? Do the Disney people know you are there?

A: We pay the regular admission and usually the Disney people do not know we are on site. Similarly, both in and out of Walt Disney World, we pay for our own meals and lodging.

Q: How often is the Unofficial Guide *revised?*

A: We publish a new edition once a year, but make minor corrections every time we go to press, usually about three times a year.

Q: What are your readers' most frequently expressed complaints and most frequently expressed compliments concerning Walt Disney World?

A: Our readers gripe more about the quality and cost of food at Walt Disney World than anything else, though in truth, most readers do not have as low an opinion of the food as we do. Second on the complaint hit parade are rude guests. Especially singled out are large and sometimes unruly tour groups from Brazil. For a couple of months each year at the *Unofficial Guide* we are inundated with "Brazil Mail." Third on the list is the difficulty Walt Disney World resort guests have making reservations from their guest rooms on the internal 55 and 56 numbers. Fourth is a whole laundry list of problems relating to the Walt Disney World transportation system. Coming in fifth are complaints about the maps of the Walt Disney World property provided to guests. Sixth is the 3 P.M. check-in time at the Disney resorts, and seventh is "not enough thrill rides."

As for compliments, there is almost universal appreciation of the courtesy, friendliness, and helpfulness of Disney cast members, especially bus drivers. The cleanliness of the parks comes in second, with a lot of comments about the nice rest rooms. Disney landscaping and the beauty of the property comes in third on the praise list. Character encounters come in fourth, with late evening fireworks shows holding down fifth. Sixth is the quality of rooms at the Disney Hotels, followed in seventh place by the creative and elaborate Disney hotel swimming areas. The quality of special Disney tours and educational programs rounds out the list.

Q: I have an old edition of the Unofficial Guide. *How much of the information [in it] is still correct?*

A: Veteran travel writers will acknowledge that 5 to 8% of the information in a guidebook is out of date by the time it comes off the press! Walt Disney World is always changing. If you are using an old edition of the *Unofficial Guide*, descriptions of attractions still existing should be generally accurate. However, many other things change with every edition, particularly the Touring Plans and the hotel and restaurant reviews. Finally, and obviously, older editions of the *Unofficial Guide* do not include new attractions or developments.

Q: How many people have you surveyed for your "age group ratings" on the attractions?

A: Since the publication of the first edition of the *Unofficial Guide* in 1985, we have interviewed or surveyed just over 10,900 Walt Disney World patrons. Even with such a large survey population, however, we continue to have difficulty with certain age groups. Specifically, we would love to hear from seniors about their experiences with Splash Mountain, Big Thunder Mountain, Space Mountain, *Alien Encounter*, Star Tours, the Tower of Terror, and *Body Wars*.

Q: Do you stay in Walt Disney World? If not, where do you stay?

A: We do stay at Walt Disney World lodging properties from time to time, usually when a new hotel opens. Since we began writing about Walt Disney World in 1982, we have stayed in over 48 different properties in various locations around Orlando, Lake Buena Vista, and Kissimmee. During our last visit we stayed at the Disney Vacation Club and liked it very much.

Q: I don't think the food at Walt Disney World is bad at all. Could it be that you are just overly picky?

A: I will acknowledge that there is certainly more mediocre food at Walt Disney World than "bad" food. As for my orientation, I target the restaurant reviews in this guide to readers with discriminating palates, in other words, to those actively seeking the most satisfying dining experience available. And, yes, I am picky, particularly at the prices we pay for food at Walt Disney World.

Q: *Why are there no photographs of the theme parks in the* Unofficial Guide*?*

A: Disney has copyrighted many identifiable buildings and structures in Walt Disney World. Any recognizable photo of Walt Disney World that we publish without Disney's permission, even if we take the picture with our own camera, could constitute copyright infringement, according to Disney's legal representatives. Walt Disney World will not grant the *Unofficial Guide* permission to publish photographs because of its relationship with Steve Birnbaum's *Official Guide to Walt Disney World*.

Q: *What can we expect in terms of new developments over the next couple of years at Walt Disney World?*

A: Disney is adding a fourth major theme park, this one with a zoological theme. At EPCOT Center, several Future World pavilions are scheduled for renovation and upgrading, and of course, rumors continue to persist concerning the possibility of a Russian, Spanish, or Israeli pavilion in the World Showcase. I should point out, however, that there have been no major additions to the World Showcase family since Norway opened about five years ago.

On the hotel scene, Disney's Boardwalk will open in 1996 and construction will commence on Disney's Coronado Springs Resort, a moderately (for Disney) priced convention hotel in the Spanish/Southwestern tradition. Other resorts on the drawing board are the Wilderness Junction Resort, a rustic lodge in the image of Disney's Wilderness Lodge, and the Mediterranean Resort. Located on the Seven Seas Lagoon between the TTC and the Contemporary Resort, the Mediterranean will be a deluxe property serviced by monorail. Besides the hotels, a large, multi-faceted International Sports Center is under construction. The center will include a baseball stadium, a fieldhouse with six basketball courts, 12 tennis courts, and a track-and-field complex. In addition to being available to resort guests, it appears that Disney plans to get into the sports camp business. The sports center is scheduled to open in 1997.

Q: *What is your favorite Florida attraction?*

A: What attracts me (as opposed to my favorite attraction) is Juniper Springs, a stunningly beautiful stream about an hour north of Orlando in the Ocala National Forest. Originating as a limestone aquifer, crystal clear water erupts from the ground and begins a ten-mile journey to the creek's mouth at Lake George. Winding through palm, cypress, and live oak, the stream is more exotic than the Jungle Cruise, and alive with birds, animals, turtles, and alligators. Put in at the Juniper Springs Recreation Area on FL 40, 36 miles east of Ocala. The seven-mile trip to the FL 19 bridge takes about four and a half hours. Canoe rentals and shuttle service are available at the recreation area. Phone (904) 625-2808 for information.

Readers' Comments

A couple from Milwaukee write:

We have been to WDW many times. Seeing it, however, this time with our 4½ year old, we were struck by how extremely loud everything is. The show at Mickey's Starland was so loud, we were afraid it would do permanent damage to all of our ears—especially our 4½ year old's. DOES ANYONE CHECK THE DECIBEL LEVELS?

On another subject, a mother from Savannah, Georgia, ventures this opinion:

The final point I would like to address is babies and small children; nothing adds to the stress of a long, hot day like the sound of crying and screaming. Even our four-year-old noticed that "those babies don't like it here." If for some reason this is the *only* time you will *ever* be able to come to Walt Disney World, I guess there is no getting around it, but in reality it would be a good idea to wait until the kids are old enough to handle the place. There is a lot more to consider than the idea that the baby would like seeing Mickey Mouse.

A Bloomington, Indiana, couple had this to say:

My wife and I are 42 years old. We took your advice on taking an afternoon break. That 2–3 hours rest time back at the [hotel] kept us refreshed for our entire stay. I think without the afternoon breaks we would have missed more and enjoyed less.

Similarly, a Michigan woman stated:

We were so glad we took the nap advice. At first we thought no way, but then thought about it and it was such good advice. I think the adults needed it more than the kids. We were all ready and willing for our afternoon naps, and had a great time when we returned [to the theme park].

A mom from Ontario, Canada, found a good meal, writing:

The best meal we had on the whole trip was the Character Breakfast in the Polynesian Resort. The food was so fresh, and there was such a good variety that it was well worth the price.

A Wilmington, Delaware, mom thinks we seriously overrate Disney thrill rides:

You are much too "wussie" when it comes to coasters. I kept waiting for Space Mountain to get scary. Big Thunder was just plain fun, and Splash Mountain didn't get me wet enough to do any good. I can't imagine Star Tours, Body Wars, and especially the Teacups getting anyone the least bit sick (well, maybe Body Wars!) I hope I'm never on the Tower of Terror with you!

A Manning, South Carolina, man had some nice things to say about Disney cast members:

My final comment is that I was stunned at how polite and helpful and accommodating all of the Disney cast members were whenever we had a special request or a problem. They are a true asset and visitors should not be afraid or reluctant to make special requests or ask questions.

A Massachusetts man took exception to our restaurant ratings:

We had just one criticism about your guide that we thought we should pass on. After reading the guide, we were terrified to eat at any of the Disney restaurants. You give the impression that the food, especially at the fast food outlets, is almost inedible. As a family with young children, we are used to eating in fast food chains across the country. To our delight, we felt that the food inside Disney was always superior to what you normally would expect from a fast food chain. The hamburgers at the cafeteria in MGM were far superior to those found in any hamburger chain. The taco salad at the fast-food Mexican cafeteria across from the Pirates of the Caribbean ride was fresh, filling, and tasteful. Additionally, they were willing and eager to customize the salads based on dietary restrictions.

A Disney World veteran traveler recalls the logic of differentiating attractions by letter category:

Your comments about each attraction in the Magic Kingdom are right on! However, I have always found it useful to describe rides in terms of the scope (marketing people call this managing expectations) by telling people whether rides used to be A, B, C, D, or E tickets in the days when you required a ticket to enter each attraction. I find that this maximizes enjoyment so that people aren't disappointed by trying to compare the old E rides (Space Mountain, for example) with lesser rides like [Snow White] or the Enchanted Tiki Birds (which I recommend as a splendid place to rest). When visitors judge each attraction within its intended scope (as measured by the old A–E tickets) I find they appreciate each attraction more. It's unfair to try to compare one to another [irrespective of scope], as your guide implies is possible.

A Claremont, New Hampshire, dad tested an Unofficial Guide *claim, writing:*

You hit it on the head when you said kids remember the pool at their motel. I waited a week before asking my 5-year old son what he remembered about his vacation: answer 1. the sandbox at the Disney Vacation Club. Last time I checked he had a sandbox in the backyard . . . Must have been the Florida sun!

On the subject of children's responses, a Plano, Texas, man contributed this:

While on the subject, some parents might benefit from two other things that we learned. First, from our use in conversation of your terms "switching off" or "baby swapping," our daughter quickly caught on to the fact that she was standing in line for a ride that was potentially terrifying for her. As a result, her own imagination-driven panic sometimes led to messy scenes in the anterooms of rides (like Body Wars) that Mom and Dad took turns experiencing but had no intention of forcing on her. Second, and more happily, it occurred to us that Dumbo, the Mad Tea Party, and the delightful *Cranium Command* (all of which we experienced multiple times) were, in effect, "thrill rides" for our five-year-old. If a flying elephant can give a small child the same gleeful exhilaration that her parents enjoy on Star Tours, then the wait in line is justified in both cases.

A Nutley, New Jersey, reader encourages other readers to stand up to the Mouse:

Last but not least, I think that it is important for Disney vacationers to write to the Walt Disney World Company to encourage them to make things affordable. I have written to them often, and have asked them to continue the dinner coupons and other specials that make it easier for a family to vacation with them. I have also reminded them that the Caribbean Beach, Port Orleans, and Dixie Landings used to be their more budget-priced family resorts, and that they should not let the prices at these resorts get out of hand. I would hope that your guide would encourage people to voice their opinions to Disney. We do have some power if we choose to use it.

A Bowling Green, Kentucky, woman paraphrased a Jimmy Buffet song, writing:

I'm home, I'm exhausted, I'm broke. My head hurts, my feet stink, and I don't love Mickey. Next year I'm only going to stay a week!

And so it goes.

Index

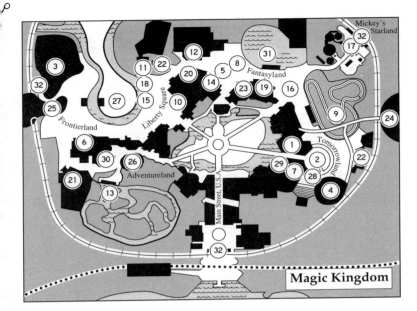

Magic Kingdom
Recommended Attraction Visitation Times

If you tour on an early entry day, move all recommended attraction visitation times up one hour. It is best to see attractions with visitation times listed as "anytime" during the more crowded middle part of the day (noon to 4 P.M.).

1. *Alien Encounter:* Before 10:30 A.M./late P.M.
2. AstroOrbiter: Before 11 A.M./late P.M.
3. Big Thunder Mountain Railroad: Before 11 A.M./late P.M.
4. *Carousel of Progress:* Before 11 A.M./after 6 P.M.
5. Cinderella's Golden Carrousel: Before 11 A.M./after 8 P.M.
6. *Country Bear Jamboree:* Before 11:30 A.M./late P.M.
7. Dreamflight: Anytime
8. Dumbo: Before 10 A.M./after 9 P.M.
9. Grand Prix Raceway: Before 11 A.M./late P.M.
10. *The Hall of Presidents:* Anytime
11. The Haunted Mansion: Before 11:30 A.M./after 8 P.M.
12. It's a Small World: Anytime
13. Jungle Cruise: Before 11 A.M./late P.M.
14. *Legend of the Lion King:* Before 11 A.M./during parades
15. Liberty Square Riverboat: Anytime
16. Mad Tea Party: Before 11 A.M./late P.M.
17. Mickey's Starland—all attractions: Anytime
18. Mike Fink Keelboats: Before 11:30 A.M. (closes at dusk)

—continued on other side—

Magic Kingdom
Recommended Attraction Visitation Times

If you tour on an early entry day, move all recommended attraction visitation times up one hour. It is best to see attractions with visitation times listed as "anytime" during the more crowded middle part of the day (noon to 4 P.M.).

—continued from other side—

19. Mr. Toad's Wild Ride: Before 11 A.M./late P.M.
20. Peter Pan's Flight: Before 10:30 A.M./late P.M.
21. Pirates of the Caribbean: Before noon/after 5 P.M.
22. Skyway: Before noon/during parades
23. Snow White's Adventures: Before 11 A.M./late P.M.
24. Space Mountain: First hour after opening/late P.M.
25. Splash Mountain: First hour after opening/late P.M.
26. Swiss Family Treehouse: Before 11:30 A.M./after 5 P.M.
27. Tom Sawyer Island: Anytime (closes at dusk)
28. Tomorrowland Transit Authority: Anytime
29. Transportarium: Anytime
30. *Tropical Serenade:* Before 11 A.M./after 3:30 P.M.
31. 20,000 Leagues Under the Sea: Before 9:30 A.M./late P.M.
32. Walt Disney World Railroad: Anytime

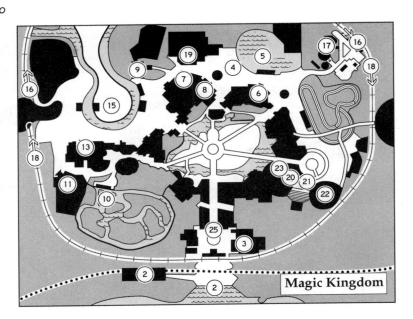

Magic Kingdom
One-Day Touring Plan, for Parents with Small Children
Pocket Outline Version

For the detailed version of this Touring Plan, see page 417.
Review the Small Child Fright Potential Chart on pages 158–161.

1. Arrive at TTC 50 min. prior to opening.
2. Take the monorail or ferry to park entrance.
3. Rent strollers (if needed) and pick up daily entertainment schedule.
4. When Fantasyland opens, ride Dumbo. (See the detailed version of this plan for special instructions on early entry days.)
5. Ride 20,000 Leagues Under the Sea.
6. Ride Mr. Toad's Wild Ride.
7. Ride Peter Pan's Flight.
8. See *Legend of the Lion King.*
9. See the Haunted Mansion.
10. Ride the Jungle Cruise.
11. Ride Pirates of the Caribbean.
12. Go to Frontierland.
13. See the *Country Bear Jamboree.*
14. Eat lunch.
15. Explore Tom Sawyer Island.
16. Take the train to Mickey's Starland.
17. See *Mickey's Starland Show* and meet Mickey. Visit Grandma Duck's petting farm.
18. Take the train to Frontierland.
19. Ride It's a Small World.
20. Go to Tomorrowland. Ride Dreamflight.
21. Ride the Tommorowland Transit Authority.
22. See *Carousel of Progress.*
23. See the *Transportarium.*
24. Enjoy live entertainment.
25. Browse along Main Street.
26. Depart Magic Kingdom.

Magic Kingdom

Magic Kingdom
Dumbo-or-Die-in-a-Day Touring Plan,
for Parents with Small Children
Pocket Outline Version

For the detailed version of this Touring Plan, see page 421.
Review the Small Child Fright Potential Chart on pages 158–161.
(Interrupt the Touring Plan for lunch, rest, and dinner.)

1. Arrive at TTC 50 min. prior to opening.
2. Ride monorail to the park entrance.
3. Rent a stroller (if needed).
4. Go to King Stefan's in the castle. (See the detailed version of this plan for special instructions on early-entry days.)
5. Make dinner reservations at the castle.
6. Ride Dumbo.
7. Ride Dumbo again.
8. Ride 20,000 Leagues Under the Sea.
9. Ride Mr. Toad's Wild Ride.
10. Ride Peter Pan's Flight.
11. Ride Cinderella's Carrousel.
12. See *Legend of the Lion King*.
13. Go to Tomorrowland.
14. Ride the Grand Prix Raceway.
15. Ride AstroOrbiter.
16. Ride Dreamflight.
17. Return to the hotel for lunch and a nap.
18. Return to the Magic Kingdom.
19. In Frontierland, go to Tom Sawyer Island.
20. See the *Country Bear Jamboree*.
21. Take the train to Mickey's Starland.
22. See *Mickey's Starland Show* and meet Mickey.
23. Visit the petting farm.
24. Enjoy the playground.
25. If you have time before dinner, ride It's a Small World.
26. See The Haunted Mansion.
27. Watch the evening parade.
28. Ride the Jungle Cruise.
29. Repeat favorite attractions.
30. Depart Magic Kingdom.

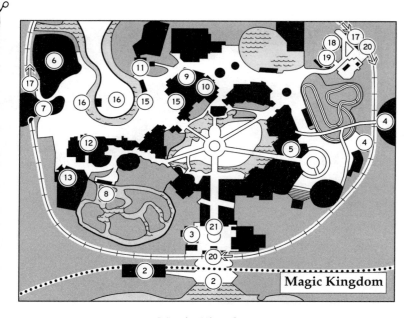

Magic Kingdom
Two-Day Touring Plan A, for When the Park Is Open Late
Pocket Outline Version

For the detailed version of this Touring Plan, see page 425.

Day One

1. Arrive at TTC 50 min. prior to opening.
2. Take the monorail or ferry to park entrance.
3. Go to City Hall for park maps and a copy of the daily entertainment guide.
4. As soon as Tomorrowland opens, ride Space Mountain. (See the detailed version of this plan for special instructions on early entry days.)
5. Experience Alien Encounter.
6. Go to Frontierland via the central hub. Ride Big Thunder Mountain.
7. Go next door and ride Splash Mountain.
8. Go to Adventureland and ride the Jungle Cruise.
9. Ride Peter Pan's Flight in Fantasyland.
10. See *Legend of the Lion King*.

11. See The Haunted Mansion.
12. Return to Frontierland. See the *Country Bear Jamboree*.
13. Ride Pirates of the Caribbean.
14. Eat lunch.
15. Ride the riverboat and see *The Hall of Presidents* in Liberty Square.
16. Explore Tom Sawyer Island.
17. Take the train from Frontierland to Mickey's Starland.
18. See *Mickey's Starland Show*.
19. Meet Mickey at the Hollywood Theater.
20. Take the train to Main Street.
21. Browse along Main Street.
22. Depart the Magic Kingdom.

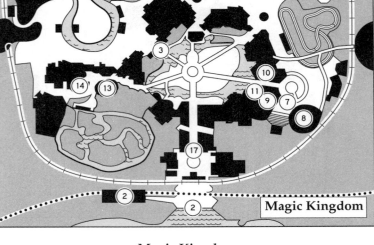

Magic Kingdom
Two-Day Touring Plan A, for When the Park Is Open Late
Pocket Outline Version

For the detailed version of this Touring Plan, see page 427.

Day Two

1. Arrive at the TTC at 2 P.M. in order to see the afternoon parade.
2. Take the monorail or ferry to park entrance.
3. Watch the parade.
4. Make dinner reservations if you want to eat in the park.
5. In Fantasyland, ride It's a Small World.
6. Go to Tomorrowland.
7. Ride the Tomorrowland Transit Authority.
8. See the *Carousel of Progress*.
9. Ride Dreamflight.
10. Experience Alien Encounter (if missed earlier).
11. See the *Transportarium*.
12. Eat dinner. (Work live shows into Touring Plan.)
13. Go to Adventureland. Explore the Swiss Family Treehouse.
14. See *Tropical Serenade*.
15. Try any rides you missed.
16. Repeat favorite attractions.
17. Browse along Main Street.
18. Depart the Magic Kingdom.

Magic Kingdom
Two-Day Touring Plan B, for Morning Touring and for When the Park Closes Early
Pocket Outline Version

For the detailed version of this Touring Plan, see page 430.

Day One

1. Arrive at TTC 50 min. prior to opening.
2. Take the monorail or ferry to park entrance.
3. Go to City Hall for park maps and a copy of the daily entertainment schedule.
4. As soon as Tomorrowland opens, ride Space Mountain.
5. Experience Alien Encounter.
6. Ride 20,000 Leagues Under the Sea.
7. Ride Dumbo
8. Ride Peter Pan's Flight.
9. See *Legend of the Lion King*

10. Ride It's a Small World.
11. In Liberty Square, see The Haunted Mansion.
12. See *The Hall of Presidents.*
13. Eat lunch.
14. Ride the riverboat.
15. In Frontierland, explore Tom Sawyer Island.
16. In Adventureland, see *Tropical Serenade.*
17. See the Swiss Family Treehouse.
18. Enjoy live entertainment.
19. Depart the Magic Kingdom.

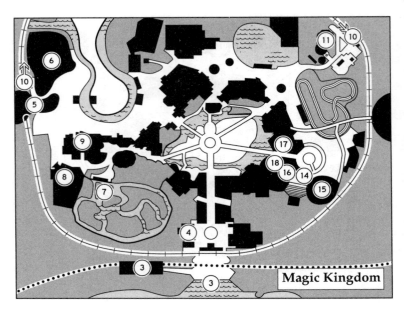

Magic Kingdom

Magic Kingdom
Two-Day Touring Plan B, for Morning Touring
and for When the Park Closes Early
Pocket Outline Version

For the detailed version of this Touring Plan, see page 432.

Day Two

1. Call (407) 824-4321 the day before your visit for the official opening time.
2. Arrive at TTC 50 min. prior to opening.
3. Take the monorail or ferry to park entrance.
4. Pick up a daily entertainment schedule. (See the detailed version of this plan for special instuctions on early entry days.)
5. In Frontierland, ride Splash Mountain.
6. Ride Big Thunder Mountain Railroad.
7. In Adventureland, ride the Jungle Cruise.
8. Ride Pirates of the Caribbean.
9. Back in Frontierland, see *Country Bear Jamboree*.

10. Take the train to Mickey's Starland.
11. See *Mickey's Starland Show* and visit Mickey.
12. Go to Tomorrowland.
13. Eat lunch.
14. Ride the Tomorrowland Transit Authority.
15. See the *Carousel of Progress*.
16. Ride Dreamflight.
17. Experience Alien Encounter
18. See the *Transportarium*.
19. Enjoy live entertainment.
20. Depart Magic Kingdom.

EPCOT Center
Recommended Attraction Visitation Times

If you tour on an early entry day, move all recommended attraction visitation times up one hour. It is best to see attractions with visitation times listed as "anytime" during the more crowded middle part of the day (noon to 4 P.M.).

1. American Adventure: Anytime
2. Body Wars (Wonders of Life): First hour after opening/late P.M.
3. *Cranium Command* (Wonders of Life): Before 11 A.M./after 3 P.M.
4. El Rio del Tiempo (Mexico): Before noon/after 3 P.M.
5. *Food Rocks* (The Land): Before 11 A.M./after 2 P.M.
6. *Harvest Theater* (The Land): Before 11 A.M./after 2 P.M.
7. *Honey, I Shrunk the Audience* (Imagination): Before 10 A.M./late P.M.
8. Horizons: Before 11 A.M./after 3 P.M.
9. *Impressions de France* (France): Before noon/late P.M.
10. Innoventions: Anytime
11. It's Fun To Be Free (World of Motion): Before noon/late P.M.
12. Journey Into Imagination Ride: Before 10:30 A.M./late P.M.
13. Living With the Land (The Land): Before 10/late P.M.
14. Living Seas: Before 10 A.M./after 3 P.M.
15. Maelstrom (Norway): Before noon/late P.M.
16. *The Making of Me* (Wonders of Life): Before 10 A.M./late P.M.
17. *O Canada!* (Canada): Anytime
18. Spaceship Earth: Before 10 A.M./late P.M.
19. Universe of Energy: Before 10:30 A.M./late P.M.
20. *Wonders of China* (China): Anytime

EPCOT Center

EPCOT Center
One-Day Touring Plan
Pocket Outline Version

For the detailed version of this Touring Plan, see page 507.
(Interrupt the Touring Plan for lunch, dinner, and IllumiNations.)

1. Arrive 45 minutes before official opening time.
2. Go to Guest Relations and make restaurant reservations.
3. Ride Spaceship Earth.
4. Ride Body Wars in the Wonders of Life pavilion.
5. Ride Living with the Land.
6. See *Honey, I Shrunk the Audience.*
7. Ride Journey into Imagination.
8. Walk to the opposite side of Future World.
9. Ride the World of Motion.
10. Go to the World Showcase.
11. Ride El Rio del Tiempo in Mexico.
12. Ride Maelstrom in Norway.
13. See *Wonders of China.*
14. Visit Italy and Germany.
15. See *The American Adventure.*
16. Visit Japan and Morocco.
17. See the film in France.
18. Visit the United Kingdom.
19. See *O Canada!*
20. Return to Future World. Ride Horizons.
21. See *Cranium Command.*
22. Ride Body Wars (if missed earlier).
23. Visit the Universe of Energy.
24. See The Living Seas.
25. See the two shows you missed earlier at The Land pavilion.
26. Enjoy IllumiNations.
27. Depart EPCOT Center.

EPCOT Center

EPCOT Center
Author's Selective One-Day Touring Plan
Pocket Outline Version

For the detailed version of this Touring Plan, see page 511.
(Interrupt the Touring Plan for lunch, dinner, and IllumiNations.)

1. Arrive 45–50 minutes before official opening time.
2. Go to Guest Relations and make restaurant reservations.
3. Ride Spaceship Earth,
4. Ride Body Wars in the Wonders of Life pavilion.
5. See Living with the Land
6. See *Honey, I Shrunk the Audience.*
7. Walk to the opposite side of Future World.
8. Ride the World of Motion.
9. Go to the World Showcase.
10. Visit Mexico.
11. Ride Maelstrom in Norway.
12. See *Wonders of China.*
13. Visit Italy and Germany.
14. See *The American Adventure.*
15. Visit Japan and Morocco.
16. See *Impressions de France.*
17. Visit the United Kingdom.
18. See *O Canada!*
19. Return to Future World. Ride Horizons.
20. See *Cranium Command.*
21. Ride Body Wars (if missed earlier).
22. Visit the Universe of Energy.
23. See The Living Seas.
24. Enjoy IllumiNations, then depart EPCOT Center.

EPCOT Center

EPCOT Center
Two-Day Touring Plan
Pocket Outline Version

For the detailed version of this Touring Plan, see page 515.
(Interrupt the Touring Plan for lunch)

Day One

1. Arrive 45–50 minutes before the official opening time.
2. Go to Guest Relations and make restaurant reservations.
3. Ride Spaceship Earth.
4. Ride Body Wars.
5. See the *Making of Me.*
6. Ride Living with the Land.
7. See *Honey, I Shrunk the Audience.*
8. Ride Journey into Imagination.
9. Go to the World of Motion pavilion.
10. Ride World of Motion.
11. Go to the World Showcase.
12. Ride El Rio del Tiempo in Mexico.
13. Ride Maelstrom in Norway.
14. See *Wonders of China.*
15. Visit Italy and Germany.
16. See *The American Adventure.*
17. Visit Japan and Morocco.
18. See *Impressions de France.*
19. Depart EPCOT Center.

EPCOT Center

EPCOT Center
Two-Day Touring Plan
Pocket Outline Version

For the detailed version of this Touring Plan, see page 517.
(Interrupt the Touring Plan for dinner and IllumiNations.)

Day Two

1. Arrive at EPCOT at 2 P.M.
2. Go to Guest Relations and make dinner reservations.
3. Go to The Living Seas.
4. See the two shows you missed yesterday at The Land.
5. Visit the Universe of Energy.
6. See *Cranium Command*.
7. Ride Body Wars and see the *Making of Me* (if missed on Day One).
8. Ride Horizons.
9. See *O Canada!*
10. Visit the United Kingdom.
11. Enjoy IllumiNations.
12. Depart EPCOT Center.

EPCOT Center

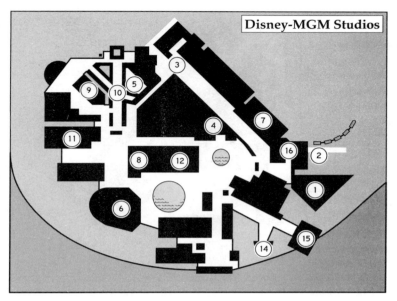

Disney-MGM Studios
Recommended Attraction Visitation Times

If you tour on an early entry day, move all recommended attraction visitation times up one hour. It is best to see attractions with visitation times listed as "anytime" during the more crowded middle part of the day (noon to 4 P.M.).

1. Animation Tour: Before 11 A.M./late P.M.
2. Backstage Tram Tour: Anytime
3. Backstage Walking Tour (Inside the Magic): Anytime
4. Great Movie Ride: Before 10 A.M./late P.M.
5. Honey, I Shrunk the Kids playground: Before 10 A.M./after dark
6. *Indiana Jones Stunt Spectacular:* First, second, or last show
7. *Making of Pocahontas:* Before noon/late P.M.
8. *Monster Sound Show:* Before 11 A.M./late P.M.
9. *MuppetVision 4-D:* Before 11 A.M./late P.M.
10. New York Street Back Lot: Anytime
11. Star Tours: First hour and a half after opening/late P.M.
12. *SuperStar Television:* Anytime after 10 A.M.
13. *Teenage Mutant Ninja Turtles:* At your convenience
14. *Theater of the Stars:* Evening
15. Tower of Terror: Before 10 A.M./late P.M.
16. *Voyage of the Little Mermaid:* Before 9:30 A.M./late P.M.

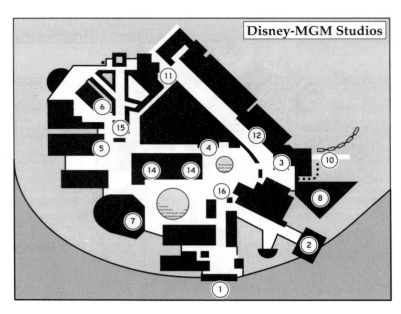

Disney-MGM Studios
One-Day Touring Plan
Pocket Outline Version

For the detailed version of this Touring Plan, see page 557.
(Before you go, check detailed itinerary for park opening procedures.)

1. Arrive 40 minutes before official opening time.
2. Ride the Tower of Terror.
3. See *Voyage of the Little Mermaid.*
4. Ride The Great Movie Ride.
5. Ride Star Tours.
6. See *MuppetVision 4-D.*
7. See *Indiana Jones.*
8. Take the Animation Tour.
9. Make meal reservations, if desired.
10. Take the tram segment of the Backstage Tour.
11. Take the walking segment of the Backstage Tour (Inside the Magic).
12. See *The Making of Pocahontas.*
13. Work live shows into Touring Plan.
14. See *The Monster Sound Show* and Superstar Television.
15. Explore the New York Street set.
16. Tour Hollywood and Sunset boulevards.
17. Enjoy live entertainment.
18. Depart the Studios.

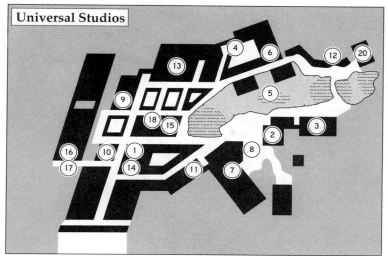

Universal Studios Florida
Recommended Attraction Visitation Times

If you tour on an early entry day, move all recommended attraction visitation times up one hour. It is best to see attractions with visitation times listed as "anytime" during the more crowded middle part of the day (noon to 4 P.M.).

1. "Alfred Hitchcock: The Art of Making Movies:" After all the rides
2. *Animal Actors Stage:* After experiencing all rides
3. Back to the Future: First thing after park opens/late P.M.
4. Beetlejuice's Rock 'N Roll Graveyard Revue: At your convenience
5. *Dynamite Nights Stunt Spectacular:* Evening
6. Earthquake: Before 11 A.M., following Kongfrontation/late P.M.
7. E.T. Adventure: Before 10 A.M., following Back to the Future
8. Fievel's Playland: Anytime
9. *Ghostbusters:* Go immediately after experiencing all rides
10. Hanna-Barbera Ride: Before 11 A.M./late P.M.
11. *The Gory Gruesome & Grotesque Horror Make-up Show:* After experiencing all rides
12. Jaws: Before 11 A.M., after experiencing E.T./late P.M.
13. Kongfrontation: Before 11 A.M., following Jaws/late P.M.
14. Lucy, a Tribute: Anytime
15. "Murder, She Wrote!" Mystery Theater: After experiencing all rides
16. Nickelodeon Studios Walking Tour: When shows are in production
17. Production Tram Tour: Late afternoon
18. *The Adventures of Rocky and Bullwinkle:* Evening
19. Street Scenes: Anytime
20. *Wild, Wild, Wild West Stunt Show:* After experiencing all the rides

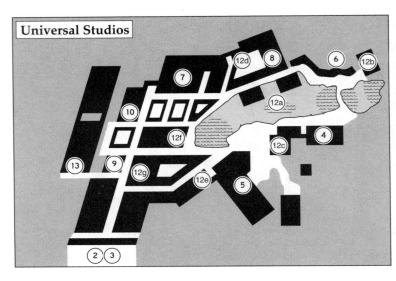

Universal Studios
One-Day Touring Plan
Pocket Outline Version

For the detailed version of this Touring Plan, see page 584.

1. Call (407) 363-8000 the day before your visit for official opening time.
2. Arrive 50 minutes before opening.
3. Ask if any rides are closed.
4. Ride Back to the Future.
5. Ride E.T. Adventure.
6. Ride Jaws.
7. Ride Kongfrontation.
8. Ride Earthquake.
9. Ride Hanna-Barbera.
10. See *Ghostbusters*.
11. This is a good time for lunch.
12. See the *Stunt Spectacular* (12a), the *Wild West Stunt Show* (12b), the *Animal Actors Stage* (12c), and *Beetlejuice* (12d), as convenient according to the daily entertainment schedule. As time permits, work the *Horror Make-up Show* (12e), and *Murder, She Wrote* (12f), which run continuously, into your schedule. See *Alfred Hitchcock* (12g) last.
13. If you are with grade-school age children, see Nickelodeon Studios.
14. See any live shows you may have missed.

Unofficial Guide Reader Survey
1996 Edition

If you would like to express your opinion about Walt Disney World or this guidebook, complete the following survey and mail it to:

Unofficial Guide Reader Survey
P.O. Box 43059
Birmingham, AL 35243

Inclusive dates of your visit _____

Did you have a car? _____ Hometown _____ State _____

Members of your party:	Person 1	Person 2	Person 3	Person 4	Person 5
Gender (M or F)					
Age					
Magic Kingdom					
Favorite Attraction					
Next Favorite Attraction					
Most Disappointing					
EPCOT Center					
Favorite Attraction					
Next Favorite Attraction					
Most Disappointing					
Disney-MGM Studios					
Favorite Attraction					
Next Favorite Attraction					
Most Disappointing					

Where did you stay?_____

Concerning accommodations, on a scale with 100 best and 0 worst, how would you rate:

The quality of your room?_____   Value for the money?_____

Did you return to your room for rest during the day?_____

On a scale with 100 best and 0 worst, rate how the Touring Plans worked:

Magic Kingdom Touring Plan: Rating _____ Name of plan _____

EPCOT Center Touring Plan: Rating _____ Name of plan _____

Disney-MGM Studios Touring Plan: Rating _____ Name of plan _____

Universal Studios Florida Touring Plan: Rating _____

Typhoon Lagoon Touring Plan: Rating _____

Pleasure Island Touring Plan: Rating _____

Favorite Restaurant in Walt Disney World_____

Most Disappointing Restaurant in Walt Disney World_____

Favorite Restaurant out of Walt Disney World_____

Most Disappointing Restaurant out of Walt Disney World_____

Did you buy this guide: Before leaving?_____   While on your trip?____

How did you hear about this guide?

Loaned or recommended by friend _____ Radio or TV talk show_____

Newspaper or magazine feature or review_____

Bookstore salesperson _____   Just picked it out on my own _____

What other guidebooks did you use?_____

On the 100 best and 0 worst scale, how would you rate them? _____

Using the same scale, how would you rate the *Unofficial Guide?*_____

Comments about your Walt Disney World vacation or about the *Unofficial Guide:* _____

_____

_____

_____

_____

Walt Disney World Restaurant Survey

Tell us about your Walt Disney World dining experiences. Listed below are the theme park full-service restaurants followed by the resort hotel restaurants on the next page. Beside each restaurant is a thumbs-up and thumbs-down symbol. If you enjoyed the restaurant enough that you would like to eat there again, circle the thumbs-up symbol. If not, circle the thumbs-down symbol.

Theme Park Full-Service Restaurants (in alphabetical order):

Akershus	Norway: EPCOT	👍 👎
Alfredo di Roma Ristorante	Italy: EPCOT	👍 👎
Au Petit Cafe	France: EPCOT	👍 👎
Biergarten	Germany: EPCOT	👍 👎
Bistro de Paris	France: EPCOT	👍 👎
Chefs de France	France: EPCOT	👍 👎
Coral Reef	Living Seas: EPCOT	👍 👎
The Garden Grill	Land Pavilion: EPCOT	👍 👎
Hollywood & Vine Cafeteria	Disney-MGM Studios	👍 👎
Hollywood Brown Derby	Disney-MGM Studios	👍 👎
King Stefan's Banquet Hall	Magic Kingdom	👍 👎
Liberty Tree Tavern	Magic Kingdom	👍 👎
Mama Melrose's Ristorante	Disney-MGM Studios	👍 👎
Marrakesh	Morocco: EPCOT	👍 👎
Nine Dragons Restaurant	China: EPCOT	👍 👎
(50's) Prime Time Cafe	Disney-MGM Studios	👍 👎
Rose & Crown	United Kingdom: EPCOT.	👍 👎
San Angel Inn	Mexico: EPCOT	👍 👎
Sci-Fi Dine-In Restaurant	Disney-MGM Studios	👍 👎
Tempura Kiku	Japan: EPCOT	👍 👎
Teppanyaki Dining Room	Japan: EPCOT	👍 👎
Tony's Town Square Restaurant	Magic Kingdom	👍 👎

Walt Disney World Hotel Restaurants (in alphabetical order):

Ariel's	Beach Club Resort	👍 👎
Arthur's 27	Buena Vista Palace	👍 👎
Artist Point	Wilderness Lodge Resort	👍 👎
Baskervilles	Grosvenor Resort	👍 👎

Walt Disney World Hotel Restaurants, cont. (in alphabetical order):

Benihana	Hilton	👍 👎
Boatwright's Dining Hall	Dixie Landings Resort	👍 👎
Bonfamille's Cafe	Port Orleans Resort	👍 👎
California Grill	Contemporary Resort	👍 👎
Cape May Cafe	Beach Club Resort	👍 👎
Cap'n Jack's Oyster Bar	Disney Village Marketplace	👍 👎
Chef Mickey's	Disney Village Marketplace	👍 👎
Cinnamon's	Polynesian Resort	👍 👎
Concourse Steakhouse	Contemporary Resort	👍 👎
Crockett's Tavern	Fort Wilderness	👍 👎
Finn's Grill	Hilton	👍 👎
Fireworks Factory	Pleasure Island	👍 👎
Fisherman's Deck	Empress Lilly Riverboat	👍 👎
Flagler's	Grand Floridian	👍 👎
Garden Grove Cafe	WDW Swan	👍 👎
Grand Floridian Cafe	Grand Floridian	👍 👎
Harry's Safari Bar & Grill	WDW Dolphin	👍 👎
Juan & Only's Bar & Jail	WDW Dolphin	👍 👎
Kimonos	WDW Swan	👍 👎
Monorail Buffet	Contemporary Resort	👍 👎
Narcoossee's	Grand Floridian	👍 👎
'Ohana Grill	Polynesian Resort	👍 👎
Olivia's Cafe	Vacation Club Resort	👍 👎
The Outback	Buena Vista Palace	👍 👎
Palio	WDW Swan	👍 👎
Planet Hollywood	Pleasure Island	👍 👎
Portobello Yacht Club	Pleasure Island	👍 👎
Sum Chows	WDW Dolphin	👍 👎
Tangaroa Terrace	Polynesian Resort	👍 👎
Victoria and Albert's	Grand Floridian	👍 👎
Whispering Canyon Cafe	Wilderness Lodge	👍 👎
Yacht Club Gallery	Yacht Club Resort	👍 👎
Yachtsman Steakhouse	Yacht Club Resort	👍 👎